CAPITAL STRUCTURE AND CORPORATE FINANCING DECISIONS

The *Robert W. Kolb Series in Finance* provides a comprehensive view of the field of finance in all of its variety and complexity. The series is projected to include approximately 65 volumes covering all major topics and specializations in finance, ranging from investments, to corporate finance, to financial institutions. Each volume in the *Kolb Series in Finance* consists of new articles especially written for the volume.

Each volume is edited by a specialist in a particular area of finance, who develops the volume outline and commissions articles by the world's experts in that particular field of finance. Each volume includes an editor's introduction and approximately 30 articles to fully describe the current state of financial research and practice in a particular area of finance.

The essays in each volume are intended for practicing finance professionals, graduate students, and advanced undergraduate students. The goal of each volume is to encapsulate the current state of knowledge in a particular area of finance so that the reader can quickly achieve a mastery of that special area of finance.

Please visit www.wiley.com/go/kolbseries to learn about recent and forthcoming titles in the Kolb Series.

CAPITAL STRUCTURE AND CORPORATE FINANCING DECISIONS

Theory, Evidence, and Practice

H. Kent Baker and Gerald S. Martin

The Robert W. Kolb Series in Finance

John Wiley & Sons, Inc.

Published by John Wiley & Sons, Inc., Hoboken, New Jersey.
Published simultaneously in Canada.

For general information on our other products and services or for technical support, please contact our Customer Care Department within the United States at (800) 762-2974, outside the United States at (317) 572-3993 or fax (317) 572-4002.

Wiley also publishes its books in a variety of electronic formats. Some content that appears in print may not be available in electronic books. For more information about Wiley products, visit our web site at www.wiley.com.

Library of Congress Cataloging-in-Publication Data:

Capital structure and financing decisions : theory, evidence, and practice / H. Kent Baker and Gerald S. Martin, editors.
p. cm.—(The Robert W. Kolb series in finance)
Includes bibliographical references and index.
ISBN 978-0-470-56952-8 (cloth); ISBN 978-1-118-02292-4 (ebk);
ISBN 978-1-118-02293-1 (ebk); ISBN 978-1-118-02294-8 (ebk)
1. Corporations—Finance. 2. Capital investments. I. Baker, H. Kent (Harold Kent), 1944– II. Martin, Gerald S. III. Title: Capital structure and corporate financing decisions.
HG4026.C2424 2011
658.15—dc22 2010045662

10 9 8 7 6 5 4 3 2 1

Contents

Acknowledgments

We extend our sincere appreciation to the many individuals involved in bringing *Capital Structure and Corporate Financing Decisions: Theory, Evidence, and Practice* from the idea stage to publication. We appreciate the support provided by Bob Kolb, the series editor, in reviewing the initial book proposal. The chapter authors deserve special thanks for their hard work in writing and revising chapters. Meghan Nesmith, who carefully reviewed each chapter and provided artful edits and comments, deserves high praise. Katharine Fredriksen also provided needed editorial assistance. Our expert publishing team at John Wiley & Sons skillfully turned the manuscript into final form. Special thanks go to Evan Burton as well as Emilie Herman, Senior Editorial Manager, and Melissa Lopez, Production Editor, all of whom demonstrated poise and professionalism. We also want to recognize the support provided by the Kogod School of Business at American University. Finally, Linda Baker deserves special thanks for her careful review of the manuscript as well as for her patience and encouragement.

CHAPTER 1

Capital Structure: An Overview

H. KENT BAKER
University Professor of Finance and Kogod Research Professor, American University

GERALD S. MARTIN
Associate Professor of Finance, American University

INTRODUCTION

According to Baker and Powell (2005, p. 4), financial management is "an integrated decision-making process concerned with acquiring, financing, and managing assets to accomplish some overall goal within a business entity." Jensen (2001) indicates that among most financial economists the criterion for evaluating performance and deciding between alternative courses of action should be maximization of long-term market value of the firm. He notes that this value maximization proposition has its roots in 200 years of research in economics and finance. For publicly-held firms, the maximization of shareholder wealth is reflected in the market price of the stock. By maximizing shareholder wealth, managers are serving the interests of the firm's owners as residual claimants. Under most circumstances, the premise of maximizing total firm value is also consistent with maximizing shareholder wealth.

This book focuses on one major aspect of financial management—how capital structure and financing decisions can contribute to maximizing the value of the firm. Financing decisions go hand in hand with investment decisions. That is, a firm needs sufficient funds to support its activities resulting from its investment decisions. *Capital structure* refers to the sources of financing employed by the firm. These sources include debt, equity, and hybrid securities that a firm uses to finance its assets, operations, and future growth. Often thought of in terms of financial leverage, a firm's capital structure is a direct determinant of its overall risk and cost of capital. The sources of capital have important consequences for the firm and can affect its value and hence shareholder wealth. For example, while debt is the least costly form of capital, the effects of increasing leverage through the use of debt simultaneously increase financial risk. Borrowing not only increases the risk of default for a firm but also increases the volatility of a firm's earnings per share and its return on equity. The benefits of a lower cost of debt decrease as leverage rises due to increasing financial risk and the likelihood of financial distress and bankruptcy. As with most financial decisions, financing decisions involve a risk-return trade-off. Given the dramatic changes that have occurred recently in the economy such as the global financial crisis, the topic of capital structure and corporate financing decisions is critically important.

Barclay and Smith (1999, p. 8) make the following observation:

> *A perennial debate in corporate finance concerns the question of optimal capital structure: Given a level of total capital necessary to support a company's activities, is there a way of dividing up that capital into debt and equity that maximizes current firm value? And if so, what are the critical factors in setting the leverage ratio for a given company?*

An *optimal capital structure* is the financing mix that maximizes the value of the firm. Yet, mixed views exist about whether an optimal capital structure actually exists. Some believe that a firm's value does not depend on its financing mix, and hence an optimal capital structure does not exist. The modern theory of capital structure started with Modigliani and Miller (1958), who pioneered the research efforts relating capital structure and the value of the firm. In their seminal work, they show that under stringent conditions of competitive, frictionless, and complete capital markets, the value of a firm is independent of its capital structure. That is, managers cannot alter firm value or the cost of capital by the capital structures that they choose. Further, business risk alone determines the cost of capital. Thus, financing and capital structure decisions are not shareholder value enhancing and are deemed to be irrelevant. In reality, these conditions rarely exist. Empirical evidence suggests that financing does matter.

Others contend that managers can theoretically determine a firm's optimal capital structure. During the last five decades, financial economists have relaxed the restrictive assumptions underlying the theory of capital structure irrelevance and have introduced capital market frictions into their models. By introducing capital market frictions, such as taxes, bankruptcy costs, and asymmetric information, they are able to explain at least some factors driving capital structure decisions. Consequently, financial economists have set forth various capital structure theories such as trade-off theory (Kraus and Litzenberger 1973), pecking order theory (Myers 1984; Myers and Majluf 1984), signaling (Ross 1977), and market timing theory (Baker and Wurgler 2002) to explain the relevance of capital structure. These theories relate directly to taxes, asymmetric information, agency problems, and bankruptcy costs. Taken separately, these theories cannot explain certain important facts about capital structure. Despite extensive research into the area of capital structure, determining the precise financing mix that maximizes the market value of the firm remains elusive.

PURPOSE OF THE BOOK

The purpose of this book is to provide an in-depth examination of important topics about capital structure and corporate financing decisions. The coverage extends from discussing basic components and existing theories to their application to increasingly complex and real-world situations. Throughout, the book emphasizes how a sound capital structure can simultaneously reduce a firm's cost of capital while increasing value to shareholders. Given the sheer volume of theoretical and empirical studies involving capital structure and financing decisions, the prospect of surveying the extant literature is a formidable task.

Although coverage is not exhaustive, the book includes a review of several hundred articles. Leading academics and researchers from around the globe provide a synthesis of the current state of capital structure and give their views about its future direction.

FEATURES OF THE BOOK

Many finance books deal with capital structure. Yet, few, if any, offer the scope of coverage and breadth of viewpoints contained in this volume. The book differs from others in several major ways. Perhaps the book's most distinctive feature is that it provides a comprehensive discussion of financial theory, empirical work, and practice involving corporate financial policies, strategies, and choices. This is an up-to-date book in terms of theoretical developments, empirical results, and practical applications.

Although the book cannot cover every topic on capital structure, given the voluminous amount of writing on the subject, it does seek to highlight some of the most important topics. The book takes a practical approach to capital structure by discussing why various theories make sense, the empirical support for them, and how firms use these theories to solve problems and to create wealth. This volume uses theoretical and mathematical derivations only when necessary to explain the topic. Although the book also reports the results of many empirical studies that link theory and practice, the objective is to distill them to their essential content so that they are understandable to the reader.

The book has six other distinguishing features.

1. The book contains contributions from numerous authors. This breadth of contributors provides a wide range of viewpoints and a rich interplay of ideas.
2. The book offers a strategic focus to help provide an understanding of how financing decisions relate to a firm's overall corporate policy. Because financial decisions are interconnected, managers must incorporate them into the overall corporate strategy of the firm.
3. The book has a global focus and examines worldwide patterns in capital structure. It reviews research not only centered on U.S. firms but also from companies around the world.
4. This volume takes both a prescriptive and descriptive perspective. Using a prescriptive approach, it examines how corporate managers should make financial decisions to improve firm value. The book's descriptive perspective discusses theories that shed light on which financial decisions managers make and analyzes the impact of these decisions on financial markets. The book also provides results from survey research describing actual financial practices of firms.
5. The book identifies areas needing future research in capital structure and financing decisions.
6. Each chapter except this introductory chapter contains a set of discussion questions to reinforce key aspects of the chapter's content. A separate section near the end of the book provides a guideline answer to each question.

INTENDED AUDIENCE

The intended audience for this book includes academics, researchers, corporate managers, students, and others interested in capital structure and corporate financing decisions. Considering its extensive coverage and focus on the theoretical and empirical literature, this book should be appealing to academics and researchers as a critical resource. Given the book's intuitive and largely nontechnical approach, it is geared toward helping corporate managers formulate policies and financial strategies that maximize firm value and policymakers in understanding capital structure choices. This volume can also stand alone or in tandem with another text or casebook for graduate and advanced undergraduate students, especially those in business or finance. This book should be especially useful in helping students develop the critical analytical skills required to understand the implications of capital structure. Finally, libraries should find this work to be suitable for reference purposes.

STRUCTURE OF THE BOOK

The remaining 23 chapters of this book are organized into four parts. A brief synopsis of each chapter follows.

Part I The Elements of Capital Structure

Chapters 2–7 provide an overview of the elements of capital structure. These chapters lay the foundation and discuss important principles and concepts involving capital structure. Chapters in this section examine the factors influencing capital structure decisions as well as the interactions among capital structure, strategy, risk, returns, and compensation. Additionally, this section identifies differences in capital structure across countries with different legal and institutional settings.

Chapter 2 Factors Affecting Capital Structure Decisions (Wolfgang Bessler, Wolfgang Drobetz, and Robin Kazemieh)

In perfect capital markets, capital structure decisions should not have any impact on the market value of a firm. However, once capital market frictions such as taxes, bankruptcy costs, and asymmetric information are introduced into the model, there are factors related to these frictions that affect capital structure decisions. This chapter provides a review of the main capital structure factors that have been identified in the literature. Survey evidence indicates that the most dominant factor that affects the decision to issue debt is maintaining financial flexibility. The major factors that determine the issuance of stock are earnings per share dilution and equity undervaluation or overvaluation. Results from regression studies using comprehensive firm-level data sets indicate that the most reliable factors for explaining corporate leverage are: market-to-book ratio (–), tangibility (+), profitability (–), firm size (+), expected inflation (+), and median industry leverage (+ effect on leverage).

Chapter 3 Capital Structure and Corporate Strategy (Maurizio La Rocca)
This chapter responds to the general call for integration between finance and strategy research by examining the relationship between capital structure decisions and corporate strategy. The literature on finance and strategy analyzes how the strategic actions of key players such as managers, shareholders, debt holders, competitors, workers, and suppliers affect firm value and its allocation between claimholders. Specifically, financing decisions can affect the value creation process by influencing efficient investment strategies due to conflicts of interest among managers, firm's financial stakeholders, and firm's nonfinancial stakeholders. In turn, the potential interactions between financial and nonfinancial stakeholders may give rise to inefficient managerial decisions or may shape the industry's competitive dynamics to achieve a competitive advantage. A good integration between finance and strategy can be tantamount to a competitive weapon.

Chapter 4 Capital Structure and Firm Risk (Valentin Dimitrov)
With market frictions, the real and financial sides of the firm are interrelated. As a result, variables such as financial leverage can have important consequences for firm risk. Prior analytical work has identified several mechanisms through which financial leverage can affect risk but has not reached a consensus on the relative importance of these mechanisms. The empirical evidence is more conclusive. When subjected to adverse economic shocks, highly leveraged firms have lower growth in sales, make fewer investments, and are less likely to survive than firms with low leverage. These findings suggest that financial leverage amplifies negative shocks; it makes firms riskier. However, shareholders of highly leveraged firms do not appear to be compensated for this higher risk. Highly leveraged firms earn lower stock returns in the cross-section. Furthermore, increases in leverage are associated with low subsequent stock returns. These return patterns present a challenge to traditional capital asset pricing models.

Chapter 5 Capital Structure and Returns (Yaz Gulnur Muradoglu and Sheeja Sivaprasad)
This chapter examines the link between stock returns and leverage. Proposition II of the Modigliani-Miller theorem on capital structure postulates that stock returns increase with leverage due to the increase in financial risk attached to debt. A limited number of studies test this association empirically and find contradictory results. Some empirical studies report that a positive relationship exists between leverage and returns, but others find a negative relationship. This chapter summarizes the theories of capital structure and then presents empirical tests. It then discusses how conflicting empirical results may be attributed to the various definitions used in measuring stock returns and leverage, and to the sample selection procedures and methodologies adopted to test this relationship.

Chapter 6 Capital Structure and Compensation (Alan Victor Scott Douglas)
This chapter examines the interactions between capital structure and compensation. It begins by reviewing the basic determinants of capital structure, particularly as related to shareholder-bondholder conflicts relating to investment decisions. Well-designed managerial compensation can maintain efficient investment incentives and significantly alter the determinants of capital structure. Complications

arise, however, from managerial risk aversion and perquisite consumption as well as from managers trying to game the compensation-setting process. The empirical evidence indicates that two characteristics of compensation—sensitivity of pay to share price and to volatility—affect both the cost of capital and leverage. The evidence also identifies other factors affecting the compensation-capital structure relationship including the use of convertible debt, the maturity structure of the firm's debt, and debt-like components of compensation. The literature has yet to fully develop the interactions, but to date characteristics of compensation may be important determinants of capital structure.

Chapter 7 Worldwide Patterns in Capital Structure (Carmen Cotei and Joseph Farhat)
Recent research in international capital structure shows that capital structure decisions are influenced not only by firm-specific and macroeconomic factors but also by legal traditions and the quality of institutions of countries in which they operate. The differences in legal traditions and institutional settings across countries have important implications for individual firms' ability to raise capital needed to finance profitable growth opportunities. Firms operating in countries with weaker institutional settings and legal systems may have difficulty overcoming the higher information asymmetry and agency costs of debt. This can affect both the ability of firms to operate at the optimal capital structure and managers to maximize firm value.

Part II Capital Structure Choice

Chapters 8–14 discuss key factors involved in capital structure choice. Chapters 8–10 focus on major capital structure theories and their empirical tests. Chapter 11 shows how to implement the insights provided by theory into estimating a firm's cost of capital. Chapter 12 discusses economic, regulatory, and industry effects on capital structure. Chapters 13 and 14 veer from traditional empirical studies that are based on large samples of financial data and provide empirical evidence from survey research. These two chapters, which discuss the results of major surveys, provide unique information about how corporate managers make financing decisions in practice.

Chapter 8 Capital Structure Theories and Empirical Tests: An Overview (Stein Frydenberg)
The findings of empirical capital structure studies are diverse, but a consensus exists stating that fixed assets, industry leverage, and size of firms have a positive effect on the debt level, while growth opportunities, profitability, and dividend payments have a negative effect. There are two main approaches to empirical tests of capital structure theory. The first is a static cross-section or a dynamic panel data approach where leverage is regressed against accounting variables that proxy for theoretical factors such as the firm's tax position, potential for agency costs, expected bankruptcy costs, asymmetric information, and transaction costs. The evidence about the determinants of capital structure is robust across firms and countries. The second is a time-series approach that examines the effects of new issues of securities on stock price returns. While the literature reaches a consensus

about the direction of effects, it is far from reaching a consensus on the size of the effects.

Chapter 9 Capital Structure Irrelevance: The Modigliani-Miller Model (Sergei V. Cheremushkin)
Much debate exists about the real-world applications of the Modigliani-Miller theory given its highly restrictive assumptions. Although subsequent research identifies relevant factors affecting capital structure, additional work is needed to create a generalized analytical framework for determining capital structure under real-world conditions. This chapter provides a simple risk-shifting explanation that helps in understanding various problems and establishes the shapes of cost of debt and equity functions of leverage. This explanation offers several insights about the integration of trade-off theory and other approaches to dealing with market imperfections. A generalized cost of equity formula and an extended decision rule for capital budgeting are also presented.

Chapter 10 Trade-Off, Pecking Order, Signaling, and Market Timing Models (Anton Miglo)
Over recent years researchers have extensively tested the trade-off and pecking order theories of capital structure. Taken separately, these theories cannot explain certain important facts about capital structure. Market timing theory emerged after the publication of Baker and Wurgler (2002) as a separate theory of capital structure. The theoretical aspects of market timing theory are underdeveloped. A popular line of inquiry has emerged based on surveys of managers about their capital structure decisions. For example, Graham and Harvey (2001) report a large gap between theory and practice. The signaling theory of capital structure lacks empirical support for some of its core predictions. However, several new theories have emerged that contradict the notion of signaling quality through debt issuance. This chapter presents an overview of the pros and cons for each theory. A discussion of major recent papers and suggestions for future research are provided.

Chapter 11 Estimating Capital Costs: Practical Implementation of Theory's Insights (Robert M. Conroy and Robert S. Harris)
This chapter focuses on the challenges of estimating a company's cost of capital. Its goal is to illustrate and improve the craft of such estimation. While theory offers sound conceptual advice, decision makers still face a host of practical choices. The chapter reports results for a wide array of publicly-traded companies and highlights areas in which best practice would especially benefit from future research. The investigation shows that analysts can benefit from using estimates from both single-company data and comparable firm averages to triangulate the cost of capital. The findings also reinforce the belief that cost of capital estimation is a craft and done best when informed by substantial knowledge and care in selecting comparable firms. Finally, the chapter suggests three areas for future attention in both research and practice: extensions to private firms, better gauges of capital structure impacts, and methods to estimate changes in equity market risk premiums over time.

Chapter 12 Economic, Regulatory, and Industry Effects on Capital Structure (Paroma Sanyal)
The purpose of this chapter is to provide a comprehensive study of the nonfinancial determinants of capital structure. This chapter focuses on three important sets of factors that influence a firm's financing decision: (1) intercountry differences, (2) interindustry differences within a country, and (3) interfirm differences within the same industry. Within interindustry differences the focus is on the financing decision of firms in nonregulated versus regulated industries. By studying firms that are regulated and those that are transitioning from a regulated to a competitive environment, this chapter provides a unique window into how changing incentive structures influence financial choices of firms. Within firm-specific factors, this chapter highlights how small startups make their financing decisions.

Chapter 13 Survey Evidence on Financing Decisions and Cost of Capital (Franck Bancel and Usha R. Mittoo)
Survey evidence shows that managers in the United States and Europe identify financial flexibility as the main driver of debt policy and earnings per share dilution as the primary concern when issuing common stock. There is moderate support for the views that firms follow the trade-off theory, target their debt ratio, and use market timing when raising capital. Most managers use the capital asset pricing model (CAPM) to estimate cost of equity but a firm-wide discount rate to evaluate different projects. In making financing decisions, managers rely primarily on informal criteria and less on theories.

Chapter 14 Survey Evidence on Capital Structure: Non-U.S. Evidence (Abe de Jong and Patrick Verwijmeren)
Financial executives are responsible for making financing decisions that optimize firms' financing arrangements. The capital structure literature has a rich set of theories that aim to prescribe optimal decisions or explain actual decisions. Most empirical research is based on publicly available data about firms' financing structures and decisions in relation to characteristics of the market, the firm, and the decision maker. In survey research, the data often comes directly from the financial executives, which allows a direct assessment of theoretical predictions and constructs. This chapter describes survey evidence from countries other than the United States and also provides avenues for future survey research based on alternative survey-based research methods.

Part III Raising Capital

Chapters 15–19 explore various aspects of raising capital. Included are discussions about the effect of recent financial crises and potential regulatory changes that may occur. Chapter 15 highlights the functions of financial intermediaries while Chapter 16 examines the importance of bank relationships and the role of collateralization. Chapter 17 explores the role of credit rating agencies and credit insurance. Chapter 18 discusses the role that securitization plays in the capital-raising process. Chapter 19 provides an analysis of sale and leasebacks, a tool that simultaneously raises capital and recapitalizes the firm.

Chapter 15 The Roles of Financial Intermediaries in Raising Capital (Neal Galpin)

This chapter reviews the literature on financial intermediation, with a focus on lending and underwriting activities. It begins by exploring the direct lending function of financial intermediaries, considering theoretically and empirically what role financial intermediaries play in providing capital. It also provides evidence on which type of financial intermediary is most appropriate for different types of borrowers. The chapter then reviews the theory and evidence on underwriting activities by financial intermediaries. With the repeal of the Glass-Steagall Act, a single intermediary can engage in both lending and underwriting, so the chapter next turns to theory and evidence on combining these services. Finally, because recent financial crises have drastically affected financial intermediaries, the chapter concludes with some recent work on crises and financial intermediation.

Chapter 16 Bank Relationships and Collateralization (Aron A. Gottesman and Gordon S. Roberts)

This chapter surveys the literature related to bank relationships and collateralization. Bank relationships are developed through the bank's generation of proprietary information. Benefits of a bank relationship include the reduction in information asymmetries, superior monitoring, and the ability to negotiate contract terms. Costs include the soft-budget constraint problem and the hold-up problem. The primary market for loans is strengthened by a secondary loan market that has experienced significant growth and is both liquid and well-integrated with other markets. Borrowers engage in bonding when they pledge collateral, as its presence benefits lenders by controlling the agency problem of asset substitution and improving default recovery rates. Collateral also benefits borrowers by reducing loan spreads and facilitating access to financing. These benefits are greater for riskier borrowers, as they are most likely to engage in secured borrowing. Consequently, secured loans remain riskier and carry higher yields than unsecured loans, despite the role of collateral in reducing risk and spreads.

Chapter 17 Rating Agencies and Credit Insurance (John Patrick Hunt)

This chapter discusses credit ratings and their importance. It reviews the mixed event-study evidence on whether ratings are informative and other empirical evidence about rating performance during the financial crisis. The chapter also reviews recent work on the interrelated issues of the roles of reputation and competition in producing high-quality ratings. Although policymakers have assumed that rating-agency competition is good, economists' theoretical conclusions and the empirical literature are mixed. In particular, models that incorporate ratings shopping often lead to the conclusion that competition is harmful. The chapter also reviews various aspects of U.S. rating-dependent financial regulation. The discussion of rating agencies concludes with a description of special legal protections the agencies claim and a review of recent proposals for reform. Finally, the chapter includes a brief discussion of bond insurance, a credit-protection mechanism that has been used extensively in the municipal and structured-finance markets.

Chapter 18 Secured Financing (Hugh Marble III)
Secured debt is often part of a firm's capital structure. While private loans are far more likely than public debt to be secured, the majority of firms use some secured debt. The explanations for the choice of security provisions are generally focused on (1) mitigating agency conflicts between bondholders and stockholders, (2) signaling or mitigating information asymmetry, (3) improving incentives to monitor and efficiently liquidate, and (4) transferring wealth from other claimants to stockholders and secured lenders. This chapter addresses the theoretical arguments and empirical support for these explanations. At least some evidence is consistent with each of the first three arguments. The use of security provisions to improve monitoring and liquidation choices has the strongest empirical support.

Chapter 19 Sale and Leasebacks (Kyle S. Wells)
A sale and leaseback is an alternative to traditional financing in which the owner of an asset contracts to sell the asset and then to lease it from the buyer. Leasebacks differ from direct leasing in that the operating assets essentially remain unchanged. A leaseback is primarily a financing decision. Although much of the literature focuses on the benefits from differential taxation, empirical research suggests other reasons that firms use leasebacks. Primary among these is utilizing hidden value in the firm's assets. This chapter discusses why a manager might choose a sale and leaseback and in what situations it could be an appropriate form of financing. The chapter also presents a summary of both the theoretical and empirical literature about leasebacks and provides anecdotal evidence of how a sale and leaseback transaction may affect a firm's cash flows and financial statements.

Part IV Special Topics

Chapters 20–24 provide a discussion of various considerations concerning capital structure choice. Chapters 20 and 21 focus on the role financial distress and bankruptcy, which is a product of capital structure choice, play on the operations and governance of the firm. Next, Chapter 22 explores the decision to lease and its implications on capital structure. Chapter 23 examines private investments in public equity (PIPE), an increasingly important source of capital for small firms and explains how hedge funds essentially use PIPEs as a means to underwrite securities offerings without following the normal underwriting process. Finally, Chapter 24 discusses how the choice of financing M&As interacts with capital structure decisions and why firms actively adjust their capital structure before and after such transactions.

Chapter 20 Financial Distress and Bankruptcy (Kimberly J. Cornaggia)
Optimal debt levels are limited by expected costs of financial distress and bankruptcy. This chapter reviews a host of methods for gauging financial risk, with attention paid to the increasing use of off-balance-sheet financing. The chapter discusses direct and indirect costs associated with distress including those observed well before any default event. Other topics include the role of economic viability of financially distressed firms and internal and external sources of risk, including those from distressed rivals, customers, and suppliers. The chapter compares the formal bankruptcy process to private workouts and explains key provisions of

the Bankruptcy Code including changes made in 2005. Particular attention is paid to the inherent conflicts of interest among parties to the bankruptcy. Finally, the chapter reviews the literature pertaining to the resolution of financial distress both in and out of bankruptcy court.

Chapter 21 Fiduciary Responsibility and Financial Distress (Remus D. Valsan and Moin A. Yahya)
A legal debate exists regarding the fiduciary duties owed by directors to creditors, especially involving the "vicinity of insolvency." Looking at the issue from a corporate finance perspective and using well-established theorems and results, the chapter shows that creditors can protect themselves. Studies show the extent to which creditors use covenants to protect themselves against opportunistic behavior by managers and shareholders. Debt can also increase the value of the firm and its shares. Therefore, the idea that shareholders use debt for opportunistic behavior is misplaced. Debt can align managerial incentives to maximize the value of the firm. Fiduciary duties should be owed to the corporation as a whole, which is essentially what happens in judicial practice.

Chapter 22 The Leave versus Buy Decision (Sris Chatterjee and An Yan)
Leasing an asset, in contrast to outright ownership, accounts for a large fraction of the market for fixed assets and durable goods. Leasing contracts exhibit many unique and complex features that provide a fertile ground for both theoretical and empirical research. This chapter provides an overview of models that try to explain why leasing can be a valuable financing option for many firms, why certain assets are more amenable to leasing as opposed to purchase, and why leasing has some special contractual features. Models are discussed that are based on taxes, asymmetric information, and incomplete contracts. The chapter also discusses some empirical findings including a review of a comprehensive test of the lease-versus-debt puzzle.

Chapter 23 Private Investment in Public Equity (William K. Sjostrom Jr.)
This chapter examines private investment in public equity (PIPE), an important source of financing for small public companies. The chapter describes common characteristics of PIPE deals, including the types of securities issued and the basic trading strategy employed by hedge funds, which are the most common investors in small company PIPEs. The chapter contends that by investing in a PIPE and promptly selling short the issuer's common stock, a hedge fund is essentially underwriting a follow-on public offering while legally avoiding many of the regulations applicable to underwriters. This regulatory arbitrage enables hedge funds to secure the advantageous terms responsible for the market-beating returns they have garnered from PIPE investments. Additionally, the chapter details securities law compliance issues with respect to PIPE transactions and explores SEC PIPE-related enforcement actions.

Chapter 24 Financing Corporate Mergers and Acquisitions (Wolfgang Bessler, Wolfgang Drobetz, and Jan Zimmermann)
Mergers and acquisitions (M&As) are major corporate investment and financing events that raise some important issues from a financial perspective. These issues

include: (1) the method of payment (i.e., paying with either stock or cash); (2) the financing of the transaction (i.e., using internal funds or issuing new equity or debt); and (3) the interaction between the financing requirements and the firm's long-term target capital structure. This chapter analyzes these financial aspects of M&As and the interactions among them. The crucial factors for the method of payment decision are generally agency problems and particularly transaction risks such as overpayment and ownership considerations. Cash payments are mostly financed with internally generated funds and by issuing new debt, whereas equity payments are mainly associated with equity offerings. Nevertheless, the financing decision may also depend on the bidder's current financial leverage. Consequently, firms often adjust their capital structure before and after an M&A to minimize deviations from their optimal capital structure. The analysis suggests that financing corporate M&As involves a complex system of dependencies and interactions among many factors.

SUMMARY AND CONCLUSIONS

Despite extensive research, financial economists still view capital structure as a puzzle in which all the pieces do not fit perfectly into place. Surveys by Graham and Harvey (2001); Bancel and Mittoo (2004); and Brounen, Dirk, de Jong, and Koedijk (2004, 2006) report gaps between theory and practice involving capital structure decisions. Although understanding in this area is incomplete and questions still remain on how firms should determine their financing mix, much theoretical and empirical evidence is available to provide guidance in unraveling the capital structure puzzle. The following chapters offer a wealth of useful information about the factors that influence capital structure and corporate financing decisions in the real world. Let's now begin our journey into one of the most controversial and highly researched topics in corporate finance.

REFERENCES

Baker, H. Kent, and Gary E. Powell. 2005. *Understanding Financial Management—A Practical Guide*. Malden, MA: Blackwell Publishing.

Baker, Malcolm, and Jeffrey Wurgler. 2002. "Market Timing and Capital Structure." *Journal of Finance* 57:1, 1–32.

Bancel, Franck, and Usha Mittoo. 2004. "Cross-Country Determinants of Capital Structure Choice: A Survey of European Firms." *Financial Management* 33:4, 103–132.

Barclay, Michael J., and Clifford W. Smith Jr. 1999. "The Capital Structure Puzzle: Another Look at the Evidence." *Journal of Applied Corporate Finance* 12:1, 8–20.

Brounen, Dirk, Abe de Jong, and Kees Koedijk. 2004. "Corporate Finance in Europe: Confronting Theory with Practice." *Financial Management* 33:4, 71–101.

Brounen, Dirk, Abe de Jong, and Kees Koedijk. 2006. "Capital Structure Policies in Europe: Survey Evidence." *Journal of Banking & Finance* 30:5, 1409–1442.

Graham, John R., and Campbell R. Harvey. 2001. "The Theory and Practice of Corporate Finance: Evidence from the Field." *Journal of Financial Economics* 60:2, 187–243.

Jensen, Michael C. 2001. "Value Maximization, Stakeholder Theory, and the Corporate Objective Function." *Journal of Applied Corporate Finance* 14:3, 8–21.

Kraus, Alan, and Robert H. Litzenberger. 1973. "A State Preference Model of Optimal Financial Leverage." *Journal of Finance* 38:4, 911–922.

Modigliani, Franco, and Merton H. Miller. 1958. "The Cost of Capital, Corporation Finance and the Theory of Investment." *American Economic Review* 48:3, 261–297.
Myers, Stewart C. 1984. "The Capital Structure Puzzle." *Journal of Finance* 39:3, 575–592.
Myers, Stewart C., and Nicholas S. Majluf. 1984. "Corporate Financing and Investment Decisions When Firms Have Information That Investors Do Not Have." *Journal of Financial Economics* 13:2, 187–222.
Ross, Stephen A. 1977. "The Determination of Financial Structure: The Incentive Signaling Approach." *Bell Journal of Economics* 8:1, 23–40.

ABOUT THE AUTHORS

H. Kent Baker is a University Professor of Finance and Kogod Research Professor in the Kogod School of Business at American University. He has held faculty and administrative positions at Georgetown University and the University of Maryland. Professor Baker has written or edited numerous books of which his most recent include *Survey Research in Corporate Finance: Bridging the Gap between Theory and Practice* (Oxford University Press, 2011), *The Art of Capital Restructuring: Creating Shareholder Value through Mergers and Acquisitions* (John Wiley & Sons, 2011), *Capital Budgeting Valuation: Financial Analysis for Today's Investment Projects* (John Wiley & Sons, 2011), *Behavioral Finance—Investors, Corporations, and Markets* (John Wiley & Sons, 2010), *Corporate Governance: A Synthesis of Theory, Research, and Practice* (John Wiley & Sons, 2010), *Dividends and Dividend Policy* (John Wiley & Sons, 2009), and *Understanding Financial Management: A Practical Guide* (Blackwell, 2005). He has more than 230 publications in academic and practitioner outlets including in the *Journal of Finance*, *Journal of Financial and Quantitative Analysis*, *Financial Management*, *Financial Analysts Journal*, *Journal of Portfolio Management*, and *Harvard Business Review*. Professor Baker ranks among the most prolific authors in finance during the past half century. He has consulting and training experience with more than 100 organizations and has presented more than 750 training and development programs in the United States, Canada, and Europe. Professor Baker holds a BSBA from Georgetown University; MEd, MBA, and DBA degrees from the University of Maryland; and MA, MS, and two PhDs from American University. He also holds both CFA and CMA designations.

Gerald S. Martin is an Associate Professor of Finance in the Kogod School of Business at American University. He previously held faculty positions at the Mays Business School at Texas A&M University. Professor Martin's research focuses on securities regulation and enforcement activities, corporate payout policy, financial distress, and Warren Buffett with articles appearing in the top scholarly journals such as *Journal of Financial Economics* and *Journal of Financial and Quantitative Analysis*. He is often engaged as a consultant to mutual and hedge funds and an expert witness in corporate malfeasance and bankruptcy cases. His research has been featured in the popular press including *BusinessWeek*, *Forbes*, the *New York Times*, the *Wall Street Journal*, and other publications throughout the world. Professor Martin has made numerous personal appearances on CNBC, Bloomberg Television, and National Public Radio. His research has directly affected the way in which damage estimates are calculated in financial fraud class action lawsuits. Before his academic career, he spent 17 years in the private sector as President and CEO of

TMI Aircraft Finance, LLC and TMI Leasing, LLC and as an executive in finance and marketing for Textron Financial Corporation and Bell Helicopter Textron Inc. During his professional career he financed more than a billion dollars in aviation equipment including corporate and commercial fixed-wing aircraft, helicopters, turbine, and piston aircraft engines in more than 40 countries. Professor Martin holds a PhD and MS degrees in finance and MBA and BBA degrees in marketing from Texas A&M University.

PART I

The Elements of Capital Structure

CHAPTER 2

Factors Affecting Capital Structure Decisions

WOLFGANG BESSLER
Professor of Finance, Center for Banking and Finance,
Justus-Liebig-University Giessen

WOLFGANG DROBETZ
Professor of Finance, Institute of Finance, University of Hamburg

ROBIN KAZEMIEH
Research Assistant and PhD Student, Institute of Finance, University of Hamburg

INTRODUCTION

In their seminal papers, Modigliani and Miller (1958) and Miller and Modigliani (1961) provide a new perspective on optimal capital structure and dividend policy. Using arbitrage arguments, they prove that under very restrictive assumptions neither capital structure nor dividend decisions matter. Therefore, such decisions should not have any impact on the market value of a firm. Because financing, capital structure, and dividend decisions do not enhance shareholder value, they are deemed to be irrelevant.

Subsequent work over the last five decades has relaxed several of the restrictive assumptions behind the irrelevance propositions and has introduced capital market frictions into the model, such as taxes, bankruptcy costs, and asymmetric information. Presumably, factors that affect capital structure decisions are related to these types of frictions. The objective of this chapter is to discuss the main factors identified in the literature that lead to deviations from the Modigliani-Miller irrelevance propositions and do affect capital structure decisions.

This chapter begins with a brief review of the three major capital structure theories: (1) the trade-off theory, (2) the pecking order theory, and (3) the market timing theory. Next, the chapter provides a discussion of survey results on capital structure decisions and how they compare to the predictions of these theories. The chapter then takes a more structured approach by defining measures of leverage and factors that are widely believed to impact capital structure decisions. These factors are connected to capital market frictions and the corresponding capital structure theories. The chapter ends with a brief discussion of econometric issues, a presentation of the most important stylized facts from empirical studies, and an illustration of the zero leverage phenomenon.

CAPITAL STRUCTURE THEORIES

Although financial economists widely agree on the notion that capital structure is not irrelevant, there exists no comprehensive model of capital structure that incorporates all empirical observations. All available models can explain but also contradict some of the known stylized facts, with different models having problems with different facts. Two well-known models are the trade-off theory and the pecking order theory. A third group of models, which has gained popularity in the literature recently, incorporates market timing activities. This section provides a brief overview of these models.

Trade-Off Theories

In the static trade-off theory, as originally introduced by Kraus and Litzenberger (1973), firms balance the tax benefits of debt against the deadweight costs of financial distress and bankruptcy. Because firms are allowed to deduct interest paid on debt from their tax liability, they favor debt over equity. The present value of the resulting gains from choosing debt over equity, the so-called tax shield, increases firm value. Without any additional and offsetting cost of debt, this tax advantage would imply full debt financing.

An obvious candidate for an offsetting cost of debt is bankruptcy. In fact, debt increases the risk of financial distress, potentially avoiding a firm's excessive debt financing. The higher a firm's debt ratio, the higher will be the associated probability of bankruptcy. The resulting costs of financial distress can be divided into direct and indirect costs (Haugen and Senbet 1978). Direct costs of bankruptcy are comprised of legal fees, restructuring costs, and credit costs, among others. Indirect costs include losses in customer confidence, declining vendor relationships, and the loss of employees.

Agency costs represent another type of costs that should be weighed against the tax advantage of debt. Jensen and Meckling (1976) argue that managers have an incentive to strive for maximization of equity value instead of total firm value. Managers of debt-financed firms tend to engage in risk-shifting strategies when they have free cash flow available. Specifically, they favor risky projects that benefit shareholders in the case of success but burden losses on bondholders in the case of failure. Rational bond investors are aware of this type of overinvestment problem, and hence they demand a risk premium and consequently a higher interest payment as a compensation for this behavior. These increased costs reduce the attractiveness for firms to issue debt. Myers' (1977) underinvestment hypothesis follows a similar line of reasoning. Managers of highly levered firms have an incentive to forgo positive net present value (NPV) projects as long as the gains from these projects accrue only to the bondholders.

Both the overinvestment and the underinvestment problem are examples for managerial moral hazard, and they tend to be most pronounced for highly leveraged firms that suffer from financial distress. However, debt can also have a moderating impact on agency conflicts. Jensen's (1986) free cash flow hypothesis posits that leverage exerts a disciplining effect. Because managers are forced to generate constant cash flows to meet their firms' debt repayments, the ability to invest in firm value–destroying but equity value–enhancing projects is reduced. In contrast to dividend payments or share repurchases, committed interest payments represent a credible signal to the market that a firm enjoys favorable prospects. Therefore, in order to arrive at optimal financing decisions, managers need to evaluate the agency costs of debt (risk shifting and underinvestment) against the agency costs of equity (free cash flow problem).

Overall, a firm is said to follow the static trade-off theory if its leverage is determined by a single period trade-off between the tax benefits of debt and the deadweight costs of bankruptcy as well as the agency costs of debt and equity. However, the static model only focuses on a single-period decision and does not contain the notion of target adjustment. More specifically, it has a solution for leverage, but there is no room for the firm ever to be anywhere but at this optimum. A natural extension is to consider multiple periods, which leads to dynamic trade-off theories. Although there may be an optimal debt ratio, keeping this ratio constant all the time will prove costly to a firm. Maintaining a fixed leverage ratio requires frequent rebalancing of debt and equity, and hence transaction costs are incurred. Kane, Marcus, and McDonald (1984) and Brennan and Schwartz (1984) were the first to argue that firms will have a debt corridor within which their debt ratio is allowed to float instead of trying to maintain a certain debt ratio. Once its debt ratio crosses the upper or lower bound of this corridor, a firm rebalances its capital structure back to the optimal level. Simulation results in Fischer, Heinkel, and Zechner (1989) indicate that even small transaction costs can lead to a delay in rebalancing and wide variations in debt ratios.

In a dynamic model with frictions, the debt ratio of most firms, most of the time, is therefore likely to deviate from the optimal debt ratio. For example, Welch (2004) and Bessler, Drobetz, and Pensa (2008) document that firm leverage when measured in market terms does not respond to short-run equity fluctuations but only to long-run value changes. Recent theoretical models by Hennessy and Whited (2005), Leary and Roberts (2005), and Strebulaev (2007), among others, incorporate such long-lived effects into dynamic trade-off theories. In these models, different types of adjustment costs lead to somewhat different capital structure dynamics. As a general result, however, the persistent effect of shocks on leverage is more likely due to adjustment costs rather than indifference toward capital structure. This notion of a dynamic trade-off theory has recently been supported empirically in a battery of studies that test target adjustment models (Leary and Roberts 2005; Alti 2006; Flannery and Rangan 2006; Hovakimian 2006; Kayhan and Titman 2007; Huang and Ritter 2009). Overall, while Chang and Dasgupta (2009) question the results from these tests because they lack power to reject alternatives, firms' capital structure policies seem largely consistent with the existence of leverage targets in the long-run. However, the speed of adjustment towards the target debt level is rather slow.

Pecking Order Theory

The pecking order theory, first proposed by Myers and Majluf (1984) and Myers (1984), is based on the notion of asymmetric information between firm insiders and outsiders and the resulting adverse selection problems. Managers will have more information about the true value of a firm's assets and future growth opportunities than outside investors, and hence investors closely observe financing decisions to infer information about a firm's prospects. In contrast to the trade-off theory, the pecking order theory has no predictions about an optimal debt ratio. It rather posits that a firm's capital structure is the result of the firm's financing requirements over time and its attempt to minimize adverse selection costs.

Managers as firm insiders tend to have superior information about the value of the firm, and hence they will be reluctant to issue new equity when they feel that the firm is undervalued because issuing new equity leads to a dilution of the shares of existing shareholders. Put differently, new shareholders would benefit at the expense of old shareholders, who are in turn likely to object to the new issue. The only time that a firm issues equity is when managers feel that it is currently overvalued. By announcing an equity issue, a firm essentially sends a signal to the market that its equity is too expensive, and one indicator for adverse selection costs is the empirically observed drop in share prices on the announcement day. Accordingly, the optimal decision for a firm to satisfy its financing needs is to use internal funds whenever available; such financing avoids all asymmetric information problems. If internal funds are depleted, a firm will next issue debt because the value of debt as a fixed claim is presumably less affected by information asymmetry than equity, which serves as a residual claim. Hybrid securities, such as junior debt or convertible debt, are the next source of financing, while equity only serves as the very last financing alternative.

The pecking order theory ranks financing sources according to the degree they are affected by information asymmetry, where internal funds exhibit the lowest and equity the highest adverse selection costs. The strict interpretation suggests that after the initial public offering (IPO), a firm should never issue equity unless debt financing has become infeasible. This leads to the concept of a debt capacity, which serves to limit the amount of debt within the pecking order and to allow for the use of equity (Shumway, 2001; Lemmon and Zender 2010). While no agreed-upon definition of debt capacity is available in the literature, the notion of a sufficiently high debt ratio that prevents further debt issues could explain the observation that firms issue too much equity (Frank and Goyal 2003) and at the wrong time (Fama and French 2005). Closely related to these observations is the time-varying adverse selection explanation of firms' financing choices, which is a dynamic analog of the pecking order theory. In fact, a less strict interpretation of the pecking order theory suggests that firms tend to issue equity when stock prices are high and when a high stock price coincides with low adverse selection costs (Lucas and McDonald 1990; Korajczyk, Lucas, and McDonald 1992). Recent empirical studies support this notion and document that temporarily low information asymmetry increases the probability of an equity issue (Bharat, Pasquariello, and Wu 2008; Autore and Kovacs 2010; Bessler, Drobetz, and Grüninger 2010).

Market Timing Theory

Baker and Wurgler (2002) document that market timing efforts—that is, issuing equity when the stock market is perceived to be more favorable and market-to-book (M/B) ratios are relatively high—have a persistent impact on corporate capital structures. They argue that neither the trade-off theory nor the pecking order theory is consistent with the persistent negative effect of a weighted average of a firm's past M/B ratios on firm leverage. Instead, the authors suggest that firms time their equity issues to stock market conditions. The capital structure changes induced by these equity issues persist because firms do not readjust their debt ratios towards the target afterwards. They contend an ad hoc theory of the capital structure, where the observed capital structure is not the result of a dynamic optimization strategy but merely reflects the cumulative outcome of past attempts to time the equity market.

Empirical studies document that market timing plays an important role in shaping financing activity and exacerbates the deviations from leverage targets in the short-run (Leary and Roberts 2005; Alti 2006; Kayhan and Titman 2007). Moreover, these studies indicate that deviations do reverse, suggesting that the trade-offs underlying the target have non-negligible effects on firm value. Overall, these findings support a modified version of the dynamic trade-off theory of the capital structure that includes market timing as a short-term factor. An alternative explanation presumes that firms with a repeated history of raising capital at high M/B ratios are likely to be growth firms. The improvement in growth prospects lowers the target debt ratio (e.g., due to higher costs of financial distress), and an equity issuance is the rational response of firms to move towards the new leverage target (Hovakimian 2006).

SURVEY EVIDENCE

One methodology to analyze whether aspects of corporate decisions are consistent with capital structure theory is to conduct surveys among financial decision makers. For example, Graham and Harvey (2001) survey more than 4,000 chief financial officers (CFOs) of U.S. firms, asking them about their financing decisions. Of the 392 CFOs who completed the survey, the majority makes capital structure decisions based on practical informal rules. On a very aggregate level, more than 80 percent of the surveyed managers indicate that they pursue some sort of flexible target debt ratio. Only 18 percent of the CFOs claim that they do not have a target debt ratio. By contrast, about 10 percent state that their firm follows a strict target debt ratio. These responses suggest that the majority of firms have flexible or somewhat tight leverage targets, providing support for some version of a dynamic trade-off theory.

Graham and Harvey (2001) further ask managers about the factors that affect the decision to issue debt. The most dominant factor is maintaining financial flexibility, which can be interpreted as preserving unused debt capacity or a target credit rating. Almost 60 percent of the respondents view financial flexibility as important or very important. Although this result seems to support the pecking order theory, responses are unrelated to the severity of information asymmetry. Specifically, CFOs of large firms and firms with high dividend payments view financial flexibility to be more important than CFOs of smaller firms and firms with low dividend payments, which is at odds with the predictions of the pecking order theory.

The second most important factor that affects the decision to issue debt is a firm's credit rating. If credit rating is viewed as a proxy for potential financial distress costs, this result can be viewed as support for the trade-off theory. Nevertheless, when asked directly about the influence bankruptcy costs and costs of financial distress have on their decision-making process, only 20 percent of the managers consider this factor as important. As expected, earnings and cash flow volatility is another relevant factor for firm's debt issues. High cash flow volatility leads to high potential costs of financial distress, and both the trade-off and the pecking order theories predict a negative relationship between volatility and leverage. Other responses support either one of the theories. For example, while the importance of insufficient internal funds for the decision to issue debt supports the pecking order theory, the relatively high number of respondents who perceive the corporate tax advantage of debt as important is in line with the predictions of the trade-off theory. Less important factors for debt issuances according to survey respondents are transaction costs, equity under- or overvaluation, industry debt levels, and customer/supplier comfort.

Another noteworthy result is that few respondents claim to time their debt issues in order to take advantage of expected changes in their credit rating, although they might reasonably have private information about their creditworthiness. In contrast, many CFOs respond that they time interest rates by issuing debt when they feel the level of market interest rates is particularly low. Assuming that interest rate parity relationships hold, this belief may simply be an illusion or the result from overconfidence in market timing abilities. Therefore, the success of interest rate timing, as empirically documented by Baker, Greenwood, and Wurgler (2003) and Henderson, Jegadeesh, and Weisbach (2006), is clearly surprising given that market interest rates constitute public information in presumably efficient capital markets.

Another question in Graham and Harvey's (2001) survey addresses the factors that affect the issuance of common stock. The two most important factors are earnings per share (EPS) dilution and equity under- or overvaluation; 69 percent and 67 percent of the respondents consider these factors as important or very important, respectively. The academic view is that earnings dilution will not affect the value of the firm and hence should not deter firms from issuing equity if two conditions are met: (1) the firm is fairly valued (based on management's view of the current prospects) at the time of the offering; and (2) the firm expects to earn the minimum required rate of return on the fresh equity raised. But if the stock is undervalued, then there is a "real" (rather than just an "accounting") dilution of value. Therefore, the importance of equity under- or overvaluation is consistent with the pecking order theory.

In fact, the pecking order is based on the premise that managers avoid issuing securities, particularly equity, when the firm is undervalued. Both the empirically observed negative market reaction upon announcement of an equity issue and undervaluation will cause a dilution of value. At the same time, managers also engage in market timing; a recent stock price increase, potentially resulting in overvaluation and providing windows of opportunity, is an important or very important driver of the equity-issuing decision for 63 percent of the responding CFOs. On the one hand, the focus on EPS may suggest that respondents focus too much on accounting and too little on economic value. On the other hand, managers may have difficulty separating accounting from real dilution, and the concern with EPS dilution is also a concern about issuing undervalued equity.

More than 50 percent of the CFOs claim that maintaining a target debt-to-equity ratio plays an important or very important role in their decision to issue equity. This finding again supports the trade-off theory, which predicts that firms pursue a target debt ratio. As expected, another important factor for an equity issue seems to be the existence of employee stock option plans.

Graham and Harvey's (2001) survey results are based on the answers from U.S. financial decision makers. Hence, whether their findings can be generalized for other countries with different financial systems is unclear ex ante. Survey studies from countries outside the United States document that corporate finance practices appear to be influenced mostly by firm size and to a lesser extent by shareholder orientation, while national differences are weak at best (Brounen, de Jong, and Koedijk 2004; Drobetz, Pensa, and Wöhle 2006).

A MORE STRUCTURED APPROACH: DEFINING CAPITAL STRUCTURE FACTORS

Having discussed what managers think (or, at least, say) is important for a firm's capital structure, the chapter now takes a more structured approach to identify factors that affect capital structure decisions. Specifically, this section introduces factors that are capable of explaining the cross-sectional and time-series variation in firms' leverage ratios. According to the early work by Harris and Raviv (1991), the consensus is that leverage increases with fixed assets, nondebt tax shields, investment opportunities, and firm size, and it decreases with volatility, advertising expenditure, the probability of bankruptcy, profitability, and uniqueness of the product. Observable leverage factors should be related to capital structure theories because they are assumed to proxy for the underlying forces that drive these theories, such as the costs of financial distress and information asymmetry. However, the expected sign of the relationship is not always unambiguous, and hence sorting out the factors that are reliably signed and economically important for predicting leverage is important. For the sake of brevity, the following discussion focuses only on factors that are frequently used in empirical capital structure research. Most of these factors are part of what Frank and Goyal (2009) call the "core model of leverage." Exhibit 2.1 provides a summary of central predictions of the trade-off theory and the pecking order theory regarding the relationship between leverage and selected capital structure factors.

Exhibit 2.1 Central Predictions of Capital Structure Theories

Factor	Trade-Off Theory	Pecking Order Theory
Tangibility	+	–
Firm size	+	–
Growth opportunities	–	+/–
Profitability	+	–
Volatility	–	–

Note: This exhibit summarizes the relationship between the leverage ratio and selected capital structure factors according to the two major capital structure theories, the trade-off theory and the pecking order theory.

Tangibility of Assets

The tangibility of assets can be interpreted as a measure for the level of collateral a firm can offer to its debtors. A high ratio of fixed-to-total assets provides debtors with a high level of security since they can liquidate assets in case of bankruptcy. In contrast, a low ratio of fixed-to-total assets leaves little collateral (assets) for debtors in case of bankruptcy.

While tangibility makes debt less risky, its influence on a firm's capital structure is not unambiguous. Galai and Masulis (1976) and Jensen and Meckling (1976) argue that stockholders of levered firms are prone to overinvest, which can lead to the classical shareholder-bondholder conflict. However, if debt can be secured against existing assets, creditors have an improved guarantee of repayment, and the recovery rate will be higher. Therefore, in the trade-off theory, the lower expected costs of distress and fewer debt-related agency problems predict a positive relationship between the proportion of tangible assets and leverage.

In contrast, Grossman and Hart (1982) argue that agency costs of managers consuming more than the optimal level of perquisites are higher for firms with lower levels of assets that can be used as collateral. Managers of highly levered firms will be less able to consume excessive perquisites because bondholders will more closely monitor such firms. Moreover, the low information asymmetry associated with tangible assets makes equity issuances less costly (Harris and Raviv 1991). The monitoring costs are generally higher for firms with less collateralizable assets, and hence they might voluntarily choose higher debt levels to limit consumption of perquisites. This notion implies a negative relationship between tangibility of assets and leverage under the pecking order theory.

Tangibility of assets can be measured using a variety of proxy variables. Examples include the ratio of net property, plant, and equipment to total assets; the ratio of research and development (R&D) expenses to sales; and the ratio of selling, general and administration expenses to sales.

Firm Size

The effect of size on leverage is also ambiguous. On the one hand, Titman and Wessels (1988) argue that large firms tend to be more diversified and fail less often. Moreover, since bankruptcy costs consist of a fixed part and a variable part, they tend to be relatively higher for smaller firms (Warner 1977; Ang, Chua, and McConnell 1982). Accordingly, the trade-off theory predicts an inverse relationship between size and the probability of bankruptcy, and hence a positive relationship between size and leverage.

On the other hand, size can be regarded as a proxy for information asymmetry between firm insiders and capital markets. For example, large firms are more closely observed by analysts, and hence they should be more capable of issuing informationally sensitive equity. Accordingly, the pecking order theory predicts a negative relationship between leverage and size, with larger firms exhibiting increasing preference for equity relative to debt.

Firm size is usually measured as the logarithm of total assets or sales. Alternatively, size can be captured by a dummy variable that takes a value of one if the firm has been listed on the Compustat database for more than five years, and zero otherwise.

Growth Opportunities

Jensen and Meckling (1976) and Myers (1977) suggest that managers of levered firms have an incentive to engage in asset substitution and underinvestment. The debt-related agency costs are higher for firms with substantial growth opportunities. Accordingly, the trade-off theory predicts that firms with more investment opportunities have less leverage because they have stronger incentives to avoid underinvestment and asset substitution that can arise from stockholder-bondholder agency conflicts. This notion is further supported by Jensen's (1986) free cash flow theory, which predicts that firms with more investment opportunities have less need for the disciplining effect of debt payments to prevent managerial squandering.

The predictions of the pecking order are not clear-cut. In its simplest form, it suggests a positive relationship between leverage and growth opportunities. Debt typically grows when investment exceeds retained earnings and falls when investment is less than retained earnings. Therefore, given profitability, book leverage is predicted to be higher for firms with more investment opportunities. However, in a more complex version of the pecking order theory, managers are concerned with future as well as current financing costs. Balancing current and future costs, firms with large expected growth opportunities can possibly maintain a low-risk debt capacity in order to avoid financing future investments with new equity offerings (or even forgoing profitable investments). Therefore, a more complex version of the pecking order theory posits that firms with larger expected investments exhibit less current leverage.

In most instances, growth opportunities are measured using the M/B ratio. Alternatively, the change in the logarithm of total assets or the ratio of capital expenditures to assets can be used to capture the growth potential.

Profitability

According to the trade-off theory, bankruptcy costs, taxes, and agency costs push more profitable firms towards higher leverage. First, expected bankruptcy costs decline when profitability increases. Second, the deductibility of interest payments for tax purposes induces more profitable firms to finance with debt. Finally, in the agency models of Jensen and Meckling (1976), Easterbrook (1984), and Jensen (1986), higher leverage helps to control agency problems by forcing managers to pay out more of the firm's excess cash. The strong commitment to use a larger fraction of pre-interest earnings for debt payments suggests a positive relationship between book leverage and profitability. This notion is also consistent with signaling models of the capital structure, where managers can use higher levels of debt to signal an optimistic future for the firm (Ross 1977).

In sharp contrast, the pecking order model predicts that higher earnings should result in less leverage. Firms prefer raising capital initially from retained earnings, then from debt, and finally from issuing new equity. This hierarchy of financing choices is due to the adverse selection costs associated with new equity issues in the presence of information asymmetries. In this case, debt grows when investment exceeds retained earnings and falls when investment is less then retained earnings. Accordingly, a negative relationship between leverage and profitability would be a strong support for the pecking order theory.

Two measures for profitability are frequently used in the literature: the return on assets and the gross margin. The return on assets is computed as the ratio of operating income before depreciation to assets, and the gross margin is defined as the ratio of operating income to sales.

Volatility

Firms with volatile cash flows (mostly approximated by the standard deviation of stock returns) experience higher expected costs of financial distress, and the debt-related agency costs are also more pronounced with increasing volatility. Additionally, more volatile cash flows reduce the probability that the tax shield will be fully utilized. Therefore, the trade-off theory implies a negative relationship between leverage and the volatility of cash flows.

The pecking order theory allows for the same prediction. According to De Angelo and Masulis (1980), investors have little ability to accurately forecast future earnings based on publicly available information for firms with high earnings volatility. The market will view these firms as "lemons" and demand a premium to provide debt. Moreover, in order to reduce the necessity of issuing new equity or else being unable to realize profitable investments when cash flows are low, firms with more volatile cash flows maintain low leverage. Accordingly, the pecking order model also predicts a negative relationship between leverage and cash flow volatility.

Industry Classification

Industry effects are important factors for capital structure decisions either because managers use industry median leverage as a benchmark for their own firm's leverage or because industry effects reflect a set of correlated but otherwise omitted factors. For example, Harris and Raviv (1991, p. 333) suggest that a firm's industrial classification is an important determinant of leverage and report "... that drugs, instruments, electronics, and food have consistently low leverage while paper, textile mill products, steel, airlines, and cement have consistently high leverage." Regulation is another factor that impacts capital structure decisions; regulated firms tend to have more stable cash flows and lower expected costs of financial distress. While this notion justifies higher leverage for firms in regulated industries, the trade-off theory nevertheless offers ambiguous predictions. In fact, managers have less discretion in regulated industries, reducing agency problems and the need for debt as a disciplinary device. As Frank and Goyal (2009) contend, in a pecking order world, industry classification should only impact capital structure choices if it serves as a proxy for a firm's financing deficit, and hence no general predictions can be inferred. Empirical studies usually exclude financial institutions and utilities from the sample because these industries are subject to specific rules and regulations, and hence exogenous factors unrelated to direct financing activities severely affect their leverage.

Tax Considerations

Firms will exploit the tax deductibility of interest payments to reduce their tax payments, and hence the trade-off theory predicts that firms tend to issue more debt when corporate tax rates are higher. However, firms with other tax shields, such as net operating loss carry-forwards, depreciation expenses, and investment tax credits, have less need to exploit the debt tax shield. Ross (1985) argues that if such firms issue excessive debt, they may become "tax-exhausted" in the sense that they are unable to use all their potential tax shields. Debt is then "crowded out," and the incentive to use debt financing diminishes as nondebt tax shields increase. Accordingly, in the framework of the trade-off theory, one would expect a negative relationship between leverage and nondebt tax shields. In contrast, Scott (1977) and Moore (1986) argue that firms with substantial nondebt tax shields should also have considerable collateral assets that can be used to secure debt. Secured debt is less risky than unsecured debt, and hence one could also hypothesize a positive relationship between leverage and nondebt tax shields.

The impact of taxes on leverage can be measured using different variables. Examples are the top statutory tax rate, the ratio of the net operating loss carry-forward to assets, the ratio of depreciation expense, and the ratio of investment tax credits to assets.

Debt Rating

Faulkender and Petersen (2006) and Lemmon and Zender (2010) suggest that firms issue less debt and finance themselves through equity issues when their access to debt markets is restricted. On the one hand, one would expect that firms with an investment-grade credit rating have easier access to debt markets than firms without such a rating, and hence these firms exhibit higher leverage. On the other hand, having a credit rating implies that a firm faces a lower degree of information asymmetry. Accordingly, the pecking order theory predicts that firms with a credit rating will use less debt and more equity. As a support for the general notion that credit ratings affect financing decisions, Kisgen (2009) documents that firms issue significantly less debt when they are close to rating changes. However, studies related to credit ratings generally suffer from measurement problems, split ratings, and reverse causality.

Debt Market Conditions

Taggart (1985) argues that high expected inflation increases the real value of tax deductions. Therefore, higher expected inflation should lead to higher leverage in the trade-off theory. The positive relationship between expected inflation and leverage can also be the result of debt market timing: managers attempt to issue debt when expected inflation is high relative to current interest rates. Supporting this notion of debt market timing, Barry, Mann, Mihov, and Rodríguez (2008) provide evidence that firms issue more debt when the current level of interest rates is low relative to historical levels. Henderson, Jegadeesh, and Weisbach (2006) also document that firms issue more long-term debt when interest rates are lower, and they time their long-term debt issues prior to future increases in interest rates.

Moreover, firms issue debt overseas when interest rates in the place of issue are lower than they are at home.

Stock Market Conditions

Welch (2004) documents that firms do not rebalance changes in the market value of equity induced by stock returns. He suggests that stock returns are the primary determinant of capital structure changes; in fact, stock returns seem even more important than all other factors, at least in the short-run. The market timing theory predicts that managers will not respond passively to counterbalance market-driven valuation effects but instead will pursue an active financing strategy and exploit "windows of opportunities" by issuing equity after stock price run-ups (Bessler, Drobetz, and Pensa 2008). Closely related is the observation that firms buying back their own shares experience the highest positive long-run excess return if the repurchase is triggered by a severe share price decline (Peyer and Vermaelen 2008).

A negative relationship between stock prices and leverage is also consistent with the time-varying adverse selection hypothesis, which is the dynamic analog to the pecking order theory. According to this hypothesis, firms tend to issue equity when stock prices are high and when a high stock price coincides with low adverse selection. If the degree of information asymmetry is time-varying, the magnitude of the resulting adverse selection costs is to some extent under the control of the firm, and hence the firm will issue equity when it expects relatively little information asymmetry and low adverse selection costs. Presumably, a price run-up will be associated with reduced information asymmetry since the gradual resolution of information asymmetry may trigger the run-up (Lucas and McDonald 1990). Another related prediction is that firms tend to announce equity issues after information releases, even if this implies costly delays of issues (Dierkens 1991; Korajczyk, Lucas, and McDonald 1991, 1992).

The observation that strong stock market performance results in a reduction of market leverage is a purely mechanical effect. Both the market timing theory and the time-varying adverse selection hypothesis predict that firms will issue equity subsequent to a price run-up, reducing market leverage even further. While firms exploit mispricing according to the market timing theory (Baker and Wurgler 2002), they take advantage of temporary low information asymmetry (e.g., as measured by low dispersion in analysts' EPS forecasts) in the dynamic version of the pecking order theory (Autore and Kovacs 2010; Bessler, Drobetz, and Grüninger. 2010). In contrast, the trade-off theory predicts that a low market debt ratio will encourage managers to issue debt in order to rebalance their firms' capital structure, which leads to increasing debt ratios following high stock returns.

Macroeconomic Conditions

Gertler and Gilchrist (1993) document that aggregate net debt issues of large firms (but not small firms) increase subsequent to recessions induced by monetary contractions. The likelihood of bankruptcy decreases, taxable income increases, and the value of collaterals also increases during expansions, all making a firm's debt less risky and leverage pro-cyclical.

In contrast, Frank and Goyal (2009) argue that agency problems are more pronounced during recessions. Therefore, if debt disciplines managers, leverage should be counter-cyclical. The pecking order theory also predicts a negative relationship between leverage and economic growth. Internal funds increase during economic booms, making firms less dependent on external debt. Finally, consistent with the notion of time-varying adverse selection, equity issues cluster when economic prospects are good (as measured by standard business cycle variables, such as the term spread and the default spread), and information asymmetry is temporarily low (Choe, Masulis, and Nanda 1993; Korajczyk and Levy 2003). Accordingly, leverage should again be counter-cyclical.

In the dynamic trade-off theory, firms adjust their debt ratio towards the target debt ratio if shocks have led to deviations from the optimum. The speed of adjustment is also dependent on macroeconomic conditions. For example, Drobetz and Wanzenried (2006) and Cook and Tang (2010) document that adjustment speed is higher when economic prospects are good. Hackbarth, Miao, and Morellec (2006) provide an overview of theoretical work in this area.

EMPIRICAL ISSUES

Having established the most important factors that are likely to explain capital structure decisions and the variation in leverage ratios, attention now focuses on how to define and measure leverage. In fact, there is no consensus on the meaning of "textbook debt" and "textbook equity." Empirical research contains many different empirical definitions of leverage. Another important issue is the choice of book or market leverage. This section starts with a discussion of these questions followed by highlighting some basic methodological issues, before presenting the most important "stylized facts" from empirical tests that relate leverage to the capital structure factors. The section ends with a brief discussion of the zero leverage phenomenon.

How to Measure Leverage?

Any empirical capital structure test needs to define what exactly is meant by *leverage*. There are many different forms of debt, equity, and mixtures of the two, and hence the appropriate definition of what debt-to-equity ratio should be used in empirical research is not obvious. For example, Rajan and Zingales (1995) use four different measures of leverage. The first and broadest definition of leverage is the ratio of total (non-equity) liabilities to total assets. This measure can be viewed as a proxy of what is left for shareholders in case of liquidation. However, it does not provide a good indication of whether the firm is at risk of default in the near future. Since total liabilities also include items such as accounts payable, which are used for transaction purposes rather than for financing, it is likely to overstate the amount of leverage. Moreover, this leverage proxy is potentially affected by provisions and reserves, such as pension liabilities.

A second definition of leverage is the ratio of short- and long-term debt to total assets. This measure of leverage only covers debt in a narrower sense (i.e., interest-bearing debt) and excludes provisions. However, it does not incorporate the fact that some assets are offset by specific nondebt liabilities. For example, an increase in the gross amount of trade credit leads to a reduction in this leverage proxy.

Because the levels of accounts payable and accounts receivable differ across industries, a third definition of leverage is the ratio of debt to net assets, where net assets are total assets less accounts payable and other current liabilities. This measure is unaffected by non-interest-bearing debt and working capital management. However, it is influenced by other factors that have nothing to do with financing. For example, assets held against pension liabilities may decrease this measure of leverage.

A fourth definition of leverage is the ratio of total debt to capital, where capital is defined as total debt plus equity. This measure of leverage looks at the "capital employed," and hence it best represents the effects of past financing decisions. Moreover, it most directly relates to the agency problems associated with debt.

Using Book Values versus Market Values

Another key question in empirical capital structure research is whether to use book leverage (debt divided by total assets) or market leverage (book debt divided by the sum of book debt plus the market value of equity). Myers (1977) argues that managers focus on book leverage because debt is better supported by assets in place than by growth opportunities. In addition, Klock and Thies (1992) and Fama and French (2002) claim that book values better reflect a firm's target debt ratio because the market value of equity strongly fluctuates and is dependent on a number of factors that are out of a firm's direct control. The survey results in Graham and Harvey (2001) also support the notion that market values may not reflect the underlying alterations initiated by managers, and hence market leverage numbers may be an unreliable guide to corporate financial policy.

Nevertheless, using book value-based measures of leverage involves some important caveats. First, the book value of equity is determined through the difference between the left-hand and the right-hand side of the balance sheet and cannot represent a firm's economic conditions appropriately. Being a mere "plug-number," as Welch (2004) refers to the book value of equity, it can even become negative. He argues that interest coverage ratios are more appropriate to measure the advantages of debt to firms. Second, international accounting rules imply that book values of equity grow with cash flows and shrink with depreciation. Therefore, the fact that profitability and asset tangibility are strong predictors of book value-based debt ratios should not be surprising (Shyam-Sunder and Myers 1999). Third, book value-based measures of leverage are less volatile than market value-based measures and tend to overstate the importance of corporate issuing activities. After all, new securities are issued at market values and not at book values. The book measure is backward looking, and it measures what has taken place. Markets are generally assumed to be forward looking. Finally, market-based debt ratios describe the relative ownership of the firm by creditors and equity holders, and hence they are an indispensable input to compute the weighted average cost of capital (WACC).

Exhibits 2.2 and 2.3 present average book and market leverage ratios, respectively, of selected countries over time. Leverage is defined as the ratio of total debt to capital. One immediate observation is that leverage ratios tend to be higher in

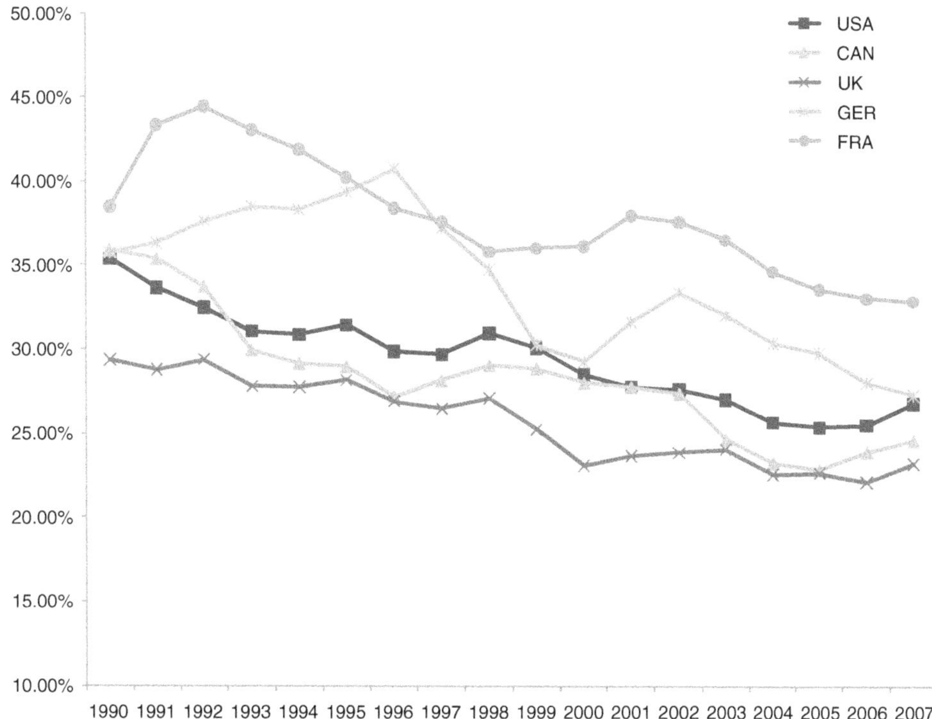

Exhibit 2.2 Book Leverage Ratios for Different Countries
Note: This figure plots the development of mean book leverage ratios for the United States (US), Canada (CAN), the United Kingdom (UK), Germany (GER), and France (FRA) based on their coverage in the Compustat Global database. The sample consists of 5,267 (USA), 874 (CAN), 2,586 (UK), 881 (GER), and 926 (FRA) firms. The leverage ratio is computed as the ratio between total debt and capital.

bank-based financial systems (such as Germany and France) compared to market-based financial systems (such as the Anglo-Saxon countries). Rajan and Zingales (1995) provide a more detailed analysis of cross-country differences in leverage ratios.

The choice between book or market leverage remains an unsettled issue. Flannery and Rangan (2006) note that the results in several recent capital structure studies are robust across different definitions of book and market leverage. The international data in Exhibits 2.2 and 2.3 also seem to support Bowman's (1980) earlier notion that a strong correlation exists between market and book value based leverage measures. In contrast, Frank and Goyal (2009) report that the main capital structure factors are not always robust to the choice of book or market leverage.

Methodological Issues

In order to examine the relationship between leverage and standard capital structure factors, the simplest empirical test runs a regression of the leverage ratio (dependent variable) on a set of capital structure factors (explanatory variables). For example, using firm-level data from the G-7 countries, Rajan and Zingales (1995)

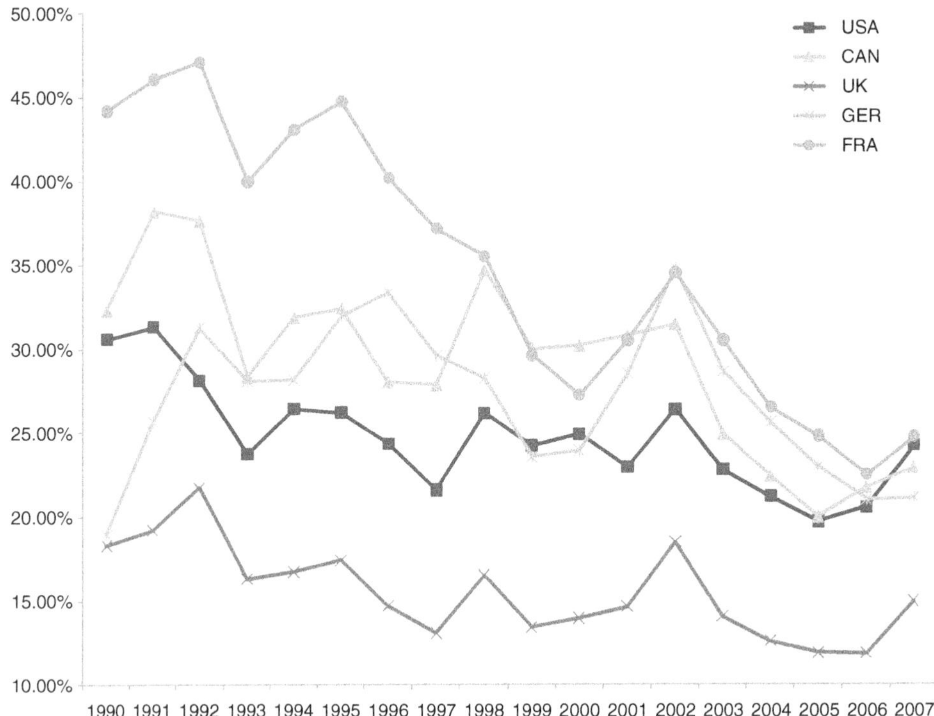

Exhibit 2.3 Market Leverage Ratios for Different Countries

Note: This figure plots the development of mean market leverage ratios for the United States (US), Canada (CAN), the United Kingdom (UK), Germany (GER), and France (FRA) based on their coverage in the Compustat Global database. The sample consists of 5,267 (USA), 874 (CAN), 2,586 (UK), 881 (GER), and 926 (FRA) firms. The leverage ratio is computed as the ratio between total debt and capital.

estimate the following cross-sectional ordinary least square (OLS) regression with four of the previously discussed factors as explanatory variables:

$$\text{Leverage (firm } i) = \alpha + \beta_1 \times \text{Tangible assets}_i + \beta_2 \times \text{Market-to-book ratio}_i + \beta_3 \times \log(\text{Sales}_i) + \beta_4 \times \text{Return on assets}_i + \varepsilon_i \quad (2.1)$$

where the left-hand side variable is leverage of firm i in a given year. All explanatory variables are past years' averages of the corresponding variables. The cross-sectional model in Equation 2.1 explains differences across firms along the four capital structure factors (tangibility, growth opportunities, size, and profitability). The interpretation of the signs of the estimated coefficients (betas) is straightforward: A positive (negative) sign indicates a positive (negative) relationship between leverage and the respective factor. Therefore, the signs of the relationships offer insight about the validity of the different theories of capital structure, as summarized in Exhibit 2.1.

While this simple specification of the relationship between leverage and capital structure factors is easy to estimate and interpret, it has several major drawbacks. Most important, factors are assumed to be exogenous but are often actually endogenous. A regressor variable is said to be endogenous if it is correlated with the error term of the data generating process. Börsch-Supan and Köke (2002) provide a detailed description of how endogeneity problems can arise from reverse causality (where the direction of causality is unclear), sample selectivity, omitted variables, or measurement errors of explanatory variables. The consequence of endogeneity is that OLS will be biased and inconsistent, which in turn implies that both the point estimates of the coefficients and inferences will be invalid.

To some extent, the endogeneity problem in Equation 2.1 is alleviated because in Rajan and Zingales (1995) the explanatory variables are taken as past years' averages of the factors. However, a more appropriate approach to tackle this problem is to use panel data. A panel data set contains repeated observations for the same firms, collected over a number of periods. The availability of repeated observations on the same firms allows estimating more realistic models than a single cross-section can do. Most important, panel data make analyzing changes in leverage on a firm-level over time possible. They are not only suitable to explain why individual firms choose different leverage ratios but also to model why a given firm has different leverage ratios at different points in time. Moreover, if the omitted variables are time invariant, a simple fixed-effects panel estimator delivers robust results. Endogeneity problems can also be addressed because panel data provide instruments (lagged variables) that are unavailable in cross-sectional data. For all these reasons, a standard approach in the empirical literature is to work with panel data.

Stylized Facts

Empirical corporate finance research has produced numerous studies attempting to identify the factors that drive the capital structures of firms. Since these studies differ greatly in terms of variable definition, sample selection, sample size, sample period, and the econometric methodology, an exhaustive account of all nuances is beyond the scope of this chapter. Exhibit 2.4 provides a summary of the results of selected previous empirical studies. Most recently, Frank and Goyal (2009) identify six major factors that are the driving forces behind capital structure decisions. Accordingly, six stylized facts emerge from their "core model of leverage":

1. *Firms with high growth opportunities tend to have low levels of leverage.* This finding supports the trade-off theory, as growth opportunities lead to an increase in the costs of financial distress that can offset the tax benefits of debt. The free cash flow theory also predicts that firms with more growth potential have less need for the disciplining effect of debt payments to prevent managerial squandering.
2. *Firms with considerable tangible assets tend to have high levels of leverage.* Again, the trade-off theory predicts this observation; having collateralizable assets makes a firm less likely to default and reduces the expected costs of bankruptcy. Since these costs offset the tax benefits of debt, their reduction leads to an increase in leverage.
3. *Large firms tend to have high levels of leverage.* This finding again supports the trade-off theory. Large firms are usually more diversified, making them less

Exhibit 2.4 Results from Selected Empirical Studies

	Frank and Goyal (2009)	Kayhan and Titman (2007)	Fan, Titman, and Twite (2003)	Goyal, Lehn, and Racic (2002)	Shyam-Sunder and Myers (1999)	Rajan and Zingales (1995)	Jensen, Solberg, and Zorn (1992)	Titman and Wessel (1988)	Kim and Sorensen (1986)
Size	+	+	+	+		+		–	
Growth opportunities	–	–	–	–		–			–
Profitability	–	–	–	–	–	–	+	–	
Tangibility	+	+	+	–	+	+	+		
Volatility					–		–		+
Taxes			–						–

Note: This exhibit reports the signs of the estimated sensitivity coefficients in selected empirical studies that regress the leverage ratio on different sets of capital structure factors. Only factors found to be significant in more than one previous empirical study are reported. Empty cells mean that the factor was either not tested or found to be insignificant.

likely to default. The offsetting costs of the tax advantage are low, and hence firms can make more extensive use of their tax shield.

4. *Profitable firms tend to have less leverage.* This finding provides strong evidence for the pecking order theory. The theory predicts that firms use internally generated funds initially to finance positive NPV projects. Accordingly, more profitable firms need less debt.
5. *When expected inflation is high, firms tend to have high levels of leverage.* This finding supports the trade-off theory, as the real value of the tax shield is positively related to inflation. This positive effect of inflation on leverage can also be explained by market timing. Since the real value of debt decreases with inflation, managers have an incentive to issue debt when expected inflation is high.
6. *Firms that belong to industries in which the median leverage ratio is high tend to have higher leverage.* One explanation for this finding is that managers use industry median leverage ratios as target ratios for their own firms. Hovakimian, Opler, and Titman (2001) also report that firms actively adjust their leverage ratios towards the industry average. Another explanation is that industry classification proxies for a set of omitted factors. For example, firms from the same industry could face similarly structured vendor relationships, which make them more or less dependent on debt.

The Zero Leverage Phenomenon

Recently, another empirical finding has gained attention in the capital structure literature. Specifically, the capital structures of many firms contain no debt and thus are fully equity-financed. All existing capital structure theories have trouble accounting for this observed phenomenon. Even more puzzling, the number of zero leverage firms is increasing. For example, Devos, Dhillon, Jagannathan, and Krishnamurthy (2008) report the percentage of U.S. firms pursuing a zero-leverage strategy increased from 8 percent in 1990 to 20 percent in 2004. Bessler, Drobetz, Haller, and Meier (2010) document that this development is also an international trend.

Minton and Wruck (2001) were the first to focus on low-leverage firms, meaning firms with less than 20 percent of debt. They argue that firms issuing no or only little debt are following some sort of pecking order. These firms often generate high cash flows or sit on large cash reserves. Most of the firms exhibiting a low leverage ratio do not consider it a long-term strategy. Minton and Wruck (2001) document that 70 percent of the firms following a conservative debt policy dismiss it over the years; half of them do so within five years. While the decision to pursue little debt is not specific to a certain industry, firms with low book-to-market ratios and firms operating in industries with high bankruptcy risks are more likely to have extremely low levels of leverage. Strebulaev and Yang (2006) focus on firms that have no external debt. They find that more than a quarter of the firms following a zero-leverage strategy keep their zero leverage ratio for at least five consecutive years, indicating a deliberate decision for conservative financing. Moreover, zero-leverage firms tend to be smaller than their industry peers, pay more dividends, and are significantly more profitable.

As elaborated in Strebulaev and Yang (2006), neither the trade-off theory nor the pecking order theory is capable of explaining the zero leverage phenomenon. Devos, Dhillon, Jagannathan, and Krishnamurthy (2008) contend that taxes, financial flexibility, or managerial entrenchment could account for the observed phenomenon. While the authors dismiss taxes and managerial entrenchment, they find empirical evidence for the hypothesis that firms pursue a zero-leverage strategy to maintain their financial flexibility. Moreover, a strong link exists between issuing debt and investment opportunities; zero leverage firms tend to raise debt in order to finance investments. Nevertheless, an open research question is why and when firms initiate and abandon a zero leverage policy.

SUMMARY AND CONCLUSIONS

Even 50 years after Modigliani and Miller's (1958) path-breaking analysis, corporate finance still lacks a unifying capital structure theory. However, the existing theories serve as analytical tools to dissect the empirical findings, but none is capable of explaining all aspects of capital structure choice. While each theory can successfully account for some of the stylized facts, it has trouble with some of the others. The current state of the literature suggests that the most reliable factors for explaining corporate leverage are market-to-book ratio (–), tangibility (+), profitability (–), firm size (+), expected inflation (+), and median industry leverage (+ effect on leverage). Frank and Goyal (2009) refer to these factors as the "core leverage factors" that affect capital structure decisions.

DISCUSSION QUESTIONS

1. What are the assumptions and predictions of the trade-off theory? How can agency problems lead to a target leverage ratio?
2. What are the assumptions and predictions of the pecking order theory? Why do empirical studies generally find a negative abnormal stock return upon the announcement of an equity issue?
3. What are possible empirical measures for leverage, and what is the rationale for using either book or market leverage ratios?
4. What are the most important stylized facts derived from empirical studies that relate leverage and capital structure factors?

REFERENCES

Alti, Aydogan. 2006. "How Persistent Is the Impact of Market Timing on Capital Structure?" *Journal of Finance* 61:4, 1681–1710.

Ang, James S., Jess H. Chua, and John McConnell. 1982. "The Administrative Costs of Corporate Bankruptcy: A Note." *Journal of Finance* 37:1, 219–226.

Autore, Don M., and Tunde Kovacs. 2010. "Equity Issues and Temporal Variation in Information Asymmetry." *Journal of Banking and Finance* 34:1, 12–23.

Baker, Malcolm, Robin Greenwood, and Jeffrey Wurgler. 2003. "The Maturity of Debt Issues and Predictable Variation in Bond Returns." *Journal of Financial Economics* 70:2, 261–291.

Baker, Malcolm, and Jeffrey Wurgler. 2002. "Market Timing and Capital Structure." *Journal of Finance* 57:1, 1–32.

Barry, Christopher B., Steven C. Mann, Vassil T. Mihov, and Mauricio Rodríguez. 2008. "Corporate Debt Issuance and the Historical Level of Interest Rates." *Financial Management* 37:3, 413–430.

Bessler, Wolfgang, Wolfgang Drobetz, and Matthias Grüninger. 2010. "Information Asymmetry and Financing Decisions." *International Review of Finance*, forthcoming.

Bessler, Wolfgang, Wolfgang Drobetz, and Pascal Pensa. 2008. "Do Managers Adjust the Capital Structure to Market Value Changes? Evidence from Europe." In Wolfgang Breuer and Marc Gürtler, eds., *Zeitschrift für Betriebswirtschaft/Special Issue—50 Years after MM: Recent Developments in Corporate Finance*, 113–145. Wiesbaden, Germany: Gabler.

Bessler, Wolfgang, Wolfgang Drobetz, Rebekka Haller, and Iwan Meier. 2010. "The Zero-Leverage Phenomenon: International Evidence," Working Paper, University of Giessen, University of Hamburg and HEC Montreal.

Bharath, Sreedhar T., Paolo Pasquariello, and Guojun Wu. 2009. "Does Asymmetric Information Drive Capital Structure Decisions?" *Review of Financial Studies* 22:9, 3211–3243.

Börsch-Supan, Axel, and Jens, Köke. 2002. "An Applied Econometricians' View of Empirical Corporate Governance Studies." *German Economic Review* 3:3, 295–326.

Bowman, Robert G. 1980. "The Importance of a Market Value Measurement of Debt in Assessing Leverage." *Journal of Accounting Research* 18:1, 242–254.

Brennan, Michael C., and Eduardo S. Schwartz. 1984. "Financial Policy and Firm Valuation." *Journal of Finance* 39:3, 593–607.

Brounen, Dirk, Abe de Jong, and Kees Koedjik. 2004. "Corporate Finance in Europe: Confronting Theory with Practice." *Financial Management* 33:4, 71–101.

Chang, Xin, and Sudipto, Dasgupta. 2009. "Target Behavior and Financing: How Conclusive Is the Evidence?", *Journal of Finance* 64:4, 1767–1796.

Choe, Hyuk, Ronald W. Masulis, and Vikram K. Nanda. 1993. "Common Stock Offerings Across the Business Cycle: Theory and Evidence." *Journal of Empirical Finance* 1:1, 3–31.

Cook, Douglas O., and Tian Tang. 2010. "Macroeconomic Conditions and Capital Structure Adjustment Speed." *Journal of Corporate Finance* 16:1, 73–87.

De Angelo, Harry, and Ronald W. Masulis. 1980. "Optimal Capital Structure under Corporate and Personal Taxation." *Journal of Financial Economics* 8:1, 3–29.

Devos, Erik, Upinder Dhillon, Murali Jagannathan, and Srinivasan Krishnamurthy. 2008. "Does Managerial Entrenchment Explain the 'Low Leverage' Puzzle? Evidence from Zero-Debt Firms and Debt Initiations." *Working Paper*. University of Texas.

Dierkens, Nathalie. 1991. "Information Asymmetry and Equity Issues." *Journal of Financial and Quantitative Analysis* 26:2, 181–199.

Drobetz, Wolfgang, and Gabrielle Wanzenried. 2006. "What Determines the Speed of Adjustment to the Target Capital Structure?" *Applied Financial Economics* 16:13, 941–958.

Drobetz, Wolfgang, Pascal Pensa, and Claudia B. Wöhle. 2006. "Kapitalstrukturpolitik in Theorie und Praxis: Ergebnisse einer Fragebogenuntersuchung" *Zeitschrift für Betriebswirtschaft* 76:3, 253–285.

Easterbrook, Frank H. 1984. "Two-Agency Cost Explanations of Dividends." *American Economic Review* 74:4, 650–659.

Fama, Eugene F., and Kenneth R. French. 2002. "Testing Tradeoff and Pecking Order Predictions about Dividends and Debt." *Review of Financial Studies* 15:1, 1–33.

Fama, Eugene F., and Kenneth R. French. 2005. "Financing Decisions: Who Issues Stock?" *Journal of Financial Economics* 76:3, 549–582.

Fan, Joseph P. H., Sheridan Titman, and Garry J. Twite. 2003. "An International Comparison of Capital Structure and Debt Maturity Choices." Working Paper, Hong Kong School of Business and Management.

Faulkender, Michael, and Mitchell A. Petersen. 2006. "Does the Source of Capital Affect Capital Structure?" *Review of Financial Studies* 19:1, 45–79.

Fischer, Edwin O., Robert Heinkel, and Josef Zechner. 1989. "Dynamic Capital Structure Choice: Theory and Tests." *Journal of Finance* 44:1, 19–40.

Flannery, Mark J., and Kasturi P. Rangan. 2006. "Partial Adjustment toward Target Capital Structures." *Journal of Financial Economics* 79:3, 469–506.

Frank, Murray Z., and Vidhan K. Goyal. 2003. "Testing the Pecking Order Theory of Capital Structure." *Journal of Financial Economics* 67:2, 217–248.

Frank, Murray Z., and Vidhan K. Goyal. 2009. "Capital Structure Decisions: Which Factors Are Reliably Important?" *Financial Management* 38-:1, 1–37.

Galai, Dan, and Ronald W. Masulis. 1976. "The Option Pricing Model and the Risk Factor of Stock." *Journal of Financial Economics* 3:1–2, 631–644.

Gertler, Mark, and Simon Gilchrist. 1993. "The Role of Credit Market Imperfections in the Monetary Transmission Mechanism: Arguments and Evidence." *Scandinavian Journal of Economics* 95:1, 43–64.

Goyal, Vidhan K., Kenneth Lehn, and Stanko Racic. 2002. "Growth Opportunities and Corporate Debt Policy: The Case of the U.S. Defense Industry." *Journal of Financial Economics* 64:1, 35–59.

Graham, John R., and Campbell R. Harvey. 2001. "The Theory and Practice of Corporate Finance: Evidence from the Field." *Journal of Financial Economics* 60:2–3, 187–243.

Grossman, Sanford J., and Oliver Hart. 1982. "Corporate Financial Structure and Managerial Incentives." In John McCall, ed., *The Economics of Information and Uncertainty*, 107–140. Chicago: University of Chicago Press.

Hackbarth, Dirk, Jianjun Miao, and Erwan Morellec. 2006. "Capital Structure, Credit Risk, and Macroeconomic Conditions." *Journal of Financial Economics* 82:3, 519–550.

Harris, Milton, and Artur Raviv. 1991. "The Theory of Capital Structure." *Journal of Finance* 46:1, 297–355.

Haugen, Robert A., and Lemma W. Senbet. 1978. "The Insignificance of Bankruptcy Costs to the Theory of Optimal Capital Structure." *Journal of Finance* 33:2, 383–393.

Henderson, Brian J., Narasimhan Jegadeesh, and Michael S. Weisbach. 2006. "World Markets for Raising New Capital." *Journal of Financial Economics* 82:1, 63–101.

Hennessy, Christopher A., and Toni M. Whited. 2005. "Debt Dynamics." *Journal of Finance* 60:3, 1129–1165.

Hovakimian, Armen. 2006. "Are Observed Capital Structures Determined by Equity Market Timing?" *Journal of Financial and Quantitative Analysis* 41:1, 221–243.

Hovakimian, Armen, Tim Opler, and Sheridan Titman. 2001. "The Debt-Equity Choice." *Journal of Financial and Quantitative Analysis* 36:1, 1–24.

Huang, Rongbing, and Jay R. Ritter. 2009. "Testing Theories of Capital Structure and Estimating the Speed of Adjustment." *Journal of Financial and Quantitative Analysis* 44:2, 237–271.

Jensen, Gerald R., Donald P. Solberg, and Thomas S. Zorn. 1992. "Simultaneous Determination of Insider Ownership, Debt, and Dividend Policies." *Journal of Financial and Quantitative Analysis* 27:2, 247–263.

Jensen, Michael C. 1986. "Agency Cost of Free Cash Flows, Corporate Finance and Takeovers." *American Economic Review* 76:2, 323–339.

Jensen, Michael C., and William H. Meckling. 1976. "Theory of the Firm: Managerial Behavior, Agency Costs and Ownership Structure." *Journal of Financial Economics* 3:4, 305–360.

Kane, Alex, Alan J. Marcus, and Robert L. McDonald. 1984. "How Big Is the Tax Advantage of Debt?" *Journal of Finance* 39:3, 841–853.

Kayhan, Ayla, and Sheridan Titman. 2007. "Firms' Histories and Their Capital Structures." *Journal of Financial Economics* 83:1, 1–32.

Kim, Wi S., and Eric H. Sorensen. 1986. "Evidence on the Impact of the Agency Costs of Debt on Corporate Debt Policy." *Journal of Financial and Quantitative Analysis* 21:2, 131–144.

Kisgen, Darren J. 2009. "Do Firms Target Credit Ratings or Leverage Levels?" *Journal of Financial and Quantitative Analysis* 44:6, 1323–1344.

Klock, Mark, and Clifford Thies. 1992. "Determinants of Capital Structure." *Review of Financial Economics* 1:2, 40–52.

Korajczyk, Robert A., and Amnon Levy. 2003. "Capital Structure Choice: Macroeconomic Conditions and Financial Constraints." *Journal of Financial Economics* 68:1, 75–109.

Korajczyk, Robert A., Deborah J. Lucas, and Robert L. McDonald. 1991. "The Effect of Information Releases on the Pricing and Timing of Equity Issues." *Review of Financial Studies* 4:4, 685–708.

Korajczyk, Robert A., Deborah J. Lucas, and Robert L. McDonald. 1992. "Equity Issues with Time-Varying Asymmetric Information." *Journal of Financial and Quantitative Analysis* 27:3, 397–417.

Kraus, Alan, and Robert H. Litzenberger. 1973. "A State Preference Model of Optimal Financial Leverage." *Journal of Finance* 38:4, 911–922.

Leary, Mark T., and Michael R. Roberts. 2005. "Do Firms Rebalance Their Capital Structures?" *Journal of Finance* 60:6, 2575–2619.

Lemmon, Michael L., and Jaime F. Zender. 2010. "Debt Capacity and Tests of Capital Structure." *Journal of Financial and Quantitative Analysis*, forthcoming.

Lucas, Deborah J., and Robert L. McDonald. 1990. "Equity Issues and Stock Price Dynamics." *Journal of Finance* 45:4, 1019–1043.

Miller, Merton H., and Franco Modigliani. 1961. "Dividend Policy, Growth, and the Valuation of Shares." *Journal of Business* 34:4, 411–433.

Minton, Bernadette A., and Karen H. Wruck. 2001. "Financial Conservatism: Evidence on Capital Structure from Low Leverage Firms." Working Paper, Ohio State University.

Modigliani, Franco, and Merton H. Miller. 1958. "The Cost of Capital, Corporation Finance and the Theory of Investment." *American Economic Review* 48:3: 261–297.

Moore, William. 1986. "Asset Composition, Bankruptcy Costs and the Firm's Choice of Capital Structure." *Quarterly Review of Economics and Business* 26:1, 51–61.

Myers, Stewart C. 1977. "Determinants of Corporate Borrowing." *Journal of Financial Economics* 5:2, 147–175.

Myers, Stewart C. 1984. "The Capital Structure Puzzle." *Journal of Finance* 39:3, 575–592.

Myers, Stewart C., and Nicholas S. Majluf. 1984. "Corporate Financing and Investment Decisions When Firms Have Information That Investors Do Not Have." *Journal of Financial Economics* 13:2, 187–222.

Peyer, Urs, and Theo Vermaelen. 2008, "The Nature and Persistence of Buyback Anomalies." *Review of Financial Studies* 22:4, 1693–1745.

Rajan, Raghuram G., and Luigi Zingales. 1995. "What Do We Know about Capital Structure? Some Evidence from International Data." *Journal of Finance* 50:5, 1421–1460.

Ross, Steve. 1977. "The Determination of Financial Structure: The Incentive Signalling Approach." *Bell Journal of Economics* 8:1, 23–40.

Ross, Stephen A. 1985. "Debt and Taxes and Uncertainty." *Journal of Finance* 40:3, 637–657.

Scott, James H. 1977. "Bankruptcy, Secured Debt and Optimal Capital Structure." *Journal of Finance* 32:1, 1–19.

Shumway, T. 2001, "Forecasting Bankruptcy More Accurately: A Simple Hazard Model." *Journal of Business* 74:1, 101–124.

Shyam-Sunder, Lakshmi, and Stewart C. Myers. 1999. "Testing Static Tradeoff against Pecking Order Models of Capital Structure." *Journal of Financial Economics* 51:1, 219–244.

Strebulaev, Ilya A. 2007. "Do Tests of Capital Structure Mean What They Say?" *Journal of Finance* 62:4, 1747–1787.

Strebulaev, Ilya A., and Baozhong Yang. 2006. "The Mystery of Zero-Leverage Firms." Working Paper, Stanford University.

Taggart, Robert A., 1985. "Secular Patterns in the Financing of U.S. Corporations." In Benjamin M. Friedman, ed., *Corporate Capital Structures in the United States*, 13–80. Chicago: University of Chicago Press.

Thies, Clifford, and Mark S. Klock. 1992. "Determinants of Capital Structure." *Review of Financial Economics* 1:1, 40–52.

Titman, Sheridan, and Roberto Wessels. 1988. "The Determinants of Capital Structure Choice." *Journal of Finance* 43:1, 1–19.

Warner, Jerold. 1977. "Bankruptcy Costs: Some Evidence." *Journal of Finance* 32:2, 337–347.

Welch, Ivo. 2004. "Capital Structure and Stock Returns." *Journal of Political Economy* 112:1, 106–131.

ABOUT THE AUTHORS

Wolfgang Bessler is Professor of Finance and Banking at the Justus-Liebig University Giessen. He holds a doctorate from the University of Hamburg and was a faculty member at Syracuse University, Rensselaer Polytechnic Institute, and the Hamburg School of Economics. His research interests are corporate finance, financial markets and institutions, and asset management. He serves as a member on the editorial board of various international finance journals including the *European Journal of Finance*.

Wolfgang Drobetz is Professor of Finance at the University of Hamburg. He holds a doctorate from the University of St. Gallen and a Habilitation from the University of Basel. His research interests are corporate finance, asset pricing, and asset management. He is a member of the editorial board of the *European Journal of Finance* and served as co-president of the European Financial Management Association (EFMA).

Robin Kazemieh is a researcher and PhD student in finance at the University of Hamburg. He graduated with distinction in business administration at the University of Hamburg and received an M.Sc. in finance from the Barcelona Graduate School of Economics at Pompeu Fabra University. His research interests are corporate finance, asset pricing, and asset management.

CHAPTER 3

Capital Structure and Corporate Strategy

MAURIZIO LA ROCCA
Assistant Professor in Business Economics and Finance, University of Calabria

INTRODUCTION

This chapter responds to the general call for integration between finance and strategy by examining how financial decisions are related to corporate strategy. Finance allows organizations to quantitatively understand how a firm's strategic initiative affects corporate value (Kochhar and Hitt 1998).

With relatively few exceptions, strategic management and finance appear to be in a schizophrenic tension, if not in direct opposition (Ward and Grundy 1996). Bettis (1983) argues that modern financial theory and strategic management are based on different paradigms resulting in opposing conclusions. The conflicting state of these two knowledge systems might not matter if managers could easily make the linkages between strategy and finance in practice (Grundy 1992). But the few empirical studies available suggest that general managers do not find these linkages easy to make.

The polarity between finance and strategy, two areas of research that traditionally are studied separately, is apparent. However, these two areas present many connections. Thus, understanding the way in which these areas function individually and interrelate is relevant.

In particular, the link between financial decisions and strategy is largely unexplored. An extremely relevant but controversial topic in the academic and business communities relates to capital structure decisions and their effects on the firm's creation of value. A firm's *capital structure* generally refers to the financing mix used to finance the firm. Debt and equity are the two major sources of financing with debt holders and shareholders representing the two types of financial investors in the firm. Each of these is associated with different levels of risk, benefits, and control. While debt holders exert lower control, they often earn a fixed rate of return and are protected by contractual obligations with respect to their investment. Shareholders are the residual claimants who bear most of the risk and correspondingly have greater control over decisions.

Financial theory suggests that in perfect and efficient markets, financing decisions may be "irrelevant" to firms' strategy (Modigliani and Miller 1958). In practice, however, such choices may differentially affect firm value because of several imperfections (Myers and Majluf 1984). Several scholars contend that financial decisions have strategic importance (Barton and Gordon 1987; Bromiley 1990). Oviatt (1988) suggests that a theoretical integration between the two disciplines is possible, and transaction cost economics and agency theory provide possible avenues. According to Barton and Gordon, corporate strategies complement traditional finance paradigms and enrich the understanding of a firm's capital structure decisions.

Based on the stylized facts about capital structure, many factors that result in benefits and costs influence the optimal mix between debt and equity. Firms that use debt as a source of finance can benefit from tax advantages as a result of the interest deductibility, reduction in asymmetric information, and managerial discipline. Some costs relate to the use of debt based on the presence of financial distress, agency problems, and loss of financial flexibility. The relationship between a firm's management and its financial and nonfinancial stakeholders generates relevant information asymmetries and agency problems at the base of costs of financial distress and differences between "real" decisions and financing decisions. Therefore, the concept of *value maximization* is important to better understand the potential interrelation between capital structure and corporate strategy.

In general, the literature on finance and strategy is concerned with the strategic actions of key players such as managers, shareholders, debt holders, competitors, workers, and suppliers that affect firm value and the allocation of value between claimholders. Providing a different role from these corporate players is possible according to how "close" they are to the core of the corporation: if they are a corporation's owners or if they are at the boundary of the core such as suppliers, competitors, and customers. Specifically, capital structure decisions can affect the value creation process influencing efficient investments strategies according to the existence of conflicts of interest between managers, the firm's financial stakeholders (shareholders and debt holders) and the firm's nonfinancial stakeholders (suppliers, competitors, and customers). Exhibit 3.1 provides an overview of the relationships between the firm and its financial and nonfinancial stakeholders.

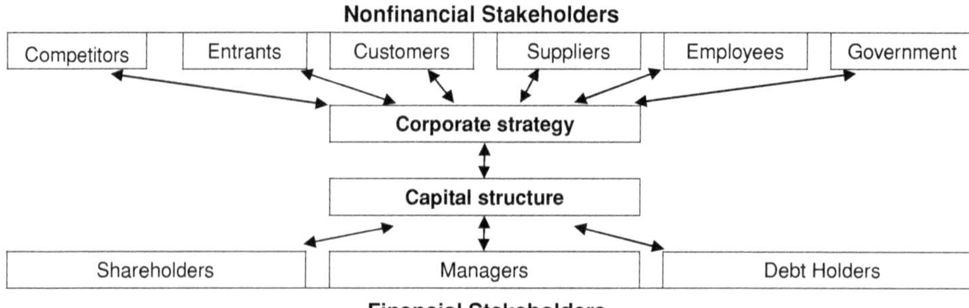

Exhibit 3.1 Overview of the Relation between Capital Structure and Financial and Nonfinancial Stakeholders

Note: Relevant interactions between capital structure and corporate strategy. Nonfinancial stakeholders, such as competitors, customers, and employees, may influence a firm's strategy and capital structure. Financial stakeholders, such shareholders, managers, and debt holders, may also influence capital structure decisions and corporate strategy.

This chapter describes the factors affecting agency problems with the financial stakeholders, explaining how debt can cause shareholders (managers) to accept projects that are too risky and reject profitable investments, but also identifying various situations in which debt holders and shareholders may disagree on the decision to liquidate firms. The interactions among managers, shareholders, and bondholders can influence the process of identifying, selecting, and choosing investment projects and, as a result, the processes of value creation. The presence of these conflicts, together with information asymmetries and incomplete contracting, can lead to suboptimal investment strategies that do not maximize the firm's value but rather benefit only a specific category of subjects.

The chapter also discusses how debt policy can affect the nonfinancial stakeholders' behavior and how competitiveness in the product market directly influences the firm's competitive strategy and consequently the processes of value creation. A new line of research has analyzed the possible connections among capital structure, stakeholder theory, market structure, and a firm's strategic behavior. First, capital structure affects the behavior of nonfinancial stakeholders, as claimants to the firm's cash flows, in addition to shareholders and bondholders. Second, the firm's debt level affects market structure, product market behaviors of rivals, and industry concentration. Third, capital structure can serve as a way to commit to a certain product-market strategy and can cause firms to behave more or less aggressively, which makes competition "tougher" or "softer." Thus, the interaction between how a corporation is financed and how its nonfinancial stakeholders view the firm suggests that capital structure decisions must be incorporated into the firm's overall corporate strategy. Therefore, the chapter describes how a firm's financial situation is likely to affect its sales, its ability to attract employees and suppliers, the competitors' market behavior, and its ability to operate profitably. In all the cases, capital structure serves to mitigate opportunistic problems and leverage the firm's competitive advantage.

This chapter discusses these interactions and the consequences for the value creation processes. Studies based on capital structure largely ignore the nature of the firm's investments and the overall environment in which it operates. This chapter considers the role of all stakeholders within the firm's environment regarding the interactions among its financial decisions, product design, employment policy, and other strategic choices.

The rest of the chapter is organized as follows. The next section highlights how the interactions among managers, shareholders, and debt holders affect capital structure and investment decisions, creating the so-called problems of overinvestment and underinvestment. The chapter then focuses on the interaction between how a corporation is financed and how its nonfinancial stakeholders view the firm, suggesting that capital structure decisions must be incorporated into the firm's overall corporate strategy. The final section presents the main conclusions and provides directions for future research.

CAPITAL STRUCTURE AND CORPORATE STRATEGY: THE ROLE OF FINANCIAL STAKEHOLDERS

The interactions among managers, shareholders, and debt holders and their related conflicts of interest influence capital structure, corporate governance activities, and strategic plans. Such influence could give rise to inefficient managerial decisions and suboptimal investments that generally fall under the categories of problems of overinvestment and underinvestment.

Problems in overinvestment deal with the possibility that management can abuse its decision-making power. This can occur by adopting unprofitable investments (managerial overinvestment) that could damage the interests of the shareholders or overly risky projects (risk shifting or asset substitution) in favor of the shareholders but against the interests of the debt holders (Jensen 1986; Jensen and Meckling 1976; Stulz 1990). Managerial overinvestment can take the well-known form of an empire-building strategy, managerial entrenchment, or overconfidence. As Jensen and Meckling discuss, overinvestment in risky projects is generated due to equity's limited liability. Overinvestment in the form of risk shifting is based on managers who, after having contracted a debt, transfer value from debt holders to shareholders and thus heightens leverage (risk shifting), which increases the risk of distress and bankruptcy. Overinvestment in the form of asset substitution is based on managers who, after having contracted a debt, transfer value from debt holders to shareholders by undertaking new investment projects that are riskier than the firm's average ones.

Underinvestment problems have to do with the agency relationship between shareholders and debt holders or between new and old shareholders. Managers can act in shareholder interest against debt holders, creating problems of underinvestment (also called *debt overhang*) as discussed by Myers (1977). Myers suggests that the presence of "risky" debt, which shows a lower market value than the nominal one, can stimulate managers to reject positive net present value (NPV) projects (underinvest) and thus decrease firm value. Shareholders of firms that have risky debt are unwilling to finance projects, thus taking on a cost that would exclusively or mostly benefit the firm's debt holders. Moreover, the presence of risky debt and high-growth opportunities can allow managers to act in the interests of the old shareholders against the new shareholders, creating problems of underinvestment in risky projects or risk avoidance. In general, high-growth and indebted firms adopt a conservative and prudent investment policy due to the fear that they may lose growth opportunities if the firm were to be offered for sale. Managers are scared about the firm's possibility to survive at least up until the time when they can take advantage of such growth opportunities. Thus, firms with good economic prospects are stimulated to underinvest and to avoid overly risky investments (risk avoidance). Exhibit 3.2 synthesizes and lists the main characteristics of such problems.

When a firm has risky debt and scarce growth opportunities, managers acting in shareholder interests could reject positive NPV investment projects (debt overhang) because the value created would be advantageous only for the firm's debt holders and would not avoid distress. Managers could also decide to promote high-risk investment policies (risk shifting) that take away value from debt holders and maximize equity value. However, if growth opportunities are high, managers may decide to choose conservative investment policies to avoid the risk of losing their control over the firm (risk avoidance). Thus, the main source of these types of distortions lies in the presence of risky debt, that is, in high levels of debt whose market value is lower than the nominal one and therefore difficult for the firm to handle (crisis situations or financial distress).

Exhibit 3.2 Problems Overinvestment and Underinvestment: Characteristics, Determining Factors, and Consequences

	Overinvestment		Underinvestment	
	Empire Building or Managerial Overinvestment (Jensen 1986; Stulz 1990)	**Risk-Shifting or Overinvestment in Risky Projects (Jensen and Meckling 1976)**	**Underinvestment or Debt Overhang (Myers 1977)**	**Risk Avoidance or Underinvestment in Risky Projects (Brito and John 2002)**
Subjects involved in agency relations	Managers against shareholders and also debt holders	Managers with shareholders against debt holders	Managers with shareholders against debt holders; present shareholders against new shareholders	Managers against shareholders (and also debt holders)
Determining factors	Leverage: Low Growth opportunities: Low Cash flow availability: High	Leverage: High Growth opportunities: Low (high risk but unprofitable growth opportunities) Cash flow availability: Low	Leverage: High Growth opportunities: Low Cash flow availability: Low	Leverage: High Growth opportunities: High Cash flow availability: Low
Type of firm	Firms that rarely make recourse to debt and that operate in sectors that have scarce growth prospects	Firms that do make recourse to debt, especially when in financial difficulty, and that operate in high risk sectors	Firms that make recourse to debt, especially when in financial difficulty and that operate in sectors with good economic potential	Both young firms with high growth potential (high tech) and mature ones (resulting from leverage buyouts)
Effect on firm value	Choice of projects with negative NPV	Choice of high-risk projects, with low probabilities of being successful or even with negative NPV	Refusal toward positive NPV investment projects	Refusal toward risky investment projects but with positive NPV
Role of debt	Reduces such problems due to its ability to discipline management	Exacerbates such problems	Exacerbates such problems	Exacerbates the problem

Note: This exhibit shows that overinvestment and underinvestment problems differ based upon the following: the subjects involved in agency relations, determining factors, firm of type, effect on firm value, and role of debt.

For firms with low debt levels, high liquidity, and low growth opportunities (as in the case of mature firms) managers could undertake negative NPV investment projects for purely opportunistic reasons such as empire building. The origins of managerial overinvestment can be found in the type of decision-making power that allows management to engage in investments for its own benefit. In this case, as Jensen (1986) and Stulz (1990) note, an increase in leverage disciplines management's behavior. In fact, the presence of debt obliges managers to pay interest rates and meet deadlines and thus increases their commitment toward more efficient company management. Although debt offers the benefit of preventing problems of managerial overinvestment, its costs lie on the possibility of exacerbating problems of underinvestment. As Stulz comments, the existence of a trade-off between the costs and benefits of debt thus becomes evident. The benefits of debt would become obvious in how management efficiently exercises its control over firm activity. On the other hand, high debt could increase the risk that the managers may reject positive NPV projects and accept excessively risky projects.

As Brito and John (2002) observe, managerial overinvestment and underinvestment concern the quantity of the resources invested in firm activity (i.e., the level of the investment the firm makes, while risk shifting and risk avoidance concern the level of risk that various investment choices can produce. Moreover, in firms that are having financial problems (such as being close to bankruptcy) but that still have high-growth opportunities, incentives for risk avoidance are the main determining factor behind suboptimal investment choices. To the contrary, in firms with low economic prospects, incentives for managerial overinvestment, risk shifting, and underinvestment become dominant, depending on whether the firm is in optimal financial shape (with much available cash) or is in financial difficulty (close to bankruptcy). Therefore, problems of incomplete contracts, information asymmetries, and conflicts of interest among managers, shareholders, and debt holders can give rise to inefficient investment strategies both when there is a high and a low level of debt.

CAPITAL STRUCTURE AND CORPORATE STRATEGY: THE ROLE OF NONFINANCIAL STAKEHOLDERS

Beside the role of financial stakeholders (shareholders and debt holders) in influencing capital structure decisions and a firm's investment strategy, financial policy is also related to nonfinancial stakeholders. They are the associates of a firm, such as customers, suppliers, employees, and the community in which the firm operates, who have no direct monetary stake in the company and no direct influence on the firm's financial policy (no decision or voting power). Nonetheless, they have a stake in the firm's financial health. Nonfinancial stakeholders are interested in the firm's financing choices because they can be hurt by its financial difficulties. Specifically, a firm's capital structure choices can affect nonfinancial stakeholders by affecting the probability of default on their explicit and implicit claims on the firm and by influencing the firm's production and pricing decisions. Consequently, firms may be forced (implicitly) to take the interests of their nonfinancial stakeholders into account in formulating financial policy.

Although financing decisions and product market decisions involve different departments in a firm, they are closely related. As Wanzenried (2003, p. 171) suggests, "How much debt should a firm raise, and how much output should it produce? At first glance, these decisions do not seem to depend on each other. While the first one is made by the firm's financial department, the second one falls in the responsibility of the marketing division. But the choice of a firm's capital structure is in fact closely related to its output market decisions." Indeed, firms can use their financial policy towards product-market participants (customers, suppliers, employees, and competitors) to solve asymmetric information and agency problems. Further, capital structure can serve as a signaling device to these nonfinancial stakeholders and thereby affect their behavior. Thus, the interrelationship between the financial and "real" decisions of firms can come from the role of financial instruments in conveying information (on a firm's profitability) to investors as well as to product-market rivals, consumers, and suppliers (Istaitieh and Rodriguez-Fernandez 2006).

The literature linking capital structure and product-market factors relates some elements of modern financial theory to stakeholder theory, industrial organization, and the strategic management of firms. Franck and Huyghebaert (2004) as well as Istaitieh and Rodriguez-Fernandez (2006) provide comprehensive surveys of theoretical and empirical works on this topic. As highlighted by Istaitieh and Rodriguez-Fernandez, the survey of Harris and Raviv (1991) on capital structure suggests that one of the distinctive categories of determinants deserving more attention concerns products and product-market characteristics. In their conclusion, Harris and Raviv (p. 351) refer to the role of these characteristics as the most promising for future research on capital structure: "In our view, models which relate capital structure to products and inputs are the most promising. This area is still in its infancy and is short on implications relating capital structure to industrial organization variables such as demand and cost parameters, strategic variables, etc."

Capital Structure and Stakeholder Theory

Stakeholder theory of capital structure concerns the important role played by a firm's nonfinancial stakeholders (customers, employees, suppliers, and government) in affecting its financial decisions. Specifically, there are indirect bankruptcy costs stemming from nonfinancial stakeholders that are relevant. Due to these costs, many large firms tend to be more conservative in capital structure policy, maintaining low debt ratios even when banks offer substantial amounts of debt at attractive rates. Nonfinancial stakeholders prefer to avoid doing business with a financially distressed firm because of its high likelihood of liquidation. The threat of future bankruptcy may lead to ending post-sale services and assistance and scare customers in the ex-ante choice to acquire its products. Thus, nonfinancial stakeholders may stop doing business with a company if its increasing leverage ratio could lead to distress in the future.

The role of nonfinancial stakeholders and the threat of financial distress can be explained by several factors. These include customers' need for a particular product or service (Titman 1984), a firm's desire to maintain a certain level of quality and services for its products (Maksimovic and Titman 1991), and the bargaining power of workers or other suppliers (Sarig 1998). In general, a firm's financial condition can affect how suppliers, customers, and employees perceive its reliability.

In his seminal paper, Titman (1984) explains the argument that customers and other nonfinancial stakeholders affect debt as follows. For firms that market durable or unique goods, their liquidation due to a financial crisis may impose costs on three parties: (1) customers, who may be unable to obtain the product, parts, and/or related services; (2) suppliers, who may have to stop doing business with the firm; and (3) employees, if the firm offers them fewer opportunities for advancement. Thus, a firm's liquidation decision may impose costs on other stakeholders, especially the customers, workers, or suppliers who make firm-specific investments. These costs might be transferred to shareholders by customers, demanding lower prices for the firm's product; by suppliers, who may be reluctant or may even stop doing business with the firm; or by potential employees who avoid seeking jobs in these firms. In particular, customers who can predict a firm's behavior from their knowledge of its financial status may be reluctant to do business with a firm that is threatened with bankruptcy or is in financial distress. Thus, customers would pay less for the firms' products in the market or for substitute products of other firms (Maksimovic and Titman 1991). Moreover, potential employees would demand higher wages, and potential suppliers would ask for higher prices. Therefore, a firm may deliberately use financial instruments to convey information to customers as well as its marketing agents and distributors about its quality. Thus, the firm might have an interest in maintaining a low debt level to avoid the probability of distress.

The previously mentioned effect is related to industry-specific features. Stakeholder views are particularly important for firms whose products need future servicing such as automobiles and computers, or whose products' quality is important but difficult to observe such as prescription drugs. Financial distress resulting from high leverage will be costly for firms requiring their employees and suppliers to invest in product-specific training and physical capital that is specialized to the firms' needs (Banerjee, Dasgupta, and Kim 2004). Moreover, suppliers in specialized industries tend to have low leverage if they depend on relatively few customers for a major proportion of their sales. This idea suggests why some firms choose not to borrow when banks are willing to provide debt financing at attractive terms or when tax shields are relevant. Yet, financial distress should be less costly for firms that produce nondurable goods such as agricultural products or services that are not particularly specialized such as hotel rooms, or whose quality can easily be assessed (Titman 1984). These firms should have relatively more debt in their capital structure.

However, financial distress related to a high level of debt in the capital structure can affect the potential viability of the firm's future prospects and can generate some benefits to the firm's "committed stakeholders." Highly levered firms and thus financial distress can benefit firms by improving their bargaining positions with their committed stakeholders. In terms of bargaining power with employees, a general assumption is that financial distress can provide a negotiation advantage to the firm because employees must consider how their wage demands affect the firm's future viability. By increasing leverage, the firm can reduce its employees' demands by exploiting their fear that a wage increase will push the firm toward bankruptcy (Dasgupta and Sengupta 1993). Without attractive alternative sources of employment, unionized employees gain less from achieving higher wages if pay raises substantially increase the probability that the firm may become bankrupt. Thus, the higher the level of debt, the lower is the union's optimal wage. More debt increases the likelihood of bankruptcy, which causes the union to lower its wage demands, thus reducing the expected cost. Hence, debt policy leads to an increase in the value of the firm threatened by unionization. For the same reasons, government can be pushed to provide subsidies such as loan guarantees to distressed firms to keep them far from failing. Thus, firms obtain financing at below-market rates that otherwise would not be possible.

By contrast, some studies (Sarig 1998) argue that skilled employees of highly levered firms can negotiate better contract terms than can employees of identical but less levered firms. This is because highly levered firms are more susceptible to employees' threats to seek alternative employment than are less levered firms. Because of debt overhang, distressed firms are generally less willing to take on new opportunities, offering fewer chances to employees for career advancement. Potential employees, especially if highly skilled, avoid distressed firms because young managers tend to value growth opportunities and search for firms with high future prospects. As a result, firms whose employees are presumably more specialized or searching for highly skilled employees use relatively little debt in their capital structure.

Capital Structure and Reputation

Reputation is a social evaluation of the public toward an organization concerning the feelings that stakeholders have about a company. It gives an indication of whether stakeholders like, admire, or trust a company and its attributes. In particular, Fombrun (1996, p. 72) defines a corporate reputation as "a perceptual representation of a company's past actions and future prospects that describes the firm's overall appeal to all of its key constituents when compared with other rivals." This intangible asset concerns (1) reputation in the product market, related to the product's quality and reliability; (2) management reputation, associated with the quality and reliability of the firm's CEO; and (3) financial reputation, related to the firm's capacity to tackle its payment commitments originating in borrowing and fulfilling its contractual obligations over a long period (Dollinger, Golden, and Saxton 1997). In general, a positive corporate reputation is taken to be a valuable resource leading to competitive advantage and contributes to organizational performance (Fombrun and Shanley 1990). Thus, a product market's observation of a firm's behavior over a long period is one of its most valuable intangible assets. Managers' willingness to preserve this intangible asset discourages opportunistic decision making.

The firm's reputation, which signals its quality, is reflected as greater ease in obtaining the required financing and thus increases its debt capacity (Diamond 1989). Consequently, firms with strong reputations and incentives to maintain a good reputation to ensure long-run profitability typically are able to obtain the necessary financing. However, firms can be short-term-oriented in spite of their good reputations (Maksimovic and Titman 1991). High-debt firms, where the probability of default is relevant, often pay more attention to the short-run survival than to the future growth opportunities related to such intangible assets as reputation. If the firm is financially distressed, it will reduce the quality of its products today to avoid bankruptcy. In this sense, managers prefer to lose reputation but keep a firm ongoing in the short run. This is because the long-run value of a good reputation may be less important to managers than the short-run need to generate enough cash to avoid bankruptcy.

Capital Structure, Corporate Strategy, and Diversification

Starting in the 1980s, some authors (Titman 1984; Barton and Gordon 1987; Oviatt 1988) studied the link between corporate strategy and capital structure focusing on a diversification strategy involving both product diversification and geographic diversification (firm's internationalization). Among many theoretical approaches, the link between diversification and capital structure choices has been mostly explained through the coinsurance effect (Lewellen 1971) and transaction cost theory (Williamson 1988), as well as by applying agency cost theory (Jensen 1986).

According to Lewellen (1971), the coinsurance effect concerns the reduction of operating risk due to the imperfect correlation between the different cash flows of a firm running diverse businesses. Thus, due to this kind of risk reduction, multibusiness or multinational firms can assume more debt. Consistent with this argument, several studies (Alonso-Menéndez 2003; Bergh 1997) find the coinsurance effect resulting from the lack of correlation between businesses to be one of the most important value-increasing sources associated with unrelated diversification. Firms that follow unrelated diversification can issue more debt and benefit from the fiscal advantages related to debt financing (Bergh 1997) because the tax liability of the diversified firm may be less than the cumulated tax liabilities of the different (single) business units.

Williamson (1988) notes that the transaction cost approach concerns the governance of contractual relations in transactions between two parties. In particular, by matching corporate finance theory and strategy theory, this approach examines a firm's financial decisions in terms of its specific assets, considering debt and equity as alternative governance structures. Firms diversify their activities in response to the presence of an excess of unutilized assets, and the kind of diversification strategy depends on the characteristics of these resources. An excess of highly specific assets is more likely to lead to related diversification because these assets can only be transferred across similar businesses. Conversely, an unrelated diversification strategy should be based on the presence of an excess of nonspecific assets. Therefore, the transaction cost approach, considering debt as a rule-based governance structure and equity as a discretionary governance device, supports using debt to finance nonspecific assets and using equity to finance specific ones. Thus, in the presence of highly specific assets (mainly associated to related-diversified firms) that keep a limited liquidation value in case of default, equity is the preferred financial instrument because the firm cannot easily re-employ such assets.

In contrast, in the presence of general purpose assets (mainly associated to unrelated-diversified firms), which are more valuable as collateral and able to retain their value in the event of liquidation/default, debt is the preferred financing tool. For instance, in the case of financial distress, a firm operating in three sectors—grocery, mechanical, and pharmaceutical—and having mainly general-purpose assets, has the opportunity to liquidate the assets easily and quickly because such assets are useable in many activities and industry sectors. Thus, the higher capacity to meet the scheduled debt payment, thanks to general-purpose asset liquidity, provides security for the loan provided, reducing the cost of capital and increasing the debt capacity.

Agency cost theory, which is rooted in the existence of conflicts of interest between shareholders and managers (Jensen and Meckling 1976), provides a further theoretical scheme that supports the influence of diversification strategy on capital structure (Kochhar and Hitt 1998). Jensen (1986) points out the disciplining role of debt on managerial behavior in that it reduces managerial discretion regarding free cash flow. Therefore, Jensen's perspective supports the positive role of debt in reducing the ability of a manager to realize detrimental diversification strategies, especially unrelated ones. Consequently, the result of diversification on the debt-equity choice can be interpreted according to the monitoring effect.

Stakeholders, especially shareholders, are assumed to be able to influence the strategic decisions of managers. In particular, shareholders will act to prevent diversification strategies, especially unrelated ones that represent opportunistic managerial behaviors. As a result, they will promote using debt as a device to discipline managerial behavior. This, in turn, limits managers from making diversification decisions especially when they engage in unrelated diversification (Jensen 1986). Therefore, debt prevents managers from using diversification to destroy value for their private benefit.

Previous empirical evidence regarding the effect of product diversification on capital structure determinants provides meaningful results. Prior studies show that multibusiness firms carry more debt than focused firms and the amount of debt increases with the degree of diversification. For example, using a sample of 249 U.S. firms, Rumelt (1974) observes that firms employing a strategy of unrelated diversification have the highest debt level. Barton and Gordon (1987), using 279 U.S. firms, and Lowe, Naughton, and Taylor (1994), using 176 Australian firms, obtain similar results. In their study of 187 U.S. firms, Kochhar and Hitt (1998) show that firms prefer equity financing for related diversification but use debt financing for unrelated diversification. La Rocca et al. (2009) show that related and unrelated diversification have opposite effects on debt. Specifically, a related-diversification strategy, which is associated with lower debt ratios, has a negative influence on leverage; by contrast, unrelated diversification, which is associated with higher debt usage, has a positive effect on debt. Anderson et al. (2000) find that 199 U.S. multibusiness firms have higher debt ratios than firms that operate in a single segment. Other authors suggest that diversified firms need to carry greater leverage to maximize firm value (Kaplan and Weisbach 1992; Li and Li 1996). As Li and Li (p. 704) note, "a combination of diversification with low leverage leads to overinvestment."

To reduce this kind of agency problem, empirical evidence shows that diversified firms carry relatively more debt than nondiversified firms (Kaplan and Weisbach 1992). However, based on the findings of Comment and Jarrell (1995), this observation does not seem to be robust. Also, Alonso-Menéndez (2003), who analyzes 480 Spanish manufacturing firms during the 1991 to 1994 period, does not find a significant relationship between leverage and diversification.

Concerning geographic diversification, prior studies suggest that multinational firms carry less debt than do domestic firms (Burgman 1996), but debt increases with the degree of internationalization (Chen et al. 1997) showing a lower cost of debt (Reeb, Mansi, and Allee 2001). Multinational firms are less sensitive to currency fluctuations than domestic firms, suggesting that multinational firms are in a better position to reduce their exposure to foreign exchange risk. Although bankruptcy costs are lower, leverage, especially long-term debt, is lower for multinational firms than domestic firms due to the higher agency costs of debt (Myers 1977).

Capital Structure, Market Structure, and Competitive Strategy

Another relevant but still undervalued stream of research, which has been the focus of studies in industrial organization, concerns how product market behavior and competitiveness in an industry is related to capital structure. This topic consists of two broad issues: (1) the way market characteristics affect corporate financing choices, and (2) the way a firm wants to alter its capital structure to affect the behavior of other firms and the kind of reaction of other firms due to a certain firm's capital structure. Thus, managers could use capital structure to reduce product market competition, making the firm stronger against their competitors, or to extract favorable behavior from other competitors. In this sense, if a firm's leverage influences the investment decisions, the incentive to take on a risky project, the liquidation choice, and thus the action of its competitors, then managers can use capital structure choice as a strategic tool that grants a competitive advantage.

A firm's capital structure may affect both market structure and the competitiveness of an industry by strategically changing financial behavior, depending on a firm's capital structure and that of its rivals. A firm's financial structure can influence production and pricing decisions as well as its precommitment to a certain strategic output or price level, but it also affects entry and exit decisions through incumbent predatory behavior.

The relationship between market structure and capital structure can be explained by considering how, during an industry recession, more highly levered firms tend to experience lower operating profits and lose more market share than their more conservatively financed competitors. Product differentiation and industry concentration exacerbate this effect (Opler and Titman 1994). Unlevered rivals can try to take advantage of the situation by using aggressive behavior to weaken the financial position of a competing firm. In an effort to drive out (highly levered) competitors vulnerable to financial distress, particularly those firms with specialized products, financially strong (unlevered) firms may take advantage of distress periods to aggressively advertise or price their products. The incentives of rivals are greater in concentrated markets because firms can make greater gains from such a strategy.

Opler and Titman (1994) suggest that highly levered firms lose market share to their less levered rivals during industry downturns for several reasons. First, distressed firms that face underinvestment problems (debt overhang) and invest less are forced to sell off assets and reduce their selling efforts. Second, highly levered firms have difficulty retaining and attracting customers who are concerned about long-term viability and product quality of product. Third, rival competitors can consider highly levered firms as a vulnerable competitor and seize the opportunity to steal customers.

Capital structure choice can also alter the incentive of who runs firms and can modify the behavior of product market rivals due to predation strategy. For example, low-debt and cash-rich firms can prey upon high-debt and cash-poor rivals. To drive a rival out of the market, predators may choose to voluntarily lose money in the short run, relative to the short-term profits they could achieve with a different strategy. By reducing competition, they hope to eventually more than recoup any short-term losses by, for example, increasing prices of their products (Joskow and Klevorick 1979). This behavior may affect strategic choices that can hurt their rival's bottom line and prospects based on such factors as low price, intense advertising, and selective price cuts.

Low-levered firms, assumed to have deep pockets, can engage in predatory practices especially in a highly competitive environment designed to financially exhaust highly levered rivals and drive them out of the market. A highly levered firm might be vulnerable to predation from low-levered competitors because low-levered competitors can purposefully reduce their prices and keep this strategy for a long time to drive the highly levered firm out of business. The highly levered firm may not survive this kind of competitive behavior if it can no longer secure financing for its operating or investment costs.

The predatory policy of a conservatively financed firm is especially effective in industries in which customers and other stakeholders are concerned about the long-term viability of the firms with which they do business and in highly concentrated industries. Moreover, this effect is higher for entrant firms. Telser (1966), who implicitly assumes capital market imperfections, argues that, as a rule, a firm entering the market has a more vulnerable financial structure than does an incumbent. With perfect financial markets this strategy cannot succeed because the entrant can always secure financing as long as its entry is profitable. Therefore, an incumbent with deep pockets can engage in predatory practices, such as engaging in a price war or increasing its output, to exhaust the entrant financially and drive it out of the market, at least temporarily (Poitevin 1989). Once again, when an incumbent firm observes the entrant's levered financial structure, it increases its output, thus lowering the latter's cash flow and making its default more likely. Predatory incentives are an increasing function of the entrant's debt level. Foresighted firms use low debt levels as a strategic instrument to signal their solvency and toughness to the market, thus deterring any predatory action and risk of aggressive behavior by rivals. Empirical work such as Chevalier (1995) verifies that debt weakens competitive position of firms.

Moreover, according to the incentive theory and the agency model, a high level of competition in the product market can replace debt as a managerial disciplinary mechanism, thereby inducing more efficient behavior. Thus, under this perspective, debt and product market competition can be considered two substitute corporate governance tools and a possible trade-off between competition and debt can exist (Nickell 1996).

Lastly, debt affects the competitive dynamics of an industry in a nontrivial way. Bankruptcy costs could change results due to the limited liability effect, that is, if a firm becomes insolvent, creditors are paid whatever operating profits are available. Thus, a high leverage level induces firms to usually act more aggressively in the product markets by increasing their sales and gaining a strategic advantage. In an industry in which the aggregate demand for a product is extremely uncertain, greater output generally increases risk because it leads to higher profits when product demand is strong, but lower profits when demand is weak. Hence, because higher leverage increases a firm's appetite for risk, the greater a firm's leverage, the greater is its incentive to produce at a high level of output (Brander and Lewis 1986). This behavior is based on the limited liability effect of debt financing. As Jensen and Meckling (1976) suggest, an increase in the firm's indebtedness induces equity holders to adopt riskier strategies due to the limited liability of debt. Thus, firms behave more aggressively in output markets compared to a situation without debt issue. High-debt firms become motivated to pursue output strategies that raise returns in good states of the economy and lower returns in bad states of the economy. Thus, competitors observing a firm's high leverage ratio will realize the firm is going to boost production.

SUMMARY AND CONCLUSIONS

Strategy and finance are growing closer together, and a strong integration between them can be tantamount to a competitive weapon. In particular, the interactions between financing and investment decisions create a situation in which high or low debt can compromise a firm's ability to take advantage of strategic options. The need to study in greater depth the relationships between real decisions and financing, with respect to interactions with financial and nonfinancial stakeholders, is a topic of interest both to academics and practitioners.

The common theme here is that a firm's financial policy and its ability to support the value creation process are affected by its relationship with (1) financial stakeholders, specifically shareholders and debt holders, and (2) nonfinancial stakeholders such as customers, employees, and suppliers. Leverage created by debt generates tax benefits and a series of responsibilities and incentives that can affect the relationship between managers and stakeholders, and consequently the process of value creation.

The first part of this chapter focused on the cost and thus the investment distortions that arise because of the conflicts of interest among management, shareholders, and debt holders. To the extent that lenders anticipate how debt distorts investment incentives, shareholders will bear the costs of the investment distortions caused by their firm's capital structure. A firm with an incentive to make investment decisions that reduce the value of its debt will be subject to higher borrowing costs and may at times be unable to obtain debt financing. Thus, firms have an incentive to design their capital structures such as to minimize these investment distortions. This chapter discusses this well-known topic based on the management and finance literature. The chapter points out the causes, determining factors, and effects that ensue in response to problems arising from the interactions between financial stakeholders.

A high-levered firm can engage in actions that are harmful to its shareholders or debt holders but also to its nonfinancial stakeholders, such as customers, employees, and suppliers. Indeed, the conflicts arising among managers, shareholders, and debt holders do not appear to be the major source of troubles with debt financing for many firms. A high-levered firm can have difficulty getting more external financing and may find that efficiently carrying out its daily business is more costly.

Thus, the second part of the chapter analyzed the role of nonfinancial stakeholders in influencing capital structure decisions. The types of products a firm sells, the nature and degree of output-market competition, uncertainty in the product market, and other aspects of the firm's overall strategy influence its capital structure, along with taxes, information asymmetries, and agency costs. At the same time, theoretical work shows an alternative, opposing relationship. Thus, depending on the underlying assumptions, corporate debt can increase or decrease a firm's aggressiveness. Furthermore, capital structure influences the probability of predation and market exit.

The chapter examines the situations where firms should limit their desire to use debt financing, and in contrast, explains why many firms choose to maintain a low debt ratio even when lenders are willing to provide debt capital at attractive terms. To summarize, the potential interactions among managers, financial stakeholders, and nonfinancial stakeholders influence capital structure, corporate governance activities, and value creation processes. These in turn, may give rise to inefficient managerial decisions, or they may shape the industry's competitive dynamics to achieve a competitive advantage.

This chapter is a prelude to further and more detailed empirical study, able to explore how strategy and finance can be welded more closely together. The research in this area until now has been largely theoretical, but the subject deserves further empirical examination. A robust research design and data set may offer relevant approaches to understanding how product-market behavior affects capital structure.

Accounting for the endogeneity problem should be important. A certain capital structure can affect product market competition, but also firms may anticipate the effect of leverage on product market behavior so the latter may influence capital structure choices. As Zingales (1998, p. 905) points out, "in the absence of a structural model we cannot determine whether it is the product market competition that affects capital structure choices or a firm's capital structure that affects its competitive position and its survival." Future research could simultaneously and empirically study a two-directional effect, considering endogeneity problems, in which the debt level affects and is affected by nonfinancial stakeholders or, in general, by the firm's strategic behavior in the product market. Moreover, most of the reports in the extant literature examine how the debt-equity mix drives these decisions, but other aspects of the financing mix may also play a role. Additional studies evaluating the role of capital structure on product-market behavior may benefit from taking into account such factors as debt mix, debt maturity structure, debt seniority structure, and covenants.

DISCUSSION QUESTIONS

1. What firm-specific factors boost underinvestment and overinvestment problems in a company? In which case does the use of debt reduce opportunism?
2. According to the stakeholder theory of capital structure, would someone prefer to work for a high-debt or a low-debt firm? Explain why.
3. What is the role of product-market reputation on financing decisions?
4. How can capital structure choice modify the behavior of product market rivals due to predation strategy?

REFERENCES

Alonso-Menéndez, Eduardo. 2003. "Does Diversification Strategy Matter in Explaining Capital Structure? Some evidence from Spain." *Applied Financial Economics* 13:6, 427–430.

Anderson, Ronald, Thomas Bates, John Bizjak, and Michael Lemmon. 2000. "Corporate Governance and Firm Diversification." *Financial Management* 29:1, 5–22.

Banerjee, Shantanu, Sudipto Dasgupta, and Yungsan Kim. 2004. *Buyer-Supplier Relationships and the Takeholder Theory of Capital Structure*. Kowloon: Hong Kong University of Science and Technology.

Barton, Sidney, and Paul Gordon. 1987. "Corporate Strategy: Useful Perspective for the Study of Capital Structure?" *Academy of Management Review* 12:1, 67–75.

Bergh, Donald. 1997. "Predicting Divestiture of Unrelated Acquisitions: An Integrative Model of Ex-Ante Conditions." *Strategic Management Journal* 18:9, 715–731.

Bettis, Richard. 1983. "Modern Financial Theory, Corporate Strategy and Public Policy: Three Conundrums." *Academy of Management Review* 8:3, 406–415.

Brander, James, and Tracy Lewis. 1986. "Oligopoly and Financial Structure: The Limited Liability Effect." *American Economic Review* 76:5, 956–970.

Brito, Jose A., and Kose John. 2002. "Leverage and Growth Opportunities: Risk Avoidance Induced by Risky Debt." Working Paper, University of New York, Salomon Center, Stern School of Business.

Bromiley, Philip. 1990. "On the Use of Financial Theory in Strategic Management." In Paul Shrivastava and Robert Lamb, eds., *Advances in Strategic Management*, vol. 6, 71–98, Greenwich, CT: JAI Press.

Burgman, Todd. 1996. "An Empirical Examination of Multinational Corporate Capital Structure." *Journal of International Business Studies* 27:3, 553–570.

Chen, Charles J. P., Agnes C. S. Cheng, Jia He, and Jawon Kim. 1997. "An Investigation of the Relationship between International Activities and Capital Structure." *Journal of Information Systems* 28:4, 563–577.

Chevalier, Judith. 1995. "Capital Structure and Product-Market Competition: Empirical Evidence from the Supermarket Industry." *American Economic Review* 85:3, 415–435.

Comment, Robert, and Gregg Jarrell. 1995. "Corporate Focus and Stock Returns." *Journal of Financial Economics* 37:1, 67–87.

Dasgupta, Sudipto, and Kunal Sengupta. 1993. "Sunk Investment, Bargaining and Choice of Capital Structure." *International Economic Review* 34:1, 203–220.

Diamond, Douglas. 1989. "Reputation Acquisition in Debt Markets." *Journal of Political Economy* 97:4, 828–862.

Dollinger, Marc, Peggy Golden, and Todd Saxton. 1997. "The Effect of Reputation on the Decision to Joint Venture." *Strategic Management Journal* 18:2, 127–140.

Fombrun, Charles. 1996. *Reputation: Realizing Value from the Corporate Image*. Boston: Harvard Business School Press.

Fombrun, Charles, and Mark Shanley. 1990. "What's in a Name? Reputation Building and Corporate Strategy." *Academy of Management Journal* 33:2, 233–258.

Franck, Tom, and Nancy Huyghebaert. 2004. "On the Interactions between Capital Structure and Product Markets: A Survey of the Literature." *Tijdschrift voor Economie en Management* 49:4, 727–787.

Grundy, Tony. 1992. *Corporate Strategy and Financial Decisions*. London: Kogan Page.

Harris, Milton, and Arthur Raviv. 1991. "Capital Structure and the Informational Role of Debt." *Journal of Finance* 45:2, 297–355.

Istaitieh, Abdulaziz, and Jose Rodriguez-Fernandez. 2006. "Factor-product Markets and Firm's Capital Structure: A Literature Review." *Review of Financial Economics* 15:1, 49–75.

Jensen, Michael. 1986. "Agency Costs of Free Cash Flow, Corporate Finance, and Take-Overs." *American Economic Review* 76:2, 323–329.

Jensen, Michael C., and William H. Meckling. 1976. "Theory of the Firm: Managerial Behavior, Agency Costs and Ownership Structure." *Journal of Financial Economics* 3:4, 305–360.
Joskow, Paul L., and Alvin K. Klevorick. 1979. "A Framework for Analyzing Predatory Pricing Policy." *Yale Law Journal* 89:2, 213–270.
Kaplan, Steven, and Michael Weisbach. 1992. "The Success of Acquisitions: Evidence for Divestitures." *Journal of Finance* 47:1, 107–138.
Kochhar, Rahul, and Michael Hitt. 1998. "Linking Corporate Strategy to Capital Structure: Diversification Strategy, Type and Source of Financing." *Strategic Management Journal* 19:6, 601–610.
La Rocca, Maurizio, Tiziana La Rocca, Dionigi Gerace, and Ciorstan Smark. 2009. "Effect of Diversification on Capital Structure." *Accounting and Finance* 49:4, 799–826.
Lewellen, Wilbur. 1971. "A Pure Financial Rationale for the Conglomerate Merger." *Journal of Finance* 26:2, 521–537.
Li, David, and Shan Li. 1996. "A Theory of Corporate Scope and Financial Structure." *Journal of Finance* 51:2, 691–709.
Lowe, Julian, Tony Naughton, and Peter Taylor. 1994. "The Impact of Corporate Strategy on Capital Structure of Australian Companies." *Managerial and Decision Economics* 15:3, 245–257.
Maksimovic, Vojislav, and Sheridan Titman. 1991. "Financial Policy and Reputation for Product Quality." *Review of Financial Studies* 4:1, 175–200.
Modigliani, Franco, and Merton Miller. 1958. "The Cost of Capital, Corporation Finance and the Theory of Finance." *American Economic Review* 48:3, 291–297.
Myers, Stewart. 1977. "Determinants of Corporate Borrowing." *Journal of Financial Economics* 5:2, 146–175.
Myers, Stewart, and Nicolas Majluf. 1984. "Corporate Financing and Investment Decision When Firms Have Information That Investors Do Not Have." *Journal of Financial Economics* 13:2, 187–221.
Nickell, Stephen. 1996. "Competition and Corporate Finance." *Journal of Political Economy* 104:4, 724–746.
Opler, Tim, and Sheridan Titman. 1994. "Financial Distress and Corporate Performance." *Journal of Finance* 49:3, 1015–1040.
Oviatt, Benjamin M. 1988. "Agency and Transaction Cost Perspectives on the Managers-Shareholder Relationship: Incentives for Congruent Interests." *Academy of Management Review* 13:2, 214–225.
Poitevin, Michel. 1989. "Financial Signalling and the 'Deep Pocket' Argument." *RAND Journal of Economics* 20:1, 26–40.
Reeb, David M., Sattar A. Mansi, and John M. Allee. 2001. "Firm Internationalization and the Cost of Debt Financing: Evidence from Non-Provisional Publicly Traded Debt." *Journal of Financial and Quantitative Analysis* 36:3, 395–414.
Rumelt, Richard. 1974. *Strategy, Structure and Economic Performance*. Cambridge: Harvard University Press.
Sarig, Oded H. 1998. "The Effect of Leverage on Bargaining with a Corporation." *Financial Review* 33:1, 1–16.
Stulz, René. 1990. "Managerial Discretion and Optimal Financing Policies." *Journal of Financial Economics* 26:1, 3–27.
Telser, Lester. 1966. "Cutthroat Competition and the Long Purse." *Journal of Law and Economics* 9:2, 259–277.
Titman, Sheridan. 1984. "The Effect of Capital Structure on a Firm's Liquidation Decision." *Journal of Financial Economics* 13:1, 137–151.
Wanzenried, Gabrielle. 2003. "Capital Structure Decisions and Output Market Competition under Demand Uncertainty." *International Journal of Industrial Organization* 21:2, 171–200.

Ward, Keith, and Tony Grundy. 1996. "The Strategic Management of Corporate Value." *European Management Journal* 14:3, 321–330.

Williamson, Oliver. 1988. "Corporate Finance and Corporate Governance." *Journal of Finance* 43:3, 567–591.

Zingales, Luigi. 1998. "Survival of the Fittest or the Fattest? Exit and Financing in the Trucking Industry." *Journal of Finance* 53:3, 905–938.

ABOUT THE AUTHOR

Maurizio La Rocca is an Assistant Professor in Business Economics and Finance at University of Calabria (Italy). He has published in journals such as the *International Small Business Journal, Small Business Economics*, and others. His teaching interests are in corporate finance, capital structure, corporate governance, and venture capital. He has won several teaching awards and a research award from the Italian Academy of Business Administration and Management in 2008. He received a PhD in Business Economics and Management from the University of Catania and was visiting at the University of Chicago's Graduate School of Business and Temple University.

CHAPTER 4

Capital Structure and Firm Risk

VALENTIN DIMITROV
Assistant Professor and Boutellier Endowed Faculty Scholar, Rutgers University

INTRODUCTION

This chapter provides an analysis of the effects of capital structure on firm risk. From the onset, those familiar with the capital structure irrelevance principle of Modigliani and Miller (1958) (hereafter MM) may object to such an analysis. After all, in capital markets with no transaction costs, financial distress costs, or taxes, capital structure affects neither the risk nor the value of the firm. In MM's world, what determines the firm's risk is the firm's earnings stream, which is taken as a given. Importantly, the real operations of the firm are assumed to be independent of the firm's financing decisions. As a result, changing the firm's capital structure shifts the risk among the firm's security holders while leaving the total risk of the firm unchanged. So, while analyzing how capital structure affects the risk to shareholders may be worthwhile, any attempt to link financing decisions to the risk of the firm is of little use.

Such objections notwithstanding, a large body of research suggests that capital structure can have important consequences for firm risk. Unlike Modigliani and Miller (1958), this research explicitly considers the interactions between the real and financial sides of the firm. The focus is primarily on the role of debt in the firm's capital structure. In imperfect capital markets, financial leverage raises the cost of external funds, especially during periods of economic distress when the firm's cash flows and net worth are low. As a result, highly levered firms in economic distress may have difficulty funding their operations, leading to further deterioration in operating performance. Alternatively, high financial leverage may motivate managers to make value-maximizing choices that they might otherwise avoid. Financial leverage may also increase managers' bargaining power with other stakeholders such as employees and suppliers. In this case, financial leverage may make firms more resilient to negative shocks. Therefore, according to theory, the overall relation between financial leverage and firm risk is likely to depend on the relative importance of these mechanisms. In contrast, the empirical evidence is more conclusive. When subjected to adverse economic shocks, highly levered firms have lower growth in sales, make fewer investments, and are less likely to survive than firms with low leverage. These findings suggest that financial leverage amplifies negative shocks; it makes firms riskier.

Does the increase in risk due to financial leverage lead to higher expected firm returns? Because data on firm expected returns are generally unavailable, most of the existing evidence on this topic examines the link between financial leverage and stock returns. An increase in financial leverage has two potential effects on the expected return to equity. First, even if the firm's operations are independent from the firm's financing decisions, an increase in financial leverage directly increases the cash flow risk to equity holders and thus raises the expected return to equity. Second, in imperfect capital markets, financial leverage can increase the expected return to equity to the extent that leverage increases the total risk of the firm. Both effects predict that financial leverage is positively associated with expected stock returns. Surprisingly, most of the evidence in the literature finds the opposite relation: High financial leverage is associated with low stock returns. Apparently, equity holders of highly levered firms are not compensated for bearing higher risk.

The goal of this chapter is not to provide a comprehensive analysis of risk in the context of capital structure choices. The literature on this topic is far too voluminous for such an undertaking. Instead, the goal is to highlight the possibility for interactions between the real and financial sides of the firm and the consequences of such interactions for the overall risk of the firm. The focus is entirely on the role of financial leverage. Distinctions between different debt securities and different classes of equity have been ignored. The papers referenced here were chosen for their contribution to the literature. However, many equally important papers have not been discussed. Interested readers are encouraged to review other available resources on this topic, including the remaining chapters in this volume.

FINANCIAL LEVERAGE AND THE REAL OPERATIONS OF THE FIRM: THE THEORY

Prior research has identified several mechanisms through which financial leverage can affect the operating risk of the firm. This section provides a brief summary of the theoretical arguments for each mechanism before discussing the relevant empirical evidence. These mechanisms are interrelated and are likely to operate simultaneously.

Positive Relation between Financial Leverage and Risk

Perhaps one of the most significant costs of high financial leverage is that it raises the cost of external funds. Specifically, because of asymmetric information between shareholders and debt holders, debt financing arrangements will entail dead-weight losses (agency costs) relative to the perfect information equilibrium. Bernanke and Gertler (1995) refer to the difference between the cost of funds raised externally and the opportunity cost of funds internal to the firm as an external finance premium. Because agency costs increase with the probability of financial distress (Jensen and Meckling 1976; Myers 1977), firms with higher financial leverage will face higher external finance premiums and will find investing more costly. Hence, financial leverage is expected to be negatively associated with investments, a prediction that is strongly supported by the results of Lang, Ofek, and Stulz (1996). Not only are highly levered firms likely to invest less in general, but their investments are also likely to be more sensitive to economic distress. Bernanke and Gertler (1989) predict that external finance premiums rise when firms are subject to adverse economic shocks that reduce cash flows and net worth. Importantly, the authors predict that external finance premiums would rise more for firms with low credit quality such as highly levered firms. The larger increase in the external finance premium of highly levered firms during economic downturns would result in a larger decrease in investment and further deterioration in performance.

Financial distress brought about by the use of high leverage may also negatively affect firms' ability to compete. Bolton and Scharfstein (1990) suggest that financially weak firms are prone to predation by deep-pocket rivals, leading to market share losses and even exit from the industry. Predation is expected to be stronger in concentrated industries, where surviving firms stand to gain more from removing a weakened competitor. Chevalier and Scharfstein (1996) develop a model in which highly levered firms increase prices during recessions in order to meet their debt obligations. To the extent that less levered rivals can maintain lower prices, the model predicts that highly levered firms would lose additional market share. Alternatively, financial distress may affect a firm's competitiveness because customers and suppliers are reluctant to do business with firms that could go bankrupt (Titman 1984; Maksimovic and Titman 1991). All of these effects are likely to be stronger during economic downturns, when highly levered firms are most vulnerable to drops in cash flows. Hence, competitive pressures may further increase the operating risk of highly levered firms.

The final argument for why financial leverage is positively associated with operating risk is based on the work of Brander and Lewis (1986). The focus is again on the conflict of interest between shareholders and debt holders. As firms take on more debt, they have an incentive to pursue riskier product market strategies that increase returns in good states and lower returns in bad states. This is because shareholders will ignore negative returns in bankrupt states when bondholders become the residual claimants. By increasing the variance of the firm's profits, shareholders increase the value of their option-like claim on the firm's future output.

Negative Relation between Financial Leverage and Risk

In contrast to the above-mentioned studies, financial leverage can make firms more resilient to negative shocks for two reasons. First, financial distress brought about by high leverage may force managers to make decisions that benefit the firm but reduce managers' private benefits. By reducing the margin for error, financial distress may also force managers to work harder to avoid bankruptcy. Essentially, high leverage may reduce the agency costs between managers and shareholders, resulting in more efficient businesses (Jensen 1986). If this is the case, highly levered firms should be able to react more quickly and more aggressively to economic downturns, resulting in better operating performance.

Second, high financial leverage may be used as a bargaining tool to force concessions from nonfinancial stakeholders such as employees and suppliers. In Perotti and Spier (1993), firms use leverage strategically when current profits are low and further investment is beneficial to employees. Because of the possibility of financial distress, highly levered firms can credibly threaten not to undertake new investments unless employees concede to wage reduction. Managers can use similar threats to force concessions from suppliers that are dependent on the firm for their own survival. Shifting costs in such a manner may help highly levered firms to better weather economic downturns.

In sum, theory provides no definitive answer as to how financial leverage affects firm risk. Fortunately, the empirical evidence reviewed in the subsequent section is much more conclusive.

FINANCIAL LEVERAGE AND THE REAL OPERATIONS OF THE FIRM: THE EVIDENCE

Testing for interactions between financial leverage and the real operations of the firm is difficult. The biggest challenge is the endogeneity of capital structure choices to firm performance and industry structure. If financial leverage affects the real operations of the firm, then the firm's financial decisions will take that into consideration. As a result, evidence on the association between financial leverage and operating performance in the cross-section is difficult to interpret. For example, finding that financial leverage is associated with inferior operating performance can indicate either that financial leverage hurts performance or that poor performance leads to higher financial leverage. Alternatively, it could be that a common factor leads to both high financial leverage and poor performance.

Several papers develop innovative research methodologies in order to minimize this endogeneity concern. The approach is to observe the relation between financial leverage and firm performance following exogenous shocks that increase the costs associated with financial leverage or alter the competitive environment of the firm. The adverse shocks that have been examined include overall industry distress (Opler and Titman 1994), industry deregulation (Zingales 1998), market entry (Khanna and Tice 2000), and economic recessions (Campello 2003; Khanna and Tice 2005). One important advantage of this approach is that these shocks can be viewed as realizations of different risks. As a result, finding that highly levered firms have different sensitivities to various exogenous shocks is also evidence that financial leverage affects the operating risk of the firm.

Financial Leverage and Industry Downturns

The study by Opler and Titman (1994) is one of the earliest to document differences in the performance of highly levered firms following adverse shocks. The shock used in the study is economic distress at the industry level. Specifically, an industry is defined as being economically distressed when its median sales growth is negative and when it experiences median stock returns below –30 percent. These criteria ensure that the negative shocks are serious enough as to affect operating performance. Importantly, the stock returns criterion also ensures that the downturns are unanticipated, which helps alleviate endogeneity concerns. Firm performance during the distress periods is measured by sales growth, stock returns, and changes in operating income relative to industry averages. The main question examined in the study is whether the effect of leverage on firm performance is more negative when industries become economically distressed. Even if financial leverage itself is endogenously determined, the differential effect of financial leverage on firm performance in times of economic distress can still be interpreted reliably.

The results of the study provide strong support for models predicting a positive relation between financial leverage and firm risk. Using a sample of 46,799 firm-years of data in the 1972 to 1991 period, Opler and Titman (1994) find a reliably negative relation between financial leverage and sales growth after controlling for other characteristics. In other words, highly levered firms lose market share to their more conservatively financed counterparts even in normal times. More importantly, the authors find that these market share losses accelerate during periods of industry distress. In distressed industries, industry-adjusted sales growth for firms in the highest leverage decile is 26.4 percent lower, on average, than for firms in the lowest leverage decile. Highly levered firms also experience greater declines in market value of equity, investment growth, and employment growth. Consistent with the predictions of Titman (1984) and Maksimovic and Titman (1991) on customer-driven losses in market share, the adverse effects are stronger for firms that sell more specialized products. The adverse effects are also stronger in concentrated industries, as predicted by the predation model of Bolton and Scharfstein (1990).

Financial Leverage and Deregulation Risk

Instead of using industry returns and sales data to identify adverse shocks, Zingales (1998) examines how financial leverage affects competitive outcomes in the trucking industry following its deregulation in 1980. Deregulation had two important effects on the trucking industry. First, it unexpectedly changed the competitive environment in which firms operated. Second, it increased the leverage of existing firms by sharply decreasing the value of the firms' operating certificates. As a result of the deregulation, a total of 4,589 trucking companies across the United States shut down between 1980 and 1985. Given these statistics, the main performance measure analyzed by Zingales is the probability of exit following deregulation. Specifically, the goal is to examine whether financial leverage (along with efficiency) affects the probability of exit following deregulation.

Data for the study come from Interstate Commerce Commission filings collected by the American Trucking Association and cover the period from 1976 to 1985. Exit is defined as liquidation (both voluntary and through bankruptcy) or a merger. The basic regression relates a firm's status (exit or survival) in 1985 to financial and operating variables in 1977. The results show that the initial level of debt reduces the firm's chances of survival. Even after controlling for the firm's profitability, size, and efficiency, an increase in leverage of one standard deviation reduces the probability of survival by 8 percent. The results are unaffected by further controls for the ex-ante risk of default. Overall, financial leverage apparently increases the risk of exit following deregulation.

Additional results provided by Zingales (1998) parallel the results in Opler and Titman (1994). The relation between financial leverage and exit is stronger in less competitive segments of the trucking industry, which is consistent with the predation-based model of Bolton and Scharfstein (1990). Because less competitive segments offer a more differentiated product, this result is also consistent with the customers-based models of Titman (1984) and Maksimovic and Titman (1991).

Consistent with the existence of financial constraints, highly levered trucking firms appear to exit in part because they cannot successfully finance new investments. Interestingly, evidence also suggests that more levered carriers are forced to discount their services, apparently to compensate customers for the increased risk of default. This finding is inconsistent with the prediction of Chevalier and Scharfstein (1996) that highly levered firms increase prices during periods of economic distress in order to avoid bankruptcy.

Financial Leverage and New Entry Risk

Khanna and Tice (2000) provide evidence on the interaction between financial leverage and the real operations of the firm following the entry of a new competitor. The focus is on the discount department industry, and the exogenous shock used in the study is the rapid expansion of Wal-Mart into numerous new markets from 1975 to 1996. The main performance measure is whether the incumbent firm chooses to expand, retrench, or not to change the number of stores following Wal-Mart's entry in the local market. If highly levered firms are unable to obtain the funds necessary to defend their market share, they may be more likely to retrench following Wal-Mart's entry.

The results reported in Khanna and Tice (2000) confirm this hypothesis. Following Wal-Mart's entry, an increase in financial leverage of 10 percent decreases the probability of expansion by 2.7 percent and increases the probability of retrenchment by 3.5 percent. These results occur despite controlling for other variables such as size, market share, and profitability. Assuming that retrenchment is bad and expansion is good, the results are consistent with financial leverage increasing the operating risk of the firm. However, this interpretation is made more difficult by the finding that highly levered firms are also more likely to retrench in markets without entry by Wal-Mart. Highly levered firms could possibly invest less aggressively, regardless of the threat posed by new entrants. While this may be one cost of financial leverage, it does not necessarily imply that highly levered firms are riskier. Alternatively, highly levered firms may be more likely to retrench in the non–Wal-Mart market because they are directing whatever little funds they have to defend their market share against Wal-Mart. In this case, the retrenchment in non–Wal-Mart markets would be further evidence that financial leverage makes firms more vulnerable to the entry of a new competitor.

Financial Leverage and Macroeconomic Shocks

The results discussed so far show that financial leverage makes firms riskier in the sense that it makes them more vulnerable to industry-specific shocks. Yet, an argument can be made that the most relevant risk for providers of capital (both shareholders and debt holders) is related to economy-wide shocks. At least in theory, industry-specific risk can be diversified away. Economy-wide shocks also fit well with the current understanding of risk. Specifically, business cycle fluctuations are beyond the control of any individual firm, are largely unpredictable, and can have a large impact on firm performance.

Campello (2003) provides extensive evidence on the sensitivity of highly levered firms to changes in economic activity. The results are similar to those based on industry-specific shocks. Following negative shocks to economic activity, highly levered firms lose market share in industries in which rivals are relatively unlevered. In terms of economic significance, the industry-adjusted sales growth of the more levered firms is nearly 1.3 percent lower than that of their unlevered rivals following a 1 percent decline in GDP. These results show that financial leverage increases operating risk and are broadly consistent with the predictions of Bolton and Scharfstein (1990) and Chevalier and Scharfstein (1996). Once again, no support exists for the alternative prediction that financial leverage helps firms gain market share during times of economic distress.

Khanna and Tice (2005) provide further evidence on the sensitivity of highly levered firms to macroeconomic shocks. Using data on department stores across a panel of cities over the 1982 to 1995 period, the authors report a series of findings that confirm the detrimental effect leverage can have on the firm's operations. The first set of results establishes that cities with more levered firms have higher department store prices during normal periods; high debt appears to reduce competition. However, the relation during recessions is reversed. In cities with a mix of high- and low-debt firms, higher debt levels have a negative effect on prices. These results are consistent with low-debt firms cutting prices to induce exit of financially weak rivals. The second set of results shows that highly levered firms are more likely to exit during recessions. This finding parallels the results of Zingales (1998) concerning firm exit following industry deregulation. But Khanna and Tice (2005) are able to extend the analysis further by showing that lower prices can increase the probability of exit for highly levered firms. They also show that efficient highly levered firms are most affected by lower prices during recessions. Apparently, low-debt firms strategically lower prices during recessions to force exit of efficient, financially weak competitors.

Limitations and Extensions

Overall, based on the evidence reviewed in this section, debt financing seems to be risky. So should firms do their best to avoid debt financing? Unfortunately, the literature still does not provide a clear answer to this question. Current studies on the link between financial leverage and the real operations of the firm focus almost exclusively on large negative shocks. Much less is known about the performance of highly levered firms during economic expansions or in industries subject to positive shocks. As discussed earlier, debt financing may reduce agency costs and increase the firm's bargaining power, and these effects may be particularly valuable during economic expansions when cash flows are high. Consequently, financial leverage may have positive effects on performance during economic expansions that are even larger than the corresponding losses during economic downturns. In other words, financial leverage may magnify both positive and negative economic shocks. Consistent with this possibility, Campello (2003) finds that highly levered firms have higher relative-to-industry growth in sales during economic expansions. Models based on credit market imperfections cannot easily explain such findings because financing frictions are less important during expansions. Clearly, more research along these lines is needed before making any strong conclusions.

Another limitation of current research is its general assumption of a monotonic relation between financial leverage and operating performance: that is, financial leverage either boosts or hurts performance. But evidence suggests that such an assumption may be inappropriate. For example, Campello (2006) allows for a non-monotonic relation between leverage and relative-to-industry sales growth. He finds that while excessive firm debt is associated with market share losses that benefit industry rivals, a moderate level of debt is associated with market share gains. These findings lend some support to models predicting that leverage may act as a commitment mechanism to increase output, such as that of Brander and Lewis (1986). These findings are also consistent with research showing improvement in firm performance and productivity following management leveraged buyouts (e.g., Kaplan 1989; Lichtenberg and Siegel 1990). Therefore, at least in some circumstances, financial leverage can improve firm performance. Whether it can also reduce the operating risk of the firm remains an open question.

The final point to emphasize is that, with the exception of Opler and Titman (1994), the studies reviewed in this section do not examine how financial leverage affects the value of the firm in times of economic distress. Instead, they focus on other measures of performance such as sales growth and survival. This makes concluding that financial leverage amplifies negative shocks more difficult. For example, the larger drop in sales for highly levered firms following market entry or during economic recessions could be the optimal response to decreases in demand. Similarly, exit (through liquidation or merger) could be the optimal response for some firms following industry deregulation. If this is the case, financial leverage may actually reduce the adverse effects of industry or economy-wide shocks. Admittedly this alternative interpretation is inconsistent with the finding that even efficient highly levered firms have lower growth in times of economic distress. Nevertheless, finding that financial leverage also reduces the value of the firm in times of economic distress would strengthen the conclusion that financial leverage increases the operating risk of the firm.

FINANCIAL LEVERAGE AND STOCK RETURNS

The positive relation between financial leverage and operating risk has important implications for the firm's required rate of return. Specifically, to the extent that the additional operating risk resulting from debt financing is systematic, the expected rate of return for the firm should be increasing in financial leverage. Because data on firm returns are generally unavailable, this section focuses on the relation between financial leverage and return on equity, as measured by realized stock returns.

Before turning to the empirical evidence, a brief review of the predicted relation between financial leverage and stock returns in the absence of any capital market imperfections may be useful. In Modigliani and Miller (1958), financial leverage has no effect on the overall risk of the firm since the firm's earnings stream is unaffected by financing decisions. However, even in this benchmark case, financial leverage increases the risk and return on equity because of the priority of debt. For example, a firm with a debt-to-equity ratio of 1, rate of return on its assets of 20 percent, and 10 percent interest on debt would earn 30 percent return on its equity. If the rate of return on its assets decreases to 15 percent (a 25 percent drop), the rate of return on equity decreases to 20 percent, dropping by 33.3 percent. In other words, financial leverage increases the expected return on equity but also makes equity riskier (it increases equity beta). If financial leverage also increases the operating risk of the firm, the positive relation between financial leverage and return on equity should be even stronger.

Surprisingly, this simple prediction finds virtually no empirical support. The evidence seems to indicate the financial leverage is associated with lower, not higher, stock returns. The following section reviews these findings and then discusses several recent papers that may shed light on this puzzling result.

Cross-Sectional Studies

The simplest approach to examine the relation between financial leverage and stock returns is to relate financial leverage to stock returns in the cross-section of firms. Specifically, each month realized stock returns are regressed on a lagged measure of financial leverage and additional control characteristics, using all firms with available data for that month. The estimated coefficients from the monthly regressions are then averaged over all the months in the study, and the average coefficient is compared to its time-series standard error for statistical inferences (Fama and MacBeth 1973). Research that follows this approach includes Bhandari (1988), Fama and French (1992), and Penman, Richardson, and Tuna (2007), among others. The main difference among these studies is the definition of financial leverage (i.e., whether it is based on market values or book values) and, more importantly, the time period for the analysis. While earlier studies find a positive relation between financial leverage and stock returns, more recent studies find a negative relation.

Bhandari (1988) provides the first large-sample evidence on the relation between financial leverage and stock returns. The study covers the period from 1948 to 1979 and focuses on market leverage. Specifically, market leverage is defined as the difference between the book value of total assets and the book value of common equity, divided by the market value of common equity. Bhandari finds that financial leverage is positively related to stock returns in the cross-section. At first look, this result is consistent with Modigliani and Miller (1958). However, Bhandari finds that financial leverage helps explain the cross-section of returns even in tests that include equity beta and size. This is a puzzling result. In MM, leverage is related to returns only because it increases equity betas; leverage does not have an independent effect on returns. The results also show that the premium associated with financial leverage is much larger in January than in other months and is consistently positive over the sample period. Bhandari acknowledges that traditional capital asset pricing models cannot easily account for these findings, and speculates that the premium associated with financial leverage may not be due to higher risk after all.

Fama and French (1992) examine the cross-section of stock returns during the more recent period from 1963 to 1990. They use both market leverage and book leverage in their tests, where market leverage is defined as the log of the ratio of book assets to market equity (ln(A/ME)) and book leverage is defined as the log of the ratio of book assets to book equity (ln(A/BE)). The results show that both variables are significantly related to average returns but with opposite signs. As in Bhandari (1988), higher market leverage is associated with higher average returns. In contrast, higher book leverage is associated with lower average returns. These results are clearly at odds with the prediction of Modigliani and Miller (1958).

The explanation offered by Fama and French (1992) is that, taken together, market leverage and book leverage proxy for the book-to-market effect. Specifically, the difference between market and book leverage is book-to-market equity:

$$\ln(\text{BE/ME}) = \ln(\text{A/ME}) - \ln(\text{A/BE})$$

Of course, in the context of traditional capital asset pricing models, the existence of a book-to-market effect is a puzzle in its own right. Fama and French maintain that the risk captured by book-to-market is related to a distress factor in returns, while others such as Lakonishok, Shleifer, and Vishny (1994) and Daniel and Titman (1997) attribute the results to market mispricing. Whatever the reason, the key point is that the relation between leverage and returns is absorbed by the book-to-market effect.

Penman, Richardson, and Tuna (2007) provide further evidence on the relation among leverage, book-to-market, and the cross-section of stock returns. They lay out a decomposition of book-to-price (i.e., book-to-market) that derives from the accounting for book value and that articulates precisely how book-to-price absorbs leverage. Book-to-price (B/P) can be decomposed into operating and leverage components. The first component, measured as the book value of net operating assets divided by their market value, pertains to business operations and serves as a proxy for operating risk under the risk explanation of the B/P effect. The second component, measured as net debt divided by the market value of equity, is a measure of leverage that captures financing risk. Using this decomposition, the authors find that the operating component of the B/P ratio is positively related to subsequent returns, consistent with the findings of Fama and French (1992). However, holding the operating component fixed, the leverage component is negatively associated with subsequent returns. The negative relation between leverage and returns is evident for firms with both high and low B/P ratios and is robust to controls for other return factors, including the B/P factor. Hence, the B/P ratio apparently cannot account for the negative relation between leverage and subsequent returns.

In sum, studies relating leverage to stock returns in the cross-section report results that are inconsistent with the idea that financial leverage increases the expected return on equity. If anything, the consensus that is emerging in the literature is that high leverage is associated with low subsequent stock returns.

Changes in Financial Leverage and Stock Returns

An alternative to the cross-sectional approach is to examine how changes in financial leverage relate to stock returns. Focusing on changes in leverage may help alleviate concerns that the level of financial leverage is correlated with omitted risk factors and that these factors drive the negative relation between financial leverage and stock returns in the cross-section. In the benchmark setting of Modigliani and Miller (1958), an increase (decrease) in financial leverage would lead to higher subsequent stock returns, all else being equal. An increase in financial leverage may also decrease equity values if it increases the operating risk of the firm.

Eckbo (1986) provides early evidence on the valuation effects of leverage increases. In a sample of 723 corporate debt offerings during the period from 1964 to 1981, Eckbo reports nonpositive price effects at the announcement of straight debt offerings and significantly negative price effects at the announcement of convertible debt offerings. These results are weakly consistent with the idea that increases in financial leverage decrease equity values. However, attributing the decrease in equity values to increases in risk alone is difficult. Equity values may also decrease if debt offerings signal poor operating performance, as in Miller and Rock (1985), or indicate that the firm's securities are overvalued, as in Myers and Majluf (1984). Although additional tests do not provide strong support for either of these alternatives, they do not give much credence to the risk explanation either. Equally troubling to proponents of the risk explanation are results showing that equity offerings are also associated with negative announcement period returns (see, e.g., Asquith and Mullins 1986; Masulis and Korwar 1986). Apparently, equity values decrease with any external financing announcement regardless of whether the transaction increases or decreases financial leverage.

Spiess and Affleck-Graves (1999) focus on long-run stock returns following debt offerings. Based on a sample of 2,229 public debt offerings over the period from 1975 to 1989, the authors show that firms issuing either straight or convertible debt underperform benchmark portfolios in the subsequent five years. In other words, increases in financial leverage are associated with lower subsequent returns. Dichev and Piotroski (1999) report similar underperformance following private debt offerings. These findings are exactly the opposite of what Modigliani and Miller's (1958) model would predict. Interpreted in the risk-return framework, the results indicate that firms increasing their financial leverage are less risky than other firms with similar characteristics.

A more plausible explanation is that overvalued firms issue both equity and debt, and investors under-react to the initial announcement of external financing. This is essentially the prediction of Myers and Majluf (1984), albeit combined with a dose of irrationality. Consistent with this explanation, Loughran and Ritter (1995) and Spiess and Affleck-Graves (1995) find that stock returns are also abnormally low after equity offerings. The results are also consistent with Miller and Rock (1985). Debt financing may signal deteriorating operating performance that gets reflected into prices only gradually. Recent findings by Dimitrov and Jain (2008) support this explanation. Specifically, they report that changes in financial leverage are strongly negatively correlated with contemporaneous changes in earnings and operating cash flows. Changes in financial leverage are also negatively correlated with both contemporaneous and subsequent stock returns, suggesting that investors react slowly to the deteriorating performance.

Explaining the Relation between Leverage and Returns

Overall, neither the levels nor the changes in financial leverage provide much evidence in support of a positive relation between leverage and expected stock returns. So even though financial leverage increases the operating risk of the firm, shareholders apparently are not compensated with higher expected returns. One way to resolve the puzzle is to attribute the findings to the market's mispricing of financial risk. But before resorting to market inefficiency arguments, considering rational explanations for these return patterns is worthwhile.

One explanation offered by George and Hwang (2010) is that firms with high distress costs choose low leverage to avoid distress. This explanation critically relies on the existence of financial distress costs. If financial distress is costly, firms with high distress costs may optimally utilize less leverage than firms with low costs. Since firms with high costs choose low leverage, low leverage firms have the greatest exposure to distress risk. Thus, leverage and expected stock returns should be negatively correlated in the cross-section. George and Hwang offer several new results to support their hypothesis. Importantly, the authors find that low leverage firms are less likely to become distressed but also suffer more in terms of operating performance once they become distressed. The results are consistent with the hypothesis that low leverage firms have higher distress costs. However, reconciling these findings with earlier studies showing that financial leverage magnifies adverse economic shocks is difficult. Thus, judging whether George and Hwang's explanation can successfully resolve the levered returns puzzle may be premature.

Gomes and Schmid (2010) offer another explanation based on financial market imperfections. They model the relation between financial leverage and stock returns in a dynamic setting where both leverage and investment are determined endogenously. The theoretical results show that leverage and investments are often strongly correlated. Highly levered firms in the model tend to be more mature firms with relatively safe book assets and fewer risky growth assets. In other words, highly levered firms in the model face less underlying asset risk and possibly less equity risk. As a result, cross-sectional studies may show that financial leverage is negatively associated with returns even if leverage by itself increases expected returns. Thus, tests that fail to control for the interdependence between leverage and investment decisions are unlikely to be very informative. Whether controlling for endogeneity can resolve the levered returns puzzle remains an open question.

SUMMARY AND CONCLUSIONS

In perfect capital markets, capital structure affects neither the risk nor the value of the firm. Markets, however, are not perfect. With market frictions, the real and financing sides are no longer independent. As a result, variables such as financial leverage can have important consequences for the risk of the firm.

Prior analytical work has identified several mechanisms through which financial leverage can affect risk. On the negative side, financial leverage may increase operating risk. It can impair the firm's access to capital and its ability to invest. Highly levered firms may fall victim to predation by financially stronger rivals and may lose market share if customers are concerned that the firm may enter bankruptcy. All of these effects are likely to be stronger during recession when credit constraints are more likely to bind. On the positive side, financial leverage can reduce agency costs between managers and shareholders, resulting in better decision making. It can also increase managers' bargaining power with nonfinancial stakeholders. These effects may reduce operating risk.

While theory provides no definitive answer as to how financial leverage affects firm risk, the empirical evidence is more conclusive. Financial leverage amplifies negative economic shocks. Highly levered firms experience disproportionate decreases in sales growth, investments, and market value of equity during industry downturns. They are less likely to survive following industry deregulation. When a new firm enters their market, highly levered firms are more likely to retrench.

Finally, such firms experience disproportionate decreases in sales during economic recessions, even if their operations are more efficient. Firms with low leverage benefit at the expense of highly levered firms.

Despite having greater operating risk, highly levered firms do not provide greater returns to their shareholders. Cross-sectional studies find that financial leverage is negatively associated with stock returns. Firm valuations drop following both increases and decreases in financial leverage, while changes in financial leverage are negatively associated with subsequent stock returns. These results are puzzling. Accounting for the endogeneity of financial leverage may help resolve the puzzle.

What lessons should managers draw from the academic literature? One implication is that conservative managers may do well to avoid excessive debt, especially if they compete in concentrated industries against rivals with low leverage. For less risk-averse managers, the implications are less clear. While financial leverage increases operating risk, higher operating risk may be in the best interest of shareholders because of the option-like properties of equity. Financial leverage can also increase the firm's operating cash flows by reducing agency costs and taxes. Further research is needed to determine whether financial leverage is worth the risk.

DISCUSSION QUESTIONS

1. Many investors and lawmakers have blamed financial leverage for the economic crisis during 2008 and 2009. Discuss whether the academic literature supports this assertion.
2. A common argument against regulation is that unfettered competition always assures the most efficient outcome. Discuss whether this argument is valid in imperfect capital markets.
3. Can financial constraints, defined as frictions that prevent the firm from funding all desired investments, ever be beneficial to the firm? If so, explain why.
4. Many empirical multifactor asset pricing models include financial leverage as an additional risk factor. Under what conditions would financial leverage be a priced risk factor? Discuss whether these conditions are met.

REFERENCES

Asquith, Paul, and David W. Mullins. 1986. "Equity Issues and Offering Dilution." *Journal of Financial Economics* 15:2, 61–89.

Bernanke, Ben, and Mark Gertler. 1989. "Agency Costs, Net Worth, and Business Fluctuations." *American Economic Review* 79:1, 14–31.

Bernanke, Ben S., and Mark Gertler. 1995. "Inside the Black Box: The Credit Channel of Monetary Policy Transmission." *Journal of Economic Perspectives* 9:4, 27–48.

Bhandari, Laxmi C. 1988. "Debt/Equity Ratio and Expected Common Stock Returns: Empirical Evidence." *Journal of Finance* 43:2, 507–528.

Bolton, Patrick, and David S. Scharfstein. 1990. "A Theory of Predation Based on Agency Problems in Financial Contracting." *American Economic Review* 80:1, 93–106.

Brander, James A., and Tracy R. Lewis. 1986. "Oligopoly and Financial Structure: The Limited Liability Effect." *American Economic Review* 76:5, 956–970.

Campello, Murillo. 2003. "Capital Structure and Product Markets Interactions: Evidence from Business Cycles." *Journal of Financial Economics* 68:3, 353–378.
Campello, Murillo. 2006. "Debt Financing: Does It Boost or Hurt Firm Performance in Product Markets?" *Journal of Financial Economics* 82:1, 135–172.
Chevalier, Judith A., and David S. Scharfstein. 1996. "Capital-Market Imperfections and Countercyclical Markups: Theory and Evidence." *American Economic Review* 86:4, 703–725.
Daniel, Kent, and Sheridan Titman. 1997. "Evidence on the Characteristics of Cross-Sectional Variation in Stock Returns." *Journal of Finance* 52:1, 1–33.
Dichev, Ilia D., and Joseph D. Piotroski. 1999. "The Performance of Long-Run Stock Returns Following Issues of Public and Private Debt." *Journal of Business Finance & Accounting* 26:9, 1103–1132.
Dimitrov, Valentin, and Prem C. Jain. 2008. "The Value-Relevance of Changes in Financial Leverage Beyond Growth in Assets and GAAP Earnings." *Journal of Accounting, Auditing & Finance* 23:2, 191–222.
Eckbo, B. Espen. 1986. "Valuation Effects of Corporate Debt Offerings." *Journal of Financial Economics* 15:2, 119–151.
Fama, Eugene F., and Kenneth R. French. 1992. "The Cross-Section of Expected Stock Returns." *Journal of Finance* 47:2, 427–465.
Fama, Eugene F., and James D. MacBeth. 1973. "Risk, Return, and Equilibrium: Empirical Tests." *Journal of Political Economy* 81:3, 607–636.
George, Thomas J., and Chuan-Yang Hwang. 2010. "A Resolution of the Distress Risk and Leverage Puzzles in the Cross-Section of Stock Returns." *Journal of Financial Economics* 96:1, 56–79.
Gomes, Joao F., and Lukas Schmid. 2010. "Levered Returns." *Journal of Finance* 65:2, 467–494.
Jensen, Michael C. 1986. "Agency Costs of Free Cash Flow, Corporate Finance, and Takeovers." *American Economic Review* 76:2, 323–329.
Jensen, Michael C., and William H. Meckling. 1976. "Theory of the Firm: Managerial Behavior, Agency Costs and Ownership Structure." *Journal of Financial Economics* 3:4, 305–360.
Kaplan, Steven. 1989. "The Effects of Management Buyouts on Operating Performance and Value." *Journal of Financial Economics* 24:2, 217–254.
Khanna, Naveen, and Sheri Tice. 2000. "Strategic Responses of Incumbents to New Entry: The Effect of Ownership Structure, Capital Structure, and Focus." *Review of Financial Studies* 13:3, 749–779.
Khanna, Naveen, and Sheri Tice. 2005. "Pricing, Exit, and Location Decisions of Firms: Evidence on the Role of Debt and Operating Efficiency." *Journal of Financial Economics* 75:2, 397–427.
Lakonishok, Josef, Andrei Shleifer, and Robert W. Vishny. 1994. "Contrarian Investment, Extrapolation, and Risk." *Journal of Finance* 49:5, 1541–1578.
Lang, Larry, Eli Ofek, and René M. Stulz. 1996. "Leverage, Investment, and Firm Growth." *Journal of Financial Economics* 40:1, 3–29.
Lichtenberg, Frank R., and Donald Siegel. 1990. "The Effects of Leveraged Buyouts on Productivity and Related Aspects of Firm Behavior." *Journal of Financial Economics* 27:1, 165–194.
Loughran, Tim, and Jay R. Ritter. 1995. "The New Issues Puzzle." *Journal of Finance* 50:1, 23–51.
Maksimovic, Vojislav, and Sheridan Titman. 1991. "Financial Policy and Reputation for Product Quality." *Review of Financial Studies* 4:1, 175–200.
Masulis, Ronald W., and Ashok N. Korwar. 1986. "Seasoned Equity Offerings: An Empirical Investigation." *Journal of Financial Economics* 15:1–2, 91–118.
Miller, Merton H., and Kevin Rock. 1985. "Dividend Policy under Asymmetric Information." *Journal of Finance* 40:4, 1031–1051.

Modigliani, Franco, and Merton H. Miller. 1958. "The Cost of Capital, Corporation Finance and the Theory of Investment." *American Economic Review* 48:3, 261–297.
Myers, Stewart C. 1977. "Determinants of Corporate Borrowing." *Journal of Financial Economics* 5:2, 147–175.
Myers, Stewart C., and Nicholas S. Majluf. 1984. "Corporate Financing and Investment Decisions When Firms Have Information That Investors Do Not Have." *Journal of Financial Economics* 13:2, 187–221.
Opler, Tim C., and Sheridan Titman. 1994. "Financial Distress and Corporate Performance." *Journal of Finance* 49:3, 1015–1040.
Penman, Stephen H., Scott A. Richardson, and Irem Tuna. 2007. "The Book-to-Price Effect in Stock Returns: Accounting for Leverage." *Journal of Accounting Research* 45:2, 427–467.
Perotti, Enrico C., and Kathryn E. Spier. 1993. "Capital Structure as a Bargaining Tool: The Role of Leverage in Contract Renegotiation." *American Economic Review* 83:5, 1131–1141.
Spiess, D. Katherine, and John Affleck-Graves. 1995. "Underperformance in Long-Run Stock Returns Following Seasoned Equity Offerings." *Journal of Financial Economics* 38:3, 243–267.
Spiess, D. Katherine, and John Affleck-Graves. 1999. "The Long-Run Performance of Stock Returns Following Debt Offerings." *Journal of Financial Economics* 54:1, 45–73.
Titman, Sheridan. 1984. "The Effect of Capital Structure on a Firm's Liquidation Decision." *Journal of Financial Economics* 13:1, 137–151.
Zingales, Luigi. 1998. "Survival of the Fittest or the Fattest? Exit and Financing in the Trucking Industry." *Journal of Finance* 53:3, 905–938.

ABOUT THE AUTHOR

Valentin Dimitrov joined Rutgers University in 2004 after spending a year as an instructor at Tulane University. Professor Dimitrov has published articles on accounting, corporate finance, and empirical asset pricing in such journals as the *Journal of Financial Economics* and *Review of Financial Studies*. He has taught classes in investments, corporate finance, and financial accounting, and has won the Rutgers Business School Junior Faculty Teaching Award. Professor Dimitrov holds a BS in Management degree and a PhD in Business Administration from Tulane University.

CHAPTER 5

Capital Structure and Returns

YAZ GÜLNUR MURADOĞLU
Professor of Finance, Cass Business School, City University

SHEEJA SIVAPRASAD
Senior Lecturer, Department of Finance and Business Law, University of Westminster

INTRODUCTION

In their seminal work on capital structure, Modigliani and Miller (1958) (hereafter, MM) formulated their Propositions I and II. Proposition I states the market value of a firm is independent of its capital structure. That is, the average cost of capital for a firm is completely independent of its capital structure, and it is equal to the capitalization rate of a pure equity stream of its class. Derived from Proposition I, Proposition II states the expected yield of a share is equal to the appropriate capitalization rate plus a premium related to financial risk equal to the debt-to-equity ratio.

Modigliani and Miller's (1958) work led to the development of different theories on capital structure. During the 1960s and 1970s, various economists introduced several theories, including trade-off theory, pecking order theory, agency theory, market timing theory, corporate control theory, and product cost theory.

The remainder of this chapter has the following organization. The first section discusses the work of MM and the theories of capital structure. Empirical work is not necessarily consistent with the MM propositions. Initial work during the 1980s and early 1990s report a positive relationship between leverage and returns, while more recent work during the past decade shows that the relationship between leverage and stock returns is negative. The next section discusses this association in detail. The discrepancies between the findings of the empirical work on the link between leverage and stock returns are mainly due to different definitions of leverage employed and the properties of the various samples and methodologies used. Methodological issues are discussed in the next to last section. The final section provides a summary and conclusions.

THEORIES OF CAPITAL STRUCTURE

Origins of the theory of capital structure go back to 1950s and the work of Modigliani and Miller (1958). MM show that financing decisions do not matter in perfect capital markets. They argue a firm's operations, and not its financing decisions, determine its total value. This work had overwhelming influence on the development of several capital structure theories. Yet, researchers have undertaken limited work designed to examine the empirical relationship between leverage and stock returns. Despite MM's assertion of the irrelevance of capital structure, practitioners believe that capital structure matters and view it as an important decision that affects a firm's performance.

The MM Theory of Capital Structure

The MM theorem is a cornerstone in corporate finance. MM start with the question "what is the cost of capital to a firm?" They argue that this question has posed an issue to three main classes of economists. Financial economists are concerned with the techniques of financing firms so as to ensure continued existence. Managerial economists focus on capital budgeting decisions while economic theorists are concerned with investment behavior at the micro and macro levels.

According to theorists of the time such as Somers (1955) and Hicks (1975), the two main decision-making criteria are maximization of profits and maximization of market value. In the case of the first criterion, a physical asset is worth acquiring if it increases the net profits of the firm. But the net profits increase only if the expected rate of returns of the asset exceeds the rate of interest. In keeping with the second criterion, an asset is worth purchasing only if it increases the value of the owners' equity (i.e., the market value of the firm).

However, MM discount the first criterion of profit maximization. They argue that what ought to be considered is the utility function (or risk preferences) of the owners. Management would have difficulty taking into consideration the risk preferences of owners when deciding on which projects to accept. Hence, the decision-making criterion that should guide managers is whether accepting the project increases the value of the firm's shares. Use of this criterion suggests adopting a market value approach.

Proposition I states the market value for a firm is independent of its financing decisions. MM built their original model based on the following assumptions:

- Investment opportunities of the firm remain fixed.
- Investors have homogeneous expectations about future corporate earnings and the volatility of these earnings.
- Capital markets are perfect, e.g., there are no transaction costs, and taxes and investors can borrow at the same rate as companies.
- There are no bankruptcy and reorganization costs.
- Debt is risk free and the interest rate on debt is the risk-free rate.
- The business risk of a firm can be measured by the standard deviation of earnings, and firms can be grouped into distinct business sectors.

In MM's theoretical model, Proposition 1 takes the following form for any firm j in class k:

$$V_j = (S_j + D_j) = \overline{X_j}, \tag{5.1}$$

where V_j = market value of firm; S_j = the market value of its common shares; D_j = the market value of the debt of the company; and X_j = expected return on the assets owned by the company.

Later, Modigliani and Miller (1963) relaxed the assumption on taxes and incorporated the tax advantage on earnings into their model. They argue that the tax advantage of debt financing is greater than originally suggested. Because debt provides the firm with a tax shield in the form of interest deductibility, the firm may benefit by issuing debt. The market values of firms in each risk class must be proportional in equilibrium to their expected returns net of taxes.

Proposition II states the rate of return on common stock of companies whose capital structure includes some debt is equal to the appropriate capitalization rate for a pure equity stream plus a premium related to financial risk, which is equal to the debt-to-equity ratio times the spread between the capitalization rate and risk-free rate. MM's Proposition II took the following form:

$$i_j = p_k + (p_k - r)D_j/E_j, \tag{5.2}$$

where i_j = the expected yield of a share of stock; p_k = the capitalization rate for a pure equity stream in the class; r = the cost of debt; and D_j/E_j = the debt-to-equity ratio.

The return on equity capital is an increasing function of leverage. This is because debt increases the riskiness of the stock, and hence equity shareholders will demand a higher return on their stocks. MM test Proposition II for electric utilities and oil and gas companies. They define returns as the sum of interest, preferred dividends, and stockholders' income net of corporate income taxes. Their results show that the beta coefficient is 0.02 for the electric utilities and 0.05 for the oil companies. MM express this result as follows:

$$\text{Electric utilities } z = 6.6 + 0.017h \tag{5.3}$$

$$\text{Oil companies } z = 8.9 + 0.051h \tag{5.4}$$

where z = the percentage of return to equity shareholders; and h = the debt-to-equity ratio.

MM also conduct linearity tests between leverage and returns. Contrary to the traditionalist theory of leverage, MM do not find a hint of a curvilinear or a U-shaped relationship between the cost of capital and leverage. MM's finding of a linear relationship between returns and leverage provides evidence of the rising costs of borrowed funds as leverage increases.

THEORIES OF CAPITAL STRUCTURE

Modigliani and Miller's (1958) seminal work led to the development of the following theories of capital structure. Chapter 10 provides additional discussion of several of these theories.

Trade-Off Theory

Trade-off theory argues that debt in a firm's capital structure is beneficial to equity investors as long as they are rewarded up to the point where the benefit of the tax deductibility of interest is offset against potential bankruptcy costs. Trade-off theory stems from Modigliani and Miller (1963). According to MM, shareholders should benefit from a firm having debt in its capital structure due to the tax advantage of debt.

Trade-off theory consists of static trade-off theory and dynamic theory. According to the static trade-off theory, using debt compared with equity has both advantages and disadvantages. Thus, firms should select an optimal capital structure that balances these at the margin (Scott 1977). Although the initial theory focused on the trade-off between tax advantages and the bankruptcy costs of debt, it was later extended to include agency costs (Jensen and Meckling 1976). The traditional view is that tax advantages to debt exist but are counter-balanced by costs associated with bankruptcy and financial distress beyond a certain level. As Scott notes, firms unable to provide collateral must pay higher interest or be forced to issue equity instead of debt. Thus, a positive relationship between tangibility of assets and leverage is predicted. Myers (1977) analyzes the link between debt financing and firm value when interest is a tax-deductible expense ignoring bankruptcy costs. He concludes that the amount of debt issued by the firm is the amount that maximizes the market value of the firm.

In their dynamic trade-off theory, Fischer, Heinkel, and Zechner (1989) find that even in a trade-off setting with a fixed cost of issuing equity, firms may stray from their target capital structure adjusting leverage only when it goes beyond extreme bounds. This occurs because when a firm earns profits, it often pays off debt, and leverage falls automatically. A firm only periodically makes large readjustments in order to capture the tax benefits of leverage. Thus, profitable firms typically use less leverage if trade-off theory is at work and adjustment costs are taken into account. Leland (1994) also presents a dynamic trade-off model. In this model, firms let their leverage fluctuate over time reflecting accumulated earnings and losses and do not adjust leverage toward the target as long as the adjustment costs exceed the value lost due to suboptimal capital structure.

The Miller (1977) model discounts the tax advantage of issuing debt because it gets offset by personal taxes. This model led to attempts to reconcile his model with the balancing theory of capital structure. DeAngelo and Masulis (1980) show the presence of a corporate tax shield substituting for debt implies a market equilibrium in which each firm has a unique capital structure. The existence of nondebt tax shields, such as depreciation deductions and investment tax credits together with an asymmetric corporate tax code that does not rebate losses, is sufficient to overturn the irrelevance of Miller. DeAngelo and Masulis contend that a substitution effect exists between the level of nondebt tax shields and the tax benefits of corporate leverage.

Kim (1982) also finds that if leverage-related costs such as bankruptcy costs and agency costs are significant and if the income from equity is untaxed, then the marginal bondholders' tax rate will be lower than the corporate rate. Further, there will be a positive net tax advantage to corporate debt financing. In his study on 5308 listed Japanese companies, Gul (1999) observes the nondebt tax shields and argues that high growth firms have lesser nondebt tax shields.

Kraus and Litzenberger (1973) examine the direct and indirect costs of bankruptcy and the tax advantage of debt. They conclude that the taxation of corporate profits and the existence of bankruptcy penalties are market imperfections that are central to a positive theory of the effect of leverage on the firm's market value. However, the authors argue that if the firm's debt obligation exceeds its earnings, the firm's value is not necessarily a concave function of its debt obligation.

Pecking Order Theory

Donaldson (1961) first suggests the pecking order theory. He conducts a study on a sample of large corporations in which management strongly favors internal generation as a source of new funds as compared to external funds. Myers (1984) develops a pecking order theory about how firms finance themselves and about the capital structures that result from these pecking order decisions. As Myers and Majluf (1984) show, if outside investors are less informed than firm insiders, equity may be mispriced by the market. If firms are required to finance new projects by issuing equity, underpricing may be so severe that new investors capture more than the net present value (NPV) of the new project resulting in a net loss to existing shareholders. In such a case, management will reject the project even if its NPV is positive. This underinvestment can be avoided if the firm can finance the new project using a security that is not so badly undervalued by the market. To avoid this distortion, managers follow what Myers called the pecking order. Managers finance projects first with retained earnings, which involves no asymmetric information, followed by low-risk debt for which the problem is negligible and then with risky debt. The firm issues equity only as a last resort when investment so far exceeds earnings that financing with debt would produce excessive leverage.

Krasker (1986) tests the pecking order model and his results are similar to those of Myers (1984). Aybar-Arias, Casino-Martinez, and Lopez-Gracia (2004) examine pecking order theory in small and medium enterprises (SMEs) and find results similar to the model. Narayanan (1988) and Heinkel and Zechner (1990) obtain results that are similar to those of Myers. Yet, they conclude that there can be overinvestment, that is, investment in negative NPV projects when the information asymmetry concerns only the value of the new project. Narayanan explains that when firms can issue debt or equity, all firms either issue debt or reject the project. Narayanan finds that new issues of debt and Heinkel and Zechner find that existing debt reduces the overinvestment problem relative to equity financing.

Other studies test pecking order theory indirectly. For example, Korajczyk, Lucas, and McDonald (1991) and Choe, Maslius, and Nanda (1993) examine if firms time equity issuance to avoid periods of greater asymmetric information problems; they find that firms are likely to issue equity in boom periods when investors have a favorable outlook on the economy while Korajczyk et al. find that firms time their equity offerings soon after they report earnings.

Helwege and Liang (1996) directly test the existence of a pecking order by examining the financing choices of small firms as they age. Their empirical results provide little support for pecking order theory. They find that the probability of obtaining external funds is unrelated to the shortfall in internal sources of cash. However, their results show that firms with surplus cash avoid the capital markets.

Frank and Goyal (2003) test pecking order theory of corporate leverage. Contrary to the theory, they find that net equity issues track the financing deficit more closely than do net debt issues. Debt financing does not dominate equity financing in magnitude. They conclude that equity is more important than debt.

Graham and Harvey (2001) find mixed results in their survey of 392 chief financial officers (CFOs) in testing the pecking order theory and very little evidence that executives are concerned about asymmetric information. Similarly, in their study on capital structure decisions of Dutch companies, De Jong and Veld (2001) do not find their results supporting the adverse selection costs of Myers and Majluf (1984). Agca and Mozumdar (2005) argue that the conflicting evidence of pecking order theory is more due to the differences between the financing practices of large and small firms, and the skewness of the firm size distribution. The authors find that the theory does not hold for small firms due to their low debt capacities that are quickly exhausted, forcing them to issue equity.

Agency Costs Theory

The models based on agency costs focus on how capital structures can help contain the agency costs by aligning the interests of the shareholders, managers, and debt holders. Jensen and Meckling (1976) identify two types of conflicts: conflicts between equity shareholders and managers, and conflicts between equity shareholders and debt holders. According to Harris and Raviv (1991), conflicts between shareholders and managers arise because they might disagree on an operating decision such as project selection. This problem cannot be solved through contracts based on cash flows and investment expenditures. Hence, debt helps to mitigate the problem by giving investors the option to force liquidation if cash flows are poor.

Jensen (1986) contends that debt payments reduce free cash flow available to self-interested managers. Therefore, managers determine capital structure by trading off the benefits versus the costs of using debt. Stulz (1990) finds that debt payments limit the amount of free cash flow available for profitable payments. According to DeAngelo and DeAngelo (2006), firms can use low leverage, substantial equity payouts, and moderate cash holdings to control agency costs while preserving financial flexibility. Although high leverage mitigates agency problems, it also reduces financial flexibility because the utilization of the current borrowing capacity translates into less availability in the future.

Conflicts between debt holders and shareholders arise because the debt contract gives shareholders an incentive to invest suboptimally. If an investment yields large returns that are well above the face value of the debt, shareholders capture most of the gains. However, if an investment turns out to be a loss, debt holders must bear the consequences. As a result, shareholders may take on very risky projects at the expense of debt holders. Thus, debt holders bear the costs of investing in value decreasing investments created by debt. This is generally called the "asset substitution effect" and is an agency cost of debt financing. According to Williamson (1988), the benefits of debt are the incentives provided to managers by the rules under which the debt holders can take over the firm and liquidate the assets. The cost of debt is that the inflexibility of the rules can result in liquidating assets when they are more valuable to the firm. Hence, Williamson concludes that firms should finance more redeployable assets with debt.

Agarwal and Mandelker (1987) find that the security holdings of managers of firms with a debt-to-equity ratio that increases are larger than those for which the ratio decreases. Thus, when firms make financing decisions, executive holdings seem to have a role in reducing agency problems. Harvey, Lins, and Roper (2004) focus on the effect of capital structure as a governance mechanism in emerging markets. They find that actively monitored debt helps to create value to firms that have potentially high agency costs, which arises from misaligned managerial incentives and overinvestment problems. Hovakimian, Opler, and Titman (2001) find the negative relationship between past stock returns and leverage increasing choices is similar with agency models when managers have incentives to increase leverage when stock prices are low. Their results are also similar with the theory that managers are reluctant to issue equity when they view their firms' stocks as being underpriced. Biais and Casamatta (1999) analyze the optimal financing of investment projects when managers must exert unobservable effort and can switch to less-profitable riskier ventures. Optimal financial contracts can be implemented by a combination of debt and equity when risk shifting is the most severe, while stock options are also needed when the problem of investing suboptimally is the most severe.

Market Timing Theory

Market timing theory primarily advocates that capital structure evolves as the cumulative outcome of past attempts to time the equity market (Baker and Wurgler 2002). Thus, firms prefer equity when the relative cost of equity is low and prefer debt otherwise. There are two versions of market timing. One version focuses on information asymmetry developed by Myers and Majluf (1984), previously discussed under pecking order theory. Korajczyk, Lucas, and McDonald (1992) examine adverse selection that varies across firms. Choe, Masulis, and Nanda (1993) study adverse selection that varies across time. They find that firms are likely to issue equity in boom periods when investors have a favorable outlook on the economy. Their results are similar to those of Korajcyzk et al. who find that firms tend to announce equity issues following releases of information that may reduce information asymmetry.

The second version of the market timing theory involves equity market timing and irrational investors or managers and time-varying mispricing. La Porta et al. (1997) find that managers issue equity when they believe its cost to be irrationally low and repurchase equity when they believe its cost is irrationally high. Here the critical assumption is that managers can time the market. Survey evidence by Graham and Harvey (2001) shows that CFOs try to time the equity market. In fact, two-thirds of the responding CFOs admit that they have issued equity depending on the amount by which their stock is undervalued or overvalued. Hovakimian, Hovakimian, and Tehranian (2004) also find evidence of market timing. Their results show that high stock returns increase the probability of equity issuance but have no effect on target leverage. Baker and Wurgler (2002) argue that the theory of capital structure is the result of equity market timing and not a quest to maintain target capital structures. Instead, they relate capital structure to past market-to-book ratios.

Corporate Control Theory

Corporate control theory studies the linkage of capital structure with takeover activities. Harris and Raviv (1988, 1991), Stulz (1988), and Israel (1991) proposed the theory of corporate control and capital structure. The insight offered by Harris and Raviv (1988) and Stulz is that capital structure affects the outcome of takeover contests through its effect on the distribution of votes between management and outside investors. Israel studies how capital structure affects the outcome of takeovers though their effect on the distribution of cash flows between voting rights and nonvoting rights.

In their study, Harris and Raviv (1988) conclude that the optimal capital structure results from a trade-off between increases in management's voting power and increases in the likelihood that the firm will go bankrupt, causing incumbent management to lose its benefits of control. Stulz (1988) shows that a higher equity fraction held by management decreases the probability of a takeover but increases the premium offered if a bid is made.

Israel (1991) explains that as the bargaining power of the target shareholders' decreases, the target optimally issues more debt, and the fraction of the takeover premium as a result falls. The author states the choice of capital structure is based on its effect on both the probability that value-increasing acquisitions will materialize and the division of the synergy gain between the various parties. Israel concludes that the optimal debt level balances a decrease in the probability of acquisition against a higher share of the synergy for the target's shareholders. His results show that the probability of firms becoming targets decreases with leverage and that the acquirers' share of the total equity gain increases with targets' leverage. Israel also finds that when a bidder initiates an acquisition, it leads to an increase in the target's stock price and debt levels and also the acquiring firm's value increases.

The basic idea is that managers select capital structure and ownership structure in order to gain advantages in future takeover battles. Israel (1992) uses debt as a mechanism that enables the incumbent management to obtain the maximum value from the rival. He shows that firm value depends on both capital and ownership structures.

Product Cost Theory

Capital structure models based on product stem from recently developed theories. Studies examine the connection between capital structure and either product market strategy or characteristics of product inputs (Harris and Raviv 1991). Brander and Lewis (1986) find that product market decisions and financial decisions are normally related. They document systematic differences across industries with respect to financial structures. These variations can be explained industry specific factors such as the varying degrees of competition. Titman (1984) observes that liquidation of a firm may impose costs on its customers (or suppliers) such as the inability to obtain the product, parts, and/or services. He shows that firms may use capital structure to commit shareholders to an optimal liquidation policy by incorporating these normally ignored costs. Singh, Davidson, and Suchard (2003) find that corporate leverage is positively related across product lines but negatively related to geographic diversification.

Campello (2003) provides firm and industry-level evidence of the effects of capital structure on product outcomes for a cross-section of industries. His results show that firms relying more heavily on external financing are more likely to reduce their investment in market share building during downturns and that the competitive outcomes resulting from such actions are jointly determined both by capital structures of the firm and its rivals. Stomper and Zulehner (2004) examine the effect of leverage on investments. They find evidence that leverage and debt maturity affect corporate strategy. Norton (1995) studies the issue of franchising and capital structure. He concludes that franchising is clearly a capital structure issue where the role of debt incurred by franchisees is a potential screening and bonding device.

Campello (2006) seeks to establish whether debt hurts a firm's product market performance. He identifies leverage as creditors' valuation of assets. Campello finds that moderate debt taking is associated with relative-to-rival sales gains but high indebtedness leads to product market underperformance. Kale and Shahrur (2007) investigate how the inclusion of suppliers and customers as stakeholders affects a firm's leverage choice. They find that a firm's leverage is negatively related to the research and development (R&D) intensities of its suppliers and customers. Their results are similar to the bargaining role for debt where they find a positive relationship between a firm's debt level and its degree of concentration in supplier/customer industries. Hence, capital structure has an impact on a firm's products and pricing policies.

These studies explore the association between capital structure and marketing strategy or characteristics of products or inputs. Studies find evidence supporting a link between capital structure and product market strategy or characteristics of product inputs. As this is a relatively new theory, more work needs to be done to substantiate the existing research evidence.

EMPIRICAL WORK ON THE RELATIONSHIP BETWEEN LEVERAGE AND RETURNS

This section discusses the limited number of studies examining the connection between leverage and returns. Some studies show that returns increase with leverage (Hamada 1972; Bhandari 1988), while others indicate the opposite relationship (Hall and Weiss 1967; Dimitrov and Jain 2008; Korteweg 2010; Muradoglu and Sivaprasad 2009). Although these studies show that leverage can explain returns, the results are contradictory. This may result from differences in methodologies, samples, and definitions of leverage.

Positive Relationship between Leverage and Returns

Hamada (1969) theoretically proves that Proposition II holds by concluding that the capitalization rate for a firm's equity, or the rate of return by investors, increases linearly with a firm's leverage ratio. The main limitation of this work is its theoretical orientation. Hamada (1972) tests the link between a firm's leverage and its common stock's systematic risk over a cross-section of all firms. He concludes that firms with debt have higher returns because of greater financial risk. He uses industry as a proxy for business risk because his sample lacks a sufficient number of firms to undertake separate analysis of different sectors. Using 304 U.S. firms from 1948 to 1967, Hamada applies the market model to test the association between leverage and stock returns and finds a positive relationship.

Masulis (1983) also shows that a change in leverage is positively related to a change in stock returns. He studies daily stock returns following exchange offers and recapitalizations where recapitalizations occur at a single time. However, his work has limitations. For example, his sample contains a group of all companies that have gone through pure capital structure changes. Because this group of companies represents a certain class of risk, assuming that characteristics of firms in this subsample are representative of all firms is unreasonable. The study analyzes short-term value changes as a result of changes in leverage brought about by exchange offers and recapitalizations.

Bhandari (1988) tests MM's Proposition II by examining whether expected common stock returns are positively related to the debt ratio in the cross-section of all firms. He adjusts returns for inflation, controls for idiosyncratic risk through size and beta, and includes all firms including financial companies, whose capital structures differ markedly from others in his sample. Bhandari conducts his tests in the cross-section of all firms without assuming different sectors as being in different risk classes. His results provide evidence that leverage has a significant positive effect on expected common stock returns.

Negative Relationship between Leverage and Returns

Arditti (1967) explores the association between leverage and returns. He defines *returns* as the geometric average of returns and *leverage* as the ratio of equity at market value to debt at book value. His sample of firms includes industrials, railroads, and utilities. He finds a negative but insignificant relationship between leverage and returns. Arditti contends that this result could be due to omitting some interfirm risk variables that are positively correlated with returns but negatively correlated with the leverage ratio. These omitted variables must relate to some non-income information because the regressions include all other information relating to income.

Hall and Weiss (1967) test the link between returns and the ratio of equity-to-assets, which is inversely related to leverage. The authors define *returns* as returns on equity on an after-tax basis. Their sample includes the top 500 largest industrial corporations. Hall and Weiss find a negative relationship between equity-to-assets ratio and returns. They argue that since large amounts of leverage (i.e., a low equity-to-assets ratio) imply high risks, one would expect a negative relationship between returns to equity holders and the equity-to-assets ratio.

In Baker's (1973) investigation of the relationship between leverage and industry returns, he measures leverage inversely as the ratio of equity-to-assets for the leading firms in an industry over the sample period. He also finds that relatively large amounts of leverage (i.e., a low equity-to-assets ratio) tend to raise industry profit rates, which implies that more leverage results in greater risks.

Nissim and Penman (2003) examine the effect of leverage on profitability. They distinguish between the profitability of operations and that of financing and between contemporaneous and future profits. When they form portfolios sorted by financial leverage, the authors find that the portfolios with the lowest financial leverage perform better than portfolios with high financial leverage. Nissim and Penman argue that this result is because firms with profitable operating assets have more operating leverage and less financial leverage than firms with less-profitable operating assets. When they examine the effect of total leverage, that is, leverage arising from operating and financing activities, the authors discover that leverage has a negative relationship with future returns

Dimitrov and Jain (2008) measure the effect of leverage changes on stock returns as well as on earnings-based measures of performance. Their results show a negative correlation between leverage and risk-adjusted stock returns. The authors study how changes in levels of debt are negatively associated with contemporaneous and future-adjusted returns. Hull (1999) measures market reaction to common stock offerings with the sole purpose of debt reduction and reports a negative immediate response—increasingly more so for firms further from the industry norm.

Korteweg (2004) tests the MM Proposition II based on pure capital structure changes (i.e., exchange offers). He controls for business risk by assuming nonzero debt betas and uses a time series approach. The author finds that returns decrease in leverage. Korteweg (2010) examines the net benefits of leverage to firms. His results show that firms that have debt in their capital structure are worth 5.5 percent more than the same firm with no debt in their capital structure. He also finds that net benefits for low-debt firms increase by taking on more leverage but decrease when leverage becomes high, implying the existence of an optimal capital structure.

George and Hwang (2009) find a significant negative relationship between leverage and stock returns. They investigate the possible explanations for this relationship and conclude that it could result from the distress costs across firms.

Muradoglu and Sivaprasad (2009a) study the link between capital structure and abnormal returns. Their evidence indicates that a firm's industry matters. Abnormal returns have a negative relationship with firm leverage. However, abnormal returns increase as the average industry leverage in a risk class increases. Separating the average level of external financing in an industry from that in a particular firm is important. Focusing on industry characteristics, they show that firms in nonregulated and competitive industries with low concentration ratios exhibit this behavior. In contrast, in the utilities' risk class, abnormal returns increase with firm leverage. Modigliani and Miller (1958) find that returns increase in leverage in the utilities sector.

In another study, Muradoglu and Sivaprasad (2009b) use the explicit valuation model of Modigliani and Miller (1958) on firms' returns and leverage and show that stock returns decline in leverage and the relationship is linear. The authors find that the negative relationship between leverage and stock returns holds for tax-paying firms and firms in competitive low-concentration industries. Muradoglu and Sivaprasad (2009c) also use an investment strategy based on firm-level capital structures. Their evidence shows that investing in low-leverage firms yields abnormal returns of 4.43 percent per annum. If an investor holds a portfolio of low-leverage and low–market-to-book ratio firms, abnormal returns increase to 16.18 percent per annum. A portfolio of low-leverage and low market risk yields abnormal returns of 6.67 percent and a portfolio of small firms with low leverage earns 5.37 percent per annum. Using the Fama and MacBeth (1973) methodology with modifications, Muradoglu and Sivaprasad confirm that portfolios based on low leverage earn higher returns in longer investment horizons.

WHY THE EMPIRICAL RELATIONSHIP BETWEEN LEVERAGE AND RETURNS DIFFERS

Previous studies on the connection between leverage and returns use various definitions for returns and leverage as well as different samples and methodologies. The following discussion examines the potential effects that result from these differences.

Definitions of Returns and Leverage

In Modigliani and Miller's (1958) tests of Proposition II, they approximate returns to shareholders by using the firm's net income. Arditti (1967) defines returns as the geometric mean return. Hall and Weiss (1967) define returns as profits after taxes and the ratio of book value of equity to assets as an indicator for leverage. Hamada (1972) calculates returns as profits after taxes and interest, which are the earnings that equity and preferred shareholders receive on their investment for the period. This approach is similar to the estimation of returns by MM. Bhandari (1988) defines stock returns as inflation adjusted. Recent work uses risk-adjusted returns and shows that higher leverage is associated with higher rates of return (Dimitrov and Jain 2008; Korteweg 2010; George and Hwang 2009; Muradoglu and Sivaprasad 2009a, 2009b, 2009c).

Researchers also use different measures of leverage. For example, Rajan and Zingales (1995) argue that the most relevant measure depends on the objective of the analysis. These authors use five different definitions as measures of leverage: (1) non-equity liabilities to total assets, (2) debt-to-total assets, (3) debt-to-net assets, (4) debt-to-capital, and (5) the interest coverage ratio (i.e., earnings before interest and taxes divided by interest expense). They take into account both the book and market measures of leverage. Rajan and Zingales explain that when analyzing the agency problems associated with debt, the relevant measure is probably the total debt to firm value. On the other hand, when measuring the distress factor associated to debt, the most appropriate measure would be the interest coverage ratio. This ratio relates to how the firm has been financed in the past and hence can be used to assess the relative claims on firm value held by debt and equity.

Schwartz (1959) proposes using the ratio of total debt to net worth as the best single measure of gross risk. He argues that using a broader definition of debt is best when debt encompasses the total of all liabilities and ownership claims. Firms in various industries have different asset structures that are financed by cash flows generated from various forms of debt and equity. Using book values of both variables ensures that capital structure is measured via the cash flows generated at the time when those assets were financed. Schwartz also contends that an optimum capital structure for a widely-held company is one that maximizes the long-run value of the common stock per share.

Modigliani and Miller (1958) define leverage as the ratio of the market value of bonds and preferred debt to the market value of all securities. Arditti (1967) defines the leverage ratio as the ratio of equity at the market value to debt at the book value. Hall and Weiss (1967) define leverage as equity to assets. Bhandari (1988) uses the book value of debt to the market value of equity to measure leverage. Korteweg (2004, 2009) defines leverage as the ratio of total debt to total capital plus total debt both in market values and does not account for the difference between the book and market values of leverage. Dimitrov and Jain (2008) measure leverage as ratio of total debt to total capital, both in market values.

Rajan and Zingales (1995) contend that the measure of leverage denoted by total debt divided by total assets fails to consider that some assets are offset by specific nondebt liabilities. By basing leverage estimations on book values, this variation between market and book values is absorbed by the market-to-book effect, a variable ignored by several studies including Modigliani and Miller (1958) and Bhandari (1988).

Penman, Richardson, and Tuna (2007) break down the book-to-price ratio into two components: enterprise book-to-price, which reflects operating risk, and a leverage, which reflects financing risk. Fama and French (1992) argue that the difference between the market and book values of leverage can be captured by using market-to-book ratio as a risk factor. Penman et al. define leverage as net debt divided by the market value of equity. George and Hwang (2009) use book value of long-term debt to the book value of assets. Muradoglu and Sivaprasad (2009a, 2009b, 2008c) base their leverage estimations on book values. They argue that the market-to-book effect, a variable ignored by several studies, absorbs this variation between market and book values.

Thus, various studies use different measures of leverage. The relevant measure depends on the objective of the analysis. Analyzing agency problems is best done using the total debt ratio (Rajan and Zingales 1995). Schwartz (1959) describes the ratio of total debt to net worth as the best single measure of gross risk. It encompasses the total of all liabilities and ownership claims. The use of book values of both variables ensures that capital structure is measured via the cash flows generated at the time those assets were financed. Using the book values of both debt and equity enables researchers to isolate the effects of cash flows used to finance the assets from market fluctuations.

Samples and Methodologies

Modigliani and Miller (1958) test the association between leverage and stock returns in the utilities and oil and gas sectors. They adopt a simple regression model and find that a positive relationship exists. Hamada (1972) tests the relationship between a firm's leverage and its common stock's systematic risk over a cross-section of all firms. He concludes that firms financed with debt have higher returns due to greater financial risk. Hamada uses industry as a proxy for business risk because his sample lacks a sufficient number of firms to undertake separate analysis of different sectors.

Bhandari's (1988) sample involves all firms, including financial companies. He uses the Fama and MacBeth (1973) methodology to test the relationship between leverage and stock returns. On examining the literature on announcements and leverage, Masulis (1983) shows that a change in leverage is positively related to a change in stock returns. His sample contains a group of all companies that have gone through pure capital structure changes. The study analyzes short-term value changes as a result of changes in leverage brought about by exchange offers and recapitalizations.

Arditti's (1967) sample of firms includes industrials, railroads, and utilities. He reports a negative but insignificant relationship between leverage and returns. Arditti contends that this finding could result from omitting some interfirm risk variables that are positively correlated with returns but negatively correlated with the leverage ratio. He notes that these omitted variables must relate to some non-income information because the regressions include all other information relating to income.

Korteweg's (2004) tests are based on pure capital structure changes (i.e., exchange offers). He controls for business risk by assuming nonzero debt betas and uses a time series approach. Korteweg (2010) classifies his sample based on industry classification. He categorizes the industries according to two-digit Standard Industrial Classics (SIC) codes and Fama and French (1992) classifications and includes insurance companies and utilities. The Fama-French classification assigns firms to 48 industries based on four-digit SIC codes. He measures the net benefits of leverage as the difference in value between a levered and unlevered firm.

Dimitrov and Jain (2008) measure the effect of leverage changes on stock returns as well as on earnings-based measures of performance in all nonfinancial firms. They exclude financial firms and regulated utilities. The authors adopt a portfolio approach using Fama and MacBeth (1973) to run a cross-sectional regression and Fama and French (1992) plus Carhart (1997) four-factor model to run a time-series regression. Dimitrov and Jain report a negative correlation between leverage and risk-adjusted stock returns. The authors study how changes in levels of debt are negatively associated with contemporaneous and future-adjusted returns.

George and Hwang (2009) test the relationship across all New York Stock Exchange, American Stock Exchange, and NASDAQ companies and exclude financial companies. They follow the Fama and MacBeth (1973) regression approach. Muradoglu and Sivaprasad (2009b, 2009c) examine the effect of leverage on returns at the firm and portfolio level. They exclude all financial companies, adopt Generalized Methods of Moments (GMM) panel estimations, and use Fama and MacBeth regressions in their estimations.

SUMMARY AND CONCLUSIONS

The main focus of this chapter is to examine the relationship between leverage and stock returns. The chapter started by examining the theoretical work of Modigliani and Miller (1958), its propositions, and implications. Next, the chapter introduced various capital structure theories that stemmed from MM theory and then reviewed the empirical work on capital structure dealing with the link between leverage and stock returns. Based on a limited number of empirical studies, the main conclusion is that leverage can explain returns but the empirical relationship is not necessarily positive. Some empirical studies show a positive association but recent work provides evidence supporting a negative relationship. The conflicting empirical evidence may result from using different definitions of leverage, stock returns, methodologies, and samples.

DISCUSSION QUESTIONS

1. Discuss MM Proposition II and its implications on stock returns.
2. What are the differences between the trade-off and pecking order theories of capital structure?
3. What is the empirical relationship between stock returns and leverage?
4. What potential reasons may explain the contradictory empirical results involving stock returns and leverage?

REFERENCES

Agarwal, Anup, and Gershon N. Mandelker. 1987. "Managerial Incentives and Corporate Investment and Financing Decisions." *Journal of Finance* 42:4, 823–837.

Agca, Senay, and Abon Mozumdar A. 2005. "Firm Size, Debt Capacity and Corporate Financing Choices." Available at http://ssrn.com/abstract=687369.

Arditti, Fred D. 1967. "Risk and Return on Equity." *Journal of Finance* 22:1, 19–36.

Aybar-Arias, Cristina, Alejandro Casino-Martinez, and Jose Lopez-Gracia. 2004. "Capital Structure and Sensitivity in SME Definition: A Panel Data Investigation." Available at http://ssrn.com/abstract=549082.

Baker, Malcolm, and Jeffrey Wurgler. 2002. "Marketing Timing and Capital Structure." *Journal of Finance* 57:1, 1–30.

Baker, Samuel H. 1973. "Risk, Leverage and Profitability: An Industry Analysis." *Review of Economics and Statistics* 55:4, 503–507.

Bhandari, Laxmi C. 1988. "Debt/Equity Ratio and Expected Common Stock Returns: Empirical Evidence." *Journal of Finance* 43:2, 507–528.

Biais, Bruno, and Catherine Casamatta. 1999. "Optimal Leverage and Aggregate Investment." *Journal of Finance* 54:4, 1291–1323.

Brander, James A., and Tracey R. Lewis. 1986. "Oligopoly and Capital Structure: The Limited Liability Effect." *American Economic Review* 76:5, 956–970.

Campello, Murillo. 2003. "Capital Structure and Product Markets Interactions: Evidence from Business Cycles." *Journal of Financial Economics* 68:3, 353–378.

Campello, Murillo. 2006. "Debt Financing: Does It Boost or Hurt Firm Performance in Product Markets?" *Journal of Financial Economics* 82:1, 135–172.

Carhart, Mark. 1997. "On Persistence in Mutual Fund Performance." *Journal of Finance* 52:1, 87–82.

Choe, Hyuk, Ronald W. Masulis, and Vikram K. Nanda. 1993. "Common Stock Offerings across the Business Cycle." *Journal of Empirical Finance* 1:1, 1–29.

DeAngelo, Harry, and Linda DeAngelo. 2006. "Capital Structure, Payout Policy, and Financial Flexibility." Available at http://ssrn.com/abstract= 916093.

DeAngelo, Harry, and Ronald W. Masulis. 1980. "Optimal Capital Structure under Corporate and Personal Taxation." *Journal of Financial Economics* 8:1, 3–27.

De Jong, Abe, and Chris Veld. 2001. "An Empirical Analysis of Incremental Capital Structure Decisions under Managerial Entrenchment. "*Journal of Banking and Finance* 25:10, 1857–1895.

Dimitrov, Valentin, and Prem C. Jain 2008. "The Value Relevance of Changes in Financial Leverage beyond Growth in Assets and GAAP Earnings." *Journal of Accounting, Auditing and Finance* 23:2, 191–222.

Donaldson, Gordon. 1961. *Corporate Debt Capacity: A Study of Corporate Debt Policy and the Determination of Debt Capacity*. Cambridge, MA: Division of Research, Harvard Graduate School of Business Administration.

Fama, Eugene F., and Kenneth French 1992. "The Cross-Section in Expected Stock Returns." *Journal of Finance* 47:2, 427–466.

Fama, Eugene F., and James D. MacBeth. 1973. "Risk, Return and Equilibrium: Empirical Tests." *Journal of Political Economy* 81:3, 607–636.

Fischer, Edwin O., Robert Heinkel, and Josef Zechner. 1989. "Dynamic Capital Structure Choice: Theory and Tests." *Journal of Finance* 44:1, 19–40.

Frank, Murray Z., and Vidhan K. Goyal. 2003. "Testing the Pecking Order Theory of Capital Structure." *Journal of Financial Economics* 67:2, 217–248.

George, Thomas J., and Chuan-Yang Hwang. 2009. "A Resolution of the Distress Risk and Leverage Puzzles in the Cross-Section of Stock Returns." *Journal of Financial Economics*, 96:1, 56–79

Graham, John R., and Campbell R. Harvey. 2001. "The Theory and Practice of Corporate Finance: Evidence from the Field. " *Journal of Financial Economics* 60:2-3, 187–243.

Gul, Ferdinand A. 1999. "Growth Opportunities, Capital Structure and Dividend Policies in Japan." *Journal of Corporate Finance* 5:2, 141–168.

Hall, Marshall, and Leonard Weiss. 1967. "Firm Size and Profitability." *Review of Economics and Statistics* 49:3, 319–331.

Hamada, Robert S. 1969. "Portfolio Analysis, Market Equilibrium and Corporation Finance." *Journal of Finance* 24:1, 13–31.

Hamada, Robert S. 1972. "The Effect of the Firm's Capital Structure on the Systematic Risk of Common Stocks." *Journal of Finance* 27:2, 435–452.

Harris, Milton, and Artur Raviv. 1988. "Corporate Control Contests and Capital Structure." *Journal of Financial Economics* 20:1, 55–86.

Harris, Milton, and Artur Raviv. 1991. "The Theory of Capital Structure." *Journal of Finance* 46:1, 297–355.

Harvey, Campbell R., Karl V. Lins, and Andrew H. Roper. 2004. "The Effect of Capital Structure When Expected Agency Costs Are Extreme." *Journal of Financial Economics* 74:1, 3–30.

Heinkel, Robert, and Josef Zechner. 1990. "The Role of Debt and Preferred Stock as a Solution to Adverse Investment Incentives." *Journal of Financial and Quantitative Analysis* 25:1, 1–24.

Helwege, Jean, and Nellie Liang. 1996. "Is There a Pecking Order? Evidence from a Panel of IPO Firms." *Journal of Financial Economics* 40:3, 429–458.

Hicks, John R. 1975. *Value and Capital: An Inquiry into Some Fundamental Principles of Economic Theory*, 2nd ed. Oxford: Oxford University Press.

Hovakimian, Armen, Tim Opler, and Sheridan Titman. 2001. "The Debt-Equity Choice." *Journal of Financial and Quantitative Analysis* 36:1, 1–24.

Hovakimian, Armen, Gayane Hovakimian, and Hassan Tehranian. 2004. "Determinants of Target Capital Structure: The Case of Dual Debt and Equity Issues." *Journal of Financial Economics* 71:3, 517–540.

Hull, Robert M. 1999. "Leverage Ratios, Industry Norms, and Stock Price Reaction: An Empirical Investigation of Stock-for-Debt Transactions." *Financial Management* 25:2, 32–45.

Israel, Ronen. 1991. "Capital Structure and the Market for Corporate Control: The Defensive Role of Debt Financing." *Journal of Finance* 46:4, 1391–1409.

Israel, Ronen. 1992. "Capital and Ownership Structures, and the Market for Corporate Control." *Review of Financial Studies* 5:2, 181–198.

Jensen, Michael C. 1986. "Agency Costs of Free Cash Flow, Corporate Finance and Takeovers." *American Economic Review* 76:2, 305–360.
Jensen, Michael C., and William H. Meckling. 1976. "Theory of the Firm: Managerial Behavior, Agency Costs and Ownership Structure." *Journal of Financial Economics* 3:4, 305–360.
Kale, Jayant R., and Husayn Shahrur. 2007. "Corporate Capital Structure and the Characteristics of Suppliers and Customers." *Journal of Financial Economics* 83:2, 321–365.
Kim, Han E. 1982. "Miller's Equilibrium, Shareholder Leverage Clienteles, and Optimal Capital Structure. " *Journal of Finance* 37:2, 301–319.
Korajczyk, Robert A., Deborah J. Lucas, and Robert L. McDonald. 1991. "The Effect of Information Releases on the Pricing and Timing of Equity Issues." *Review of Financial Studies* 4:4, 685–708.
Korajczyk, Robert A., Deborah J. Lucas, and Robert L McDonald. 1992. "Equity Issues with Time-Varying Asymmetric Information." *Journal of Financial and Quantitative Analysis* 27:3, 397–418.
Korteweg, Arthur G. 2004. "Financial Leverage and Expected Stock Returns: Evidence from Pure Exchange Offers." Available at http://ssrn.com/abstract=597922.
Korteweg, Arthur G. 2010. "The Net Benefits to Leverage." *Journal of Finance* 65 (6), 2137-2170.
Krasker, William. 1986. "Stock Price Movements in Response to Stock Issues under Asymmetric Information." *Journal of Finance* 41:1, 93–105.
Kraus, Alan, and Robert H. Litzenberger. 1973. "A State Preference Model of Optimal Financial Leverage. " *Journal of Finance* 28:4, 911–922.
La Porta, Rafael, Josef Lakonishok, Andrei Shleifer, and Robert Vishny. 1997. "Good News for Value Stocks: Further Evidence on Market Efficiency." *Journal of Finance* 52:2, 859–874.
Leland, Hayne. 1994. "Corporate Debt Value, Bond Covenants and Optimal Capital Structure." *Journal of Finance* 49:4, 1213–1252.
Masulis, Ronald W. 1983. "The Impact of Capital Structure Change on Firm Value: Some Estimates." *Journal of Finance* 38:1, 107–126.
Miller, Merton H. 1977. "Debt and Taxes." *Journal of Finance* 32:2, 261–275.
Modigliani, Franco, and Merton H. Miller. 1958. "The Cost of Capital, Corporation Finance and the Theory of Investment." *American Economic Review* 48:3, 261– 297.
Modigliani, Franco, and Merton H. Miller. 1963. "Corporate Income Taxes and the Cost of Capital: A Correction." *American Economic Review* 53:3, 433–443.
Muradoglu, Gulnur, and Sheeja Sivaprasad. 2009a. "An Empirical Analysis of Capital Structure and Abnormal Returns." Available at http://ssrn.com/abstract=948393.
Muradoglu, Gulnur, and Sheeja Sivaprasad. 2009b. "Leverage, Stock Returns, Taxes, Industry Concentration." Available at http://ssrn.com/abstract=1031987.
Muradoglu, Gulnur, and Sheeja Sivaprasad. 2009c. "Using Firm Leverage as an Investment Strategy." Available at http://ssrn.com/abstract=1031198.
Myers, Stewart C. 1977. "Determinants of Corporate Borrowing." *Journal of Financial Economics* 5:2, 147–175.
Myers, Stewart C. 1984. "The Capital Structure Puzzle." *Journal of Finance* 39:3, 575–592.
Myers, Stewart C., and Nicholas S. Majluf. 1984. "Corporate Investment and Financing Decisions When Firms Have Information That Investors Do Not Have." *Journal of Financial Economics* 13:2, 187–221.
Narayanan, M. P. 1988. "Debt Versus Equity Under Asymmetric Information." *Journal of Financial and Quantitative Analysis* 23:1, 39–51.
Nissim, Doron, and Stephen H. Penman. 2003. "Financial Statement Analysis of Leverage and How It Informs About Profitability and Price-to-Book Ratios." *Review of Accounting Studies* 8:4, 531–560.
Norton, Seth W. 1995. "Is Franchising a Capital Structure Issue?" *Journal of Corporate Finance* 2:1, 75–101.

Penman, Stephen H., Scott A. Richardson, and Irem Tuna. 2007. "The Book-to-Price Effect in Stock Returns: Accounting for Leverage." *Journal of Accounting Research* 45:2, 427–467.
Rajan, Raghuram, and Luigi Zingales. 1995. "What Do We Know about Capital Structure? Some Evidence from International Data." *Journal of Finance* 50:5, 1421–1460.
Schwartz, Eli. 1959. "Theory of the Capital Structure of the Firm." *Journal of Finance* 14:1, 18–39.
Scott, Jr. James H. 1977. "Bankruptcy, Secured Debt and Optimal Capital Structure." *Journal of Finance* 32:1, 1–19.
Singh, Manohar, Wallace N. Davidson III, and Jo-Ann Suchard. 2003. "Corporate Diversification Strategies and Capital Structure." *Quarterly Review of Economics and Finance* 43:1, 147–167.
Somers, Herman. M. 1955. "Cost of Money as the Determinant of Public Utility Rates." *Buffalo Law Review* 4: Spring, 289–316.
Stomper, Alex, and Christine Zulehner. 2004. "Why Leverage Distorts Investment?" Available at http://ssrn.com/abstract=527982.
Stulz, René M. 1988. "Managerial Control of Voting Rights: Financing Policies and the Market for Corporate Control." *Journal of Financial Economics* 20:1, 25-54.
Stulz, René M. 1990. "Managerial Discretion and Optimal Financing Policies." *Journal of Financial Economics* 26:1, 3–27.
Titman, Sheridan. 1984. "The Effect of Capital Structure on a Firm's Liquidation Decision." *Journal of Financial Economics* 13:1, 137–151.
Williamson, Oliver E. 1988. "Corporate Finance and Corporate Governance." *Journal of Finance* 43:3, 567–591.

ABOUT THE AUTHORS

Gulnur Muradoglu is a Professor of Finance at Cass Business School of City University, London. She has worked for Cass as the Director of PhD Program and for Manchester Business School as the Director of MSc. Finance. She has been at the Wharton School of the University of Pennsylvania as a Fulbright Scholar and at Warwick Business School as a Visiting Fellow. Her research interests are in corporate finance, behavioral finance, and emerging markets. She is the director of the Behavioral Finance Working Group. Professor Muradoglu has been an Associate Editor of *Emerging Markets Finance and Trade* and on the editorial boards of *Comparative Economic Systems, International Journal of Behavioral Accounting and Finance, Finance Letters,* and *Frontiers of Finance and Economic*. She has published more than 30 articles in such journals as the *Journal of Behavioral Finance, Journal of Economics and Business, European Journal of Finance, Multinational Finance Journal,* and *Applied Financial Economics.*

Sheeja Sivaprasad is a Senior Lecturer at the University of Westminster, United Kingdom. She received a B.Com and M.Com from the University of Kerala, India, and an MSc in Investment Management and a PhD in Finance from Cass Business School, City University. Her teaching interests are in corporate finance, security analysis, and principles of finance, portfolio theory, research methods, and accounting.

CHAPTER 6

Capital Structure and Compensation

ALAN VICTOR SCOTT DOUGLAS
Associate Professor and Robert Harding Research Leadership Fellow,
University of Waterloo

INTRODUCTION

The purpose of this chapter is to examine the interactions between capital structure and compensation. How a firm finances its assets is of paramount importance in capitalist economies. Moreover, compensation schemes guide these fundamental decisions. The dollar value of compensation packages provides an indication of the importance of these decisions and has attracted the attention of academics, the media, Wall Street, and Main Street.

The literature analyzing capital structure is voluminous (Harris and Raviv 1991; Parsons and Titman 2008). The chapter begins with a basic review of capital structure and compensation to position the discussion that follows. Similar to capital structure, extensive literature also exists on compensation plans (Murphy 1999). Compensation plans induce desired actions by linking an employee's monetary payments to performance. Different measures of performance are appropriate in diverse situations such as for various employees (board members, top management, departmental managers, and front-line employees) and for different components of an individual's compensation package (annual bonuses based on accounting performance versus option grants based on capital market performance).

This chapter mainly focuses on the incentives relating to top management compensation because top management makes the investment decisions that are related to the determinants of capital structure. Compensation plans influence these decisions as well as other managerial decisions, such as effort levels and perquisite consumption. Some analyses are highly theoretical, focusing on the mathematical form of the optimal compensation function (the function linking compensation payments to performance). Other contributions take a more practical approach, restricting attention to the optimal use of one or more of the components of observed compensation plans such as salary, bonus, shares, and options. Still others, particularly empirical studies, abstract from optimal compensation altogether and focus on the interaction between observed compensation and capital structure. Although each approach enters the discussion below, the discussion mainly focuses on studies that provide strong integration with the more practical, empirical literature.

The goal of this chapter is to provide an overview of the main theoretical interactions between capital structure and compensation, to examine the empirical evidence relating to these interactions, and to identify areas for potential contributions. The chapter is organized as follows. First, the basic theoretical determinants of capital structure that are likely to be related to executive (top management) compensation are outlined. Next, managerial incentives and the role of compensation are introduced. After discussing the main theoretical interactions between capital structure and compensation, the evidence in empirical literature is examined. This discussion begins with studies linking capital structure and compensation choices, and then considers the additional insights from studies linking compensation to the yield on corporate debt (i.e., the cost of debt capital). Some debt-like features of compensation are discussed as well as the effects of capital structure on employee compensation.

CAPITAL STRUCTURE AND COMPENSATION: ANALYSIS

A voluminous theoretical literature analyzes both capital structure and managerial compensation. This section of the chapter begins with a discussion of the mainstream issues in the theoretical capital structure literature and then relates these issues to managerial incentives from a theoretical perspective.

Capital Structure Basics

Capital structure refers to the mix of financial securities issued by a firm to finance its assets. Typically, these securities are categorized as debt or equity securities, although there can be different types of both debt and equity securities (e.g., short- and long-term debt, junior and senior debt, convertible debt, preferred shares, common shares, and voting and nonvoting shares). This chapter generally takes a generic view of capital structure, in which *capital structure* refers to the proportion of assets financed with straight debt and common equity. The chapter periodically goes into slightly more detail, considering convertible and short-term debt and dual class shares to provide useful insights into the relationship between capital structure and compensation.

Much of the capital structure literature focuses on the firm's value-maximizing or optimal capital structure. A common starting point when considering optimal capital structure is the seminal paper published by Nobel Prize–winning authors Modigliani and Miller (1958) (hereafter MM). MM illustrate that with perfect capital markets (full information and no taxes, bankruptcy costs, transactions costs, or contracting costs), the firm's capital structure should not affect value because it does not influence the overall opportunities available to individual investors in well-functioning debt and equity markets. While this "irrelevance" result may not seem helpful, their analysis is highly illuminating because it indicates where not to look for the determinants of optimal capital structure.

To determine an optimal capital structure requires introducing features of the firm or capital markets that cause investor returns to depend on capital structure. Taxes and bankruptcy costs are straightforward examples. Interest payments are deductible when calculating the firm's taxable income, so taxes create a benefit to financing with debt (although this corporate tax benefit may be offset on the personal tax side, where interest is often more highly taxed than equity returns). Potential bankruptcy costs, such as legal fees (or more general costs of financial distress including distracted management, reputation costs, and customer concern with warranties) reduce the expected returns of investors and make debt more costly.

In addition to the effect on taxes and financial distress, capital structure can influence the firm's investment decisions. The differing payoff structure of bondholders and shareholders (bondholders are paid before shareholders) can influence investment incentives. In particular, if the firm employs a high debt-to-equity ratio such that the debt becomes risky, shareholders have an incentive to choose investments with greater risk (Fama and Miller 1972). This is termed the *asset substitution* problem: shareholders have an incentive to substitute riskier investments because they receive the upside, while bondholders bear the downside. Shareholders also have an incentive to pass up investments that increase debt value (Myers 1977). This is termed the *underinvestment* problem: shareholders forgo investments in which the benefits accrue to bondholders by increasing their payments in bankruptcy (or avoiding bankruptcy altogether). These investment distortions reduce the returns available for investors and therefore decrease the optimal level of debt in the firm's capital structure.

Capital structure can also affect firm value when there is asymmetric information regarding the value of the firm's assets. When a firm knows it is underpriced, it may forgo investments that would be financed on unfavorable terms. Since equity is more susceptible to mispricing than debt (equity payoffs are more volatile than debt payments), this problem is more severe for equity financing. Firms facing this information environment can engage in more value-increasing investments by using debt rather than equity (Myers and Majluf 1984). Finally, firms may attempt to alleviate mispricing effects by conveying their true value to the market. When defaulting on a debt payment is costly and the ability to make payments is positively related to the value of the firm's assets, issuing debt can serve as a credible signal of firm value. In this environment, firms can again increase value by using more debt in the capital structure (Ross 1977).

Managerial Incentives and Capital Structure

This review illustrates how the interaction between investment and financing decisions can cause the capital structure decision to affect value. Of course, top management rather than shareholders makes or at least influences these decisions. Therefore, capital structure should reflect not only managerial interests but also those of shareholders and bondholders.

Shareholder and bondholder interests are relatively straightforward, as both parties are outside investors who care primarily about their monetary payoffs. Introducing a third player, managers who care about their own monetary payoffs, is enough to complicate the picture and give the firm's compensation plan an important role in what is often termed the "shareholder-manager agency conflict." Further, recognizing that managerial interests can include nonpecuniary benefits (e.g., reduction in effort, perquisite consumption, elevated social status, and empire building) helps to clarify that the relationship between capital structure and compensation may reflect complex multilevel interactions between the various agency conflicts.

Jensen and Meckling (1976) present a pioneering analysis of these interactions, beginning with the manager's preference for perquisite consumption. Perquisites are anything that benefits the manager but not outside shareholders. For example, as Jensen and Meckling (p. 312) note, perquisites include "physical appointments of the office, the attractiveness of the secretarial staff, the level of employee discipline, the kind and amount of charitable contributions, personal relations (such as love and respect) with employees, a larger than optimal computer to play with, purchase of production inputs from friends, etc." The authors link management's perquisite consumption to the pecuniary rewards they receive from their share ownership. Jensen and Meckling illustrate that managers are likely to cut back on perquisites when they face greater pay-sensitivity (own a greater share of the firm's equity). This occurs because managers bear a greater opportunity cost when they are entitled to a greater share of the firm's profits.

The relationship between share ownership and perquisite consumption is also related to capital structure. Leverage helps control perquisites because, for a given level of managerial wealth, the manager can own a greater share of the equity in a levered firm. Leverage is also costly, because it increases the asset substitution incentive illustrated by Fama and Miller (1972). The firm's optimal capital structure combines debt as well as internal and external equity to minimize total agency costs (i.e., the costs of perquisite consumption and asset substitution).

Jensen and Meckling's (1976) pioneering study recognizes the interactions between the manager-shareholder and shareholder-bondholder conflicts, and illustrates how these interactions determine the firm's optimal capital structure. The setting, however, is that of a combined manager-entrepreneur, and as such, their analysis is best applied to entrepreneurial firms in which the manager is also a substantial shareholder.

Managerial compensation plays a more prominent role in settings where managers serve as "agents" for the firm's owners (principals). In this principal-agent setting, managers typically own a small fraction of the firm's equity, and their monetary rewards are closely tied to their compensation contract (of course, the agent's ownership increases if the compensation plan includes stock or option grants). This setting is more applicable to large corporations whose securities trade on the major financial exchanges with managerial ownership in the neighborhood of 1 percent of the firm's equity.

John and John (1993) present an illustrative analysis of the relationship between capital structure and compensation in this setting. They begin with the shareholder-bondholder asset substitution conflict, which itself would limit leverage as in Jensen and Meckling (1976). They illustrate that when managers make investment decisions based on the rewards in their compensation plan, the compensation plan can be designed to dissuade asset substitution, thereby reducing this agency cost of debt and relaxing the limitations of leverage. Specifically, the compensation scheme includes an equity component (an equity share), a salary, and a penalty if the firm goes bankrupt. The penalty causes the manager to prefer safer investments, while the equity share causes the manager to prefer riskier investments, similar to shareholders. Compensation with an appropriate equity share, therefore, can induce efficient risk taking.

Designing such a compensation plan is in the shareholders' interest because debt value is computed under rational expectations, taking into account the investment choices induced by the compensation contract, and the expected compensation level is set equal to the manager's reservation wage. The shareholders, therefore, ultimately bear any agency costs.

As leverage becomes more desirable, perhaps due to the tax advantage, the shareholders' asset substitution incentive is exacerbated. The shareholders, however, can counteract this effect on managerial incentives by reducing the equity share in the compensation contract so that the manager's investment choices remains efficient. John and John (1993) find that the sensitivity of the manager's pay to equity value is negatively related to firm leverage. The authors also illustrate that the negative relationship between pay sensitivity and leverage is mitigated for convertible debt because convertible debt does not exacerbate the asset substitution incentive. That is, if the firm chooses riskier investments that benefit shareholders at the bondholders' expense, convertible debt holders can simply convert their debt to equity.

John and John (1993) provide a highly tractable model with straightforward empirical implications (tests of the model are discussed below). The theoretical literature illustrates that the relationship between capital structure and compensation may be more complicated. John and John show that the convexity of the payoffs on stock and options align the manager's risk preferences with shareholders. The concavity of a risk-averse manager's utility function, however, can upset this result because it implies that the value of stock and options in the market differs from the value of the same stock and options to a risk-averse manager. For example, the manager cannot hedge the performance of her own firm, or her securities are nontransferable or have not vested, or she is concerned with signaling or control. Lewellen (2006) illustrates that stock and deep in-the-money options can actually reduce the manager's incentives to increase leverage because risk aversion outweighs the increase in the market value of the options.

In another theoretical study, Dybvig and Zender (1991) illustrate that the idea in John and John (1993), which shows that an appropriately designed compensation contract can alleviate shareholder-bondholder agency costs, is quite general. Indeed, they show that such contracts can again render capital structure irrelevant in a Modigliani and Miller (1958) setting that is extended to include agency and information concerns.

Persons (1994) takes the analysis one step further, illustrating that the arguments in John and John (1993) and Dybvig and Zender (1991) hinge on the ability to use the compensation plan as a commitment device. Unfortunately, the ability to do so is questionable as shareholders appear to be able to alter the management's compensation contract just as easily as they can take the expropriating actions contained in the original analyses. While Persons's analysis suggests that agency costs remain an important consideration, it provides little guidance on the links between compensation and capital structure. That is, Persons's analysis illustrates that the relationships between capital structure and compensation in John and John as well as Dybvig and Zender are not equilibrium relationships; he does not, however, illustrate what the equilibrium relationships might be.

Douglas (2006) takes a step in this direction, showing that the shareholders' ability to adjust compensation contracts ex-post can induce managers to adjust investment choices ex-ante. Shareholders recognize this and use the capital structure as a commitment to implement compensation that penalizes the manager for opportunistic investment choices. In equilibrium, managers avoid opportunistic investments, and shareholders implement efficient compensation schemes.

The managerial opportunism in Douglas (2006) stems entirely from the manager's pursuit of information advantages, and the link between capital structure and compensation is implemented by a perfectly functioning board of directors. One further branch of the literature examines managerial opportunism in poorly governed firms with entrenched management. In such firms, managers have an incentive to use free cash flow for pet projects or empire building; they prefer low leverage because debt commitments can interfere with empire building (Jensen 1986; Novaes and Zingales 1995; Zwiebel 1996; Morellec 2004).

If entrenched managers faced no discipline, the inefficiencies would lead to low market valuation. This could attract a hostile takeover. To deter this, management allows for some leverage in their capital structure as a commitment to run the firm more efficiently and keep hostile takeovers at bay. The debt commitments improve managerial incentives by allowing lenders to monitor, reducing the free cash flow available to managers (via interest payments), and forcing managers to focus on creating sufficient value to avoid default or bankruptcy (Grossman and Hart 1982; Stulz 1990). This role of leverage presents a further dimension to the relationship between managerial incentives and capital structure.

CAPITAL STRUCTURE AND COMPENSATION: EMPIRICAL EVIDENCE

A growing literature investigates the empirical relationship between capital structure and managerial rewards. This part of the chapter discusses the empirical literature. It begins with a discussion of earlier studies that link capital structure to the managerial rewards associated with equity ownership, as well as more recent studies that incorporate a more comprehensive definition of compensation, including salary, bonus, stock, and option holdings. Subsequently, this section considers additional insights from studies linking compensation to the yield on corporate debt (i.e., the cost of debt capital), those that focus on the debt-like features of some components of compensation, and studies that link capital structure to managerial entrenchment and broader levels of employee compensation.

Compensation and Capital Structure

Early studies investigating the empirical relationship between managerial rewards and capital structure focus on the incentives associated with managerial shareholdings and find mixed results regarding the relationship with capital structure. Friend and Lang (1988) find no significant relationship between book leverage and the proportion of the firm's equity owned by top management. Using a slightly larger data set, Mehran (1992) finds a significant relationship for both stock ownership and the fraction of compensation awarded as options. Following Jensen and Meckling (1976), he concludes that higher ownership aligns manager and shareholder incentives, while greater option compensation increases the manager's willingness to take risks.

Recently, more comprehensive details of compensation components have become available in the form of Standard & Poor's ExecuComp database. ExecuComp contains data on salary, cash bonuses, stock, and option components of compensation, and allows researchers to compute the following: (1) the amount paid directly to managers each year, termed "flow compensation"; (2) the executives' holdings of stock in their own companies; and (3) the executives' holdings of unexercised options on their companies' stock. Flow compensation includes salary, annual bonus, other annual compensation (such as recordable perquisites and tax reimbursements), long-term incentive plans, the value of restricted stock granted, the Black–Scholes value of new stock options granted, and other payments such as pension contributions and severance payments. The stock and option holdings are self-explanatory and have grown rapidly in recent years (Hall and Liebman 1998; Murphy 1999; Bergstresser and Philippon 2006), so that stock and options now comprise the lion's share of the manager's firm-specific wealth. New grants are included in the flow compensation category each year, whereas existing holdings of stock and options are included separately in (2) and (3), as described above.

As an indication of the incentives associated with the three categories, average annual flow compensation in the United States during the period 1993 to 1999 was $2.7 million, the average annual change in the value of stock holdings was $3.6 million, and the average annual change in the Black–Scholes value of chief executive officers' (CEOs) options held was $1.75 million (Ortiz-Molina 2007; financial sector excluded). The sum of these gives an all-inclusive compensation measure, termed the "change in firm-specific wealth." The change in firm-specific wealth averages $8 million in this period, and ranges from a loss of $122.8 million to a gain of $596 million; the high end is a remarkable level of annual compensation and helps to explain the considerable media coverage of top executive compensation.

The change in the above manager's firm-specific wealth is used to compute two important features of managerial compensation plans, each of which potentially affects capital structure decisions. The first feature measures the sensitivity of CEO wealth to stock returns, termed *delta*. Formally, delta is defined as the change in the manager's firm-specific wealth due to a 1 percent change in the firm's equity value. Some debate exists, however, regarding the use of the percentage change versus the dollar change in equity value (Aggarwal and Samwick 1999; Core and Guay 2002). Delta, therefore, is commonly referred to as the degree of pay-sensitivity or pay-for-performance in the manager's compensation scheme. The second measure is the sensitivity of CEO wealth to stock return volatility, termed *vega*. Formally, vega is defined as the change in the manager's firm specific wealth due to a 1 percent change in the *standard deviation* of the firm's stock price. Both measures are related to the incentive conflicts between managers, shareholders, and bondholders outlined above, and as such, both are likely to be related to capital structure. In particular, delta is closely related to the manager's incentives for perquisite consumption or empire building and avoiding financial distress, while vega is closely related to the manager's risk-taking incentives, and therefore the asset substitution conflict between shareholders and bondholders.

Studies focus on the pay-for-performance measure, delta, and find that it is negatively related to the amount of debt firms employ in their capital structure. Ortiz-Molina (2007) further addresses the causality of this relationship, concluding that causality runs from capital structure to compensation. That is, firms with more debt in their capital structure implement compensation plans with lower pay sensitivity.

Numerous possible explanations exist for the negative relationship between delta and debt. First, it could reflect that compensation and leverage are substitute methods of controlling the agency costs of equity (i.e., manager-shareholder conflicts). A higher delta increases the sensitivity of the manager's wealth to changes in shareholder wealth, so actions that decrease shareholder wealth, such as perquisite consumption or investing in pet projects, become more costly to the manager (Jensen and Meckling 1976), and wealth-increasing actions are more rewarded. Increasing delta, therefore, is one way to mitigate shareholder-manager conflicts. Another way is to increase the debt in the firm's capital structure. Debt commitments can align manager incentives by reducing the free cash flow available for pet projects, focusing managers on avoiding default, and inducing lenders to monitor, as discussed above. Putting these two methods of controlling manager-shareholder conflicts together, a possible explanation for the negative relationship between delta and debt is that they are substitute methods of mitigating the agency costs of equity: a lower delta is needed when the manager faces greater debt commitments.

A second explanation for the negative relationship is that compensation is used to mitigate the agency costs of debt, specifically, to offset shareholder-bondholder conflicts. In particular, the shareholders' asset substitution incentive increases with the debt-equity ratio, so firms must reduce the alignment between managers and shareholders to convince bondholders they will invest efficiently (John and John 1993). If delta represents the alignment of manager and shareholder preferences, a lower delta is again needed as the debt-equity ratio increases.

To help distinguish between these two explanations and further investigate the agency costs of debt explanation, Ortiz-Molina (2007) examines the effect of different types of debt in the firm's capital structure. He finds that the negative relationship between leverage and delta weakens for convertible debt. This is again consistent with the second explanation: the conversion option itself protects against asset substitution, so less protection is needed through the compensation plan, again as predicted by John and John (1993).

John, Mehran, and Qian (2006) take the investigation one step further by introducing monitoring by regulators and nondepository (subordinated) debt holders in the banking industry. They find that delta again decreases with leverage but increases with the intensity of monitoring. The authors argue that this finding is consistent with the agency costs of debt explanation in John and John (1993) because monitoring helps to control the adverse incentives created by delta. The finding is inconsistent with the agency cost of equity explanation, however, where monitoring would be an alternative way to mitigate manager-owner conflicts.

In a somewhat different approach, Coles, Daniel, and Naveen (2006) examine how investment and financing policies depend on the characteristics of managerial compensation. Again, they examine the incentives associated with the changes in the manager's firm-specific wealth from Compustat ExecuComp, but they focus on the sensitivity of managerial wealth to stock return volatility, vega, controlling for the pay-sensitivity effects in delta. The authors find that vega is positively related to leverage. Vega is also positively related to riskier investment choices (greater research and development, fewer lines of business, less plant and equipment), and ultimately to riskier stock returns. Because their results hold for lagged values of vega, the authors interpret a causal effect from compensation to policy choices: greater compensation for risk implements higher leverage and riskier investment choices.

Coles, Daniel, and Naveen (2006) conclude that firms increase the sensitivity of managerial wealth to risk, that is, increase vega, when inducing more risk (including higher leverage) is optimal. That is, higher vega causes higher leverage. In contrast, Ortiz-Molina (2007) concludes that firms increase the sensitivity of managerial wealth to stock price. That is, firms increase delta when less leverage is optimal in its capital structure. Thus, lower leverage causes higher delta.

In part, the differing conclusions reflect the focus on different measures, delta versus vega, although Coles et al. (2006) also find that delta is negatively related to leverage. The authors focus on vega because their main interest is managerial risk choices. In contrast, Ortiz-Molina (2007) considers both risk and perquisite choices because perquisites are a driver of the agency costs of equity. However, the hypothesis concerning agency costs of debt receives more support in Ortiz-Molina due to the additional evidence obtained from convertible debt. In the agency costs of debt hypothesis, lower pay-sensitivity reduces the alignment between managers and shareholders, and therefore the manager's asset substitution incentive. That is, a lower delta is interpreted as a lower risk-taking incentive, and the risk-taking incentive is negatively related to leverage. This conclusion conflicts with Lewellen's (2006) finding that stock and deep-in-the-money options actually reduce the manager's incentive to increase risk. It also conflicts with Coles et al.'s conclusion that risk-taking incentives are positively related to leverage. Since Ortiz-Molina's conclusions relate to risk-taking incentives, incorporating vega directly into his analysis could be interesting. Again, vega seems more closely related to managerial risk choices while delta seems more closely related to the manager's effort and perquisite choices.

The conclusions also differ in terms of causality. Coles et al. (2006) conclude that causality runs from compensation to capital structure while Ortiz-Molina (2007) concludes the opposite. Causality is conceptually important but difficult to establish empirically, especially given that compensation and leverage may be simultaneously determined. To address the empirical issues relating to causality and simultaneity, Coles et al. use lagged values of vega and delta, predicted (instrumental) values of vega and delta, and simultaneous regression techniques. They also find evidence of a positive "feedback effect" from leverage to vega. Ortiz-Molina also uses simultaneous equations and predicted values of leverage but addresses causality in a different way. He examines the firm's choice of stock and option grants, given the capital structure in place. Ortiz-Molina finds that that option grants are more common in firms with lower straight debt and higher convertible debt, which is consistent with capital structure leading compensation in the agency costs of debt hypothesis.

Causality also seems to run both ways elsewhere in the literature. For example, Cohen, Hall, and Viceira (2000) find that vega drives both leverage and stock price volatility, whereas Core and Guay (1999) find that leverage is a determinant of delta. Lewellen (2006) finds evidence that compensation both affects and explains leverage choices. Lewellen, Loderer, and Martin (1987) find that option grants are positively related to leverage, while Mehran (1995) finds no effect, and Bryan, Hwang, and Lilien (2000) find that new option (stock) grants are negatively (positively) related to leverage. Given the number of studies that draw different conclusions, a rigorous evaluation of each method to determine which best establishes causality could be of interest.

The evidence above establishes a strong relationship between top management compensation and capital structure choices, particularly with respect to delta and vega. Some question remains, however, regarding the precise nature of these interactions. To shed additional light and get a feel for the economic importance of the relationship, some studies examine the link between compensation and the firm's cost of capital. If compensation affects the manager's incentives to take actions that affect the value of the firm's debt, this should be reflected in the pricing of the debt and the cost of debt capital.

Compensation and the Cost of Debt

Substantial literature documents that managerial incentives are related to the firm's cost of debt, as measured by the yield on corporate bonds. Bagnani et al. (1994) show that managerial ownership increases the cost of debt (bond yield) in the 5 to 25 percent ownership range, but it has no effect at higher ownership levels. Ortiz-Molina (2006) finds a similar effect of managerial stock ownership and illustrates that the effect on yield increases for managerial stock options.

As above, some recent studies tend to focus on the risk-taking incentive represented by the vega of top management compensation. As expected, the potentially adverse effects of risk-taking on the firm's bondholders create a positive relationship between vega and borrowing costs (the yield on the firm's debt). These studies also tend to find opposite effects of delta and vega consistent with the argument that managerial risk aversion outweighs the risk-taking incentives in delta but not vega (Billet and Liu 2008; Billet, Mauer, and Zhang 2010; Brockman, Martin, and Unlu 2010). These findings are consistent with the conclusions of Coles et al. (2006).

Carlson and Lazrak (2010) take a different approach. They argue that compensation is likely to affect the firm's cost of debt capital but that the manager's aversion to low pay levels drives investment decisions. If compensated with risky stock alone, managers avoid risk. The inclusion of cash compensation establishes a minimum pay level that relaxes the manager's aversion to risky investments. As cash compensation increases, managers are more likely to pursue investments that reduce bondholder wealth. The proportion of cash-to-stock in CEO compensation, therefore, drives leverage and the cost of debt capital. Carlson and Lazrak present evidence consistent with both predictions, using the yield spread on corporate credit default swaps during 2001 to 2006 to estimate the cost of debt capital. They find that credit default swap (CDS) spreads increase with the cash-to-stock ratio in compensation plans.

The idea that managerial risk-taking incentives increase the cost of debt is also consistent with the statements of debt ratings agencies. Brockman et al. (2010, p. 1) note that a 2007 Moody's Investors Service Special Comment states: "Executive pay is incorporated into Moody's credit analysis of rated issuers because compensation is a determinant of management behavior that affects indirectly credit quality." The report by Moody's Investor Service (2007, p. 4) later clarifies that the "primary interest in analyzing pay is to gain insight into the compensation committee's intent regarding the structure, size and focus of incentives." A study by Moody's Investor Service (2005, p. 8) concludes that "pay packages that are highly sensitive to stock price and/or operating performance may induce greater risk taking by managers, perhaps consistent with stockholders' objectives, but not necessarily bondholders' objectives." Brockman et al. find similar statements regarding CEO incentives and credit analysis in Standard & Poor's reports.

To shed additional light on the effects of capital structure, Brockman et al. (2010) examine the interaction between the effects of delta and vega on bond yield, and the firm's debt maturity choice. They argue that firms use the maturity structure of their debt to offset the adverse effects of managerial incentives. Shorter-term debt can reduce managerial incentives to increase risk because the debt becomes due before returns are realized, providing creditors with additional flexibility to monitor managers (Barnea, Haugen, and Senbet 1980; Leland and Toft 1996; Stulz 1990). Brockman et al. find that greater managerial incentives to increase risk, implemented through a higher vega and a lower delta, increase the yield on the firm's debt. They also find that firms with higher vegas and lower deltas have more short-term debt in their capital structure, using the shorter maturity to mitigate the cost associated with risk-taking incentives.

Further evidence is provided by examining the announcement effects of incentive-changing events. Using a relatively small sample from 1978 to 1982, DeFusco, Johnson, and Zorn (1990) find that option grants are associated with a positive stock price reaction and a negative bond price reaction. Billet, Mauer, and Zhang (2010) provide an updated analysis using a relatively large sample of first-time stock and option grants from the ExecuComp database. These initial grants induce a positive stock price reaction and a negative bond price reaction. Further, the price reactions depend on the delta and vega measures associated with the grants: Stock reactions decrease with the change in delta but increase with the change in vega, while the opposite occurs with bond reactions. The negative correlation between stockholder and bondholder wealth effects, particularly when the grant affects vega, suggests that the market recognizes a potential wealth transfer effect similar to the asset substitution effect illustrated by Fama and Miller (1972).

Managerial Entrenchment

The previous section establishes that managerial incentives affect the cost of debt. A related question is whether these effects are related to the possibility of managerial entrenchment. Billet and Liu (2008) incorporate potential entrenchment effects by distinguishing the cash flow rights and the control rights associated with dual class shares (all shares have cash flow rights, but some have superior voting rights). They find that yield spreads increase with managerial voting rights and decrease with managerial cash flow rights. The magnitude of the effect is substantial:

Moving from the first to third quartile of managerial voting rights increases the cost of debt by 46 basis points and is associated with a lower credit rating. Interestingly, Billett and Liu also find that leverage increases with managerial voting rights and decreases with cash flow rights, which at first glance seems surprising given the higher cost of debt. However, this result can be explained if the divergence of manager and shareholder interests is associated with greater managerial perquisites, such as empire building, which reduce equity and debt values. Since equity is the residual claim, the cost of equity may increase more than the cost of debt increases. One way to investigate this possibility would be to examine the effect of the divergence between voting and cash flow rights on total firm value (the value of debt plus equity). The explanation above suggests that entrenchment has substantial effects on firm value.

While pinpointing the effects of managerial entrenchment is somewhat difficult, Berger, Ofek, and Yermack (1997) contribute by employing multiple measures to capture managerial entrenchment and/or monitoring: manager tenure, board size, board composition, excess compensation (i.e., the residual in a log wage equation), direct stock ownership (as a percent of common shares), options held (as a percent of common shares), and the presence of a major block holder.

In general, Berger et al. (1997) document that firms with weak managerial incentives avoid high levels of leverage. For example, managers with longer tenures, larger boards, and lower stock and option holdings choose lower leverage. They also show that entrenchment-decreasing events, such as takeover threats, managerial replacement, and a new block holder, lead to increases in leverage. In sum, the relationship between managerial incentives and leverage, including compensation and managerial entrenchment, has many dimensions.

Debt-Like Components of Compensation

Recognizing that some components of managerial compensation have debt-like features is important. Indeed, Sundaram and Yermack (2007) illustrate that debt-like compensation (promised cash payments in the future), in the form of defined benefit pensions and deferred compensation, is a significant component of overall compensation, especially in larger, older firms. When Jack Welch left General Electric in 2001, the firm owed him $84 million in pension benefits and $25 million in deferred compensation. Sundaram and Yermack point out that this component of compensation may significantly affect the size and composition of firm payouts, the firm's cost of debt, the choice of new securities to be issued (debt vs. equity), project choice, capital expenditure choice, and the incentive to pursue diversifying mergers. Debt-like compensation appears to be another important dimension in the relationship between managerial incentives and capital structure.

Yermack and Wei (2009) conduct an event study of stockholders' and bondholders' reactions to companies' initial reports of their CEOs' inside debt positions, as required by Securities and Exchange Commission (SEC) disclosure regulations that became effective early in 2007. When CEOs have sizeable pensions or deferred compensation, the disclosure causes a rise in bond prices, a fall in equity prices, and a reduction in the volatility of both securities. These results indicate a transfer of value from equity to debt, as well as an overall destruction of enterprise value when a CEO's inside debt holdings are large.

Capital Structure and Employee Compensation

While the focus of this chapter is top management (executive) compensation, recognizing that capital structure can also be related to the compensation of other parties affiliated with the firm, such as rank-and-file employees, is important. Berk, Stanton, and Zechner (2010) examine the relationship between employee compensation (wages) and leverage in a setting where the firm bears the risk associated with labor productivity. Because shareholders can diversify this risk away, the firm can efficiently offer a labor contract that commits to retain workers when their productivity falls below their wage. The firm's ability to make this commitment depends on its capital structure since it cannot uphold the commitment in bankruptcy. Recognizing this, workers demand higher wages to compensate for higher leverage. In equilibrium, firms with higher leverage pay higher wages and attract employees who are more tolerant toward risk. Chemmanur, Cheng, and Zhang (2008) test this prediction and find a positive relationship between firm leverage and average firm wages as well as CEO compensation. Also, the matching of risk-tolerant employees and firm leverage could help explain the persistent heterogeneity in capital structures documented by Lemmon, Roberts, and Zender (2008). Finally, since equity markets enable shareholders to diversify better than all other factors of production, this result potentially extends to the compensation paid to all factors.

SUMMARY AND CONCLUSIONS

This chapter examines the many interactions between capital structure and top management (executive) compensation. The chapter focuses on top management as the makers of decisions of interest to shareholders and bondholders. Managerial compensation can mediate the conflicting preferences of shareholders and bondholders regarding investment and financing decisions including the shareholders' asset substitution incentive. Also, capital structure can mitigate the conflicting preferences of managers and owners, particularly in the presence of information asymmetries or managerial entrenchment. For example, higher debt commitments can curtail perquisite consumption and focus managers on generating sufficient cash flow to avoid default.

Executive compensation has many components including salary, cash bonuses, stock, and options. Recent empirical studies attempt to incorporate the incentives from all components into two measures: delta and vega, which measure the manager's pay-sensitivity to shareholder returns and shareholder risk, respectively. Strong evidence suggests that vega is positively related to leverage and that delta is negatively related to leverage.

A full explanation of this evidence does not yet exist. At present, the leading explanation appears to be risk related. In particular, the manager's personal risk aversion appears to outweigh the shareholder's asset substitution (risk-taking) incentive contained in delta. In contrast, the risk-taking incentive contained in vega appears to outweigh the manager's personal risk aversion. Delta, therefore, tends to encourage safer investments and lower leverage, while vega encourages the opposite. To the extent that delta is driven by stock and deep-in-the-money options while vega is driven by out-of-the-money options, this may reflect Lewellen's

(2006) finding that stock and deep-in-the-money options actually reduce risk taking due to the concavity of the manager's utility function. This explanation of the opposite effects of delta and vega on risk-taking incentives also appears consistent with the finding that vega increases and delta decreases the cost of debt capital.

While these are intriguing results, they are far from conclusive. Some authors (Carlson and Lazrak 2010) argue that the ratio of cash to stock in compensation, rather than delta and vega, drives leverage and the cost of debt capital. Further, conflicting evidence exists regarding the causality in the relationship between compensation and capital structure. The evidence also shows that other factors are important in the relationship between compensation and capital structure including the use of convertible debt, the maturity structure of the firm's debt, and debt-like components of compensation. The literature has yet to fully investigate the interactions, but to date the characteristics of compensation appear likely to be a significant determinant of capital structure. Moreover, following Berk, Stanton, and Zechner's (2010) arguments and recognizing the importance of long-term stock and option holdings, compensation variables may be relatively persistent and help to explain the persistent heterogeneity in capital structure documented by Lemmon, Roberts, and Zender (2008).

DISCUSSION QUESTIONS

1. Modigliani and Miller (1958) illustrate that with perfect capital markets, capital structure is irrelevant for total firm value, so managers need not worry about the firm's capital structure. Why has this result received so much attention? Could earning-based compensation "upset" this result?
2. In analyzing the relationship between capital structure and managerial incentives, studies employ substantially different settings. For example, Jensen and Meckling (1976) focus on the incentives associated with a combined manager-owner; John and John (1993) focus on a principal-agent setting, where the manager is an employee facing a compensation contract designed by a well-functioning board of directors; and Zwiebel (1996) focuses on entrenched managers in firms with poorly functioning boards. What are the implications of these different settings for the conclusions of their analyses?
3. Some authors argue that in the 1980s, managers had weak monetary incentives that led to stagnant firm values. For example, Jensen (1986) argues that managers have access to free cash flow and face little discipline in how they use it, except for the threat of a hostile takeover. Jensen and Murphy (1990) argue that the degree of pay for performance in managerial compensation is weak, finding that managerial wealth changed by approximately $3.25 per $1000 change in shareholder wealth. This degree of pay for performance provides little incentive to invest free cash flow efficiently. How has the situation facing managers changed since the 1980s?
4. The large corporation in which managers serve as agents for the firm's owners is a classic example of the principal-agent relationship. In general, the firm's owners are its investors, who include both shareholders and bondholders. Despite this, compensation contracts are usually designed to maximize the wealth of shareholders in the principal-agent model. Is this consistent with bondholders being owners?

REFERENCES

Aggarwal, Rajesh K., and Andrew A. Samwick. 1999. "The Other Side of the Trade-Off: The Impact of Risk on Executive Compensation." *Journal of Political Economy* 107:1, 65–105.

Bagnani, Elizabeth Strock, Nikolaos T. Milonas, Anthony Saunders, and Nickolaos G. Travlos. 1994. "Managers, Owners, and the Pricing of Risky Debt: An Empirical Analysis." *Journal of Finance* 49:2, 453–477.

Barnea, Amir, Robert A. Haugen, and Lemma W. Senbet. 1980. "A Rationale for Debt Maturity Structure and Call Provisions in the Agency Theoretic Framework." *Journal of Finance* 35:5, 1223–1234.

Berger, Philip G., Eli Ofek, and David L. Yermack. 1997. "Managerial Entrenchment and Capital Structure." *Journal of Finance* 52:4, 1411–1438.

Bergstresser, Daniel, and Thomas Philippon. 2006. "CEO Incentives and Earnings Management." *Journal of Financial Economics* 80:3, 511–529.

Berk, Jonathan, Richard Stanton, and Josef Zechner. 2010. "Human Capital, Bankruptcy, and Capital Structure." *Journal of Finance* 65:3, 891–926.

Billett, Matthew T., and Yixin Liu. 2008. "Shareholder-Manager Alignment and the Cost of Debt." Available at http://ssrn.com/abstract=958991.

Billett, Matthew T., David C. Mauer, and Yilei Zhang. 2010. "Stockholder and Bondholder Wealth Effects of CEO Incentive Grants." *Financial Management*. Forthcoming.

Brockman, Paul, Xiumin Martin, and Emre Unlu. 2010. "Executive Compensation and the Maturity Structure of Corporate Debt." *Journal of Finance* 65:3, 1123–1161.

Bryan, Stephen, LeeSeok Hwang, and Steven Lilien. 2000. "CEO Stock-based Compensation: An Empirical Analysis of Incentive Intensity, Relative Mix, and Economic Determinants." *Journal of Business* 73:4, 661–693.

Carlson, Murray, and Ali Lazrak. 2010. "Leverage Choice and Credit Spread When Managers Risk Shift." *Journal of Finance*. Forthcoming.

Chemmanur, Thomas J., Yingmei Cheng, and Tianming Zhang. 2008. "Capital Structure and Employee Pay: An Empirical Analysis." Working Paper, Boston College.

Cohen, Randolph B., Brian J. Hall, and Luis M. Viceira. 2000. "Do Executive Stock Options Encourage Risk-taking?" Working Paper, Harvard Business School.

Coles, Jeffrey L., Naveen D. Daniel, and Lalitha Naveen. 2006. "Managerial Incentives and Risk Taking." *Journal of Financial Economics* 79:2, 431–468.

Core, John E., and Wayne R. Guay. 1999. The Use of Equity Grants to Manage Optimal Equity Incentive Levels." *Journal of Accounting and Economics* 28: 2, 151–184.

Core, John and Wayne Guay. 2002. "The Other Side of the Tradeoff: The Impact of Risk on Executive Compensation —Revised Comment." Working Paper, University of Pennsylvania.

DeFusco, Richard A., Robert R. Johnson, and Thomas S. Zorn. 1990. "The Effect of Executive Stock Option Plans on Stockholders and Bondholders." *Journal of Finance* 45:2, 617–627.

Douglas, Alan. 2006. "Capital Structure, Compensation and Incentives." *Review of Financial Studies* 19:2, 605–632.

Dybvig, Phillip, and Jaime Zender. 1991. "Capital Structure and Dividend Irrelevance with Asymmetric Information." *Review of Financial Studies* 4:1, 201–219.

Fama, Eugene F., and Merton H. Miller. 1972. *The Theory of Finance*. New York: Holt, Rinehart, and Winston.

Friend, Irwin, and Larry H. P. Lang. 1988. "An Empirical Test of the Impact of Managerial Self-Interest on Corporate Capital Structure." *Journal of Finance* 43:2, 271–281.

Grossman, Sanford J., and Oliver D. Hart. 1982. "Corporate Financial Structure and Managerial Incentives." In John McCall, ed., *The Economics of Information and Uncertainty*, 107–140. Chicago: University of Chicago Press.

Hall, Brian J., and Jeffrey B. Liebman, 1998. "Are CEOs Really Paid Like Bureaucrats?" *Quarterly Journal of Economics* 113:3, 653–691.

Harris, Milton, and Artur Raviv. 1991. "The Theory of Capital Structure." *Journal of Finance* 46:1, 297–355.

Jensen, Michael C. 1986. "Agency Costs of Free Cash Flows, Corporate Finance, and Takeovers." *American Economic Review* 76:3, 323–339.

Jensen, Michael C., and William H. Meckling. 1976. "Theory of the Firm: Managerial Behavior, Agency Costs and Ownership Structure." *Journal of Financial Economics* 3:4, 305–360.

Jensen, Michael C., and Kevin J. Murphy. 1990. "Performance Pay and Top-Management Incentives." *Journal of Political Economy* 98:2, 225–264.

John, Kose, Hamid Mehran, and Yiming Qian. 2006 "Incentive Features in CEO Compensation: The Role of Regulation and Monitored Debt." NYU Working Paper No. CLB-06-018. Available at http://ssrn.com/abstract=1291606.

John, Teresa A., and Kose John. 1993. "Top-management Compensation and Capital Structure." *Journal of Finance* 48:3, 949–974.

Leland, Hayne E., and Klaus Bjerre Toft. 1996. "Optimal Capital Structure, Endogeneous Bankruptcy, and the Term Structure of Credit Spreads." *Journal of Finance* 51:3, 987–1019.

Lemmon, Michael L., Michael R. Roberts, and Jaime F. Zender. 2008. "Back to the Beginning: Persistence and the Cross-Section of Corporate Capital Structure." *Journal of Finance* 63:4, 1575–1608.

Lewellen, Katharina. 2006. "Financing Decisions When Managers Are Risk Averse." *Journal of Financial Economics* 82:3, 551–589.

Lewellen, William G., Claudio Loderer, and Kenneth Martin. 1987. "Executive Compensation and Executive Incentive Problems: An Empirical Analysis." *Journal of Accounting and Economics* 9:3, 287–310.

Mehran, Hamid. 1992. "Executive Incentive Plans, Corporate Control, and Capital Structure." *Journal of Financial and Quantitative Analysis* 27:4, 539–560.

Mehran, Hamid. 1995. "Executive Compensation Structure, Ownership and Firm Performance." *Journal of Financial Economics* 38:2, 163–184.

Modigliani, Franco, and Merton Miller. 1958. "The Cost of Capital, Corporation Finance, and the Theory of Investments." *American Economic Review* 48:3, 261–297.

Moody's Investor Service. 2005. "Special Comment: CEO Compensation and Credit Risk." July, 1–10. Available at www.moodys.com.

Moody's Investor Service. 2007. "Special Comment: A User's Guide to the SEC's New Rules for Reporting Executive Pay." April 1–14. Available at www.moodys.com.

Morellec, Erwan. 2004. "Can Managerial Discretion Explain Observed Leverage Ratios?" *Review of Financial Studies* 17:2, 257–294.

Murphy, Kevin J. 1999. "Executive Compensation." In Orley Ashenfelter and David Card, eds., *Handbook of Labor Economics*, 1st ed., vol. 3, 2485–2563. Princeton, NJ: North Holland.

Myers, Stuart C. 1977. "Determinants of Corporate Borrowing." *Journal of Financial Economics* 5:2, 147–175.

Myers, Stuart C., and Nicholas Majluf. 1984. "Corporate Financing and Investment Decisions When Firms Have Information Investors Do Not Have." *Journal of Financial Economics* 13:2, 187–221.

Novaes, Walter, and Luigi Zingales. 1995. "Capital Structure Choice When Managers Are in Control: Entrenchment Versus Efficiency." Working Paper, University of Chicago.

Ortiz-Molina, Hernan. 2006. "Top-Management Incentives and the Pricing of Corporate Public Debt." *Journal of Financial and Quantitative Analysis* 41:3, 317–340.

Ortiz-Molina, Hernan. 2007. "Executive Compensation and Capital Structure: The Effects of Convertible Debt and Straight Debt on CEO Pay." *Journal of Accounting and Economics* 43:1, 69–93.

Parsons, Christopher, and Sheridan Titman. 2008. "Empirical Capital Structure: A Review." *Foundations and Trends in Finance* 3:1, 1–93.

Persons, John C. 1994. "Renegotiation and the Impossibility of Optimal Investment." *Review of Financial Studies* 7:2, 419–449.

Ross, Stephen. 1977. "The Determination of Financial Structure: The Incentive Signalling Approach." *Rand Journal of Economics* 8:3, 23–40.

Stulz, René. 1990. "Managerial Discretion and Optimal Financing Policies." *Journal of Financial Economics* 22:1, 3–28.

Sundaram, K. Rangarajam, and David L. Yermack. 2007, "Pay Me Later: Inside Debt and Its Role in Managerial Compensation." *Journal of Finance* 62:4, 1551–1588.

Yermack, L. David, and Chenyang Wei. 2009. "Stockholder and Bondholder Reactions to Revelations of Large CEO Inside Debt Holdings: An Empirical Analysis." NYU Working Paper No. FIN-09-020. Available at http://ssrn.com/abstract=151925.

Zwiebel, Jeremy. 1996. "Dynamic Capital Structure under Managerial Entrenchment." *American Economic Review* 86:5, 1197–1215.

ABOUT THE AUTHOR

Alan Victor Scott Douglas is an Associate Professor of Finance and a Robert Harding Research Leadership Fellow in the School of Accounting and Finance at the University of Waterloo. Previously, he was a faculty member at Clemson University in South Carolina and Queen's University at Kingston, Ontario. His main expertise is in the areas of corporate financial policy, managerial compensation, corporate control, and performance. Professor Douglas has published in leading finance and accounting journals such as the *Journal of Corporate Finance*, *Contemporary Accounting Review*, *Review of Financial Studies*, and *Journal of Empirical Finance*. He received a PhD in Financial Economics from Queen's University.

CHAPTER 7

Worldwide Patterns in Capital Structure

CARMEN COTEI
Assistant Professor of Finance, University of Hartford

JOSEPH FARHAT
Associate Professor of Finance, Central Connecticut State University

INTRODUCTION

While most of the empirical research on capital structure has been done in a single country context, usually the United States, recent research focuses on identifying differences in capital structure across countries with different legal and institutional settings. Studies by La Porta et al. (1997, 1998, 2000a, 2000b), Demirgüç-Kunt and Maksimovic (1999), Claessens and Klapper (2005), and Alves and Ferreira (2007) highlight the presence of systematic differences in the capital structure and dividend policy across countries. These studies show that legal systems and financial market development play an important role in how firms are financed. For example, countries with lower protection of creditor and equity shareholder rights—civil law countries—have less-developed financial markets, and firms use equity markets less frequently to raise capital. Rajan and Zingales (1995) demonstrate the importance of a well-developed financial market to fulfill the external financing needs of corporations. Demirgüç-Kunt and Maksimovic analyze the relationship between firm financing choices and the level of development of financial markets. They find a negative relationship between stock market development and the ratios of both long- and short-term leverage. The literature also establishes that a relationship exists between the legal system and the development of the financial markets. Countries with a civil law tradition tend to have undeveloped financial markets and a propensity for bank-based systems, whereas common law countries tend to be more market-based and have financially developed markets (Demirgüç-Kunt and Levine 1999).

The goal of this chapter is to provide a synthesis of relevant studies that highlight the main issues and viewpoints regarding capital structure across countries. The papers referenced represent important contributions on capital structure theories and emphasize how well these theories explain leverage ratios in an international context.

The remainder of the chapter has the following organization. The first section discusses determinants of capital structure and makes cross-country comparisons. This is followed by a review of the impact of legal traditions on capital structure. The next two sections examine international evidence involving partial adjustment to a target capital structure and the pecking order theory. The final section provides a summary and conclusions.

DETERMINANTS OF CAPITAL STRUCTURE: CROSS-COUNTRY COMPARISONS

Several studies examine the role of firm-specific factors, macroeconomic factors, and institutional settings on capital structure decisions. Recently, a growing body of research has started to employ cross-country comparisons to test capital structure theories. By investigating how firm features relate to capital structure across many countries, these studies attempt to identify the economic forces underlying leverage factors and to reveal information about the strengths and shortcomings of a particular theory. For example, Rajan and Zingales (1995) examine whether the factors identified as explaining the firm leverage in the United States also explain the leverage ratios across G7 industrialized nations and find that the same factors are correlated with leverage in all countries analyzed.

Antoniou, Guney, and Paudyal (2008) identify the firm-specific and macroeconomic factors that managers consider in their capital structure choices in Group of Five (G5) nations (two capital market-oriented economies—the United States and the United Kingdom—and three bank-oriented economies—Germany, Japan, and France) and measure their speed of adjustment to optimal leverage. They find that the leverage ratio is positively related to tangibility of assets and firm size and negatively related to profitability, growth opportunities, interest rates, and share price performance in both types of economies. However, across all five countries analyzed, asset tangibility, equity premium, profitability, and effective tax rate vary, suggesting that differences in institutional environments and traditions contribute to capital structure decisions. For example, profitability is inversely related to market leverage in all countries studied but Japan.

The sizes of the coefficients of profitability also vary across countries with U.S. firms having the largest (in absolute terms). Among European countries analyzed, France has the largest coefficient for profitability. Antoniou, Guney, and Paudyal (2008) explain this result by the preference of French managers for retaining a high proportion of earnings in order to maintain a closely-held ownership structure and also by the strategic informational advantage French managers have over creditors. Among the G5 nations, British firms have the highest payout ratio, which impacts the hierarchy of financing strategies. British firms use less internal financing and more external financing. In Germany the tax rate on dividends is lower than on retained earnings, which explains why German firms have a higher payout ratio (28.8 percent) relative to French firms (6.5 percent). When controlling for macroeconomic factors, a negative relationship exists between the term-structure of interest rates and leverage in all G5 countries except Germany. This is consistent with the fact that when interest rates are high, firms are reluctant to issue debt capital, especially long-term debt. As a result, when the term-structure of interest rates widens, managers prefer to issue equity, consistent with the wealth-maximizing hypothesis. Mergers and acquisitions (M&As) appear to influence the capital structure decisions in Japan, the United Kingdom, and the United States but have no effect on French and German firms. These results are consistent with the view that hostile takeovers are more frequent in market-based economies relative to bank-based economies.

Booth et al. (2001) analyze the capital structure choices of firms from 10 developing countries and find that the same variables (size, tangibility, and profitability) affect these decisions as in developed countries. However, systematic differences exist in the way country variables such as gross domestic product (GDP) growth rate, inflation rate, and development of capital markets affect debt ratios.

The main theories of capital structure (trade-off, pecking order, and market timing) make precise statements regarding how leverage relates to observable firm attributes (Titman and Wessels 1988; Shyam-Sunder and Myers 1999; Baker and Wurgler 2002). For U.S. firms, Frank and Goyal (2009) document that the main factors that statistically affect leverage across many treatments of data are industry median leverage, market-to-book assets ratio, tangibility, profits, firm size, and inflation. Similarly, for major industrialized G7 countries, Rajan and Zingales (1995) report that the dominant factors explaining the leverage ratios are the market-to-book assets ratio, tangibility, profitability, and firm size.

A natural question is whether these factors are equally important in a large panel of countries with different institutional features, as well as special circumstances that arise from differences in the quality of institutions governing their country. Oztekin and Flannery (2010) examine a panel of 37 countries with different institutional environments and show that among the factors affecting leverage proposed by Frank and Goyal (2009) and Rajan and Zingales (1995), only industry median leverage, tangibility, and firm size have consistent signs and statistical significance across a large number of countries, using both book and market definitions of leverage. In addition to these factors, the results highlight past leverage as the most significant factor in all sample countries. Consistent with the dynamic trade-off theory, past leverage can capture 70 percent of the total variation in leverage compared to 5 percent captured by the remaining traditional determinants.

The prior literature (La Porta et al. 1997, 1998, 2000a, 2000b, 2002; Demirgüç-Kunt and Maksimovic 1999; Bancel and Mittoo 2004) shows that capital structure decisions are influenced not only by firm-specific characteristics but also by country-specific institutional characteristics such as legal traditions and quality of institution. Different institutional features in various countries may impact the trade-off between bankruptcy costs and tax benefits as well as the information asymmetry costs for firms. For example, in countries with weak institutional settings that are subject to high bankruptcy and agency costs of debt, firms find the tax benefits of debt more valuable (Oztekin and Flannery 2010). Also, firms operating in countries with higher distress costs need more collateral relative to firms operating in lower distress costs environments. In higher distress costs countries, lenders can repossess collateral or enforce debt contracts to reduce the bankruptcy and agency costs of debt. Therefore, firm-specific characteristics as well as the financial environment and traditions in which firms operate influence capital structure decisions.

THE IMPACT OF LEGAL TRADITIONS ON CAPITAL STRUCTURE

Although no two countries have identical legal systems, legal scholars identify two broad legal traditions: civil law and common law. Within the civil law tradition, commercial laws originate from three major families: French, German, and Scandinavian. Civil laws offer investors weaker legal rights than do common laws. Relatively speaking, common law countries offer both shareholders and creditors the strongest protection and French civil law countries offer the weakest protection, with the Scandinavian and German-civil law countries falling between the two extremes (La Porta et al. 1997, 1998). Francis, Khurana, and Pereira (2001) find that national accounting standards are more transparent in common law countries. This leads to a higher bankruptcy rate in these countries (Claessens and Klapper 2005) and therefore a higher cost of financial distress. Frankel and Montgomery (1991) argue that differences in bankruptcy laws can explain the variation in aggregate debt levels across countries.

As noted in the introduction, the differences in legal systems should lead to different capital structures across countries. Exhibit 7.1 shows the classification of 37 countries by legal system (civil versus common) and market development (developed versus emerging). The fourth column reports the total leverage ratio, the fifth the long-term debt ratio, and the last column the short-term debt ratio. While there is no major difference in the total leverage between civil and common law countries, maturity structure seems to matter with long-term and short-term debt ratios varying markedly across countries with different legal systems.

Exhibit 7.2 reports the balance sheet presentation of corporate assets and liabilities across all civil-law countries versus common-law countries. Total liabilities (current liabilities, short-term and long-term debt, and other liabilities) in civil-law countries are around 60 percent of total assets, which is about 2 percentage points higher than in common-law countries.

Looking into the components of total debt, long-term and short-term debt ratios vary significantly across different legal systems. Firms in common law countries tend to have significantly more long-term debt and less short-term debt relative to firms in civil law countries. In civil law countries, the proportion of long-term debt in total debt is 48 percent, while in common law countries long-term debt accounts for about 66 percent of total debt. Lower bondholders' protection rights, higher agency cost for long-term bondholders (La Porta et al. 1998), and higher information asymmetry can explain the debt maturity structure in civil law countries. Since financing with short-term debt requires continuous renegotiation, a higher short-term debt ratio potentially eliminates the overinvestment problem by giving creditors more control over managers and thus reducing the risk-shifting problems. Firms in civil law countries depend more on internally generated funds to finance their investments. In contrast, firms in common law countries have a higher financing deficit and rely more on external financing, with an emphasis on equity over debt to close the financing gap. When firms in civil law countries have a financing deficit, they use more debt, particularly more short-term debt, to close their financing gap. The short-term debt financing represents 54 percent of total debt issued in civil law countries. In contrast, the short-term debt financing represents only 37 percent of total debt issued in common law countries.

Exhibit 7.1 Legal Systems and Debt Ratios

Country	Legal System	Market	Total Debt Ratio	Long-Term Debt Ratio	Short-Term Debt Ratio
Argentina	Civil	Emerging	0.339	0.161	0.178
Austria	Civil	Developed	0.258	0.126	0.132
Belgium	Civil	Developed	0.275	0.139	0.136
Brazil	Civil	Emerging	0.297	0.154	0.143
Chile	Civil	Emerging	0.268	0.157	0.111
China	Civil	Emerging	0.304	0.048	0.256
Denmark	Civil	Developed	0.271	0.140	0.131
Finland	Civil	Developed	0.247	0.151	0.097
France	Civil	Developed	0.239	0.119	0.120
Germany	Civil	Developed	0.225	0.099	0.126
Greece	Civil	Developed	0.301	0.134	0.167
Italy	Civil	Developed	0.264	0.109	0.155
Japan	Civil	Developed	0.289	0.113	0.176
Korea	Civil	Emerging	0.336	0.122	0.214
Mexico	Civil	Emerging	0.290	0.162	0.128
Netherlands	Civil	Developed	0.267	0.144	0.123
Norway	Civil	Developed	0.308	0.231	0.077
Philippines	Civil	Emerging	0.290	0.133	0.157
Portugal	Civil	Developed	0.315	0.151	0.164
Spain	Civil	Developed	0.236	0.086	0.150
Sweden	Civil	Developed	0.218	0.135	0.083
Switzerland	Civil	Developed	0.256	0.158	0.098
Taiwan	Civil	Emerging	0.278	0.087	0.191
Turkey	Civil	Emerging	0.237	0.086	0.151
Average	**Civil**		**0.275**	**0.131**	**0.144**
Australia	Common	Developed	0.234	0.176	0.058
Canada	Common	Developed	0.272	0.216	0.056
Hong Kong	Common	Developed	0.225	0.105	0.12
India	Common	Emerging	0.313	0.214	0.099
Ireland	Common	Developed	0.274	0.222	0.052
Israel	Common	Emerging	0.296	0.185	0.111
Malaysia	Common	Emerging	0.286	0.120	0.166
New Zealand	Common	Developed	0.310	0.254	0.056
Singapore	Common	Developed	0.228	0.109	0.119
South Africa	Common	Emerging	0.188	0.116	0.072
Thailand	Common	Emerging	0.291	0.158	0.133
United Kingdom	Common	Developed	0.218	0.147	0.071
United States	Common	Developed	0.283	0.229	0.054
Average	**Common**		**0.263**	**0.173**	**0.090**

Note: The sample consists of all nonfinancial firms listed on WorldScope database during the period 1990 to 2004. The legal system classification (civil versus common) follows La Porta et al. (1998). The level of market development (developed versus emerging) follows the Morgan Stanley Capital International standards. The ratios are defined as follows: total debt ratio = (long-term + short-term debt)/total assets; long-term debt ratio = long-term debt/total assets; and short-term debt ratio = short-term debt/total assets.

Exhibit 7.2 Financing Patterns across Countries with Different Legal Systems

Panel A. Common-Size Balance Sheet	**Civil**	**Common**	**Differences**
Current assets	0.483	0.451	0.032**
Net property, plant, and equipment	0.355	0.376	−0.021**
Other assets	0.162	0.179	−0.017*
Current liabilities	0.298	0.261	0.037**
Short-term debt	0.144	0.090	0.055**
Long-term debt	0.131	0.173	−0.042**
Total debt	0.275	0.263	0.012**
Other liabilities	0.026	0.054	−0.028*
Stockholders' equity	0.401	0.428	−0.027**
Panel B. Corporate Cash Flows	**Civil**	**Common**	**Differences**
Investments	0.066	0.083	−0.017**
Cash dividends	0.011	0.016	−0.005*
Change in working capital	0.005	0.004	0.001
Internal cash flow	0.060	0.036	0.024**
Financing deficit (surplus)	0.023	0.067	−0.045**
Net equity issued/Total assets	0.011	0.058	−0.047**
Net debt issued/Total assets	0.012	0.010	0.002
Long-term debt issued/Total debt issued	0.458	0.627	−0.170**

Note: The sample consists of all nonfinancial firms listed on WorldScope database during the period 1990 to 2004. The value of each balance-sheet item is calculated as a percentage of the book value of total assets. Other assets are defined as investments and advances + intangibles. Current liabilities exclude short-term debt. Other liabilities are defined as deferred taxes + minority interest. The value of each item in the cash flow statements is calculated as a percentage of the book value of total assets. Financing deficit (surplus) is defined as the sum of cash dividends, investments and change in working capital minus internal cash flow divided by total assets. **, * indicate that the coefficient is statistically different from zero at the 0.01 and 0.05 levels, respectively.

The evidence presented in Exhibit 7.2 is consistent with the argument that countries with stronger legal protection, higher legal enforcement, more active capital markets, and higher accounting standards improve investors' confidence in securities markets. These factors also reduce the severity of the information asymmetry problem, thus prompting the use of external funding and a move toward equity financing rather than debt financing.

PARTIAL ADJUSTMENT TO A TARGET CAPITAL STRUCTURE: INTERNATIONAL EVIDENCE

The trade-off theory of capital structure predicts that firms seek to maintain an optimal capital structure by balancing the benefits and costs of debt. The benefits include the tax shield, the reduction of free cash flow problems, and other potential conflicts between managers and shareholders, whereas the costs include expected financial distress costs, costs associated with underinvestment, and asset substitution problems. The trade-off theory predicts that firms have an optimal capital structure and adjust their leverage toward the optimum over time (Taggart 1977; Opler and Titman 1994).

To the degree that legal and institutional features affect the benefits and costs of debt, variation in these factors should influence the speed of adjustment. Empirical evidence shows that firms in common law countries adjust to optimal capital structure significantly more quickly than firms in civil law countries (Cotei, Farhat, and Abugri 2009). The contribution of long-term debt in the speed of adjustment also varies with legal system. In civil law countries, long-term debt accounts for about 51 percent of the rate of adjustment, while in common law countries long-term debt shows a contribution of more than 64 percent in the rate of adjustment.

Oztekin and Flannery (2010) link the quality rankings of institutions as implied by the legal system to the adjustment speed. They show that firms in countries with a higher quality of institutions have higher speed of adjustments. For a sample of 37 countries, the evidence suggests that firms in countries with common law traditions adjust more quickly toward an optimal capital structure (27 percent), followed by Scandinavian (25 percent), German (22 percent), and finally French civil law (15 percent) firms.

Several other studies show evidence of target behavior in foreign countries. Nivorozhkin (2005) documents the determinants of capital structure and the speed of adjustment in five European Union (EU) accession countries from central and eastern Europe. The estimated average speed of adjustment across all countries is 17 percent, compared to 20 percent per year reported in Banerjee, Heshmati, and Wihlborg (2004) for a sample of UK firms. This is consistent with the stylized fact that firms in countries with developed capital markets have higher adjustment speeds relative to those with emerging economies. Nivorozhkin shows that the speed of adjustment varies substantially across both the countries analyzed and differently sized firms. Relatively smaller firms tend to adjust 4 to 9 percent faster than larger firms. The speed of adjustment ranges from 8 percent in the Czech Republic to 24 percent in Romania.

Wanzenried (2002) shows a much higher speed of adjustment for a sample of developed countries (continental Europe and the United Kingdom). Across all firms analyzed, the adjustment speed is as high as 45.6 percent for continental European countries and 48.3 percent for the United Kingdom. Using Spanish data, De Miguel and Pindado (2001) report that Spanish firms face lower adjustment costs than do U.S. firms. The lower the adjustment costs, the higher is the speed of adjustment. Antoniou, Guney, and Paudyal (2008) find that firms in G5 countries (the United States, United Kingdom, France, Germany, and Japan) adjust their debt ratios to attain target capital structures but at different speeds. The speed of adjustment is fastest in French firms, followed by American, British, German, and Japanese firms, respectively. For German and Japanese firms, the cost of being off target relative to the cost of adjustment is low. The result is consistent with the fact that in bank-based economies (German and Japanese), firms have close ties with their creditors, and therefore they adjust slowly to their target leverage without incurring substantial agency costs.

Overall, the results for G5 countries are consistent with a dynamic framework for capital structure decisions in which managers trade off the cost of adjustment and the cost of being off target. The speed of adjustment depends not only on the legal traditions but also on the country's financial orientation and corporate governance traditions. The role of the financial orientation of the economy (market-based versus banked-based economy) on the firms' capital structure decisions is extremely important because of the direct implications on the sources of funds available to corporations.

Some studies show a positive relationship between market-based financial systems and strong protection of shareholders' rights, good accounting standards, and a low level of corruption (Demirgüç-Kunt and Levine 1999). Therefore, the opportunities in a developed capital market induce firms to issue equity. As a result, firms operating in market-based economies should have lower leverage ratios relative to those in bank-based economies. The speed of adjustment is higher in market-based economies because a market-based structure imposes lower adjustment costs and higher benefits of adjusting to optimal capital structure (Oztekin and Flannery 2010). Specifically, for a sample of 37 countries, firms in market-based financial systems adjust at an average rate of 23 percent, while firms in banked-based financial systems adjust at an average rate of 20 percent, using a book leverage measure.

To evaluate the impact of easier capital market access on the adjustment speed, researchers use various proxies such as shareholders' and creditors' rights and the quality of their enforcement. The evidence shows that the adjustment is faster in countries with stronger shareholders'/creditors' rights and better enforcement of these rights. This is consistent with La Porta et al. (1997, 1998), who suggest that enforcement of investors' rights is an effective mechanism that reduces external financing costs.

The standard partial adjustment model used in the literature to examine the adjustment process toward a leverage target relies on the changes in the debt that is partially absorbed by the difference between debt target, $Lev_t{}^*$, and lagged debt, Lev_{t-1}. If the cost function of recapitalization and the cost function of being away from the optimal debt can be approximated by quadratic terms, then the total loss function can be written as follows:

$$\ell = \phi\left(Lev_t - Lev_t^*\right)^2 + \varphi\left(Lev_t - Lev_{t-1}\right)^2 \tag{7.1}$$

The first term measures the cost of being away from the target and the second term measures the cost of adjustment (recapitalization). Taking the first derivative to minimize the loss function leads to the following:

$$\frac{\partial \ell}{\partial Lev_t} = 2\varphi\left(Lev_t - Lev_t^*\right) + 2\phi\left(Lev_t - Lev_{t-1}\right) = 0$$

$$Lev_t - Lev_{t-1} = \frac{\phi}{\phi + \varphi}\left(Lev_t^* - Lev_{t-1}\right)$$

$$Lev_t - Lev_{t-1} = \alpha_1\left(Lev_t^* - Lev_{t-1}\right)$$

The adjustment rate coefficient α_1 depends on the ratio of marginal cost of being away from the target to marginal cost of adjustment. Obviously, the higher the adjustment cost, the slower is the rate of adjustment. A full adjustment will occur if the cost of adjustment is too low or the cost of being away from the target is too high. Further, firms will not adjust their debt toward the optimal leverage if the cost of being away from the optimal leverage is zero. Thus, the model can be written as follows:

$$Lev_t - Lev_{t-1} = \alpha_0 + \alpha_1 (Lev_t^* - Lev_{t-1}) + \varepsilon_t \tag{7.2}$$

where:

Lev_t Total leverage at time t
$Lev_t{}^*$ Optimal leverage level at time t
α_1 Adjustment rate coefficient
ε_t Error term.

where:

$\alpha_1 = 0$ (reflects no adjustment to the target)
$0 < \alpha_1 < 1$ (reflects partial adjustment to the target due to the cost of adjustment)
$\alpha_1 = 1$ (reflects a full adjustment to the target (the adjustment is costless))

The parameter α_1 may be interpreted in terms of the relative cost of being away from the optimal leverage and the cost of recapitalization (adjusting).

Panel A of Exhibit 7.3 reports the rates of adjustment by country, and Panel B shows the differences in speed of adjustments across civil law and common law countries. Compared to firms in civil law countries, those in common law countries have a significantly higher rate of adjustment toward the target leverage. The results imply that across all countries firms adjust toward the target leverage but with a significantly different rate of adjustment depending on their institutional environments. This result supports the conjecture that stronger investor protection, higher transparency, and well-developed financial markets in common law countries reduce the cost of recapitalization.

THE PECKING ORDER THEORY: INTERNATIONAL EVIDENCE

The pecking order theory (Myers and Majluf 1984; Myers 1984) and its extensions (Lucas and McDonald 1990) are based on the idea of asymmetric information between managers and investors. Managers know more about the true value of the firm and the firm's riskiness than less informed outside investors. If the information asymmetry results in underpricing of the firm's equity and the firm needs to finance a new project by issuing equity, the underpricing may be so severe that new investors capture most of the net present value (NPV) of the project, resulting in a net loss to existing shareholders. Thus, managers who work in the best interest of the current shareholders will reject the project. To avoid the underinvestment problem, managers will seek to finance the new project using a security that is not undervalued by the market such as internal funds or riskless debt. This affects the choice between internal and external financing. The pecking order theory can explain why firms tend to depend on internal sources of funds and prefer debt to equity if external financing is required. Therefore, a firm's leverage is not driven

Exhibit 7.3 Partial Adjustment Model across Countries with Different Legal Systems

Panel A. Partial Adjustment Model across Countries

Country Yes	α_1	R^2
Argentina	0.435*	0.27
Australia	0.468**	0.37
Austria	0.249*	0.21
Belgium	0.289*	0.19
Brazil	0.279*	0.14
Canada	0.393**	0.22
Chile	0.243*	0.13
China	0.438**	0.33
Denmark	0.298*	0.17
Finland	0.282*	0.17
France	0.290**	0.16
Germany	0.222**	0.11
Greece	0.281*	0.14
Hong Kong	0.358**	0.20
India	0.291**	0.17
Ireland	0.474**	0.31
Israel	0.439*	0.33
Italy	0.249*	0.13
Japan	0.191**	0.11
Korea	0.444**	0.26
Malaysia	0.325**	0.20
Mexico	0.364**	0.21
Netherlands	0.310**	0.17
New Zealand	0.327*	0.17
Norway	0.455**	0.36
Philippines	0.315*	0.18
Portugal	0.357*	0.21
Singapore	0.401**	0.22
South Africa	0.402**	0.33
Spain	0.374*	0.20
Sweden	0.311**	0.17
Switzerland	0.238**	0.14
Taiwan	0.477**	0.31
Thailand	0.311**	0.20
Turkey	0.440*	0.50
United Kingdom	0.325**	0.17
United States	0.380**	0.21

Panel B. Partial Adjustment Model across Different Legal Systems

Legal System	α_1	R^2
Civil	0.307**	0.190
Common	0.372**	0.210
Civil-Common	−0.072*	

Note: The sample consists of all nonfinancial firms listed on WorldScope database during the period 1990 to 2004. The partial adjustment model is: $Lev_t - Lev_{t-1} = \alpha_0 + \alpha_1 \left(Lev_t^* - Lev_{t-1}\right) + \varepsilon_t$. The dependent variable is the change in total debt ratio. The independent variable is the deviation from the target leverage. **, * indicate that the coefficient is statistically different from zero at the 0.01 and 0.05 level, respectively.

by the trade-off theory but is simply the cumulative result of a firm's attempts to mitigate information asymmetry.

The pecking order theory predicts that a financing deficit is the main determinant of debt issue and that firms use external financing only if internal funds are insufficient to finance their growth opportunities. If external funds are needed, the pecking order theory predicts that:

- Firms will issue the safest security possible, given that the cost of financial distress is ignored. A safe security is defined as one unaffected by the revelation of managers' inside information (Shyam-Sunder and Myers 1999). This implies that firms will first issue debt and then equity.
- Firms will issue equity when the cost of financial distress is high.

In civil law countries, where the market tends to have a bank-based structure and the capital market is less developed, less information is available about firms and therefore higher information asymmetry exists. This could be the result of the lack of good corporate government standards, low accounting standards, and low protection to shareholders and creditors. In the context of the pecking order theory, this makes firms more reliant on internal funds and debt (secured and unsecured) in order to close their financing deficit.

Diamond (1984) and Boyd and Prescott (1986) point out that banks can easily overcome informational asymmetries. Thus, the costs of acquiring and processing information about corporations and managers may be reduced in bank-based systems. Morck, Yeung, and Yu (2000) show that countries with less-developed financial systems and poorer investor protection have a higher local market volatility and higher R^2 due to the increase in market risk and lack of transparency. Thus, firms in less-developed capital markets are expected to have a higher cost of raising equity and a lower cost of financial distress due to opaqueness, illiquid capital markets, and lower protection of creditors. This encourages firms to rely more on internally generated funds or on borrowing from the banking system to meet their external financing needs. Therefore, a positive relationship should exist between the debt ratio and the financing deficit. Across different institutional settings and controlling for the deviation from the target leverage, firms in civil law countries, emerging economies, and bank-based countries should exhibit a higher magnitude of financing deficit coefficient in the pecking order model of financing.

An important question emerges from the above discussion: Does the pecking order theory provide a better explanation of the changes in capital structure, relative to the trade-off theory, in countries with higher information asymmetry? This question is examined by adding the financing deficit variable to the partial adjustment model. This leads to the following:

$$Lev_t - Lev_{t-1} = \alpha_0 + \alpha_1 (Lev_t^* - Lev_{t-1}) + \alpha_2 FIN_t + \varepsilon_t \tag{7.3}$$

where:

Lev_t Total leverage at time t
Lev_t^* Optimal leverage level at time t

α_1 Adjustment rate coefficient
FIN Firms' financing deficit-surplus of *i*th firm

If firms follow pecking order behavior, the financing deficit variable should absorb the changes in debt. Thus, a lower speed of adjustment or a nonsignificant speed of adjustment at most should be observed. Using this model to test the pecking order theory across countries with different legal systems and institutional settings, Exhibit 7.4 reports the variables that explain the changes in total debt by country (Panel A) and legal system (Panel B).

When controlling for the deviation from the target leverage ($Lev_t^* - Lev_{t-1}$), the financing deficit coefficient shows a significant positive sign across countries with different legal traditions and institutional settings. Yet, the financing deficit cannot explain all the changes in debt ratios. Although the deficit adds some information to explain the changes in debt, it does not rule out the targeting behavior. The coefficient of the speed of adjustment is not significantly lowered after controlling for the financing deficit, but it improves the model's ability to explain changes in debt by increasing the coefficient of determination.

SUMMARY AND CONCLUSIONS

Capital structure decisions vary considerably around the world in terms of the particular mix of equity, short-term debt, and long-term debt across different legal systems, financial structures, and economic development levels. These differences are important because they affect the cost of capital for firms operating in various countries and implicitly the required rates of returns for investors.

Evidence shows that firm-specific factors identified as main determinants of leverage ratios for U.S. firms influence the leverage ratios for non–U.S. firms. Leverage ratios are positively related to tangibility of assets and firm size and negatively related to profitability, growth opportunities, interest rates, and share price performance. However, some determinants vary across countries, such as the equity premium, effective tax rates, and payout ratios. This suggests that factors other than a firm's attributes affect capital structure decisions.

The legal traditions and financial market structures also have a significant influence on how firms choose to finance their investment opportunities. Evidence shows that firms in the United States and the United Kingdom have very different levels of debt but similar capital markets and financial institutions. On the contrary, firms in Japan and the United States have very similar levels of debt, yet they have very diverse legal systems and institutions. A natural question is: Why do the debt levels vary so much across countries with different legal systems and financial market structures? Research shows that common law countries offer both shareholders and creditors the strongest protection, while civil law countries offer the weakest investor protection. On average, firms in common law countries tend to have significantly more long-term debt and less-short term debt relative to firms in civil law countries. The difference in maturity structure of debt across various legal systems is explained by higher information asymmetry, higher agency costs for long-term bondholders, and lower protection rights present in countries with a civil law system. These legal features also explain why firms in civil law countries

Exhibit 7.4 The Pecking Order Model across Countries with Different Legal Systems

Panel A. The Pecking Order Model across Countries

Country	α_1	α_2	R^2
Argentina	0.340*	0.395*	0.320
Australia	0.464**	0.066*	0.371
Austria	0.249*	−0.040	0.208
Belgium	0.268*	0.222*	0.284
Brazil	0.273*	0.167*	0.161
Canada	0.384**	0.111*	0.233
Chile	0.220*	0.304*	0.224
China	0.435**	0.109*	0.341
Denmark	0.282*	0.214*	0.221
Finland	0.262*	0.344*	0.306
France	0.286**	0.164*	0.194
Germany	0.218**	0.183*	0.155
Greece	0.243*	0.332*	0.253
Hong Kong	0.353**	0.169*	0.224
India	0.272**	0.413**	0.316
Ireland	0.483**	0.090*	0.320
Israel	0.422*	0.223*	0.360
Italy	0.250**	0.147*	0.161
Japan	0.187**	0.263**	0.155
Korea	0.430**	0.341**	0.320
Malaysia	0.315**	0.322*	0.245
Mexico	0.350**	0.275*	0.253
Netherlands	0.293**	0.319**	0.297
New Zealand	0.325*	0.396*	0.309
Norway	0.449**	0.101*	0.370
Philippines	0.294*	0.312*	0.236
Portugal	0.328*	0.202*	0.251
Singapore	0.389**	0.257*	0.270
South Africa	0.405**	0.093*	0.336
Spain	0.307*	0.494*	0.314
Sweden	0.290**	0.216*	0.255
Switzerland	0.217*	0.257*	0.208
Taiwan	0.467**	0.278**	0.364
Thailand	0.275**	0.336**	0.268
Turkey	0.439*	0.238*	0.534
United Kingdom	0.318**	0.160**	0.206
United States	0.375**	0.160**	0.238

Panel B. The Pecking Order Model across Different Legal Systems

Legal System	α_1	α_2	R^2
Civil	0.298**	0.231**	0.231
Common	0.366**	0.161*	0.239
Civil-Common	−0.068**	0.071**	

Note: The sample consists of all nonfinancial firms listed on WorldScope Database during the period 1990 to 2004. The model is: $Lev_t - Lev_{t-1} = \alpha_0 + \alpha_1 (Lev_t^* - Lev_{t-1}) + \alpha_2 FIN_t + \varepsilon_t$. The dependent variable is the change in total debt ratio. The independent variables are the deviation from the target leverage, and financing Deficit/Surplus. The Deficit/Surplus is defined as the sum of cash dividends, investments, and change in working capital minus internal cash flow divided by total assets. **, * indicate that the coefficient is statistically different from zero at the 0.01 and 0.05 level, respectively.

rely more on internally generated funds to finance their investment opportunities, while firms in common law countries use more external financing, especially equity over debt, to close their financing gap.

The target behavior predicted by the trade-off theory is an important feature present in firms operating in countries with different legal systems and institutional environments. Studies show that firms in common law countries adjust much more quickly to an optimal capital structure than do firms in civil law countries (Cotei, Farhat, and Abugri 2009; Oztekin and Flannery 2010). Additionally, the speed of adjustment is higher in market-based economies relative to bank-based economies (Antoniou, Guney, and Paudyal 2008). Firms that operate in market-based economies have lower adjustment costs and higher benefits of adjusting to an optimal capital structure. The closer a firm's debt ratio to an optimal ratio, the higher is the firm's value and the lower is the cost of capital. Thus, a firm's valuation is significantly influenced not only by the firm's attributes but also by the legal and financial systems in which it operates.

DISCUSSION QUESTIONS

1. Identify and discuss the impact of firm-specific and macroeconomic factors on capital structure decisions around the world.
2. Prior research establishes that a firm's capital structure is not only influenced by firm-specific factors but also by a country's legal traditions. Discuss how legal systems affect firms' capital structure across countries.
3. The trade-off theory of capital structure predicts that firms have optimal (target) debt ratios. Discuss the differences in the rate of adjustment toward optimal capital structure across countries with different legal traditions and financial structure systems.
4. Does the pecking order theory explain the changes in capital structure across countries with different information asymmetry? Why or why not?

REFERENCES

Alves, Paulo F. Pereira, and Miguel A. Ferreira. 2007. "Capital Structure and Law around the World." Working Paper, ISCTE Business School, Lisbon.

Antoniou, Antonios, Yilmaz Guney, and Krishna Paudyal. 2008. "The Determinates of Capital Structure: Capital Market-Oriented Versus Bank-Oriented Institutions." *Journal of Financial and Quantitative Analysis* 43:1, 59–92.

Baker, Malcolm, and Jeffrey Wurgler. 2002. "Market Timing and Capital Structure." *Journal of Finance* 57:1, 1–32.

Bancel, Franck, and Usha R. Mittoo. 2004. "Cross-Country Determinants of Capital Structure Choice: A Survey of European Firms." *Financial Management* 33:4, 103–132.

Banerjee, Saugata, Almas Heshmati, and Clas Wihlborg. 2004. "The Dynamics of Capital Structure." *Research in Banking and Finance* 4:1, 275–297.

Booth, Laurence, Varouj Aivazian, Asli Demirgüç-Kunt, and Vojislav Maksimovic. 2001. "Capital Structure in Developing Countries." *Journal of Finance* 56:1, 87–130.

Boyd, John H., and Edward C. Prescott. 1986. "Financial Intermediary-Coalitions." *Journal of Economic Theory* 38:2, 211–232.

Claessens, Stijn, and Leora F. Klapper. 2005. "Bankruptcy around the World: Explanations of Its Relative Use." *American Law and Economics* 7:1, 253–283.

Cotei, Carmen, Joseph Farhat, and Benjamin Abugri. 2009. "Testing Trade-off and Pecking Order Models under Different Institutional Environments." Available at www.papers.ssrn.com/sol3/papers.cfm?abstract_id=1404596.

De Miguel, Alberto, and Julio Pindado. 2001. "Determinants of the Capital Structure: New Evidence from Spanish Data." *Journal of Corporate Finance* 7:1, 77–99.

Demirgüç-Kunt, Asli, and Ross Levine. 1999. "Bank-Based and Market-Based Financial Systems: Cross-Country Comparison." Working Paper, World Bank.

Demirgüç-Kunt, Asli, and Vojislavy Maksimovic. 1999. "Institutions, Financial Markets and Firm Debt Maturity." *Journal of Financial Economics* 54:3, 295–336.

Diamond, Douglas W. 1984. "Financial Intermediation and Delegated Monitoring." *Review of Economic Studies* 51:3, 393–414.

Francis, Jere, Inder Khurana, and Raynolde Pereira. 2001. "Investor Protection Laws, Accounting and Auditing around the World." Working Paper, University of Missouri at Columbia.

Frank, Murray Z., and Vidhan K Goyal. 2009. "Capital Structure Decisions: Which Factors Are Reliably Important?" *Financial Management* 38: 1, 1-37.

Frankel, Allen B., and John D. Montgomery. 1991. "Financial Structure: An International Perspective." In George L. Perry and William C. Brainard, eds., *Brookings Papers on Economic Activity* 1991:1, 257–310. Washington, DC: Brookings Institution Press.

La Porta, Rafael, Florencio Lopez-de-Silanes, Andrei Shleifer, and Robert W. Vishny. 1997. "Legal Determinants of External Finance." *Journal of Finance* 52: 3, 1131–1150.

La Porta, Rafael, Florencio Lopez-de-Silanes, Andrei Shleifer, and Robert W. Vishny. 1998. "Law and Finance." *Journal of Political Economy* 106:6, 1113–1155.

La Porta, Rafael, Florencio Lopez-de-Silanes, Andrei Shleifer, and Robert W. Vishny. 2000a. "Agency Problems and Dividend Policies around the World." *Journal of Finance* 55:1, 1–33.

La Porta, Rafael, Florencio Lopez-de-Silanes, Andrei Shleifer, and Robert W. Vishny. 2000b. "Investor Protection and Corporate Governance." *Journal of Financial Economics* 58:1–2, 3–27.

La Porta, Rafael, Florencio Lopez-de-Silanes, Andrei Shleifer, and Robert W. Vishny. 2002. "Investor Protection and Corporate Valuation." *Journal of Finance* 57:3, 1147–1170.

Lucas, Deborah J., and Robert L. McDonald. 1990. "Equity Issues and Stock Price Dynamics." *Journal of Finance* 45:4, 1019–1043.

Morck, Randall, Bernard Yeung, and Wayne Yu. 2000. "The Information Content of Stock Markets: Why Do Emerging Markets Have Synchronous Stock Price Movements?" *Journal of Financial Economics* 58:1, 215–260.

Myers, Stewart C. 1984. "The Capital Structure Puzzle." *Journal of Finance* 39:3, 575–592.

Myers, Stewart C., and Nicholas S. Majluf. 1984. "Corporate Financing and Investment Decisions When Firms Have Information That Investors Do Not Have." *Journal of Financial Economics* 13:2, 187–221.

Nivorozhkin, Eugene. 2005. "Financing Choices of Firms in EU Accession Countries." Working Paper, Gothenburg University.

Opler, Tim C., and Sheridan Titman. 1994. "The Debt-Equity Choice: An Analysis of Issuing Firms." Working Paper, Boston College.

Oztekin, Ozde, and Mark J. Flannery. 2010. "Partial Adjustment toward Optimal Capital Structure Around the World." Midwest Finance Association Meeting, Las Vegas, 2010.

Rajan, Raghuram G., and Luigi Zingales. 1995. "What Do We Know about Capital Structure? Some Evidence from International Data." *Journal of Finance* 50:5, 1421–1460.

Shyam-Sunder, Lakshmi, and Stewart C. Myers. 1999. "Testing Static Trade-Off against Pecking Order Models of Capital Structure." *Journal of Financial Economics* 51:2, 219–244.

Taggart, Robert A., Jr. 1977. "A Model of Corporate Financing Decisions." *Journal of Finance* 32:5, 1467–1484.

Titman, Sheridan, and Roberto Wessels. 1988. "The Determinants of Capital Structure Choice." *Journal of Finance* 43: 1, 1–19.
Wanzenried, Gabrielle. 2002. "Capital Structure Dynamics in UK and Continental Europe." Working Paper, University of Berne.

ABOUT THE AUTHORS

Carmen Cotei is an Assistant Professor of Finance at the University of Hartford. She specializes in empirical corporate finance. Her primary research interests are equity issues, capital structure, and analysts' forecasts. Other interests are small business finance, particularly small business survival and financing sources. Professor Cotei's teaching interests are corporate finance, mergers and acquisitions, and financial markets and institutions. She won the Barney School of Business Excellence in Teaching Award in 2008. Professor Cotei holds a B.S. in Finance from the Academy of Economic Studies and a PhD in Financial Economics from the University of New Orleans.

Joseph Farhat is an Associate Professor of Finance at Central Connecticut State University (CCSU). Before joining CCSU, he was an Assistant Professor of Finance at Southern Connecticut State University, Investment Consultant for the Social Security Investment Commission in Jordan, Assistant Professor at the Hashemite University-Jordan, and Adjunct Professor of Financial Economics at the University of Jordan. Professor Farhat is the recipient of the 2002 Toussaint Hocevar Outstanding PhD Student Award for his academic achievement and the 2006 Best Paper in Corporate Finance Award from the Southwestern Finance Association for his scholarly activities. He was placed on the CCSU Excellence in Teaching Honor Roll in 2007, 2008, and 2009. Professor Farhat is the Editor of the *Banking and Finance Review*, a biannual, peer-reviewed international research journal. He holds a PhD in Financial Economics from the University of New Orleans.

PART II

Capital Structure Choice

CHAPTER 8

Capital Structure Theories and Empirical Tests: An Overview

STEIN FRYDENBERG
Associate Professor, Trondheim Business School

INTRODUCTION

The central theme in capital structure literature is whether an optimal or at least a target capital structure exists. An *optimal capital structure* is defined by a relation between debt and equity that minimizes cost of capital and consequently maximizes the value of the firm. A *target capital* structure is the form of financing toward which firms move their capital structure over time. The target capital structure can be modelled as average historic capital structure or by a regression equation contingent on firm-specific variables. The starting point for all modern treatments of this subject is the irrelevance proposition of Modigliani and Miller (1958) (hereafter MM). In a perfect world with no capital market imperfections and no possibility of an arbitrage trade if there are imperfections, capital structure is independent from the value of the firm.

The perfect market assumptions underlying Modigliani and Miller (1958) differ from the real world in which firms operate. The absence of the assumptions of the MM theorem gives reasons for capital structure relevance in the real world. Jensen and Meckling (1976) introduce the asset substitution problem and the agency problem that arise in a debt-financed firm where the entrepreneurs do not bear the full consequence of suboptimal investment policy. Jensen (1986) suggests that management overspending can be controlled by forcing debt repayment each year, which is a positive effect of debt financing. The capital structure literature discusses the imperfections and their possible consequence for capital structure decisions.

The capital structure literature contains two main theories: the trade-off theory and the pecking order theory (Myers 1984). In the static trade-off theory, the firm's benefits and costs of debt are weighed against each other by adjusting to its optimal capital structure. The main theoretical benefit of debt is the tax shield on interest paid on debt. The main adverse consequence is the cost of financial distress (Scott 1976). The extended trade-off theory also incorporates product market commitments, asymmetric information costs, and agency costs. The firm should adjust the capital structure to the point where marginal cost of debt equals marginal cost of equity.

The pecking order theory, which can be motivated by both asymmetric information and transaction costs, offers a distinction between internal and external capital. Asymmetric information may exist both between the company and shareholders and between the company and its lenders. The effect on the debt ratio depends on whether uncertainty exists about risks or return. Meza and Webb (1987) argue that equity is the preferred means of financing when there is asymmetric information about risks.

Myers and Majluf (1984) find that uncertainty about future returns gives debt a positive role as a signal in a separating equilibrium between high- and low-quality firms. Stockholders in overvalued firms can benefit by issuing equity, which can send negative signals to the stock market. Transaction costs will favor retained earnings and then debt before costly external equity. The pecking order theory proposes that firms finance their investments with internally generated funds before debt and then external equity. The firm's debt ratio will reflect the cumulative requirement for external funding (Myers 1984) and marginal costs at the time of the capital structure adjustment.

In a review paper, Harris and Raviv (1991) find the three main hypotheses used to explain differences in capital structure among companies are the transaction-cost hypothesis, the asymmetric-information hypothesis, and the tax hypothesis. They report that leverage increases with fixed assets, nondebt tax shields, investment opportunities, and firm size. By contrast, leverage decreases with volatility, advertising expenditure, probability of bankruptcy, profitability, and uniqueness of the product. This consensus of capital structure determinants still holds in simple cross-section analysis, but is contested by the market timing theory of Baker and Wurgler (2002) and the findings of Welch (2004). Welch finds that previous leverage and stock market return are more important than all the traditional capital structure factors together.

As the academic discussion on trade-off versus pecking order theory by Shyam-Sunder and Myers (1999) and Fama and French (2002) continues, ascertaining which of the two main theories best describe capital structure adjustments is difficult. In a reconciliation of these two theories, Kayhan and Titman (2007) claim that short-term movements are governed by pecking order theory, while a long-term target is determined by a trade-off between costs and benefits of debt and equity. The purpose of this chapter is to present an overview of recent directions in capital structure research. The remainder of the chapter first discusses common capital structure determinants. Next, the chapter presents the two main theories of capital structure choice and how they can be studied in a dynamic regression equation framework. Evidence from event studies and surveys on capital structure decisions is presented. The final section offers a summary and conclusions.

CAPITAL STRUCTURE DETERMINANTS

Both recent and historic studies have tried to find the determinants of capital structure. Titman and Wessels (1988) use the amount of tangible assets, nondebt tax shields, growth, uniqueness of the firm, industry, size, volatility of revenue, and profitability to explain leverage in a latent variable model. They find that both the long-term debt and short-term debt-to-equity ratio are negatively related to uniqueness. They interpret the uniqueness finding as support for the Titman

(1984) product market commitment model. They also find that size and profitability have a negative effect on short-term debt. This difference in financing reflects the high transaction costs that small firms face when they issue long-term debt or equity. Titman and Wessels do not find any significant effect from volatility, asset structure, or nondebt-tax shields on either short-term or long-term debt in their factor analytic model, which could be a result of the initial correlation between variables. For example, in the factor collateral value they include both intangible assets with a negative weight and inventory, and plant and equipment with a positive weight. The effect from these two variables could cancel out an effect from collateral on the debt ratios.

Empirical Methods

The empirical literature is extensive and fragmented into several research perspectives. The two approaches to empirical tests of capital structure are governed by the data used in the analysis. The first is a cross-section or panel data approach where leverage is regressed against variables such as nondebt tax shields, size, volatility of earnings, tangible assets, research and development (R&D) expenditures, and earnings. The second is a time-series approach, in which effects of new issues of securities on stock price returns are studied. Welch (2007) discusses problems with choice of leverage proxy, the nonlinearity of leverage ratio, and survivorship biases. There is also the simultaneity problem, which involves the simple one-equation model often used in empirical research. Many of the explanation variables in cross-section leverage regression functions are possibly endogenous, especially lagged debt ratio, bankruptcy risk, dividends and earnings before taxes, interest, and depreciations and amortization (EBITDA). Using lagged variables as instruments can alleviate the simultaneity problem.

As Barclay and Smith (1995) note, within-estimators are used because firm-specific characteristics that are not measurable in accounting ratios are important for capital structure choice. Using a real options model, Lambrecht and Myers (2008) show that under risky debt each firm will have a unique debt ratio; the optimal debt level is dependent on the firm value at closure and not on its going concern value. This model prediction could explain why managers use book debt ratio values as targets. A firm's book equity value can represent the liquidation value of the firm. Within estimators, demeaned or differenced variables, can solve the omitted variables problem and show a higher degree of explanation than levels regressions. Excluded variables that are correlated with the included variables may cause misleading conclusions because the effects of these excluded variables are transmitted through the included variables.

However, regressing on the information set within the firm is different from regressing on the full set of information between and within firms. A size variable can be a proxy for less asymmetric information and less bankruptcy risk in large firms. Not obvious is the fact that a small increase in size within the firm compared to size differences between firms should be interpreted as a reduction in asymmetric information. The firm may increase in size over a few years but still be opaque. The interpretation of the variables should reflect this distinction. Robust estimates of standard errors due to the heterogeneity problem are becoming more standard. Panel data regressions have the problem that residuals across the sample of firms can be correlated, that is, a time effect that affects all the firms. Residuals can also be correlated across years, which is an unobserved firm effect. Recent papers may use difference Generalized Method of Moments (GMM) or system GMM (Arrelano and Bond 1991; Blundell and Bond 1998) to correct for the correlation between lagged dependent variable and the error term. Windmeijer (2005) introduces finite sample adjustments of standard errors that can correct for underestimation of standard errors in two-step GMM. Fama and MacBeth (1973) estimate standard errors that can alleviate underestimation bias of standard errors in panel data. Petersen (2008) finds that many estimation methods used in the literature also include estimators that are not robust to the dependence in the error terms, which can produce too narrow confidence intervals. This may exacerbate the problem of inconsistent findings in the capital structure literature.

Tax-Related Factors

Higher debt and interest payments will lead to less tax in a classical tax system. The empirical evidence for this conjecture has been difficult to find because taxes are correlated with higher profitability. Information of the firm's marginal tax rates is also hard to obtain. Information on an investor's personal tax rates is private and varies between investors. Graham (2000) finds that a firm can double its debt level before the value of the tax shield is reduced, which makes the relatively low debt ratio a puzzle for many firms. Graham (1996) simulates a firm's marginal tax rate using simulated income paths and tax schedules. He interprets differences in present value of tax shields for different income paths as a firm's marginal tax rate for an extra dollar of income. Graham finds that firms with higher marginal tax rates issue more debt, which is consistent with the trade-off theory.

Fama and French (2002) find that firms with more depreciation and R&D have less book leverage. Hovakimian, Opler, and Titman (2001) find that net operating loss carry-forwards reduce the probability of firms issuing debt. Similar findings tend to support the trade-off theory of optimal capital structure. Bradley, Jarrell, and Kim (1984), however, find a positive relation between nondebt-tax shields and leverage. This finding contradicts the a priori belief that focuses on the substitutability between nondebt-tax shields and debt-tax shields. A possible explanation is that nondebt-tax shields are also proxies for the tangibility of assets.

Bankruptcy Costs

Costs of expected financial distress are projected to reduce the debt level. Warner (1977) finds that direct bankruptcy costs have been calculated to be trivial, ranging from 1 percent of firm value seven years before bankruptcy to 5 percent in the year of bankruptcy. Altman (1984) estimates the indirect bankruptcy costs to be 8.1 percent three years before bankruptcy and 10.5 percent in the year during bankruptcy. The total costs are thus substantial before and during a bankruptcy. Expected bankruptcy costs increase when the likelihood of bankruptcy increases. As the firm's expected bankruptcy costs increase, a new equilibrium between bankruptcy costs and tax advantages of debt will settle at a lower level of leverage.

Weiss (1990), who studied 99 bankruptcies for firms listed on the New York Stock Exchange (NYSE) and the American Stock Exchange (AMEX), finds that average costs of bankruptcy are 20.6 percent of the market value of equity. Thorburn (2000) studies Swedish firms undergoing auction bankruptcies and finds the costs of this system to be lower compared to the American Chapter 11 reorganization procedure. She finds direct costs in percent of prefiling book value of assets at an average of 6.4 percent across the sample of firms undergoing auctions in bankruptcy. Thorburn reports direct costs of 3.7 percent for the largest firms in her sample. The firms in her sample are much smaller than public firms undergoing Chapter 11, which lead to the conclusion that auction bankruptcies are cost efficient. Indirect bankruptcy costs are closely tied to the recovery rate of debt. Low recovery rates, especially for unsecured debt, make the creditors nervous when borrowers experience financial distress. Thorburn finds that secured debt holders receive on average 69 percent of their claims while junior unsecured creditors receive an average of only 2 percent. These recovery rates are even lower for firms with a greater fraction of intangible assets and in years with a general economic downturn.

Andrade and Kaplan (1998) estimate the cost of financial distress to be 10 to 20 percent of firm value. Bankruptcy costs can be represented by earnings. Increased earnings will reduce bankruptcy costs and should increase the debt ratio. Instead, studies usually find a negative relationship between leverage and profitability, which does not support the bankruptcy cost hypothesis. A firm with higher volatility of cash flow is more likely to have higher expected bankruptcy costs. Bradley, Jarrell, and Kim (1984) find that leverage decreases with return volatility. They indicate that volatility of firm earnings is an important inverse determinant of firm-leverage ratios. Kisgen (2006) finds that firms take action to improve credit ratings when firm fundamentals are close to inducing a rating change. Credit ratings represent the likelihood of default and are connected to the cost of debt. Kisgen's findings therefore support the relevance of expected bankruptcy costs for capital structure decisions.

Real Options and Growth Opportunities

According to the debt overhang theory of Myers (1977), debt can make firms forgo positive net present value (NPV) investments if they have to share future proceeds with creditors in place. Growth firms should therefore be more equity financed. The growth variable should be forward looking because Myers describes firms with growth opportunities as less prone to debt financing. Kamath (1997) finds that 82 percent of NYSE firm managers would depart from target debt ratio to pursue a growth opportunity.

Long and Malitz (1985) find that intangible, firm-specific, and unobservable growth opportunities tend to reduce the effectiveness of bond covenants. Owners of firms with a high proportion of intangible investments opportunities must then control agency costs through a limit on the outstanding risky debt.

According to Barclay and Smith (1995), firms that have few growth options and that are large or regulated have more long-term debt in their capital structure. Shortening the effective maturity of the firms' debt reduces the incentive problem described in Myers (1977). Managers of regulated firms have more restrictions on future investment decisions than managers of unregulated firms. This reduction in managerial discretion reduces the adverse-incentive effects of long-term debt. Barclay and Smith conclude the most important systematic determinant of a firm's capital structure and dividend yield is its investment opportunities. Kim and Sorensen (1986) find support for Myers's (1977) growth theory because high-growth firms use less debt.

Studies using the market-to-book value of equity variable as a growth proxy find a negative relation between leverage and market-to-book value of equity. In line with Tobin's q-theory, the market-to-book ratio can be interpreted as the investment possibilities or the growth possibilities of the firm but can also be explained as an effect of market timing equity issues (Baker and Wurgler 2002).

MacKay (1999) examines real flexibility and financial structure. He tests whether real flexibility increases debt capacity by either lowering default risk or decreasing debt capacity by letting stockholders risk-shift. He measures real flexibility as the sensitivity of marginal production and investment decisions to variations in the economy surrounding the firm. His evidence shows that leverage and debt maturity are inversely related to real flexibility. Where there are more possibilities for the risk-shifting incentive by the stockholders, both debt and the maturity of debt are reduced.

Industry Effects

An industry dummy variable can model the effect of the interindustry differences in capital structure. Firms belonging to the same industry face the same economic conditions. Bradley, Jarrell, and Kim (1984) find significant differences in capital structure between firms in different industries.

A relation can exist between the industry average debt ratio and firms' debt ratios due to industry competition. Models of competition set up firm aggression as a function of financial and operational leverage. Chevalier (1995) finds that firms increase their prices after a leveraged buyout (LBO) if other firms in the industry also have high leverage. If the other firms in the industry have little debt or are concentrated, they can afford to be more aggressive in pricing policy towards an entrant with higher leverage. Firms will therefore look to industry averages as a benchmark and may even use them as a target debt ratio.

Industry can have a two-way effect on capital structure. MacKay and Phillips (2005) find industry effects on financing and a connection between a firm's natural hedge, its capital-labor ratio, and financial leverage in competitive industries but not in concentrated industries. Firms that deviate from the median capital intensity also deviate from median industry capital structure. Between-industry and intra-industry variation in production technology could warrant an inclusion of industry code as an independent variable.

Asgharian (1997) analyzes the relation between capital structure and industry classification in Sweden. He finds that highly leveraged firms in distressed industries experience relatively larger setbacks than firms with less leverage.

Talberg et al. (2008) estimate debt functions per industry and find that these regression equations are not equal across industries, with differences for core variables such as tangibility, profitability, and a market-to-book growth variable. The industry dummy variables in a pooled regression are significant, indicating industry effects on leverage.

The intra-industry differences in capital structure can be taken as a measure of different risk levels in industries. A business with higher risk should have less debt according to the theory of bankruptcy costs. Managers may fear losing their jobs and will reduce the leverage in a high-risk industry. Industries may exhibit different degrees of asymmetric information, which can cause varying risk premiums for debt capital in the industries.

Industry may also proxy for other omitted variables such as technology, regulation, and asset types of firms in the industry. Almazan and Molina (2002) find that different technology leads to different capital structures. Using an industry variable may therefore cleanse the other variables from the noise of omitted factors, and the industry variable is likely to represent several factors that can affect capital structure.

Uniqueness of Firm

Titman (1984) introduces uniqueness of a firm's products as a possible explanation for capital structure choice. Stakeholder theory predicts that firms with unique products, such as computer and automobile manufacturers, should have lower leverage. In case of bankruptcy, unique firms may turn over costs to employees, suppliers, and customers. These costs will ultimately be borne by the stockholders of the leveraged firm, which can reduce leverage in the first place.

Long and Malitz (1985) focus on moral hazard effects by regressing leverage on advertising, capital expenditures, and unleveraged beta. Advertising, R&D, and unleveraged beta have a significantly negative effect on leverage while capital expenditures have a significantly positive effect on leverage. Bradley et al. (1984) find the intensity of R&D and advertising expenditures are inversely related to leverage. Titman and Wessels (1988) also find that firms with unique products have low debt ratios. Kovenock and Phillips (1995) study product-market rivalry and how it affects capital structure. They present evidence of interaction between capital structure decisions and product market behavior using plant-level data from the U.S. Bureau of Census from 1979 to 1990. They find that firms are more likely to recapitalize when they have individual plants of low productivity, operate in a highly concentrated industry, and have low industry capitalization.

Tangibility

The positive relationship between fixed assets and interest-bearing debt ratios is one of the more robust findings in the capital structure studies (Titman and Wessels 1988; Rajan and Zingales 1995; Frank and Goyal 2003). Studies find a positive effect between tangible assets and long-term debt level. The factor is motivated by agency costs, asymmetric information, and bankruptcy costs, which all have the same positive effect on the debt level. Having secured loans, the lender is not so concerned with the possible costs of agency, asymmetric information, and bankruptcy. Collateral will reduce the lender's required return of debt and potentially increase debt attractiveness compared to equity.

Size

Small firms are subject to a higher bankruptcy risk than large companies because they usually are not as diversified as the large companies. A measure of size is often defined either as the natural logarithm of revenues or total assets, both of which bring the same results. The empirical findings on the size effect of listed firms are a positive relationship between size and leverage (Hovakimian and Li 2009). However, Brav (2009) finds that privately-held firms in the United Kingdom rely more on debt financing and less on external capital markets. Higher relative bankruptcy costs for small firms lead to the hypothesis that size is negatively related to bankruptcy probability. Van der Wijst and Thurik (1993) study small businesses of the retail trade and find that theoretical determinants of capital structure appear relevant. The influences, however, appear far less straightforward than the theory suggests. The authors find influences on total debt to be a net effect of opposite influences on long- and short-term debt.

In small nonlisted firms, investors have to rely on annual accounting reports and the information they might obtain from personal contact with the firm's management. If small firms are rationed in the market for external equity, a positive relationship is expected. Hence, a contradiction exists: small firms should have less debt due to bankruptcy costs, but they should have more debt due to asymmetric information, which leads to a rationing of the external equity. Small firms are not often listed on stock exchanges and, when they are, the stock price reaction to news is often greater and the buy-sell price spread is larger than for large companies. Both symptoms indicate that small firms have a relatively higher degree of asymmetrical information.

Profitability

Return-on-assets measures the economic performance of the firm. The effect of a high return on assets is less debt (Rajan and Zingales 1995; Baker and Wurgler 2002; Welch 2004). This solid finding has its economic rationale in the pecking order hypothesis where firms prefer retained earnings to debt. The negative effect on debt from return on assets is evidence for the Myers and Majluf (1984) pecking order theory, in which firms prefer retained earnings. The free cash flow argument of Jensen (1986) is not confirmed. Profitable firms could increase their debt to take advantage of higher tax shields, but this is contrary to the empirical findings. The negative effect from profitability to the debt level is a serious argument against the validity of the trade-off theory.

Myers and Majluf (1984) predict that profitability explains leverage since the pecking order hypothesis suggests that retained earnings are a less costly type of financing than debt and new equity. Asymmetric information arguments motivate this variable because high earnings reduce the necessity of issuing underpriced debt or equity. In this argument, the causal relation runs from return to debt. A negative coefficient for the return variable is predicted because retained earnings represent a less-expensive way of funding compared to debt and new equity.

Jensen (1986) claims that firms with a high degree of free cash flow will tend to use these funds on empire building and other nonpositive NPV projects, for instance, perquisites such as an airplane for the firm and expensive office-space for management. Free cash flow is cash not needed for profitable investment projects. In the Jensen's theory of free cash flow, debt has an important bonding role that trims the firm of unnecessary dead-weight. In this argument, the causality runs from debt to profitability, and more debt leads to higher profitability. This theory predicts a positive coefficient for the return variable.

International Differences in Capital Structure Determinants

Factors such as managerial preferences, quality of corporate governance, and agency costs can vary among countries. La Porta et al. (1998) measure country differences and find that firms in countries with higher investor protection have less debt. La Porta et al. point to differences between firms financed by banks and firms financed mainly in the bond market. The institutional setting can partly explain differences between countries and can also affect the within-country cross-sectional correlation between leverage and factors such as firm profitability and firm size. Bank debt can result in lower agency costs, assuming that asymmetries of information are less of a problem between a bank and a firm than between the single investor in the bond market and the firm.

Rajan and Zingales (1995) examine evidence from international data using balance sheet data from the United States, Japan, Germany, France, Italy, the United Kingdom, and Canada (G-7 countries). The findings show that firms are levered fairly similarly across the G-7 countries. Their findings seem to support the institutional view. That is, their evidence shows that firms in countries that better protect creditors have less leverage than firms in other countries. For instance, firms in the United Kingdom and Germany have less debt to capital, adjusted for accounting differences, than the other G-7 countries. Rights of the creditors are so protected in the United Kingdom that a reorganization of a firm is difficult, which may lead to more liquidation of firms in financial distress. Booth et al. (2001) study 10 developing countries as well as firms from developed countries. The developing countries have substantially lower amounts of long-term debt, but the long-term debt ratio is affected by the same variables as in more developed countries. They conclude that modern finance can explain some of the capital structure internationally, but the institutional features of each country are also important because of country differences.

Summary of Capital Structure Determinants

In addition to firm characteristics, there exists a unique firm-specific effect that materializes in fixed-effects regression using a dummy variable for each firm or a demeaning of the variables. In these regressions, the usual R^2 is higher than in pooled regressions. The increase in degree of explanation from pooled regressions to fixed effects regression indicates that most leverage regressions omit important explanation variables. Kayhan and Titman (2007) find each firm's history of cash flows, investment expenditures, and stock prices to be important for determining capital structure.

Takeover targets can also use debt as an acquisition deterrent because a buyout often requires an ex-post increase in debt. Safieddine and Titman (1999) find that takeover targets increase their debt ratios after an unsuccessful takeover offer. Subsequently, they reduce investments, sell assets, and reduce the number of employees. The former takeover targets experience increased cash flow and share prices outperforming benchmarks in the next five years. Higher leverage helps the former takeover candidates to make adjustments that would have been done by the potential new owners. Higher leverage commits managers to making improvements that keep the firm independent.

The core findings of determinants of capital structure are relatively robust across firms and over time periods. An early study by Friend and Hasbrouck (1988) finds an economically significant positive effect from fixed assets and a negative effect from return on assets to the debt-to-book assets ratio. Titman and Wessels's (1988) significant findings are a positive effect from growth and a negative effect from uniqueness and size. Rajan and Zingales (1995) report significant negative effects from return and market-to-book ratios and significant positive effects from fixed assets and size.

DYNAMIC CAPITAL STRUCTURE AND TESTS OF PECKING ORDER THEORY VERSUS TRADE-OFF THEORY

Dynamic capital structure studies are defined by using the lagged debt ratio as an explanatory variable, which according to Welch (2004) has a large influence on next-period debt ratio. Using a dynamic perspective can provide possible reasons for capital structure relevance.

Dynamic Capital Structure Choice

A positive change in capital structure that leads to less risk taking and underinvestment in the future could lead to a change in cash flows to the firm. The expected cash flow from investment projects and their distribution is assumed to be constant in Modigliani and Miller (1958), but in the real, dynamic world the cash flow is likely to change in the future if capital structure changes investment policy. Fischer, Heinkel, and Zechner (1989) argue that the relation is dynamic and make allowances for dynamic adjustments in the firm's capital structure. They claim that costs of recapitalization prevent firms from adjusting their capital structure continuously and propose that any ratio within a set of boundaries is optimal, so similar firms may have different leverage ratios at a given point in time.

Bevan and Danbolt (2000) analyze the dynamics of capital structure for UK. companies. They find significant changes in the relative importance of the various debt elements over time, as well as changes in the relation between gearing (leverage) and the level of growth opportunities, size, profitability, and fixed assets. The authors claim that credit markets have changed in the United Kingdom during the 1990s with large companies using less bank finance and banks lending more to smaller firms. Bank debt seems to be more closely related to corporate profitability and collateral values.

The sum of total long-term and total current liabilities is explained by the log of sales, market-to-book ratio, and EBITDA scaled by assets. Companies with high levels of growth opportunities tend to use more long- and short-term debt. These companies have shifted from debt towards equity finance in the sample period.

Baker and Wurgler (2002) construct a market timing variable by weighting the market-to-book ratio for a given year with the amount of debt and equity issued during the same year divided by total debt and equity issue. The regression results show that leverage is negatively related to the external finance weighted market-to-book variable. This allows the authors to argue that firms issue securities at times when they have high market-to-book ratios, that is, when firms may be overvalued by the stock market. They also document time trends with increasing equity issues and less retained earnings during the market boom in the late 1990s.

Pecking Order versus Trade-Off Theory

Several arguments can motivate the pecking order of financing observed by Donaldson (1961). Transactions costs, asymmetric information, and tax reasons favor retained earnings compared to new external debt and equity. Myers and Majluf (1984) model a situation where the market considers new equity negative news from the company. The debt overhang of Myers (1977) also predicts a preference for retained earnings versus debt in a growth company.

Frank and Goyal (2003) test the pecking order theory against the static trade-off theory. They find robust evidence of mean reversion in leverage but do not find support for the pecking order theory. Frank and Goyal do not include both theories in the regressions but run a conventional leverage regression and a separate deficit model to test the pecking order hypothesis. They use a conditional target-adjusting framework. The authors find that leverage is more persistent at lower levels, which indicates that firms readjust more from high debt levels. Frank and Goyal find that dependence between debt and dividends is contingent on firm size where larger firms increase debt as dividends increase but small firms decrease debt as dividends increase. Pooling small and large firms creates numerically unstable coefficients. This motivates testing the theory on homogenous firms. Frank and Goyal conclude that work remains to be done because all the financial factors put together account for less than the previous level of leverage. Fama and French (2005) study firms that make net stock issues and find pecking order violations in a majority of the firms. They claim that firms can issue stock with less asymmetric information costs to employees and current stockholders. The pecking order alone cannot explain financing choices.

Hovakimian, Opler, and Titman (2001) study debt issuance. The findings confirm that firms are most likely to issue equity after experiencing a share price increase. This appears inconsistent with trade-off models of the debt-equity choice because in an earnings-driven capital structure, adjustment debt or equity issuance is seen as way to offset the adjustment made by earnings. For example, assume that a firm has a target debt ratio. If this firm starts to earn more money, the equity will increase. Thus, to maintain the target debt ratio predicted by trade-off models, the firm must issue debt to compensate for the increased equity. The equity issue after share price run-up is therefore a puzzle not explained well by the trade-off theory. Yet, the market timing theory of Baker and Wurgler (2002) can explain this observation.

Shyam-Sunder and Myers (1999) find that simple pecking order models explain much more of the time-series variance in actual debt ratios than a target adjustment model based on the static trade-off theory. They find that a target-adjustment equation predicts gradual adjustment to target ratios where each firm's target is measured by its average debt ratio. Over the period 1971 to 1989, they find a 30 percent closing of the gap between current debt and the debt target each year. This finding is robust for several estimators as a variance-component model with two-way random effects, first-order serial correlation, and dummy variables for each year of the model. The dependent variable is change in debt ratio, and the independent variable is the difference between target debt ratio and last year's debt ratio. The adjustment towards a debt target is also significant. Commenting on the power of their test, Shyam-Sunder and Myers postulate that the target-adjustment model can produce significant results even when it is false. They simulate data using Monte Carlo simulation. The authors produce one series of data where firms issue debt when there is a deficit, hence following a pecking order, and one data series that simulates firms following a trade-off path with specified adjustment coefficients. Testing the estimated model on both actual and simulated data, the authors find the trade-off model lacks power to reject, but the pecking order model has statistical power to reject the null of no pecking order adjustments. Later Chirinko and Singha (2000) criticize their model setup and claim the coefficients are biased because the firms could be following other financing strategies than the pure pecking order or trade-off behavior that are simulated.

Fama and French (2002) present a similar model to Shyam-Sunder and Myers (1999) and find that debt ratios contain mean reversion but at a slow speed. Fama and French find that the shared predictions of the pecking order and the trade-off theory perform well. Increased volatility of net cash flow reduces leverage. Yet, they find contradictions in which more profitable firms have less leverage, consistent with the pecking order model but not with the trade-off model. Low leverage nonpayers of dividends issue relatively more equity when they have higher investments, which is not consistent with pecking order theory. Studies on financing in privately-held firms have seen renewed interest such as Brav (2009). Brav finds that privately-held firms in the United Kingdom compared to public firms have more persistent debt ratios, less equity financing, and higher sensitivity to profitability and tangibility capital structure determinants. Privately-held firms are worthwhile to study as a supplement to the studies made on public firms.

Fama and French (2002) ask whether the firms form a target debt ratio after book or after market values. They find leverage to have mean reversion in a regression of change in book leverage versus target leverage. However, the pace is slow. Why is looking at the book values of the firms relevant and not only the market values? After all, Modigliani and Miller (1958) established the irrelevance of capital structure in relation to market values of assets, debt, and equity. Fama and French argue the predictions of the trade-off and pecking order model are related to the book value of leverage, but some of the predictions also concern the market value of leverage. Lambrecht and Myers (2008) contend that book values can proxy for salvage value and firms therefore relate their debt ratio to this minimum valuation of the firm.

Agency costs, taxes, and bankruptcy costs should induce firms to increase their debt ratios whenever earnings increase. Scaling both debt and profits by total assets should enable measuring a positive relationship between return on assets and book leverage (debt to assets). Market leverage, however, may remain constant because the market value of equity increases with profitability. Since higher profitability usually means a higher market value of assets, the ratio of debt-to-market value of assets may remain relatively constant. This may result in failing to get the postulated positive relationship between profitability and leverage when using market leverage. In sum, even if the trade-off model predicts a positive relationship between profitability and leverage, this is relevant for book leverage only in most cases. Neither of the two main theories can be rejected. Nevertheless, the negative relationship between profits and leverage found in several papers is often interpreted as support for the pecking order theory.

SPEED OF ADJUSTMENT TO TARGET CAPITAL STRUCTURE

If firms have a target capital structure, the speed of adjustment at which they move towards their target could determine whether they follow a trade-off theory or a pecking order theory when making financial decisions.

Target Capital Structure

A target capital structure measured as a contingent debt ratio over several years will necessarily measure the average cost of debt and equity over the years. In the pecking order theory, the marginal cost of debt and equity at the time of security issue determines whether the firm chooses debt or equity. Even though the average cost of debt is less than the average cost of equity—that is, the firm has less debt than the target debt ratio—the firm could still issue equity if the marginal cost of equity is less than the marginal cost of debt at the time of the issue. This requires that the slope of the equity cost curve be less than the slope of the debt cost curve as indicated by Modigliani and Miller (1958) in their Figure 2 for high debt ratios. This measurement problem between marginal and average cost of capital could be a reason for the firm's slow adjustment to the target observed by a small speed of adjustment. Firms can follow a pecking order pattern in the short term, but trade-off theory may draw the debt ratio towards a target debt ratio in the long run.

Kayhan and Titman (2007) find that firms have a target debt ratio and move towards it, but variation in cash flow, investment expenditures, and stock price effect can have important short-term effects on the movement towards the target debt ratio. The authors take the difference in variables at year one to five and then five to ten year time spans and find that recent history has more influence on leverage change than the distant history. Byoun (2008) estimates target adjustment models for firms above and below the target debt ratio and controls for financial deficit or surplus. His results are that most of the adjustments occur when firms are above target with a financial surplus or below target debt with a financial deficit.

Speed of Adjustment

Auerbach (1985) finds empirical estimates for the importance of different characteristics of the firm for influencing the debt ratio and the choice between short-term and long-term debt. His partial adjustment model shows rapid speeds of adjustment (SOA), particularly for short-term debt. The regression equation is differenced, and the negative sign of lagged debt therefore indicates that an increase in one year has a negative effect on the change next year. He finds a positive coefficient for a cash flow deficit variable as expected, based on the pecking order hypothesis. Firms borrow when internal funds are insufficient to cover the capital expenditures.

Studying the SOA involves moving beyond finding determinants of the target debt ratio to showing whether the target debt ratio has any relevance for capital structure adjustments. According to Leary and Roberts (2005), the SOA can show support for either the trade-off theory or the pecking order theory. If firms show no SOA different from zero, then claiming that a target debt ratio exists would be difficult. Instead, a zero SOA could be supportive of either market timing or the pecking order theory. Iliev and Welch (2010) claim there is a bias in recent SOA estimates. The rationale behind SOA estimates is a prediction that firms will move towards their optimal debt ratios estimated as a target debt ratio. Under transaction costs, this adjustment can be slow.

A choice exists between using observed and target debt ratio conditioned on firm-specific variables. The conditional target debt ratio will be forward-looking and adjustable, while the observed target debt ratio is an average of historical debt ratios. The theory is based on a trade-off towards an optimal capital structure. A conditional target debt ratio should be a better proxy because current firm characteristic can be used to predict future target debt ratio.

The estimates of SOA show some variation, from 7 percent in Fama and French (2002) and 8 percent in Kayhan and Titman (2007) to 36 percent in Flannery and Rangan (2006) and 32 percent in Antoniou, Guney, and Paudyal (2008). These estimates are based on regressions with market value of equity. Using book value of equity, the estimates in some studies are slightly higher and in other studies lower but no obvious trend is visible. Huang and Ritter (2009) use a long differencing estimator to find estimates of SOA that are less biased than system GMM estimates if the autoregressive parameter of lagged leverage is close to one. The authors find a SOA of 21 percent when they subtract the four-year lagged value from the current value of the variables. The parameter estimates are robust for changes in the time dimension of the long differencing process. Cook and Tang (2010) find that macroeconomic determinants influence the SOA being higher in good economic periods. If a reasonable estimate of the SOA is 25 percent, the firm will use 2.4 years to adjust half of the deviation from the target debt ratio. This cannot be called a rapid adjustment, and the trade-off theory is therefore dominated by pecking order theory in the short term. However, a conditional target debt ratio may represent a long-term target for a firm's capital structure.

SURVEYS AND EVENTS STUDIES

The hypotheses of capital structure are difficult to measure. What are the driving factors behind management adjustment of capital structure? Surveys are a contrast to the papers based on objective measures as market values and accounting records.

Surveys

Surveys try to find the hidden motivation behind financing choices and have the advantage that they can question difficult-to-measure and complex factors such as the degree of asymmetric information and financial flexibility. Kamath (1997) surveys a sample of NYSE firms to learn more about the managerial opinions and practices with debt financing. The results confirm the pecking order theory because the respondents report relying on a hierarchy of financing options. The firms following financial hierarchies find past profits, average debt ratio in the industry, and past growth to be important determinants of their capital structure.

Financial managers report greater flexibility with capital structure than with dividend decisions. Firms attempting to adopt a target debt ratio find that industry average is a useful benchmark for their own debt ratio. When presented with a hypothetical good investment opportunity, the responding managers indicate that they would invest and deviate from their target capital structure but that they are reluctant to cut dividends. Therefore, capital structure appears to be a more flexible issue compared to investment and dividend decisions.

In another survey, Graham and Harvey (2001) attempt to learn about the views and actions of managers. For capital structure, 44 percent of the responding firms report having a somewhat tight and strict target debt ratio. According to the respondents, the most important factors affecting debt policy are financial flexibility (59.4 percent), credit rating (57.1 percent), cash flow volatility (48.1 percent), insufficient cash flow (46.8 percent), and tax deduction (46.4 percent). Factors not considered important are the firm's future prospects, personal tax cost, takeover deterrent, threat of competitors, incentive for management, and accumulation of past profits. Asset-liability maturity match governs the maturity structure of the debt. Firms issue long-term financing to avoid refinancing in a recession. The underinvestment theory of Myers (1977) finds less support in Graham and Harvey perhaps because the managers are governed by practical rules as credit rating, earnings per share dilution, and financial flexibility in their choice of capital structure. If managers behave according to such hypotheses in the capital structure literature as asset substitution, asymmetric information, transactions costs, or personal taxes, they apparently do so unknowingly.

Bancel and Mittoo (2004) find that 87.9 percent of the responding managers in their survey consider financial flexibility important. Managers achieve this financial flexibility by timing the issue to the stock exchange market value for the firm. The managers find that having access to financing at any time is important, regardless of the economic activity and prospects for the future. This evidence is consistent with the Leland and Pyle (1977) hypothesis that management times the firm's security issues.

Respondents rank credit ranking as important for capital structure choice. In fact, more than 72 percent of the managers consider credit rankings as important. Interest tax savings (59.6 percent) and volatility of earnings (50.9 percent) are also factors behind debt policy. Between 20 percent and 40 percent of the chief executive officers and chief financial officers in the survey view customer or supplier concerns over excess debt, transaction costs, expected bankruptcy costs, and debt levels in the industry as of moderate importance.

Personal tax cost on interest income, incentive to make managers work hard, take-over deterrence, industry price strategies, and concessions from employees are of little concern in the surveyed firms. Bancel and Mittoo (2004) find that managers are concerned about not only the real financial economic consequences but also about the impact of their decisions on financial statements. Finally, the authors find little evidence that firms follow industry norms of capital structure.

The research design behind surveys involves directly asking managers about what they think is important. Surveys generally support the more practical reasons for capital structure adjustments such as financial flexibility, credit rating, cash flow volatility, and tax issues. Managers do not report that more complex factors including asymmetric information, agency costs, and stakeholder theories are important for their choice of capital structure. Still, arguments involving debt overhang and agency costs may surface in areas such as financial flexibility because added flexibility increases managers' discretion over firm funds.

Event Studies

Regarding the fundamental question of whether a firm's capital structure matters, event studies explore possible stockholder wealth effects of capital structure decisions. If the signaling hypothesis of Myers and Majluf (1984) has some effect, announcement effects of corporate securities should be possible to detect. Issuing securities that raise the debt ratio should be a positive signal that increases the stock price. According to Masulis (1980, 1983), events that both increase leverage and provide a favorable signal of firm prospects such as debt for common stock exchange offers and stock repurchases seem to give the largest positive announcement effect.

Event studies use the time-series approach and study extended series of returns in the stock market. Any sign of significant abnormal yield on an investment in stocks in a time window around a security issue can be taken as evidence in one direction or the other depending upon the design of the test. Initial public offerings offer a substantial discount on stocks and reduce leverage. After an abnormal stock price appreciation, firms seem to issue equity. This fact can be taken as evidence for the market timing hypothesis where firms issue equity when they are overvalued. Seasoned equity offerings, studied by Mikkelson and Partch (1986), indicate that the market considers the issuance of seasoned equity as bad news.

Masulis (1980) studies exchange offers, which change a firm's financial structure and not the structure of its assets. A leverage-increasing debt offer can damage value for the original debt holders if they have imperfect protective covenants in their debt contracts. The market views an increase in leverage as good news but regards a leverage decreasing exchange offer as bad news. Billingsley, Smith, and Lamy (1994) find that issuances of securities are influenced by where a firm's capital structure is relative to the industry average. Stockholders' reactions to the announced plan to issue and to the issuance of securities are influenced by whether the issue moves the firm away from or closer to the average capital structure in the industry. Bayless and Chaplinsky (1991) investigate how investors' expectations about the type of security to be issued influence the market reaction to debt and equity offers. Markets react negatively when firms that are expected to issue debt issue equity instead. Event studies show that capital structure changes can have stock price effects. For a firm that has stock value maximization as an objective, the capital structure changes must be considered carefully.

SUMMARY AND CONCLUSIONS

The theories of capital structure do not give definitive answers to everyday questions about how firms should be financed. However, Frank and Goyal (2009) separate the most important factors from the less important ones. They find that a core model of capital structure does a good job explaining capital structure. Starting with 25 factors, they initially find an R^2 of 0.29, which is not much higher than an R^2 of 0.26 from a 6-factor core model. They eliminate several minor factors by using Bayesian information criteria. The core model is composed of a positive relation to median industry debt ratio, tangible assets, size, and expected inflation, in addition to a negative relation to market-to-book, profitability, and dividends.

Frank and Goyal (2009) conclude that there is no unified theoretical model of leverage that can account for all these factors but the factors are already included in theoretical models in the literature. Financial economists interpret significant industry variables as support for several hypotheses. For example, such variables can proxy for the degree of transparency in one industry and hence the asymmetric information in this industry. Frank and Goyal are skeptical about a single hypothesis interpretation of capital structure and claim that industry can proxy for many factors. Therefore, they conclude that an industry variable can have more than one interpretation.

Based on this review of capital structure, one conclusion is that there are some common findings and answers to questions about what determines capital structure choice and how firms develop their capital structure over time. A simple question from practitioners as to whether their firms are overleveraged or underleveraged can be answered by a target debt ratio prediction. The literature has reached a consensus about the direction of effects, but it is far from reaching a consensus on the size of the effects as the discussion on speed of adjustments illustrates. The search for a model that explains corporate capital structure remains in progress. The future will hopefully bring models that integrate the empirical findings and the partial theoretical models into a more comprehensive framework for practical capital structure decisions.

DISCUSSION QUESTIONS

1. What are the main firm-specific determinants of corporate capital structure?
2. How has the capital structure literature evolved since 1958?
3. What underlying hypotheses may explain capital structure choice?
4. Is the trade-off theory or the pecking order theory the main theory behind capital structure decisions?
5. How can a significant positive speed of adjustment of capital structure determine whether pecking order or market timing is the more prominent theory?
6. Which effects can capital structure adjustments have on firm value, competitiveness, and relation to shareholders?

REFERENCES

Almazan, Andres, and Carlos A. Molina. 2002. "Intra-Industry Capital Structure Dispersion." McCombs Research Paper Series No. FIN-11-02. Available at http://ssrn.com/abstract=292699 or doi:10.2139/ssrn.292699.

Altman, Edward I. 1984. "A Further Empirical Investigation of the Bankruptcy Cost Question." *Journal of Finance* 39:4, 1067–1089.

Andrade, Gregor, and Steven Kaplan. 1998. "How Costly Is Financial (Not Economic) Distress? Evidence from Highly Leveraged Transactions That Became Distressed." *Journal of Finance* 53:5, 1443–1493.

Antoniou, Antonios, Yilmaz Guney, and Krishna Paudyal. 2008. "The Determinants of Capital Structure: Capital Market Oriented versus Bank Oriented Institutions." *Journal of Financial and Quantitative Analysis* 43:1, 59–92.

Arellano, Manuel, and Stephen Bond. 1991. "Some Tests of Specification for Panel Data: Monte Carlo Evidence and an Application to Employment Equations." *Review of Economic Studies* 38:2, 277–297.

Asgharian, Hossein. 1997. "*Essays on Capital Structure.*" Lund Economic Studies nr. 64. Doctoral Thesis, Department of Economics, Lund University, Sweden.

Auerbach, Alan J. 1985. "Real Determinants of Corporate Leverage." In Benjamin M. Friedman, ed., *Corporate Capital Structures in the United States*, 301–324. Chicago: University of Chicago Press.

Baker, Malcolm, and Jeffrey Wurgler. 2002. "Market Timing and Capital Structure." *Journal of Finance* 57:1, 1–32.

Bancel, Franck, and Usha R. Mittoo. 2004. "The Determinants of Capital Structure Choice: A Survey of European Firms." *Financial Management* 33:4, 103–134.

Barclay, Michael J., and Clifford W. Smith Jr. 1995. "The Maturity Structure of Corporate Debt." *Journal of Finance* 50:2, 609–631.

Bayless, Mark, and Susan Chaplinsky. 1991. "Expectations of Security Type and the Information Content of Debt and Equity Offers." *Journal of Financial Intermediation* 1:3, 195–214.

Bevan, Alan, and Jo Danbolt. 2000. "Dynamics in the Determinants of Capital Structure in the UK." Working Paper, University of Glasgow. Available at http://ssrn.com/abstract=233551.

Billingsley, Randall S., David. M. Smith, and Robert E. Lamy. 1994. "Simultaneous Debt and Equity Issues and Capital Structure Targets." *Journal of Financial Research* 17:4, 495–516.

Blundell, Richard, and Stephen Bond. 1998. "Initial Conditions and Moment Restrictions in Dynamic Panel Data Models." *Journal of Econometrics* 87:1, 115–143.

Booth, Laurence, Varouj Aivazian, Asli Demirgüc-Kunt, and Vojislav Maksimovic. 2001. "Capital Structure in Developing Countries." *Journal of Finance* 56:1, 87–130.

Bradley, Michael, Gregg A. Jarrell, and E. Han Kim, 1984. "On the Existence of an Optimal Capital Structure: Theory and Evidence." *Journal of Finance* 39:3, 857–878.

Brav, Omer. 2009. "Access to Capital, Capital Structure, and the Funding of the Firm." *Journal of Finance* 64:1, 263–306.

Byoun, Soku. 2008. "How and When Do Firms Adjust Their Capital Structures towards Targets?" *Journal of Finance* 63:6, 3069–3096.

Chevalier, Judith A. 1995. "Do LBO Supermarkets Charge More? An Empirical Analysis of the Effects of LBOs on Supermarket Pricing." *Journal of Finance* 50:4, 1095–1112.

Chirinko, Robert S., and Anuja R. Singha. 2000. "Testing Static Tradeoff against Pecking Order Models of Capital Structure: A Critical Comment." *Journal of Financial Economics* 58:3, 417–425.

Cook, Douglas O., and Tian Tang 2010. "Macroeconomic Conditions and Capital Structure Adjustment Speed." *Journal of Corporate Finance* 16:1, 73–87.

Donaldson, Gordon. 1961. *Corporate Debt Capacity: A Study of Corporate Debt Policy and the Determination of Corporate Debt Capacity*. Boston. Division of Research, Harvard Business School Harvard University. Reprint: Beard Books, Washington, D.C. 2000.

Fama, Eugene, and Kenneth R. French. 2002. "Testing the Trade-off and Pecking Order Predictions about Dividend and Debt." *Review of Financial Studies* 15:1, 1–34.

Fama, Eugene, and Kenneth R. French. 2005. "Financing Decisions: Who Issues Stocks?" *Journal of Financial Economics* 76:3, 549–582.

Fama, Eugene, and James MacBeth. 1973. "Risk, Return and Equilibrium: Empirical Tests." *Journal of Political Economy* 81:3, 607–636.

Fischer, Edwin O., Robert Heinkel, and Josef Zechner. 1989. "Dynamic Capital Structure Choice: Theory and Tests." *Journal of Finance* 44:1, 19–40.

Flannery, Mark, and Kasturi Rangan. 2006. "Partial Adjustment towards Target Capital Structures." *Journal of Financial Economics* 79:3, 469–506.

Frank, Murray Z., and Vidhan K. Goyal, 2003. "Testing the Pecking Order Theory of Capital Structure." *Journal of Financial Economics* 67:2, 217–248.

Frank, Murray Z., and Vidhan K. Goyal 2009. "Capital Structure Decisions: Which Factors Are Reliably Important?" *Financial Management* 38:1, 1–37.

Friend, Irwin, and Joel Hasbrouck. 1988. "Determinants of Capital Structure." In Andy Chen, ed., *Research in Finance*, vol. 7, 1–19. New York: JAI Press, Inc.

Graham, John R. 1996. "Debt and the Marginal Tax Rate." *Journal of Financial Economics* 41:1, 41–74.

Graham, John R. 2000. "How Big Are the Tax Benefits of Debt?" *Journal of Finance* 55:5, 1901–1941.

Graham, John R., and Campbell R. Harvey. 2001. "The Theory and Practice of Corporate Finance: Evidence from the Field." *Journal of Financial Economics* 60:2–3, 187–243.

Harris, Milton, and Arthur Raviv. 1991. "The Theory of Capital Structure." *Journal of Finance* 46:1, 297–355.

Hovakimian, Armen, and Guangzhong Li. 2009. "Do Firms Have a Unique Target Debt Ratio to Which They Adjust? Available at http://ssrn.com/abstract=1138316.

Hovakimian, Armen, Tim Opler, and Sheridan, Titman. 2001. "The Debt-Equity Choice: An Analysis of Issuing Firms." *Journal of Financial and Quantitative Analysis* 36:1, 1–24.

Huang, Rongbing, and Jay R. Ritter. 2009. "Testing Theories of Capital Structure and Estimating the Speed of Adjustment." *Journal of Financial and Quantitative Analysis* 44:2, 237–271.

Iliev, Peter, and Ivo Welch. 2010. "Reconciling Estimates of Speed of Adjustments of Leverage Ratios." Working Paper, Pennsylvania State University and Brown University. Available at http://www.ssrn.com/abstract=1542691.

Jensen, Michael. 1986. "Agency Costs of Free Cash Flow, Corporate Finance and Takeovers." *American Economic Review* 76:2, 323–329.

Jensen, Michael, and William Meckling. 1976. "Theory of the Firm: Managerial Behavior, Agency Costs and Capital Structure." *Journal of Financial Economics* 3:4, 305–360.

Kamath, Ravindra R. 1997. "Long Term Financing Views and Practices of Financial Managers of NYSE Firms." *Financial Review* 32:2, 350–356.

Kayhan, Ayla, and Sheridan Titman. 2007. "Firms' Histories and Their Capital Structures." *Journal of Financial Economics* 83:1, 1–32.

Kim, Saeng W., and Eric H. Sorensen. 1986. "Evidence on the Impact of the Agency Costs of Debt on Corporate Policy." *Journal of Financial and Quantitative Analysis* 21:2, 131–143.

Kisgen, Darren J. 2006. "Credit Ratings and Capital Structure." *Journal of Finance* 61:3, 1035–1072.

Kovenock, Dan, and Gordon Phillips. 1995. "Capital Structure and Product-Market Rivalry: How Do We Reconcile Theory and Evidence?" *American Economic Review* 85:2, 403–408.

La Porta, Rafael, Florencio Lopez-de-Silanes, Andrei Shleifer, and Robert Vishny. 1998. "Law and Finance." *Journal of Political Economy* 106:6, 113–1155.

Lambrecht, Bart, and Stewart Myers. 2008. "Debt and Managerial Rents in a Real Options Model of the Firm." *Journal of Financial Economics* 89:2, 209–231.

Leary, Mark T., and Michael R. Roberts. 2005. "Do Firms Rebalance Their Capital Structure?" *Journal of Finance* 60:6, 2575–2619.

Leland, Hayne, and David Pyle. 1977. "Informational Asymmetries, Financial Structure and Financial Intermediation." *Journal of Finance* 32:2, 371–387.

Long, Michael S., and Ileen B. Malitz. 1985. "The Investment-Financing Nexus: Some Empirical Evidence." *Midland Corporate Finance Journal* 3:3, 53–59.

MacKay, Peter. 1999. "Real Flexibility and Financial Structure: An Empirical Analysis." Working Paper, Center for Economic Studies, U.S. Bureau of the Census.

MacKay, Peter, and Gordon Phillips. 2005. "How Does Industry Affect Firm Financial Structure?" *Review of Financial Studies* 18:4, 1431–1466.

Masulis, Ronald W. 1980. "The Effect of Capital Structure Change on Security Prices." *Journal of Financial Economics* 8:2, 139–178.

Masulis, Ronald W. 1983. "The Impact of Capital Structure Change on Firm Value: Some Estimates." *Journal of Finance* 38:1, 107–126.

Meza, David D., and David C. Webb. 1987. "Too Much Investment: A Problem of Asymmetric Information." *Quarterly Journal of Economics* 102:2, 281–292.

Mikkelson, Wayne H., and M. Megan Partch. 1986. "Valuation Effects of Security Offerings and the Issuance Process." *Journal of Financial Economics* 15:1–2, 31–60.

Modigliani, Franco, and Merton H. Miller. 1958. "The Cost of Capital, Corporation Finance and the Theory of Investment." *American Economic Review* 48:3, 655–669.

Myers, Stewart C. 1977. "Determinants of Capital Borrowing." *Journal of Financial Economics* 5:2, 147–175.

Myers, Stewart C. 1984. "The Capital Structure Puzzle." *Journal of Finance* 39: 3, 575–592.

Myers, Stewart C., and Nicholas S. Majluf. 1984. "Corporate Financing and Investment Decisions When Firms Have Information Investors Do Not Have." *Journal of Financial Economics* 13:2, 187–222.

Petersen, Mitchell A. 2008. "Estimating Standard Errors in Finance Panel Data Sets: Comparing Approaches." *Review of Financial Studies* 22:1, 435–480.

Rajan, Raghuram G., and Luigi Zingales. 1995. "What Do We Know about Capital Structure: Some Evidence from International Data." *Journal of Finance* 50:5, 1421–1460.

Safieddine, Assem, and Sheridan Titman. 1999. "Leverage and Corporate Performance: Evidence from Unsuccessful Takeovers." *Journal of Finance* 54:2, 547–580.

Scott, James H. 1976. "The Theory of Optimal Capital Structure." Bell Journal of Economics 7:1, 33–54.

Shyam-Sunder, Lakshmi, and Stewart Myers. 1999. "Testing Static Tradeoff against Pecking Order Models of Capital Structure." *Journal of Financial Economics* 51:2, 219–244.

Talberg, Magnus, Christian Winge, Stein Frydenberg, and Sjur Westgaard. 2008. "Capital Structure across Industries." *International Journal of the Economics of Business* 15:2, 181–200.

Thorburn, Karin. 2000. "Bankruptcy Auctions: Costs, Debt Recovery, and Firm Survival." *Journal of Financial Economics* 58:3, 337–368.

Titman, Sheridan. 1984. "The Effect of Capital Structure on a Firm's Liquidation Decision." *Journal of Financial Economics* 13:1, 137–151.

Titman, Sheridan, and Robert Wessels. 1988, "The Determinants of Capital Structure Choice." *Journal of Finance* 43:1, 1–19.

Van der Wijst, Nico, and Roy Thurik. 1993. "Determinants of Small Firm Debt Ratios: An Analysis of Retail Panel Data." *Small Business Economics* 5:1, 55–65.

Warner, Jerold B. 1977. "Bankruptcy Costs: Some Evidence." *Journal of Finance* 32:2, 337–347.

Weiss, Lawrence A. 1990. "Bankruptcy Resolution, Direct Costs and the Violation of Priority of Claims." *Journal of Financial Economics* 27:2, 285–314.
Welch, Ivo. 2004. "Capital Structure and Stock Returns." *Journal of Political Economy* 112:1, 106–131.
Welch, Ivo. 2007. "Common Flaws in Empirical Capital Structure Research." Working Paper, Brown University. Available at http://ssrn.com/paper=931675.
Windmeijer, Frank. 2005. "A Finite Sample Correction for the Variance of Linear Efficient Two Step GMM Estimators." *Journal of Econometrics* 126:1, 25–51.

ABOUT THE AUTHOR

Stein Frydenberg is Associate Professor at Trondheim Business School and Norwegian University of Science and Technology (NTNU). He has a Master's degree in business economics from the Norwegian School of Economics and Business Administration and a Master's in science from NTNU. He has worked in the armed forces, construction companies, and the university sector. His work has been published in *Journal of Investing, Journal of Property Research, International Journal of the Economics of Business, International Journal of Managing Projects in Business,* and *Scandinavian Journal of Business Research.* His current research interests include hedge fund performance, capital structure in privately-held and listed companies, and investment analysis.

CHAPTER 9

Capital Structure Irrelevance: The Modigliani-Miller Model

SERGEI V. CHEREMUSHKIN
Assistant Professor, Mordovian State University

INTRODUCTION

Before Modigliani and Miller's (1958) (hereafter MM) seminal article, the conventional finance wisdom was that a moderate amount of debt increases the value of a firm's common stock because debt is less expensive than equity, which implies U-shaped cost of capital function of leverage. In contrast, MM assert that without taxes the value of the firm is completely independent of its capital structure. Thus, all capital structures are equivalent because the cost of capital in their model remains unchanged, regardless of the capital structure. MM also explain the reasons for this independence. When considering corporate income tax results, they recognize that firm value increases with financial leverage.

Modigliani and Miller (1958) pose the following question: What is the cost of capital to a firm in a world in which it uses funds to acquire assets whose yields are uncertain? They assert that under certainty the two criteria of rational decision making—the maximization of profits and the maximization of market value—are equivalent. Under uncertainty, however, this equivalence vanishes. According to MM, using debt instead of equity to finance a given venture may increase the expected return to the owners but only at the cost of increased dispersion of the outcomes. As Modigliani and Miller (p. 263) state, "Under these conditions the profit outcomes of alternative investment and financing decisions can be compared and ranked only in terms of a subjective 'utility functions' of the owners which weighs the expected yield against other characteristics of the distributions [of outcomes]."

Accordingly, Modigliani and Miller (1958) ask several other questions: How is management to ascertain the risk preferences of its stockholders and to compromise among their tastes? How can economists build a meaningful investment function in the face of the fact that any given investment opportunity might or might not be worth exploiting, depending on precisely who happens to be the owner of the firm at the moment? By answering these questions, MM establish the principles that govern the rational investment and financial policy in a world of uncertainty. Namely, they suggest the market value maximization criterion provides a workable theory of investment. Modigliani and Miller (p. 264) assert the following:

> *Under this approach any investment project and its concomitant financing plan must pass only the following test: Will the project, as financed, raise the market value of the firm's shares? If so, it is worth undertaking; if not, its return is less than the marginal cost of capital to the firm. Note that such a test is entirely independent of the tastes of current owners, since market prices will reflect not only their preferences but those of all potential owners as well. If any current stockholder disagrees with management and the market over the valuation of the project, he is free to sell out and reinvest elsewhere, but will still benefit from the capital appreciation resulting from management's decision.*

This is the conceptual basis for further research and may be recognized as the origin of the value-based management paradigm.

This chapter does not provide a comprehensive survey of the literature on the capital structure theory. Instead, it provides a summary of major issues and viewpoints regarding the underlying assumptions of capital structure relevance-irrelevance for capital budgeting purposes and suggests a simple approach to extend MM's model to imperfect market conditions. The chapter has the following organization. The next section discusses MM's capital structure propositions and underlying assumptions and explores the interactions between the cost of debt and equity functions of leverage. Next follows a section on the influence of corporate income tax and the cost of financial distress both on the value of a firm and on the cost of its equity. Subsequent sections offer an extended analytical framework for finding optimal capital structure under various market imperfections. The final section summarizes and concludes.

MM CAPITAL STRUCTURE PROPOSITIONS AND THEIR INTERPRETATIONS

Rubinstein (2003) credits Williams (1938) as the first to introduce the capital irrelevance proposition. According to the law of the conservation of investment value, Williams (p. 73) states, "Bonds could be retired with stock issues, or two classes of junior securities could be combined into one, without changing the investment value of the company as a whole." Nonetheless, Modigliani and Miller (1958) provide the first formal analysis of capital structure irrelevance.

Proposition I, which provides the essence of the Modigliani and Miller (1958) model, states that under perfect capital markets and in the absence of taxes, the market value of any firm is independent of its capital structure and is given by capitalizing its expected return at the cost of unlevered equity. To establish this proposition, MM assume the law of one price for absolute substitutions, arbitrage possibilities, and the opportunity for investors to put the equivalent leverage in their portfolio directly by borrowing on their personal account (also known as homemade leverage). MM introduces various simplifications to make these proofs possible. First, they sort firms into risk classes and assume that firms in one class are perfect substitutes for one another, differing only by a scale factor. The authors also assume the following: (1) individual investors have homogenous expectations about the firm's future returns; (2) perfect capital markets under conditions of atomistic competition and the rationality of economic agents; and (3) the firm issues debt of no risk. The model also implies static equilibrium and perpetuities.

Modigliani and Miller (1958) use a proof by contradiction. If Proposition I does not hold, then investors could exploit arbitrage opportunities and ensure a costless, instantaneous increase in their wealth by short-selling overpriced stock and buying equivalent underpriced stock representing identical income streams in all respects except price. Having the possibility to replicate or cancel any corporate structure, investors should not value leverage.

The first wave of MM criticism concerns controversies about the arbitrage proof. Some question the ability of individual investors to replicate a corporate portfolio of stock and debt. A counterargument concerns the unlimited liability of individuals in contrast to limited liability of corporations. This gap is usually filled with the corporations' greater ability to exploit arbitrage opportunities than individual investors.

Durand (1959), the first formal critic of Modigliani and Miller (1958), criticizes the restrictive assumptions and discusses some deficiencies in the MM argument. He points out that the model does not consider closely-held businesses such as proprietorships, partnerships, and hybrid firms that issue marketable securities. The owners of these firms cannot easily buy or sell their stake in capital as is possible in corporations. Also, the no-arbitrage argument is not fully applicable to such firms. So actual capital markets cannot behave as specified in the MM model. Durand also questions whether individuals have equal access to capital markets and can borrow or lend at the same terms as firms.

In fact, individuals cannot borrow on the same terms as firms and encounter constraints in the amount of credit. Subsequent research ignores these complications because such constraints simply could not exist in a perfect capital market. But this redirects the debate to the applicability of Modigliani and Miller (1958) world constructs for an analysis of real-world situations.

The Modigliani and Miller (1958) model is static, whereas the real world probably follows a dynamic equilibrium where deviations from the model are commonly observed as intraday variability of prices. At the firm level, managers should account for various costs of financial alternatives. Also, investors encounter considerable transaction costs and regulatory restrictions in real-world firms. Durand (1959) views MM's model as inappropriate because it does not reflect reality. In contrast to MM who claim financial policy generally does not influence a firm's value, he believes that corporations should exploit arbitrage opportunities whenever possible. His advice is to adjust a firm's capital structure by taking profits resulting from market fluctuations. In their reply to Durand's criticism, Modigliani and Miller (1959) argue the capital structure irrelevance proposition describes the central tendency of the real-world capital market given that mechanisms exist to promote equilibrium. But this does not exclude temporary deviations from the equilibrium. However, as price dynamics are almost unpredictable, a firm should not focus on price speculations or try to outwit the market by frequently rearranging its capital structure. Instead, a firm should focus on investment opportunities and not concern itself with the slippery possibilities of unexpected gains.

Miller (1988) later expresses regret for not suggesting a more constructive approach and emphasizing what actually matters in practice. He notes that when formulating capital structure irrelevance, MM focus on proving the inconsistency of a U-shaped cost of capital function and convincing people that the cost of equity is a linear increasing function of the leverage and the weighted average cost of capital (WACC) remains the same no matter what combination of financing sources the firm chooses.

Stiglitz (1969) relaxes the assumption of risk classes and homogeneous expectations and shows that the Modigliani and Miller (1958) propositions hold for a generalized equilibrium model if firms do not issue so much debt that they incur a positive probability of bankruptcy. Later, Stiglitz (1974) shows the invariance of the maturity structure of debt and any other aspects of a firm's financial policy. In equilibrium, the market value of the firm is implied by an optimal capital structure, irrespective of the financial policies chosen by the firm. Even if the firm does not choose the optimal capital structure, investors can apply homemade leverage to obtain the optimal proportions.

The acceptability of the arbitrage proof is no longer disputed, and such proofs are now widespread. For example, Black and Scholes (1973) use the arbitrage proof in deriving their famous option pricing formula, as does Sharpe (1964) in developing the capital asset pricing model (CAPM). Finally the arbitrage proof, though slightly modified, has become a standard for financial analysis. Yet, skepticism still exists about the validity of the assumptions and the applicability of practical implications for corporate finance.

The practical implications of the MM theory are known as Propositions II and III. Proposition II claims the cost of levered equity is equal to the cost of unlevered equity, plus a premium related to financial risk equal to the debt-to-equity ratio times the spread between the cost of unlevered equity and the cost of debt. In the absence of taxes, the cost of unlevered equity is written as follows:

$$K_e = K_u + (K_u - d)\,\frac{VD}{VLE} \tag{9.1}$$

where K_e = the cost of equity; K_u = the cost of an unlevered firm; VD = the value of debt; and VLE = the value of levered equity.

Proposition III, the most controversial of the propositions, states that to act in the best interests of the shareholders, a firm should exploit an investment opportunity if and only if the rate of return on the investment is as large as or larger than the cost of unlevered equity. The independence of the cost of capital is identical to the assertion that the firm's cash flow is discounted at a weighted average rate. This rate actually splits the cash flows into parts and discounts them at their respective costs. Modigliani and Miller (1958) use an analogy of the price of milk after skimming off some butter fat to illustrate why a firm cannot reduce a cost of capital by issuing cheaper debt instead of equity. Under a perfect market, a dairy farmer cannot consistently earn more for the milk by skimming some of the butter fat and selling it separately. MM assert that a dairy farmer cannot typically earn more for selling milk parts separately because the gain from the high-priced butter fat would be lost in selling the low-priced residue of thinned milk. Later, they provide a more intuitive example using a "pie-slicing" exercise. Both analogies explain the redistribution of the risky cash flow among stakeholders.

The Risks-Shifting Interpretation of the MM Model

Examining redistribution of risk between shareholders and creditors reveals the nature of capital structure irrelevance. If debt has no risk, then financial leverage simply reallocates the entire risk of an all-equity financed firm to the residual cash flow of shareholders after the interest expense. If the investors apply a constant price to a unit of risk, as is implied by the CAPM, they recognize even the smallest increase in risk redistributed to equity as the debt-to-equity ratio increases. The value of the levered equity will decrease proportionately. This explains the linear relationship between the cost of levered equity and the debt-to-equity ratio.

Let V_U represent the market value of all-equity financed firm, D equal the market value of debt, r be the risk-free rate, and E_L represent the value of levered equity. By repaying rD on debt periodically, the firm detaches a certain cash flow for the benefit of creditors at the expense of owners. Shareholders value this cash flow at a risk-free rate as D. Because a monetary unit of residual value to shareholders E_L is riskier than that of V_U and the unit of risk is valued at the same price, E_L is equal to $V_U - D$. The combined value of equity and debt cannot exceed the value of an unlevered firm because the total cash flow and the total risk do not change.

Relaxing the assumption of risk-free debt does not rule out the implications of redistribution of risk between equity and debt. Under limited liability of a firm, the risk for lenders benefits shareholders. Lenders accept a portion of risk in all-equity financed cash flow. Their risk is bounded by a default event and increases as the debt coverage ratio falls. In the absence of bankruptcy costs, owners are released from this portion of risk. They will evaluate debt as lenders do. Again, E_L is equal to $V_U - D$. Thus, even though debt is cheaper than equity, leverage does not reduce a firm's average cost of capital. Debt only allocates risk between shareholders and lenders increasing the cost of levered equity. This result occurs only under perfect market conditions and assuming a fixed investment policy. The possibility of uncertain future investment opportunities and discretionary manager's choice involves additional complexity that may be resolved only by means of option pricing theory. This possibility will be discussed later.

As Morton (1954, p. 442) writes, "If one individual owned all the various types of securities issued, his risk would be the same." Nevertheless, Morton does not explain how the risk is redistributed between shareholders and creditors. MM address this issue in their skimmed milk analogy. Modigliani and Miller (1958, p. 271) also mention that "visualizing the equilibrating mechanism in terms of switchers by investors between stocks and bonds as the yields of each get out of line with their 'riskiness' . . . is an argument quite different from the pure arbitrage mechanism." An alternative way to prove capital structure irrelevance, which takes into consideration reallocation of risk, is to explain why the price for a unit of risk is fixed under perfect market conditions. The MM arbitrage argument under a single risk class assumption is a roundabout way to prove this as a corollary from capital structure irrelevance and avoids problems associated with defining risk. But the stability of the objective price for risk is a more general rule that allows solving much of the controversy both under perfect and imperfect capital markets.

Capital structure will be relevant if shareholders value cash flows on debt in a different way compared to lenders. Although this difference is impossible under perfect capital markets, it may occur in the case of closely-held firms or under various market imperfections. Even the risk-free rate may differ between owners and lenders because of governmental regulations, size of their wealth, their location, informational asymmetry, stock issuing and debt issuing expenses (e.g., underwriter's commissions and discounts, promotion, and professional expenses), and other factors. If debt does not generate additional cash flows, the value of levered equity under any of these conditions is determined by deducting the value of debt from the shareholders' viewpoint from the value of the unlevered firm. Particularly, nondiversified owners value debt differently from diversified lenders such as banks.

Incorporating the Cost of Debt Dependence on Leverage

Reallocating a firm's risk is also useful in understanding the shapes of the cost of debt and equity functions of leverage. In addressing this issue, Modigliani and Miller (1958) provide an incorrect picture of the dependencies between costs. Under MM Proposition II with risk-free debt, the risk of a firm worth $1 billion could be allocated to only $1 value of equity. If the leverage tends to infinity and the debt somehow carries no risk to lenders, then the cost of levered equity will be large. However, this may take place only under unlimited liability of a firm, which is inconsistent with the initial premises of MM.

A purely mathematical interpretation of Proposition II leads to a senseless result: The cost of levered equity tends to decline after the cost of debt exceeds the cost of unlevered equity. But this situation is obviously impossible in an ideal MM world after examining it through the logical instrumentality of a risk-shifting framework presented in a previous subsection. The credit risk is the risk of loss due to a debtor's nonpayment and, therefore, by definition it may be only a portion of the risk of an all-equity financed firm. At the extreme, when a firm is completely financed with debt, the cost of levered equity is equal to the cost of unlevered equity. However, if this is the case, lenders become owners. The formula for the cost of levered equity as proposed by MM cannot represent this extreme case because it encounters the division-by-zero problem in the denominator. Asserting that a firm's cost of debt can exceed its cost of unlevered equity is unrealistic under perfect capital markets.

If debt is risky, then its risk will not be independent of leverage but should increase as the debt coverage ratio reduces with leverage. That is, under limited liability, the more debt a firm has, the greater is the probability of a credit default event and subsequent losses for lenders. The implications of this are expressed in two opposing ways: (1) the cost of debt increases and (2) the value of debt decreases because of lower expected payments compared to the promised amount and the greater cost of debt. With increased leverage (in terms of the promised amount), the reduction in the value of the debt implies a slowing down in the growth of debt-to-equity ratio (a measure of leverage taken by MM), which partly masks the increase in risk.

As Modigliani and Miller (1958, p. 273) note, "economic theory and market experience both suggest that the yield demanded by lenders tends to increase with the debt-equity ratio." Although they mention a "rising supply curve for borrowed funds" as a reason for this phenomenon, it cannot have significant effects for a firm under their assumption of atomistic competition. No matter how much debt an individual firm has, it will be unable to influence supply or demand curves at a macro level. The most obvious reason for the interest rate on debt to increase markedly with leverage is due to the increasing probability of default and, therefore, the risk for lenders resulting from the reduction in the debt coverage ratio. Subsequent research shows the model also holds if the debt is risky (Stiglitz 1969; Fama and Miller 1972; Merton 1973; Rubinstein 1976; Fama 1978).

Relaxing the assumption of a constant interest rate on debt, Modigliani and Miller (1958) incorrectly portray an exponentially increasing cost of debt as a function of the debt-to-equity ratio. Modigliani and Miller (p. 275) argue that if the interest rate on debt increases with leverage, the cost of levered equity "will still tend to rise, but at a decreasing rather than a constant rate," and "beyond some high level of leverage, depending on the exact form of the interest function" the cost of levered equity "may even start to fall."

Brewer and Michaelsen (1965) object to the description being inconsistent with implicitly assumed risk aversion, which follows from the assumption of the cost of risky equity being higher than the risk-free cost of debt. That is, risk-neutral investors require a risk-free rate of return for both risk-free and risky assets, while risk lovers apply a risk discount and not a premium for risky assets compared to risk-free assets. Risk aversion in turn implies the cost of levered equity greater than risk-free rate everywhere and hence a monotonically increasing cost of levered equity curve.

Berlingeri (2006), who provides an extensive mathematical analysis of the cost of debt as a function of leverage, concludes that a cost of debt function is concave and bounded from above by the cost of unlevered equity. He also states that if the first derivative of the cost of debt function tends to infinity (the point where a firm is all-debt financed), then the cost of levered equity function will also tend to infinity.

Estimating the precise form of dependence between the cost of debt and leverage is difficult. Presumably, it is described as a concave or, under protective covenants, as an S-shaped function bounded from above by the cost of unlevered equity. The cost of unlevered equity serves as an asymptote, as the cost of debt may reach this value only if a firm is all-debt financed, but then, as the equity becomes a zero value, the debt-to-equity ratio turns to infinity. Here a qualitative change occurs where mathematics loses its explanative power.

Analysts often use credit risk models to determine a probability of default and, therefore, the risk premium and the cost of debt function for creditors under various degrees of leverage. These models are usually classified as structural models, implied credit risk models, rating models, statistical models (logit regressions and discriminant analysis), and hybrid models. A credit risk model is also a necessary element in estimating the current value of costs of financial distress, which is contingent on the credit default event or expectation of its coming occurrence. Probabilistic simulation may also be effective because it deals with the uncertainty of fundamental variables such as the prices of equity and debt or cash flows.

Simple computer simulations within the CAPM framework indicate the shape of the cost of levered equity function appears as presented in Exhibit 9.1. The cost of debt function (*CD*) is bounded from above by the cost of unlevered equity curve (*CUE*). This result is consistent with the conclusions of Berlingeri (2006). The cost of levered equity function (*CLE*) is much lower compared to the MM line, which is

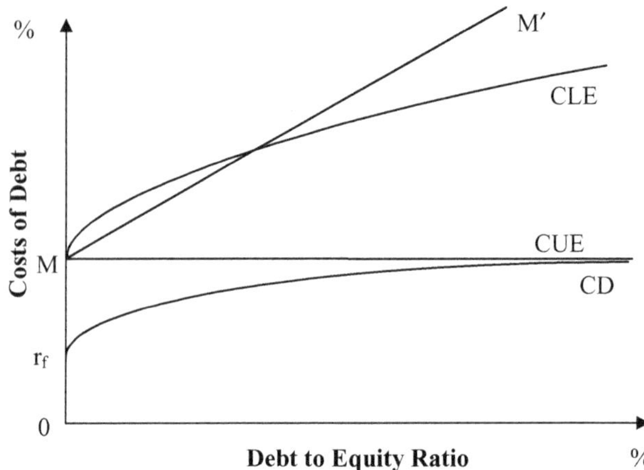

Exhibit 9.1 True Functions of the Cost of Levered Equity Function When the Cost of Debt Increases with Leverage (According to Monte-Carlo Simulations under the CAPM)

Note: The exhibit demonstrates that in the absence of covenants and collateral the cost of debt (*CD*) is a concave function of leverage bounded from above with the cost of unlevered equity (*CUE*). The cost of levered equity (*CLE*) function starts from the cost of unlevered equity at the point of zero leverage and increases similarly to cost of debt lying above the MM line at low leverage and significantly below the MM line at high leverage. A gap exists between the risk-free rate and the cost of unlevered equity. Modigliani and Miller (1958) mistakenly picture all functions departing from the point of risk-free rate (r_f). If this were true, all functions would coincide and lie horizontally. The risk of an unlevered firm determines the curves.

valid only under a constant interest rate on debt. The growth rate of both the cost of debt and equity slows down as the leverage increases.

Comparing Exhibit 9.1 and Modigliani and Miller's (1958, p. 275) figure, the striking difference is that MM picture the cost of debt and levered equity functions as departing from one point. This implies that the unlevered firm is risk free, but if it were so, then leverage would not add any risk, and the cost of debt and equity functions would be equal to a risk-free rate at any amount of debt. The functions differ only if the firm is risky. As the risk increases, so does the difference between the cost of levered equity and the cost of unlevered equity, and between the cost of debt and the cost of unlevered equity.

Debt becomes risky even at the smallest possible degree of leverage. Nonetheless, using protective covenants and collateral, firms can maintain the debt at almost no risk, unless leverage reaches a point where covenants are no longer effective. Under these conditions the cost-of-debt function presumably becomes S-shaped as presented in Exhibit 9.2. This result is consistent with Merton's (1974) risky structure of interest rates.

The cost functions presented here should be considered in valuation and capital budgeting. Specifically, they are needed in sensitivity analysis to search for an optimal capital structure by trading off tax benefits and bankruptcy costs, planning highly leveraged transactions, and in many other financial applications.

Despite complexities in the dependencies between the cost of debt and equity, the WACC remains constant unless additional cash flows or risks are associated with leverage. The following sections explore cases where these additional effects

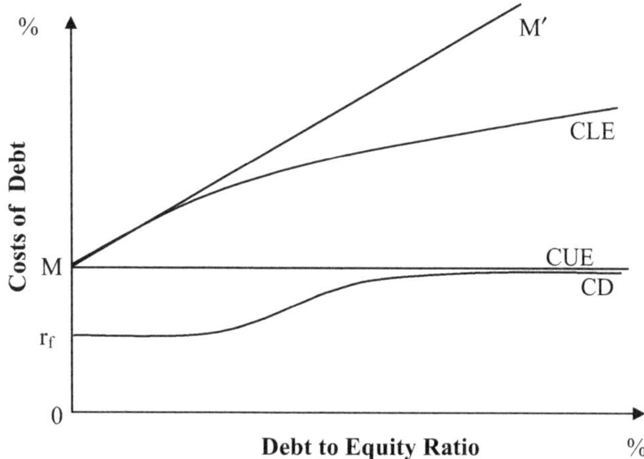

Exhibit 9.2 True Functions of the Cost of Levered Equity Function When the Cost of Debt Increases with Leverage and Using Protective Covenants.

Note: This exhibit demonstrates that under protective covenants the cost of debt (CD) starts out as a convex function of leverage, passes through an inflexion point where it becomes concave and approaches the limiting value of cost of unlevered equity asymptotically as the debt-to-equity ratio tends to infinity. The cost of levered equity (CLE) is determined by increasing the cost of debt in accordance with Proposition II.

arise. To bring the model closer to reality, taxes and default troubles are the first issues considered.

THE TRADE-OFF BETWEEN TAX ADVANTAGES AND BANKRUPTCY COSTS

This section examines issues involving taxes and bankruptcy. Specifically, it shows that a trade-off exists between the tax advantages of debt and bankruptcy costs.

Confusion Surrounding Corporate Income Tax

The influence of tax benefits on a firm's market value is a subject of much debate and controversy among financial economists. Because of the tax deductibility of interest expense on debt, financial leverage creates a flow of tax savings, which adds to a firm's value benefiting shareholders.

Modigliani and Miller (1958) put forward the first version of the cost of equity formula for a levered firm that implicitly assumes tax savings are discounted at cost of unlevered equity, which is shown in Equation 9.1. However, MM do not provide sufficient justification for this assumption. In their corrected version, Modigliani and Miller (1963) explicitly assume that the tax savings are discounted at the cost of debt and the cost of levered equity formula changes as follows:

$$K_e = K_u + (K_u - d)(1 - T)\frac{VD}{VLE} \tag{9.2}$$

where T = the effective corporate income tax rate. This time MM, retaining the assumption of risk-free debt, decide that the tax savings are a sure stream that carries no risk. This formula still implies a positive linear relationship between the cost of equity and leverage but increases the estimate of the tax advantages of debt financing.

Actually, there is no mistake in the original Modigliani and Miller (1958) version. The key issue concerns the assumptions about the riskiness of the tax savings. Their riskiness results from the possibility of profits falling below contractual interest, changes in the tax code, loss of nondebt tax shields, unanticipated changes in future interest rates, changes in financing policies, and firm-specific effects of tax law provisions (e.g., loss carry-backs and carry-forwards and investment tax credits). So, the assumption about the risk-free discount rate for tax savings is invalid even for an ideal MM world.

Modigliani (1988) expresses regret for not presenting the basic valuation formula in a general form with an arbitrary discount rate for tax savings. This rate may vary from the risk-free cost of capital to the cost of unlevered equity or even higher, depending on the riskiness of the tax savings as a function of debt-to-equity ratio. Modigliani and Miller (1963) suggest the incremental tax advantage of borrowing declines as the firm issues more debt and interest tax shields become less certain.

Rao and Stevens (2007) develop a formalized model explaining how risky debt affects the firm's depreciation and interest tax shields. They recognize that leverage increases the probability tax shields will be unusable because of the increase in the cost of debt. However, Rao and Stevens use a set of simplifying assumptions and do not try to estimate the shape of the cost of tax savings function. Applying WACC in a traditional way, they stumble upon circularity in the calculations. In other words, the discount rate for the tax savings is not fixed but increases with leverage because the possibility of profits falling below contractual interest and the probability of unused nondebt tax shields increase as leverage rises. Discounting the tax savings, using the cost of debt, is reasonable if the debt-to-equity ratio is low, but if leverage is high, the cost of tax savings might be even greater than the cost of unlevered equity. However, determining the form of the relationship between financial leverage and the appropriate cost of tax savings is difficult because of the specificity of the relevant factors, especially tax regulations and nondebt tax shields. Today, researchers can use probabilistic simulations to solve the problem.

Unfortunately, Equation 9.2 is widely used in practice without appropriately considering its limitations. This equation not only assumes the cost of debt for discounting tax savings but also is designed specifically for perpetuities. Thus, this equation is invalid for finite cash flows (usually analyzed in capital budgeting and financial modeling) and implies a constant amount of debt.

Equation 9.2 should not be used to evaluate investment projects or firms with finite cash flows because this equation does not properly account for changing debt payments and tax savings. Vélez-Pareja and Burbano-Pérez (2005) suggest a generalized formulation of the cost of capital for any type of cash flow using an arbitrary cost of tax savings, which is represented by Equation 9.3:

$$K_e = K_u + (K_u - d)\frac{VD}{VLE} - (k_u - \psi)\frac{VTS}{VLE} \tag{9.3}$$

where:

ψ = the cost of tax savings; and VTS = the value of tax shield. This formula can be rearranged to a more intuitive form of the weighted average of specific discount rates:

$$K_e = K_u \frac{VUE}{VLE} - d\frac{VD}{VLE} + \psi\frac{VTS}{VLE} \tag{9.4}$$

where VUE = the value of unlevered equity. Equation 9.4 allows formulating a generalization of Proposition II. That is, the cost-of-equity formula is nothing more than a weighted average of specific discount rates, where the weights are the values of unlevered equity, debt, tax shield, and other components of capital structure, all divided by the value of levered equity. This rule may be generalized even further for any cost of capital including WACC. The only special feature of traditional WACC is that it is designed to value a firm on the basis of unlevered cash flow without tax savings and the effect of tax savings is added through the WACC. According to Vélez-Pareja and Burbano-Pérez, the generalized WACC formula is (Equation 9.5):

$$\text{WACC} = K_e\frac{VLE}{VLF} + d\frac{VD}{VLF} + \psi\frac{VTS}{VLF} - \frac{TS}{VLF} \tag{9.5}$$

where:

TS = the periodic tax savings; and VLF = the value of a levered firm.

Myers (1974), researching interactions between corporate financing and investment decisions, derives a general adjusted present value (APV) rule for capital budgeting decisions. He assumes that a firm's value consists of all-equity financing plus the present value of tax savings. Although Modigliani and Miller (1958) explicitly use this approach, they stress the insignificance of the tax advantages on debt. Myers identifies inconsistencies in, and a lack of general standards associated with, the WACC-based approach to valuation and uses a mathematical programming formulation of the problem. Generally speaking, an extended version of this approach may be described as discounting by components (D-by-C) approach. This approach consists of applying specific discount rates for valuing underlying cash flows and then adding those values to get the value of the firm in the same manner as the underlying cash flows are added in order to find the total cash flow to the firm. In other words, the cash flow's additivity is fully transferred to the values of cash flows. Another concern is to maintain consistency in the viewpoints because shareholders and lenders under market anomalies may value the same cash flow differently. If properly constructed, the WACC is nothing more than another mathematical representation of the D-by-C rule. However, because WACC involves greater complexities in calculation, it may lead to confusion.

Costs of Financial Distress

Tax-adjusted propositions rule out the financing policy irrelevance and revive the idea of an optimal capital structure. With the tax-deductibility of interest expense, the value of the firm is evidently not independent of financial leverage. This leads to a paradoxical conclusion to the firm's financial policy: Managers should increase debt to produce as many tax benefits as possible. As Miller (1988, p. 112) exclaims: "The optimal capital structure might be all debt!" But conventional finance wisdom warns against reckless leveraging.

Yet, Miller (1977) argues that in equilibrium the value of a firm is still independent of its capital structure despite the tax deductibility of interest payments. He believes equilibrium market prices and returns for securities already account for distortions imposed by personal and corporate taxes and the firm cannot improve its performance simply by changing its debt-to-equity ratio. According to Miller (p. 269), "companies following a no-leverage or low leverage strategy ... would find a market among investors in the high tax brackets; those opting for a high leverage strategy ... would find the natural clientele for their securities at the other end of the scale." But this construction contradicts the previous assertion that assets with identical returns in a homogeneous risk class must sell at one price. Because firms with different amounts of leverage provide unequal tax benefits on debt with comparably little additional risk, why investors should not value those benefits is unclear. The substantial presence of leverage buyouts (LBOs) in the 1980s suggests the relevance of the corporate income taxes.

Miller (1988) recognizes the tax advantages of debt and partly agrees with the existence of an optimal capital structure. Recent research and empirical evidence also confirms the relevance of the tax-deductibility of interest for firm valuation. Yet, counterbalancing costs such as the transaction costs associated with bankruptcy may offset the tax advantages of debt. Kraus and Litzenberger (1973) develop a simple trade-off model between tax savings and the cost of financial distress. Jensen and Meckling (1976) provide further analysis of these costs. The costs of financial distress may be direct (e.g., legal, consulting, and restructuring expenses) or indirect (e.g., lost sales and profits, broken contracts, poor credit terms, increased costs of issuing debt to refinance current obligations, and employee turnover).

Miller (1977) recognizes the existence of bankruptcy costs and agency costs but still argues that these costs seem disproportionately small relative to the tax savings they supposedly balance and suggests ignoring them. In contrast, Ju et al. (2005) calculate optimal capital structures under a dynamic trade-off framework. They refute Miller's argument that despite the large tax advantage of debt, firms tend to use too little leverage in practice. Their estimate of the optimal debt-to-total capital ratio for a typical S&P firm was 15.29 percent versus an actual ratio of 22.62 percent in 2000.

Recent empirical evidence reveals the costs of financial distress are too large to ignore. Altman and Hotchkiss (2006) provide a survey of the estimates of the direct costs of formal bankruptcy proceedings in the United States since the 1950s. They report the direct costs to be around 4 percent of a firm's market value as estimated by most researchers, and at the extreme these costs approach 10 percent. Altman (1984) finds that indirect costs average 10.5 percent of firm value measured just before bankruptcy. The combined direct and indirect costs average 16.7 percent of firm value. Andrade and Kaplan (1998), studying 31 highly leveraged transactions of the 1980s that subsequently become financially distressed, estimate the combined direct and indirect costs of financial distress as 10 to 20 percent of firm value with an upper bound not exceeding 23 percent of firm value.

Almeida and Philippon (2005) explain why firms appear conservative when using debt. They compute the present value of costs of financial distress using risk-adjusted default probabilities derived from corporate bond spreads and show risk-adjusted costs of financial distress are 4.5 percent of predistress firm value. In contrast, a valuation of distress costs that ignores risk premium produces an estimate of 1.4 percent.

Graham (2000) assumes that tax shields are as risky as the debt that generates them. He estimates the capitalized tax benefit of debt is 9.7 percent of firm value (or as low as 4.3 percent, net of personal taxes). Surprisingly, he discovers that even firms with low expected costs of financial distress use debt conservatively and underemploy tax benefits from debt. He reports 44 percent of the sample firms could double interest deductions and still expect to realize full tax benefits from their tax deductions. Levering up to the kink (the point where a firm's marginal benefit function of interest deductions becomes downward sloping), the typical firm could add 15.7 percent to firm value or 7.3 percent after considering the personal tax penalty.

Although varying considerably in detail, empirical findings demonstrate the costs of financial distress are too large to ignore. A key concern is to how to develop practical methods that model these costs. Doing so is likely to improve a firm's financial management. The trade-offs between the tax benefits of debt and the costs of financial distress lead to the existence of an optimal capital structure.

EXTENSION OF THE MM MODEL

A frequent criticism of the MM model concerns its simplified assumptions relative to a real-world setting. Although extensive research exists on the validity of the MM propositions under imperfect market conditions and on the implications of different market anomalies, no unified approach exists for treating these imperfections.

Jensen and Meckling (1976) extend their analysis of capital structure to include debt incentives for managers to engage in future investment opportunities. Having discovered that debt engenders agency costs, which depend not only on the debt-to-equity ratio but also on the fraction of the equity held by managers, the authors suggest a theory of corporate ownership structure. They explain that once a firm issues debt it may undertake more uncertain investments, which in turn may redistribute wealth from bondholders to its owners. Such redistribution occurs under limited liability because owners receive most of the gains if the risky project succeeds while creditors bear most of the losses if it does not.

As Merton (1973) notes, equity in a levered firm may be viewed as a call option on the total value of the firm with an exercise price equal to the face value of the debt. As is well known, the value of the option increases with uncertainty and the exercise price. Because more debt implies a higher exercise price for a call option on the total value of the firm, the value of the levered equity rises as the firm's total cash flow becomes more volatile and its debt-to-equity ratio rises. Thus, bondholders presume managers choose riskier investments and ask for an appropriate price for debt that results in reducing a firm's value.

Jensen and Meckling (1976) consider this reduction as one of the possible forms of agency costs associated with debt. If creditors undertake actions to prevent managers from engaging in risky investments, they incur monitoring and binding costs (on writing and enforcing restrictive provisions) and experience reduced profitability because of the limited ability of managers to exploit favorable and unfavorable opportunities. The authors also regard the costs of financial distress in a single bundle with agency costs of debt. Because outside equity also generates agency costs, the search for an optimal ownership structure is a compromise between agency costs of debt and outside equity. Jensen and Meckling, however, ignore the problem of a lack of diversification for wholly-owned firms.

Conventional methods used to estimate the risk premium of a project or a firm assume that the owner holds only a small fraction of his wealth in the firm. This assumption is typically valid for widely-held corporations but may be inappropriate for closely-held firms. To value closely-held firms, Long and Bryant (2007) recommend starting with the conventional valuation for a public firm and making adjustments for the lack of the owner's diversification by including unsystematic risk in the discount rate and by applying a discount for low liquidity. Although the authors tend to put all those adjustments into the discount rate, this approach is prone to errors. Most of the adjustments can be applied directly to the specific cash flows rather than to discount rates. This approach separates risk from other factors that may influence firm value.

Myers and Majluf (1984) breathe new life into the pecking order framework. The term "pecking order" originally referred to a hierarchical system of social organization in chickens, where pecking is used as a measure of dominance. In finance, this framework states that firms adhere to a hierarchy of financing sources, recognizing the advantages of using internal financing before external financing, and of using debt before external equity. Those advantages stem from various sources including adverse selection due to informational asymmetry and agency costs problems.

Frank and Goyal (2007) provide an extensive survey of trade-off and pecking order theories and related evidence. They conclude that interpreting the evidence remains difficult. According to Frank and Goyal, the pecking order theory predicts that debt grows when investments exceed earnings and debt falls when earnings exceed investments. Empirical studies contradict this prediction. Evidence shows that firms adjust their debt frequently, but such adjustments hold for large firms that might be expected to face the least severe adverse selection problem. Curiously, small firms, for which information asymmetry is presumably an important problem, do not change debt policies often.

Although the recent evidence provides some support for the trade-off theory, the prevailing view is that the amounts of debt across companies seem to exceed the reasonable levels as predicted by theory. However, Ju et al. (2005) raise an objection, saying that the issue hinges on the realistic parameters for calculating an optimal capital structure as a proper benchmark for empirical testing.

Such explanations offer insights into making capital budgeting decisions and valuing a firm. The risk-shifting explanation presented in this chapter provides some insights into how to combine the various imperfections into a single model. The following steps may be helpful in constructing such a model:

- Construct a model under assumptions of perfect market.
- Identify relevant market imperfections.
- Analyze the redistribution of risk between stakeholders stemming from the most important imperfections.
- Adjust specific discount rates for component cash flows according to the implications of the previous step.
- Consider additional cash flows resulting from debt and other sources of financing.

Distinguishing between two possible implications of imperfect conditions is important: (1) identifying the actual or potential cash flows to shareholders (e.g., tax savings, costs of financial distress, and issuing expenses on equity and debt); and (2) accepting additional risks or reducing a portion of the risk on the residual cash flow to equity after servicing and repaying debt.

To properly account for risk shifting, the MM model (namely, Proposition II) needs a subtle modification: both debt and equity should be valued from the shareholders' viewpoint. In Equation 9.6, the basic model in the absence of taxes may be reformulated as follows:

$$CLE = CUE + (CUE - CDsh)\frac{VDsh}{VLE} \tag{9.6}$$

where:

$CDsh$ = the cost of debt to shareholders; and $VDsh$ = the value of debt to shareholders.

In Equation 9.7, the cost of debt to shareholders may be expressed as follows:

$$CDsh = RFCEsh + RPopp - RPEXsh \tag{9.7}$$

where:

$RFCEsh$ = the risk-free rate for shareholders

$RPopp$ = the premium for risks of lenders that at the same time turn to the benefit of shareholders

$RPEXsh$ = the premium for shareholders for their exclusive risks and costs on debt, which are neutral for lenders and not reflected in the market value of debt

In contrast, the cost of debt to lenders is found as follows (Equation 9.8):

$$CDcr = RFCDcr + RPopp + RPEXcr + RPLIQcr \tag{9.8}$$

where:

$RFCDcr$ = the risk-free rate for lenders
$RPEXcr$ = the premium for lenders for their exclusive risks and costs, which are neutral for shareholders
$RPLIQcr$ = the premium for liquidation costs for lenders

Additional cash flows associated with debt should be valued separately. Their specific discount rates are added to the cost of levered equity function according to their weights in the value of levered equity. Particularly, the value of the tax savings is accounted for as (Equation 9.9):

$$-CTS\frac{VTS_{t-1}}{VLE_{t-1}}, \tag{9.9}$$

where:

CTS = cost of tax shield.

The cost of financial distress is added as (Equation 9.10):

$$+\frac{VFD_{t-1} - VFD_t}{VLE_{t-1}}, \tag{9.10}$$

where:

VFD = the value of financial distress.

Then the resulting cost of equity function may be presented as follows (Equation 9.11):

$$\begin{aligned} CLE_t &= CUE_t + (CUE_t - CDsh_{t-1})\frac{VDsh_{t-1}}{VLE_{t-1}} \\ &\quad - CTS_{t-1}\frac{VTS_{t-1}}{VLE_{t-1}} + \frac{VFD_{t-1} - VFD_t}{VLE_{t-1}}. \end{aligned} \tag{9.11}$$

Under imperfect markets, the possibility of the interest rate on debt exceeding the cost of unlevered equity is not ruled out. This may occur if lenders incur additional costs (e.g., suing, liquidation, control, and collection) or if lenders are price setters while firms are price takers (then lenders may set a monopolistic premium). But this interest rate does not influence the cost of the levered equity formula because the inputs of this formula should be the cost and value of debt from the viewpoint of shareholders. Debt could not be so beneficial for owners that they should discount it at a rate higher than the cost of unlevered equity. By definition, cash flow to debt is a deduction from an all-equity financed cash flow and cannot increase or decrease the risk of the latter but can only reallocate this risk to a residual (levered) cash flow to shareholders.

Suppose that cost of unlevered equity is 10 percent. Because the leverage is extremely high, lenders set a 12 percent cost of debt. Estimating the portion of risks accepted by lenders, managers estimate the true cost of debt from the shareholders' viewpoint to be only 9 percent. The cost of debt cannot exceed 10 percent unless debt generates extra benefits for shareholders. Tax benefits are treated separately. The value of debt from the shareholders' viewpoint (apart from tax savings) is calculated by discounting the expected cash flow to debt at a 9 percent discount rate. As a result, the value of debt for shareholders is greater than the distorted market value of debt monopolistically set by lenders at a 12 percent rate. If shareholders incurred risk on debt, it should be accounted for with a negative risk premium according to Equation 9.7.

The hurdle rate to accept or reject an investment is calculated as a simple weighted average of specific costs of component cash flows with regard to the value of levered equity from the stakeholders' viewpoint. This is a generalized decision rule for capital budgeting.

SUMMARY AND CONCLUSIONS

Although many are skeptical about the Modigliani and Miller (1958) model, they still continue using formulas (e.g., the cost of equity and WACC) derived from their work. More than a decade ago, Stulz (1999) remarked that the MM framework, despite numerous corrections to real-world conditions, was the conventional approach to the teaching and practice of capital budgeting. However, adjustments are needed to increase the practicality of this framework. For example, in identifying an optimal capital structure, a useful approach is to consider the trade-off between the marginal increase in tax benefits and the marginal decrease in costs of financial distress, agency costs, and transaction costs. Other considerations may be relevant for a specific firm. Although calculations are trivial, estimating the inputs into an extended model presents a challenge.

DISCUSSION QUESTIONS

1. Explain the probable forms of the cost-of-debt function and the reasons for a specific relationship between the cost of debt and levered equity.
2. Consider tax savings and financial distress costs in estimating the effect of financial leverage on firm value. What role does the discount rate of the tax savings play in the MM model? Discuss practical ways to calculate the appropriate discount rate for the tax savings.
3. What complications exist when valuing investment projects of closely-held firms? Describe the conventional approach to determining the appropriate risk premium for such firms and discuss if the arbitrage argument is valid for them.
4. Propose and discuss methods to account for persistent market imperfections in capital budgeting decision making. Explain how such imperfections affect the MM model.

REFERENCES

Almeida, Heitor, and Thomas Philippon. 2005. "The Risk-Adjusted Cost of Financial Distress." *Journal of Finance* 62:6, 2557–2586.

Altman, Edward I. 1984. "A Further Empirical Investigation of the Bankruptcy Cost Question." *Journal of Finance* 39:4, 1067–1089.

Altman, Edward I., and Edith S. Hotchkiss. 2006. *Corporate Financial Distress and Bankruptcy*. Hoboken, NJ: John Wiley & Sons.

Andrade, Gregor, and Steven N. Kaplan. 1998. "How Costly Is Financial (Not Economic) Distress? Evidence from Highly Leveraged Transactions That Became Distressed." *Journal of Finance* 53:5, 1443–1493.

Berlingeri, Hugo Oscar. 2006. "U-Shaped Cost of Equity Function? Digging Into Modigliani-Miller (1958) Mistake." Available at http://ssrn.com/abstract=934550.

Black, Fischer, and Myron Scholes. 1973. "The Pricing of Options and Corporate Liabilities." *Journal of Political Economy* 81:3, 637–654.

Brewer, Dawson, and Jacob Michaelsen. 1965. "The Cost of Capital, Corporation Finance, and the Theory of Investment: Comment." *American Economic Review* 55: 4, 638–639.

Durand, David. 1959. "The Cost of Capital, Corporation Finance, and the Theory of Investment: Comment." *American Economic Review* 49:4, 639–655.

Fama, Eugene F. 1978. "The Effects of a Firm's Investment and Financing Decisions on the Welfare of Its Security Holders." *American Economic Review* 68:3, 272–284.

Fama, Eugene F., and Merton H. Miller. 1972. *The Theory of Finance*. New York: Holt, Rinehart and Winston.

Frank, Murray Z., and Vidhan K. Goyal. 2007. "Trade-Off and Pecking Order Theories of Debt." Available at http://ssrn.com/abstract=670543.

Graham, John R. 2000. "How Big Are the Tax Benefits of Debt?" *Journal of Finance* 55:5, 1901–1942.

Jensen, Michael C., and William H. Meckling. 1976. "Theory of the Firm: Managerial Behavior, Agency Costs and Ownership Structure." *Journal of Financial Economics* 3:4, 305–360.

Ju, Nengjiu, Robert Parrino, Allen M. Poteshman, and Michael S. Weisbach. 2005. "Horses and Rabbits? Trade-Off Theory and Optimal Capital Structure." *Journal of Financial and Quantitative Analysis* 40:2, 259–281.

Kraus, Alan, and Robert H. Litzenberger. 1973. "A State-Preference Model of Optimal Financial Leverage." *Journal of Finance* 28:4, 911–922.

Long, Michael S., and Thomas A. Bryant. 2007. *Valuing the Closely Held Firm*. New York: Oxford University Press.

Merton, Robert C. 1973. "Theory of Rational Option Pricing." *Bell Journal of Economics and Management Science* 4:1, 141–183.

Merton, Robert C. 1974. "On the Pricing of Corporate Debt: The Risk Structure of Interest Rates." *Journal of Finance* 29:2, 449–470.

Miller, Merton H. 1977. "Debt and Taxes." *Journal of Finance* 32:2, 261–275.

Miller, Merton H. 1988. "The Modigliani-Miller Propositions after Thirty Years." *Journal of Economic Perspectives* 2:4, 99–120.

Modigliani, Franco. 1988. "MM—Past, Present, Future." *Journal of Economic Perspectives* 2:4, 149–158.

Modigliani, Franco, and Merton H. Miller. 1958. "The Cost of Capital, Corporation Finance, and the Theory of Investment." *American Economic Review* 48:3, 261–297.

Modigliani, Franco, and Merton H. Miller. 1959. "The Cost of Capital, Corporation Finance, and the Theory of Investment: Reply." *American Economic Review* 49:4, 655–669.

Modigliani, Franco, and Merton H. Miller. 1963. "Corporate Income Taxes and the Cost of Capital: A Correction." *American Economic Review* 53:3, 433–443.

Morton, Walter A. 1954. "The Structure of the Capital Market and the Price of Money." *American Economic Review* 44:2, 440–454.

Myers, Stewart C. 1974. "Interactions of Corporate Financing and Investment Decisions: Implications for Capital Budgeting." *Journal of Finance* 29:1, 1–25.

Myers, Stewart C., and Nicholas S. Majluf. 1984. "Corporate Financing and Investment Decisions When Firms Have Information That Investors Do Not Have." *Journal of Financial Economics* 13:2, 187–221.

Rao, Ramesh K. S., and Eric C. Stevens. 2007. *A Theory of the Firm's Cost of Capital: How Debt Affects the Firm's Risk, Value, Tax Rate, and the Government's Tax Claim*. Singapore: World Scientific Publishing Co.

Rubinstein, Mark E. 1976. "The Valuation of Uncertain Income Streams and the Pricing of Options." *Bell Journal of Economics and Management Science* 7:2, 407–425.

Rubinstein, Mark E. 2003. "Great Moments in Financial Economics: II. Modigliani-Miller Theorem." *Journal of Investment Management* 1:2, 7–13.

Sharpe, William F. 1964. "Capital Asset Prices: A Theory of Market Equilibrium under Conditions of Risk." *Journal of Finance* 19:3, 425–42.

Stiglitz, Joseph E. 1969. "A Re-Examination of the Modigliani-Miller Theorem." *American Economic Review* 59:5, 784–793.

Stiglitz, Joseph E. 1974. "On the Irrelevance of Corporate Financial Policy." *American Economic Review* 64:6, 851–866.

Stulz, René M. 1999. "What's Wrong with Modern Capital Budgeting?" *Financial Practice and Education* 9:2, 7–11.

Vélez-Pareja, Ignacio, and Antonio Burbano-Pérez. 2005. "A Practical Guide for Consistency in Valuation: Cash Flows, Terminal Value and Cost of Capital." Available at http://ssrn.com/abstract=466721.

Williams, John Burr. 1938. *The Theory of Investment Value*. Cambridge, MA: Harvard University Press.

ABOUT THE AUTHOR

Sergei Cheremushkin graduated from Mordovian State University in 2001 with distinction. He holds a degree of candidate in economic sciences and has been an assistant professor since June 2005. He has taught a wide variety of topics in finance, social and economic forecasting, and public administration and has published articles in corporate finance in Russian journals and over the Internet. His research interests are in corporate finance, financial modeling, and innovative economy. He has won numerous research grants including the grant of President of Russian Federation for young scholars.

CHAPTER 10

Trade-Off, Pecking Order, Signaling, and Market Timing Models

ANTON MIGLO
Associate Professor, University of Bridgeport

INTRODUCTION

The modern theory of capital structure began with the famous proposition of Modigliani and Miller (1958) that described the conditions of capital structure irrelevance. Since then, many financial economists have altered these conditions to explain the factors driving capital structure decisions. Harris and Raviv (1991) synthesize the major theoretical literature in the field and suggest promising avenues for future research. They argue that asymmetric information theories of capital structure are less promising than control-based or product-based theories.

The financial crisis during 2008 and 2009 forced financial economists to look critically at capital structure theory because the problems faced by many companies stemmed from their financing policies. Corporate managers appeared to lack an understanding of the role of asymmetric information and agency problems. The market for mortgage-backed securities, which many believe was at the core of financial crisis, involved asymmetric information between investors and issuers. Various scandals, such as the one involving Bernie Madoff, illustrate the depth of agency problems in finance. Financial economists failed to give sufficient attention to the links among taxes, bankruptcy costs, and capital structure until recent surveys of managers revealed their importance.

This chapter surveys four major capital structure theories: trade-off, pecking order, signaling, and market timing. These theories directly relate to asymmetric information, agency problems, taxes, and bankruptcy costs. After presenting the basic model and ideas underlying each theory, the chapter discusses their consistency with observed evidence. The chapter also discusses the main foci of current and future research on capital structure.

TRADE-OFF THEORY

In contrast to dividends, interest paid on debt reduces the firm's taxable income. Debt also increases the probability of bankruptcy. Trade-off theory suggests that capital structure reflects a trade-off between the tax benefits of debt and the expected costs of bankruptcy (Kraus and Litzenberger 1973).

Model and Empirical Evidence

Consider a firm that generates a random cash flow R that is uniformly distributed between 0 and $\overline{R}$. The firm faces a constant tax rate T on corporate income. If the earnings are insufficient to cover the promised debt payment, D, there is a deadweight loss of kR that is used up in the process. This loss can include direct bankruptcy costs such as fees paid to lawyers and indirect bankruptcy costs such as losses due to general lack of confidence in the firm. If earnings are large enough ($R > D$), equity holders receive $(R–D)(1–T)$. Otherwise, they receive nothing. The market value of debt V_d equals $\frac{\overline{R}-D}{\overline{R}}D + \frac{D}{\overline{R}}\frac{D(1-k)}{2}$. Here $\frac{\overline{R}-D}{\overline{R}}$ is the probability that $R > D$ and $\frac{D}{\overline{R}}$ is the probability of default. If $R > D$, the creditors receive D and they receive on average $\frac{D(1-k)}{2}$ if the firm defaults. The market value of equity V_e equals $\frac{\overline{R}-D}{\overline{R}}(\frac{\overline{R}+D}{2} - D)(1 - T)$. The firm's value V equals

$$V_d + V_e = \frac{\overline{R} - D}{\overline{R}}D + \frac{D}{\overline{R}}\frac{D(1-k)}{2} + \frac{\overline{R} - D}{\overline{R}}\left(\frac{\overline{R} + D}{2} - D)(1 - T\right) \tag{10.1}$$

The firm's choice of leverage is determined by maximizing V. The first-order condition with respect to D is

$$D = \frac{T\overline{R}}{T + 1 - k} \tag{10.2}$$

Expected Bankruptcy Costs and Debt

If k is higher in Equation 10.2, the equilibrium level of D should be lower. As the expected bankruptcy costs increase, the advantages of using equity also increase. This result has several interpretations. Large firms should have more debt because they are more diversified and have lower default risk. Tangible assets suffer a smaller loss of value when firms go into distress. Hence, firms with more tangible assets, such as airplane manufacturers, should have higher leverage compared to those that have more intangible assets, such as research firms. Growth firms tend to lose more of their value than nongrowth firms when they go into distress. Thus, theory predicts a negative relationship between leverage and growth. Empirical evidence by Rajan and Zingales (1995); Barclay, Morellec, and Smith (2006); and Frank and Goyal (2007) generally supports the above predictions.

Taxes and Debt

When T increases in Equation 10.2, debt should also increase because higher taxes lead to a greater tax advantage of using debt. Hence, firms with higher tax rates should have higher debt ratios compared to firms with lower tax rates. Inversely, firms that have substantial nondebt tax shields such as depreciation should be less likely to use debt than firms that do not have these tax shields. If tax rates increase over time, debt ratios should also increase. Debt ratios in countries where debt has a much larger tax benefit should be higher than debt ratios in countries whose debt has a lower tax benefit.

The evidence, however, is mixed. Graham (1996) finds some support for tax factors. Titman and Wessels (1988) find that nondebt tax shields and the use of debt are positively correlated. According to Wright (2004), leverage in the corporate sector was remarkably stable between 1900 and 2002 despite large differences in tax rates. A survey of 392 CFOs by Graham and Harvey (2001) finds that 45 percent of the respondents agree that tax considerations play an important role in their capital structure choices.

Debt and Profitability

As suggested in Equation 10.2, if $\overline{R}$ increases, D should also increase. Thus, more profitable firms should have more debt. Expected bankruptcy costs are lower and interest tax shields are more valuable for profitable firms. Empirical studies typically find a negative relationship between profitability and leverage (Titman and Wessels, 1988; Rajan and Zingales, 1995; Fama and French, 2002; Frank and Goyal, 2007).

Debt Conservatism

Although trade-off theory predicts that the marginal tax benefit of debt should be equal to the marginal expected bankruptcy cost, the empirical evidence is mixed. Some researchers argue that the former is greater than the latter because direct bankruptcy costs are small and the level of debt is below optimal (Miller 1977; Graham 2000). Others find that indirect bankruptcy costs can total as much as 25 percent to 30 percent of assets value and are thus comparable with tax benefits of debt (Molina 2005; Almeida and Philippon 2007). Additionally, including personal taxation in the basic model can reduce the tax advantage of debt (Green and Hollifield 2003; Gordon and Lee 2007) because tax rates on the return from equity such as dividends or capital gain are often reduced.

Target Debt Level

Debt changes should be dictated by the difference between current level and the level of debt predicted by Equation 10.2. In the recent literature, the continuous process of adjusting capital structure toward the target ratio has been called "target reversion" or "mean reversion" (Shyam-Sunder and Myers 1999; Frank and Goyal 2003). The evidence usually confirms mean reversion (Fama and French 2002; Kayhan and Titman 2007). Different opinions exist about the speed of capital structure adjustments. Some researchers find that these adjustments are too slow (Fama and French 2002) while others contend that large adjustments are costly (Altinkilic and Hansen 2000). Deviations from the target can then be gradually removed over time (Leary and Roberts 2005). Conducting econometric research on mean reversion remains challenging. The major difficulty is that the target debt-to-equity ratio is unobservable. Chang and Dasgupta (2007) show, for example, that even purely random financing can lead to mean reversion in simulated data.

Including Agency Costs in the Basic Framework

Agency costs arise because managers do not necessarily act in the best interests of shareholders who also may not act in the best interests of creditors. Including agency costs in the basic model can help to explain some problems of trade-off theory discussed above such as debt conservatism. If an investment yields large returns, equity holders capture most of the gains. If, however, the investment fails, debt holders bear the consequences. As a result, equity holders may benefit from investing in highly risky projects, even if the projects are value decreasing. Jensen and Meckling (1976) call this the "asset substitution effect." Debt holders can correctly anticipate equity holders' future behavior. This leads to a decrease in the value of debt and reduces the incentive to issue debt. Myers (1977) observes that when firms are likely to go bankrupt in the near future, equity holders may have no incentive to contribute new capital to invest in value-increasing projects. Equity holders bear the entire cost of the investment, but the returns from the investment may be captured mainly by the debt holders ("debt overhang").

On the other hand, some agency theories favor higher debt. For example, Jensen (1986) argues that debt improves the discipline of an entrenched manager. The evidence confirms that firms use leverage as a disciplinary device for managers. For example, firms reduced their leverage after the Sarbanes–Oxley Act (2004) that required more reliable financial information and hence reduced the extent of agency problems (Bertus, Jahera, and Yost 2008). Jensen and Meckling (1976) contend that choosing debt instead of equity allows for the insiders' fraction of equity to remain high and thus improves their incentive to work in the interests of shareholders. Malmendier, Tate, and Yan (2005) and Hackbarth (2008) present behavioral models in which an overconfident manager chooses higher debt levels than does a rational manager. The overall effect of agency problems on debt level is difficult to quantify. Additionally, the general importance of the asset substitution problem is under debate (Parrino and Weisbach 1999). In their survey of chief financial officers (CFOs), Graham and Harvey (2001) find this problem unimportant.

The above analysis leads to the following conclusions. First, empirical evidence usually confirms that leverage is inversely related to the expected bankruptcy costs and that firms adjust their capital structures toward target ratios. Second, mixed evidence exists about the importance of tax factors for capital structure and the sensitivity of capital structure to tax changes. The evidence is also ambiguous about whether firms' leverage is too low and whether they move toward a target ratio quickly enough. Third, evidence showing a negative correlation between debt and profitability does not support trade-off theory.

Dynamic Extensions

Although the basic model ignores retained earnings and transaction costs, these factors are important in a dynamic setting. For example, profitable firms may prefer to retain earnings in order to reduce the cost of raising funds in the future. This may lead to lower leverage as compared to static theory. Consider a two-period model. The first-period earnings are R_1. The firm must determine the amount of dividends d and retained earnings $I = R_1 - d$. This decision determines the financing structure for the period 2 investment projects that cost $C - I + D$, where D denote debt. The projects generate earnings R_2. The firm faces costs zD when raising external funds. Investors are assumed to be risk-neutral and the risk-free interest rate equals 0. The shareholders' payoff V equals the sum of first- and second-period dividends $d + (R_2 - D - zD)(1 - T)$. This can be written as $d + (R_2 - (1 + z)(C - R_1 - d))(1 - T)$.

The derivative of V with respect to d is $1 - (1 + z)(1 - T)$. If z is sufficiently high, this derivative is negative and thus optimal $d = 0$.

Hence, a firm with high profit in period 1 should not distribute dividends and use retained earnings to finance investment in period 2. A firm with low profit that has insufficient funds to finance the project internally will use debt. This leads to a situation where low-profit firms have more debt than high-profit firms (negative correlation between debt and profitability). This also contributes to the debt conservatism discussion because high-profit firms have a debt level below that prescribed by Equation 10.2. By adding bankruptcy costs and equity financing in the model, the results do not change: High-profit firms do not use external financing although the debt-to-equity ratio for low-profit firms depends on the level of bankruptcy costs as compared to tax benefits.

Researchers have addressed similar ideas in several recent papers. Hennessy and Whited (2005) analyze a model with equity flotation costs and show that under some plausible values of parameters, a negative correlation between debt and profitability can be observed. Ju et al. (2005) provide estimates of optimal capital structures based on a calibrated contingent-claims model where long-term creditors can force bankruptcy if the firm's value is too low. The authors show that firms are not underlevered relative to the predictions of their model. Strebulaev (2007), who analyzes a model where firms in distress have to sell their assets at a discount, shows that the debt level is below that predicted by the static models. In Tserlukevich's (2008) model, investments are irreversible and "fixed investment cost" depends on the existing stock of capital. The model can replicate a negative relationship between leverage and profitability. Morellec (2004) analyzes a contingent claims model with manager-stockholder conflicts. The model can generate low debt ratios. Titman and Tsyplakov (2007) consider a model where the firm can maximize the equity value or the claim holders' value depending on whether contracts can be costlessly written. The model can explain slow adjustment toward the target debt level. Cook and Kieschnick (2009) argue that a dynamic model with boundedly rational managers can explain capital structure partial adjustments toward a target ratio.

Dynamic trade-off models are likely to provide an important contribution to trade-off theory. Empirical results and simulated results apparently dominate theoretical results. New theoretical results are expected.

PECKING ORDER THEORY

Myers and Majluf (1984) set forth pecking order theory. The key element of pecking order theory is asymmetric information between a firm's insiders and outsiders.

The Basic Model and Evidence

Information asymmetries exist in almost every facet of corporate finance and complicate managers' ability to maximize firm values. Managers of good-quality firms face the challenge of directly convincing investors about the true quality of their firm, especially if this concerns future performance. As a result, investors try to incorporate indirect evidence in their valuation of firm performance by analyzing information-revealing actions including capital structure choice.

Consider a firm that is raising funds for an investment project. The investment cost is C. There are two types of firms. For type g, the project brings cash flow θ_g and for type b it is θ_b, $\theta_g > \theta_b$. The fraction of type g firms is f. The initial capital structure is 100 percent equity with n shares outstanding. The firm's managers know the firm's type, which is publicly unavailable. The managers maximize the wealth of the initial shareholders. The firm has internal funds I, $I > C$. To finance the project, the firm may use internal funds or issue equity.

Pecking Order

If g decides to use internal funds, the shareholders' profit is

$$\theta_g - C + I \tag{10.3}$$

If, on the other hand, g were to issue equity, it would be mimicked by b because the value of shares issued by g will be greater than that of b. The shares of g will be mispriced. More specifically, investors will require a fraction of equity s such that $s(I + f\theta_g + (1 - f)\theta_b) = C$. This means that the profit of initial shareholders for g is

$$(1 - s)(I + \theta_g) = I + \theta_g - \frac{C(I + \theta_g)}{I + f\theta_g + (1 - f)\theta_b} \tag{10.4}$$

which is less than the amount determined by Equation 10.3 because $\theta_g > \theta_b$. Therefore g should use internal funds to finance the project. In this case b is indifferent between internal funds and equity. In either case the shareholders' payoff for type b is $\theta_b - C + I$.

Equity is dominated by internal funds in this model. Low-quality firms use equity as much as internal funds but high-quality firms prefer internal funds. Similarly debt dominates equity. Suppose that the firm can finance the project with risk-free debt. Then g can issue debt to avoid any mispricing. If debt issued by the firm is risky, the situation does not change appreciably. Debt suffers from misvaluation less than equity. The same holds if the firm has available assets-in-place. Hence a "pecking order" emerges: internal funds, debt, and equity (Myers and Majluf 1984).

The empirical evidence on pecking order theory is mixed. Shyam-Sunder and Myers (1999), Lemmon and Zender (2007), and a survey of New York Stock Exchange firms by Kamath (1997) find support for pecking order while Chirinko and Singha (2000) and Leary and Roberts (2010) do not. Frank and Goyal (2003) show that the greatest support for pecking order occurs among large firms.

Share Price Reaction to Equity Issue Announcements

After the market learns that the firm has a valuable investment project (but before the financing decision is made), the true value of g is $I + \theta_g - C$, and the true value of b is $I + \theta_b - C$. Thus the share price is $\frac{f(I + \theta_g - C) + (1 - f)(I + \theta_b - C)}{n}$. However after the issue is announced, the share price is $\frac{I + \theta_g - C}{n}$. The share price has decreased because investors have figured out that the issuer's type is b. The announcement of issuing stock drives down the stock price. Empirically, the announcements of equity issues result in significant negative stock price reactions (Masulis and Korwar 1986; Antweiler and Frank 2006).

Negative Correlation between Debt and Profitability

Good-quality firms tend to use internal funds for financing as much as possible. Because low-quality firms do not have as much profits and retained earnings as high-quality firms, they use external sources, usually debt, more frequently. This helps to explain the puzzle about the negative correlation between debt and profitability.

The Extent of Asymmetric Information and Pecking Order

Pecking order theory predicts that a higher extent of asymmetric information reduces the incentive to issue equity. For example, if in the basic model $\theta_g = \theta_b$, firms can issue equity without the risk of being misvalued. In this case, there is no negative reaction to equity issues announcements.

The evidence, however, is ambiguous. D'Mello and Ferris (2000) and Bharath, Pasquariello, and Wu (2008) support the prediction that pecking order theory is more likely to hold when the extent of asymmetric information is large. Choe, Masulis, and Nanda (1993) find that equity issues are more frequent when the economy is doing well and information asymmetry is low. Yet, Frank and Goyal (2003) find the greatest support for pecking order theory among large firms that are expected to face the least severe adverse selection problems because they receive better coverage by equity analysts.

The following summarizes the above analysis. The evidence supports predictions of the pecking order theory such as the negative correlation between debt and profitability, negative share price reaction on equity issue announcements, and better share price reaction on debt issues than on equity issues. The evidence is mixed about whether firms always follow a pecking order hierarchy and whether the extent of asymmetric information reduces the incentive to issue equity.

Extensions with Different Types of Asymmetric Information

A rich set of new predictions can arise when analyzing an environment with staged investments. In this setting, investors may have private information about both a firm's short-term and long-term earnings. Firms with positive information about short-term earnings may have negative information about long-term earnings and vice versa. Halov (2006) proposes a model that considers a firm without internal funds where the choice of security depends not only on the current adverse selection cost of security but also on the future information environment and future financing needs of the firm. Debt issues today make future security issues more sensitive to the degree of asymmetric information in the issuance period. Halov finds that future adverse selection costs negatively affect the debt component of new external financing and positively affect the cash reserves of the firm. He explains why companies may prefer equity to debt and provides an idea about why the incentive for issuing equity depends both on the extent of asymmetric information in the current period and in future periods.

Miglo (2009) considers a firm with a two-stage investment project. Asymmetric information exists about both the firm's quality and its growth potential. If the extent of asymmetric information is higher for quality than for growth, an equilibrium where high-quality firms issue equity does not exist that is consistent with pecking order theory. If the extent of asymmetric information regarding quality is small but is high for growth, a firm's behavior will differ from what pecking order theory predicts. These results can help to explain why firms in growing industries do not follow pecking order theory. These industries are characterized by a high degree of uncertainty about the rates of growth.

Information asymmetry may also exist about a firm's risk. Consider the basic model where investment projects are risky and firm types differ in the probability of a project's success and in the amount of profit generated in the case of success. There are two types of firms. For type g, the project brings cash flow g_h if successful and g_l otherwise. The probability of success is θ_g. The same parameters for type b are b_h, b_l and θ_b. Assume $g_h > b_h$ and no internal funds. To see why high-quality type firms can issue both debt and equity, consider two situations. First, suppose that $\theta_g = \theta_b$ (firms have the same risk and thus no asymmetric information exists about risk) and $g_l > b_l$. Halov and Heider (2006) show that the mispricing of equity issued by g (high-quality type) will be greater than that of debt. Thus, g would prefer debt to equity, which is consistent with pecking order theory. The second case is when $g_h\theta_g + g_l(1-\theta_g) = b_h\theta_b + b_l(1-\theta_b) = m$. Firms have the same average value so there is no asymmetric information about the firm's value. In this case, firms can issue equity that has the same value for each type and avoid mispricing. For both firm types, insiders require a fraction of equity s such that $sm = C$.

Halov and Heider (2006) predict that a firm should issue more equity and less debt if risk plays a larger role in the adverse selection problem of external financing. This helps to explain why large mature firms tend to issue debt and young small firms tend to issue equity. Outside investors presumably know less about the risk of an investment for a small, young, non–dividend-paying firm than for a large, mature, dividend-paying firm.

SIGNALING

In the pecking order model, good-quality firms have to use internal funds to avoid adverse selection problems and losing value. These firms cannot signal their quality by changing their capital structure. The following section discusses models in which capital structure serves as a signal of private information (Ross 1977).

Basic Model, Major Predictions, and Evidence

Consider a firm that is raising funds for an investment project. The investment cost is C. The project brings cash flow H if successful and 0 otherwise, $H > C$. There are two types of firms. For type g, the probability of success is 1 and for type b it is θ_b, $\theta_b < 1$. The fraction of high-quality firms is f. The initial capital structure is 100 percent equity with n shares outstanding. To finance the project, the firm can issue debt or equity. The firm's manager knows the firm's type, which is publicly unavailable. The manager's objective function is $aR - (1-a)K$. This means that the manager chooses the capital structure to maximize a weighted average of the shareholders payoff R net of a penalty K for bankruptcy. The higher a is, higher is the weight of shareholders' payoff in the manager's objective function. An example of penalty for bankruptcy is loss of reputation. If g were to issue equity, the firm would be mimicked by b. If the manager of b benefits from getting a higher price of shares without any risk of bankruptcy, the shares of g are undervalued. Now suppose that g signaled its type by issuing debt with a face value C. If b would issue debt, the expected value of manager's objective function is $a\theta_b(H - C) - (1 - a)(1 - \theta_b)K$. If b would issue equity, then the expected value is $a(\theta_b H - C)$. The manager issues equity if $a(\theta_b H - C) > a\theta_b(H - C) - (1 - a)(1 - \theta_b)K$. This can be simplified to:

$$(1 - a)K > aC. \tag{10.5}$$

This means that if the bankruptcy penalty is high enough and if the manager is sufficiently "bankruptcy-averse" (a is sufficiently low), a signaling equilibrium is possible where g issues debt and b issues equity.

Share Price Reaction and Securities Issues

After the market learns that the firm has a valuable investment project (in cases when signaling equilibrium exists), the true value of g is $H - C$ and the true value of b is $\theta_b H - C$. Thus the share price is $\frac{fH+(1-f)\theta_b H-C}{n}$. However, after the debt issue is announced, the share price is $\frac{H-C}{n}$. The share price has increased because investors have figured out that the issuer type is g. Thus, the market reaction on debt issues (more generally, on leverage-increasing transactions such as issuing convertible debt, repurchasing shares, and debt for equity swaps) is positive. Similarly, the market reaction on equity issues (or leverage-decreasing transactions) is negative. Leland and Pyle (1977) obtain the same results by using managerial risk aversion instead of a bankruptcy penalty.

A negative share price reaction on the announcement of equity issues is usually consistent with empirical evidence, as discussed in the previous section (similar for leverage-decreasing transactions). Evidence on the positive market reaction on leverage-increasing transactions (with the exception of debt issues) also supports signaling theory (Masulis 1980; Antweiler and Frank 2006; Baker, Powell, and Veit 2003). The evidence on the announcement of debt issues does not support signaling theories. Eckbo (1986) as well as Antweiler and Frank find insignificant changes in stock prices in response to straight corporate debt issues.

Firm Performance and Securities Issues

If a separating equilibrium exists, high-quality firms issue debt, and low-quality firms issue equity. The empirical prediction is that firm value (or profitability) and the debt-to-equity ratio is positively related. The evidence, however, is ambiguous. Most empirical studies report a negative relationship between leverage and profitability as discussed earlier. In a similar spirit, some studies document the superior absolute performance of equity-issuing firms before and immediately after the issue (Jain and Kini 1994; Loughran and Ritter 1997). Several studies examine long-term firm performance following capital structure changes. Shah (1994) reports that business risk falls after leverage-increasing exchange offers but rises after leverage-decreasing exchange offers. Jain and Kini (1994), Mikkelson, Partch, and Shah (1997), and Loughran and Ritter (1997) document the long-run operating underperformance of equity-issuing firms compared to non-issuing firms.

The above analysis leads to the following conclusions. First, the empirical evidence supports such predictions of signaling theory as a negative market reaction on leverage-decreasing transactions and a positive reaction on leverage-increasing transactions (excluding debt issues). Second, the evidence does not support a positive market reaction to debt issues. The negative correlation between debt and profitability also contradicts signaling theory. Third, the evidence is mixed regarding the predictions of signaling theory about firms' operating performance after issuing equity. Long-term underperformance of firms issuing equity compared to non-issuing firms supports the theory while better operating performance of firms issuing equity shortly after the issue compared to non-issuing firms does not support the theory.

Many explanations exist as to why managers of high-quality firms may use leverage-decreasing transactions as a signal. These explanations include issuing equity to signal low variance of earnings (Brick, Frierman, and Kim 1998), retiring existing debt to signal earnings quality (Brennan and Kraus 1987), and signaling based on a model that combines asymmetric information with agency problems (Noe and Rebello 1996). A challenge for researchers today is to find a model that can explain several major empirical phenomena simultaneously. Two possible directions for future research involve dynamic extensions of signaling models and security design models.

Dynamic Extensions of Signaling Models

Dynamic models such as Miglo (2007, 2009) allow for focusing on a firm's performance profile over time and its effect on leverage. Consider a firm that invests in a project that costs C in each of two periods, $t = 1, 2$. In each period the project may be successful or unsuccessful. A firm's insiders have private information about the probability of success in each stage. The firms are of two types, type g and type b, with respective probabilities of success θ_{gt} and θ_{bt} in stage t.

Suppose g issues equity for each stage of investments and distributes period earnings as dividends. In stage 2, investors require a fraction of equity s_2 such that: $s_2\theta_{g2} = C$. In stage 1, investors require a fraction of equity s_1 such that: $s_1\theta_{g1} + s_1(1 - s_2)\theta_{g2} = C$. Now consider the payoff of shareholders of b in case b decides to mimic g. This equals $(1 - s_1)\theta_{b1} + (1 - s_1)(1 - s_2)\theta_{b2}$. If a signaling equilibrium exists, the shareholders' payoff for type b is $\theta_{b1} + \theta_{b2} - 2C$ (the true value of b). Thus, a separating equilibrium exists if $(1 - s_1)\theta_{b1} + (1 - s_1)(1 - s_2)\theta_{b2} < \theta_{b1} + \theta_{b2} - 2C$. This can be simplified to:

$$\frac{\theta_{g1} + \theta_{g2} - 2C}{\theta_{b1} + \theta_{b2} - 2C} < \frac{\theta_{g1} + \theta_{g2} - C}{\theta_{b1} + \theta_{b2}(1 - C/\theta_{g2})} \tag{10.6}$$

If the extent of asymmetric information regarding firms' total values is sufficiently small and if $\theta_{g1} > \theta_{b1}$and $\theta_{g2} < \theta_{b2}$, then Equation 10.6 holds. In an extreme case, for example, when $\theta_{g1} + \theta_{g2} - 2C = \theta_{b1} + \theta_{b2} - 2C$, Equation 10.6 becomes $\theta_{g2} < \theta_{b2}$. Here, the value of shares in period depends on the firm's total value and not on the firm's performance in a particular period, while the value of shares in period 2 depends on period 2's performance. The firm with low overall value can benefit from overvaluation in period 1 but can have a loss from period 2 undervaluation. When asymmetric information about a firm's overall value is relatively small and information about the timing of earnings is high, the latter effect can dominate.

The separating equilibrium described above implies that firms issuing equity have better operating performance at the moment of issue or soon after the issue. These firms also have lower operating performance in the long run. Leverage is negatively correlated with profitability because firms with higher profits in the first period issue equity. Miglo (2007) also explains why firms with a low rate of earnings growth issue equity and firms with a high rate of earnings growth issue debt (Mohamed and Eldomiaty 2008; Chichti and Bougatef 2010).

Hennessy, Livdan, and Miranda (2010) develop a dynamic model of the firm under repeated hidden information. In equilibrium, firms signal positive information by substituting debt for equity, which explains the inverse relationship between leverage and net worth. Firms with negative private information are unlevered, which is consistent with debt conservatism.

Security Design, Informed Investors, and Information Production

Investors such as banks can sometimes obtain information on a firm's quality and produce analytical information. Fulghieri and Lukin (2001) show that good firms want to partition their securities so that some claims are informationally sensitive. If the cost of becoming informed is low and the degree of asymmetric information is high, firms may prefer a higher information-sensitive security to promote information production by "specialized" outside investors. This explains the negative correlation between debt and firm value because firms with low profitability do not need to issue equity, which is sensitive to a firm's value. Fulghieri and Lukin also predict that younger firms with good growth opportunities are more likely to be equity financed. These firms can be especially interested in information production by outside investors.

Inderst and Mueller (2006) analyze a model where outside investors are better informed than insiders. The firm finances safe projects that are likely to break even based on easily verifiable (hard) information with debt but finances risky projects that are less likely to break even based on hard information with equity. This explains why high-growth firms are financed with equity.

MARKET TIMING

The decision to issue equity depends on stock market performance (Lucas and McDonald 1990; Korajczyk, Lucas, and McDonald 1992). This idea did not become a major capital structure theory, called "market timing," until Baker and Wurgler (2002).

The Basic Model, Major Results, and Evidence

Consider a firm that raises equity for an investment project. The investment cost is C. The cash flow from the project equals M. There are two types of firms. Type g has assets in place that generate a cash flow I in addition to the cash flow from the project. The assets in place of type b do not generate any cash flow. The publicly available parameter M depends on the macroeconomic situation. The firm's type is its private information. The initial capital structure is 100 percent equity. Three situations are possible

1. $M < C$. In this case, neither firm issues equity nor undertakes the project. Both types of firms have negative net present value (NPV) projects.
2. $C \leq M < \frac{C+\sqrt{C^2+4I}}{2}$. In this case, b issues equity and invests in the project and g does not. Investors require fraction s of b's equity such that $sM = C$. If g mimics b and issues equity, then the shareholders' payoff is $(1 - s)(I + M)$. To sustain an equilibrium, this should be less than I. Equilibrium holds if

$$M < \frac{C + \sqrt{C^2 + 4I}}{2} \tag{10.7}$$

3. $M \geq \frac{C+\sqrt{C^2+4I}}{2}$. Both firm types issue equity and undertake the project in which g is undervalued and b is overvalued.

Equity Issues and the Business Cycle

The model predicts that when the economy is bad (M is low), firms do not issue equity. When the economy has average performance, some firms will issue equity. When the economy is booming (M is high), equity issues are large. Empirical work by Choe, Masulis, and Nanda (1993), Bayless and Chaplinsky (1996), and Baker and Wurgler (2002) suggests a positive relationship between equity issues and the business cycle.

Share Price and Equity Issue

When $C \leq M < \frac{C+\sqrt{C^2+4I}}{2}$, g has positive NPV projects but is undervalued if the firm decides to issue equity. If $M \geq \frac{C+\sqrt{C^2+4I}}{2}$, g is also undervalued but the undervaluation is less severe. In the latter case, b is overvalued. One interpretation is that overvalued firms always issue equity. Undervalued firms may wait until the cost of misvaluation is low enough to be outweighed by the benefits from new projects.

Empirical evidence supports the prediction that share price performance is important for equity issues decisions (Rajan and Zingales 1995; Kamath 1997; Graham and Harvey 2001; Baker and Wurgler 2002). Mixed evidence exists about whether investors overpay for shares. Some researchers maintain that investors tend to be overly optimistic during new issues, analyst forecasts are excessively high, and managers manipulate earnings before going public (Teoh, Welch, and Wong 1998; Baker and Wurgler 2002). Other researchers argue in favor of an efficient market version of the market timing argument (Hansen and Sarin 1998; Knill and Lee 2006). Still other researchers suggest that market timing is not based on good market performance as compared to a firm's predicted performance. Instead, it is based on the market performance before the issue, called "pseudo-market timing" (Schultz 2003; Butler, Grullon, and Weston 2005).

Ritter and Welch (2002) provide evidence that stock returns of companies issuing new shares underperform in the long run compared to that of non-issuing firms. This new-issue puzzle suggests that investors purchasing shares of initial public offerings or seasoned equity offerings are irrational because they have lower returns compared to investments in shares of non-issuing firms. Eckbo, Masulis, and Norli (2007) and Carter, Dark and Sapp (2009) note, however, that one needs to estimate the risk of those firms to provide a correct interpretation of long-term underperformance of newly issued stocks.

Stock Returns before Equity Issue

If the arrival of growth opportunities is independent of price history, then overvalued firms will experience average performance before the issue. Undervalued firms will have above-average performance as they wait for the price to improve before they issue equity. Thus, on average, positive abnormal returns precede equity issues. The evidence confirms this prediction (Korajczyk, Lucas, and McDonald 1990; Loughran and Ritter 1995).

Extent of Asymmetric Information and Equity Issues

In the basic model, the extent of asymmetric information can be measured by parameter I. A large I means that a sizeable difference exists between firm's types. As follows from Equation 10.7, the model suggests that high I makes equity issues less frequent because equilibrium is unlikely when both types of firms issue equity. This result has several interpretations. Because asymmetric information should be reduced after information release, this should be a good time to conduct equity issues. As time passes, managers receive new information, and the degree of asymmetry increases. Thus, the magnitude of the price decline associated with a stock issue announcement should be positively related to the time between the last information release and the issue. Korajczyk, Lucas, and McDonald (1991) find that equity issues tend to cluster early within a quarter, which is consistent with the release of quarterly earnings announcements, and that issues trail off near the end of the quarter. Also, few firms issue equity before releasing their annual report, and larger firms, which suffer less from asymmetric information, tend to issue equity later.

Chang, Dasgupta, and Hillary (2006) argue that information asymmetry affects a firm's incentives to time the market. They show that firms with low information asymmetries (those with greater analyst coverage) have lower incentives to time the market. Firms followed by fewer analysts tend to make infrequent but large issues of equity.

In summary, evidence generally supports the market timing theory. Evidence shows that managers wait before issuing equity until the stock market conditions get better. Also, stocks tend to have high returns before the issue of equity. Further, firms tend to window-dress or improve their performance before issuing securities. Mixed evidence exists about whether investors overpay for shares. Only a few theoretical models exist on market timing. As a result, authors sometimes have different views about the interpretation of market timing. To be comparable with trade-off theory or pecking order theory, market timing models should be able to explain a broader set of phenomena about capital structure than currently exists.

SUMMARY AND CONCLUSIONS

This section summarizes the analysis of major theories of capital structure presented above and provides concluding remarks. Empirical evidence usually confirms the main prediction of trade-off theory: Leverage should be inversely related to expected bankruptcy costs. The major weakness of trade-off theory is the negative correlation between debt and profitability. The only theory that provides a straight explanation for this phenomenon is pecking order theory. Pecking order theory also helps to explain negative share price reaction on equity issue announcements. Signaling theory is useful in explaining the negative market reaction to a broad range of leverage-decreasing transactions and the positive reaction for some leverage-increasing transactions. It also predicts the positive market reaction on debt issues which does not have empirical support. Evidence mostly supports market timing theory, in that managers wait until the market conditions get better before issuing securities. Evidence also shows that stocks tend to have high returns before new equity issues. Some recent papers address problems associated with trade-off theory such as debt conservatism and the low sensitivity of debt regarding tax changes. Recent research helps to explain why growing and risky firms issue equity based on an asymmetric information approach suggested by pecking order and signaling theories.

Several major conclusions emerge from the development of capital structure theory over the past 20 years. First, researchers have extensively tested trade-off and pecking order theories. Taken separately, these theories cannot explain certain important facts about capital structure. In the future, financial economists need to continue developing dynamic versions of each theory or to develop new models that incorporate both trade-off and pecking order ideas. Second, market timing theory emerged after the publication of Baker and Wurgler (2002) as a separate theory of capital structure. Compared to trade-off and pecking order theories, theoretical aspects of market timing theory are underdeveloped. Third, a popular line of inquiry has emerged based on surveys of managers about their capital structure decisions. For example, Graham and Harvey (2001) report a large gap between theory and practice. Fourth, signaling theory of capital structure lacks empirical support regarding some of its core predictions. However, several new theories have emerged that contradict the notion of signaling quality through debt issuance. More research may be required to create new models that can compete with trade-off and pecking order theories.

DISCUSSION QUESTIONS

1. Explain the long-term underperformance of firms issuing equity.
2. Explain the mean reversion of capital structure. What is the difficulty of conducting econometric research on mean reversion? What is the problem with taking a firm's historical average debt-to-equity ratio as its target debt-to-equity ratio?

3. Propose and discuss the potential capital structure–related impact of government response to the corporate scandals during 2000 and 2003 and the financial crisis during 2008 and 2009. Discuss the effect of more disclosure requirements by the Sarbanes–Oxley Act (2004).
4. Explain why Microsoft and some other large profitable firms in the software industry use practically zero debt in their capital structure. How should Microsoft's capital structure change if it expands globally?

REFERENCES

Almeida, Heitor, and Thomas Philippon. 2007. "The Risk-Adjusted Cost of Financial Distress." *Journal of Finance* 62:6, 2557–2586.

Altinkilic, Oya, and Robert Hansen. 2000. "Are There Economies of Scale in Underwriting Fees? Evidence of Rising External Financing Costs." *Review of Financial Studies* 13:1, 191–218.

Antweiler, Werner, and Murray Z. Frank. 2006. "Do U.S. Stock Markets Typically Overreact to Corporate News Stories?" Working Paper, University of British Columbia and University of Minnesota.

Baker Kent H., Gary E. Powell, and E. Theodore Veit. 2003. "Why Companies Use Open-Market Repurchases: A Managerial Perspective." *Quarterly Review of Economics and Finance* 43:3, 483–504.

Baker, Malcolm, and Jeffrey Wurgler. 2002. "Market Timing and Capital Structure." *Journal of Finance* 57:1, 1–32.

Barclay, Michael J., Erwan Morellec, and Clifford W. Smith Jr. 2006. "On the Debt Capacity of Growth Options." *Journal of Business* 79:1, 37–59.

Bayless, Mark, and Susan Chaplinsky. 1996. "Is There a Window of Opportunity for Seasoned Equity Issuance?" *Journal of Finance* 51:1, 253–278.

Bertus, Mark, John S. Jahera Jr., and Keven Yost. 2008. "Capital Structure, Corporate Governance, and the Effect of Sarbanes–Oxley." *Corporate Ownership and Control*. Forthcoming.

Bharath, Sreedhar, Paolo Pasquariello, and Guojun Wu. 2008. "Does Asymmetric Information Drive Capital Structure Decisions?" *Review of Financial Studies* 22:8, 3211–3243.

Brennan, Michael, and Alan Kraus. 1987. "Efficient Financing under Information Asymmetry." *Journal of Finance* 42:5, 1225–1243.

Brick, Ivan E., Michael Frierman, and Yu K. Kim. 1998. "Asymmetric Information Concerning the Variance of Cash Flows: The Capital Structure Choice." *International Economic Review* 39:3, 745–761.

Butler Alexander W., Gustavo Grullon, and James P. Weston. 2005. "Can Managers Forecast Aggregate Market Returns?" *Journal of Finance* 60:2, 963–986.

Carter, Richard B., Rick H. Dark, and Travis Sapp. 2009. "Characterizing the Risk of IPO Long-Run Returns: The Impact of Momentum, Liquidity, Skewness, and Investment." Available at http://papers.ssrn.com/sol3/papers.cfm?abstract_id=1463015.

Chang, Xin, and Sudipto Dasgupta. 2007. "Target Behavior and Financing: How Conclusive Is the Evidence?" *Journal of Finance* 64:4, 1767–1796.

Chang, Xin, Sudipto Dasgupta, and Gilles Hillary. 2006. "Analyst Coverage and Financing Decisions." *Journal of Finance* 61:6, 3009–3048.

Chichti, Jamel, and Khemaies Bougatef. 2010. "Equity Market Timing and Capital Structure: Evidence from Tunisia and France." Available at http://www.tn.refer.org/CEAFE/Papiers_CEAFE10/Fina_marche/Bougatef.pdf.

Chirinko, Robert, and Anuja Singha. 2000. "Testing Static Trade-off Against Pecking Order Models of Capital Structure: A Critical Comment." *Journal of Financial Economics* 58:3, 417–425.

Choe, Hyuk, Ronald Masulis, and Vicram Nanda. 1993. "Common Stock Offerings across the Business Cycle." *Journal of Empirical Finance* 1:1, 1–29.

Cook, Douglas, and Robert Kieschnick. 2009. "On the Evolution of Capital Structure." Working Paper, University of Alabama and University of Texas at Dallas.

D'Mello, Ranjan, and Stephen P. Ferris. 2000. "The Information Effects of Analyst Activity at the Announcement of New Equity Issues." *Financial Management* 29:1, 78–95.

Eckbo, B. Espen. 1986. "Valuation Effects of Corporate Debt Offerings." *Journal of Financial Economics* 15:1, 119–151.

Eckbo, B. Espen, Ronald Masulis, and Oyvind Norli. 2007. "Security Offerings." In B. Espen Eckbo (ed.), *Handbook of Corporate Finance: Empirical Corporate Finance*, vol. 1, 233–373. Amsterdam: Elsevier/North-Holland.

Fama, Eugene, and Kennett R. French. 2002. "Testing Trade-Off and Pecking Order Predictions about Dividends and Debt." *Review of Financial Studies* 15:1, 1–33.

Frank, Murray, and Vidhan Goyal. 2003. "Testing the Pecking Order Theory of Capital Structure." *Journal of Financial Economics* 67:2, 217–248.

Frank, Murray, and Vidhan Goyal. 2007. "Capital Structure Decisions: Which Factors Are Reliably Important?" Working Paper, University of Minnesota and Hong Kong University of Science and Technology.

Fulghieri, Paolo, and Dmitry Lukin. 2001. "Information Production, Dilution Costs, and Optimal Security Design."*Journal of Financial Economics* 61:1, 3–42.

Gordon, Roger, and Young Lee. 2007. "Interest Rates, Taxes and Corporate Financial Policies." *National Tax Journal* 60:1, 65–84.

Graham, John R. 1996. "Debt and the Marginal Tax Rate." *Journal of Financial Economics* 41:1, 41–73.

Graham, John R. 2000. "How Big Are the Tax Benefits of Debt?" *Journal of Finance* 55:5, 1901–1941.

Graham, John R., and Campbell R. Harvey. 2001. "The Theory and Practice of Corporate Finance: Evidence from the Field." *Journal of Financial Economics* 60:2, 187–243.

Green, Richard, and Burton Hollifield. 2003. "The Personal-Tax Advantages of Equity." *Journal of Financial Economics* 67:2, 175–216.

Hackbarth, Dirk. 2008. "Managerial Traits and Capital Structure Decisions." *Journal of Financial and Quantitative Analysis* 43:4, 843–881.

Halov, Nikolay. 2006. "Dynamics of Asymmetric Information and Capital Structure." Working Paper, New York University.

Halov, Nikolay, and Florian Heider. 2006. "Capital Structure, Risk and Asymmetric Information." Working Paper, New York University and European Central Bank.

Hansen, Robert S., and Atulya Sarin. 1998. "Are Analysts Over-Optimistic Around Seasoned Equity Offerings." Working Paper, Tulane University.

Harris, Milton, and Artur Raviv. 1991. "The Theory of Capital Structure." *Journal of Finance* 46:1, 297–356.

Hennessy, Christopher, Dmitry Livdan, and Bruno Miranda. 2010. "Repeated Signaling and Firm Dynamics Signal." *Review of Financial Studies* 23:5, 1981–2023.

Hennessy, Christopher A., and Tony A. Whited. 2005. "Debt Dynamics." *Journal of Finance* 60:3, 1129–1165.

Inderst, Roman, and Holger Mueller. 2006. "Informed Lending and Security Design." *Journal of Finance* 61:5, 2137–2162.

Jain, Bharat, and Omesh Kini. 1994. "The Post-Issue Operating Performance of IPO Firms." *Journal of Finance* 49:5, 1699–1726.

Jensen, Michael C. 1986. "Agency Costs of Free Cash Flow, Corporate Finance, and Takeovers." *American Economic Review* 76:2, 323–329.

Jensen, Michael C., and William H. Meckling. 1976. "Theory of the Firm: Managerial Behavior, Agency Costs and Ownership Structure." *Journal of Financial Economics* 3:4, 305–360.

Ju Nengjiu, Robert Parrino, Allen M. Poteshman, and Michael S. Weisbach. 2005. "Horses and Rabbits? Trade-Off Theory and Optimal Capital Structure." *Journal of Financial and Quantitative Analysis* 40:2, 259–281.

Kamath, Ravindra. 1997. "Long-Term Financing Decisions: Views and Practices of Financial Managers of NYSE Firms." *Financial Review* 32:2, 331–356.

Kayhan, Ayla, and Sheridan Titman. 2007. "Firms' Histories and Their Capital Structures." *Journal of Financial Economics* 83:1, 1–32.

Knill, April M., and Bong-Soo Lee, 2006. "Market Timing or Pseudo-Market Timing: An International Examination." Working Paper, Available at http://papers.ssrn.com/sol3/papers.cfm?abstract_id=908800.

Korajczyk, Robert A., Deborah Lucas, and Robert McDonald. 1990. "Understanding Stock Price Behavior around the Time of Equity Issues." In R. Glenn Hubbard (ed.), *Asymmetric Information, Corporate Finance, and Investment*, 257–278. Chicago: University of Chicago Press.

Korajczyk, Robert A., Deborah Lucas, and Robert McDonald. 1991. "The Effect of Information Releases on the Pricing and Timing of Equity Issues." *Review of Financial Studies* 4:4, 685–708.

Korajczyk, Robert A., Deborah Lucas, and Robert McDonald. 1992. "Equity Issues with Time-Varying Asymmetric Information." *Journal of Financial and Quantitative Analysis* 27:3, 397–417.

Kraus, Alan, and Robert H. Litzenberger. 1973. "A State-Preference Model of Optimal Financial Leverage." *Journal of Finance* 28:4, 911–922.

Leary, Mark T., and Michael R. Roberts. 2005. "Do Firms Rebalance Their Capital Structures?" *Journal of Finance* 60:6, 2575–2619.

Leary, Mark T., and Michael R. Roberts. 2010. "The Pecking Order, Debt Capacity, and Information Asymmetry." *Journal of Financial Economics* 95:3, 332–355.

Leland, Hayne E., and David H. Pyle. 1977. "Information Asymmetries, Financial Structure, and Financial Intermediation." *Journal of Finance* 32:2, 371–378.

Lemmon, Michael L., and Jaime F. Zender. 2008. "Debt Capacity and Tests of Capital Structure Theories." Working Paper, University of Utah and University of Colorado.

Loughran, Tim, and Jay R. Ritter. 1995. "The New Issues Puzzle." *Journal of Finance* 50:1, 23–51.

Loughran, Tim, and Jay R. Ritter. 1997. "The Operating Performance of Firms Conducting Seasoned Equity Offerings." *Journal of Finance* 52:5, 1823–1850.

Lucas, Deborah, and Robert McDonald. 1990. "Equity Issues and Stock Price Dynamics." *Journal of Finance* 45:4, 1019–1043.

Malmendier, Ulrike, Geoffrey A. Tate, and Jun Yan. 2005. "Corporate Financial Policies with Overconfident Managers." Working Paper, Stanford University and University of Pennsylvania.

Masulis, Ronald W. 1980. "The Effects of Capital Structure Change on Security Prices: A Study of Exchange Offers." *Journal of Financial Economics* 8:2, 139–177.

Masulis, Ronald, and Ashok Korwar. 1986. "Seasoned Equity Offerings: An Empirical Investigation." *Journal of Financial Economics* 15:1, 91–118.

Miglo, Anton. 2007. "Debt-Equity Choice as a Signal of Earnings Profile over Time." *Quarterly Review of Economics and Finance* 47:1, 69–93.

Miglo, Anton. 2009. "Multi-stage Investment, Long-Term Asymmetric Information and Pecking Order Revisited." Working Paper, University of Bridgeport and University of Guelph. Available at http://papers.ssrn.com/sol3/papers.cfm?abstract_id=1107240.

Mikkelson, Wayne H., M. Megan Partch, and Kshitij Shah. 1997. "Ownership and Operating Performance of Companies that Go Public." *Journal of Financial Economics* 44:2, 281–307.

Miller, Merton H. 1977. "Debt and Taxes." *Journal of Finance* 23:2, 261–275.

Modigliani, Franco, and Merton H. Miller. 1958. "The Cost of Capital, Corporate Finance and the Theory of Investment." *American Economic Review* 48:3, 261–297.
Mohamed, Ehab K. A., and Tarek I. Eldomiaty. 2008. "Is Debt Governance Structure Relevant to Firm Operating Performance in Egypt? A Dynamic Approach." *International Journal of Accounting and Finance* 1:2, 216–249.
Molina, Carlos A. 2005. "Are Firms Underleveraged? An Examination of the Effect of Leverage on Default Probabilities." *Journal of Finance* 60:3, 1427–1459.
Morellec, Erwan. 2004. "Can Managerial Discretion Explain Observed Leverage Ratios?" *Review of Financial Studies* 17:1, 257–294.
Myers, Stewart C. 1977. "Determinants of Corporate Borrowing." *Journal of Financial Economics* 5:2, 147–175.
Myers, Stewart C., and Nicolas S. Majluf. 1984. "Corporate Financing and Investment Decisions When Firms Have Information That Investors Do Not Have." *Journal of Financial Economics* 13:2, 187–221.
Noe, Thomas H., and Michael J. Rebello. 1996. "Asymmetric Information, Managerial Opportunism, Financing, and Payout Policies." *Journal of Finance* 51:2, 637–660.
Parrino, Robert, and Michael S. Weisbach. 1999. "Measuring Investment Distortions Arising from Stockholder-Bondholder Conflicts." *Journal of Financial Economics* 53:1, 3–42.
Rajan, Raghuram, and Luigi Zingales. 1995. "What Do We Know about Capital Structure? Some Evidence from International Data." *Journal of Finance* 50:5, 1421–1460.
Ritter, Jay R., and Ivo Welch. 2002. "A Review of IPO Activity, Pricing, and Allocations." *Journal of Finance* 57:4, 1795–1828.
Ross, Stephen A. 1977. "The Determination of Financial Structure: The Incentive Signaling Approach." *Bell Journal of Economics* 8:1, 23–40.
Sarbanes–Oxley Act. 2004. Available at http://www.gpo.gov/fdsys/pkg/PLAW-107publ204/pdf/PLAW-107publ204.pdf.
Schultz, Paul H. 2003. "Pseudo Market Timing and the Long-Run Performance of IPOs." *Journal of Finance* 58:2, 347–381.
Shah, Kshitij. 1994. "The Nature of Information Conveyed by Pure Capital Structure Changes." *Journal of Financial Economics* 36:2, 89–126.
Shyam-Sunder, Lakshmi, and Stewart C. Myers. 1999. "Testing Static Tradeoff against Pecking Order Models of Capital Structure." *Journal of Financial Economics* 51:2, 219–244.
Strebulaev, Ilya A. 2007. "Do Tests of Capital Structure Theory Mean What They Say?" *Journal of Finance* 62:4, 1747–1787.
Teoh, Siew H., Ivo Welch, and T. J. Wong. 1998. "Earnings Management and the Underperformance of Seasoned Equity Offerings." *Journal of Financial Economics* 50:1, 63–99.
Titman, Sheridan, and Sergey Tsyplakov. 2007. "A Dynamic Model of Optimal Capital Structure." *Review of Finance* 11:3, 401–451.
Titman, Sheridan, and Roberto Wessels. 1988. "The Determinants of Capital Structure Choice." *Journal of Finance* 43:1, 1–21.
Tserlukevich, Yuri. 2008. "Can Real Options Explain Financing Behavior?" *Journal of Financial Economics* 89:2, 232–252.
Wright, Stephen H. 2004. "Measures of Stock Market Value and Returns for the US Nonfinancial Corporate Sector, 1900–2002." *Review of Income and Wealth* 50:4, 561–584.

ABOUT THE AUTHOR

Anton Miglo is an Associate Professor of economics and finance at the School of Business, University of Bridgeport. Previously, he was an assistant professor in the department of economics at the University of Guelph. Professor Miglo has authored 15 academic publications, two book chapters, and numerous conference proceedings. His recent publications appear in the *Quarterly Review of Economics and Finance*, *Journal of Economics and Business*, *Manchester School*, and *Journal of Economics*. Professor Miglo's areas of expertise include corporate finance and the economics of contracts and information. He obtained his PhD with excellence in financial economics from the University of Quebec in Montreal. During his studies, he was awarded a prestigous scholarship from the Canadian Council of Social Science Research.

CHAPTER 11

Estimating Capital Costs: Practical Implementation of Theory's Insights

ROBERT M. CONROY
J. Harvie Wilkinson, Jr. Professor, Darden Business School, University of Virginia

ROBERT S. HARRIS
C. Stewart Sheppard Professor, Darden Business School, University of Virginia

INTRODUCTION

Even for practical purposes theory generally turns out the most important thing in the end.
—Justice Oliver Wendell Holmes

General propositions do not decide concrete cases.
—Justice Oliver Wendell Holmes

Good decisions result from a blend of sound reasoning and good implementation. Finance theory provides a useful lens on a firm's decisions and their impact on financial market value. As is often the case, however, solid theoretical underpinning still leaves many unanswered questions for practitioners.

The first portion of this chapter reviews the basic notion of a weighted average cost of capital (WACC) and its uses. The discussion then turns to applying guidance from theory to estimating capital costs. Such a project inevitably involves a combination of useful guidelines and professional judgment. To illustrate this blend, the chapter examines data available to outside analysts. Companies in the S&P 500 are examined to illustrate the implications of different choices in making estimates. For instance, what are implications of looking at company-specific data versus industry averages? This analysis informs conclusions about likely impacts of applying certain practices across a range of companies. Along the way, the chapter draws on recommendations from finance scholars, best practice revealed in surveys, and experience in the field. The chapter ends by providing conclusions and suggestions for practice. The chapter stresses that best practice requires professional judgment even when using the best of general procedures.

THE WEIGHTED AVERAGE COST OF CAPITAL

This section investigates the basic idea underlying WACC and examines its major components. It also illustrates the calculation of WACC.

The Basic Idea

The concept and theory of the WACC is straightforward. It is a means for managers to capture investor perspectives and use them to shape a firm's decisions. Most firms use a mix of funding sources, primarily common equity and various forms of debt. As a consequence, thinking of an average cost of these sources is useful. The firm's overall WACC is thus the cost of raising funds, given the financing mix the firm has chosen. Further, this cost to the firm is importantly the rate of return investors require to supply that pool of funds to the firm. As a result, WACC can be used to benchmark financial performance. A firm creates value for investors only if its earned returns can exceed investors' requirements.

The WACC benchmark return shows up in two primary settings: (1) valuing investment opportunities or companies using discounted cash flow (DCF) techniques and (2) estimating capital charges for performance measures such as economic profit. In these applications, a critical concept is that a firm's existing WACC only measures the rate of return investors require from a company, given the firm's existing business risk and financial strategy. If the firm were to move into more risky ventures, then its current WACC would reflect neither the investors' reaction to the increased risk nor the appropriate benchmark for existing investments (e.g., a project or division) if that investment's use of funds did not fit the firm's average risk profile. A better risk-adjusted benchmark would be the WACC for another company, which is primarily in the riskier (safer) line of operations.

In addition to its common sense appeal, a great virtue of the WACC framework is that it fits the realities of decentralized decision making in companies. Often capital is allocated from a corporate pool as investment proposals compete for funding. Since WACC incorporates all financing in the discount rate, DCF evaluation of investments using WACC calls for cash flow estimates that are free of financing (free cash flows). The framework thus focuses managers on an investment's business case as reflected in free cash flows available to all suppliers of capital. This organizational separation can take advantage of the relative expertise of different individuals in the company (e.g., treasury specialists in estimating WACC and operational managers in evaluating the business case) and focuses decisions on business issues rather than financing details. After all, a typical firm's primary engine for value creation is expertise in particular business settings, not in fine-tuning cost of capital estimates. Not surprisingly, surveys of corporate managers such as Burns and Walker (2009) reveal widespread application of the WACC framework.

The WACC's useful "separation" of financing and investment cash flows can be relaxed in settings such as real estate investments, private equity, and project finance, where investment-specific financing can be an important source of value creation and may not be well approximated by an average mix of funds. Those refinements are, however, beyond the scope of the current discussion.

Components of the Weighted Average Cost of Capital

Equation 11.1 shows the simplest portrayal of WACC, which is common to financial texts. Here WACC is calculated as the after-tax weighted average of the required returns (costs) on equity (K_e) and debt (K_d), where the weights are the proportion of financing done by equity (W_e) and debt (W_d), and T is the corporate tax rate.

$$\text{WACC} = W_e K_e + W_d K_d (1 - T) \tag{11.1}$$

The cost of debt is adjusted to its after-tax equivalent to reflect the corporate tax deductibility of interest payments. Financing weights add to 1.0 since the entire firm is financed from either debt or equity sources. These are long-term weights reflecting the firm's plans going forward. Accounts payable, accruals, and other short-term liabilities arising in the natural course of doing business are not included as part of capital for WACC calculations. These liabilities normally pay no interest and, rather than being included in the discount rate, are captured in free cash flows as part of the firm's operating model. In essence, "capital" funds are assets minus these short-term items. On the other hand, short-term interest-bearing debt would be part of the debt weight in Equation 11.1 when the firm considers such short-term funding as a permanent part of financing. In assessing the "long-term" cost of short-term debt, however, one cannot simply use the current short-term interest rate, which is in effect for only a short period. A more typical assessment is that continually rolling over short-term debt (or having a floating interest rate) will expose the firm to long-term costs similar to those of long-term debt. This leads to applying the cost of long-term debt to all debt financing.

Since essentially all the major estimation issues occur even in the simple formulation shown in Equation 11.1, this equation is used to frame discussion. A straightforward extension is to include additional funding components such as different seniorities of debt or preferred stock.

To illustrate a calculation of WACC, consider FMG Inc., a hypothetical company that has a financing mix of 0.73 equity and 0.27 debt at a time when its costs of debt and equity are 5.60 percent and 11 percent, respectively. The chapter will later discuss how to estimate all of these values. Assuming that the corporate marginal tax rate is 35 percent, each dollar of interest generates a tax savings, or interest tax shield, of $0.35. The after-tax cost of debt is calculated simply by multiplying K_d times $(1 - T)$, where T is the tax rate. In this case, this after-tax cost of debt would be $5.60\% \times (1 - 0.35) = 3.64\%$. Substituting all these values in Equation 11.1 shows a WACC around 8.5 percent: $\text{WACC} = 0.73(11\%) + 0.27(5.60\%)(1 - 0.35) = 8.57\%$ or approximately 8.50%.

If all of the assumptions were precisely correct, the calculated WACC of 8.57 percent would be the right financial benchmark for FMG's average risk profile investment. In practice, inevitable measurement errors in estimation dictate that a more thoughtful interpretation is that FMG's cost of capital is around 8.5 percent. Avoiding false precision is important.

GUIDELINES FOR ESTIMATION FROM FINANCE THEORY

Estimating WACC requires four choices: (1) choosing the cost of debt, (2) specifying the tax rate, (3) calculating financing weights, and (4) picking the cost of equity. How do practitioners proceed? Burns and Walker (2009) examine a large set of surveys looking at the capital budgeting process in U.S. corporations over the last quarter century. While their mandate is broader than choice of a hurdle rate, Burns and Walker report that the WACC is the dominant discount rate used by companies and shed light on how practitioners estimate its components. They report that firms use after-tax market costs of debt based on marginal tax rates, not average rates. Moreover, firms typically use market value or target weights, not book value weights. In tackling the more difficult task of estimating the cost of equity, the vast majority of firms (as much as 93 percent in one survey) use the capital asset pricing model (CAPM), which builds in direct forward-looking information from market interest rates as part of the calculations. The CAPM is discussed in more detail later.

The CAPM is also used in the utility sector; however, variants of the dividend growth model are the most commonly employed approach in regulatory cases (Cross 2008). Dividend growth models can incorporate forward-looking growth rates from analysts, but their use is typically limited to stable, lower-growth businesses such as utilities with a large number of comparable companies. Based on these observations about practice, there is much good news about the alignment of the practice of estimating capital costs and the underlying theory. Exhibit 11.1 captures guidelines flowing from theory.

Applying such conceptual guidelines need not involve complex mathematics, but markets and real data do not always cooperate to make things simple. Two practical and vital issues stand out. First, measurement error is a fact of life. Statistics indicate that appropriate averages provide better estimates than reliance on a single calculation. But finding comparable observations to average is often a challenge. Trade-offs between the quantity and comparability of data used invariably involve professional judgments. Second, capital costs change over time. Not surprisingly, investors can and do change their views on a company and on markets. Ultimately, estimating capital costs is a craft informed by theory with substantial judgment required. Exhibit 11.2 offers guidelines to improve that craft.

The Thorny Issue of Estimating the Cost of Equity

Since the cost of equity is the most difficult item to estimate for WACC, it demands special attention. The heart of the problem is that, unlike yields to maturity in the bond market, prices in equity markets do not directly reveal a good proxy for shareholder return requirements. As a consequence, resorting to theory leaves significant implementation questions unanswered. The most commonly used theory is the CAPM, which posits that the required return on any stock, K_e, is the sum of a risk-free rate and a stock's risk premium as shown in Equation 11.2.

$$K_e = R_f + \beta(R_m - R_f) \text{ or } R_f + \beta(\text{MRP}) \tag{11.2}$$

Exhibit 11.1 Estimating Components of the Weighted Average Cost of Capital

Component	Guidance from Theory	Suggestion for Implementation
Cost of debt (pretax), K_d	Forward-looking market rate based on risk	Use the long-term rate for all interest costs to reflect the long-term horizon Yield to maturity on traded debt of company or similar risk debt (e.g., same bond rating)
Tax rate, T	Forward-looking rate capturing tax benefits of debt financing	Use a forward-looking marginal rate based on company circumstances
Weights of equity and debt, W_e, W_d	Market value, which is also the target ratio for future	Use all interest-bearing debt Forward-looking weights based on market value targets Separate categories only for significant forward-looking sources
Cost of equity, K_e	Forward-looking market rate based on risk	Incorporate data from comparable companies Use models such as the Capital Asset Pricing Model Use tests of reasonableness by comparing to interest rates

Note: This exhibit summarizes guidance for estimating the components of the weighted average cost of capital: WACC = $W_eK_e + W_dK_d(1 - \text{T})$.

Exhibit 11.2 Guidelines in Estimating Capital Costs

- **Match risks** from the use of capital to the right benchmark. A company's WACC fits the particular average risk profile for that company.
- **Use financial market data** to estimate required rates of return since they reflect opportunities available to investors.
- **Use forward-looking data** that reflect investor expectations since expectations (not history) drive financial markets.
- **Use risk-adjusted required returns** when appropriate since investors' required rates of return include a risk premium. This also means using debt and equity costs consistent with the financing weights. If the debt weight changes materially, both lenders and shareholders will change their view of risk and adjust their return requirements.
- **Pay attention to statistical issues.** For instance, appropriate averages provide better final estimates than reliance on a single calculation. Trade-offs between the quantity and comparability of data used invariably involve professional judgments.
- **Look for shifts in investors' views** of risk and required return, since these can change over time and will drive changes in capital costs.

R_f is the risk-free rate of return; R_m is the return on the market; β is beta, which measures the relative risk of the individual stock also called systematic risk; and MRP is the equity market risk premium. Equation 11.2 shows that the risk premium on an individual stock is just the stock's beta times the market risk premium. That MRP is itself the extra return that investors require to hold a broad market portfolio of risky securities ("the market") rather than the risk-free asset. In essence, beta just scales the stock's risk premium up or down depending on whether the stock is above ($\beta > 1$), below ($\beta < 1$), or of average ($\beta = 1$) risk.

To illustrate, suppose FMG's stock has an estimated beta of 1.10, the market risk premium is 6 percent, and the risk-free rate is 4.4 percent. Using Equation 11.2, FMG's cost of equity is as follows:

$$\begin{aligned} K_e &= 4.4\% + (1.1)(6\%) \\ &= 4.4\% + 6.6\% = 11\% \end{aligned}$$

Note that the CAPM adds a risk premium of 6.6 percent to calculate FMG's cost of equity. This risk premium is higher than the market risk premium of 6 percent because FMG is riskier than the average stock in the market (i.e., $\beta > 1$).

Proxy for a Risk-Free Rate

Since most applications of WACC focus on longer-term decisions, analysts typically use the yield to maturity on long-term U.S. government bonds as a proxy for R_f. While U.S. government bonds are not risk-free, they are perhaps the least risky of long-term investments. Using government bond yields has the benefit of incorporating investors' expectations (as revealed in the bond market) about macroeconomic conditions such as inflation. Bruner et al. (1998) find that maturities of 10 or more years are best practice choices. For the purpose of estimates in this chapter, the yield to maturity on a 20-year U.S. Treasury bond is used, which was 4.4 percent at the time market data were gathered. In some applications with very long planning horizons (e.g., electric utilities), analysts often use 30-year maturities.

Estimating the Market Risk Premium

While the CAPM calls for a forward-looking market risk premium, recommendations on its level vary significantly. One source of advice is the academy. In a survey of hundreds of professors, Fernandez (2009a) finds 6.3 percent as the average market premium in the United States that professors recommended in 2008. Behind that average is a wide array of opinion. Fernandez (2008) reviews 100 textbooks and finds the recommended market premium ranges from 3 percent to 10 percent with an average of 6.6 percent.

Looking at an array of practitioner advice on the market risk premium also yields substantial variation. For instance, Pratt and Grabowski (2008) conclude that as of the beginning of 2007 a reasonable estimate of the normal (unconditional) market premium is in the range of 3.5 percent to 6.0 percent. Rosenbaum and Pearl (2009) suggest a market risk premium of 7.1 percent but also note estimates from Wall Street practitioners that range from 4 percent to 8 percent. Writing for McKinsey & Company Inc., Koller, Goedhart, and Wessels (2005) suggest 4.5 percent to 5.5 percent. This evidence echoes results of prior surveys. For instance,

Bruner et al. (1998) report the following on the market risk premium: "We polled various investment banks and academic studies on the issue . . . and got anywhere between 2% and 8%, but most were between 6% and 7.4%." Initial estimates in this chapter assume a market risk premium of 6 percent, which fits average perceptions revealed in surveys and texts. Implications of different assumptions are discussed at the end of the chapter.

Estimating Beta

Beta should capture forward-looking risk as perceived by investors. In practice, however, its estimation relies heavily on past data. Guidance from financial texts is strong on conceptual foundation but gives relatively little attention to choices facing a practitioner. Most finance textbooks discuss estimating beta using regression analysis. To the extent that authors get into details, a common suggestion is to start with five years of data. The discussion is typically accompanied by cautionary notes such as the need to discard past data that are not representative of the future (e.g., in the case of a company that just made a major divestiture). Fernandez (2009b) offers perspective from a survey on how professors justify betas they use to calculate the cost of equity. Of the more than 1791 respondents using beta, 71 percent cite regressions, 50 percent note web sites and databases, and 22 percent mention textbooks or papers. But the academy finds no consensus on a specific method. Some texts suggest using industry betas given the statistical issues inherent in any single-company regression. Some promote using an average unlevered beta for the industry and then relevering to a firm's beta using the company's financial mix. Some advocate relying on published betas from financial advisors. In general, texts point out that the analyst must use judgment and not rely blindly on past data.

Practitioner-driven books such Koller, Goedhart, and Wessels (2005) from McKinsey & Company Inc. and Pratt and Grabowski (2008) provide more concrete guidance and reveal part of the craft in estimating beta. For example, Koller et al.'s (pp. 307–308) advice includes these particulars:

- "Raw regressions should use at least 60 data points (e.g., five years of monthly returns). Rolling betas should be graphed to examine any systematic changes in a stock's risk."
- "Raw regressions should be based on monthly returns. Using shorter return periods, such as daily and weekly returns, leads to systematic biases."
- "Company stock returns should be regressed against a value-weighted, well diversified portfolio, such as the SP500 or MSCI World Index."

They also note that betas can be improved by using industry averages or versions of beta smoothing that mollify the impact of measurement errors. Pratt and Grabowski discuss similar issues and also note that betas may be affected by firm size, which is an important issue for smaller firms.

As a practical matter, choosing a beta is part art and part science. The next section examines the extent to which the different approaches provide different results.

APPROACH AND DATA

This section provides evidence on how much estimates differ by applying alternative, commonly recommended approaches to cost of capital estimation across a large set of firms. This large-scale application sacrifices the additional layer of professional judgment that would be applied if the focus were on a handful of companies. On the other hand, it provides evidence to inform analysts' choices about method. In practice, even the best methods do not obviate the need for careful attention to the particulars. Koller, Goedhart, and Wessels (2005) and Pratt and Grabowski (2008) provide useful details on specific applications.

Studying S&P 500 firms permits addressing two sets of questions. The first set speaks to the relative values of estimates: How large are differences in cost of capital estimates when firm-specific versus industry average data are used? Do the results differ depending on whether historic or Value Line betas are employed? The intent is to gauge the impact of methods that deal with the trade-off between measurement error and comparability of data. Choices on these methods affect the analyst's assessment of the relative capital costs among firms. The second set of questions focuses on assumptions about the market risk premium. If the CAPM is applied, that figure is the same for all firms; therefore, no amount of averaging across companies will reduce its impact. How large are differences in cost of capital estimates? How do the magnitudes compare to differences among firms?

Starting with all firms in the S&P 500, firms in the financial sector are eliminated as their business models are not well suited to the WACC framework, which separates financing from the business cash flows. Theory calls for incorporating the most recent information available to investors. In practice, there are inevitable compromises on the timing of data available. For instance, audited annual financial statements appear but once a year. Since the objective is to analyze all industrial firms in the S&P 500, this chapter uses large research data sets that are updated only periodically. The analysis uses financial statements, stock market prices, and betas as of the year-end 2008, the date of the most recent Chicago Research in Security Prices (CRSP) information. Each firm is assigned to an industry according to Value Line industry classifications. Yields to maturity for both government and corporate bonds come from January 2010 and bond ratings from June 2009. The calculations focus on the impacts of different methods over a large set of companies. When analysts look at specific companies, any past data (e.g., from an annual statement) should be checked to make sure that material changes have not occurred. Financial market data should be current as of the date of the analysis.

Following the guidelines in Exhibit 11.1, debt is defined as the sum of all interest-bearing debt, and its interest cost is based on the company's bond rating. Lacking ready access to debt market values, the market value of debt is approximated with its book value. Analysts often use this approximation because deviations of market and book values for debt are much less pronounced than in the case of equity. Extra effort to gather market values of debt is warranted in situations where a company's debt has been downgraded and/or the company is experiencing financial difficulty. Equity is measured at market value.

An additional judgment concerns the tax rate. The full marginal statutory U.S. corporate tax rate of 35 percent is used for current estimates. In practice, complexities of the tax laws such as tax-loss carry-forwards and carry-backs, investment tax credits, state taxes, and international tax treatments complicate the situation. For instance, if a company expects to use interest tax shields in the future via carry-forwards, the present value of those shields will fall short of the 35 percent from an immediate tax benefit. Koller, Goedhart, and Wessels (2005) from McKinsey & Company Inc. advocate using the full statutory rate for investment-grade companies but also discuss possible refinements. Graham and Mills (2008) estimate effective marginal tax rates and provide insights to sharpen the analysis. While most companies in their sample hit the statutory marginal rate, the average effective marginal tax rate is about 5 percent lower.

The cost of equity comes from the CAPM. Three methods are used to estimate beta:

- Historical betas are estimated from regressions using five years of monthly data and the S&P 500 as a market proxy. This regression standard does not incorporate any analyst judgment.
- Betas reported by Value Line, an oft-cited provider of financial data, explicitly adjust for known statistical issues. Quoting Value Line (2010), "The 'Beta coefficient' is derived from a regression analysis of the relationship between weekly percentage changes in the price of a stock and weekly percentage changes in the NYSE Index over a period of five years. In the case of shorter price histories, a smaller time period is used, but two years is the minimum. The Betas are adjusted for their long-term tendency to converge toward 1.00."
- Relevered betas incorporate an industry average measure of business risk (an unlevered beta), which is then adjusted upward (relevered) to reflect the financial risk created by the firm's financing mix. This process is discussed in more detail later.

As shown in Exhibit 11.3, historic beta estimates vary substantially depending on whether one proxies the market with an equally weighted or value-weighted index. For instance, the sample average historic beta is only 0.87 using an equally weighted index, well below figures that result from using a value weighted index.

Exhibit 11.3 Beta Estimates for Sample Companies Using Different Stock Indices and Using Value Line. Indices used are the CRSP Equally Weighted Index (CRSP EW), CRSP Value Weighted Index (CRSP VW), and the S&P 500.

Betas	**5-Year Historic (Monthly Returns)**			**Value Line**
Index	**CRSP EW**	**CRSP VW**	**S&P 500**	
Total firms	412	412	412	412
Number of betas	411	411	411	403
Mean	0.87	1.10	1.17	1.04
Median	0.82	1.05	1.11	1.00
Standard deviation	0.43	0.51	0.52	0.28

Note: This exhibit displays betas that result from different estimation approaches applied to industrial firms in the S&P 500.

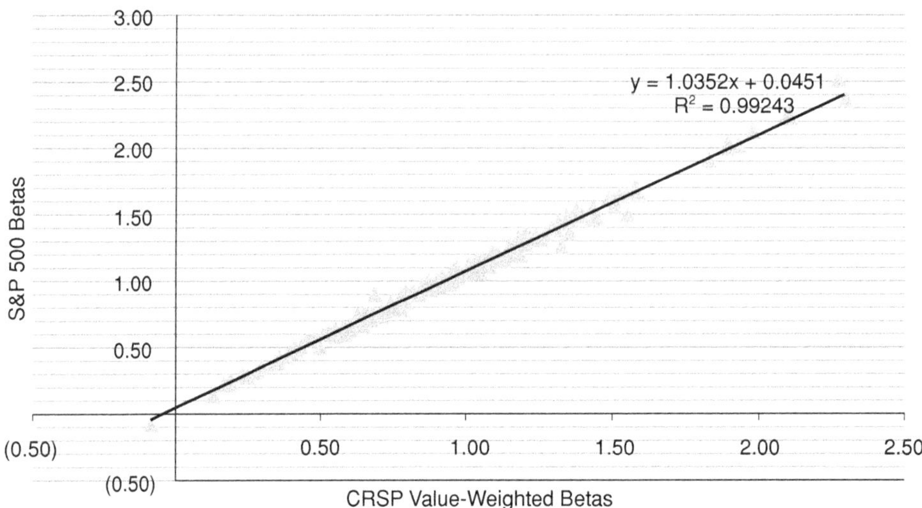

Exhibit 11.4 Plot of Historical Betas Using Two Different Value Weighted Market Indices
Note: This exhibit plots the relationship between two sets of beta estimates for S&P 500 companies using five years of historic data. Betas using the S&P 500 Index as a proxy for the market are plotted on the vertical axis. Betas using the CRSP Value Weighted Index as a proxy for the market are plotted on the horizontal axis. The exhibit also reports the results of regression analysis of the two sets of betas where y represents the vertical axis and x the horizontal axis.

On the other hand, as illustrated in Exhibit 11.4 both the value-weighted CRSP index and the S&P 500 (also value weighted) yield very similar beta estimates. These sample results illustrate the importance of choosing a value-weighted index (theory's suggestion) in estimating historic betas. The choice among broadly diversified value weighted indices is less critical. We adopt historic betas using the S&P 500 to estimate capital costs.

Historic betas do not, however, mirror those from Value Line. Exhibit 11.3 shows that Value Line betas have much less cross-sectional variation than the historic figures. This comes as no surprise given that historic estimates, unlike Value Line's approach, involve no input from analysts. Value Line's adjustments also appear informed by more than the type of simple smoothing done by Bloomberg, which uses the following formula: adjusted beta = historic beta (0.67) + 0.33. Exhibit 11.5 plots the distribution for historic, Value Line, and adjusted betas using Bloomberg's formula applied to the historic betas. Exhibit 11.5 conveys a key message for analysts: be wary of blindly using historic betas from individual company data. The tails of the distribution for historic betas contain significant measurement error. A clear advantage of Value Line betas (or those from other providers who do more than just historical regressions) is that they reflect professional judgment and attention to statistical detail. Moreover, they are data directly available to and used by investors. The objective is to capture investors' views of future risk. As various estimates of WACC are presented, the difference that the choice of beta makes, including using industry averages to reduce measurement error, is examined.

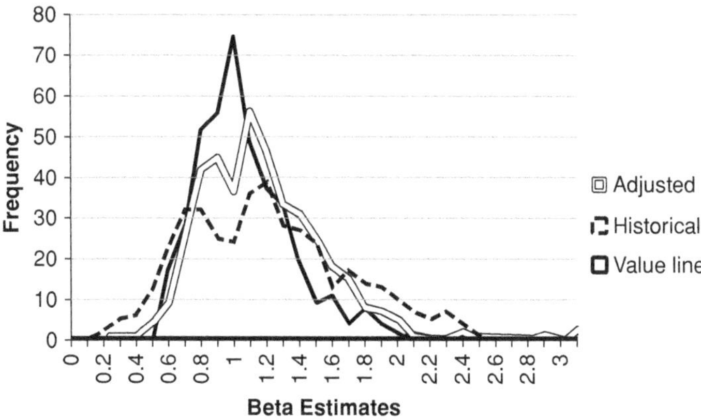

Exhibit 11.5 Frequency Distribution of Value Line, Historic, and Adjusted Historic Betas
Note: The exhibit plots the frequency of betas across the sample firms using different estimation methods. Historical betas use five years of data with the S&P 500 index as a proxy for the market. Adjusted betas are historical betas converted using the Bloomberg adjustment discussed in the text. Value Line betas come from Value Line.

THREE APPROACHES TO USING DATA FROM COMPARABLE FIRMS

Recognizing that measurement error is a fact of life, good practice in cost of capital estimation calls for gathering data on comparable firms. A recommended approach is to match firm on business risk and to look at capital structure and size. An in-depth treatment would arm the analyst with details of each company's businesses. This chapter uses all firms in an industry. The analysis focuses on three methods of estimating a company's WACC, two of which take advantage of data from other firms comparable in risk to the company.

"Single" Company Estimates of WACC

An initial step is to calculate a "single company" WACC based solely on data for the company. This may be the analyst's only resort if no good comparables can be found. As always, the most difficult ingredient to estimate is the cost of equity even if adopting the CAPM. Using Equations 11.1 and 11.2, a single company WACC is estimated for each firm in the sample. As a point of reference, the calculations for FMG earlier in the chapter roughly parallel the average characteristics of the sample firms. For instance, the average debt weight across companies was 0.27.

Industry Average WACC

Many analysts stop with a standalone calculation, but this is not advisable. Much can be learned from the other companies. One straightforward step is to calculate a single company WACC for each firm and then average across the industry. This average helps mollify the impacts of measurement error. Moreover, it is an especially useful benchmark for a business that is not publicly traded, such as a division of a larger company or a privately-held firm operating in this industry.

WACC Using Relevered Betas

Another way to take advantage of data from comparable firms is to separate the business and financial risk that affect a company's beta. First, the analyst uses appropriate theory to unlever the betas of a set of comparable firms. This creates measures of pure business risk: the unlevered betas. Next, the analyst averages the unlevered betas to reduce measurement error in any individual company estimate. Finally, the analyst reverses the same theory to transform the average unlevered beta into a beta for the company's stock (a relevered beta) that fits the firm's own mix of debt and equity. This relevered beta thus reflects both the business and financial risks facing the firm's shareholders. The logic of this approach is compelling and seems to capture the best of both worlds: statistical advantages of averages and controls for the impacts of debt equity mix on shareholder risks. Later some of the limitations of this method are discussed. Koller et al. (2005) advocate the unlevering formula shown in Equation 11.3.

$$\beta_u = \beta_{lev}/(1 + D/E) \tag{11.3}$$

Once beta is relevered, the analyst can calculate an individual company's cost of equity and its WACC.

DIFFERENCES IN COST OF CAPITAL ESTIMATES APPLYING ALTERNATE APPROACHES

The first challenge for an analyst lies in finding comparable firms. Of the sample firms, 73 percent are classified in industries with five or more companies in the sample. In these cases the good news is a reasonable start for finding comparable firms. But not all firms in an industry will be good business matches once the analyst looks more closely. For some industries, the analyst will have the luxury of a double-digit list to winnow, but only 31 percent of firms are classified in industries with 10 or more companies. At the other end of the spectrum, 11 percent of the companies had one or no other firms in the industry. Of course, the list of comparable firms can be expanded by going outside the S&P 500. As analysts broaden the search for comparables, however, they need to pay closer attention to issues related to firm size discussed later in the chapter. What about differences in estimates using alternate methods?

To compare methods, the difference between a firm's single company WACC and the average WACC for its industry is calculated. In parallel fashion, the difference between a firm's WACC using a relevered beta and the industry average WACC is calculated. Results are reported using both Value Line and historic betas. The mean absolute value of these differences indicates the typical size of the spread between estimates.

The intent is to show the magnitudes of judgmental trade-offs facing an analyst. Given concerns about measurement error in any single company WACC estimate, a simple standard is to resort to an industry average. That estimate requires adopting no theory about how betas should be relevered yet still takes advantage of statistical benefits of averaging. Another approach to taking advantage of averaging is to shoot for an estimate individualized to a company using relevered betas, but that requires assuming a particular theory of relevering. If all three approaches yield similar estimates in practice, the analyst's choice among the methods would make little difference.

Single Company versus Industry Average WACC

Exhibit 11.6 shows mean absolute deviations across each industry with at least seven companies. This section starts with results using Value Line betas. For the food processing industry, for instance, Exhibit 11.6 shows 52 basis points as the mean absolute deviation of single company WACCs from the industry average. This falls below the average figure of 82 basis points for all the industries displayed and is one of the lowest mean deviations for an industry. Some industries have mean absolute deviations well over 100 basis points. Thus, an analyst looking at companies in the food processing industry likely has an easier task than is the case in many other industries. The additional challenges call for the analyst to take a particularly close look at matching comparables. Being classified in the same industry does not necessarily ensure similar business risks.

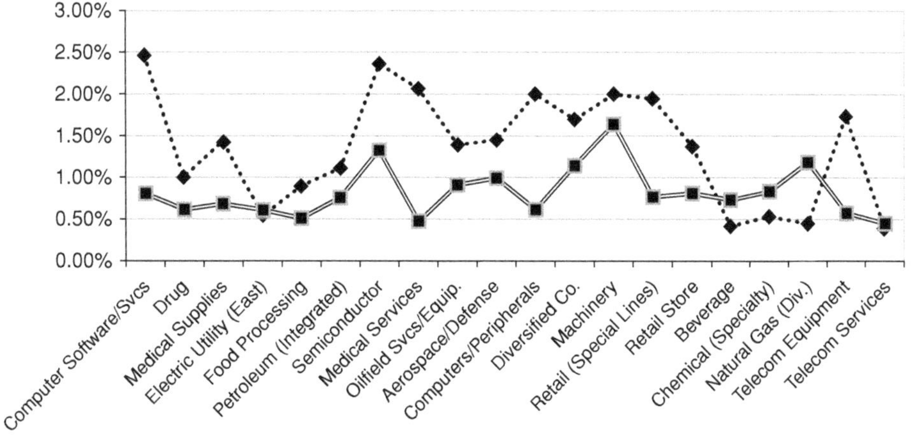

Exhibit 11.6 Mean Absolute Difference between Cost of Capital Estimates Using Single Company Estimates and the Industry Average Cost of Capital by Industry

Note: The exhibit plots the mean absolute difference for the industry between firm-level single company estimates of cost of capital and the industry average cost of capital. Industries displayed have seven or more firms.

Turning to results with historic betas, Exhibit 11.6 shows much a larger difference in the estimates. For all industries shown, the mean absolute deviation averages 136 basis points. In many industries the deviations are 150 basis points and higher. This echoes earlier concerns about use of historic betas in estimating a company's WACC. Single company historic betas contain too much measurement error to provide reliable cost of capital estimates. The wisdom of averages and using analyst judgment is critical. Value Line betas (or other adjusted betas) are recommended over historic betas in any standalone calculation.

WACC Using Relevered Betas versus Industry Average WACC

Exhibit 11.7 reveals that relevered betas create estimates that are typically quite close to the industry average. For many industries the mean absolute difference is almost zero, and the average deviation in Exhibit 11.7 is less than 25 basis points using either Value Line or historic beta estimates. These differences are a fraction of the numbers shown in Exhibit 11.6 when single company estimates are used. The reduction is especially notable using historic betas since the approach averages unlevered betas to mollify measurement errors in historic betas. The reduction for Value Line betas is less dramatic since these betas already benefit from some attention to measurement error.

One way to interpret Exhibit 11.7 is that relevering betas typically does not create an estimate very different from just using the industry average WACC. In part, this results from clustering of capital structures in an industry leading to

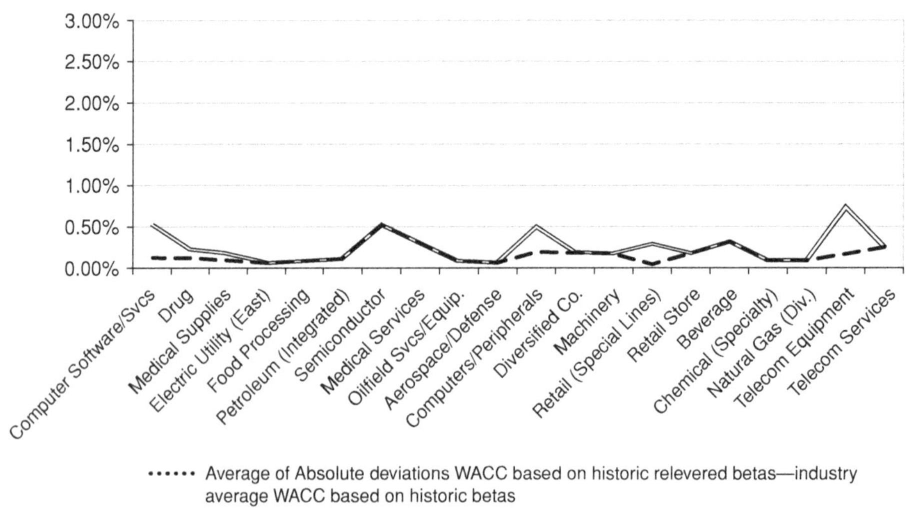

Exhibit 11.7 Mean Absolute Difference between Cost of Capital Estimates Using Relevered Betas and the Industry Average Cost of Capital by Industry

Note: The exhibit plots the mean absolute difference for the industry between the firm-level estimates of cost of capital using relevered betas and the industry average cost of capital. Industries displayed have seven or more firms.

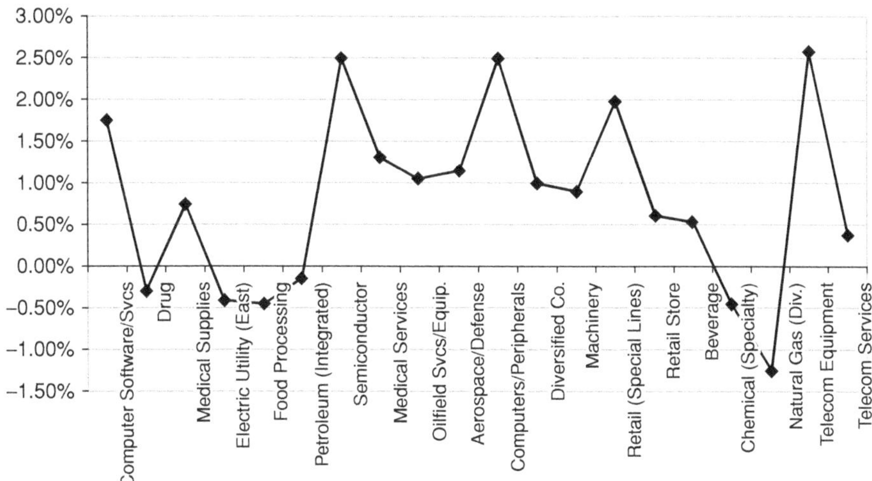

Exhibit 11.8 Differences in Level of Cost of Capital Estimates Depending on Choice of Betas by Industry

Note: This exhibit plots the difference between the industry average WACC using historic betas and the industry average WACC using Value Line betas. Industries displayed have seven or more firms.

little variation in relevered betas. On the other hand, there are instances in which the difference will be material. How much confidence the analysts puts into that difference will depend on the analyst's belief in the theory used in the relevering process. As discussed later, this is an area in which analysts could benefit from new research.

Differences in Levels of WACC Using Value Line and Historic Betas

While the differences in Exhibit 11.7 are similar whether using Value Line or historic betas, this does not mean that the level of the estimates will be the same. Remember that the source of beta estimates will also affect the industry average. While the average beta in the market should be equal to one no matter how measured, this need not be true by industry. Exhibit 11.8 compares the levels of industry average WACCs using Value Line and historic betas. Differences in these levels will not be eliminated by averaging unlevered betas and then relevering.

Exhibit 11.8 shows substantial differences in estimates at the industry level. In some industries the difference exceeds 2 percent. Exhibit 11.8 reinforces the importance of analyst judgment in selecting ways to estimate betas. Simply averaging historic betas to reduce measurement error does not mean that they will provide good estimates.

Summary of Differences in Cost of Capital Estimates

Overall, the results comparing alternate methods illustrate the constant tension faced by an analyst in making trade-offs between the statistical benefits of averaging and matching risks across firms. Using adjusted betas (such as those supplied by Value Line) and taking advantages of averages is critical for good practice. These methods help the analyst, but good estimates also require professional judgment that can only take place by close examination of the data at hand.

IMPACT OF ASSUMPTIONS ABOUT THE MARKET RISK PREMIUM

The results above are useful in understanding how to assess relative capital costs among firms. In that sense, they serve a vital role in understanding capital allocation and valuation. But what about the general level of capital costs? Recall that at any point in time all CAPM estimates embed an identical assumption about the market risk premium. The estimates so far in this chapter used a 6 percent equity market risk premium consistent with many text and survey recommendations. Many authors and respondents, however, often cite a market risk premium characterizing "normal" market conditions in the interests of conveying a durable conceptual framework. In practice, both intuition and research suggest that equity market risks and risk premiums change over time. As earlier discussion revealed, substantial disagreement exists on what to use as a market risk premium. To illustrate, consider the summary comments of a leading corporate finance textbook after careful review of much evidence. Brealey, Myers, and Allen (2008, p. 180) "have no official position on the issue, but we believe that a range of 5% to 8% is reasonable for the risk premium in the United States." Since average betas approximate 1 and the average financing mix for our sample firms is 0.73 equity, a 300 basis point increase in the market risk premium increases the sample average cost of equity by about 300 basis points and the weighted average cost of capital by just over 200 basis points (300(0.73) = 219).

Exhibit 11.9 illustrates the consequences in more detail by displaying two distributions of single company WACCs using Value Line betas. One distribution assumes a market risk premium of 5 percent, and the other adopts 8 percent. Using the 8 percent market risk premium, less than a fifth of the firms have cost of capital estimates below the median WACC estimate at a 5 percent market risk premium.

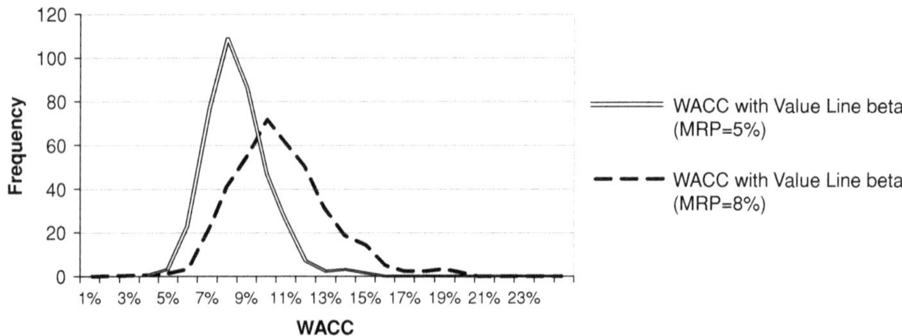

Exhibit 11.9 Distributions of Cost of Capital Estimates for Alternate Assumptions about the Equity Market Risk Premium (MRP)

Note: This exhibit plots the frequency of cost of capital estimates (WACC) for the sample firms based on assuming alternatively a 5 percent market risk premium and an 8 percent market risk premium.

These substantial differences in estimated capital costs are larger than those driven by the alternate methods covered earlier. One route for practitioners to gauge estimates of the market risk premium is to look at companies (such as utilities) where they can apply both the CAPM and variations of the dividend growth model. Such an approach can provide a reasonableness check on the market risk premium that might be used more broadly. Practice would benefit from future research to provide better ways to gauge the market risk premium.

AREAS FOR GUIDANCE FROM FUTURE RESEARCH

This section highlights three areas in which future research could provide important guidance to improve practice. A brief discussion of each area follows.

Capital Structure and Shareholder Required Returns and Risk

Since extra debt exposes shareholders to more risk, looking for ways to gauge capital structure's impact on the cost of equity is only natural. While using unlevered betas has its appeal, the method comes with baggage. First is the challenge that capital structure choices are not likely independent of business risk even within an industry. Such a pattern can clearly emerge within an industry if firms with higher business risk target a particular bond rating by using less debt. Some analysts steer clear of averaging unlevered betas across companies based on this concern. A second concern is the mechanics of unlevering. The formulas rely on theory that captures debt's tax advantages but does not deal well with some of the offsetting costs (such as financial distress). Moreover, disagreements exist on which version of the theory to apply. Equation 11.3 follows from the assumption that future interest tax shields carry the same risk as the firm's underlying business. This is consistent with future debt levels being targeted as a percent of the firm's market value, which is itself subject to risk. The illustrations in this chapter adopted Equation 11.3 because this assumption is likely closer to the truth than the leading alternative. The alternative approach assumes that interest tax shields are no more risky than the interest payments on current known debt and modifies Equation 11.3 by multiplying D/E by 1 minus the tax rate. Equation 11.3 also assumes the beta of debt is zero, which may be a reasonable approximation for investment-grade companies but would not fit highly levered situations. The specific formula used is especially important if one extrapolates to beta levels far from debt levels seen in an industry. Standard finance texts such as Ross, Westerfield, and Jaffee (2010) and Brealey, Myers, and Allen (2008) derive unlevering formulas, whereas Chaplinsky and Harris (1997) contrast different versions. Research to investigate these methods and suggest better ones for modeling capital structure effects would be a boon to practice.

Private Companies and Size Effects

Because this chapter deals with publicly-traded S&P 500 companies, the added challenges when a firm is small or investors have limited liquidity stay in the background. Private firms typically face both of these related issues. Using highly liquid public firms matched to a private firm's industry provide an important input for estimating a private firm's capital cost, but questions remain. Practitioners often make ad hoc upward adjustments for liquidity or firm size risk. Best practice would benefit from future research to help guide this process. Bowman and Bush (2006) and Pratt and Grabowski (2008) provide additional discussion of this issue.

Changes in Capital Costs over Time

Fortunately, incorporating interest rate changes in WACC calculations is straightforward since readily available data on market rates captures changes in the government debt market and in spreads between corporate and government debt. At the time of this writing, U.S. interest rates are low due to monetary policy addressing a recession, and these low rates are built into the estimates presented in the chapter.

Accounting for changes in equity market conditions over time is more difficult. Zenner et al. (2008.), who are part of a J.P. Morgan team, provide an informative look at estimating forward-looking market risk premiums using a number of methods. The results show substantial changes over time. As of May 2008, J. P. Morgan concludes that the premium is in the 5 to 7 percent range, consistent with the 6 percent figure used in this chapter. By early 2009, however, Connor, Zenner, and Janek (2009) of J. P. Morgan cite a market risk premium of 9 percent reflecting heightened uncertainty and market risk in the wake of fall 2008. As illustrated earlier, such differences in market risk premium assumptions have major effects on capital cost estimates. Damodaran (2009) and Koller, Goedhart, and Wessels (2005) discuss additional approaches to estimating forward-looking risk premium. Harris and Marston (2001) find that that the market risk premium tends to be higher in low interest rate environments and when bond credit spreads and stock market volatility are high.

The authors of this chapter conclude that the market risk premium does change over time. The low government rates and higher stock market volatility after fall 2008 point to a market risk premium at the time of this writing that is higher than historical norms. Readers can adapt the results presented to fit their view of the market risk premium. The hope is that future research in this area will provide more agreement on best practice to deal with changes in the market risk premium.

SUMMARY AND CONCLUSIONS

The WACC provides a useful lens to understand how investors assess a firm and many of its key decisions. As is often the case, however, solid theoretical underpinning still leaves many unanswered questions. This chapter addresses issues faced by a practitioner armed with sound conceptual advice but still left with a host of practical choices. Using data for publicly-traded firms, the chapter focuses on how ways to make these choices affect cost of capital estimates. The chapter also suggests three areas for future attention in both research and practice: (1) extensions to private firms, (2) better gauges of capital structure impacts, and (3) methods to estimate changes in equity market risk premiums over time.

Based on examining S&P 500 firms across a range of industries, the chapter shows that differences in WACC estimates are particularly sensitive to the choice of beta and to the use of single company versus industry average data. Moreover, these differences vary by industry. Employing adjusted betas (e.g., from Value Line) provides more consistent and reasonable estimates than those using historical betas. The results also show that analysts can benefit from using estimates from both single company data and comparable firm averages to triangulate on the cost of capital. The findings recall and reinforce the view that cost of capital estimation is a craft and done best when informed by substantial knowledge and care in selecting comparable firms.

DISCUSSION QUESTIONS

1. Is a firm's WACC always the appropriate hurdle rate for its investments? If not, why not?
2. What factors might analysts use to select comparable firms?
3. Why is the WACC typically based on market value weights of debt and equity?
4. What is the disadvantage of using a market risk premium based on historical averages of past returns?
5. What are the practical difficulties of using the CAPM to estimate the cost of equity?
6. What are the advantages and disadvantages of unlevering betas and then relevering them in estimating the cost of capital?

REFERENCES

Bowman, Robert, and Susan Bush. 2006. "Using Comparable Companies to Estimate the Betas of Private Companies." *Journal of Applied Finance* 16:2, 71–81.

Brealey, Richard A., Stewart C. Myers, and Franklin Allen. 2008. *Principles of Corporate Finance*, 9th ed. New York: McGraw-Hill Irwin.

Bruner, Robert F., Kenneth M. Eades, Robert S. Harris, and Robert C. Higgins. 1998. "Best Practices in Estimating the Cost of Capital: Survey and Synthesis." *Financial Practice and Education* 8:1, 13–28.

Burns, Richard M., and Joe Walker. 2009. "Capital Budgeting Surveys: The Future Is Now." *Journal of Applied Finance* 19:1/2, 78–90.

Chaplinsky, Susan, and Robert S. Harris. 1997. "The Effects of Debt Equity Policy on Shareholder Return Requirements and Beta." UVA-F-1168, Charlottesville, VA: Darden Business Publishing.

Connor, Ian, Marc Zenner, and Evan Janek. 2009. "Challenges Ahead: Building a New Power Infrastructure in Today's Financial Paradigm." New York: J. P. Morgan Capital Structure Advisory and Solutions.

Cross, Phillip S. 2008. "2008 ROE Survey: Rates, Risks & Regulators." *Public Utilities Fortnightly* 146:11, 24–31.

Damodaran, Aswath. 2009. "Equity Risk Premiums (ERP): Determinants, Estimation and Implications: A Post-crisis Update." Working Paper, Stern School of Business, New York University.

Fernandez, Pablo. 2008. "The Equity Premium in 100 Textbooks." Working Paper, IESE School of Business.

Fernandez, Pablo. 2009a. "Market Risk Premium Used in 2008 by Professors: A Survey with 1400 Answers." Working Paper, IESE School of Business.

Fernandez, Pablo. 2009b. "Betas Used by Professors: a Survey with 2,500 Answers." Working Paper, IESE School of Business.

Graham, John R., and Lillian F. Mills. 2008. "Using Tax Return Data to Simulate Corporate Marginal Tax Rates." *Journal of Accounting and Economics* 46:2–3, 366–380.

Harris, Robert S., and Felicia C. Marston. 2001. "The Market Risk Premium: Expectational Estimates Using Analysts' Forecasts." *Journal of Applied Finance* 11:1, 6–16.

Koller, Tim, Marc Goedhart, and David Wessels. 2005. *Valuation: Measuring and Managing the Value of Companies*, 4th ed. Hoboken, NJ: John Wiley & Sons.

Pratt, Shannon P., and Roger J. Grabowski. 2008. *Cost of Capital: Applications and Examples* 3rd ed. Hoboken, NJ: John Wiley & Sons.

Rosenbaum, Joshua, and Joshua Pearl. 2009. *Investment Banking: Valuation, Leveraged Buyouts, and Mergers and Acquisitions*. Hoboken, NJ: John Wiley & Sons.

Ross, Stephen A., Randolph W. Westerfield, and Jeffrey Jaffe. 2010. *Corporate Finance*, 9th ed. New York: McGraw-Hill Irwin.

Value Line. 2010. "Glossary of Investment Terms." Available at http://www.valueline.com/sup_glossb.html.

Zenner, Marc, Scott Hill, John Clark, and Nishant Mago. 2008. "The Most Important Number in Finance: The Quest for the Market Risk Premium." New York: J. P. Morgan Capital Structure Advisory and Solutions.

ABOUT THE AUTHORS

Robert M. Conroy is the J. Harvie Wilkinson, Jr. Professor of Business Administration, and has served as Associate Dean for MBA Education at the University of Virginia's Darden School of Business in Charlottesville, Virginia. A professor in the finance area, Professor Conroy has published numerous articles and authored dozens of cases on capital markets. Much of his recent research focuses on Japanese financial markets. He has taught at the International University of Japan in Niigata, Helsinki School of Economics, and IESE Business School in Spain. Before coming to Darden in 1988, Professor Conroy taught at the University of North Carolina and Duke University.

Robert S. Harris is the C. Stewart Sheppard Professor at the University of Virginia's Darden School of Business, which he joined in 1988. A graduate of Davidson College (summa cum laude), Professor Harris received his PhD (Economics) from Princeton University and has served on the faculties of the University of Pennsylvania (Wharton School), University of North Carolina (Kenan Flagler School), and as a visitor at London Business School and Oxford University (Said School of Business). His teaching and writing focus on corporate finance and financial markets. Professor Harris has been active in management roles and serves an advisor to corporate and not-for-profit organizations. He has served as Darden's Dean and as Chief Learning Officer and vice president of United Technologies Corporation.

ACKNOWLEDGMENT

The authors thank Michael Bailey for excellent research assistance.

CHAPTER 12

Economic, Regulatory, and Industry Effects on Capital Structure

PAROMA SANYAL
Economist, Data for Decisions

INTRODUCTION

Capital structure decisions are at the core of a firm's financial strategy and have important long-term implications for firm behavior. Cash-constrained firms can either use equity or debt financing when they borrow from the capital market to finance their investments. Each choice has associated costs and benefits, and influences risk-taking and investment behavior (Kale and Noe 1995; Norton 1985; Spiegel 1996; Kühn 2002a, 2002b; Mauer and Sarkar 2005; Hirth and Uhrig-Homburg 2010), agency issues (Baumol 1965; Jensen and Meckling 1976; Myers 1977, 1984, 2001; Myers and Majluf 1984; Shleifer and Vishny 1989; Childs, Mauer, and Ott 2005), and research and development (R&D), innovation and technology adoption decisions (Himmelberg and Peterson 1994; Hall, Berndt, and Levin 1990; Spiegel 1997). Hence, understanding a firm's capital structure choice is a crucial step to comprehending how a firm evolves and survives in a given environment. Leverage (total debt to total assets) is perhaps the most common variable used to characterize a firm's capital structure choice (Bradley, Jarrell, and Kim 1984; Titman and Wessels 1988; Rajan and Zingales 1995; Fama and French 2002).

A large body of literature studies the capital structure decisions of nonregulated manufacturing firms and investigates why the financing mix (i.e., the internal and external sources of financing and the debt-to-equity ratio) of various firms differs. In their seminal work in this area, Modigliani and Miller (1958) show that in perfect capital markets, the choice between debt and equity financing does not affect firm value or the cost of capital. However, their results hold only under stringent conditions of competitive, frictionless, and complete capital markets where capital flows to its most efficient use and the costs of capital are determined by business risk alone. These conditions are not often found in reality, and empirical evidence suggests that financing does matter.

Several classical theories help to explain the observed capital structure choices of firms (Harris and Raviv 1991). The trade-off theory posits that firms "trade-off" between value-enhancing tax savings and the potential for financial distress when determining the mix of debt and equity financing, and predicts moderate debt levels for firms. The problem with this theory, however, is that it cannot explain the existence of very low debt levels in highly profitable companies (Myers 1984). If the interest tax shield is indeed enough motivation to hold more debt, then a negative relationship should exist between leverage and profits.

The pecking order theory (Myers 1984; Myers and Majluf 1984) attempts to explain this empirical regularity and posits that firms have a preference ordering. That is, firms use internal funds first, followed by debt, and then use external equity as a last resort. However, overall evidence for this theory has been mixed (Helwege and Liang 1996; Shyam-Sunder and Myers 1999; Frank and Goyal 2003). Moreover, Myers (2001) argues that this theory does not show how information asymmetry affects the financing choices of firms and why firms do not use other available alternatives to alleviate such information problems.

The trade-off and pecking order theories assume that the incentives of managers are aligned with that of shareholders through the use of optimal incentive contracts. Yet, even the best crafted incentive contracts cannot perfectly align interests and cannot entirely prevent managers from taking action according to their self-interests. Jensen's (1986) free cash flow theory takes this into account when explaining a firm's capital structure decision. This theory holds that a firm with large amounts of free cash flow, that substantially exceeds its profitable investment opportunities, may hold higher levels of debt. In this case, debt forces managers to pay out the extra cash instead of investing it in inefficient *empire-building*, which is the investment in projects that enhance the manager's power within the firm without necessarily increasing firm value. Under these circumstances, higher debt may increase the firm's value, despite the higher risk of bankruptcy associated with high leverage. Together, these three theories—trade-off, pecking order, and free cash flow—provide valuable insights into a nonregulated firm's financing behavior. More recently, the trend has been to combine the insights of all three models into a unified theory of capital structure.

Titman (2001, p. 23) notes the following:

> *Corporate treasurers do occasionally think about the kind of tradeoffs between tax savings and financial distress costs that we teach in our corporate finance classes. However, since this tradeoff does not change much over time, the balancing of the costs and benefits of debt financing that we emphasize so much in our textbooks is not their major concern. They spend much more thinking about changes in market conditions and the implications of these changes on how firms should be financed.*

Differences in the development of capital markets, legal systems, bankruptcy laws, changes in the regulatory environment, such as imposition of new regulations or deregulating an industry to usher in competition, dramatically change the landscape in which firms operate. The traditional theories of capital structure fail to adequately explain even nonregulated firm behavior in these cases. The next section briefly surveys the evidence on how intercountry variations in economic and institutional factors influence the capital structure decision of nonregulated firms.

ECONOMIC AND INSTITUTIONAL FACTORS: AN INTERNATIONAL PERSPECTIVE

A large body of empirical work indirectly investigates the link between legal and regulatory systems and financing by focusing on cross-country institutional factors for developed countries (Stonehill et al. 1975; Kester 1986; Burgman 1996; Shleifer and Vishny 1997; La Porta et al. 1998; Bancel and Mittoo 2004; Delcoure 2006). These studies draw comparisons between British, European, and Scandinavian legal systems, or between the Anglo-Saxon countries such as the US and UK, and non–Anglo-Saxon countries such as Japan. Specifically, based on a sample of 49 developed countries with different legal systems, La Porta et al. find that firms in countries with stronger legal safeguards have more external debt and equity financing available to them. An important related question is the following: Do firms in developing countries make different capital structure decisions than their counterparts in the developed world? Most papers find that although certain basic similarities exist between developed and developing countries so do major differences (Mayer 1990; Atkin and Glen 1992; Singh et al. 1992; Glen and Pinto 1994; Singh 1995; Demirguc-Kunt and Maksimovic 1996; Wald 1999; Booth et al. 2001; Desai, Foley, and Hines 2004; Bas, Muradoglu, and Phylaktis 2009).

Singh et al. (1992) and Singh (1995) find that firms located in developing economies rely more heavily on equity than on debt and on external rather than internal finance relative to their counterparts in the developed countries. Glen and Pinto (1994) and Demirguc-Kunt and Maksimovic (1996) find that firms display a higher leverage in countries with strong legal institutions and more developed capital markets. Desai, Foley, and Hines (2004) confirm these findings and report that firms rely less on external debt and more on internal sources in countries with underdeveloped capital markets and poor creditor protections. However, developing countries are not a monolithic block and evidence by Atkin and Glen (1992) shows considerable heterogeneity in corporate capital structure even among developing nations.

Two related strands in this literature attempt to explain the differences between developing nations. One explanation traces the dissimilarities between counties to the differences in institutional and legal frameworks such as disparities in the institutional and regulatory environment. These include differences in bankruptcy laws and availability of various financing opportunities (Booth et al. 2001), better creditor protection (Fan, Titman, and Twite 2008), information asymmetries, creditor conflict resolution policies, tax policies, and agency problems (Wald 1999), variations in the national culture of countries (Chui, Lloyd, and Kwok 2002), and government policies such as privatization, financial liberation that have increased real interest rates, and the declining cost of equity capital due to rising price-earnings ratios (Singh 1995).

A second related explanation is provided by Glen and Pinto (1994) and Demirguc-Kunt and Maksimovic (1996), who emphasize the development of capital markets, the strength of the banking sector, and effectiveness of legal systems. Firms display a higher leverage in countries with more developed capital markets and strong legal institutions. Studying the affiliates of multinational firms, Desai, Foley, and Hines (2004) find that capital market conditions and tax incentives of the host country have a large influence on an affiliate's capital structure. Firms rely less on external debt and more on internal sources in countries with underdeveloped capital markets and poor creditor protections.

One weakness of a majority of these intercountry studies is that differences in the institutional and legal environment as well as accounting practices make comparing financial data across countries difficult. According to Rajan and Zingales (1995), institutional differences between the G-7 countries cannot adequately explain the observed variation in capital structure across these countries. Surveying managers in 16 European and Scandinavian countries, Bancel and Mittoo (2004) echo the above findings. Thus, besides focusing on intercountry differences in economic and regulatory factors, there is a need to study interindustry differences within a country to determine how industry-specific factors influence the capital structure decision of firms.

INDUSTRY EFFECTS AND CAPITAL STRUCTURE

Industry and firm characteristics have important implications for the capital structure choice of firms. Conceivably, a firm in a competitive landscape versus one in a concentrated setting, an entrant versus an incumbent, or a technology leader versus a laggard may follow different financial paths. A long line of literature explains how the real and the financial side of firm structure interact with each other. That is, this literature examines how leverage influences a firm's competitive position, investment decisions, asset structure, workforce restructuring, and strategic behavior, and conversely how the product market and firm-specific forces affect capital structure (Bhattacharya and Ritter 1983; Titman 1984; Rotemberg 1984, 1988; Brander and Lewis 1986; Gertner, Gibbons, and Scharfstein 1988; Maksimovic 1988; Bolton and Scharfstein 1990; Rotemberg and Scharfstein 1990; Maksimovic and Zechner 1991; Ofek 1993; Chevalier and Scharfstein 1996; Fries, Miller, and Perrsudin 1997; Sarig 1998; Khanna and Tice 2000; Istaitieh and Rodríguez-Fernández 2006; Banerjee, Dasgupta, and Kim 2008). This section focuses on the latter effect, that is, how industry characteristics such as the market environment, competitive landscape, and firm-specific characteristics within an industry influence the capital structure decision of firms.

Aggregate industry-level factors such as market concentration, product market competition, and industry characteristics can influence the financing decision of firms. Gertner, Gibbons, and Scharfstein (1988) develop a "two-audiences signaling" game-theoretic model where the informed firm signals to two uninformed parties, the product market, and the capital market. They show that the product market fundamentally affects the type of equilibrium in the capital market. In the same spirit, Rotemberg and Scharfstein (1990) explain how firms alter their capital structure to affect their competitive position in the product market. In their theoretical model, Brander and Lewis (1986) show how market structure, mode of competition within the industry, such as price or quantity competition, R&D races, and other dimensions of competition and uncertainty, all influence the mix of financing options that firms use. They find that the strategic factors that influence debt, such as using it as a commitment mechanism, apply primarily to oligopolies, and not to monopolies or perfectly competitive markets. Brander and Lewis also show that under Cournot competition, where firms decide independently the amount of output they produce, firms choose a positive debt level irrespective of whether they face cost or demand uncertainty. Showalter (1995), however, reaches a different conclusion. He shows that if firms are engaged in Bertrand competition, where the firms act independently of each other and compete in prices, then the type of uncertainty matters. When costs are uncertain, firms do not use debt because it does not confer a strategic advantage, while demand uncertainty increases leverage.

The effect of industry concentration and firm financial leverage is complex and depends on the degree of competition within the industry. On the one hand, concentrated industries with "intense rivalry" are more likely to have low financial leverage, while lack of competition may lead to a high leverage. Istaitieh and Rodríguez-Fernández (2006) point to two related arguments that can help explain the inverse relationship between leverage and market concentration; that is, high concentration leads to low leverage. The first explanation is based on strategic behavior on part of the firms. Firms with a lower leverage may prey on highly leveraged firms in order to drive them out of business. This effect may be stronger in concentrated industries where the gain in market share is larger. Foreseeing this, firms in concentrated industries would hold a lower leverage to signal their "toughness" to the market and other competitors (Brander and Lewis 1986). The second explanation is based on agency theory. If strong competition exists among firms in a concentrated industry structure, then product market competition would discipline managers, and debt would not serve as a disciplining mechanism as Jensen (1986) argues in his theory of "free cash flows."

If, on the other hand, concentrated industries are collusive, a positive relationship may exist between industry concentration and firm leverage. A low level of competition may lead to high and stable profits. In such cases, debt may serve as a disciplining mechanism to prevent managers from using the free cash flow to finance negative net present value projects. Additionally, secure profits reduce bankruptcy risk and may induce firms to hold greater debt. Finally, Istaitieh and Rodríguez-Fernández (2006) argue that since firms are typically larger in concentrated industries and large firms are more diversified and better organized, such firms have a low probability of financial distress. This leads to more borrowing and thus higher levels of debt (Titman and Wessels 1988; Bolton and Scharfstein, 1996).

Other industry effects, such as whether the firm is high or low tech and the existence of tariffs, influence a firm's financing decision. Based on a sample of small U.S. startup firms, Sanyal and Mann (2010) find that the financial structure of hi-tech and non–hi-tech startups differs significantly. Baggs and Brander (2006) find that decreases in import tariffs tend to increase leverage while decreases in export tariffs generally decrease leverage. However, industry factors can only partially explain the observed differences in leverage among firms. Several authors (Bowen, Daley, and Huber 1982; Maksimovic and Zechner 1991; MacKay 2003; MacKay and Philips 2005) argue that firm-specific characteristics may be of greater importance than the aggregate industry-level factors. Based on 343 competitive manufacturing industries in the United States, MacKay and Philips find that industry-fixed effects only explain 13 percent of the variation in capital structure among firms. Rather, firm-fixed effects account for 53 percent of the variation in capital structure, while 34 percent can be attributed to within-firm variations. The next section outlines some of the firm-specific factors that encourage or deter firms from taking on more debt.

FIRM CHARACTERISTICS AND CAPITAL STRUCTURE

Complex interactions exist between industry and firm attributes and shape the capital structure decision of firms. MacKay and Phillips (2005, p. 1435) posit that the relative position of the firm within the industry, such as "the similarity of a firm's capital-labor ratio to the industry median, the actions of industry peers, and its status as an entrant, incumbent, or exiting firm" have important implications for capital structure. They confirm Maksimovic and Zechner's (1991) finding that within competitive industries, firms that diverge from the median industry capital-to-labor ratio use more debt relative to firms whose capital-to-labor ratios are more in line with industry medians. Fries, Miller, and Perraudin (1997) find that firms increase their leverage after entering an industry. Besides the position of firms vis-à-vis their peers, other factors such as the nature of assets under governance determine both the availability and use of different forms of financing.

MacKay (2003) finds that firm-specific factors, such as flexibility on the production and investment side, have significant implications for the financial structure of firms. He reports that firms able to adjust their production aspects, such as factor intensity or product level or mix, without much difficulty generally use less debt. He also suggests that such production flexibility may lead to ex-post opportunism by equity holders, and by anticipating such behavior, bondholders demand greater returns, raising the cost of debt. This lowers the amount of debt that such firms use. Additionally, a firm with a large proportion of intangible and/or specific assets should also have low debt levels. According to the transaction costs framework, firms with specific assets suffer from a higher transaction cost in the event of a bankruptcy, as such assets are tailored to the specific needs of the firm and cannot be easily redeployed outside the firm. This low liquidation value leads to higher bankruptcy costs, which, in turn, increases the cost of debt (Williamson 1975, 1985; Klein, Crawford, and Alchian 1978; Balakrishna and Fox 1993; Kochar 1996; Vincente-Lorente 2001).Thus such firms are financed primarily through equity as it reduces the transaction costs by limiting the opportunistic behavior of managers, as equity holders can exercise greater control over the firm's operations (Bradley, Jarrell, and Kim 1984; Long and Malitz 1985; Williamson 1988; Močnik 2001; Vilasuso and Minkler 2001). Sanyal and Mann (2010) confirm this finding for small startups. They report that new firms with high asset specificity, such as those with a small tangible asset base, are less likely to be financed through debt. However, the opposite effect is observed for firms that show investment flexibility. Greater investment flexibility, such as high amount of liquid assets, increases financial leverage (Mackay, 2003).

Titman (1984) and Titman and Wessels (1988) make a similar argument about bilateral buyer-supplier relationships and unique products (especially in durable goods industries). They argue that industries where firms produce unique products or in lines of business where a particular firm is central to its customers or suppliers, very high costs of bankruptcy are present. In such cases, firms carry low levels of debt. Banerjee, Dasgupta, and Kim (2008) investigate a similar issue with their focus on relation-specific investment. The authors argue that suppliers with relation-specific assets may be concerned about the difficulty of redeploying their own specific assets should the customer fail, rather than about the effect of the supplier's own leverage on the incentive of customers to invest in the relation-specific asset that Titman and Wessels (1988) suggest. In such cases, the supplier would prefer to maintain a low debt ratio and would want the same for the principal customer as this would make the customer less prone to bankruptcy risk. Based on firms in Compustat, Banerjee, Dasgupta, and Kim (2008) show that in durable goods industries, customer firms that buy a high percentage of their inputs from "dependent suppliers" and the "dependent producer" both have lower financial leverage. This effect is dependent on the proportion of inputs that come from the "dependent supplier." As expected, this effect is non-existent in nondurable manufacturing industries.

Other firm attributes such as the newness of a firm or its size also fundamentally influence the capital structure choice of firms. Small firms are more likely to suffer from greater information asymmetry making external financing more expensive and imposing credit constraints on smaller new ventures (Avery, Bostic, and Samolyk 1998; Berger and Udell 1995; Paulson and Townsend 2004). The scale of the venture may also influence the issuance of public equity, which is an option primarily open to large firms. The empirical literature mostly finds that large firms use more debt (Cosh and Huges 1994; Cassar 2004; Sanyal and Mann, 2010). Additionally, the legal organization of the firm affects its capital structure. Although earlier literature suggests a positive relationship between debt levels and firm incorporation (Coleman and Cohn 2000), Cassar (2004) fails to find such a relationship.

For new startups, entrepreneur attributes play a very important role in a firm's financing decisions. Entrepreneur characteristics such as their education (Bates 1990; Chandler and Hanks 1998; Baum and Silverman 2004; Astebro and Bernhardt 2005; Sanyal and Mann 2010), race and ethnic ties (Bates 1997a, 1997b; Smallbone et al. 2003; Sanyal and Mann 2010); gender (Fay and Williams 1991; Verheul and Thurik 2001); strategic alliances and networks (Petersen and Rajan 1994; Baum and Silverman 2004; Chang 2004); the owner's risk-return preferences (Scherr, Sugrue, and Ward 1993); and experience of the founding team (Delmar and Shane 2006) influence the use of different forms of financing and hence the capital structure of the firm.

Besides the above factors, other informational and strategic considerations influence the financing decision of firms. Both theoretical and empirical studies show that firms alter their leverage decisions when attempting to signal information to outside investors (Ross 1977; Leland and Pyle 1977; Masulis 1980; Talmor 1981; Dann 1981; Gertner et al. 1988; Israel, Ofer, and Siegel 1988; Poitevin 1990; Ravid and Sarig 1991; MacKay 2003). Sanyal and Mann (2010) show that debt is an unlikely source of financing for small startups characterized by high information opacity.

One major difference between various firms is whether they are subject to some form of regulation by the government, specifically rate regulation. Rate regulation implies that the firm is not free to set market prices and some external regulatory body determines the rate the firm charges its customers. On the upside, the firm is guaranteed a rate of return and shielded from bankruptcy concerns and cost shocks. On the downside, the risk of regulatory intervention in the market is pervasive (Lewiner and Easton 2004), and regulators may engage in wealth-shifting from equity holders and rate payers. Regulation changes the types and nature of risks that regulated firms face (Norton 1985; Grout and Zalewska 2006). Thus, the factors that influence the financing decision of regulated firms, such as utilities, airlines, and telecommunication, vis-à-vis their nonregulated counterparts are different. Because these are large industrial segments, understanding their capital structure decisions is important given their economy-wide implications. The next section briefly outlines existing theories that explain the capital structure choice of regulated firms.

THEORIES EXPLAINING THE CAPITAL STRUCTURE OF REGULATED FIRMS

The capital structure choices of regulated firms differ substantially from those of nonregulated firms. Regulation appears to increase leverage. The prevailing wisdom is that regulated firms choose high debt levels to induce rate (price) increases (Taggart 1981, 1985; Besley and Bolten 1990; Chen and Fanara 1992; Dasgupta and Nanda 1993; Rao and Moyer 1994; Spiegel and Spulber 1994, 1997; Klein, Phillips, and Shiu 2000; Resende 2010). This assumes that the capital structure decisions are exogenous to regulators; that is, the firm decides on its capital structure to influence the price set by the regulator who takes the capital structure as given. Besley and Bolten (1990), who survey both utilities and regulators, find that 60 percent of those surveyed believe that a high leverage ratio leads to higher prices. High debt levels induce regulators to set high rates that account for the firm's costs including the cost of debt, thereby insuring the firm against possible financial distress.

Taggart (1985), who challenges this traditional view to some extent, attributes the high debt levels primarily to the "safer business environment" created by regulation. However, the author cannot reject a "price-influence effect"; that is, regulators increase the rate of highly levered firms to avoid the risk of bankruptcy. Taggart argues that the higher leverage of regulated firms cannot solely be a product of firms using a higher leverage to obtain higher prices from regulators (although he admits that some evidence supports this notion). He cites evidence from the early twentieth-century regulation of electric utilities to show that although such gaming may have taken place in the early days of regulation, regulators soon became aware of the situation and took steps to combat them. Taggart shows that the statutes governing the financial structure of regulated utilities clearly display this awareness on the part of the regulators. He argues that regulation provides stability to a firm's cash flow, and the debt-capacity model would predict an increase in leverage in this environment.

More recently, the use of debt financing as a strategic tool by regulated firms, in an environment where regulators treat the firm's capital structure as exogenous, has once again gained credence. Spiegel and Spulber (1997) argue that a regulated firm faces two opposing incentives while choosing its capital structure. On the one hand, the firm wants to increase leverage to prevent rate decreases from regulators.

High leverage signals to regulators that this is a high cost firm. In order to prevent a possible bankruptcy and the associated deadweight loss, regulators can be induced to undertake future rate increases. On the other hand, a regulated firm wants lower leverage, which signals to the capital market that it is a low cost, high valued firm. Spiegel and Spulber's theoretical model shows that the equilibrium choice of capital structure of a regulated firm ultimately depends on the size of the investment. For large projects, firms use debt first or solely depending on the size of the investment, followed by equity.

All the above explanations assume that the capital structure of the regulated firm is exogenous to the regulator, who reacts passively to the given mix of debt and equity while setting prices. De Fraja and Stones (2004) provide an alternative explanation for high leverage ratios in regulated firms. They contend that the assumption of exogeneity of the capital structure decision may be suited to the U.S.-style rate of return regulation where the regulated firms are long established and regulators react passively to the given capital structure. But in countries such as the United Kingdom, where state-owned utilities have been newly privatized and regulated, the exogeneity assumption is incorrect. De Fraja and Stones maintain that regulators may induce firms to hold more debt because this reduces the cost of capital and allows for price reductions.

They model the regulator's price setting behavior under two assumptions: (1) when the utility's capital structure is exogenous and (2) when regulator decisions can influence such financing choices. They show a trade-off between lower prices and higher price volatility as debt levels increase. When the capital structure is endogenous, a social welfare maximizing regulator sets a low price that is subject to some volatility. This implies that the optimal capital structure is one with higher debt levels, given that debt finance is cheaper than equity. De Fraja and Stones argue that this is the case in countries such as the United Kingdom, where regulatory actions induce firms to hold higher levels of debt (sometimes 70 to 80 percent) when compared to U.S. utilities (35 to 40 percent), where regulators typically take the capital structure as given.

The above discussion indicates that no unified theory is available that can explain the high debt levels held by regulated firms and the explanations depend on assumptions about the institutional and regulatory systems to which the firms are subject. Thus, the effect of regulation on the capital structure decision of firms remains largely an empirical question.

INTER-INDUSTRY EMPIRICAL EVIDENCE ON REGULATED INDUSTRIES

In the United States, empirical evidence from several industries shows that regulated firms display higher leverage than unregulated firms. In their classic study of 25 industries spanning the period 1962 to 1981, Bradley, Jarrell, and Kim (1984) find that firms in regulated industries such as electricity, gas, airlines, and telephone consistently display a higher leverage when compared to nonregulated firms. Sanyal and Bulan (2009) show that in a sample of Compustat firms from 1990 to 2001, debt is 22 percent of assets for nonregulated manufacturing firms compared to 34 percent for regulated utilities. The evidence from non-U.S. countries is similar. British energy company National Grid Group Plc, the Spanish telecom company Telefonica de Espana, and the Italian transport company Autostrade per l'Italia, all increased their leverage when they became private regulated companies (Bortolloti et al. 2007). For regulated utilities, where debt levels influence prices, the incentives for holding debt are different from those of nonregulated firms. The literature contains two alternative hypotheses designed to explain the level of debt held by regulated firms.

In fact, MacKay and Phillips (2005) find that most of the variation in firm financial structure is due to intra-industry variation. Focusing on a single industry can isolate the effect of specific regulatory and market factors that influence a firm's capital structure. Moreover, this enables explicit identification of firm and industry characteristics that directly affect the choice of debt, rather than controlling for these factors using industry and firm fixed effects as is done in a majority of inter-industry studies. Focusing on a single industry enables exploiting the considerable variation in regulatory policies and firm-specific factors to get a more powerful test of the determinants of a firm's capital structure. In their study of the insurance industry, Klein, Phillips, and Shiu (2000) find that tighter and more pervasive regulatory control leads to higher debt levels. In his study of U.S. local exchange carriers in the telecommunications market, Resende (2010) finds empirical evidence supporting the view that regulated firms carry higher debt levels to induce higher rates for regulators.

Most studies, however, explain how and why regulated firms hold higher debt levels than their unregulated counterparts, and how the move from a competitive environment to a regulated one increases leverage. Few papers investigate the reverse issue; that is, what happens to a firm's capital structure when a regulated industry is deregulated and subject to competitive forces. Extending the logic from the earlier studies, the change from a regulated and hence safer environment, to a competitive and uncertain one should result in more conservative financial choices for the firm and lead to a decline in leverage. Dewenter and Malatesta (2001), who compare state-owned and private firms, support this view by finding that government-backed firms lower their debt levels following privatization.

Ovtchinnikov (2010) reports a similar conclusion. Based on a sample of all nonfinancial firms in Compustat from 1966 to 2006, he finds that deregulation changes the operating environment of firms, affecting their competitive landscape, profitability, growth opportunities, and bankruptcy probability. These factors combined lead to a decline in leverage. In his sample, regulated firms, on average, decreased their leverage from 42.3 percent in the regulated phase to 31.9 percent in the post-deregulated phase.

The deregulation of the U.S. electric utility industry provides a unique "natural experiment" that allows one to study this precise question and observe financing choices for the same firm in both the regulated and competitive regimes. Focusing on a single industry during a time when the institutional environment changed permits isolating the effects of specific regulatory and market factors on firm leverage. By exploiting the considerable variation in interstate deregulation speed and modality one obtains a more powerful test of the determinants of a firm's capital structure.

THE U.S. ELECTRIC UTILITY INDUSTRY: A CASE STUDY

The electric utility industry in the United States has been traditionally organized as a vertically integrated regulated monopoly with for-profit, investor-owned utilities wielding service monopolies in particular geographical regions that were overseen by the Federal Energy Regulatory Commission (FERC) and state regulators. The primary purpose of regulating the utilities was to set prices based on the "cost of service ratemaking" principle in which rates are fixed and cannot be changed without regulator authorization. Rate regulation has typically been associated with high leverage ratios. This has been attributed to several factors. The predominant cause for high leverage ratios is attributed to utilities attempting to influence regulators to set higher rates (Hagerman and Ratchford 1978; Dasgupta and Nanda 1993; Spiegel and Spulber 1994). Conversely, others have argued that regulators implicitly incentivize utilities to carry more debt since it is cheaper than equity and allows the regulators to decrease rates (De Fraja and Stones 2004). Other explanations point to utility managers reacting to unfavorable regulation (Rao and Moyer 1994), a safer business environment under regulation that implies a greater debt capacity for firms (Taggart 1985), and regulatory quality inducing greater debt (Rao and Moyer 1994).

This regulatory structure changed during the 1980s and 1990s when "cost-based" regulation paradigms gave way to competitive electricity markets (Hogan 1995; Joskow 1997, 1999). The Energy Policy Act (EPAct) of 1992 and FERC Orders 888 and 889 in 1996 fundamentally changed the stable operating environment of utilities by altering regulatory conditions and the market environment. This engendered two types of uncertainties: (1) regulatory risk arising from uncertainties about the emerging institutional structure and the policy environment, and (2) market uncertainties arising from demand fluctuations, price competition, and threats to market share. The onset of restructuring altered the nature of financial distress costs by increasing bankruptcy probability. Additionally, the market may also have undervalued these firms under transition. Both factors are expected to reduce leverage after deregulation.

Based on available data for all regulated electric utilities between 1990 and 2001, Sanyal and Bulan (2009) find that leverage decreases between 25 and 27 percent post-deregulation. They show that any policy that decreases earnings stability, or increases competition and threatens market share, lowers debt levels. Specifically, utilities in states that encouraged divestiture of generation assets reduced leverage, and firms facing higher market uncertainty have lower leverage. However, if utilities expected to exercise greater market power in the future, they were more likely to take on higher debt when compared to utilities in states where there was no potential for exercising market power. Sanyal and Bulan also find that more profitable firms rely less on debt to finance investments, and those with greater tangible assets display higher debt levels. The negative coefficient on asset growth lends support to the hypothesis that firms with high growth opportunities are more likely to forgo profitable investments if they are highly levered.

Bulan and Sanyal (2009) offer another important finding that highlights the difference in capital structure decisions between nonregulated and regulated firms.

Existing theories suggest that a firm's growth opportunities (i.e., its discretionary future investments), are an important determinant of its capital structure. The common prediction from empirical and theoretical literature (Myers 1977) is a negative relationship between leverage and growth opportunities. Yet, Bulan and Sanyal find that the relationship between leverage and growth opportunities in the electric utility industry can be positive or negative depending on the exact nature of the growth opportunity. When growth opportunity is measured by the potential market that a utility may gain due to a lack of default provider policies in neighboring states, the impact on leverage is positive. When the growth opportunity is characterized by the opportunity of gaining access to potential markets due to divestiture policies in neighboring states, the effect is negative. Most empirical research documents this latter result. Their findings highlight the complexities surrounding financing decisions and show that conventional cross-country or cross-industry leverage regressions cannot fully capture the dynamics of firm financing activities.

SUMMARY AND CONCLUSIONS

Substantial research investigates the financial determinants of capital structure of nonregulated firms with somewhat less emphasis on the financing decisions of regulated firms. This chapter provides a comprehensive study of the nonfinancial determinants of capital structure. It focuses on three important sets of factors that influence a firm's financing decision: (1) intercountry differences; (2) inter-industry differences within a country; and (3) interfirm differences within the same industry. One important focus of inter-industry differences is the regulatory status of the firm. This chapter brings together the existing literature in the field to provide a thorough understanding of the determinants of capital structure in a regulated environment. By studying firms that are transitioning from a regulated to a competitive environment, this chapter provides a unique window into how changing incentive structures influence financial choices of firms. The chapter also briefly examines the capital structure of small startups. Whereas substantial theory and research underpins the analysis of the financial structure of existing large firms, little theory and virtually no research focuses on small startup financial structure, which is an area for potential future research.

DISCUSSION QUESTIONS

1. What theories explain the capital structure decisions of regulated versus nonregulated firms?
2. What are the industry and firm-specific nonfinancial characteristics from a theoretical and empirical perspective that significantly influence the financing decision of firms?
3. What does empirical evidence say about the similarity of the capital structure decisions of firms across counties?
4. Why did the regulated electric utilities display higher leverage compared to nonregulated manufacturing firms? How and why did this change after deregulation of the U.S. electricity market?

REFERENCES

Astebro, Thomas, and Irwin Bernhardt. 2005. "The Winner's Curse of Human Capital." *Small Business Economics* 24:1, 63–78.

Atkin, Michael, and Jack Glen. 1992. "Comparing Corporate Capital Structures around the Globe." *International Executive* 349:5, 369–387.

Avery, Robert B., Raphael W. Bostic, and Katherine A. Samolyk. 1998. "The Role of Personal Wealth in Small Business Finance." *Journal of Banking and Finance* 22:6, 1019–1061.

Baggs, Jen, and James A. Brander. 2006. "Trade Liberalization, Profitability, and Financial Leverage." *Journal of International Business Studies* 37:2, 196–211.

Balakrishna, Srinivasan, and Isaac Fox. 1993. "Asset Specificity, Firm Heterogeneity and Capital Structure." *Strategic Management Journal* 14:1, 3–16.

Bancel, Franck, and Usha Mittoo. 2004. "Cross-Country Determinants of Capital Structure Choice: A Survey of European Firms." *Financial Management* 33:4, 103–132.

Banerjee, Santanu, Sudipto Dasgupta, and Yungsun Kim. 2008. "Buyer–Supplier Relationships and the Stakeholder Theory of Capital Structure." *Journal of Finance* 63:5, 2507–2552.

Bas, Tugba, Gulnur Muradoglu, and Kate Phylaktis. 2009. "Determinants of Capital Structure in Developing Countries." Working Paper, Cass Business School.

Bates, Timothy. 1990. "Entrepreneur Human Capital Inputs and Small Business Longevity." *Review of Economics and Statistics* 72:4, 551–559.

Bates, Timothy. 1997a. "Financing Small Business Creation: The Case of Chinese and Korean Immigrant Entrepreneurs." *Journal of Business Venturing* 12:2, 109–124.

Bates, Timothy. 1997b. "Unequal Access: Financial Institution Lending to Black- and White-Owned Small Business Start-Ups." *Journal of Urban Affairs* 19:4, 487–495.

Baum, Joel A. C., and Brian S. Silverman. 2004. "Picking Winners or Building Them? Alliance, Intellectual, and Human Capital as Selection Criteria in Venture Financing and Performance of Biotechnology Startups." *Journal of Business Venturing* 19:3, 411–436.

Baumol, William J. 1965. "The Stock Market and Economic Efficiency." New York: Fordham University Press.

Berger, Alan M., and Geoffrey F. Udell. 1995. "Relationship Lending and Lines of Credit in Small Firm Financing." *Journal of Business* 68:3, 351–381.

Besley, Scott, and Steven E. Bolten. 1990. "What Factors are Important in Establishing Mandated Returns? A Survey of Utilities and Regulators." *Public Utilities Fortnightly* 125:1, 26–30.

Bhattacharya, Sudipto, and Jay R. Ritter. 1983. "Innovation and Communication: Signalling with Partial Disclosure." *Review of Economic Studies* 50:2, 331–346.

Bolton, Patrick, and David S. Scharfstein. 1990. "A Theory of Predation Based on Agency Problems in Financial Contracting." *American Economic Review* 80:1, 93–106.

Bolton, Patrick, and David S. Scharfstein. 1996. "Optimal Debt Structure and the Number of Creditors." *Journal of Political Economy* 104:1, 1–25.

Booth, Laurence, Varouj Aivazian, Asli Demirguc-Kunt, and Vojislav Maksimovic. 2001. "Capital Structures in Developing Countries." *Journal of Finance* 56:1, 87–130.

Bortolotti, Bernardo, Carlo Cambini, Laura Rondi, and Yossi Spiegel. 2007. "Capital Structure and Regulation: Does Ownership Matter?" Working Paper, Fondazione Eni Enrico Mattei.

Bowen, Robert M., Lane A. Daley, and Charles C. Huber, Jr. 1982. "Evidence on the Existence and Determinants of Inter-Industry Differences in Leverage Robert." *Financial Management* 11:4, 10–20.

Bradley, Michael, Gregg A. Jarrell, and E. Han Kim. 1984. "On the Existence of an Optimal Capital Structure: Theory and Evidence." *Journal of Finance* 39:3, 857–878.

Brander, James A., and Tracy Lewis, 1986. "Oligopoly and Financial Structure: The Limited Liability Effect." *American Economic Review* 76:5, 956–970.

Bulan, Laarni T., and Paroma Sanyal. 2009. "Is There Room For Growth? Debt, Growth Opportunities and the Deregulation of U.S. Electric Utilities." Working Paper, Brandeis University.

Burgman, Todd. 1996. "An Empirical Examination of Multinational Corporate Capital Structure." *Journal of International Business Studies* 27:3, 553–570.

Cassar, Gerald. 2004. "The Financing of Business Start-Ups." *Journal of Business Venturing* 19:2, 261–283.

Chandler, Gaelyn N., and Steven H. Hanks. 1998. "An Examination of the Substitutability of Founders Human and Financial Capital in Emerging Business Ventures." *Journal of Business Venturing* 13:5, 353–369.

Chang, Sea J. 2004. "Venture Capital Financing, Strategic Alliances, and the Initial Public Offerings of Internet Startups." *Journal of Business Venturing* 19:1, 721–741.

Chen, Chao Chen, and Philip Fanara, Jr. 1992. "The Choice among Long-Term Financing Instruments for Public Utilities." *Financial Review* 27:3, 431–465.

Chevalier, Judith A., and David S. Scharfstein. 1996. "Capital-Market Imperfections and Countercyclical Markups: Theory and Evidence." *American Economic Review* 86:4, 703–725.

Childs, Paul D., David Mauer, and Steven H. Ott. 2005. "Interactions of Corporate Financing and Investment Decisions: The Effects of Agency Conflicts." *Journal of Financial Economics* 76:3, 667–690.

Chui, Andy C. W., Alison E. Lloyd, and Chuck C. Y. Kwok. 2002. "The Determination of Capital Structure: Is National Culture a Missing Piece to the Puzzle?" *Journal of International Business Studies* 33:1, 99–127.

Coleman, Susan, and Richard Cohn. 2000. "Small Firms' Use of Financial Leverage: Evidence from the 1993 National Survey of Small Business Finances." *Journal of Business Entrepreneurship* 12:3, 81–98.

Cosh, Andy, and Alan Hughes. 1994. "Size, Financial Structure and Profitability: UK Companies in the 1980s." In Alan Hughes and David John Storey (eds.), *Finance and Small Firms*, 18–63. London: Routledge.

Dann, Larry Y. 1981. "Common Stock Repurchases: An Analysis of Returns to Stockholders and Bond Holders." *Journal of Financial Economics* 9:2, 113–138.

Dasgupta, Sudipto, and Vikram Nanda. 1993. "Bargaining and Brinkmanship—Capital Structure Choice by Regulated Firms." *International Journal of Industrial Organization* 11:4, 475–497.

De Fraja, Gianni, and Clive Stones. 2004. "Risk and Capital Structure in the Regulated Firms." *Journal of Regulatory Economics* 26:1, 69–84.

Delcoure, Natalya. 2006. "The Determinants of Capital Structure in Transitional Economies." *International Review of Economics and Finance* 16:3, 400–415.

Delmar, Frédéric, and Scott Shane. 2006. "Does Experience Matter? The Effect of Founding Team Experience on the Sales of Newly Founded Firms." *Strategic Organization* 4:3, 215–247.

Demirguc-Kunt, Asli, and Vojislav Maksimovic. 1996. "Stock Market Development and Financing Choices of Firms." *World Bank Economic Review* 10:2, 341–369.

Desai, Mihir A., C. Fritz Foley, and James R. Hines, Jr. 2004. "Multinational Perspective on Capital Structure Choice and Internal Capital Markets." *Journal of Finance* 59:6, 2451–2487.

Dewenter, Kathryn L., and Paul H. Malatesta. 2001. "State-Owned and Privately Owned Firms: An Empirical Analysis of Profitability, Leverage, and Labor Intensity." *American Economic Review* 91:1, 320–334.

Fama, Eugene F., and Kenneth R. French. 2002. "Testing Trade-Off and Pecking Order Predictions about Dividends and Debt." *Review of Financial Studies* 15:1, 1–33.

Fan, Joseph P. H., Sheridan Titman, and Garry Twite. 2008. "An International Comparison of Capital Structure and Debt Maturity Choices." Working Paper, Chinese University of Hong Kong. Available at http://papers.ssrn.com/sol3/papers.cfm?abstract_id=423483.

Fay, Michael, and Lesley Williams. 1991. "Sex of Applicant and the Availability of Business 'Start-Up' Finance." *Australian Journal of Management* 16:1, 65–72.

Frank, Murray Z., and Vidhan K. Goyal, 2003. "Testing the Pecking Order Theory of Capital Structure." *Journal of Financial Economics* 67:3, 217–224.

Fries, Stephen, Marcus Miller, and William Perraudin. 1997. "Debt in Industry Equilibrium." *Review of Financial Studies* 10:1, 39–67.

Gertner, Robert, Robert Gibbons, and David S. Scharfstein. 1988. "Simultaneous Signalling to the Capital and Product Markets." *RAND Journal of Economics* 19:2, 173–190.

Glen, Jack, and Brian Pinto. 1994. "Debt and Equity? How Firms in Developing Countries Choose." Discussion Paper #22, The World Bank and International Finance Corporation.

Grout, Paul A., and Anna Zalewska. 2006. "The Impact of Regulation on Market Risk." *Journal of Financial Economics* 80:1, 149–184.

Hagerman, Robert L., and Brian T. Ratchford. 1978. "Some Determinants of Allowed Rates of Return on Equity to Electric Utilities." *Bell Journal of Economics* 9:1, 46–55.

Hall, Bronwyn H., Ernst Berndt, and Richard C. Levin. 1990. "The Impact of Corporate Restructuring on Industrial Research and Development." *Brookings Papers on Economic Activity—Microeconomics*, 85–124.

Harris, Milton, and Arthur Raviv. 1991. "The Theory of Capital Structure." *Journal of Finance* 46:1, 297–355.

Helwege, Jean, and Nellie Liang. 1996. "Is There a Pecking Order? Evidence from a Panel of IPO Firms." *Journal of Financial Economics* 40:3, 429–458.

Himmelberg, Charles P., and Bruce C. Petersen. 1994. "R&D and Internal Finance: A Panel Study of Small Firms in High-Tech Industries." *Review of Economics and Statistics* 76:1, 38–51.

Hirth, Stefan, and Marliese Uhrig-Homburg. 2010. "Investment Timing When External Financing Is Costly." *Journal of Business Finance and Accounting*. Forthcoming.

Hogan, William W. 1995. "A Competitive Electricity Market Model." Working Paper, Harvard Electricity Policy Group. Available at http://ksghome.harvard.edu/~whogan/transvis.pdf.

Israel, Ronen, Aharon R. Ofer, and Daniel R. Siegel. 1989. "The Information Content of Equity-for-debt Swaps: An Investigation of Analyst Forecasts of Firm Cash Flows." *Journal of Financial Economics* 25:2, 349–370.

Istaitieh, Abdulaziz, and José M. Rodríguez-Fernández. 2006. "Factor-Product Markets and Firm's Capital Structure: A Literature Review." *Review of Financial Economics* 15:1, 49–75.

Jensen, Michael. 1986. "The Agency Costs of Free Cash Flow, Corporate Finance and Takeovers." *American Economic Review* 76:2, 323–329.

Jensen, Michael, and William Meckling. 1976. "Theory of the Firm: Managerial Behavior, Agency Costs and Ownership Structure." *Journal of Financial Economics* 3:4, 305–360.

Joskow, Paul. 1997. "Restructuring, Competition, and Regulatory Reform in the U.S. Electric Sector." *Journal of Economic Perspectives* 11:3, 119–138.

Joskow, Paul. 1999. "Deregulation and Regulatory Reform in the U.S. Electric Power Sector." Working Paper, Brookings AEI Conference on Deregulation in Network Industries.

Kale, Jayant R., and Thomas H. Noe. 1995. "Dilution Costs, Underinvestment, and Utility Regulation under Asymmetric Information." *Journal of Regulatory Economics* 7:2, 177–197.

Kester, W. Carl. 1986. "Capital and Ownership Structure: A Comparison of United States and Japanese Manufacturing Corporations." *Financial Management* 15:1, 5–16.

Khanna, Naveen, and Sheri Tice. 2000. "Strategic Responses of Incumbents to New Entry: The Effect of Ownership Structure, Capital Structure, and Focus." *Review of Financial Studies* 13:3, 749–779.

Klein, Benjamin R., Robert G. Crawford, and Armen A. Alchian. 1978. "Vertical Integration, Appropriable Rents and the Competitive Contracting Process." *Journal of Law and Economics* 21:2, 297–326.

Klein, Robert W., Richard D. Phillips, and Wenyan Shiu. 2000. "The Capital Structure of Firms Subject to Price Regulation: Evidence from the Insurance Industry." *Journal of Financial Services* 21:1, 79–100.

Kochar, Rahul. 1996. "Explaining Firm Capital Structure: The Role of Agency Theory vs. Transaction Cost Economics." *Strategic Management Journal* 17:9, 713–728.

Kühn, Kai-Uwe. 2002a. "Technology Choice and Capital Structure under Rate Regulation: A Comment." *International Journal of Industrial Organization* 20:2, 269–278.

Kühn, Kai-Uwe. 2002b. "Technology Choice and Capital Structure under Rate Regulation: Rejoinder." *International Journal of Industrial Organization* 20:2, 283–284.

La Porta, Rafael, Florencio Lopez-de-Silanes, Andrei Shleifer, and Robert W. Vishny. 1998. "Law and Finance." *Journal of Political Economy* 106:6, 1113–1155.

Leland, Hayne E., and David H. Pyle. 1977. "Informational Asymmetry, Financial Structure and Financial Intermediation." *Journal of Finance* 32:2, 371–387.

Lewiner, Colette, and Bill W. Easton. 2004. "Deregulation: Meeting the Delivery and Sustainability Challenges." Capgemini Utilities Research Program. Available at http://www.au.capgemini.com/resources/thought_leadership/deregulation_meeting_the_delivery_and_sustainability_challenges/.

Long, Michael, and Ileen Malitz. 1985. "The Investment-Financing Nexus: Some Empirical Evidence." *Midland Corporate Finance Journal* 3:3, 53–59.

MacKay, Peter. 2003. "Real Flexibility and Financial Structure: An Empirical Analysis." *Review of Financial Studies* 16:4, 1131–1165.

MacKay, Peter, and Gordon M. Phillips. 2005. "How Does Industry Affect Firm Financial Structure?" *Review of Financial Studies* 18:4, 1433–1466.

Maksimovic, Vojislav. 1988. "Capital Structure in Repeated Oligopolies." *RAND Journal of Economics* 19:3, 389–407.

Maksimovic, Vojislav, and Joseph Zechner. 1991. "Debt, Agency Costs, and Industry Equilibrium." *Journal of Finance* 46:5, 1619–1643.

Masulis, Ronald W. 1980. "The Effect of Capital Structure Change on Security Prices: A Study of Exchange Offers." *Journal of Financial Economics* 8:2, 139–178.

Mauer, David C., and Sudipto Sarkar. 2005. "Real Options, Agency Conflicts and Optimal Capital Structure." *Journal of Banking and Finance* 29:6, 1405–1428.

Mayer, Colin. 1990. "Financial Systems, Corporate Finance and Economic Development." *Asymmetric Information, Corporate Finance and Investment*, R. Glenn Hubbard (ed.), 307–332. Chicago: University of Chicago Press.

Močnik, Dijana. 2001. "Asset Specificity and a Firm's Borrowing Ability: An Empirical Analysis of Manufacturing Firms." *Journal of Economic Behavior and Organization* 45:1, 69–81.

Modigliani, Franco, and Merton H. Miller. 1958. "The Cost of Capital, Corporation Finance and the Theory of Investment." *American Economic Review* 48:3, 261–297.

Myers, Stewart C. 1977. "Determinants of Corporate Borrowing." *Journal of Financial Economics* 5:2, 147–175.

Myers, Stewart C. 1984. "The Capital Structure Puzzle." *Journal of Finance* 39:3, 575–592.

Myers, Stewart C. 2001. "Capital Structure." *Journal of Economic Perspectives* 15:2, 81–102.

Myers, Stewart C., and Nicholas S. Majluf. 1984. "Corporate Financing and Investment Decisions When Firms Have Information That Investors Do Not Have." *Journal of Financial Economics* 13:2, 187–221.

Norton, Seth W. 1985. "Regulation and Systemic Risk: The Case of Electric Utilities." *Journal of Law and Economics* 28:3, 671–868.

Ofek, Eli. 1993. "Capital Structure and Firm Response to Poor Performance: An Empirical Analysis." *Journal of Financial Economics* 34:1, 3–30.

Ovtchinnikov, Alexei V. 2010. "Capital Structure Decisions: Evidence from Deregulated Industries." *Journal of Financial Economics* 95:2, 249–274.

Paulson, Anna L., and Robert Townsend. 2004. "Entrepreneurship and Financial Constraints in Thailand." *Journal of Corporate Finance* 10:2, 229–262.
Petersen, Mitchell A., and Raghuram G. Rajan. 1994. "The Benefits of Lending Relationships: Evidence from Small Business Data." *Journal of Finance* 49:1, 3–37.
Poitevin, Michel. 1990. "Strategic Financial Signaling." *International Journal of Industrial Organization* 8:4, 499–518.
Rajan, Raghuram, and Luigi Zingales. 1995. "What Do We Know about Capital Structure? Some Evidence from International Data." *Journal of Finance* 50:5, 1421–1460.
Rao, Ramesh, and Charles R. Moyer. 1994. "Regulatory Climate and Electrical Utility Capital Structure Decisions." *Financial Review* 29:1, 97–124.
Ravid, S. Abraham, and Oded H. Sarig. 1991. "Financial Signaling by Committing to Cash Outflows." *Journal of Financial and Quantitative Analysis* 26:2, 165–180.
Resende, Marcelo. 2010. "Capital Structure and Regulation in U.S. Local Telephony: An Exploratory Econometric Study." *Economics Bulletin* 30:1, 392–404.
Ross, Stephen A. 1977. "The Determination of Financial Structure: The Incentive Signaling Approach." *Bell Journal of Economics* 8:1, 23–40.
Rotemberg, Julio J. 1984. "Financial Transaction Costs and Industrial Performance." Working Paper 1554-84, Sloan School of Management.
Rotemberg, Julio J. 1988. "Short Investor Horizon and Industrial Performance." Working Paper 1554-84, Sloan School of Management.
Rotemberg, Julio J., and David S. Scharfstein. 1990. "Shareholder-Value Maximization and Product-Market Competition." *Review of Financial Studies* 3:3, 367–391.
Sanyal, Paroma, and Laarni T. Bulan. 2009. "Regulatory Risk, Market Uncertainties, and Firm Financing Choices: Evidence from U.S. Electricity Market Restructuring." Working Paper, Brandeis University.
Sanyal, Paroma, and Catherine L. Mann. 2010. "Asset Specificity, Information Asymmetry and New Firm Financing." Working Paper, Brandeis University.
Sarig, Oded H. 1998. "The Effect of Leverage on Bargaining with Corporation." *Financial Review* 33:1, 1–16.
Scherr, Frederick C., Timothy F. Sugrue, and Janice B. Ward. 1993. "Financing the Small Firm Startup: Determinants of Debt Use." *Journal of Small Business Finance* 1:2, 179–183.
Shleifer, Andrei, and Robert W. Vishny. 1989. "Management Entrenchment: The Case of Manager Specific Investments." *Journal of Financial Economics* 25:1, 123-139.
Shleifer, Andrei, and Robert W. Vishny. 1997. "A Survey of Corporate Governance." *Journal of Finance* 52:2, 737–783.
Showalter, Dean M. 1995. "Oligopoly and Financial Structure: Comment." *American Economic Review* 85:3, 647–653.
Shyam-Sunder, L., and Stewart C. Myers. 1999. "Testing Static Tradeoff against Pecking Order Models of Capital Structure." *Journal of Financial Economics* 51:2, 219–244.
Singh, Ajit. 1995. "Corporate Financial Patterns in Industrializing Economies: A Comparative International Study." Technical paper #2, International Finance Corporation, Washington, DC.
Singh, Ajit, Javed Hamid, Bahram Salimi, and Y. Nakano. 1992. "Corporate Financial Structures in Developing Countries." Technical Paper #1, International Finance Corporation, Washington, DC.
Smallbone, David, Monder Ram, David Deakins, and Robert Baldock. 2003. "Access to Finance by Ethnic Minority Businesses in the UK." *International Small Business Journal* 21:3, 291–314.
Spiegel, Yossef. 1996. "The Role of Debt in Procurement Contracts. " *Journal of Economics and Management Strategy* 5:3, 379–407.
Spiegel, Yossef. 1997. "The Choice of Technology and Capital Structure under Rate Regulation." *International Journal of Industrial Organization* 15:2, 191–216.

Spiegel, Yossef, and Daniel F. Spulber. 1994. "The Capital Structure of a Regulated Firm." *RAND Journal of Economics* 25:3, 424–440.

Spiegel, Yossef, and Daniel F. Spulber. 1997. "Capital Structure with Countervailing Incentives." *RAND Journal of Economics* 28:1, 1–24.

Stonehill, Arthur, Theo Beckhuisen, Richard Wright, Lee Remmers, Norman Toy, Antonio Pares, Alan Shapiro, Douglas Egan, and Thomas Bates. 1975. "Financial Goals and Debt Ratio Determinants: A Survey of Practice in Five Countries." *Financial Management* 4:3, 27–41.

Taggart, Robert A., Jr. 1981. "Rate of Return Regulation and Utility Capital Structure Decision." *Journal of Finance* 36:2, 383–393.

Taggart, Robert A., Jr. 1985. "Effects of Regulation on Utility Financing: Theory and Evidence." *Journal of Industrial Economics* 33:3, 257–276.

Talmor, Eli. 1981. "Asymmetric Information, Signaling, and Optimal Financial Decisions." *Journal of Financial and Quantitative Analysis* 16:4, 413–435.

Titman, Sheridan. 1984. "The Effect of Capital Structure on a Firm's Liquidation Decision." *Journal of Financial Economics* 13:1, 137–151.

Titman, Sheridan. 2001. "The Modigliani and Miller Theorem and Market Efficiency." Working Paper #8641, National Bureau of Economic Research.

Titman, Sheridan, and Roberto Wessels. 1988. "The Determinants of Capital Structure Choice." *Journal of Finance* 43:1, 1–19.

Verheul, Ingrid, and Roy A. Thurik. 2001. "Start-Up Capital: Differences between Male and Female Entrepreneurs." *Small Business Economics* 16:4, 329–345.

Vilasuso, Jon, and Alanson Minkler. 2001. "Agency Cost, Asset Specificity, and the Capital Structure of the Firm." *Journal of Economic Behavior and Organization* 44:1, 55–69.

Vincente-Lorente, José David. 2001. "Specificity and Opacity as Resource-Based Determinants of Capital Structure: Evidence from Spanish Manufacturing Firms." *Strategic Management Journal* 22:2, 157–177.

Wald, John K. 1999. "How Firm Characteristics Affect Capital Structure: An International Comparison." *Journal of Financial Research* 22:2, 161–187.

Williamson, Oliver E. 1975. *Market and Hierarchies: Analysis and Antitrust Implications*. New York: Free Press.

Williamson, Oliver E. 1985. *The Economic Institutions of Capitalism*. New York: Free Press.

Williamson, Oliver E. 1988. "Corporate Finance and Corporate Governance." *Journal of Finance* 43:3, 567–591.

ABOUT THE AUTHOR

Paroma Sanyal is an economist with Data for Decisions, an economic consulting firm in the Boston area. Previously, she was a faculty member at the Economics Department and the International Business School at Brandeis University. Her main expertise is in the area of industrial organization, corporate finance, and the energy sector. She has worked extensively on issues relating to the effects of regulation on the financial structure and innovation strategy of firms, on the effects of executive compensation and governance on various facets of firm performance, and on the capital structure of startups. She has published in well-regarded economics and finance journals such as the *Review of Economics and Statistics*, *Journal of Economics and Business*, *Annals of Finance*, *International Review of Economics and Finance*, *Journal of Regulatory Economics*, *Annales d'Economie et de Statistique*, and the *Energy Journal*. She received her PhD in Economics from the University of California, Irvine.

CHAPTER 13

Survey Evidence on Financing Decisions and Cost of Capital

FRANCK BANCEL
Professor, ESCP Europe

USHA R. MITTOO
Bank of Montreal Professor of Finance, University of Manitoba

INTRODUCTION

Most of the chapters in this book include findings from traditional empirical studies that are based on large samples of financial data. Empirical studies are the norm in financial research, as they allow researchers to conduct time-series and cross-sectional tests using powerful statistical analysis. This chapter and the next instead focus on survey studies that have a long tradition but are less common in finance. Surveys of managers provide unique information to understand how managers make corporate financing decisions. Some surveys have led to the development of new theories and the most important and influential research articles ever published in finance. For example, Lintner's (1956) seminal paper on how managers make dividend decisions is based on a field study of U.S. managers. Similarly, Pilcher's (1955) survey paper provided insights into why firms issue convertible debt that led to several theoretical and empirical studies on convertible debt decisions.

More recently, Graham and Harvey (2001) conduct a comprehensive survey of U.S. managers that provides valuable insights into the theory and practice of corporate finance covering cost of capital, capital budgeting, and capital structure decisions. Their paper has attracted much attention of both academics and practitioners and has spurred survey research across different countries around the world. Several recent studies rely on surveys to investigate how managers make decisions across countries on several corporate finance issues including international listings, initial public offerings, capital structure, convertible debt issuance, and dividend policy. These surveys have brought a new set of knowledge and increased understanding of financial practices across countries.

The survey method has several unique advantages and complements traditional empirical studies. The main advantage is that surveys allow researchers to ask direct questions on both the assumptions and implications of financial theories to validate or modify existing theories, and motivate new ones. Second, the survey method is a particularly useful tool in making cross-country comparisons. Financial data needed to conduct empirical studies might not be easily available or even comparable across countries. For example, differences in disclosure and reporting requirements make comparing financial statement and accounting data across countries difficult. Survey studies can partly overcome this problem by asking similar questions to managers around the world. To the extent that a country's institutions affect a firm's financing structure, their impact should be reflected in managerial policies and practices in that country. By comparing responses from multiple countries simultaneously, these studies provide valuable insights into which factors underlying corporate decisions are portable across countries and which are unique to a country. Finally, surveys have an advantage when timing of information collection is crucial for making informed decisions. Traditional empirical studies generally use historical data and are limited in their ability to deal with qualitative issues. Surveys facilitate the collection of both qualitative and quantitative data in a timely fashion. Managers also find surveys useful in learning about the practices of their peers. For example, survey studies conducted during the 2008 global financial crisis about the impact of the crisis provided valuable information to both corporate managers and policymakers in better understanding and dealing with the crisis.

Of course, the survey method has several limitations. A major drawback is that surveys measure beliefs—and not necessarily actions—of managers. Survey analysis also faces the risk that the respondents are not representative of the population and nonresponse bias could influence the results. Another limitation is that managers may not understand some questions, give a wrong or "politically correct" answer, or simply make decisions on different criteria than asked in survey questions. Despite these limitations, surveys are a valuable complementary method to empirical studies, and their use in finance is growing.

The goal of this chapter is to present survey evidence on cost of capital and financing decisions for U.S. and European managers. The remainder of the chapter consists of the following sections. The next section provides survey evidence on how managers compute the firm's cost of capital and account for risk factors in the cost of capital. The following section presents findings on the major determinants of managers' debt, equity, and convertible debt policies and examines differences across different legal system countries. The next section discusses some examples where theory and practice differs and discusses some plausible explanations and implications of these differences. The final section summarizes and concludes.

This chapter is not a comprehensive review of survey research on corporate financing issues. Instead, it focuses on the findings of a few surveys with the goal of providing a clear summary of the major determinants of U.S. and European managers' financing decisions. The next chapter complements this chapter by providing a more in-depth analysis of the country-specific factors in capital structure decisions. The reader interested in an in-depth study of survey research will find several useful references in both these chapters. Also, Baker, Singleton, and Veit (2010) provide a synthesis of survey research in corporate finance.

WHAT SURVEYS TELL ABOUT THE COST OF CAPITAL

How managers calculate the cost of capital is important in understanding their financing decisions. For example, managers can choose different sources of financing to minimize the firm's cost of capital and to manage additional risk factors associated with specific projects.

The Cost of Capital Estimation

While calculating the cost of debt is straightforward, computing the cost of equity is more complex. The corporate finance literature suggests several methods to compute the firm's cost of equity capital such as the capital asset pricing model (CAPM), a multi-beta CAPM (with extra risk factors in addition to the market beta), average historical returns, or a dividend discount model.

Exhibit 13.1 shows the results of several surveys involving the methods that firms use to calculate the cost of equity capital. In practice, the CAPM appears to be the most popular method. Graham and Harvey (2001) find that 73.5 percent of U.S. managers responding to their survey report that they always or almost always use the CAPM. The second and third most popular methods are average stock returns and a multi-beta CAPM, respectively. Only a small number of firms back the cost of equity out from a dividend discount model. Other criteria based on average historical returns on common stocks or including some extra "risk factors" to the CAPM are only marginally used. Bruner et al. (1998) also show that about 80 percent of U.S. corporations and financial advisors in their sample use the CAPM to estimate the cost of equity (not tabulated).

The findings of recent surveys contrast sharply with surveys conducted in the 1980s. For example, Gitman and Mercurio (1982) report results from 177 Fortune 1000 firms and find that only 22.6 percent of firms report using the CAPM compared to 26.0 percent who report using a version of the dividend model to establish their cost of capital. This evidence suggests that the use of CAPM has increased over time and the practice of finance has slowly converged with new techniques recommended in finance textbooks.

The use of CAPM, however, differs across countries. Brounen, de Jong, and Koedijk (2004) report that although the CAPM is the most popular method in Europe, only about 43 percent of European managers responding to their survey say that they always or almost always use CAPM. The average historical returns and some version of a multi-beta CAPM are the second and third most popular methods in European countries, but a relatively smaller percentage of European managers employ these methods relative to their U.S. peers. In sharp contrast to the U.S. and European evidence, the CAPM appears to be less popular in Canada. Baker, Dutta, and Saadi (2009) report that a majority of Canadian firms responding to their survey report using subjective judgment for cost of equity or using the cost of debt plus an equity premium. Less than 37 percent of Canadian firms indicate that they use the CAPM to calculate the cost of capital.

Major differences also exist across firms, especially between large and small firms. Large firms tend to use more sophisticated techniques and criteria (divisional

Exhibit 13.1 Cost of Equity Capital

	Gitman and Mercurio (1982)	Graham and Harvey (2001)	Baker et al. (2009)	Brounen et al. (2004)			
	United States		Canada	UK	Netherlands	Germany	France
	Used by responding firms (%)	Always or almost always (%)	% of Often or Always	Always or almost always (%)	Always or almost always (%)	Always or almost always (%)	Always or almost always (%)
Using the CAPM (market return adjusted for risk)	22.6	73.49	36.8	47.06	55.56	33.96	45.16
Average historical returns on common stock		39.41		31.25	30.77	18.00	27.27
CAPM with extra risk factors		34.29		27.77	15.38	16.07	30.30
Earnings/price (E/P) ratio	15.8		21.8				
Dividend/earnings growth model	26.0	15.74	12.9	10.0	10.71	10.42	10.34
Judgment			60.3				
Cost of debt plus a premium	13.0		52.3				
Return required by investors	35.6		20.0				

Note: This exhibit presents survey evidence about the cost of equity capital for the United States, Canada, and Europe. Data come from Gitman and Mercurio (1982), Graham and Harvey (2001), Baker, Dutta, and Saadi (2009), and Brounen, de Jong, and Koedijk (2004).

discount rates, each component of cash flow that has a different risk) to compute the cost of capital in both the United States and Europe. According to Graham and Harvey (2001), large firms, low leverage firms, and public firms are more likely to use CAPM. Brounen, de Jong, and Koedijk (2004) also report that the CAPM is more popular among large firms and among firms with substantial foreign sales. Bancel and Mittoo (2004a) survey large publicly-listed European firms and find that 60 percent of responding firms report using the CAPM, consistent with other survey findings.

Although the CAPM is a popular method, the evidence suggests that it may not be applied properly in practice. Bruner et al. (1998) show that the estimation of parameters, such as risk-free rate or market risk premium, differs markedly from one firm (or an adviser) to another. For example, some firms use a 90-day Treasury bill yield whereas others use a long-term Treasury bond yield to estimate risk-free rate. Gitman and Mercurio (1982) find that the firm's cost of capital estimates range between "less than 5 percent" to "higher than 25 percent" at a time where government bonds were 12.4 percent, indicating that the use of methods is not standardized.

Cost of Capital Adjustments for Risk Factors

The finance literature distinguishes between project risk and firm risk and suggests that the cost of capital should reflect the riskiness of the project. A unique firm-specific weighted average cost of capital (WACC) is appropriate only if the investment project has the same risk as the firm.

The practice appears to differ substantially from the prescribed theory as most managers use a company-wide discount rate to evaluate different projects. Based on their survey evidence, Graham and Harvey (2001) report that 58.8 percent of the U.S. managers responding to their survey say that they would always or almost always use the company-wide discount rate to evaluate projects with different risk characteristics, whereas 51 percent of these managers report using a risk-matched discount rate.

The findings about the reported use of WACC are similar across countries. According to Brounen, de Jong, and Koedijk (2004), most European firms responding to their survey also report using a company-wide discount rate to evaluate projects, including foreign projects, and less than one-third employ a risk-matched discount rate. Baker, Dutta, and Saadi (2009) report that 63.6 percent of Canadian firms responding to their survey report using the company's overall discount rate, and only 36.6 percent of Canadian firms indicate using a risk matched discount rate.

Bruner et al. (1998) find that discount rates are adjusted when the firm can establish benchmarks in the financial market, identify peer companies that allow data collection, and measure risk premiums. When estimating the firm-specific risk is difficult, managers adjust cash flows. They also find that while most of the U.S. companies and financial advisers responding to their survey report using the WACC to discount cash flows, almost all financial advisers indicate using different WACC for individual project valuation. This difference might be explained by the fact that financial advisers are specialized in finance and are more familiar with the methods presented in finance textbooks.

The survey evidence also shows that managers appear to account for several additional risk factors when evaluating investment projects. Graham and Harvey (2001) report that interest rate risk, size, inflation risk, and foreign exchange rate risk are the most important factors for the calculation of discount rates. Only a few firms adjust for book-to-market, distress, or momentum risk factors suggested in several academic theories. Brounen, de Jong, and Koedijk (2004) also report that the majority of European firms responding to their survey do not take specific risk factors into account when evaluating individual investment projects. For the calculation of discount rates, the most important factors are interest rate risk, size, inflation risk, and foreign exchange rate risk.

Again sharp differences exist between firms based on firm size and chief executive officer (CEO) characteristics. Large firms focus on different risk factors than small firms. Large firms focus more on foreign exchange risk, business cycle risk, commodity price risk, and interest rate (in addition to market risk), whereas small firms care more about interest rate risk. The findings for European firms are largely similar. Brounen, de Jong, and Koedijk (2004) also find that large firms are more concerned with foreign exchange risk, business cycle risk, commodity price risk, and interest rate risk and small firms with interest rate risk. Firms with a substantial level of foreign sales are more sensitive to exchange rate fluctuations.

WHAT SURVEYS TELL ABOUT FINANCING DECISIONS

Exhibits 13.2 and 13.3 summarize survey evidence on the major determinants of the U.S. and European Financial Executives' financing decisions and across different legal system countries. The U.S. and European results in these exhibits are based on Graham and Harvey (2001) and Bancel and Mittoo (2004a), respectively. Both surveys ask similar questions and request managers to rank the importance of factors on a scale of 0 (not important) to 4 (very important).

Debt Policy

Panel A in Exhibit 13.2 summarizes managers' responses on how firms choose the appropriate amount of debt. Both U.S. and European managers cite the desire for financial flexibility as the most important factor in their corporate debt decisions. Of the responding U.S. managers, 59 percent say that financial flexibility is important (rating of 3) or very important (rating of 4) (Panel A, mean rank = 2.59). The European managers assign an even higher ranking to this factor. In fact, 91 percent of European managers responding to the survey consider financial flexibility as important or very important in their debt financing decisions (Panel A, mean rank = 3.39). The concern about the firm's credit rating is the second most important determinant of debt level both in both U.S. and Europe (Panel A, mean rank = 2.46 and 2.78 for the United States and Europe, respectively).

Based on survey results, managers care about factors prescribed in standard trade-off theory but these appear to be second-order concerns. Less than half of U.S. managers consider tax advantage of debt (Panel A, mean rank = 2.07) and the volatility of earnings and cash flow (Panel A, mean rank = 2.32) as important

Exhibit 13.2 Factors Affecting Firm Debt Policy

	Graham and Harvey (2001)		Bancel and Mittoo (2004a)					
	United States		European Countries					
	Important or Very Important (%)	Mean	Important or Very Important (%)	Mean (all Europe)	English Law	French Law	German Law	Scandinavian Law
Panel A								
Financial flexibility.	59.38	2.59	90.80	3.39	3.00	3.48	3.43	3.43
Our credit rating (as assigned by rating agencies).	57.10	2.46	73.17	2.78	2.58	2.58	3.14	2.92
The tax advantage of interest deductibility.	44.85	2.07	58.14	2.59	2.92	2.87	2.33	1.93
The volatility of our earnings and cash flows.	48.08	2.32	50.00	2.33	2.00	2.42	2.3	2.42
The transactions costs and fees for issuing debt.	33.52	1.95	33.33	1.94	1.41	2.05	2.29	1.57
We limit debt so our customers/suppliers are not worried about our financial stability.	18.72	1.24	32.56	1.97	1.17	2.18	2.10	1.86
The potential costs of bankruptcy or near bankruptcy financial distress.	21.35	1.24	30.95	1.76	1.58	1.87	1.35	2.23
The debt levels of other firms in our industry.	23.40	1.49	23.26	1.84	1.67	1.85	1.9	1.86

(Continued)

Exhibit 13.2 *(Continued)*

	Graham and Harvey (2001)		Bancel and Mittoo (2004a)					
	United States		European Countries					
	Important or Very Important (%)	Mean	Important or Very Important (%)	Mean (all Europe)	English Law	French Law	German Law	Scandinavian Law
Panel B								
With the use of debt, we try to minimize the weighted average cost of capital.	NA	NA	69.77	2.80	2.33	3.00	2.81	2.62
We issue debt when interest rates are low.	46.35	2.22	44.83	2.10	1.17	2.15	2.62	2.00
We use debt when our equity is undervalued by the market.	30.79	1.56	43.68	2.08	1.92	2.23	1.86	2.14
We issue debt when our recent profits are not sufficient to fund our activities.	46.78	2.13	24.14	1.56	1.00	1.80	1.57	1.36
Panel C								
Matching the maturity of our debt with the life of our assets.	63.25	2.60	77.01	3.10	2.48	3.43	3.19	2.93
We issue long-term debt to minimize the risk of having to finance in "bad times."	48.83	2.15	69.77	2.83	2.42	2.95	2.76	2.92
We issue short-term when we are waiting for long-term market interest rates to decline.	35.94	1.78	31.03	1.85	1.00	1.80	2.52	1.71

Note: This exhibit presents survey evidence about U.S. and European firm debt policy. Data come from Graham and Harvey (2001) and Bancel and Mittoo (2004a). Respondents are asked to rate on a scale of 0 (not important) to 4 (very important). The exhibit reports the overall mean as well as the percent of respondents that answered 3 and 4 (important and very important).

in choosing the amount of debt. Less than one-fourth of U.S. managers consider potential cost of bankruptcy or financial distress as an important factor in debt financing decisions (Panel A, mean rank = 1.24). The European managers' views on trade-off theory factors are largely similar to their U.S. peers although a relatively higher percentage of European managers consider these factors important compared to their U.S. peers.

The cost-of-capital considerations also appears to influence debt policy (Panel B of Exhibit 13.2). About 70 percent of European managers agree that they try to minimize the WACC (mean rank = 2.80). Both U.S. and European managers also try to time the market to minimize their financing costs. More than 40 percent of managers issue debt when interest rates are low (Panel B, mean rank = 2.22 and 2.10 in U.S. and Europe, respectively) or when the firm's equity is undervalued by the market (Panel B, mean rank = 1.56 and 2.08 in the United States and Europe, respectively). About one-third of responding managers also say that they issue short-term debt when they are waiting for the long-term interest rates to decline (Panel C, mean rank = 1.78 and 1.85 in the United States and Europe, respectively).

Firms also try to manage risk when making financing choices. Hedging considerations play a major role in managers' choices between short-term and long-term debt. Of the responding managers to various surveys, about 63 percent of U.S. managers and 77 percent of European managers match the maturity of debt with that of the assets financed (Panel C, mean rank = 2.60 and 3.10 in the United States and Europe, respectively). About half of U.S. managers and 70 percent of European managers also say that they issue long-term debt to minimize the risk of refinancing in bad times (Panel C, mean rank = 2.15 and 2.83 in the United States and Europe, respectively). Hedging considerations are very important when issuing debt abroad. More than two-thirds of U.S. and European managers say that to provide a natural hedge against foreign currency devaluation and to keep the source of funds close to its use are important or very important factors in issuing foreign debt (not tabulated).

Survey results provide little evidence that managers follow their industry peers as less than one-fourth of U.S. and European managers agree that debt levels of other firms in the industry influence their debt level decisions (not tabulated). The support for financial theories based on factors such as signaling, transaction costs, asymmetric information, agency costs, and product market considerations is even weaker as these factors are considered unimportant.

Significant differences exist between large and small firms on some dimensions. Large firms are more likely to follow target debt ratios and use market timing than small firms. Providing a natural hedge is more important for large public firms with foreign exchange exposure whereas matching maturity of assets and liabilities is more important for small firms.

Common Stock Policy

Exhibit 13.3 (Panel A) presents managers' views on the determinants of their firm's common stock policy. Both U.S. and European managers identify earnings per share (EPS) dilution as the most important factor in their equity issuance decision. Of the survey respondents, about 69 percent of U.S. managers and 66 percent of European managers consider EPS dilution as an important or very important factor (mean

Exhibit 13.3 Factors Affecting Firm Decisions about Issuing Common Stock and Convertible Debt

	Graham and Harvey (2001)		Bancel and Mittoo (2004a)					
	United States		European Countries					
	Important or Very Important (%)	Mean	Important or Very Important (%)	Mean (all Europe)	English Law	French Law	German Law	Scandinavian Law
Panel A								
Earnings per share dilution.	68.55	2.84	66.04	2.72	3.2	2.96	2.87	1.56
Maintaining a target debt-to-equity ratio.	51.59	2.26	59.26	2.67	1.40	2.8	2.73	2.89
If our stock price has recently risen, the price at which we can issue is "high."	62.20	2.53	59.26	2.61	2.60	2.88	2.53	2.00
The amount by which our stock is undervalued or overvalued by the market.	66.94	2.69	53.7	2.44	3.20	2.44	2.40	2.11
Providing shares to employee stock option plan.	53.28	2.34	44.44	2.07	1.50	2.11	2.40	2.11
Whether our recent profits have been sufficient to fund our activities.	30.40	1.76	32.08	1.94	1.00	2.00	2.21	1.89
Diluting the holdings of certain shareholders.	50.41	2.14	29.63	1.67	1.00	1.76	1.80	1.56
Using a similar debt/equity ratio as is used by other firms in our industry.	22.95	1.45	27.78	1.85	1.40	1.84	2.13	1.67
Stock is our "least risky" source of funds.	30.58	1.76	25.93	1.50	2.40	1.72	1.13	1.00

Panel B								
Convertibles are an inexpensive way to issue "delayed" common stock.	58.11	2.49	57.14	2.45	2.67	2.67	2.5	1.20
Ability to "call" or force conversion of convertible debt if/when we need to.	47.95	2.29	54.76	2.43	1.75	2.57	2.10	3.00
Our stock is currently undervalued.	50.68	2.34	51.16	2.40	2.25	2.46	2.3	2.40
Avoiding short-term equity dilution.	45.83	2.18	51.16	2.16	2.75	2.33	2.22	0.80
Convertibles are less expensive than debt.	41.67	1.85	35.71	1.86	2.33	1.86	2.00	1.20
To attract investors unsure about the riskiness of our firm.	43.84	2.07	26.83	1.68	1.00	1.69	1.50	2.75

Note: This exhibit presents survey evidence about common stock and convertible debt issuance of U.S. and European firms. Data come from Graham and Harvey (2001) and Bancel and Mittoo (2004a). Respondents are asked to rate on a scale of 0 (not important) to 4 (very important). The exhibit reports the overall mean as well as the percent of respondents that answered 3 and 4 (important and very important).

rank = 2.84 and 2.72, respectively). The importance of earnings dilution is surprising and is in sharp contrast to the academic view. This point is discussed more fully in the next section.

The U.S. managers consider the amount of stock overvaluation or undervaluation as the second important factor (mean rank = 2.69) and a rise in the firm's stock price (mean rank = 2.53) as the third most important factor in their equity issuance decisions. This evidence supports the findings in numerous empirical studies that managers select the timing of financing decisions opportunistically to take advantage of attractive stock prices. For example, Kim and Weisbach (2008) show that firms around the world use market timing in their initial public offering (IPO) and seasoned equity offering (SEO) decisions. Baker and Wugler (2002) find that market timing has a persistent effect on firms' capital structure and argue that market timing is probably the single most important determinant of a firm's dynamic capital structure. Maintaining a target debt-to-equity ratio is ranked as the next important factor (mean rank = 2.26). European managers also agree with their U.S. peers about the importance of these three factors but assign slightly different rankings to them. European managers rank target debt ratio as the second most important factor (mean rank = 2.67), and stock price rise and under or overvaluation of stock as the third and fourth most important factors (mean rank = 2.61 and 2.44, respectively). Another interesting difference concerns the dilution of the holdings of certain shareholders when issuing stock. About 50 percent of the U.S. survey respondents consider such dilution important compared to less than 30 percent for their European counterparts (not tabulated). These differences could be explained partly by the sample differences since Bancel and Mittoo's (2004a) sample consists of large publicly-listed firms for which the dilution of certain shareholders may not be a major issue.

Other considerations for issuing equity include employee stock option plans (mean rank = 2.34 and 2.07 in the United States and Europe, respectively) when a firm has insufficient profits to finance investment activities (mean rank = 1.76 and 1.94 in United States and Europe, respectively). Other issues such as "capital gains tax rates faced by investors (relative to tax rates on dividends)" or debt-to-equity ratios of their industry peers are unimportant (not tabulated).

Other differences exist between large and small firms. For example, concern about EPS dilution is strong among large firms and dividend-paying firms. Large firms are also more likely to have target debt ratios compared to small firms.

Convertible Debt Policy

Why firms issue convertible debt has both intrigued and puzzled financial researchers. Several theories have been proposed to explain the rationale for convertible issuance. Most theories contend that convertible debt is an alternative to debt or equity and resolves a financing or investment problem facing the firm because of asymmetric information or agency problems (Brennan and Kraus 1987; Brennan and Schwartz 1988; Stein 1992; Mayers 1998).

The U.S. and the European convertible debt markets have several distinctive features. The U.S. convertible market is a well-developed and mature market and represents about 40 percent of the global convertible market. The U.S. convertible debt issuers are small, high-growth firms with high risk levels (Essig 1991; Lewis,

Rogalski, and Seward 1999, 2003). In contrast, European convertible debt issuers tend to be very large, financially healthy, and mature companies (Bancel and Mittoo 2004b).

Despite these differences, Exhibit 13.3 (Panel B) shows that U.S. and European managers consider similar factors when issuing convertible debt. About 60 percent of the U.S. and European managers responding to the survey value convertible debt as an inexpensive way to issue "delayed" common stock (mean rank = 2.49 and 2.45 in the United States and Europe, respectively). The option to issue convertible debt when equity is undervalued (mean rank = 2.34 and 2.40 in the United States and Europe, respectively) and avoiding short-term equity dilution are also cited as important advantages of issuing convertible debt (mean rank = 2.18 and 2.16 in the United States and Europe, respectively) and are consistent with the responses on common stock policy. Respondents also consider the "ability to call" or the flexibility to force conversion of convertible debt as an important advantage in issuing convertible debt (mean rank = 2.29 and 2.43 in the United States and Europe, respectively). However, few managers agree with the statement that convertibles are less expensive than debt.

Bancel and Mittoo (2004b) conduct an in-depth survey of European managers about why they issue convertibles. They also confirm that a majority of responding firms issue convertibles as "debt sweetener" and as an inexpensive way to issue "delayed" common stocks (and implicitly to postpone equity dilution). The authors also find strong evidence that managers attempt to time the market when issuing convertibles. European managers consider that a combination of low interest rates and high stock market volatility provides a good "window of opportunity" for issuing convertibles. Bancel and Mittoo find mixed support for most theories and conclude that the popularity of convertibles appears to be driven primarily by their flexibility in adjusting convertible design to fit the financing needs of individual firms and the investment needs of different institutional investors. This evidence is consistent with the need for financial flexibility mentioned by managers in issuing debt.

Comparisons across Legal Systems

Several studies examine the role of different legal systems and financial institutions in explaining leverage differences across countries. The premise is that the English legal system provides the strongest investor protection followed by German and Scandinavian systems with French legal system providing weakest protection. La Porta et al. (1997, 1998) hypothesize that the legal system is the primary determinant of the availability of external financing in a country and test this hypothesis in 49 countries around the world. They show that the size and breadth of capital markets vary systematically and positively with the quality of legal systems across countries. Other researchers highlight the differences in the market-based and bank-based system countries. Demirguc-Kunt and Maksimovic (1999) argue that both financial and legal institutions influence firms' financing choices and find evidence consistent with this prediction in a comparison of debt maturity across 30 countries. Demirguc-Kunt and Maksimovic (2002) argue that the legal systems in different countries can have different comparative advantages in supporting a quality banking system or quality securities markets.

Bancel and Mittoo (2004a) compare the responses of European managers across different legal system countries. Columns 5–8 in Exhibits 13.2 and 13.3 present these comparisons and show that rankings of most factors are strikingly similar across legal systems. However, there are also some notable differences on some dimensions even across systems of similar quality. For instance, despite similar quality of investor protection, managers' concern about the potential cost of bankruptcy is significantly higher in Scandinavian-system countries compared to their German-system peers (Exhibit 13.2, Panel A, mean rank = 1.35 versus 2.23). Firms in countries with low protection of creditors' rights are also more concerned about earnings volatility and financing in bad times, as expected.

Some evidence suggests that the financial system might influence the ranking of some factors. Further, firms in English system countries care less about financial flexibility and more about earnings dilution compared to their peers in other legal systems. This finding may partly be explained by market-based system since English system countries also tend to be market-based countries. Brounen, de Jong, and Koedijk (2004) also report that the concern for earnings dilution is higher in market-oriented countries. Overall, the evidence provides moderate support for the view that debt policy factors vary systematically with the quality of legal system but the determinants of equity policy appear to be related more with market-based financial systems. Further, the influence of firm-specific factors, such as firm size and ownership structure, is stronger than that of legal or financial system factors in explaining variation across countries.

THE GAP BETWEEN THEORY AND PRACTICE

The survey research discussed in the previous two sections shows that the practice of finance generally differs from that prescribed by financial theories. Some support exists for the trade-off and pecking order theories but little support for theories based on other factors such as asymmetric information or agency costs. The fact that most firms tend to use the CAPM for cost of equity and consider cost of capital in their financing decisions is reassuring. However, the evidence that managers rely primarily on financial flexibility and EPS dilution for their debt and equity decisions shows a wide gap in theory and practice of finance. Some plausible explanations for these findings and their implications for current theory and practice of corporate finance are discussed more fully below.

Financial Flexibility

Managers identify the need for financial flexibility as the main driver of their financing decisions. This finding is confirmed across countries and legal systems as well as in both earlier and more recent surveys such as Pinegar and Wilbricht (1989) and Graham and Harvey (2001). Bancel and Mittoo (2009) report that European managers also cite financial flexibility as a major factor in the IPO decision.

Two managerial surveys conducted during the recent global financial crisis also highlight the value of financial flexibility for firms around the world. Campello, Graham, and Harvey (2010) survey 1,050 chief financial officers (CFOs) in the United States, Europe, and Asia in December 2008 about the impact of the crisis on real corporate decisions. They ask respondents directly about their firm's financial constraints and find that small, private, speculative "constrained" firms were more severely affected by the credit crisis. The authors also report that financially constrained firms plan to cut more investment, research and development (R&D), marketing, and employment relative to financially unconstrained firms during the crisis.

Bancel and Mittoo (2010) survey managers of French firms in June 2009 about the impact of the global financial crisis. They ask questions on the firm's degree of financial flexibility and its debt and equity policies, both before and during the global crisis. The authors find that the crisis intensity is strongly negatively related to the firm's degree of financial flexibility. Bancel and Mittoo report that firms with high degree of internal financing tend to be more financially flexible as they tend to have low leverage, low trade credit, and high cash holdings. Their evidence also shows that financially flexible firms are less likely to say that banks are reluctant to lend and that financially flexible firms also tend to have more business flexibility.

In sum, strong evidence exists that managers perceive that their primary mission is to obtain financing for the firm, no matter what the economic conditions might be. Their focus on financial flexibility also suggests that in practice the access to financing is more difficult and complex than theories assume. Some managers state explicitly that they remain flexible in the sense of minimizing interest obligations so that they do not need to shrink their business in case of an economic downturn (Graham and Harvey 2001) or that to "negotiate financing when you don't need it" is really important (Bancel and Mittoo 2004a).

Despite its importance for managers, financial flexibility has received little attention in the academic literature. Traditional financing theories such as pecking order theory and trade-off theories assign little or no role to financial flexibility. Thus, why financial theories do not highlight financial flexibility is intriguing. One plausible explanation for this gap could be that financial flexibility is unobservable and difficult to measure. Financial flexibility is the ability of a firm to respond effectively to its cash flow and investment opportunity shocks. Some researchers define it as "untapped borrowing power," while others use debt and cash ratios to measure financial flexibility (e.g., Denis and Sibilkov 2009). However, in practice, firms can use several different sources such as bank credit lines and commercial paper to enhance their financial flexibility. Financial flexibility is also likely to depend on several other factors such as access to different sources of financing, access to foreign markets (e.g., foreign listing in the United States), and short-term trading credit. More importantly, financial flexibility could also be the part of the firm's business strategy requiring an efficient risk management and a capacity to signal to investors positive net present value (NPV) projects and to seize market opportunities. In that sense, financial flexibility is an integrating concept for major corporate finance theories.

Several recent empirical studies also provide evidence supporting this view. Graham (2000) finds that firms use their "financial flexibility (i.e., preserve debt capacity) to make future expansions and acquisitions but they appear to retain much unused flexibility even after expanding. Denis and Sibilkov (2009) conclude that the need for financial flexibility appears to drive debt decisions of firms. Other researchers note that the trade-off and pecking order theories cannot explain several observed phenomena about firms' financing behavior. For example, why many profitable firms maintain low debt and why equity issues are commonplace and not exclusively the financing vehicle of last resort (Fama and French 2005) cannot be explained by these theories.

DeAngelo and DeAngelo (2007) argue that financial flexibility is the critical missing link for an empirically viable theory of capital structure. They argue that traditional theory fails to recognize the intertemporal dependencies in the firm's financing activity since firms will select ex-ante financial policies that ex-post provide flexibility to access capital markets. DeAngelo and DeAngelo develop an intertemporal capital structure model that incorporates components of both pecking order and trade-off theory. Gamba and Triantis (2008) develop a dynamic model of the value of financial flexibility that focuses on the strategic management of corporate liquidity and its relation with the firm's financing and investment policies. Survey research has motivated development of new theories based on financial flexibility and this trend is likely to continue in the near future.

EPS Dilution

The financial theory suggests that equity dilution should not be a major concern if the new equity is invested in positive NPV projects, because it will increase firm value. The debt issuance could increase EPS if the number of a firms' shares outstanding remains constant. However, with additional risk equity will become riskier, and firm value will remain the same, all else equal. But this is not what financial managers report. Equity dilution is the most important decision criterion in issuing equity for both U.S. and European managers. Managers also report that avoiding short-term equity dilution is an important advantage of issuing convertible debt (Graham and Harvey 2001; Bancel and Mittoo 2004a).

Why equity dilution is important for managers remains a puzzle for academics. Some plausible explanations for this gap could be as follows. First, the importance of EPS dilution could partly reflect the focus of financial analysts' on EPS for stock valuation. Moreover, computing the impact on the firm's EPS is easier than computing the project NPV that requires detailed project-specific information, which is generally unavailable publicly. The evidence that EPS dilution is more important in the capital market–oriented countries is consistent with this view. Second, financial analysis and managers might focus on short-term financial activities whereas most financial theories are based on long-term time horizons. The financial community and managers may accept the idea that long-term planning is very difficult and use short-term criteria based on EPS for stock valuation. Finally, business schools are good at teaching some concepts better than others. Graham and Harvey (2001) report that EPS dilution is less important when CEOs have an MBA degree than when they do not, supporting this view.

SUMMARY AND CONCLUSIONS

This chapter summarizes the evidence on the major determinants of the firm's financing and cost of capital decisions based on surveys of financial executives in the United States and Europe. Although survey studies are less common in finance, they provide valuable insights into the link between theory and practice of finance.

The survey research shows that managers use different criteria in making financing decisions from those prescribed in theories but adhere more closely to the textbook teachings when making cost of capital decisions. Managers rely primarily on informal criteria in making financing decisions. In particular, managers identify financial flexibility as the main driver of their debt policy and EPS dilution as their primary concern in issuing common stock. Both of these factors are not emphasized in major financial theories.

Moderate support exists that firms follow the trade-off theory and use target debt ratio but less support for theories based on other factors such as asymmetric information or agency costs. Managers care about cost of capital and trade-off the costs and benefits of financing, but these are secondary-level concerns. Managers try to use "windows of opportunity" when raising capital and consider recent stock price appreciation as the most important factors influencing equity issuance decision. Firms use convertibles as "backdoor equity" or a "debt sweetener," and market timing factors are also dominant in convertible debt issuance decisions.

Managers also try to manage risk factors when raising capital. Survey evidence shows that most responding managers match the maturity of debt with the length of the project and hedge foreign exchange risk by matching sources of financing with the project. Most survey respondents also report using the CAPM to estimate cost of equity, and its popularity has increased over time, although they may not use it properly. Managers adjust for some risk factors but do not adjust for project risk. Survey evidence suggests that most managers use a company-wide discount rate to evaluate projects even when investing abroad.

Sharp differences exist across firms, especially between small and large firms. Firm size, CEO education, and level of development of financial markets are major variables in cost of capital and financing decisions. Small firms rely more on informal criteria for their cost of capital decisions. Also, small firms generally are less sophisticated when evaluating risky projects than large firms. Large firms use classical finance textbook criteria. Compared with small firms, they are more concerned about earnings dilution, credit rating, and target debt-to-equity ratios. Managers with an MBA are more likely to use sophisticated financial techniques than those without this degree.

Finally, managers' views on the major determinants of financing policy are strikingly similar across countries, but some evidence suggests that legal and country-specific factors play a role. A country's financial system can explain some differences. For example, managers in market-based systems have lower concern about financial flexibility and higher concern about earnings dilution compared to their peers in bank-based systems.

In sum, managers' criteria for their financing decisions do not match with theoretical factors. This gap between theory and practice could be due to several reasons. First, academic theories might make strong assumptions that may not apply in the "real" world. For example, several theories assume that a firm can easily raise financing in capital markets to invest in its positive NPV projects. In practice, this access is not guaranteed. In the "real world," the access to capital markets might be restricted especially for small and private firms. This reason could potentially explain why managers highly value financial flexibility, and why access to financing to meet unanticipated cash flow shocks or investment opportunities is their major concerning financing decisions. The financial crisis has shown that managers may not be wrong.

Another reason could be that theories do not provide sufficient guidance in how to measure different parameters to apply in practice. Welch (2000) finds that the estimation of the market risk premium differs significantly among both firms and financial economists. For example, the CAPM estimation could differ widely across firms because of differences in the choice of the market risk premium and beta estimation. Another reason could be that managers might devote more time to short-term financial activities while textbook and academic theories emphasize long-term financial perspective. Finally, managers may act consistently with some theoretical predictions, but this effect may be difficult to observe at an individual firm level. For example, the debt may increase the pressure on firm managers for performance as predicted in some theories based on agency cost, but it may not be obvious at the individual level. However, the relation between debt and performance may hold in empirical studies that use large aggregate firm-level data. Thus, survey studies should be viewed as complementary to empirical studies relying on secondary data.

Despite these limitations, the survey approach allows researchers to collect qualitative data that would be difficult to obtain otherwise. What chief financial officers (CFOs) have in mind and what criteria they use in making cost of capital and financing decisions are important for corporate finance research. Survey evidence can enhance understanding of current theories and motivate new theories.

DISCUSSION QUESTIONS

1. What are the major limitations of the survey method, and how can researchers address them?
2. Survey evidence shows striking differences in the responses of large and small firms? What factors might explain these differences?
3. Does a country's institutional and legal system play a major role in corporate financing decisions? If so, how?
4. Briefly discuss the survey evidence on market timing in financing decisions. Is survey evidence consistent with findings in empirical studies?

REFERENCES

Baker, H. Kent, Shantanu Dutta, and Samir Saadi. 2009. "Corporate Finance Practices in Canada: Where Do We Stand?" Working Paper, University of Ontario Institute of Technology.

Baker, H. Kent, J. Clay Singleton, and E. Theodore Veit. 2010. *Survey Research in Corporate Finance: Bridging the Gap between Theory and Practice.* New York and Oxford: Oxford University Press.

Baker, Malcolm, and Jeffrey Wurgler. 2002. "Market Timing and Capital Structure." *Journal of Finance* 57:1, 1–32.

Bancel, Franck, and Usha Mittoo. 2004a. "Cross-Country Determinants of Capital Structure Choice: A Survey of European Firms." *Financial Management* 33:4, 103–132.

Bancel, Franck, and Usha Mittoo. 2004b. "Why Do European Firms Issue Convertible Debt?" *European Financial Management* 10:2, 339–374.

Bancel, Franck, and Usha Mittoo. 2009. "Why Do European Firms Go Public?" *European Financial Management* 15:4, 844–884.

Bancel, Franck, and Usha Mittoo. 20010. "Financial Flexibility and the Impact of Global Financial Crisis: Evidence from France." Working Paper, ESCP Europe and University of Manitoba. Available at http://papers.ssrn.com/sol3/papers.cfm?abstract_id=1587302.

Brennan, Michael J., and Alan Kraus. 1987. "Efficient Financing under Asymmetric Information." *Journal of Finance* 42:5, 1225–1243.

Brennan, Michael J., and Eduardo S. Schwartz. 1998. "The Case for Convertibles." *Journal of Applied Corporate Finance* 1:2, 55–64.

Brounen, Dirk, Abe de Jong, and Kees Koedijk. 2004. "Corporate Finance in Europe: Confronting Theory with Practice." *Financial Management* 33:4, 71–101.

Bruner, F. Robert, Kennes E. Eades, Robert S. Harris, and Robert C. Higgins. 1998. "Best Practices in Estimating the Cost of Capital: Survey and Synthesis." *Financial Practice and Education* 8:1, 13–28.

Campello, Murillo, John R. Graham, and Campbell R. Harvey. 2010. "The Real Effects of Financial Constraints: Evidence from a Financial Crisis." *Journal of Financial Economics,* forthcoming. Available at http://papers.ssrn.com/sol3/papers.cfm?abstract_id=1318355.

DeAngelo, Harry, and Linda DeAngelo. 2007. "Capital Structure, Payout Policy and Financial Flexibility." Working Paper, Marshall School of Business, No. FBE 02-06.

Demirguc-Kunt, Asli, and Vojislav Maksimovic. 1999. "Institutions, Financial Markets and Firm Debt Maturity." *Journal of Financial Economics* 54:3, 295–336.

Demirguc-Kunt, Asli, and Vojislav Maksimovic. 2002. "Funding Growth in Bank-Based and Market-Based Financial Systems: Evidence from Firm-Level Data." *Journal of Financial Economics* 65:3, 337–363.

Denis, David J., and Valeriy Sibilkov. 2009. "Financial Constraints, Investment, and the Value of Cash Holdings." *Review of Financial Studies* 23:1, 247–269.

Essig, Stuart. 1991. "Convertible Securities and Capital Structure Determinants." PhD Dissertation, Graduate School of Business, University of Chicago.

Fama, Eugene, and Kenneth R. French. 2005. "Financing Decisions: Who Issues Stock?" *Journal of Financial Economics* 76:3, 549–582.

Gamba, Andréa, and Alexander Triantis. 2008. "The Value of Financial Flexibility." *Journal of Finance* 63:5, 2263–2296.

Gitman, Lawrence J., and Vincent A. Mercurio. 1982. "Cost of Capital Techniques Used by Major U.S. Firms: Survey and Analysis of Fortune's 1000." *Financial Management* 11:4, 21–29.

Graham, John R. 2000. "How Big Are the Tax Benefits of Debt?" *Journal of Finance* 55:5, 1901–1941.

Graham, John R., and Campbell R. Harvey. 2001. "The Theory and Practice of Corporate Finance: Evidence from the Field." *Journal of Financial Economics* 60:2/3, 187–243.

Kim, Woojin, and Michael S. Weisbach. 2008. "Motivations for Public Equity Offers: An International Perspective." *Journal of Financial Economics* 87:2, 281–307.

La Porta, Rafael, Florencio Lopez-de-Silanes, Andrei Shleifer, and Robert W. Vishny. 1997. "Legal Determinants of External Finance." *Journal of Finance* 52:3, 1131–1150.

La Porta, Rafael, Florencio Lopez-de-Silanes, Andrei Shleifer, and Robert W. Vishny. 1998. "Law and Finance." *Journal of Political Economy* 106:6, 1113–1155.

Lewis, Craig M., Richard J. Rogalski, and James K. Seward. 1999. "Is Convertible Debt a Substitute for Straight Debt or for Common Equity?" *Financial Management* 28:3, 5–27.

Lewis, Craig M., Richard J. Rogalski, and James K. Seward. 2003. "Industry Conditions, Growth Opportunities and Market Reactions to Convertible Debt Financing Decisions." *Journal of Banking and Finance* 27:1, 153–181.

Lintner, John. 1956. "Distribution of Incomes of Corporations among Dividends, Retained Earnings and Taxes." *American Economic Review* 46:2, 97–113.

Mayers, David. 1998. "Why Firms Issue Convertible Bonds: The Matching of Financial and Real Investment Options." *Journal of Financial Economics* 47:1, 83–102.

Pilcher, James C. 1955. *Raising Capital With Convertible Securities*. Ann Arbor, MI: University of Michigan Press.

Pinegar, Michael J., and Lisa Wilbricht. 1989. "What Managers Think of Capital Structure Theory: A Survey." *Financial Management* 18:4, 82–91.

Stein, Jeremy C. 1992. "Convertible Bonds as Backdoor Equity Financing." *Journal of Financial Economics* 32:1, 3–21.

Welch, Ivo. 2000. "Views of Financial Economists on the Equity Premium and on Professional Controversies." *Journal of Business* 73:4, 501–537.

ABOUT THE AUTHORS

Franck Bancel is Professor at ESCP Europe (France). He received a PhD (Grenoble II) and his "Habilitation à Diriger des Recherches" (Paris IX Dauphine). Professor Bancel has published several books including *Fusions d'Entreprises* (Eyrolles 2008), *Choix des Investissements* (Economica 2002), and articles in academic journals such as *Financial Management*, *European Financial Management*, and *Revue d'Economie Financière*. He has published several articles with Professor Mittoo comparing European firm financial practices with their U.S. peers and measuring distances between theories and practices. Professor Bancel was Associate Dean for research from 2002 to 2006 and Director of the ESCP Europe PhD program of the Paris campus from 2003 to 2006.

Usha R. Mittoo is the Bank of Montreal Professor of Finance at the I. H. Asper School of Business, University of Manitoba, Canada. She received her PhD in Finance from the University of British Columbia. Her main research interests concern international capital markets and corporate finance areas with a focus on cross-country studies. She has published papers in several top academic journals including *Journal of Finance* and *Journal of Corporate Finance*, and in practitioner-oriented journals such as the *Journal of Applied Corporate Finance*. Professor Mittoo is currently serving on the editorial boards of several academic journals. She has won several awards and honors for her teaching, research, and service activities including several CMA merit awards for excellence in teaching and research.

CHAPTER 14

Survey Evidence on Capital Structure: Non-U.S. Evidence

ABE DE JONG
Professor of Corporate Finance, Erasmus University and Professor of Financial Accounting, University of Groningen

PATRICK VERWIJMEREN
Lecturer, University of Melbourne

INTRODUCTION

From large multinational companies to small entrepreneurial firms, financing decisions are important because they influence the value of the firm, enable or disable access to financing future growth, and co-determine the survival chances of the firm. Decision makers are aware of the importance of the choice between debt, equity, and intermediate instruments, as well as of the relevance of the leverage—the relative amount of debt—of their companies. This chapter provides a discussion of capital structure choice from the decision maker's perspective and documents survey evidence about financing choice for non-U.S. companies.

In his address to the American Finance Association, Myers (1984, p. 575) posed the following question: "How do firms choose their capital structures?" and answered this with: "We don't know." In this book many chapters discuss theoretical insights in optimal capital structure choices of companies or present models that aim to explain capital structure decisions in firms from the perspectives of managerial self-interest or even behavioral finance. So far, the theoretical literature has not converged on a single encompassing theoretical framework for optimal financing choice. Instead, the literature is characterized by a large number of more or less independent theories about financing decisions.

Empirical research serves to rigorously test the capital structure theories. The need for this testing is best evidenced by Myers (1984, p. 576): "Given time and imagination, economists can usually invent some model that assigns apparent economic rationality to any random event." Using such methodologies as cross-sectional or panel data regression models and event studies, many studies test relations between variables, which approximate (i.e., are "proxies" for) theoretical constructs. These tests provide many important stylized facts about capital structure decisions and often meaningful connections between these facts and theory are made. Although most empirical results pertain to U.S. data sets, several studies provide international evidence. Following the study of Rajan and Zingales (1995) for G7 countries, Wald (1999) and De Jong, Kabir, and Nguyen (2008) are examples of studies in which large numbers of countries relate standard proxy variables to capital structure variables. Interestingly, these studies find very similar effects across countries as well as significant differences. This result hints at the co-existence of both fundamental capital structure determinants and institutional influences and makes further international comparative work highly relevant.

Survey research is typically motivated by the fact that indirect tests of the decision makers' intentions and considerations via proxy variables neither allow unambiguous tests of theory nor provide undisputable answers to Myers's (1984) initial question. Survey-based research can add to the body of knowledge about capital structure choice. In survey research, financial decision makers are directly approached with standard questions and provide their views on these questions. Although many fields of scientific research mainly rely on this empirical technique, in corporate finance relatively few studies are based on survey evidence. However, since the extensive survey by Graham and Harvey (2001) among U.S. chief financial officers (CFOs), there is a renewed interest in survey research. This chapter describes non-U.S. survey evidence, starting from the earliest work by Stonehill et al. (1975) until the most recent studies, building on the survey by Graham and Harvey.

In addition to the standard approach in corporate finance surveys, where the researcher asks for opinions about actual practices and the relevance of specific considerations, this chapter also provides a discussion of alternative research methods based on survey-based data. The aim is to provide an overview of the added value of empirical research based on survey data. The chapter is not intended to be exhaustive but discusses selective studies. The chapter excludes surveys that only collect information that is available via public sources for other firms: especially for small and medium-sized companies, researchers typically collect balance sheets and profit-and-loss statements via surveys (e.g., Cassar and Holmes 2003).

The structure of the chapter is as follows. The chapter first discusses the evidence from capital structure surveys. Next, it discusses studies using alternative approaches with survey data. Finally, the chapter presents ideas for future research and conclusions.

EVIDENCE FROM CAPITAL STRUCTURE SURVEYS

This section discusses the earliest capital structure surveys. It then presents the evidence for European countries because most non-U.S. studies focus on this region, and then reviews papers from other regions.

Early Studies

Early studies surveyed financial managers before the pecking order theory, static trade-off theory, and market timing theory were well-developed. Stonehill et al. (1975) is an early study that uses survey data to examine the determinants of capital structure. The authors report results based on a 1972–1973 survey of financial executives in 87 firms in France, Japan, the Netherlands, Norway, and the United States. Interestingly, their survey questions already relate to capital structure theories that had not been formally developed in the literature at that point in time. For example, their questions include the statement "we try to maintain a debt ratio equal to the debt ratios of other firms," which hints towards the potential importance of a target debt ratio. Also, another statement—"we take advantage of favorable financing opportunities to issue either debt or equity as they occur"—indicates the potential importance of market timing. Both statements receive some support in their study. Overall, the authors conclude that financial executives are more concerned with financial risk and the availability of capital than its cost. This evidence highlights the importance of financial flexibility that is confirmed in later surveys.

Stonehill et al. (1975) not only use survey data on the determinants of capital structure but also examine countries from three different continents. In fact, the country differences are an important motivation for the study. The authors argue that an important decision for financial executives of multinational firms is whether or not to allow foreign subsidiaries to use debt ratios typical in their host countries. Allowing these debt ratios may lead to a debt ratio on the consolidated balance sheet that is abnormal to the multinational's home country. Stonehill et al. find various differences in managers' perceptions among countries. Most notably, the tax advantages of debt are ranked very highly in the Netherlands but not in the four other countries.

Stonehill et al. (1975) do not directly ask questions on a financing hierarchy of firms. Fawthrop and Terry (1975), who survey senior financial executives of 54 large U.K. firms in 1974, focus on financing preferences. Their study builds on the work of Donaldson (1961). Donaldson's description of firms' financing preferences mirrors Myers's (1984) pecking order theory: Firms' managers prefer internal financing over debt financing and only use equity financing when the debt capacity is reached. Fawthrop and Terry report that this financing order appears to be the opinion of the large majority of financial executives. Regarding the debt capacity, the authors note that many executives mention a 40 percent limit of debt financing but none who could explain why 40 percent should be the 'magic figure'.

European Evidence

As mentioned in the introduction, Graham and Harvey (2001) have renewed interest in survey evidence. Surveys allow for comparisons across countries. A problem in nonsurvey cross-country research is typically that differences in accounting and disclosure practices make comparing and interpreting financial data difficult across countries. Survey evidence can add to the understanding of cross-country differences simply by asking managers about their views in different institutional settings. Bancel and Mittoo (2004) and Brounen, de Jong, and Koedijk. (2004, 2006) survey CFOs in European countries. Bancel and Mittoo include more countries (Austria, Belgium, Greece, Denmark, Finland, Ireland, Italy, France, Germany, the Netherlands, Norway, Portugal, Spain, Switzerland, Sweden, and the United Kingdom) than Brounen, de Jong, and Koedijk (who study the United Kingdom, the Netherlands, France and Germany). Yet, Brounen, de Jong, and Koedijk have a substantially larger sample size (313 CFOs versus 87 CFOs in Bancel and Mittoo). These studies allow for a two-way analysis of how institutional environments affect managers' views. First, a comparison can be made between the results in

Europe and results obtained by Graham and Harvey in the United States. Second, country differences within Europe can be exploited.

Similar to Graham and Harvey (2001), both studies find that financial flexibility and credit ratings are very important determinants of firms' financing policies. As in Stonehill et al. (1975), Brounen, de Jong, and Koedijk's (2004, 2006) results show that managers in the Netherlands value tax deductions more than managers in most other countries, but the difference is relatively small. Bancel and Mittoo (2004) find that the legal system has an effect on capital structure. Their evidence shows that concern for financial flexibility is higher in civil law systems, which could possibly be explained by the dearth of available external financing in these systems. Overall, however, the studies conclude the rankings of most factors in Europe are strikingly similar to those in the United States. Although there are differences across countries and legal systems, the same factors apparently drive most of the capital structure decisions in the United States and Europe.

Bancel and Mittoo (2004) and Brounen, de Jong, and Koedijk (2006) use the same questions as Graham and Harvey (2001) in order to draw a comparison between results. Although these questions provide strong insight into firms' financing decisions, they do not explicitly ask about the pecking order theory. Beattie, Goodacre, and Thomson (2006) survey 198 managers in the United Kingdom and do ask directly about firms' financing hierarchy. They report that 60 percent of the respondents claim to follow a financing hierarchy, while 51 percent of the respondents seek to maintain a target debt level. Their results indicate that respondents do not view having a target debt level and having a financing hierarchy as mutually exclusive: 32 percent claim to follow both the pecking order theory and the static trade-off theory, and 22 percent follow neither. For 80 percent of the respondents that do have a target debt ratio, the target debt-assets ratio is 50 percent or lower, indicating an increase compared to Fawthrop and Terry's (1975) finding of 40 percent. Beattie et al. further report that "ensuring the long-term survivability of the company" is the main determinant of capital structure, which seems very similar to valuing financial flexibility or financial conservatism.

Evidence from Other Countries

The impact of institutional environments can be studied further by focusing on countries outside the United States and Europe. A relatively early study of Allen (1991) focuses on Australia. Allen uses semistructured interviews with financial executives of 48 Australian listed companies. He reports that 40 respondents indicate having a policy of maintaining spare debt capacity. As interviewees also note that this policy improves credit ratings, Allen's findings foreshadow Graham and Harvey's (2001) findings on the relevance of financial flexibility and credit ratings. Allen concludes that his findings in Australia are very supportive of Donaldson's (1961) description of firms' financing policy. As he held his interviews around the 1987 market crash, Allen (p. 119) not surprisingly also finds evidence that managers believe "in the existence of a capital market window which opens and shuts at times outside their control."

A survey by Cohen and Yagil (2007) covers 140 managers in the United States, the United Kingdom, Germany, Canada, and Japan. As could be expected, the responses of the managers in these countries also point toward the importance of financial flexibility. Although credit ratings are also perceived as important, the average ranking of credit ratings in Cohen and Yagil is lower than in Graham and Harvey (2001), for example. In Japan, Cohen and Yagil find credit ratings to be more important than financial flexibility. As described in the next subsection, Allen (2000) also reports this reduced importance of financial flexibility. In a follow-up study, Cohen and Yagil (2010) examine sectorial differences in managers' views. They find various differences across sectors. For example, a typical manager in the banking and finance industry finds the corporate tax rate substantially more important than a typical manager in the technology sector.

So far, the chapter has focused on studies that mainly describe developed markets. Kester et al. (1998) survey executive officers in a range of Asia-Pacific countries in the period 1990 to 1996. These countries—Australia, Hong Kong, Indonesia, Malaysia, the Philippines, and Singapore—have varying levels of stock market development. The authors use the same questionnaire that is used by Pinegar and Wilbricht (1989) in the United States. Pinegar and Wilbricht survey 176 large U.S. firms and conclude that pecking order predictions are more descriptive of the respondents' answers than the static trade-off theory.

Kester et al. (1998) find that pecking order predictions are overall far more predictive of capital structure decisions than the static trade-off theory in Asia-Pacific countries. As in most surveys, however, the pecking order theory is presented as a financing hierarchy, and the survey questions do not require that information asymmetry drive the hierarchy. Ensuring long-term survivability and financial flexibility are the two most important factors in the Asia-Pacific countries according to Kester et al., whose results show a great resemblance to the results in the United States and Europe. In general, the strongest country differences in their sample can be observed between Australia and the Asian countries. These differences likely follow from the relatively well-developed market in Australia, as the other countries have more emerging markets. Kester et al. report that 43.1 percent of Australian managers believe that their securities are rightly priced more than 80 percent of the time. By contrast, Pinegar and Wilbricht (1989) report that 47.2 percent of U.S. managers believe that their prices are right more than 80 percent of the time. The percentages in the other countries are all below 20 percent. In Singapore, only 4.8 percent of the managers believe that the stock price is right more than 80 percent of the time.

Fan and So (2004) survey Hong Kong managers both in 1994 (before the 1997 Asian crisis) and in 1999 (after the crisis). Before the crisis, the authors find that more than three-quarters of managers prefer the pecking order theory over the static trade-off theory. After the crisis, less than half the managers prefer the pecking order theory. More than 77 percent of the managers indicate that the Asian financial crises have made equity look more favorable relative to debt as a source of capital. Fan and So's study shows that managers' views can change fairly rapidly. As such, a survey of managers' views on capital structure after the global financial crisis would be very interesting.

ALTERNATIVE SURVEY APPROACHES

In standard empirical finance research, the use of proxy variables for unobservable theoretical constructs is an important issue. As described in the previous section, survey results can bridge the gap between the practical considerations of decision makers such as CFOs and abstract finance theory.

All papers in the previous section directly ask executives for opinions. However, this approach suffers from a major weakness, which is best explained via an example. Graham and Harvey (2001) ask CFOs whether they are more likely to issue equity after an increase in the stock price by asking CFOs for their (dis)agreement with the following statement about motives for an equity issue: "If our stock price has recently risen, the price at which we can sell is 'high.'" In their tables a score of 1.83 on a 0–4 scale is presented in the sample of private firms. Where this question aims to measure a market timing motivation for equity issues, this is unlikely to be relevant for nonlisted firms. This example shows that CFOs have difficulty reflecting on theoretical mechanisms. Obviously, CFOs have superior knowledge about the characteristics of their firms. However, this does not imply that they are also the best judge of the rationales for relations between these characteristics. The remainder of this section discusses papers in which relatively simple questions are posed about firm characteristics and the researchers use empirical tools to measure the relations between these characteristics and answers to the other survey questions as a test of capital structure theory.

The seminal paper in this area is Ang and Jung (1993). For a sample of South Korean firms, Ang and Jung test Myers's (1984) pecking order theory. This theory predicts that information asymmetries between managers and outsiders drive incremental financing choices. A unique feature of survey data is that superior informed managers are the ones who complete the survey. Therefore, a survey instrument is capable of capturing the (perceived) information advantage of the insiders, whereas other data sources, such as annual reports, press releases, and analyst reports, relate to objective information provided to the information-disadvantaged party. Ang and Jung pose four questions, each capturing a different aspect of information asymmetry, such as "Will you not provide extra information at all in an attempt to alleviate the lender's underestimation of the future prospect of your company?" Based on the scores for these four questions, they distinguish high and low information asymmetry firms. All respondents are also asked to rank their preferences for types of funding, including bank loans, retained earnings, trade credit, straight bonds, and new stock. The results of a Mann-Whitney U-test show no significant difference in the financial preferences of the two groups of firms, which contradicts Myers's theory. A related paper with a similar structure is Ang, Fatemi, and Tourani-Rad (1997) for Indonesian firms. This also does not find asymmetric information to be an important determinant of capital structure preferences.

Allen (2000) uses a sample of 252 Australian, British, and Japanese companies to examine the extent to which firms maintain spare borrowing capacity. In Britain, 88 percent of the respondents admit to following a policy of maintaining spare borrowing capacity, like using lines of credit and bill facilities. In Australia this percentage is 56 percent, while only 32 percent of the Japanese respondents maintain spare borrowing capacity. The authors use cross-sectional differences to try to explain this low percentage in Japan. For example, one factor might be that Japanese firms are often a member of a business group, that is, a *keiretsu*. When firms are members of a group with a close relation to a main bank, they may be less concerned with high debt ratios and be less likely to have pre-arranged borrowing capacity. Allen does not find conclusive evidence on group membership. Regression analyses show that spare borrowing capacity is linked to company size.

In later studies researchers use more elaborate models. De Jong and Van Dijk (2007) use confirmatory factor analysis with structural modeling, which is an empirical model commonly used in business studies. This approach is often referred to as LISREL, which is the software used for estimations. The approach requires four steps. First, a model is designed, based on theory, in which relations between relevant variables (called constructs) are hypothesized and for each variable a set of simple characteristics is defined (called indicators). For example, based on the disciplinary role of leverage, the construct free cash flow is hypothesized to have a positive effect on the construct leverage. The indicators needed to measure free cash flow are the absence of investment opportunities and the presence of internal funds. Second, a questionnaire is designed in which for each indicator at least one simple question or statement is posed, where respondents can typically answer on a 7-point Likert scale. For example, "My firm has ample opportunity to carry out new, profitable projects." Third, questions/indicators related to the same construct are in a confirmatory factor analysis combined into factors, which measure the construct. This allows for an assessment of the quality of the survey instrument and measures the construct as a weighted average of its indicators. Fourth, the relations between the constructs are measured in a structural regression model. The key advantage of this approach is that the empirical model estimates the relations between variables, as in the cross-sectional models with proxy variables, while the CFOs only have to respond to simple questions about the characteristics of their firms. The main disadvantage is that estimates have only statistical, and not economic meaning, when compared to standard cross-sectional models.

De Jong and Van Dijk (2007) conducted a survey among Dutch CFOs of exchange-listed companies and received 102 responses. Based on the survey information, they first conduct a confirmatory factor analysis followed by a set of regression models. In the main analysis, three explained variables are included: leverage, overinvestment, and underinvestment. The regressions show that leverage is mainly explained by the marginal tax rate, collateral value of assets, and risk. These findings corroborate tax and bankruptcy theories. Overinvestment, in which managers are likely to waste internal funds to grow the company despite the negative value of investments, is driven by free cash flow and reduced by several governance-related variables. Interestingly, leverage is not related to overinvestment, which is evidence against the disciplinary role of debt. The authors only find underinvestment or debt overhang to be related to short-term debt, not to leverage. This application of survey research shows the added value of surveys because the constructs such as agency problems and information differences can be measured and explicitly modeled.

A similar paper is Romano, Tanewski, and Smyrnios (2000), providing a test of capital structure theories for a sample of Australian family firms. The authors, however, first use an exploratory factor analysis in order to find common dimension in the variables. Then the authors test a structural model using LISREL. Unfortunately, the relation between the exploratory factor analysis and the confirmatory factor analysis in LISREL, as well as the variables used to measure each of the constructs, remain unclear.

So far, the chapter has provided a discussion of survey papers solely based on questionnaire data. The survey outcomes cannot be validated using nonsurvey data as the surveys are anonymous. An important motivation for anonymity is that anonymous surveys are more likely to yield truthful answers and higher response rates. An exception is a study by De Jong and Verwijmeren (2010). This paper starts with a data set of publicly available information taken from a set of U.S., Canadian, and European firms from WorldScope, including firm and CFO names, addresses, and proxy variables used in capital structure studies. To these CFOs, the authors pose a simple question: Which description of capital structure policy fits your firm best? There are five potential responses: (1) we have a flexible target range for our debt ratio; (2) we have a somewhat tight target range for our debt ratio; (3) we have a strict target range for our debt ratio; (4) we finance new investments first from internal funds, then from new debt issues, and as a last resort from new equity issues; and (5) other. A marketing bureau administered the survey. Using a marketing bureau guaranteed anonymity to the respondents but allowed the researchers to receive a data set with the response to the question and the public data, without firm or CFO identifiers. Using this setup, the authors combine the strengths of public data (objectivity and availability) and private data (the use of otherwise unobservable information).

De Jong and Verwijmeren (2010) find that 130 of the 235 responding firms (55 percent) indicate having a target, whereas 83 firms (35 percent) follow the pecking order theory. This distinction is relevant because various papers have empirically tested the static trade-off model, the pecking order model, or both models. However, in these papers, which of the sample firms have a target debt ratio and which firms follow the pecking order without having a target is not known *a priori*. Because "pecking order firms" do not act according to the static trade-off theory, a better approach would be to exclude these firms in determining how basic static trade-off variables can explain a firm's debt level. The same applies for pecking order models, where "static trade-off firms" influence the estimation. Thus, a fundamental problem in other empirical studies is the inability to determine whether firms have a target debt ratio from public data.

De Jong and Verwijmeren (2010) use their survey instrument to distinguish "static trade-off firms" from "pecking order firms." In their paper, the authors show that empirical static trade-off models perform better for the appropriate subsample of firms, that is, when excluding pecking order firms. For firms with a target, the debt ratio is positively related to size and tangibility, which is in line with the predictions of the static trade-off model. For firms that indicate following the pecking order, size and tangibility have less influence on the debt ratio. Instead, the leverage of pecking order firms is influenced by the firm's profitability and market-to-book ratio: Both of these variables decrease leverage.

FUTURE RESEARCH

Based on the recent revival of survey-based research in the corporate finance literature (e.g., Graham and Harvey 2001; Brounen, de Jong, and Koedijk 2004, 2006), using questionnaires is a valuable addition to the toolbox of empirical researchers. For the future, three important issues seem relevant to survey research.

First, because most surveys in corporate finance use relatively complex questions, knowing how respondents interpret the questions is unclear. A good example is the notion of financial flexibility used in several studies. The approach of using relatively complex questions dates from the 1970s. In most other areas of business research, particularly strategy and marketing, and in other academic disciplines where survey research is widespread, especially psychology and sociology, researchers no longer use this approach. Therefore, survey researchers in finance may find taking into consideration developments in survey research in other fields to be of value.

The second issue is that using standardized survey instruments allows a comparison between surveys. By using the same survey in the same population over time, survey researchers may find changes in the respondent's opinions. Similarly, using literal translations of a survey in international research may facilitate comparisons between different regions. In other disciplines, particularly in psychology, the use of standard surveys is a widely-accepted practice, where subsequent studies serve to validate the survey instrument. As such, data obtained via a survey can be very valuable to other researchers. An example is the data of the Graham and Harvey (2001) study, which is available on the Internet (see Graham and Harvey 2003) and has been re-used in Brounen, de Jong, and Koedijk (2004, 2006) to compare the results for U.S. respondents with their European survey. Therefore, to facilitate future research, editors of academic journals may want to ask authors of survey studies to publish their data.

Finally, survey evidence could be combined with public data such as in De Jong and Verwijmeren (2010). Distributing the survey by a third party, such as a marketing bureau, guarantees the anonymity of respondents while allowing the researchers to receive a data set with the responses to the survey questions together with public data on the firm. Further studies can strongly benefit from this approach as it combines the strengths of public and private data.

SUMMARY AND CONCLUSIONS

The capital structure literature is characterized by a broad set of theories. The majority of the empirical research is based on publicly available data about firms' financing structures and decisions. In financing decisions, the financial executives of firms are responsible for the actual financing arrangements. Thus, an obvious approach for empirical research is to use survey research, allowing a direct assessment of theoretical predictions and constructs. This chapter describes survey studies about CFOs' opinions from countries other than the United States. Overall, these studies conclude that the findings for U.S. firms are also very relevant for non-U.S. firms. For example, findings on the importance of financial flexibility and credit ratings are widespread among surveys all over the world. Nonetheless, important differences exist between the United States and other countries. Survey evidence also indicates relevant differences across non-U.S. countries and legal systems.

Alternative survey-based research methods provide avenues for future survey research. Survey data have the potential of complementing other research methods. In fact, survey evidence can provide strong rationales for conducting nonsurvey research on particular topics. For example, survey evidence on the importance of financial flexibility has motivated many nonsurvey studies to focus on modeling and empirically testing the importance of financial flexibility, such as DeAngelo and DeAngelo (2007) and Gamba and Triantis (2008). In short, surveys are a very valuable addition to the toolbox of researchers.

DISCUSSION QUESTIONS

1. What are the strengths and weaknesses of survey research when compared to other empirical research methods in the corporate finance literature?
2. Titman (1984) argues that the liquidation of a firm may impose costs on both customers and employees. As a result, they demand risk premiums on products and wages when leverage increases. These costs are transferred to the shareholders. However, if the shareholders commit to liquidate only when the gains exceed all costs, including those of customers and employees, this would increase the cost of capital. Titman shows that managers can use their firm's capital structure to control these risk premiums. He argues that firms with higher liquidation costs to customers and employees will have less debt. Design a survey question or a set of questions to test Titman's theory.
3. Fan and So (2004) use surveys as a tool to measure changes in managers' beliefs about capital structure. Describe the study of Fan and So (2004) and discuss why managers may have changed their opinions from 1994 to 1999.

REFERENCES

Allen, David E. 1991. "The Determinants of the Capital Structure of Listed Australian Companies: The Financial Manager's Perspective." *Australian Journal of Management* 16:2, 103–128.

Allen, David E. 2000. "Spare Debt Capacity: Company Practices in Australia, Britain, and Japan." *Australian Journal of Management* 25:3, 299–326.

Ang, James S., Ali Fatemi, and Alireza Tourani-Rad. 1997. "Capital Structure and Dividend Policies of Indonesian Firms." *Pacific-Basin Finance Journal* 5:1, 87–103.

Ang, James S., and Minje Jung. 1993. "An Alternative Test of Myers' Pecking Order Theory of Capital Structure: The Case of South Korean Firms." *Pacific-Basin Finance Journal* 1:1, 31–46.

Bancel, Franck, and Usha R. Mittoo. 2004. "Cross-Country Determinants of Capital Structure Choice: A Survey of European Firms." *Financial Management* 33:4, 103–132.

Beattie, Vivien, Alan Goodacre, and Sarah Jane Thomson. 2006. "Corporate Financing Decisions: UK Survey Evidence." *Journal of Business Finance and Accounting* 33:9/10, 1402–1434.

Brounen, Dirk, Abe de Jong, and Kees Koedijk. 2004. "Corporate Finance in Europe: Confronting Theory with Practice." *Financial Management* 33:4, 71–101.

Brounen, Dirk, Abe de Jong, and Kees Koedijk. 2006. "Capital Structure Policies in Europe: Survey Evidence." *Journal of Banking & Finance* 30:5, 1409–1442.

Cassar, Gavin, and Scott Holmes. 2003. "Capital Structure and Financing of SMEs: Evidence from Australia." *Accounting & Finance* 43:2, 123–147.

Cohen, Gil, and Joseph Yagil. 2007. "A Multinational Survey of Corporate Financial Policies." *Journal of Applied Finance* 17:1, 57–69.

Cohen, Gil, and Joseph Yagil. 2010. "Sectorial Differences in Corporate Financial Behavior: An International Survey." *European Journal of Finance*, forthcoming.

De Jong, Abe, Rezaul Kabir, and Thuy Thu Nguyen. 2008. "Capital Structure around the World: The Roles of Firm- and Country-specific Determinants." *Journal of Banking & Finance* 32:9, 1954–1969.
De Jong, Abe, and Ronald van Dijk. 2007. "Determinants of Leverage and Agency Problems: A Regression Approach with Survey Data." *European Journal of Finance* 13:6, 565–593.
De Jong, Abe, and Patrick Verwijmeren. 2010. "To Have a Target Debt Ratio or Not: What Difference Does It Make?" *Applied Financial Economics* 20:1–3, 219–226.
DeAngelo, Harry, and Linda DeAngelo. 2007. "Capital Structure, Payout Policy, and Financial Flexibility." Working paper, University of Southern California. Available at http://ssrn.com/abstract=916093.
Donaldson, Gordon. 1961. *Corporate Debt Capacity*. Boston: Division of Research, Graduate School of Business Administration, Harvard University.
Fan, Dennis K. K., and Raymond W. So. 2004. "What Managers Think of Capital Structure: The Evidence from Hong Kong." *Journal of Asian Economics* 15:4, 817–830.
Fawthrop, R. A., and Brian Terry. 1975. "Debt Management and the Use of Leasing Finance in UK Corporate Financing Strategies." *Journal of Business Finance & Accounting* 2:3, 295–314.
Gamba, Andrea, and Alexander Triantis. 2008. "The Value of Financial Flexibility." *Journal of Finance* 63:5, 2263–2296.
Graham, John R., and Campbell R. Harvey. 2001. "The Theory and Practice of Corporate Finance: Evidence from the Field." *Journal of Financial Economics* 60:2, 187–243.
Graham, John R., and Campbell R. Harvey. 2003. "The Theory and Practice of Corporate Finance: The Data." Working Paper, Duke University. Available at http://ssrn.com/abstract=395221.
Kester, George W., Rosita P. Chang, Erlinda S. Echanis, Mansor M. Isa, Michael T. Skully, Susatio Socdigno, and Kai-Chong Tsui. 1998. "Executive Views on Dividends and Capital Structure Policy in the Asia-Pacific Region." In J. Jay Choi and John A. Doukas (eds.), *Emerging Capital Markets: Financial and Investment Issues*, 113–135. Westport, CT: Quorum Books.
Myers, Stewart C. 1984. "The Capital Structure Puzzle." *Journal of Finance* 39:3, 575–592.
Pinegar, J. Michael, and Lisa Wilbricht. 1989. "What Managers Think of Capital Structure Theory: A Survey." *Financial Management* 18:4, 82–91.
Rajan, Raghuram G., and Luigi Zingales. 1995. "What Do We Know About Capital Structure? Some Evidence from International Data." *Journal of Finance* 50:5, 1421–1460.
Romano, Claudio A., George A. Tanewski, and Kosmas X. Smyrnios. 2000. "Capital Structure Decision Making: A Model for Family Business." *Journal of Business Venturing* 16:3, 285–310.
Stonehill, Arthur, Theo Beekhuisen, Richard Wright, Lee Remmers, Norman Toy, Antonio Pares, Alan Shapiro, Douglas Egan, and Thomas Bates. 1975. "Financial Goals and Debt Ratio Determinants: A Survey of Practice in Five Countries." *Financial Management* 4:3, 27–41.
Titman, Sheridan. 1984. "The Effect of Capital Structure on a Firm's Liquidation Decision." *Journal of Financial Economics* 13:1, 137–151.
Wald, John K. 1999. "How Firm Characteristics Affect Capital Structure: An International Comparison." *Journal of Financial Research* 22:2, 161–187.

ABOUT THE AUTHORS

Abe de Jong is a Professor of Corporate Finance at Rotterdam School of Management, Erasmus University and Professor of Financial Accounting at the University of Groningen. He obtained his Master's and PhD degrees at Tilburg University, the Netherlands. Professor de Jong's research is in the field of empirical corporate finance and particularly capital structure choice. He has co-authored several papers based on surveys among CFOs of large companies. Professor de Jong is one of the initiators of a quarterly survey among European CFOs (see www.ceosurveyeurope.org). His work has been published in such journals as the *Journal of Financial Economics, Financial Management, Journal of Banking & Finance,* and *Journal of Corporate Finance.*

Patrick Verwijmeren is a Lecturer at the Department of Finance of the University of Melbourne. He obtained both his Master's and PhD at the Rotterdam School of Management, Erasmus University. Part of his Master's program was fulfilled in an exchange with the Copenhagen Business School, and part of his PhD was fulfilled at Owen Graduate School of Management, Vanderbilt University. Professor Verwijmeren specializes in convertible securities, short sales, and testing capital structure theories. He has published in the *Journal of Financial Economics, Financial Management, Journal of Banking & Finance, Urban Studies,* and *Applied Financial Economics,* among others. Professor Verwijmeren has also been involved in writing a report for the Dutch Ministry of Finance, dealing with the influence of hedge funds and private equity in the Netherlands.

PART III

Raising Capital

CHAPTER 15

The Roles of Financial Intermediaries in Raising Capital

NEAL GALPIN
Assistant Professor, Texas A&M University

HEUNGJU PARK
PhD Candidate, Texas A&M University

INTRODUCTION

In the Federal Reserve Board's April 2008 quarterly survey of senior loan officers, more than 50 percent of respondents reported a tightening of lending standards for loans to all sizes of firms (Board of Governors of the Federal Reserve 2008). More than 90 percent of respondents cite a "less favorable or more uncertain economic outlook" as at least somewhat important in their decision to tighten standards. According to the Securities Industry and Financial Markets Association (2008), between 2007 and 2008, long-term corporate debt issues fell from $1,203.9 billion to $737.2 billion, the lowest issuance year since 2000. Total equity issues also fell from $247.5 billion to $242.6 billion over the same time period, with initial public offering (IPO) activity falling by more than 85 percent.

To understand the importance of these declines requires knowing the functions of banks and other financial intermediaries. Though financial intermediaries serve a wide range of purposes, this chapter focuses on activities that directly provide capital to firms. Thus, the chapter excludes credit rating agencies that indirectly provide access to financing even though these are clearly important economic activities.

Financial intermediaries provide firms direct access to capital through lending or underwriting. Commercial banks, insurance companies, and pension funds, for example, primarily move capital from depositors or customer payments to borrowers. Investment banks historically acted mainly as underwriters, assisting corporations in locating investors for stock and bond issues without investing their own funds. Although the repeal of the Glass–Steagall Act in 1999 means that banks can perform both lending and underwriting activities at the same time, lending activities and underwriting activities are not perfect substitutes.

This chapter updates and extends previous surveys of the literature on financial intermediation. Gorton and Winton (2003) review bank-like financial intermediation and its importance in the real economy, while Strahan (2008) focuses on how bank structure affects the quality of lending. Ritter (2003) and Eckbo, Masulis, and Norli (2007) review evidence on investment bank and security issuance, while Ljungqvist (2007) provides special focus on a particular cost of raising capital, namely, IPO underpricing. Drucker and Puri (2007) and Gande (2008) provide surveys of banks' involvement with other capital market activities. These last two surveys are closely related to this chapter, describing the theoretical arguments and empirical evidence about merging banks' traditional lending services with services such as underwriting. Rather than argue policy or detail the inner workings of financial intermediaries, this chapter focuses on how financial intermediaries directly get capital into firms and balances theory with empirics where possible.

The reminder of the chapter is organized as follows. It begins by exploring the direct lending function of financial intermediaries and provides evidence about why firms choose particular financial intermediaries for their borrowing needs. The chapter then describes underwriting activities including the services performed by intermediaries and the combination of lending and underwriting activities within an intermediary and how this combination affects costs of borrowing. Because recent financial crises have drastically affected financial intermediaries, the chapter provides some discussion of some recent work on crises and financial intermediation. The final section offers a summary and conclusions.

LENDING BY FINANCIAL INTERMEDIARIES

The United States has some of the most developed and active public stock and bond markets in the world. Nonetheless, bank and nonbank loans and advances are extremely important sources of external financing. According to the Federal Reserve's Flow of Funds March 2009 release, such loans financed an average of 13 percent of capital expenditures by nonfarm, nonfinancial corporate businesses between 2004 and 2008 (Board of Governors of the Federal Reserve 2009). Corporate bonds financed 16 percent over the same period. Net new equity issues were negative every year over the same time period, implying that firms did not rely on external equity issues to fund investment.

These aggregate numbers are somewhat misleading, however. Small, privately-held companies with little access to public debt and equity markets benefit most from lending from banks and other private lenders. Moreover, the existence of bank loans can help increase the availability of other types of funding. This section first describes why financial intermediaries make loans to firms rather than households directly lending to firms. It then reviews evidence concerning whether banks are "special" relative to other types of financing arrangements as well as the types of firms that choose certain types of loans.

How Do Financial Intermediaries Help Lenders and Borrowers?

Why do households deposit funds with intermediaries instead of lending to corporations directly? One of the earliest answers involves transaction costs. Financial intermediaries provide reduced-cost methods of contracting between households and firms. A related answer involves information asymmetries. Financial intermediaries have information advantages relative to households and thus make borrowing and lending easier. This section reviews financial intermediaries in general as well as some results specific to one important type of financial intermediary, namely, banks.

Transactions Costs

A role of financial intermediaries in the corporate capital-raising process is to lower transaction costs. As their name suggests, transaction costs are any costs associated with transactions between economic agents. For example, assume a large number of households. Lending requires finding a potential borrower, which is costly with respect to time even if no other costs are involved. Without intermediation, every household would expend effort in finding and transacting with a borrower. Intermediaries act as a single point of contact for lenders and borrowers, reducing the search costs. Even if searching is relatively costless, writing contracts that spell out plans in all future states in a way enforceable by a court can be extremely costly or even impossible.

Screening and Monitoring

The two major costs of information asymmetry are adverse selection and moral hazard. Adverse selection costs arise when low-quality and high-quality firms both want to borrow funds but lenders cannot distinguish between them. Moral hazard arises when firm's incentives are worsened after receiving a loan. Banks and other lenders can reduce these problems through screening (reviewing a firm before making a loan) and monitoring (reviewing a project after making a loan).

Lenders gather relevant information about the prospects and the creditworthiness of the borrower before providing capital. This information resolves the information asymmetry between the lender and the borrower. Such an argument does not explain, however, why large financial intermediaries arise rather than potential borrowers approaching households directly. Boyd and Prescott (1986) show that pooling funds in a financial intermediary allows for cross-subsidization, decreasing the returns for good types and increasing the returns for bad types in such a way that each agent truthfully reveals the type of her project. A small lender cannot pool enough projects to offer this service. Gorton and Pennacchi (1990) emphasize the relative information quality possessed by different investors. By offering a deposit-like investment opportunity to uninformed investors, banks prevent uninformed traders from losing out to informed traders. This helps reduce the costs of transacting for uninformed lenders. Moreover, lenders who produce information can have a multiplier effect on firms' ability to borrow. Leland and Pyle (1977), for example, argue that intermediaries can put their own capital at risk to credibly reveal information they produce about a firm's assets.

Lenders can also monitor those firms that borrow. Diamond (1984) provides an early examination of the monitoring role of banks. He argues that a large intermediary can minimize the costs of monitoring borrowers. By diversifying the loan portfolio, the monitor can promise payments that are close to risk-free for individual lenders. The only way for the bank to meet these obligations is by keeping its promise of monitoring. Calomiris and Kahn (1991) argue that demandable deposits can discipline bank managers by giving depositors an option to force liquidation.

Chemmanur and Fulghieri (1994) expand on this monitoring role and suggest that banks or bank-like lenders have the appropriate incentives to monitor and make better renegotiation versus liquidation decisions. Bondholders do not have the correct incentives for monitoring. Boot and Thakor (1997) also develop a model that compares banks with other sources of financing. However, they do not start with assumptions about the roles of markets and institutions. Rather, they argue that a bank's investors cooperate, whereas market investors compete. Markets provide a feedback loop (prices influence real decisions by firms), whereas banks provide better protection against asset substitution.

Recent empirical papers examine whether bank relationships affect banks' role as monitors. Carletti (2004) examines how the number of bank relationships influences banks' monitoring incentives and how this decision affects loan rates and a firm's choice between single and multiple bank relationships. She finds that the multiple bank lending monitors less but do not necessarily require higher loan rates than the single bank lending. Carletti, Cerasi, and Daltung (2007) analyze banks' incentives of multiple bank lending relationship when they are subject to moral hazard and when monitoring is important. Sufi (2007) analyzes the syndicated loan market and finds that lead banks retain a larger share of loans when borrowers require more intense monitoring and due diligence. When information asymmetry between the borrowers and lenders is severe, participant lenders are closer to borrowers both geographically and in terms of previous lending relationships. Dass and Massa (2010) find that stronger borrower-lender relationships improve bank monitoring, leading to better corporate governance, but they increase adverse selection for the other market participants and lowers the firm's stock liquidity, which implies that the trade-off affects the firm value.

Further, the information production of financial intermediaries is increased as they interact with borrowers repeatedly. As financial intermediaries develop repeated relationships with their borrowers, the cost of information production declines, which solidifies their roles as efficient producers of information.

Petersen and Rajan (1994) analyze how lending relationships affect the availability and costs of funds to the firm using a survey data of small firms. They find that the prior lending relationships increase the ability of firms to borrow, though the relationships do not appear to reduce the yield on debt. Berger and Udell (1995) examine the role of relationship lending in small firm finance and show that a longer bank relationship lowers interest rates and collateral requirements on loan commitments, which implies that banks share with their clients the benefits of their privileged information. Degryse and Van Cayseele (2000) use detailed contract information of small Belgian firms and show interest rates increase with the length of the lending relationship. At the same time, the scope of the relationship, defined by significant account activity as well as the purchase of at least two other bank products, reduces the interest rates of loans. Schenone (2010) uses a firm IPO as an information event and shows that a U-shaped relationship exists between borrowing rates and relationship intensity before the IPO, while after the IPO interest rates are decreasing in relationship intensity.

Liquidity Provision

Banks are an interesting financial intermediary because of the structure of their assets and liabilities. Bank assets tend to be illiquid, while demand deposits are, as their name implies, available upon demand. Therefore, the bank provides liquidity, insuring borrowers against liquidity shocks to lenders. Diamond and Dybvig (1983) use the mismatch between liquidity of assets and demand deposits to explain bank runs. Diamond and Rajan (2000) argue that demandable deposits actually allow banks to commit to monitoring because they make the bank vulnerable to a destructive run. Berger and Bouwman (2009a) find that bank liquidity creation increased every year between 1993 and 2003. Moreover, liquidity creation is positively related to bank value. In the other camp, Deep and Shaefer (2004) show that the gap between liquid assets and liquid liabilities is not very large at most banks. Thus, they conclude that the importance of liquidity creation of banks may be overstated by theory.

A second question springing from liquidity provision involves why banks fund loans with demand deposits. Pyle (1971) uses a portfolio problem to show how correlations between deposits and loans can explain why a bank-like intermediary relies on deposits as sources of funds to make loans. Kashyap, Rajan, and Stein (2002) contend that banks provide liquidity to borrowers in both the lending and deposit-taking sides of their business. The authors suggest that banks create liquidity off the balance sheet through loan commitments and similar claims to liquid funds. Consistent with Kashyap, Rajan, and Stein's results, Harjoto, Mullineaux, and Yi (2006) find that commercial banks are more likely than investment banks to provide loan commitment contracts that expose the lender to potential liquidity risk.

Choices between Sources of Debt: Are Banks Special?

A large strand of literature considers the different roles played by sources of funds. According to Fama (1985), a bank loan provides accreditation for a firm's ability to generate a certain level of cash flows in future. Diamond (1991) suggests that banks provide monitoring for young borrowers without the benefit of a strong reputation. Once firms develop a reputation, they switch to other debt sources that do not monitor. Rajan (1992) argues that firms must trade off the benefit of bank flexibility against the cost of hold-up problems when deciding between banks and other sources. Berlin and Mester (1992) also contend that the riskiest firms choose banks over other intermediaries but focus on the renegotiations afforded by bank loans with stringent covenants.

James (1987) starts a stream of literature focusing on the effect of bank loan announcements on the firm's other security holders. He finds that bank loan announcements significantly increase stock prices while announcements of privately placed and public issues of debt experience zero or negative firm stock price reactions. Lummer and McConnell (1989) maintain that bank monitoring is more important than screening, as they show the positive response is solely due to loan renewals. Slovin, Johnson, and Glascock (1992) find significantly positive share price reactions for both initiation and renewal of loans but only for small firms. Best and Zhang (1993) show banks provide the most information where analysts provide only noisy information. Billet, Flannery, and Garfinkel (1995) find evidence that banks' credit ratings determine the level of the borrowers' stock price reaction, while Preece and Mullineaux (1994) find no statistical difference in the firms' stock price reactions to loan announcements from different lenders. Dahiya, Puri, and Saunders (2003) document a negative stock price reaction to loan sales, which suggests that banks play some monitoring role. Fields et al. (2006) show that equity price reactions to bank loan announcements have considerably decreased over time, possibly due to increased competition and the changing nature of the banking sector. Ongena et al. (2008) examine bond and equity price reaction to bank loan announcements and find that bank loan announcements transfer wealth from bondholders to equity holders but the transfer appears concentrated in smaller, riskier firms.

Another strand of empirical studies for bank loan uniqueness focuses on firms' choice of banks versus other lending sources. Houston and James (2001) show bank dependent firms are smaller, younger, less highly levered, and more likely to hold liquid assets than firms with public debt outstanding. Krishnaswami, Spindt, and Subramaniam (1999) show larger firms and firms with larger average issue sizes rely more on public debt financing, while reliance on private borrowing is positively related to the extent of a company's growth opportunities. Denis and Mihov (2003) find that firms with the highest credit quality borrow from public sources, firms with medium credit quality borrow from banks, and firms with the lowest credit quality borrow from nonbank private lenders.

UNDERWRITING BY FINANCIAL INTERMEDIARIES

This section reviews literature related to underwriting activities of financial intermediaries. Underwriting actually has several definitions depending on use. This chapter views the term *underwrite* as meaning to agree to purchase (as security issue) usually on a fixed date at a fixed price with a view to public distribution and to guarantee financial support of the issue.

Intermediaries can underwrite many different securities for firms such as common or preferred stock, straight bonds, and convertibles. The choice of security is left to other reviews because this section instead focuses on what the underwriter does in each case. The only implication for security choice is to report relative costs of underwriting by different types of security offered.

The largest difference between lending and underwriting involves what Bhattacharya and Thakor (1993) call *qualitative asset transformation.* This means that the liabilities of the bank (demand deposits) are qualitatively different from the assets of the bank (loans). In underwriting, the assets of the lender and the liabilities of the borrower match. For example, a household owns a share of stock, and a firm has obligations consistent with a share of stock after an equity offering.

Costs of Underwriting

Underwriting contracts are generally one of two types: firm commitment or best efforts. In a firm commitment contract, the underwriter purchases securities from the firm and then sells them to other investors. The spread between the price paid to the firm and the price received from investors, called the *underwriter spread*, provides compensation to the underwriter. In a best efforts contract, the underwriter brokers the deal but receives a guaranteed fee from the firm rather than bearing risks about the offer price. Several underwriters may form a syndicate to reduce risk or pool resources. Here, one intermediary serves as the lead manager with the responsibility for all aspects of the issue and others in the syndicate help to sell the securities.

Firms face two basic types of costs in underwriting arrangements: direct costs such as underwriter fees and indirect costs such as underpricing. Underpricing refers to the fact that security issues often see large positive first-day returns. This suggests that the firm could have received a higher price for that security. Lee et al. (1996) document the different costs of equity and debt offerings. Equity issues are relatively costly. IPOs have the highest costs with 11 percent of proceeds going to direct costs and indirect costs of underpricing around 12 percent of proceeds. Seasoned equity offerings (SEOs) have a much smaller cost of around 7.3 percent of proceeds. Direct costs of non–investment-grade bonds are around 3.5 percent of proceeds with investment grade bonds seeing costs of 1 percent (straight bonds) to 2 percent (convertible bonds).

Many empirical studies use these figures as a starting point, using theory to explain the cross-section of issuance costs. The chapter now turns to theories and evidence about what intermediaries do for firms in underwriting. In a sense, this chapter is asking what firms buy in paying for underwriting services.

Underwriting Services

This section reviews some of the major services underwriters provide during and after a security issue. Generally speaking, underwriters provide screening and monitoring before an issue. Underwriters also assist markets for new securities in the time immediately following the offer.

Screening and Monitoring

When the firm issues new securities, the underwriter reviews the firm's affairs. The underwriter may develop a reputation as an effective screener, monitor, or both. The underwriter uses this reputation to extract rents in securities issues.

Ramakrishnan and Thakor (1984) present a model in which firms issuing new shares to the public can hire an agent to produce information about their quality. An intermediary with a contract resembling that of a firm commitment offering, where the underwriter buys shares from the firm before selling to other investors, induces screening. Consistent with the information role of underwriters, Ritter (1987) shows costs of IPOs are drastically higher for best efforts IPOs than for firm commitment IPOs. Thus, when underwriters commit their own capital to the underwriting process, markets appear to require less compensation for uncertainty.

A large literature focuses on underpricing and information problems in equity IPOs. For example, Beatty and Ritter (1986) document more underpricing when investor uncertainty about the value of an issue is greater. They also propose that underwriters can develop a reputation for fairness by underpricing neither too much (which hurts firms) nor too little (which hurts investors). Carter and Manaster (1990) model the importance of exogenously determined underwriter reputation and find that underwriter prestige is negatively related to the magnitude and variation of post-IPO price run-ups. Cai, Helwege, and Warga (2007) also show evidence of underpricing in initial debt offerings. As with equity initial offerings, uncertainty also appears to increase the underpricing of debt offerings.

Interestingly, Altinklic and Hansen (2003) and Corwin (2003) provide underpricing evidence in SEOs, offerings by firms that already have publicly-traded stocks. Cai, Helwege, and Warga (2007) also show such underpricing in seasoned debt offerings. Underpricing magnitudes are lower in SEOs than IPOs and also increase with uncertainty. This is intriguing because during a seasoned offering, investors can see market prices of the firm's securities. The evidence suggests a role for intermediaries' information production even when markets already trade a firm's securities.

Underwriters may also provide monitoring to firms after a security issue. Hansen and Torregrosa (1992) argue that banks receive rents from their reputations for monitoring and show the reputation costs of shirking make monitoring optimal for an underwriter. Jain and Kini (1999) argue that demand exists for third-party monitoring in the IPO market and find a positive relationship between investment bank reputation and post-issue performance.

Empirically, the evidence for post-issue monitoring is at best mixed. Michaely and Womack (1999) find that stocks recommended by underwriter-affiliated analysts underperform. Das, Guo, and Zhang (2006) report that IPOs with high coverage from nonaffiliated analysts outperform relative to those with low coverage. Fang and Yasuda (2009) find that the severity of conflicts of interest has a negative effect on the performance of lower-ranked analysts regardless of bank reputation. Without a risk-based story, none of these papers provides much evidence in favor of post-issue monitoring by underwriters.

As in lending relationships, investment banks obtain information concerning firms' operations and management that is useful in underwriting subsequent offerings. Thus, the underwriters possess valuable relationship-specific information that cannot be transferred easily. Such information is especially important when a firm goes public due to the substantial uncertainty about the firm's value.

James (1992) argues that underwriters have durable relationship-specific information similar to that of commercial banks and auditors. He reports lower spreads for firms that make subsequent issues and less underwriter switching when the time between an IPO and subsequent equity issues is smaller. James and Wier (1990) show that firms with inside debt at the time of the IPO exhibit lower IPO underpricing. Krigman, Shaw, and Womack (2001) find that while client loyalty had declined, 70 percent of firms completing a SEO within three years of their IPO select the same lead underwriter.

Price Stabilization

A lead underwriter plays an important role in pricing and distributing an IPO. However, the importance of the underwriter continues beyond the IPO date through the underwriter's post-issuance activities. One important post-issue service involves price stabilization. The underwriter often offers to buy back securities offered if the price falls, acting as a market maker for the newly traded stock when liquidity is otherwise likely to be weak.

Several empirical studies focus on stabilization of share prices after IPOs. Ruud (1993) finds that the high average level of underpricing is offset by the value of price support, though price support has only a temporary effect on prices. Hanley, Kumar, and Sequin (1993) argue that price stabilization by underwriters provides dealers with a put option reducing dealers' costs. In a similar vein, Schultz and Zaman (1994) find that underwriters generally quote the highest active bids and so support the price of less-successful IPOs. Aggarwal, Prabhala, and Puri (2002) contend that underwriters provide price support as a credible commitment to reduce informational asymmetry problems in the IPO markets. Specifically, they find that stabilization enables the underwriter to reduce the ex-ante price risk of IPOs. Ellis, Michaely, and O'Hara (2000) present evidence on the first few months post-IPO and find that the lead underwriter becomes a market maker and takes a substantial inventory position in the stock. Lewellen (2006) examines the price effects and determinants of price support, finding substantial stabilization activities, done by large underwriters protecting their reputation with investors.

UNIVERSAL BANKING

Banks that perform both commercial and investment banking activities are called universal banks. In many countries, commercial banks routinely conduct investment banking activities such as helping their customers in bringing new debt and equity issues to the market. After the Glass–Steagall Act of 1933, commercial banks were not allowed to underwrite securities in the United States. In November 1999, the Financial Modernization Act of 1999 repealed the Glass–Steagall Act and removed restrictions about underwriting securities. This section summarizes the theoretical and empirical evidence on the trade-offs in combining lending with underwriting of securities.

Universal Banking: Theory

Combining lending with underwriting can be more efficient than providing the services separately. The reason is that both commercial and investment banking are heavily based on information production. Universal banks uncover firms' private information from lending activities, and banks can use the information to underwrite new issues of the firms. Just as lending relationships help with subsequent loans, such relationships can also help with subsequent security issues. Traditional investment banks expend costly resources to produce information on the firms, duplicating the efforts of lenders. If a fixed-cost component is present to both lending and underwriting of securities for the same firm, combining two functions lowers the total cost. Thus, financial intermediation can provide economies of scope.

The main costs of combining lending with underwriting are conflicts of interest and information monopoly rents. Rajan (1992) suggests that lending relationships might create hold-up problems for lenders. The hold-up problems refer to the possibilities that a relationship bank uses the superior private information about the firm to extract rents, thus distorting managerial incentives and causing inefficient investment choices. Lending and underwriting relationships together create similar problems. Moreover, combining lending and underwriting can reduce lender incentives to monitor. A lender could, for example, underwrite a security issue to provide funds for a firm to pay off the original loan. If this is possible, the lender has little reason to screen or monitor in the first place.

One argument for universal banking is that, if it is inefficient, banks will choose to specialize. Thus, there is no need for such a law. Rajan (2002) asserts that underwriting can allow banks to extract rents generated from prior lending activities. In this case, a commercial bank may choose to become a universal bank even if it is not as efficient as underwriting. Puri (1999) models the trade-off between commercial banks' potential to be better certifiers of firm value and the cost that can arise from the bank misrepresenting the value of a firm's securities in order to use the proceeds to repay bank loans. She argues that this potentially stronger certification benefit has to be weighed against the conflicts-of-interest cost. Kanatas and Qi (2003) model the information scope economies, where information costs incurred in learning about a firm in the process of underwriting their securities need not be fully incurred again when making a bank loan to the same firm. They show that the informational economies of scope can lower transaction costs and can theoretically reduce underwriting fees if banks pass along costs savings to firms. Universal banking may or may not benefit firms that use universal banks for financing needs in theory. The next section therefore turns to the evidence.

Universal Banking: Evidence

The evidence on universal banking is generally favorable. Costs of raising debt and equity appear to fall under universal banking, while the quality of securities placed remains high.

Debt Underwriting

The biggest question from a borrower's perspective is whether universal banking reduces the costs of raising debt and equity. However, such a question also requires controlling the quality of services provided. This section focuses on the quality and cost of debt issues underwritten by commercial banks.

The conflicts-of-interest effect suggests that commercial banks have incentives to place low-quality bonds during underwriting. This does not appear to be the case, however. Ang and Richardson (1994) find that the default rates are similar for investment bank- and commercial bank–underwritten securities. Kroszner and Rajan (1994) examine the relative performance of industrial bonds that are underwritten by commercial banks with those that are investment bank–underwritten. Their evidence shows that commercial bank–underwritten issues perform better than similar, investment–bank underwritten issues, which is inconsistent with commercial banks succumbing to conflicts of interest. Puri (1994) also examines the long-run default performance of bank-underwritten issues and supports the view that banks are not exploiting conflicts of interest.

From a borrower's perspective, the important question is whether universal banking reduces the costs of borrowing or allows greater access to credit. Puri (1996) examines the ex-ante pricing of industrial bonds and preferred stock during the pre–Glass–Steagall period of January 1927 through September 1929. She finds that, relative to investment bank issues, commercial bank–underwritten issues have a significantly lower yield, which is consistent with commercial banks having a net certification effect. Gande et al. (1997) use a relaxation of Glass–Steagall in 1987, which allowed some banks to set up subsidiaries with underwriting ability, to show benefits of universal banking. They find that commercial bank subsidiaries primarily underwrite small issues. Also, when underwriting where the bank has existing lending exposure, the commercial bank subsidiaries have significantly lower yields for lower credit-rated issues but no difference on the less informationally sensitive, higher-rated issues. The authors argue that potential conflicts of interest exist only when the proceeds of a debt issue are being used to refinance existing bank debt and the underwriter is a commercial bank whose loans are being refinanced.

Gande, Puri, and Saunders (1999) use a further relaxation of Glass–Steagall in 1997 to examine competitive effects of commercial bank entry and show that market concentration, underwriter spreads, and yields fall with the benefits mainly garnered by small, lower-rated debt issues. Roten and Mullineaux (2002) find the benefits of bank underwriting show up in reduced underwriting fees rather than in net yields. Yasuda (2005) examines the value of banking relationships for the firm's underwriter choice in the corporate bond market and finds that existing bank relationships have positive and statistically significant effects on a firm's underwriter choice. Overall, smaller, riskier borrowers appear to gain substantially from commercial bank entry into underwriting.

Equity Underwriting

As with debt, equity underwriting by commercial banks appears to help firms issue securities. Hebb (2002) shows that prior banking relationships with underwriters significantly reduce the underpricing of commercial bank–underwritten IPOs. Fields, Fraser, and Bhargava (2003) find that the total issuance costs are significantly lower for commercial bank IPOs than for non–commercial bank–underwritten IPOs and commercial bank-underwritten issues have superior long-run performance to non–commercial bank–underwritten IPOs. Schenone (2004) also finds that IPOs underwritten by a firm's relationship bank are less underpriced than IPOs where the firm does not have lending relationships with any potential underwriter. Benzoni and Schenone (2010) examine the long-run performance of equity issues that are underwritten by the firms' relationship banks relative to those issues that are underwritten by other commercial bank and investment bank underwriters. The authors find that IPOs underwritten by relationship banks perform no better or worse than issues underwritten by outside commercial or investment banks, which is inconsistent with relationship banks misrepresenting the quality of the firms that they underwrite.

Narayanan, Rangan, and Rangan (2004) find that the total issuance costs with SEO underwriting data are lower when a lending bank co-manages the issue with a reputable investment bank. Drucker and Puri (2005) find that when a financial intermediary concurrently lends to an issuer and underwrites the firm's SEO, the issuer benefits through lower financing costs and through receiving lower underwriter fees and lower loan yield spreads. They show that concurrent lending also helps underwriters build relationships, increasing the probability of receiving current and future business.

Once again, the bulk of the evidence suggests that universal banks provide high-quality, low-cost underwriting services to firms. This is not to say that universal banking involves no costs. On net, however, universal banking appears to benefit firms, especially small, risky firms.

FINANCIAL CRISES

The recent financial crisis had strong effects on lending activity of financial intermediaries. Ivashina and Scharfstein (2010) find that banks sharply curtailed lending to the corporate sector during the financial crisis. Puri, Rochell, and Steffen (2009) also find evidence of a supply effect whereby German banks affected by the crisis tighten lending to retail customers significantly more than non-affected banks, controlling for loan demand and loan applicant qualify. This reduction of lending also has real effects. Duchin, Ozbas, and Sensoy (2010) find a decline in corporate investments as a consequence of tightened credit supply. Tong and Wei (2008), who focus on explaining stock price changes following the financial crisis, find that stock price declines are more severe for more financially constrained firms. Campello, Graham, and Harvey (2010) survey corporate managers and find evidence that firms forgo profitable investment opportunities during the crisis as a result of binding external financing constraints.

Gatev and Strahan (2006) argue that during periods of market crisis, investors become less willing to hold risky debt and commercial paper spreads widen, which leads firms to draw funds from backup lines of credit from banks. They show that the supply of deposits to banks increases and most of these inflows are concentrated in transaction deposits. Gatev, Schuermann, and Strahan (2006) find that among banks those with the largest transaction deposit base experience the greatest inflows of funds and the banks can offer liquidity insurance. Berger and Bouwman (2009b) examine the connection between financial crisis and bank liquidity creation. They find that liquidity creation increased substantially during normal times and financial crises. The authors also report that both the share of large banks in aggregate liquidity creation and the fraction of liquidity created off the balance sheet increased over the time period.

Other crises have similar effects both in the United States and around the world. Chava and Purnanandam (2010) show that during the Russian crisis of 1998, affected banks reduced their supply of credit and worsened the terms. Moreover, borrowers dependent on those banks saw reduced valuations as a result of the crisis. Klingebiel, Kroszner, and Laeven (2007) and Dell'Ariccia, Detragiache, and Rajan (2008) provide similar evidence at the macro level. They show that output falls most during a banking crisis in industries most reliant on external financing.

SUMMARY AND CONCLUSIONS

Financial intermediaries allocate capital to businesses and consumers efficiently and can expedite the flow of credit through economies. This chapter deals with the roles of financial intermediaries in corporate capital raising process and focuses on two important activities: lending and underwriting. Though the mechanics and details of explanations differ somewhat, information problems are incredibly important in carving out an important place for financial intermediaries. Both theory and evidence point to screening and monitoring roles for lenders and underwriters to help reduce the costs of these information problems. In a general sense, the ability of financial intermediaries to produce information makes them an integral part of the economy.

Combining lending with underwriting provides trade-offs between benefits and costs of universal banking. On one hand, the combination plays off economies of scale and scope in information production. On the other hand, relationships in lending and underwriting increase the potential for hold-up problems and other conflicts of interest. Empirically, universal banking benefits appear to outweigh the costs, providing relatively high-quality, low-cost capital to small, risky borrowers.

Finally, financial crises provide interesting and important shocks to the financial system. These shocks appear to have large effects on the ability of intermediaries to provide capital to firms. Moreover, financial crises open up discussion by policymakers and others about the role and importance of financial intermediaries in the overall economy. Observing the reaction of policymakers to recent financial crisis and following up on the long-run effects of these policies should prove fertile ground for understanding how firms raise capital and why it matters.

DISCUSSION QUESTIONS

1. Rajan (1992) trades off the monitoring benefits of banking relationships against the hold-up costs. Suppose a firm borrows to pay off a bank loan. Is this good news or bad news for shareholders? Why?
2. How could conflicts of interest in universal banking lead to reduced costs of borrowing for firms? What evidence is against this particular conflict of interest?
3. Following the collapse of much of the banking sector in 1933, the Glass–Steagall Act separated banks based on their types of business. Why might price stabilization contribute to financial crises?
4. Why might relationships between banks and firms push the government to protect banks from failure in times of economic uncertainty?

REFERENCES

Aggarwal, Reena, Nagpurnanand R. Prabhala, and Manju Puri. 2002. "Institutional Allocation in Initial Public Offerings: Empirical Analysis." *Journal of Finance* 57:3, 1421–1442.

Altinklic, Oya, and Robert S. Hansen. 2003. "The Discounting and Underpricing in Seasoned Equity Offers." *Journal of Financial Economics* 69:2, 285–323.

Ang, James S., and Terry Richardson. 1994. "The Underwriting Experience of Commercial Bank Affiliates Prior to the Glass–Steagall Act: A Re-examination of Evidence for Passage of the Act." *Journal of Banking and Finance* 18:2, 351–395.

Beatty, Randolph P., and Jay R. Ritter. 1986. "Investment Banking, Reputation, and the Underpricing of Initial Public Offerings." *Journal of Financial Economics* 15:1, 213–232.

Benzoni, Luca, and Carola Schenone. 2010. "Conflict of Interest or Certification: Long-Term Performance and Valuation of U.S. IPOs Underwritten by Relationship Banks." *Journal of Financial Intermediation* 19:2, 235–254.

Berger, Allen N., and Christa H. S. Bouwman. 2009a. "Bank Liquidity Creation." *Review of Financial Studies* 22:9, 3779–3837.

Berger, Allen N., and Christa H. S. Bouwman. 2009b. "Bank Liquidity Creation, Monetary Policy, and Financial Crises." Working Paper, University of South Carolina.

Berger Allen N., and Gregory Udell. 1995. "Relationship Lending and Lines of Credit in Small Firm Finance." *Journal of Business* 68:3, 351–382.

Berlin, Mitchell, and Loretta J. Mester. 1992. "Debt Covenants and Renegotiation." *Journal of Financial Intermediation* 2:2, 95–133.

Best, Ronald, and Hang Zhang. 1993. "Alternative Information Sources and the Information Content of Bank Loans." *Journal of Finance* 48:4, 1507–1522.

Bhattacharya, Sudipto, and Anjan V. Thakor. 1993. "Contemporary Banking Theory." *Journal of Financial Intermediation* 3:1, 2–50.

Billet, Matthew, Mark Flannery, and Jon Garfinkel. 1995. "The Effect of Lender Identity on a Firm's Equity Return." *Journal of Finance* 50:2, 699–718.

Board of Governors of the Federal Reserve. 2008. "The April 2008 Senior Loan Officer Opinion Survey on Bank Lending Practices." Available at http://www.federalreserve.gov/boarddocs/snloansurvey/200805/fullreport.pdf.

Board of Governors of the Federal Reserve. 2009. "Flow of Funds Accounts of the United States." Available at http://www.federalreserve.gov/releases/z1/20090312/.

Boot, Arnoud W. A., and Anjan V, Thakor. 1997. "Financial System Architecture." *Review of Financial Studies* 10:3, 693–733.

Boyd, John, and Edward Prescott. 1986. "Financial Intermediary Coalitions." *Journal of Economic Theory* 38:2, 211–232.

Cai, Nianyun, Jean Helwege, and Arthur Warga. 2007. "Underpricing in the Corporate Bond Market." *Review of Financial Studies* 20:6, 2021–2046.

Calomiris, Charles, and Charles Kahn. 1991. "The Role of Demandable Debt in Structuring Optimal Banking Arrangements." *American Economic Review* 81:3, 497–513.

Campello, Murillo, John R. Graham, and Campbell R. Harvey. 2010. "The Real Effects of Financial Constraints: Evidence from a Financial Crisis." *Journal of Financial Economics* 97:3, 470–487.

Carletti, Elena. 2004. "The Structure of Relationship Lending, Endogenous Monitoring and Loan Rates." *Journal of Financial Intermediation* 13:1, 58–86.

Carletti, Elena, Vittoria Cerasi, and Sonja Daltung. 2007. "Multiple Bank-Lending: Diversification and Free-Riding in Monitoring." *Journal of Financial Intermediation* 16:3, 425–451.

Carter, Richard B., and Steven Manaster. 1990. "Initial Public Offerings and Underwriter Reputation." *Journal of Finance* 65:4, 1045–1067.

Chava, Sudheer, and Amiyatosh Purnanandam. 2010. "The Effect of Banking Crisis on Bank-Dependent Borrowers." *Journal of Financial Economics.* Forthcoming.

Chemmanur, Thomas J., and Paolo Fulghieri. 1994. "Reputation, Renegotiation, and the Choice between Bank Loans and Publicly Traded Debt." *Review of Financial Studies* 7:3, 475–506.

Corwin, Shane. 2003. "The Determinants of Underpricing for Seasoned Equity Offers." *Journal of Finance* 58:5, 2249–2279.

Dahiya, Sandeep, Manju Puri, and Anthony Saunders. 2003. "Bank Borrowers and Loan Sales: New Evidence on the Uniqueness of Bank Loans." *Journal of Business* 76:4, 563–582.

Das, Somnath, Re-Jin Guo, and Huai Zhang. 2006. "Analysts' Selective Coverage and Subsequent Performance of Newly Public Firms." *Journal of Finance* 61:3, 1159–1185.

Dass, Nishant, and Massimo Massa. 2010. "The Impact of a Strong Bank-Firm Relationship on the Borrowing Firm." *Review of Financial Studies.* Forthcoming.

Deep, Akash, and Guido Schaefer. 2004. "Are Banks Liquidity Transformers?" Working Paper, Harvard University.

Degryse, Hans, and Patrick Van Cayseele. 2000. "Relationship Lending within a Bank-Based System: Evidence from European Small Business Data." *Journal of Financial Intermediation* 9:1, 90–109.

Dell'Ariccia, Giovanni, Enrica Detragiache, and Raghuram Rajan. 2008. "The Real Effect of Banking Crises." *Journal of Financial Intermediation* 17:1, 89–112.

Denis, David, and Vassil Mihov. 2003. "The Choice among Bank Debt, Non-bank Private Debt, and Public Debt: Evidence from New Corporate Borrowings." *Journal of Financial Economics* 70:1, 3–28.

Diamond, Douglas. 1984. "Financial Intermediation and Delegated Monitoring." *Review of Economic Studies* 51:3, 393–414.

Diamond, Douglas. 1991. "Monitoring and Reputation: The Choice between Bank Loans and Directly Placed Debt." *Journal of Political Economy* 99:4, 689–721.

Diamond, Douglas, and Philip Dybvig. 1983. "Bank Runs, Deposit Insurance, and Liquidity." *Journal of Political Economy* 91:3, 401–419.

Diamond, Douglas, and Raghuram Rajan. 2000. "A Theory of Bank Capital." *Journal of Finance* 55:6, 2431–2465.

Drucker, Steven, and Manju Puri. 2005. "On the Benefits of Concurrent Lending and Underwriting." *Journal of Finance* 60:6, 2763–2799.

Drucker, Steven, and Manju Puri. 2007. "Banks in Capital Markets: A Survey." In B. Espen Eckbo, ed. *Handbook of Corporate Finance: Empirical Corporate Finance*, 189–232. Amsterdam: North Holland/Elsevier.

Duchin, Ran, Oguzhan Ozbas, and Berk A. Sensoy. 2010. "Costly External Finance, Corporate Investment, and the Subprime Mortgage Credit Crisis." *Journal of Financial Economics* 97:3, 418–435.

Eckbo, B. Espen, Ronald W. Masulis, and Oyvind Norli. 2007. "Security Offerings." In B. Espen Eckbo, ed. *Handbook of Corporate Finance: Empirical Corporate Finance*, 233–373. Amsterdam: North Holland/Elsevier.

Ellis, Katrina, Roni Michaely, and Maureen O'Hara. 2000. "When the Underwriter Is the Market Maker: An Examination of Trading in the IPO Aftermarket." *Journal of Finance* 55:3, 1039–1074.

Fama, Eugene. 1985. "What's Different about Banks?" *Journal of Monetary Economics* 15:1, 239–249.

Fang, Lily, and Ayako Yasuda. 2009. "The Effectiveness of Reputation as a Disciplinary Mechanism in Sell-Side Research." *Review of Financial Studies* 22:9, 3735–3777.

Fields, Paige, Donald Fraser, Tammy Berry, and Steven Byers. 2006. "Do Bank Loan Relationships Still Matter?" *Journal of Money, Credit, and Banking* 38:5, 1195-1209.

Fields, Paige, Donald Fraser, and Rahul Bhargava. 2003. "A Comparison of Underwriting Costs of Initial Public Offerings by Investment and Commercial Banks." *Journal of Financial Research* 26:4, 517–534.

Gande, Amar. 2008. "Commercial Banks in Investment Banking." In Anjan V. Thakor and Arnoud W. A. Boot, eds. *Handbook on Financial Intermediation and Banking*, 163–188, Amsterdam: North Holland/Elsevier.

Gande, Amar, Manju Puri, and Anthony Saunders. 1999. "Bank Entry, Competition and the Market for Corporate Securities Underwriting." *Journal of Financial Economics* 54:2, 165–195.

Gande, Amar, Manju Puri, Anthony Saunders, and Ingo Walter. 1997. "Bank Underwriting of Debt Securities: Modern Evidence." *Review of Financial Studies* 10:4, 1175–1202.

Gatev, Evans, Til Schuermann, and Philip. E. Strahan. 2006. "How Do Banks Manage Liquidity Risk? Evidence from the Equity and Deposit and Markets in the Fall of 1998." In Mark Carey and René Stulz, eds. *Risks of Financial Institutions*, 105–127. Chicago: University of Chicago Press.

Gatev, Evans, and Philip E. Strahan. 2006. "Bank's Advantage in Hedging Liquidity Risk: Theory and Evidence from the Commercial Paper Market." *Journal of Finance* 61:2, 867–892.

Gorton, Gary, and George Pennacchi. 1990. "Financial Intermediaries and Liquidity Creation." *Journal of Finance* 45:1, 49–72.

Gorton, Gary, and Andrew Winton. 2003, "Financial Intermediation." In George Constantinides, Milton Harris, and René Stulz, eds. *Handbook of the Economics of Finance*, 431–552. Amsterdam: North Holland.

Hanley, Kathleen Weis, A. Arun Kumar, and Paul J. Sequin. 1993. "Price Stabilization in the Market for New Issues." *Journal of Financial Economics* 34:2, 177–197.
Hansen, Robert. S., and Paul Torregrosa. 1992. "Underwriter Compensation and Corporate Monitoring." *Journal of Finance* 47:4, 1537–1555.
Harjoto, Maretno, Donald J. Mullineaux, and Ha-Chin Yi. 2006. "Loan Pricing at Investment versus Commercial Banks." *Financial Management* 35:4, 49–70.
Hebb, Gregory M. 2002. "Conflict of Interest in Commercial Bank Equity Underwriting." *Financial Review* 37:2, 185–205.
Houston, Joel, and Christopher James. 2001. "Do Relationships Have Limits? Banking Relationships, Financial Constraints, and Investments." *Journal of Business* 74:3, 347–374.
Ivashina, Victoria, and David Scharfstein. 2010. "Bank Lending during the Financial Crisis of 2008." *Journal of Financial Economics*. Forthcoming.
Jain, Bharat, and Omesh Kini. 1999. "On Investment Banker Monitoring in the New Issues Market." *Journal of Banking and Finance* 23:1, 49–84.
James, Christopher. 1987. "Some Evidence on the Uniqueness of Bank Loans." *Journal of Financial Economics* 19:2, 217–233.
James, Christopher. 1992. "Relationship-Specific Assets and the Pricing of Underwriter Services." *Journal of Finance* 47:5, 1865–1885.
James, Christopher, and Peggy Wier. 1990. "Borrowing Relationships, Intermediation, and the Cost of Issuing Public Securities." *Journal of Financial Economics* 28:1, 149–171.
Kanatas, George, and Jianping Qi. 2003. "Integration of Lending and Underwriting: Implications of Scope Economies." *Journal of Finance* 58:3, 1167–1191.
Kashyap, Anil K., Raghuram G. Rajan, and Jeremy C. Stein. 2002. "Banks as Liquidity Providers: An Explanation for the Coexistence of Lending and Deposit-Taking." *Journal of Finance* 57:1, 33–73.
Klingebiel, Daniela, Randall Kroszner, and Luc Laeven. 2007. "Banking Crises, Financial Dependence, and Growth." *Journal of Financial Economics* 84:1, 187–228.
Krigman, Laurie, Wayne Shaw, and Kent L. Womack. 2001. "Why Do Firms Switch Underwriters?" *Journal of Financial Economics* 60:2, 245–284.
Krishnaswami, Sudha, Paul A. Spindt, and Venkat Subramaniam. 1999. "Information Asymmetry, Monitoring and the Placement Structure of Corporate Debt." *Journal of Financial Economics* 51:3, 407–434.
Kroszner, Randall S., and Raghuram G. Rajan. 1994. "Is the Glass–Steagall Act Justified? A Study of the U.S. Experience with Universal Banking before 1933." *American Economic Review* 84:4, 810–832.
Lee, Inmoo, Scott Lochhead, Jay R. Ritter, and Quanshui Zhao. 1996. "The Costs of Raising Capital." *Journal of Financial Research* 19:1, 59–74.
Leland, Hayne E., and David H. Pyle. 1977. "Informational Asymmetries, Financial Structure, and Financial Intermediation." *Journal of Finance* 32:2, 371–387.
Lewellen, Katharina. 2006. "Risk, Reputation, and IPO Price Support." *Journal of Finance* 61:2, 613–653.
Ljungqvist, Alexander. 2007. "IPO Underpricing." In B. Espen Eckbo, ed. *Handbook of Corporate Finance: Empirical Corporate Finance*, 375–422. Amsterdam: North Holland/Elsevier.
Lummer, Scott, and John McConnell. 1989. "Further Evidence on the Bank Lending Process and the Capital Market Responses to Bank Loan Agreements." *Journal of Financial Economics* 25:1, 99–122.
Michaely, Roni, and Kent Womack L. 1999. "Conflict of Interest and the Credibility of Underwriter Analyst Recommendations." *Review of Financial Studies* 12:4, 653–686.
Narayanan, Rajesh P., Katuri Rangan, and Nanda K. Rangan. 2004. "The Role of Syndicate Structure in Bank Underwriting." *Journal of Financial Economics* 72:3, 555–580.

Ongena, Steven, Viorel Roscovan, Wei-Ling Song, and Bas Werker. 2008. "Banks and Bonds: The Impact of Bank Loan Announcement on Bond and Equity Prices." Working Paper, Tilburg University.

Petersen, Mitchell A., and Raghuram Rajan. 1994. "The Benefits of Lending Relationships: Evidence from Small Business Data." *Journal of Finance* 49:1, 3–37.

Preece, Dianna, and Donald Mullineaux. 1994. "Monitoring by Financial Institutions: Bank vs. Nonbanks." *Journal of Financial Services Research* 8:3, 191–200.

Puri, Manju. 1994. "The Long-Term Default Performance of Bank Underwritten Security Issues." *Journal of Banking and Finance* 18:2, 397–418.

Puri, Manju. 1996. "Commercial Banks in Investment Banking: Conflict of Interest or Certification Role?" *Journal of Financial Economics* 40:3, 373–401.

Puri, Manju. 1999. "Commercial Banks as Underwriters: Implications for the Going Public Process." *Journal of Financial Economics* 54:2, 133–163.

Puri, Manju, Jorg Rochell, and Sascha Steffen. 2009. "The Impact of the U.S. Financial Crisis on Global Retail Lending." Working Paper, Duke University.

Pyle, David H. 1971. "On the Theory of Financial Intermediation." *Journal of Finance* 26:3, 737–747.

Rajan, Raghuram. 1992. "Insiders and Outsiders: The Choice between Informed and Arm's-Length Debt." *Journal of Finance* 47:4, 1367–1400.

Rajan, Raghuram. 2002. "An Investigation into the Economics of Extending Bank Powers." *Journal of Emerging Market Finance* 1:2, 125–156.

Ramakrishnan, R. T. S., and Anjan V. Thakor. 1984. "Information Reliability and a Theory of Financial Intermediation." *Review of Economic Studies* 51:3, 415–432.

Ritter, Jay R. 1987. "The Costs of Going Public." *Journal of Financial Economics* 19:2, 269–281.

Ritter, Jay R. 2003. "Investment Banking and Securities Issuance." In George Constantinides, Milton Harris, and René Stulz, eds. *Handbook of the Economics of Finance*, 255–306. Amsterdam: North Holland.

Roten, Ivan C., and Donald J. Mullineaux. 2002. "Debt Underwriting by Commercial Bank-Affiliated Firms and Investment Banks: More Evidence." *Journal of Banking and Finance* 26:4, 689–718.

Ruud, Judith S. 1993. "Underwriter Price Support and the IPO Underpricing Puzzle." *Journal of Financial Economics* 34:2, 135–151.

Schenone, Carola. 2004. "The Effect of Banking Relationships on the Firm's IPO Underpricing." *Journal of Finance* 59:6, 2903–2958.

Schenone, Carola. 2010. "Lending Relationships and Information Rents: Do Banks Exploit Their Information Advantages." *Review of Financial Studies* 23:3, 1149–1199.

Schultz, Paul H., and Mir A. Zaman. 1994. "Aftermarket Support and Underpricing of Initial Public Offerings." *Journal of Financial Economics* 35:2, 199–219.

Securities Industry and Financial Markets Association. 2008. "Research Quarterly." Available at http://www.sifma.org/uploadedFiles/Research/ResearchReports/2009/CapitalMarkets_ResearchQuarterly_200903_SIFMA.pdf.

Slovin, Myron, Shane Johnson, and John Glascock. 1992. "Firm Size and the Information Content of Bank Loan Announcements." *Journal of Banking and Finance* 16: 6, 1057–1071.

Strahan, Philip E. 2008. "Bank Structure and Lending: What We Do and Do Not Know." In Anjan V. Thakor and Arnoud W. A. Boot, eds. *Handbook on Financial Intermediation and Banking*, 107–131. Amsterdam: North Holland/Elsevier.

Sufi, Amir. 2007. "Information Asymmetry and Financing Arrangement: Evidence from Syndicated Loans." *Journal of Finance* 62:2, 629–668.

Tong, Hui, and Shang-Jin Wei. 2008. "Real Effects of the Subprime Mortgage Crisis: Is It a Demand or a Finance Shock?" Working Paper, Columbia Business School.

Yasuda, Ayako. 2005. "Do Bank Relationships Affect the Firm's Underwriter Choice in the Corporate Bond Underwriting Market?" *Journal of Finance* 60:3, 1259–1292.

ABOUT THE AUTHORS

Neal Galpin joined the Mays Business School at Texas A&M University in 2006. His research appears in the *Journal of Law and Economics, Journal of Financial and Quantitative Analysis,* and other journals. His research interests include the role of conflicts of interest in corporate financing and investment decisions as well as the effect of financial institutions on economic growth. Professor Galpin teaches corporate finance. He received a BBA in finance from St. Bonaventure University in 1999, an MBA from University of Cincinnati in 2000, and a PhD from Indiana University in 2006.

Heungju Park is a PhD candidate in the Department of Finance of the Mays Business School at Texas A&M University. His research areas include the roles of financial intermediaries in asset markets and corporate investments. He was a research analyst at the Korea Deposit Insurance Corporation and Korea National Information and Credit Evaluation, Inc. He received a BBA in 2000 and an MS in finance from Korea University in 2002.

CHAPTER 16

Bank Relationships and Collateralization

ARON A. GOTTESMAN
Associate Professor of Finance, Lubin School of Business, Pace University

GORDON S. ROBERTS
CIBC Professor of Financial Services, Schulich School of Business, York University

INTRODUCTION

This chapter surveys the literature on bank relationships and bank loans, with a focus on the use of collateral in bank loans. The chapter consists of two sections. The first section explores bank relationships while the second explores collateralization.

The first section addresses the following questions: What does it mean to have a "bank relationship"? What are the benefits and costs associated with such a relationship? Do the benefits outweigh the costs? How are loan contract terms, borrower characteristics, and lender characteristics related to each other? What are the characteristics of the secondary loan market, and what has driven the growth of this market?

The first section shows how a bank relationship is developed through the bank's generation of proprietary information about the borrower in multiple interactions. Key benefits of a bank relationship are the reduction of information asymmetries and facilitation of monitoring, as well as the ability of the bank and borrower to negotiate contract terms. Yet, a bank relationship can be costly to both lenders and borrowers. Some early event studies show that markets initially react positively to the announcement of bank loans, suggesting the benefits outweigh the costs. However, some debate exists as to whether markets continued to react positively after the 1980s. The first section also explores the literature related to the trade-off across loan contract terms and concludes with a survey of the secondary loan market.

Prior research has documented the widespread use of collateral in bank loans in the United States. For both small business loans and large syndicated loans, around 80 percent carry collateral as security (Berger et al. 2007; Gottesman and Roberts 2004). Collateral plays an important role in bank loans in Italy, Germany, and Spain, as well as in more than 60 developing and developed countries (Pozzolo 2002; Jiménez, Salas, and Saurina 2008; Hainz, Weill, and Godlewsk 2008). In the second section, the discussion focuses on the role of collateral in bank loans with occasional reference to selected studies on collateral in bonds and asset-backed securities. The discussion is organized around two perspectives: those of borrowers and of lenders (Jiménez, Salas, and Saurina 2008).

While this chapter surveys research on banking relationships and collateralization, the coverage is not meant to be exhaustive. Rather, the goal is to review relevant papers in order to identify and summarize major issues and to provide perspective on mainstream and dissenting views. Following from this approach, the inclusion of a paper in this chapter signals an important contribution to a significant strand of research.

BANK RELATIONSHIPS

Ongena and Smith (2000a, p. 224) define a bank relationship as "the connection between a bank and customer that goes beyond the execution of simple, anonymous, financial transactions." A bank relationship develops over the course of multiple interactions with individual clients and is characterized by the information that the bank gathers through these interactions. Boot (2000) details three conditions that indicate the presence of a bank relationship. First, the information gathered is not readily available public information. Second, the information is gathered through multiple interactions such as the provision of financial services. Third, the information that is gathered remains proprietary. Boot notes that the term "bank relationship" is commonly applied to any financial intermediary that forms a relation and is not strictly limited to banks. Further, bank relationships can extend to other services provided by the financial intermediary such as investment banking, though the focus is typically on lending.

Benefits and Costs of Bank Relationships

A key benefit associated with a bank relationship is that the lender generates proprietary information about the borrower over the course of the relationship. This benefit has been explored by early studies on the impact of deposit relationships on bank loans such as Hodgman (1961) and Kane and Malkiel (1965), and later research such as Black (1975), Campbell (1979), Yosha (1995), and Bhattacharya and Chiesa (1995), among others. A lender typically faces an adverse selection problem as borrowers have information that lenders do not. The borrower is reluctant to disclose information publicly as competitors could benefit. In a bank relationship, the bank generates proprietary information that is not publicly disclosed. For example, Mester, Nakamura, and Renault (2002) provide detailed evidence regarding how banks use checking account information to evaluate borrower credit risk and to set an appropriate level of monitoring. From the bank's perspective, the costs associated with generating such information are compensated through the ability to be the dominant lender and through the reuse of the information over the course of the relationship.

Ongena and Smith (2000a) observe that the importance of the bank relationship is a function of the length and scope of the relation. They argue that lenders in longer-term relationships learn more than lenders in shorter-term relationships and make greater use of private information, have greater flexibility, and can more credibly build their reputation. Further, the authors contend that when the bank provides more services, the lender has a greater opportunity to learn. The bank and borrower can lengthen or widen the scope of the relation through concessions in one time period or service in order to gain opportunities in another.

According to Fama (1985), the reserve requirements banks face suggest that the rate of interest that borrowers pay for bank loans will be higher than other borrowing. If so, why are borrowers willing to pay these higher rates? Fama argues that while the banks face reserve requirements, borrowers choose banks over alternative lenders due to a competitive advantage. To explain the nature of the competitive advantage, Fama distinguishes between inside debt, such as bank loans, in which the lender gets access to private information, and outside debt, such as publicly-traded bonds, for which the lender relies on publicly available information. Fama contends that inside debt holders have lower information costs when monitoring their contracts, resulting in lower rates. Further, short-term inside debt bank loans send a signal to the rest of the market about the borrower's creditworthiness, which can lead to lower rates associated with other contracts. Fama notes that his distinction between inside and outside debt is similar to the distinction between inside and outside equity made by Jensen and Meckling (1976) (see also Leland and Pyle 1977; Diamond 1984; Ramakrishnan and Thakor 1984; Boyd and Prescott 1986; Ongena and Smith 2000a).

One way in which loans can be monitored is through the covenants associated with the loans. Covenants require that the borrowers communicate information to the lender, both financial and nonfinancial. They also require the borrower to comply with restrictions designed to limit the lender's risk. Examples of financial covenants are maximum debt to earnings before interest, taxes, depreciation, and amortization (EBITDA) ratios and minimum net worth requirements, while examples of nonfinancial covenants are dividend restrictions and asset sales sweep (Allen and Gottesman 2006). Bradley and Roberts (2004) provide evidence that loans to small, highly levered or high growth firms are more likely to include covenants, as are syndicated loans, loans made by investment banks, loans during recessions, and loans with high credit spreads.

Another benefit of bank relationships is the ability to negotiate contract terms that enhance the positions of the lender, borrower, and the relationship (Boot 2000). The flexibility to renegotiate contracts is valuable and may allow implicit long-term contracting. Covenants associated with contracts smooth over conflicts of interest and agency costs. Collateralization is another important characteristic of contracts, to be discussed in the collateralization section of this chapter.

From the bank's perspective, one cost associated with a bank relationship is the *soft-budget constraint problem*. When the borrower faces default, a relationship lender may be compelled to provide additional credit to protect its previous loans. This can lead the borrower to engage in behaviors in which it would not engage without the protection provided through the ongoing relationship (see Bolton and Scharfstein 1996; Boot 2000; Dewatripont and Maskin 1995).

Another cost, designated the *hold-up problem*, is driven by the information monopoly that the bank acquires due to its superior knowledge of the borrower (Wood 1975; Sharpe, 1990). This information monopoly can lead to higher rates or to the borrower's failure to exploit investment opportunities as a result of the borrower's unwillingness to borrow from the relationship bank due to monopolization fears. While the hold-up problem can be mitigated through multiple bank relationships, this can impact the availability of credit and the rates that borrowers pay (Rajan 1992; Petersen and Rajan 1995; Von Thadden 1995; Thakor 1996; Ongena and Smith 2000a, 2000b; Degryse and Ongena 2001).

Boot (2000) explores how competition impacts relationship banking. Competition can weaken relationship banking when banks exert less effort to develop relationships as the length of the relationship is expected to be shorter with more competition. Alternatively, competition can strengthen the bank's investment in the relationship as the bank uses the relationship to maintain ties with borrowers who might otherwise consider other lenders.

Empirical evidence using pre-1990s data suggests that the benefits associated with bank loans outweigh the costs. Multiple event studies show that announcement of bank loans results in a positive market reaction, (e.g., James 1987; Billett, Flannery, and Garfinkel, 1995). A follow-up study by Billett, Flannery, and Garfinkel (2006) reexamines the sample of loan announcements from the 1980s and provides evidence that firms announcing bank loans experience negative returns over the subsequent three years. Less clear is whether the positive market reaction is exclusive to renewals and the associated positive signal the renewal sends, or whether positive market reaction occurs for loan initiations as well. Lummer and McConnell (1989) provide evidence that the positive market reaction is limited to renewals, while other studies (e.g., Slovin, Johnson, and Glascock 1992; Billett et al. 1995) find a positive market reaction for both loan initiations and renewals. Ongena and Smith (2000a) provide a summary of event study in their Table 1.

There has been debate as to whether bank loans continue to generate positive market reaction today. Fields et al. (2006) present evidence that while bank loan announcements generated positive market reaction in the 1970s and 1980s neither loan initiations nor renewals generated positive market reaction during the period 2000 to 2003 and experienced diminished market reaction during the period 1990 to 1999. Fields et al. argue that the diminishment of positive market reaction is due to structural changes in financial markets, such as the greater use of information technology. However, Lee and Sharpe (2009) present evidence of positive market reaction during the period 1995 to 1999, similar to the reaction observed for studies of the 1970s and 1980s.

Loan Contract Terms and Trade-Offs

Loan contract terms differ across loans. Melnik and Plaut (1986) present a model where the loan contract is described as a function of loan size, maturity, the rate spread, the loan commitment fee rate, and collateral. They provide empirical evidence of trade-off by loan contract terms; for example, the rate spread is larger if the loan size is larger. Evidence suggests other trade-offs. For example, loans with performance-pricing covenants, which reset spreads if the borrower's financial ratios or bond rating change, are associated with lower rate spreads (Asquith, Beatty, and Weber 2005). Evidence also shows a negative relationship between promised yield and the presence of covenants (Bradley and Roberts 2004).

Other trade-offs are less straightforward, such as the relationship between loan maturity and rate spreads as well as between collateralization and rate spreads. One could argue that from the borrower's perspective, longer-maturity loans are more desirable as they limit refinancing costs, while lenders prefer shorter-term loans to minimize agency costs. This suggests that a positive relationship should be observed between maturity and spreads. Alternatively, one could posit that lower-risk borrowers are directed to longer-maturity loans, which suggests that a negative relationship should be observed. The empirical evidence is mixed. For example, Strahan (1999) and Dennis, Nandy, and Sharpe (2000) find evidence of a negative association while Helwege and Turner (1999) and Coleman, Esho, and Sharpe (2002) report a positive association. Gottesman and Roberts (2004) find evidence that the negative relation exists at the portfolio level and the positive relation exists at the individual firm level. The collateralization section of this chapter provides information about the relationship between collateralization and rate spreads.

A sole lender or a syndicate of lenders may provide loans. Syndicates are headed by a single lead arranger or multiple lead arrangers. The lead arranger typically holds a large stake and is usually a relationship bank (Allen and Gottesman 2006), facilitating its role in screening and monitoring. Sufi (2004) finds that when the borrower requires more investigation and monitoring, the lead arranger will keep a larger portion of the loan, form more concentrated syndicates, and choose syndicate participants that are geographically closer to the borrower and with whom the borrower is more likely to have had a previous relationship. Sufi argues that the larger stake by the lead arranger is an attempt to guarantee due diligence, while the participant characteristics are intended to minimize information asymmetries.

In a syndicated loan, the lead arranging bank has substantial power to influence syndicate and loan characteristics such as syndicate formation, size, composition, fees, and covenants. These decisions will affect the value of the contract. For example, larger syndicates are associated with costlier renegotiation due to the need for consent across a greater number of participants. Smaller syndicate size may therefore be preferable for riskier firms that are more likely to renegotiate the loan (Lee and Mullineaux 2001). Further, as discussed earlier, multiple bank relationships may be preferred to mitigate the hold-up problem. Also, larger syndicate size increases the likelihood that proprietary information will be leaked, suggesting that borrowers with more proprietary information will prefer smaller syndicates (Bhattacharya and Chiesa 1995). In countries where legal enforcement mechanisms are weak, evidence suggests that loan syndicates are larger (Esty and Megginson 2003).

Secondary Market

As Rule 144A securities, bank loans can be sold on the secondary market to Qualified Institutional Buyers (QIBs), an example of which are institutions with at least $100 million in investible assets (Securities Act of 1933). The secondary market for loans has grown significantly. Allen and Gottesman (2006) attribute this growth to three factors. First, secondary sales remove loans from bank balance sheets in response to constraints introduced by the Basel Capital Accords. Second, there was growth of demand for investments in Collateralized Loan Obligations (CLOs), which are composed on individual loans. Unsurprisingly, this increased demand for loans makes secondary market sale of these positions attractive to debt holders. Third, documentation and settlement standardizations introduced by the Loan

Syndication and Trade Association (LSTA) enable market liquidity and trading efficiency.

Kamstra, Roberts, and Shao (2010) observe that the secondary loan market has developed from a primarily interbank market to a market with broad institutional investor participation. They further note that the proportion of nonpar loans (i.e., those loans trading below 90 percent of principal) has increased noticeably over time. These researchers also find that ex-ante riskier loans are sold on the secondary market. Other research suggests that banks sell safer loans and that loan arrangers retain larger shares of riskier loans when syndicating (Dennis and Mullineaux 2000; Sufi 2004; Panyagometh and Roberts 2010). Dahiya, Puri, and Saunders (2003) note that the secondary market for loans is comprised of two broad categories: the trading of syndicated loan positions by syndicated loan participants and the loan sale market, where banks sell nonsyndicated loans that they hold. They present evidence that loan sale announcements result in negative market reaction, which they argue is due to the negative certification that the sale signals to the market.

While less liquid than equity markets (Allen and Gottesman 2006), the secondary loan market is comparable to others, such as the high yield bond market (Thomas and Wang 2004). Allen and Gottesman provide evidence that despite liquidity differences, equity and loan markets are highly integrated. Going one step further, Altman, Gande, and Saunders (2010) provide evidence that the secondary loan market attains a higher level of efficiency based on their finding that returns in this market "Granger cause" bond returns. They do not find the reverse to be true. They interpret this as support for the view that the monitoring advantage of loans remains, as described by Fama (1985), even when the loans trade on secondary markets. Indeed, as Allen and Gottesman find, lead arrangers typically hold the largest share of the syndicated loans; on average, the lead arranger holds a 27 percent share while other participants hold on average less than three percent. According to Altman et al., these holdings ensure the lead arranger retains its motivation to monitor in the secondary market.

Kamstra, Roberts, and Shao (2010) relate loan spreads to loan sales and identify two effects. First, they find that spreads increase with higher ex-ante probability of loan resale on the secondary market. They argue that the reduced monitoring associated with loan resale drives the increased cost of borrowing. Second, the authors identify increased liquidity as a further effect of loan sales and show that this lowers spreads. The net effect of loans sales is a lowering of spreads. This is consistent with the results of Güner (2006), who contends that the lower cost of borrowing compensates the borrower for the complexity and negative information costs associated with loan resale.

COLLATERALIZATION

Research on collateral has established two empirical regularities. First, the presence of collateral is associated with higher yields for small business loans in the United States (Berger and Udell 1990, 1995) and Europe (Degryse and Van Cayseele 2000), for large syndicated loans in the United States (Dennis, Nandy, and Sharpe 2000; Gottesman and Roberts 2007) as well as for a broad range of loans in Spain (Jiménez, Salas, and Saurina 2006a), Germany (Harhoff and Korting 1998), and Italy (Pozzolo 2002). Consistent with their higher spreads, loans with collateral carry a higher probability of default (Jiménez, Salas, and Saurina 2006a). Second, riskier borrowers are more likely to pledge collateral and to do so in greater amounts than safer borrowers. Gonas, Highfield, and Mullineaux (2004) characterize higher-quality firms as having a credit rating, larger sales, and U.S. headquarters. All of these quality measures are associated with a lower probability of collateralized debt. Other papers report similar results (Carey, Post, and Sharpe 1998; Roberts and Siddiqi 2004; Jimenez et al. 2006a). The empirical regularities also hold for U.S. public bonds (John, Lynch, and Puri 2003).

Role of Collateral: Borrower-Based Theories and Tests

The decision to employ collateral depends on the ex-ante credit risk of the borrower, and the presence of collateral impacts credit risk. Common to a wide range of theoretical models in this area is the idea that, by offering collateral, borrowers address adverse selection problems that can arise from information asymmetry between themselves and lenders regarding the borrower's credit quality. As Benmelech and Bergman (2007) point out, models focusing on adverse selection generally lead to the counterfactual prediction that higher-quality borrowers should pledge security as a signal of their lower credit risk while riskier companies borrow unsecured.

In this framework, such borrowers can offer collateral more cheaply than riskier borrowers since default (and loss of collateral) carries a lower probability. Moral hazard or agency conflicts between borrowers and lenders are at the heart of a set of models giving rise to the two empirical regularities noted above. Pledging collateral is understood as a bonding activity undertaken by borrowers in order to control the risk of asset substitution: a borrower cannot sell secured assets and switch to riskier investments without permission (Smith and Warner 1979). Underinvestment is a related agency cost of debt in which stockholders decline positive net present value projects because they must share the benefits with existing bondholders. Issuing secured debt to finance a new investment makes investing more attractive because this type of financing allows shareholders to sell part of the payoffs from the new project as opposed to sharing them with existing bondholders (Stulz and Johnson 1985). Financing with collateral also reduces lender losses should bankruptcy occur because security increases the recovery rate.

To illustrate, a recent study of recovery rates on defaulted bank loans over the period 1982 to 2008 finds a recovery rate of 62.1 percent for loans rated senior secured and 41.0 percent for senior unsecured (Moody's Investors Service 2009a). Such agency problems are likely to be more severe as loan maturity increases because conflicts take time to unfold, and, as a result, collateral is more commonly employed in longer-term lending (Gonas, Highfield, and Mullineaux 2004). Further, only riskier borrowers are required to pledge collateral consistent with the second empirical regularity.

Even with security in place, riskier borrowers are still of lower credit quality than high-quality firms that can borrow unsecured. This gives rise to the first empirical regularity: secured debt carries higher yields (Berger and Udell 1990; Pozzolo 2002, Jiménez et al. 2006a; Gottesman and Roberts, 2007). A competing explanation rejects the bonding framework and claims instead that collateral heightens agency conflicts between managers and lenders, accounting for the higher yield of secured debt. John, Lynch, and Puri (2003) document this yield differential in tests on a sample of U.S. public debt issues and argue that managers of the borrowing firm with a stake in its equity have an incentive to shift value from secured to unsecured assets. This incentive arises because increasing the value of unsecured assets leaves more value for equity in the case of bankruptcy. As such, managers could underinvest in insurance or maintenance for secured assets.

While the choice between these two conceptual frameworks for explaining collateral and spreads has not been fully resolved, the bonding approach has merit for several reasons. First, the finding that secured debt carries higher yields does not refute the bonding argument that the introduction of security reduces spreads. Because security is offered by riskier firms, econometric tests of its impact may be confounded by selection bias; the higher spreads associated with collateral likely arise from greater risk of the companies borrowing with security that are unobservable to the econometrician (e.g., Gottesman and Roberts 2004). Supporting this interpretation, Roberts and Viscione (1984) implement a paired matching technique to control for selection bias and report that security reduces bond yield. Similarly, Booth and Booth (2006) implement a two-stage model to control for the probability that a firm will borrow with collateral and find that collateral reduces yield.

Second, the bonding hypothesis is consistent with the way that practitioners, bond rating agencies, and lenders assess credit risk. For example, Moody's Investors Service (2009b) evaluates a borrower's business risk and leverage to establish a rating for a company's principal class of unsecured debt. It then examines debt features increasing "control afforded to creditors," including security, and will apply a "rating uplift" of one or more "notches" if these factors are effective. Raters may at times apply this approach too generally and fail to appreciate the nuances in types of collateral (John, Lynch, and Puri 2003). Further, raters may deviate from best practices in order to boost business as is widely believed to have happened in the period before the credit crisis of 2007 and 2008. However, the point remains that the rater's stated best practices apply the bonding approach. Further, empirical research supports the view that rating agencies recognize distinctions among classes of collateral. Benmelech and Bergman (2007) demonstrate that, consistent with best practices under the bonding hypothesis, bond rating agencies assign higher ratings to U.S. airlines offering more liquid collateral in the form of aircraft that are more redeployable to other airlines in the event of bankruptcy. Anecdotal evidence further supports the view of collateral as a bonding mechanism. While teaching a course on credit risk analysis to commercial lenders, one of the authors of this chapter was told by a banker: "When I don't understand the borrower, I ask for collateral."

Lender-Based Theories and Tests

To this point, the discussion has focused on incentive and agency issues related to borrowers. Since such issues exist on both sides of a loan contract, incentive conflicts facing lenders may also motivate the use of collateral. When a loan contract is written, the lender undertakes to monitor the borrower's ongoing credit risk and to take corrective actions should the borrower's credit quality deteriorate. Such actions include pressuring the borrower to seek additional equity or to sell assets, and in the extreme case to call the loan and force the borrower into bankruptcy.

An agency problem will arise should the lender fail to perform properly in its role as a delegated monitor on behalf of other stakeholders in the borrower. Institutional investors, customers, and suppliers, among others, all benefit from lender monitoring, which steers the borrower clear of financial shipwreck. In the case of syndicated loans, if the lead bank shirks its monitoring responsibility, harm may result to the other banks and stakeholders. Rajan and Winton (1995) view monitoring and collateral as complements. They argue that the incentive to monitor will be enhanced if a loan is secured because the lender has the ability to demand more collateral if credit risk increases. In addition to imposing an added constraint on the borrower, a bank's demand for more collateral sends a signal to other stakeholders that the borrower's financial condition has deteriorated. Consistent with the bonding hypothesis, such monitoring and actions are important as riskier companies in need of greater monitoring are more likely to borrow with collateral.

More generally, as discussed above, under the bonding hypothesis, collateral and monitoring are substitutes. As a result, there is likely an incentive to monitor less actively when loans carry security (Manove, Padilla, and Pagano 2001). While securitized, asset backed lending (which featured so prominently in the 2007–2008 credit crisis) is not the focus of this chapter; research in this area is relevant in establishing that collateral may substitute for monitoring. Keys et al. (2008) report greater default risk for loans more likely to be securitized resulting from reduced screening by lenders. In the same vein, Ashcraft and Santos (2007) document that only the least risky borrowers have enjoyed a reduction in debt costs with the introduction of credit default swaps (CDSs). For the average borrower, information advantages are more than offset by diminished incentives for monitoring. On the other side of the ledger, Benmelech, Dlugosz, and Ivashina (2009) find that this effect does not hold for corporate collateralized loan obligations.

In addition to differing degrees of diligence in monitoring, lending banks may differ in their types of lending relationships: long-term relationship lending versus transaction lending as described above. In a long-term lending relationship, collateral can serve as a smoothing device that allows the lender to tax or subsidize the borrower through adjusting collateral requirements. According to Boot and Thakor (1994), efficiencies achieved over a long relationship should lead to a lower average level of collateral. Further, lending relationships of longer duration and wider scope (encompassing a greater number of bank services) provide the lender with valuable information, which substitutes for collateral. Empirical tests support this substitution effect for U.S. small business loans (Berger and Udell 1995) and for European loans (Degryse and Cayseele 2000). Chakraborty and Hu (2006) categorize information garnered from lending relationships as "soft" (borrower's reputation for hard work and honesty) versus "hard" (verifiable information such as historical sales or profits). They report that "soft" information is valuable for lines of credit, while hard information is associated with reduced collateral in term loans.

Collateral has traditionally been important in small business loans, and this role has changed with technological advances in lending. Credit scoring models based on hard information allow banks to enter distant markets to compete with local banks. Inderst and Mueller (2007) develop a model predicting that, as entry by distant banks (employing scoring) makes markets more competitive, local banks will react by employing greater collateral. Since collateral substitutes for expensive monitoring activities, local banks can protect the thinner margins arising from competition. Berger et al. (2007) examine the impact of hard information in the form of credit scoring models. Consistent with the findings of Chakraborty and Hu (2006), they find that lenders adopting scoring reduce their use of collateral in small business loans. The results in Berger et al. are also consistent with the prediction of Inderst and Mueller that when distant transactions lenders using scoring (based on hard information) enter a market, any increase in collateral use accompanying enhanced competition will come from local banks as they replace more expensive monitoring (based on soft information).

More generally, collateral use appears to be an efficient response to competition: Market power allows banks to subsidize riskier loans making credit available to riskier borrowers (Petersen and Rajan 1995). Collateral plays the same role in the model of Inderst and Mueller (2007). From this perspective, market power and collateral are substitutes and banks should intensify their use of collateral as competition increases. Jiménez, Salas, and Saurina (2006a, 2006b) conduct tests supporting this effect of competition on a sample of Spanish bank loans over the period 1984 to 2002. They find that a Herfindahl Index of concentration carries a significantly negative coefficient in their logit model predicting the presence of collateral. Their tests include controls for the impact of bank relationships through variables measuring the number of operations each customer has with the lender as well as the number of lenders. In a follow-up paper, Jiménez, Salas, and Saurina (2008) examine collateral use by distant versus local banks defined by the distance between the branch serving customers and the bank head office. As predicted by Inderst and Mueller, they find that local banks are more likely to use collateral and that this use intensifies as markets become more competitive.

The impact of competition on collateral use remains open to debate. In contrast with the studies reviewed above, Hainz, Weill, and Godlewski (2008) argue that with greater competition, banks reduce their use of collateral. They agree that monitoring is a more expensive substitute for collateral but posit the reverse effect for competition. Rather than pressuring banks to cut costs associated with risk controls by replacing expensive monitoring with cheaper collateral as in Inderst and Mueller (2007), Hainz, Weill, and Godlewski hold that banks that enjoy market power prefer to use collateral because it is cheaper. With increased competitive pressures, banks are forced to switch to more expensive monitoring and reduce collateral. Preliminary empirical logit tests predicting the presence of collateral in a sample of bank loans from 70 countries employ the Lerner index of excess profits as well as the Herfindahl index to measure competition. The results support their contrasting hypothesis on the impact of competition on collateral, challenging the findings of Jimenez et al. (2006a); however, the samples in the two studies differ greatly. While Jiménez, Salas, and Saurina (2006a, 2006b, 2008) studied variation of competition across different markets within one developed country (Spain), the sample in Hainz et al. encompasses developed countries (including the United States and Spain) as well as developing countries. This leaves open to questioning whether the impact of competition on collateral use may be different between these two data sets drawn from contrasting financial systems.

Collateral and Economic Development

Law and economics variables reflecting conditions in the economy and banking system can also help explain differences in the use of collateral internationally. Qian and Strahan (2007) examine the features of loan contracts in 43 countries excluding the United States and report that stronger creditor rights making collateral more effective are associated with greater use of collateral particularly for borrowers with more tangible assets. Drawing on a unique dataset of loans from a multinational bank (and thus holding lender effects constant), Liberti and Mian (2009) measure the cost of collateral in different countries by the "collateral spread" defined to capture the increased collateral required for high-risk loans over that for low-risk loans. They find that the collateral spread is reduced for higher levels of financial development. Further, the authors report that, in addition to offering lower levels of collateral, riskier borrowers enjoy enhanced flexibility in being allowed to pledge firm-specific rather than more general liquid assets.

SUMMARY AND CONCLUSIONS

This chapter provides a detailed survey of the literature on bank relationships, bank loans, and the role of collateral in bank loans. The discussion reveals that bank relationships are developed through the bank's generation of proprietary information about the borrower through multiple interactions. The proprietary information is engendered through mechanisms such as checking account information as well as through information transmission mandated by loan covenants. A key benefit of a bank relationship is that the bank's access to proprietary information allows for the reduction of information asymmetries and facilitates monitoring. A further benefit is the ability of the bank and borrower to negotiate contract terms.

Bank relationships also involve costs. This chapter explores two costs identified by the literature: the soft-budget constraint problem that the lender may face and the hold-up problem that the borrower may face. A review of the empirical literature indicates that early event studies find that markets react positively to bank loans, which suggests that the benefits associated with bank relationships outweigh the costs. However, some debate exists as to whether markets continue to react positively or whether the positive market reaction is limited to periods of time before structural change in the loan market. Nonetheless, the reduction of information asymmetry attendant on relationships brings benefits that outweigh the costs.

This chapter also explores the literature related to the trade-off across loan contract terms. Some tradeoffs are complex such as the relation between loan maturity and rate spreads. The chapter also examines the role of the lead arranger and the relation between the lead arranger and loan characteristics. This chapter further provides a survey of the literature that describes and investigates the secondary loan market.

Bank lenders possess limited information about borrowers and as a result face moral hazard and agency problems when they extend loans. Offering collateral is a bonding activity by borrowers that reduces monitoring costs for lenders and lowers bankruptcy costs by increasing recoveries in the event of liquidation. Secured borrowing also attenuates agency costs of asset substitution and underinvestment. For these reasons, a borrower with a choice of either a secured or unsecured bank loan would find the secured loan offered at a lower spread. However, if a shift occurs from comparing two loans to a single borrower to examining the difference between two pools of loans, one secured and the other unsecured, the result is the opposite. Pledging collateral is an activity associated with riskier borrowers, many of whom would not qualify for unsecured bank borrowing. As result, loans with collateral are riskier and offer higher yields than unsecured borrowing.

Research on collateral in bank loans contains useful prescriptions for both corporate financial managers and bankers. Financial officers of smaller, unrated, riskier companies without established bank relationships should expect to be asked to pledge collateral when borrowing from a bank. For such companies, collateral reduces risk and monitoring costs, creating access to bank financing that might otherwise not be available on an unsecured basis. Larger, more established companies with bond ratings generally have a choice between borrowing unsecured or offering collateral. When these borrowers issue secured bonds or borrow with collateral they create shareholder value by expanding their investment set (avoiding the agency costs of underinvestment), as well as by accessing lower-cost financing. Rating agencies and lenders recognize the role of collateral in reducing necessary monitoring and lowering bankruptcy costs and as a result, for a given borrower, debt with collateral generally carries a higher rating and a lower yield than unsecured borrowing.

Turning to the bankers' perspective, the prevalent use of collateral is moderating in small business loans with the widespread use of credit scoring technology. In particular, scoring technology offers a low-cost way for banks headquartered outside a market to compete with local lenders. When facing such competition, local bankers may find controlling monitoring costs by taking collateral advantageous. Bankers also need to take a flexible approach to collateral as borrowers are likely to expect to pledge greater amounts at the start of a bank relationship when information asymmetry is high and to reduce collateral over time as the bank gains more confidence in information provided by the borrower.

DISCUSSION QUESTIONS

1. Both benefits and costs are associated with forming bank relationships. How can a bank relationship prove costly to the bank? How can it prove costly to the borrower?
2. The empirical evidence is mixed as to whether the relationship between loan maturity and rate spreads is positive or negative. What explanations exist for either finding?
3. Bankers and bond rating agencies state that when a borrower pledges collateral, the result is lower risk on a loan. Empirical research documents that, on average, secured loans carry higher yield spreads than do unsecured loans. Explain the rationale for the belief of bankers and rating agencies. How can this belief be reconciled with the findings of empirical research?
4. When a loan market becomes more competitive due to the entry of new banks headquartered in other markets, how does this affect the use of collateral?

REFERENCES

Allen, Linda, and Aron A. Gottesman. 2006. "The Informational Efficiency of the Equity Market as Compared to the Syndicated Bank Loan Market." *Journal of Financial Services Research* 30:1, 5–42.

Altman, Edward, Amar Gande, and Anthony Saunders. 2010. "Bank Debt versus Bond Debt: Evidence from Secondary Market Prices." *Journal of Money, Credit, and Banking*. Forthcoming.

Ashcraft, Adam B., and Joao A. C. Santos. 2007. "Has The CDS Market Lowered the Cost of Corporate Debt?" Available at http://ssrn.com/abstract=995728.

Asquith, Paul, Anne Beatty, and Joseph Weber. 2005. "Performance Pricing in Debt Contracts." *Journal of Accounting and Economics* 40:1, 101–128.

Benmelech, Effi, and Nittai Bergman. 2007. "Collateral Pricing." AFA 2008 New Orleans Meetings Paper. Available at http://ssrn.com/abstract=960787.

Benmelech, Effi, Jennifer Dlugosz, and Victoria Ivashina. 2009. "Securitization without Adverse Selection: The Case of CLOs." AFA 2010 Atlanta Meetings Paper. Available at http://ssrn.com/abstract=1344068.

Berger, Allen N., Marco Espinosa-Vega, W. Scott Frame, and Nathan Miller. 2007. "Why Do Borrowers Pledge More Collateral? New Empirical Evidence on the Role of Asymmetric Information." Working Paper 2006-29a, Federal Reserve Bank of Atlanta.

Berger, Allen N., and Gregory F. Udell. 1990. Collateral, loan quality and bank risk. *Journal of Monetary Economics* 25, 21-42.

Berger, Allen N., and Gregory F. Udell. 1995. "Relationship Lending and Lines of Credit in Small Firm Finance." *Journal of Business* 68:3, 351–381.

Bhattcharya, S., and Chiesa, G. 1995. Proprietary information, financial intermediation, and research incentives. *Journal of Financial Intermediation* 4, 328-357.

Billett, Matthew, Mark Flannery, and Jon Garfinkel. 1995. "The Effect of Lender Identity on a Borrowing Firm's Equity Return." *Journal of Finance* 50:2, 699–718.

Billett, Matthew, Mark Flannery, and Jon Garfinkel. 2006. "Are Bank Loans Special? Evidence on the Post-Performance of Bank Borrowers." *Journal of Financial and Quantitative Analysis* 41:4, 733–752.

Black, Fischer. 1975. "Bank Funds Management in an Efficient Market." *Journal of Financial Economics* 2: 4, 323–339.

Bolton, Patrick, and David S. Scharfstein. 1996. "Optimal Debt Structure and the Number of Creditors." *Journal of Political Economy* 104:1, 1–25.

Boot, Arnoud W. 2000. "Relationship Banking: What Do We Know?" *Journal of Financial Intermediation* 9:1, 7–25.

Boot, Arnoud W., and Anjan V. Thakor. 1994. "Moral Hazard and Secured Lending in an Infinitely Repeated Credit Market Game." *International Economic Review* 35:4, 899–920.

Booth, James R., and Lena C. Booth. 2006. "Loan Collateral Decisions and Corporate Borrowing Costs." *Journal of Money, Credit and Banking* 38:1, 67–90.

Boyd, John H., and Edward C. Prescott. 1986. "Financial Intermediary Coalitions." *Journal of Economic Theory* 38:2, 211–232.

Bradley, Michael, and Michael R. Roberts. 2004. "The Structure and Pricing of Corporate Debt Covenants." Working Paper, Duke University.

Campbell, Tim S. 1979. "Optimal Investment Financing Decisions and the Value of Confidentiality." *Journal of Financial and Quantitative Analysis* 14:2, 232–257.

Carey, Mark, Mitch Post, and Steven A. Sharpe. 1998. "Does Corporate Lending by Banks and Finance Companies Differ? Evidence on Specialization in Private Debt Contracting." *Journal of Finance* 53:3, 845–878.

Chakraborty, Atreya, and Charles Hu. 2006. "Lending Relationships in Line-of-Credit and Nonline-of-Credit Loans: Evidence from Collateral Use in Small Business." *Journal of Financial Intermediation* 15:1, 86–107.

Coleman, Anthony D. F., Neil Esho, and Ian G. Sharpe. 2002. "Do Bank Characteristics Influence Loan Contract Terms?" Working Paper, University of New South Wales.

Dahiya, Sandeep, Manu Puri, and Anthony Saunders. 2003. "Bank Borrowers and Loan Sales: New Evidence on the Uniqueness of Bank Loans." *Journal of Business* 76:4, 563–582.

Degryse, Hans, and Steven Ongena. 2001. "Bank Relationships and Firm Profitability." *Financial Management* 30:1, 9–34.

Degryse, Hans, and Patrick Van Cayseele. 2000. "Relationship Lending within a Bank-Based System: Evidence from European Small Business Data." *Journal of Financial Intermediation* 9:1, 90–109.

Dennis, Steven A., and Donald J. Mullineaux. 2000. "Syndicated Loans." *Journal of Financial Intermediation* 9:4, 404–426.

Dennis, Steven A., Debarshi Nandy, and Ian G. Sharpe. 2000. "The Determinants of Contract Terms in Bank Revolving Credit Agreements." *Journal of Financial and Quantitative Analysis* 35:1, 87–110.

Dewatripont, Mathias, and Eric S. Maskin. 1995. "Credit and Efficiency in Centralized and Decentralized Economies." *Review of Economic Studies* 62:4, 541–555.

Diamond, Douglas W. 1984. "Financial Intermediation and Delegated Monitoring." *Review of Economic Studies* 51:3, 393–414.

Esty, Benjamin C., and William L. Megginson. 2003. "Creditor Rights, Enforcement, and Debt Ownership Structure: Evidence from the Global Syndicated Loan Market." *Journal of Financial and Quantitative Analysis* 38:1, 37–59.

Fama, Eugene F. 1985. "What's Different about Banks?" *Journal of Monetary Economics* 15:1, 5–29.

Fields, L. Paige, Donald R. Fraser, Tammy L. Berry, and Steven Byers. 2006. "Do Bank Loan Relationships Still Matter?" *Journal of Money, Credit, and Banking* 38:5, 1195–1209.

Gonas, John S., Michael J. Highfield, and Donald J. Mullineaux. 2004. "When Are Commercial Loans Secured?" *Financial Review* 39:1, 79–99.

Gottesman, Aron A., and Gordon S. Roberts. 2004. "Maturity and Corporate Loan Pricing." *Financial Review* 38:1, 55–77.

Gottesman, Aron A., and Gordon S. Roberts. 2007. "Loan Rates and Collateral." *Financial Review* 42:3, 401–427.

Güner, A. Burak. 2006. "Loan Sales and the Cost of Corporate Borrowing." *Review of Financial Studies* 19:2, 687–716.

Hainz, Christa, Laurent Weill, and Christophe J. Godlewski. 2008. "Bank Competition and Collateral: Theory and Evidence." Bank of Finland Research Discussion Paper No. 27/2008. Available at http://ssrn.com/abstract=1316379.

Harhoff, Dietmar, and Tim Korting. 1998. "Lending Relationships in Germany: Empirical Evidence from Survey Data." *Journal of Banking and Finance* 22:10, 1317–1353.

Helwege, Jean, and Christopher M. Turner. 1999. "The Slope of the Credit Yield Curve for Speculative-Grade Issuers." *Journal of Finance* 54:5, 1869–1884.

Hodgman, Donald R. 1961. "The Deposit Relationship and Commercial Bank Investment Behavior." *Review of Economics and Statistics* 41:3, 257–268.

Inderst, Roman, and Holger M. Mueller. 2007. "A Lender-Based Theory of Collateral." *Journal of Financial Economics* 84:3, 826–859.

James, Christopher. 1987. "Some Evidence on the Uniqueness of Bank Loans." *Journal of Financial Economics* 19:2, 217–235.

Jensen, Michael C., and William H. Meckling. 1976. "Theory of the Firm: Managerial Behavior, Agency Costs, and Ownership Structure." *Journal of Financial Economics* 3:4, 306–360.

Jiménez, Gabriel, Vicente Salas, and Jesus Saurina. 2006a. "Determinants of Collateral." *Journal of Financial Economics* 81:2, 255–281.

Jiménez, Gabriel, Vicente Salas, and Jesus Saurina. 2006b. "Credit Market Competition, Collateral and Firms' Finance." Banco de Espana Research Paper No. WP-0612. Available at http://ssrn.com/abstract=904303.

Jiménez, Gabriel, Vicente Salas, and Jesus Saurina. 2008. "Organizational Distance and Use of Collateral for Business Loans." Available at http://ssrn.com/abstract=1233582.

John, Kose, Anthony W. Lynch, and Manju Puri. 2003. "Credit Ratings, Collateral and Loan Characteristics: Implications for Yield." *Journal of Business* 76:3, 371–409.

Kamstra, Mark J., Gordon S. Roberts, and Pei Shao. 2010. "Loan Resales, Asset Selection and Borrowing Cost." Working Paper, York University.

Kane, Edward J., and Burton G. Malkiel. 1965. "Bank Portfolio Allocation, Deposit Variability, and the Availability Doctrine." *Quarterly Journal of Economics* 79:1, 113–134.

Keys, Benjamim J., Tanmoy Mukherjee, Amit Seru, and Vikrant Vig. 2008. "Did Securitization Lead to Lax Screening? Evidence from Subprime Loans." Available at http://ssrn.com/abstract=1093137.

Lee, Kwang-Won, and Ian G. Sharpe, 2009. "Does a Bank's Loan Screening and Monitoring Matter?" *Journal of Financial Services Research* 35:1, 33–52.

Lee, Sang W., and Donald J. Mullineaux. 2001. "The Size and Composition of Commercial Lending Syndicates." Working Paper, University of Kentucky.

Leland, Hayne E., and David H. Pyle. 1977. "Informational Asymmetries, Financial Structure, and Financial Intermediation." *Journal of Finance* 32:2, 371–387.

Liberti, Jose Maria, and Atif R. Mian. 2009. "Collateral Spread and Financial Development." Available at http://ssrn.com/abstract=1117738.

Lummer, Scott L., and John J. McConnell. 1989. "Further Evidence on the Bank Lending Process and the Capital Market Response to Bank Loan Agreements." *Journal of Financial Economics* 25:1, 99–122.

Manove, Michael, A. Jorge Padilla, and Marco Pagano. 2001. "Collateral vs. Project Screening: A Model of Lazy Banks." *Rand Journal of Economics* 32:4, 726–744.

Melnik, Arie L., and Steven E. Plaut. 1986. "Loan Commitment Contracts, Terms of Lending, and Credit Allocation." *Journal of Finance* 41:2, 425–435.

Mester, Loretta J., Leonard I. Nakamura, and Micheline Renault. 2002. "Checking Accounts and Bank Monitoring." Working Paper, Federal Reserve Bank of Philadelphia.

Moody's Investors Service. 2009a. "Corporate Default and Recovery Rates, 1920–2008." Available at moodys.com.

Moody's Investors Service. 2009b. "Rating Methodology, Global Infrastructure Finance, Global Regulated Water Utilities." Available at moodys.com.

Ongena, Steven, and David C. Smith. 2000a. "Bank Relationships: A Review." In Stavros A. Zenios and Patrick T. Harker, eds., *Performance of Financial Institutions*, 221–258. Cambridge: Cambridge University Press.

Ongena, Steven, and David C. Smith. 2000b. "What Determines the Number of Bank Relationships? Cross-Country Evidence." *Journal of Financial Intermediation* 9:1, 26–56.

Panyagometh, Kamphol, and Gordon S. Roberts. 2010. "Do Lead Banks Exploit Syndicate Participants? Evidence from Ex Post Risk," *Financial Management* 39:1, 273–299.

Petersen, Mitchell A., and Raghuram G. Rajan. 1995. "The Effect of Credit Market Competition on Lending Relationships." *Quarterly Journal of Economics* 110:2, 407–443.

Pozzolo, Alberto F. 2002. "Secured Lending and Borrowers' Riskiness." Available at http://ssrn.com/abstract=302124 or doi:10.2139/ssrn.302124.

Qian, Jun, and Philip E. Strahan. 2007. "How Laws and Institutions Shape Financial Contracts: The Case of Bank Loans." *Journal of Finance* 62:6, 2803–2834.

Rajan, Raghuram G. 1992. "Insiders and Outsiders: The Choice between Informed and Arm's-Length Debt." *Journal of Finance* 47:4, 1367–1400.

Rajan, Raghuram G., and Andrew Winton. 1995. "Covenants and Collateral as Incentives to Monitor." *Journal of Finance* 50:4, 1113–1146.

Ramakrishnan, Ram T. S., and Anjan V. Thakor. 1984. "Information Reliability and a Theory of Financial Intermediation." *Review of Financial Economics* 51:3, 415–432.

Roberts, Gordon S., and Nadeem Siddiqi. 2004. "Collateralization and the Number of Creditors in Private Debt Contracts: An Empirical Analysis." *Research in Finance* 21:1, 229–252.

Roberts, Gordon S., and Jerry A. Viscione. 1984. "The Impact of Seniority and Security Covenants on Bond Yields: A Note." *Journal of Finance* 39:5, 1597–1602.

Sharpe, Steven A. 1990. "Asymmetric Information, Bank Lending and Implicit Contracts: A Stylized Model of Customer Relationships." *Journal of Finance* 45:4, 1069–1087.

Slovin, Myron B., Shane A. Johnson, and John L. Glascock. 1992. "Firm Size and the Information Content of Bank Loan Announcements." *Journal of Banking and Finance* 16:1, 35–49.

Smith, Jr. Clifford W., and Jerold B. Warner. 1979. "Bankruptcy, Secured Debt, and Optimal Capital Structure: Reply." *Journal of Finance* 35:1, 247–251.

Strahan, Phillip E. 1999. "Borrower Risk and the Price and Nonprice Terms of Bank Loans." Working Paper, Federal Reserve Bank of New York.

Stulz, René, and Herb Johnson. 1985. "An Analysis of Secured Debt." *Journal of Financial Economics* 14:4, 501–521.

Sufi, Amir. 2004. "Agency and Renegotiation in Corporate Finance: Evidence from Syndicated Loans." Working Paper, Massachusetts Institute of Technology.

Thakor, Anjan V. 1996. "Capital Requirements, Monetary Policy and Aggregate Bank Lending: Theory and Empirical Evidence." *Journal of Finance* 51:1, 279–324.

Thomas, Hugh, and Zhiqiang Wang. 2004. "The Integration of Bank Syndication Loan and Junk Bond Markets." *Journal of Banking and Finance* 28:2, 299–329.

Von Thadden, Ernst L. 1995. "Long-Term Contracts, Short-term Investment and Monitoring." *Review of Economic Studies* 62:4, 557–575.

Wood, John H. 1975. *Commercial Bank Loan and Investment Behavior*. London and New York: John Wiley & Sons.

Yosha, Oved. 1995. "Information Disclosure Costs and the Choice of Financing Source." *Journal of Financial Intermediation* 4:1, 3–20.

ABOUT THE AUTHORS

Aron Gottesman is an Associate Professor of Finance at the Lubin School of Business at Pace University. He holds a PhD and MBA in Finance and a BA in Psychology, all from York University. His research interests include financial markets, financial intermediation, and asset management. He has published articles in academic journals such as the *Journal of Banking and Finance*, *Journal of Empirical Finance*, and *Journal of Financial Markets*, among others, and has co-authored several books. His research has been cited in newspapers and popular magazines including the *Wall Street Journal*, the *New York Times*, *Forbes Magazine*, and *Business Week*. Besides teaching graduate and undergraduate courses on managerial finance, investment analysis, and capital markets, Professor Gottesman lectures and consults to financial institutions. He has received research grants and scholarships including both a research grant and doctoral fellowship from the Canadian Social Sciences and Humanities Research Council.

Gordon S. Roberts is CIBC Professor of Financial Services at York University's Schulich School of Business. He received a BA in Economics from Oberlin College and earned his PhD at Boston College. Professor Roberts has held visiting positions and lectured in 15 countries, most recently in the Schulich India MBA in Mumbai. An active researcher in the areas of corporate finance, bond investments, and financial institutions, he is author or co-author of more than 50 journal articles and three corporate finance textbooks. Roberts has served or is serving on editorial boards including the *Canadian Journal of Administrative Studies* and the *Journal of Banking and Finance*, among others. He has provided policy research and advice to financial regulators and deposit insurers and is also experienced in preparing evidence for utility rate of return hearings.

CHAPTER 17

Rating Agencies and Credit Insurance

JOHN PATRICK HUNT
Acting Professor, University of California, Davis School of Law

INTRODUCTION

Most publicly-offered debt carries a rating from a credit rating agency. Ahmed (2010) provides data suggesting that about two-thirds of corporate debt receives such a rating. The three largest credit rating agencies—Moody's, Standard & Poor's (S&P), and Fitch—maintain at least three million ratings on corporate, structured-finance, and government debt (U.S. Securities and Exchange Commission 2009). Revenues for the three large agencies, which collectively employ more than 3,500 credit analysts, total $3.5 billion. Despite widely publicized doubts about the quality of credit ratings, ratings continue to be embedded in financial regulations as well as in private arrangements such as trading agreements and investment guidelines. Debt issuers, who in most cases are the ones who pay for the ratings, do not appear to have lost interest in buying them.

Moody's and Standard & Poor's have a U.S. market share, based on the number of ratings outstanding, of 36 and 40 percent, respectively, while Fitch has 22 percent (U.S. Securities and Exchange Commission 2009). The three large, U.S.-based rating agencies dominate the global market, but many smaller agencies, mostly serving non-U.S. markets, also exist. One recent count indicates 150 rating agencies globally (Langohr and Langohr 2009) of which 10 are designated by the Securities and Exchange Commission (SEC) as "nationally recognized statistical rating organizations" (NRSROs). The NRSRO designation causes an agency's ratings to satisfy some regulatory rules and is often interpreted as the mark of an "official" rating agency. The NRSROs include Moody's, S&P, and Fitch (the Big 3), plus A.M. Best, DBRS (formerly Dominion Bond Rating Services), Japan Credit Rating Agency, Rating and Investment Information, Egan-Jones, LACE Financial, and Realpoint. Three of the smaller firms, Egan-Jones, LACE, and Realpoint, with a collective market share of just below 1 percent, operate under a subscriber-pays model. The others operate under an issuer-pays model (U.S. Securities and Exchange Commission 2009).

Exhibit 17.1 Major Agency Rating Scales

Category	S&P Scale	Moody's Scale	Fitch Scale
Investment Grade	AAA	Aaa	AAA
	AA+	Aa1	AA+
	AA	Aa2	AA
	AA–	Aa3	AA–
	A+	A1	A+
	A	A2	A
	A–	A3	A–
	BBB+	Baa1	BBB+
	BBB	Baa2	BBB
	BBB–	Baa3	BBB–
Speculative or "Junk"	BB+	Ba1	BB+
	BB	Ba2	BB
	BB–	Ba3	BB–
	B+	B1	B+
	B	B2	B
	B–	B3	B–
	CCC+	Caa1	CCC+
	CCC	Caa2	CCC
	CCC–	Caa3	CCC–
	CC	Ca	CC
Nonperforming	C	C	C
	D	WR	DDD
			DD
			D

Note: This exhibit shows the main rating scales for each of the three major agencies with breakpoints between commonly recognized credit-quality levels indicated.

What Do Credit Ratings Mean?

Credit ratings are assessments of creditworthiness that are arranged on an ordinal scale. Exhibit 17.1 presents the main scale used by each of the three major credit rating agencies. The agencies state that the scale is just a rank ordering of credit risk. An "AAA" rating should carry less credit risk than an "AA" rating, but the agencies assign no quantitative benchmarks to their scales. Likewise, steps do not reflect equal increases in credit risk. For example, there may be a greater increase in risk in going from BBB to BB than in going from AAA to AA. Important breakpoints include those between investment-grade and speculative and between speculative and nonperforming as indicated in the exhibit.

The meaning of the scale varies from agency to agency. Credit risk can be viewed as having two components: probability of default and loss given default. Expected loss is the product of these two components. For example, imagine that someone knew that a particular $1,000 bond carries an 80 percent chance of not defaulting (and thus losing $0), a 10 percent chance of losing $500, and a 10 percent chance of losing $1,000. In this example, the probability of default (credit-risk loss greater than $0) is 20 percent, and the expected loss given default is $750 (if the bond defaults, there is an equal chance of losing $500 and $1000, so the expected loss is $750). In this example, the product of probability of default and loss given default is an expected loss of $150.

According to documents on the major rating agencies, web sites as of mid-2010, Moody's ratings reflect the expected loss, and S&P's ratings reflect the risk of default (Standard & Poor's 2010; Moody's Investors Service 2010). S&P also publishes separate "recovery ratings" for some instruments that reflect the expected severity of loss in the event of default. Fitch's ratings on corporate obligations incorporate a measure of loss given default, but its ratings on structured, project, and public finance obligations measure default risk (Fitch Ratings 2010).

Although the agencies' ratings differ in what they measure, all major agencies strive for a measure of consistency across categories of instruments in their own ratings. Moody's states that its ratings have the same meaning across categories of instruments, with the exception of municipal bonds, which are graded more stringently and carry a lower credit rating for the same assessment of credit risk (Moody's Investors Service 2010). Standard & Poor's (2010, p. 2) states that its rating scale is the same for all instruments it rates: "[C]omparable credit opinions are likely to result in reasonably similar average default rates for each rating category across sectors, regions, and asset classes." Although the agencies do not assert that their ratings are comparable across agencies, regulations and users often treat ratings as comparable.

Slight confusion may occur when the statements "a BBB rating means the same thing for all instruments" and "a BBB rating does not correspond to any particular quantified level of risk" are taken together. For example, Benmelech and Dlugosz (2009b) find evidence that S&P designed its structured-finance rating model so that an A-rated structured-finance instrument would have the same probability of default as an A-rated corporate bond. In so doing, S&P necessarily embraced a specified default probability for each rating level, although it did not publicly endorse these specified probabilities.

Special Types of Ratings

The agencies publish ratings on issuers as well as individual instruments. When a firm has many different debt obligations, the issuer rating refers to the credit risk on the issuer's senior unsecured obligations for Moody's and S&P. According to Fitch Ratings (2010, p. 8), its issuer ratings refer to "the financial obligations whose non-payment would best reflect the uncured failure" of the issuer.

Ratings on sovereigns, banks, and insurance companies are special cases. The major agencies' issuer ratings on sovereigns follow the main rating scale, and the agencies provide ratings for both local-currency and foreign-currency debts. Sovereigns are thought to be more likely to repay local-currency than foreign-currency debts, particularly because most sovereigns can simply print local currency to repay debts if necessary. Thus, local-currency ratings are often higher. The agencies issue financial strength ratings for banks and insurance companies in addition to issuer credit ratings. For banks, the agencies issue financial strength ratings on a scale of A (high) to E (low) and reflect the bank's ability to meet its obligations without government support. The agencies base a bank's issuer credit rating on an assessment of the actual likelihood and extent of default losses. Thus, the rating takes into account the possibility that the bank will receive government support if it goes into distress. As recent events show, the difference can be important. For insurance companies, the agencies issue financial strength ratings on the main rating scale. These ratings reflect an assessment of how likely the company is able to honor its obligations to policyholders, as opposed to lenders. However, the issuer credit rating reflects the assessment of the lenders' exposure to risk.

Another specialized set of ratings are the "short-term" debt ratings that the agencies provide for many issuers. These ratings, which are arranged on a separate scale, reflect an assessment of the issuer's ability to meet its commitments over the next year. Short-term ratings may be particularly important for issuers that rely on short-term funding such as commercial paper.

THE THEORETICAL BASIS FOR CREDIT RATINGS

The conventional explanation for the existence of rating agencies is that they provide useful information to investors, and that they can generate this useful information more cheaply than investors. Specifically, this is often phrased in terms of asymmetric information. Without a rating agency, the issuer knows more than the investor about the instrument's quality. The investor knows this and therefore demands a high return to compensate for the possibility that the instrument is of low quality. If a rating agency can credibly certify that the instrument is of high quality, the investor should demand a lower return, which benefits the issuer. Ratings enable sellers of high-quality instruments to offer lower rates of return on debt than they could otherwise, or prevent the market from completely breaking down because of borrowers' shunning all risky instruments. Langohr and Langohr (2009) offer one version of this explanation. Although their analysis does not consider the possibility that investors could perform their own research, or that rating agencies might make errors or act strategically, other theoretical work discussed below incorporates such extensions into the basic agency-as-information-provider story.

A contrary view suggested by Partnoy (1999, 2001) is that rating agencies no longer serve the purpose of reducing information asymmetries but instead exist in their current form because the regulatory system incorporates their ratings. Although this view is based on an important insight, the widespread private use of ratings suggests that it overstates the case.

EMPIRICAL EVIDENCE ON THE PERFORMANCE OF CREDIT RATINGS

Several approaches are available to assess the performance of credit ratings. The approach favored by the rating agencies is to compute an *accuracy ratio*, which is a number that summarizes the extent to which realized defaults are concentrated among low-rated bonds. This approach maps well to ratings' stated purpose of arranging default risk along an ordinal scale. It does not, however, address whether rating agencies provide new information to the market. For example, assigning ratings solely on the basis of market spreads would probably achieve a decent accuracy ratio but would not provide any new information. Moreover, because defaults are rare and take a long time to materialize, accuracy ratios are not necessarily well-suited to understanding rating performance over short time horizons.

This section focuses on two bodies of scholarly literature addressing rating quality: (1) the decades-long series of event studies designed to find out whether corporate bonds rating changes are informative in the sense of affecting market prices, and (2) the small but growing set of papers evaluating the performance of ratings on structured products during the financial crisis that began in 2007.

Empirical Evidence on Corporate Bond Rating Performance

Norden and Weber (2004) provide an overview of the research on the effects of rating changes on stock and bond prices. The research can best be described as conflicting. Studies finding that rating changes are not associated with market price changes and may lag market price changes include Weinstein (1977), who finds that bond prices move in the direction expected with a rating change in the period from 19 months before the change to six months before the change but not thereafter. He interprets this to mean that the market incorporates the information leading to the rating change before the rating agencies do. Pinches and Singleton (1978) find that stock prices anticipate but do not react to credit-rating changes.

Hull, Predescu, and White (2004) analyze credit default swap (CDS) quotes on corporations, sovereigns, and quasi-sovereigns from 1998 to 2002 and find that CDS prices anticipate both rating changes and announcements of reviews for ratings downgrades. They find that announcements of reviews for ratings downgrades are associated with CDS price changes but rating changes themselves are not. They interpret this to mean that only review announcements, not rating changes, contain significant new information.

Studies find that rating changes are associated with simultaneous or subsequent abnormal returns, so that they may provide information to the market. Hand, Holthausen, and Leftwich (1992), who examine Moody's and S&P bond rating changes from 1977 to 1982, find significant bond and stock price reactions upon announcement of the rating change. Hite and Warga (1997) examine industrial-firm bonds issued from 1985 to 1995 and find significant bond price changes in the period six months before and in the month of rating changes. Dichev and Piotroski (2001), examining Moody's bond rating changes from 1970 to 1997, find significant abnormal stock price changes in response to rating changes. They also find evidence that stock prices overshoot when downgrades are announced.

Various studies (Hite and Warga 1997; Dichev and Piotroski 2001; Hand, Holthausen, and Leftwich 2002; Hull, Predescu, and White 2004) find that downgrades have a larger effect on prices than upgrades ("downgrade asymmetry"). Likewise, some studies such as Hite and Warga find that rating changes that cross the investment-grade boundary are associated with greater abnormal returns than changes within the investment-grade or speculative categories or the so-called investment-grade boundary effect.

Jorion and Zhang (2007), who examine the effect of rating changes on stock prices, can explain most of the downgrade asymmetry and all of the investment-grade boundary effect by considering the prechange rating. They consider a sample of rating changes on U.S. corporate bonds from 1996 to 2002 and find significant same-day stock-price effects for both upgrades and downgrades. Noting that historical data indicate that a one-step downgrade is associated with larger and larger increments in default probability going down the rating scale, they incorporate the prechange rating into the regression and find that doing so reduces the difference between the effect of upgrades and downgrades. Considering the prechange rating also eliminates the "investment-grade boundary" effect; crossing the investment-grade boundary no longer has a significant effect on stock price.

Performance of Structured-Finance Credit Ratings in Financial Crisis Beginning 2007

The financial crisis that started in 2007 focused attention on the quality of credit ratings on structured products. Empirical research conducted over the past few years generally is consistent with the popular conception that rating agencies did a poor job of assessing credit risk on financial products that were novel, complex, and/or exposed to the U.S. housing market. In particular, the research suggests that the agencies failed to appreciate fully a decline in credit quality of mortgages written in the mid-2000s. The research is inconclusive, however, partly because there is no universally accepted way of defining a "poor job" and partly because insufficient time has elapsed to get a complete picture of defaults on these products.

Benmelech and Dlugosz (2009a) analyze data from Moody's Structured Finance Default Risk Services, which contains Moody's rating histories for all structured finance products issued since 1982. They find a large increase in the number and severity of downgrades of structured-finance instruments as a class in 2007 and the first three quarters of 2008. One might expect downgrades of any instruments in a recession, but the authors find that structured-finance instruments did much worse than corporate bonds during this period. Relative to corporate bonds, structured-finance instruments experienced a greater increase in the rate of downgrades, more severe downgrades, and more asymmetry in rating changes. Rating changes for structured products are more likely to be downgrades than upgrades.

Within the structured-finance category, Benmelech and Dlugosz (2009a) find that 62 percent of the structured-finance downgrades are of securities backed by first mortgages or what Moody's calls "home equity loans," a category that includes subprime first-lien loans as well as second-lien loans. They also find that the majority of severe downgrades are of securities backed by mortgages or asset-backed security collateralized debt obligations (ABS CDOs), which are tranche structured-finance instruments where the underlying collateral pools are themselves structured-finance instruments. Their study might be considered merely suggestive because it measures downgrades instead of defaults, but it suggests problems with rating on residential mortgage-based and complex products.

Ashcraft, Goldsmith-Pinkham, and Vickery (2010) analyze a sample of 3,144 subprime and Alt-A mortgage-backed securities (MBS) deals issued between January 2001 and December 2007. They use a model based on risk factors known at the time of the deal to estimate the riskiness of the collateral pool for each deal and compare this to the rating agencies' evaluation of the riskiness, as measured by the percentage of the collateral subordinated to the lowest tranche of a particular rating. The more subordination the agency requires for a particular rating, the more risky the agency perceives the deal to be. The authors find that ratings are informative in that deals that appeared risky according to their ex-ante model received more conservative credit ratings. Moreover, deals that the agencies perceived as risky experienced higher eventual levels of realized default and loss on the underlying mortgages.

However, Ashcraft, Goldsmith-Pinkham, and Vickery (2010) also find that ratings are unstable. While deals became more risky according to the ex-ante measure between 2005 and 2007, the amount of subordination the agencies required for a given rating did not increase by a corresponding amount; thus ratings became more generous. Deals with a high proportion of low and no-documentation loans performed particularly poorly relative to their ratings. The authors also find evidence that ratings are not informationally efficient because the ex-ante model could forecast eventual defaults and losses, as well as ratings downgrades, after controlling for the initial rating. If ratings were informationally efficient, forecasting any of this should be impossible.

To investigate whether RMBS investors relied solely on ratings, Adelino (2009) considers 67,412 securities from 5,712 residential mortgage-backed securities (RMBS) issues, drawing on a JP Morgan internal MBS database that covers approximately 80 percent of all RMBS issued in the United States from 2003 to 2007. He finds that in general yield spreads at the time of issuance predicted the probabilities both of downgrade and of default after taking into account all information contained in ratings. For AAA-rated securities, however, Adelino finds that yield spreads have no statistically significant predictive power for future performance. The author interprets these results as suggesting that investors, other than investors in AAA-rated securities, did not rely solely on credit ratings. He posits that AAA investors' heavy reliance on ratings might result from rating-dependent capital regulation.

Stanton and Wallace (2010) examine a comprehensive sample of commercial MBS from 1996 to 2008, attempting to explain widespread writedowns of commercial mortgage-backed securities (CMBS) at financial institutions and the subsequent collapse of the CMBS market. They find evidence of declining rating-agency standards over the period 1996 to 2007 as subordination levels fell. Unlike the residential market, Stanton and Wallace also find no evidence of changes in underlying loan quality or pricing and that realized defaults on commercial loans are no worse in the 2007–2009 crises than in previous downturns. The authors conclude that agencies required unrealistically low subordination levels for CMBS by 2005 and that this explains the collapse.

Any poor performance of ratings during the crisis may have been due to bad luck or honest error. For example, Hill (2009) argues that agencies gave unjustified high ratings to subprime securitized securities because they "drank the Kool-Aid" and believed, along with their clients, that only relatively small amounts of subordination were needed to justify high ratings.

THEORETICAL WORK ON REPUTATION AND COMPETITION

The major rating agencies' issuer-pays business model and the conflict of interest presented when an evaluator is paid by the entity whose product is being evaluated have been a major focus of policy discussions of rating agencies. Much of the theoretical economic literature, however, dispenses with this debate and proceeds based on the assumption that agencies will be paid by issuers, addressing the conditions under which issuer-paid agencies can achieve good outcomes. In this vein, scholars have addressed two related subjects: whether agencies' concern for their reputations leads to high quality and whether competition among rating agencies can help promote quality.

Theoretical Work on Agency Reputation and Rating Quality

Rating agencies typically argue that their desire to maintain good reputations provides the right incentives for them to issue high-quality ratings. Various commentators agree (Schwarcz 2002).

Economists have not focused on explicit models of reputation to the extent one might expect. Mathis, McAndrews, and Rochet (2009) consider rating-agency reputation in the context of a multiperiod model of a profit-maximizing monopolist rating agency deciding whether to rate complex instruments, which can be good or bad. The agency can decide whether to give a good rating (and be paid) or to deny a rating for each instrument. The agency may be of two types: one that always tells the truth about product quality, or one that opportunistically maximizes profits. Investors are unsure about the agency's type; reputation is measured by investors' perception that the agency is of the truth-telling type. The authors model market discipline for poor-quality ratings by assuming that the agency has a source of income other than the complex-product ratings and that the agency will lose this income if it is caught issuing good ratings to bad complex products.

If the agency observes instrument quality only imperfectly, Mathis, McAndrews, and Rochet (2009) find that the agency has no incentive to rate honestly because investors cannot tell whether the agency inflated ratings or made an honest mistake. If the agency itself makes perfect determinations of instrument quality, the authors show that whether an agency lies depends on the amount of noncomplex rating business at stake, the agency's discount rate, and its reputation. A stronger reputation leads to a greater immediate temptation to lie because there is more to gain in the short term by cashing in on that reputation. The model suggests the existence of "reputation cycles." That is, an agency that starts out with a weak reputation will build its reputation by telling the truth, only to sell out that reputation by lying once its reputation is strong enough.

Hunt (2009a) questions the effectiveness of reputation in constraining agencies from issuing ratings on novel products when they do not know what they are doing, a separate and distinct problem from conscious rating inflation. He posits that rating failure on a novel product will not cause a loss of reputation in rating traditional products because the agency's inability to rate a new product does not signal inability to rate existing products.

Theoretical Work on Competition and Rating Quality

Lizzeri (1999) proposes a model in which competition improves rating performance. He assumes that certification intermediaries (rating agencies) that are paid by sellers (issuers) choose strategically how much of their information to reveal.

He assumes that the intermediary commits to a disclosure rule. In this framework, a monopoly rating agency will under some circumstances certify only that quality is above some minimum standard. For example, the agency might simply have the category "investment grade," where buyers would infer that unrated issuers would not qualify as "investment grade," even if they were to pay for a rating. But when the number of agencies grows to infinity, this possibility disappears, and all agencies reveal all the information they have. Lizzeri's one-period model does not consider reputation explicitly. Coffee (2006) reaches a conclusion consistent with that suggested by Lizzeri's analysis, as Coffee identifies high concentration as a major problem with the credit-rating market. Ahmed (2010) uses a model that is somewhat similar to Lizzeri's to explain why agencies issue unsolicited ratings. He proposes that they do so in order to prevent unrated issuers from issuing debt, thereby making it impossible for unrated issuers to participate in the market and increasing the value of ratings.

If rating competition is good, then regulatory barriers to entry presumably are bad. White (2002) identifies the SEC's NRSRO designation as such a barrier. The Credit Rating Agency Reform Act of 2006 sharply reduced any regulatory barrier to entry in the market by instructing the SEC to grant NRSRO status promptly upon an agency's showing that it meets objective and fairly modest criteria (15 U.S.C. § 78o-7(a); see United States Code (U.S.C.) Annotated 2010). In contrast to this focus on the NRSRO designation as a regulatory barrier to entry, Stolper (2009) suggests that regulatory certification of agencies has a role: the threat of decertification can counter agencies' temptation to inflate ratings. He presents a model wherein issuers seek high ratings, and an approving authority initially licenses two agencies and threatens to withdraw the license of the agency with the higher default rate on its highest rating class. White assumes that agencies are "immune to legal challenge," so liability is impossible, and does not include a private reputation mechanism whereby the market could punish agencies for poor quality.

Although recent U.S. policy has tilted toward promoting rating-agency competition, scholars have suggested some reasons to doubt that this is a good idea. For example, a tension may exist between the level of competition and the effectiveness of reputation. A good reputation may be of little value in a highly cost competitive market (Klein and Leffler 1981).

Moreover, if issuers can shop for ratings (purchase, or choose to reveal only those that they like) or if rating agencies may inflate ratings to please issuers, increased competition may lead to worse outcomes. The issue of rating shopping has come to the fore in the recent crisis. For example, Benmelech and Dlugosz (2009a) find "suggestive evidence" of rating shopping: CDO tranches rated solely by one agency, S&P in particular, are more likely to be downgraded, and that tranches rated solely by one agency suffered more severe downgrades.

Bolton, Freixas, and Shapiro (2009) consider rating inflation in a model in which issuers can shop for ratings and pay more for higher ratings and agencies deciding whether to inflate ratings trade off the immediate benefit of pleasing issuers and the long-term reputational costs of rating inflation. The authors assume that reputational costs, which are determined exogenously, are incurred if and only if an agency gives a high rating to an instrument that defaults.

Bolton, Freixas, and Shapiro (2009) conclude that conscious rating inflation is more likely when the market contains a large fraction of investors who take ratings at face value and when reputational costs are lower. They find that monopoly is more efficient than duopoly because duopoly facilitates ratings shopping. Their evidence also shows that rating agencies' understanding of the quality of their own ratings has an ambiguous effect on rating inflation. When agencies have a good idea whether their ratings will turn out to be right, agencies may enjoy greater immediate profits from inflating ratings. However, a countervailing effect is present because each instrument that the agency thinks is bad when it consciously inflates is in fact more likely to default and impose reputational costs.

Even without conscious inflation by rating agencies, if issuers disclose only the ratings they like, competition can be harmful by giving issuers more ratings from which to choose. Skreta and Veldkamp (2009) model this situation and note that the scope for selective disclosure is greatest for products where ratings agencies are more likely to disagree, including perhaps complex structured products.

Faure-Grimaud, Peyrache, and Quesada (2009) present a model showing that rating-agency competition may induce issuers to hide ratings. When ratings convey information to the issuers about their own quality, the issuers will desire the option to hide the rating because the rating may turn out to be worse than expected. In Faure-Grimaud et al.'s model, a monopolist rating agency will not offer this option. A competitive rating agency may offer its customers the option to hide the ratings, and some of them will take it. Moreover, a monopolist rating agency rates more firms because losses on rating firms that are of low value and are thus unwilling to pay much for a rating are offset by the increased charge that the monopolist can levy on the higher-value firms when it expands coverage. Such cross-subsidization is impossible in a competitive market. Thus, they find that competition reduces the number of ratings produced. The authors do not address the possibility of conscious rating inflation, assuming that reputational concerns will prevent this.

Damiano, Li, and Suen (2008) model competition among agencies in a way that suggests that competition is good when credit quality is strongly correlated across issuers and bad when rating quality is weakly correlated. When quality is weakly correlated, economies of scale dominate. When quality is strongly correlated, incentives to inflate ratings dominate in the monopoly case and competition blunts those incentives.

The empirical evidence on whether competition promotes rating quality is mixed. Becker and Milbourn (2009) study corporate bonds from 1995 to 2006. They find that their proxy for competition (the market share of Fitch, which grew from around to 10 percent to around 30 percent over the period) is associated with higher ratings from Moody's and S&P, lower correlation between ratings and bond yields, and larger drops in equity price on bond downgrades. The authors interpret these results as suggesting that increased competition reduced rating quality.

On the other hand, Doherty, Kartasheva, and Phillips (2009) examine the entry of Standard & Poor's into the insurance company rating market, which they note had been served only by A. M. Best for 100 years. Consistent with the results of a model they propose in which buyers value precise ratings, they find that the entrant S&P applied more stringent standards than the incumbent Best, and that higher-than-average-quality issuers in each rating category were the ones that chose to obtain an additional rating from S&P. Although the authors do not expressly draw this conclusion, their results seem to suggest that S&P's entry resulted in investors' having access to more precise information.

RATING-DEPENDENT REGULATION

Regulations may require or encourage either that issuers obtain ratings or that investors hold instruments with ratings, especially instruments with high ratings. This could create demand for ratings that persists even if the ratings themselves do not contain valuable information about credit risk (Partnoy 1999). Opp, Opp, and Harris (2010) provide a formal model for this idea, finding that if the regulatory use of ratings creates a large enough premium on high ratings, then rating agencies will simply give high (and meaningless) ratings to everything they rate. Hunt (2009b) points out that external credit ratings may be the least unacceptable alternative available to financial regulators who need a measure of credit risk, even if rating-dependent regulation does reduce rating quality by some amount.

The foregoing debate over rating-dependent regulation focuses on government's use of credit ratings to regulate private markets. Sinclair (2005) identifies the mirror-image issue, pointing out that private markets use rating agencies to "regulate" governments by relying on rating agencies to set the terms of governments' access to capital markets. Sinclair (p. 177) further describes rating agencies as the "nominally private makers of a global public policy."

A study by the Bank for International Settlements' Joint Forum (2009), based on an international survey of bank, insurance, and securities regulators, is the most comprehensive effort to date to survey rating-dependent regulation, but its coverage is incomplete. For example, the study does not address rating-dependent regulation at the state level in the United States. What is presented here is a summary of a sample of noteworthy U.S. rating-dependent regulations. The SEC's three-part proposal to reduce its reliance on ratings, U.S. Securities and Exchange Commission (2008a, 2008b, 2008c), gives a detailed overview of that particular agency's use of NRSRO ratings.

The status of rating-dependent regulation in the United States is in flux. As of late July 2010, Congress had just enacted the Dodd–Frank Wall Street Reform and Consumer Protection Act, section 939A of which appears to instruct all federal regulatory agencies to eliminate references to credit ratings in their regulations within one year. How or whether all agencies would accomplish that task was unclear (United States Congress 2010). The SEC proposed rule changes to reduce its reliance on credit ratings in June 2008 but had not taken action on the most important parts of this proposal as of mid-2010.

Capital Regulation and Deposit Insurance Assessments

Capital regulation presents probably the most important regulatory use of ratings. In the United States, ratings are used for capital regulation of broker-dealers, insurance companies, and banks. In each case, the regulated firm's capital requirements are based on a measure of the riskiness of the firm's assets, and the regulated firm may or must use credit ratings as the measure of some or all of the risk for some or all of the assets.

For broker-dealers, the basic rules require using NRSRO credit ratings as a measure of assets' risk (17 C.F.R. § 240.15c3-1; see United States Code of Federal Regulations (C.F.R.) 2010). However, these rules did not apply to the major Wall Street banks, which opted into a now-terminated capital regulation program based on internal credit assessments. For insurance companies, rules promulgated by the National Association of Insurance Commissioners (NAIC) and applied nationally provide that insurance companies may use ratings from "approved rating organizations" (the same entities as the NRSROs), or they may have their assets rated by the Securities Valuation Office, an arm of the NAIC.

For banks, current regulatory use of ratings in capital regulation is limited. Under rules in effect as of mid-2010, rating-agency ratings are used for computing risk weights only of specified exposures, including asset or mortgage-backed securities, off-balance sheet items, and securities issued by securities firms (12 C.F.R. Part 3 App. A §§ 3(a)(4)(iii), 3(b), and 3(a)(2)(xiii)(C)). The picture is clouded here by the uncertain status of the implementation of the Basel II accords, which incorporate ratings as a measure of credit risk for less-sophisticated banks, and by negotiations currently going on for a "Basel III" framework.

Ratings are also used in the related area of deposit-insurance assessments. The Federal Deposit Insurance Corporation (FDIC) determines deposit insurance assessments on well-capitalized large depository institutions using three equally weighted factors, one of which is the institution's long-term issuer rating from Fitch, Moody's, or Standard & Poor's (12 U.S.C. § 1817(b)(1)(E)(i); 12 C.F.R. §§ 327.8(i); and 327.9(d)(2)).

Limitations on Permitted Investments

Many regulations are designed to assure that firms hold only "safe" instruments. In such cases, high ratings from recognized credit-rating agencies may permit instruments to qualify as "safe." National banks in the United States may hold only "investment securities." *Investment securities* are defined as those that are rated "investment grade" by NRSROs or are the credit equivalent of investment-grade securities (12 C.F.R. §§ 1.2-1.3). Similarly, insurance companies are required by law in some U.S. states to hold instruments at or above minimum credit ratings. For example, New York's insurance law restricts investments in unsecured obligations of American institutions to those that are rated A or higher by an agency recognized by the state Superintendent of Insurance, are insured by a AAA-rated insurer, or receive the highest rating from the NAIC's Securities Valuation Office (New York Insurance Law 2010, § 1404(a)(2)). In these cases the regulated firm may but does not have to use rating agencies' ratings to satisfy the requirement.

High credit ratings are both necessary and sufficient to meet other requirements. Money market funds can hold only instruments that have high enough ratings from two NRSROs or from the single NRSRO providing a rating (17 C.F.R. § 270.2a-7). Rules limit the commercial paper, corporate bonds, and state and local bonds that federal savings associations (thrifts) may own to those with high enough ratings (12 C.F.R. §§ 560.40(a)(1), 560.40(a)(2), and 560.42). Likewise, many states require that funds of government entities be invested only in high-rated instruments.

Conflict-of-Interest Rules

Underwriters use ratings to satisfy conflict-of-interest rules promulgated under the Employee Retirement Income Security Act of 1974 (ERISA), which covers most private pension plans. These rules forbid an ERISA plan from entering into purchase and sale transactions with an entity that provides services to the plan (29 U.S.C. § 1106(a)). An underwriter needs an exemption from this rule to be secure in its ability to sell structured securities to an ERISA plan while remaining able to provide other services, such as brokerage services, to the plan. The Department of Labor has exempted underwriters of structured securities from the conflict-of-interest provisions, as long as the underwritten securities meet certain requirements, including having high credit ratings (U.S. Department of Labor 2002). These rules seem to be the origin of the common perception that pension funds can invest only in high-rated instruments.

Permitted Activities

Another type of rating-dependent regulation uses credit ratings to determine the types of activities in which a regulated firm may engage. For example, national banks may conduct activities through financial subsidiaries only if they meet certain minimum requirements (12 U.S.C. § 24a; 12 C.F.R. § 5.34(g)(3)).

Empirical Studies of the Effects of Rating-Dependent Regulation

Kisgen and Strahan (2009) find that bond yields for firms rated higher by DBRS than by other rating agencies decreased significantly in the year after the SEC designated DBRS an NRSRO. They interpret their results as suggesting that yields are affected by rating-dependent regulation in which the highest or second-highest rating is the one that "counts" for regulatory purposes, such as the money-market rules or the NAIC's insurance capital rules. The SEC's recognition means that regulatory requirements could be satisfied by high DBRS ratings, expanding the pool of buyers for firms that enjoyed such ratings.

Bongaerts, Cremers, and Goetzmann (2009) find that whether Fitch rates an issue is predicted by whether the Moody's and S&P ratings are on opposite sides of the investment-grade line, rather than by proxies for asymmetric information or dispersion of information. They interpret this as evidence that Fitch ratings serve a certification function. That is, Fitch ratings are solicited because they may permit a bond to qualify as investment grade for regulatory purposes, rather than for informational content or because issuers are shopping for ratings.

THE FIRST AMENDMENT AND RATING AGENCIES

The major credit rating agencies assert that they are "members of the media" and that their ratings are "opinions" on "matters of public concern." Thus, they argue, the First Amendment protects them from liability and, presumably, from other types of control. Some courts have accepted the arguments of the rating agencies. In some recent cases involving privately-placed rated instruments, the courts rejected the argument finding that the agencies are unlike members of the media because they disseminate the ratings narrowly. In any event, the First Amendment does not protect the agencies from liability for fraud. Fraud is the theory underlying most current actions against rating agencies. Courts continue to struggle to define fraud in the context of the agencies' predictive judgments, however.

THE FUTURE OF CREDIT RATING AGENCIES

In addition to reinvigorating the idea of reducing rating-dependent regulation, the financial crisis and the apparent failure of credit ratings on structured products brought forth a welter of proposals for rating-agency reform (Partnoy 2009). Many such proposals focus on conflicts of interest and rating inflation. Mathis, McAndrews, and Rochet (2009) conclude that policymakers cannot rely on the reputation mechanism to induce agencies to tell the truth, so that a central platform should allocate instruments to rating agencies and pay for the ratings. In a similar vein, Manns (2009) suggests a "user-fee" approach to rating agencies, wherein agencies would be paid via an SEC-administered fund. The Dodd–Frank Act requires the SEC to study adoption of a central-platform system for initial ratings on structured-finance products. Listokin and Taibleson (2010) suggest another approach to combating rating inflation, proposing that agencies be paid using the debt that they rate. The Dodd–Frank Act contains provisions intended to mitigate the conflicts of interest that rating agencies face, such as a requirement that ratings be separated from sales and marketing (15 U.S.C. § 78o-7(d)(3)). The act also addresses more aggressive ideas through studies, including studies of adopting a central-platform system for structured-finance ratings (U.S. Congress 2010, § 939F), of alternative business models for agency compensation (U.S. Congress 2010, § 939D), and of strengthening rating agency independence (U.S. Congress 2010, § 939C).

Other approaches focus on ex-post discipline of rating agencies. Langohr and Langohr (2009) suggest the creation of a code of conduct for rating agencies and a mechanism by which ratings users rate the agencies' compliance with each item on the code of conduct. The intent is to enable the market to impose reputational costs on rating agencies that abuse their reputation. Hunt (2009a) proposes an administrative system to force disgorgement of profits earned on novel-product ratings that turn out to be of low quality. The Dodd–Frank Act provides for revocation of an agency's NRSRO designation based on poor performance but does not authorize any monetary remedy or penalty (15 U.S.C. § 78o-7(d)(2)).

Another approach is based on transparency. Gerding (2009) advocates requiring rating agencies to disclose the models and data used to arrive at ratings. The idea is that this "open source" approach will permit market participants to assess and troubleshoot flaws in agency models. The Dodd–Frank Act has provisions apparently intended to increase the transparency of rating agency methodology and underlying data (15 U.S.C. § 78o-7(r)-(s)), but exactly what these broadly worded provisions require is unclear, and their significance very much depends on future SEC rulemaking.

CREDIT INSURANCE

In a "credit insurance" or bond insurance transaction, a bond issuer pays a premium to an insurer in exchange for a guarantee that bond purchasers will receive promised payments on the bond in the event the issuer defaults. Usually the premium is a single lump sum paid up front for a guarantee that covers the life of the bond.

Four bond insurers—Ambac, MBIA, FSA, and Assured Guaranty—wrote 70 to 80 percent of the industry's business in the 2000s up until the credit crisis (Drake and Neale 2010). Financial guarantee insurers are required to operate as a "monoline" insurer where they are not permitted to offer other types of insurance. Jaffee (2009) explains this as reflecting recognition that losses on such insurance are "fat-tailed" and cannot be rendered predictable by writing numerous policies because of the risk of a catastrophic economy-wide shock that causes many simultaneous failures. If financial guarantors were permitted to offer other types of insurance, policyholders on the nonfinancial lines would be exposed to the risk of nonpayment because of a catastrophic shock to the financial guarantee business.

Bond insurance has been concentrated in the municipal and structured-finance sectors and appears to be quite rare in the corporate sector. Between 2000 and the beginning of the financial crisis, about 40 to 50 percent of newly issued municipal bonds were typically insured. Although there appears to be no regulatory bar to bond insurance on corporate debt, such insurance appears quite rare. Nanda and Singh (2004) argue that insurance is an attractive form of credit enhancement in the municipal sector because insurance maintains the promised payment schedule in the event of default, thus satisfying the test under U.S. law for the payments to continue receiving the tax advantages accorded municipal bonds. Another proposed explanation for the existence of bond insurance is that issuers indicate their superior quality by being willing to pay for insurance. Thakor (1982) proposes such a signaling model for bond insurance assuming that credit ratings are impossible.

Bond insurance has been used for senior and mezzanine tranches of structured-finance offerings. Rating agencies apparently treat tranches insured (or "wrapped") by an AAA-rated bond insurer as being AAA-rated themselves. One estimate, which is based on European issuances, is that around 10 percent of structured-finance issuance is so insured, with bond insurance common for nonprime RMBS, CDOs, transport-related, and whole business securitizations (Robbé 2008).

Bond insurers came under intense pressure starting in 2007. The industry suffered large losses on outstanding insurance contracts and credit default swaps on structured products, particularly CDOs. Bond insurers also suffered losses on investments in structured products and a decline in new business as structured-finance issuance declined. Most bond insurers lost their AAA rating in 2008. Drake and Neale (2010) review the origin of the industry's problems and the regulatory response as of mid-2009.

As of mid-2010, the future of legacy bond insurers was in doubt. Ambac announced that it might not make interest payments during the second quarter of 2010 and was considering a bankruptcy filing. MBIA, which had undergone a reorganization to segregate its structured-finance business from its public-finance business, faced legal challenges aimed at unwinding the reorganization on the ground that it was a fraudulent transfer that left the structured-finance unit insolvent while MBIA's holding company itself held a speculative-grade credit rating. Of the largest insurers, only Assured, which acquired FSA in July 2009, retained its AAA financial strength rating. In the same period, there was entry into the industry, including the creation of Berkshire Hathaway Assurance in December 2007. Some players retained confidence in the underlying concept of bond insurance despite the travails of the existing major players.

SUMMARY AND CONCLUSIONS

Despite the recent financial crisis and the inconclusive literature on whether rating agencies bring valuable information to market, credit ratings are likely to continue to be important. Rating agencies must have the right incentives. Unfortunately, little consensus exists on how to accomplish this. This is due in part because the credit-rating market has so many interacting peculiarities: the issuer-pays business model, limited competition, rating-dependent regulation, and rating agencies' liability exemptions, to name a few. Efforts are currently underway to make changes on all these fronts simultaneously. Some unintended consequences are virtually guaranteed, but that is a characteristic of any course of action, including doing nothing.

DISCUSSION QUESTIONS

1. Given that future events are inherently difficult to predict, and that the ways in which predictions can fail also are unpredictable, is speaking of the quality of credit ratings and of the reputation of a credit rating agency meaningful? Explain.
2. In what ways do users rely on credit ratings? Should their reliance be reduced? Why or why not?
3. Do the various regulatory uses of credit ratings make sense? Why or why not?
4. Explain whether competition in ratings should be encouraged or discouraged?

REFERENCES

Adelino, Manuel. 2009. "Do Investors Rely Only on Ratings? The Case of Mortgage-Backed Securities." Working Paper, Massachusetts Institute of Technology, Sloan.

Ahmed, Javed I. 2010. "Credit Rating Solicitation and Access to Public Debt." Working Paper, University of California at Berkeley.

Ashcraft, Adam, Paul Goldsmith-Pinkham, and James Vickery. 2010. "MBS Ratings and the Mortgage Credit Boom." Staff Report, Federal Reserve Bank of New York. Available at http://www.newyorkfed.org/research/staff_reports/sr449.html.

Bank of International Settlements' Joint Forum. 2009. *Stocktaking on the Use of Credit Ratings.* Basel: Bank for International Settlements.

Becker, Bo, and Todd Milbourn. 2009. "Reputation and Competition: Evidence from the Credit Rating Industry." Working Paper, Harvard University.

Benmelech, Efraim, and Jennifer Dlugosz. 2009a. "The Credit Rating Crisis." Working Paper 15045. Cambridge, MA: National Bureau of Economic Research.

Benmelech, Efraim, and Jennifer Dlugosz. 2009b. "The Alchemy of CDO Credit Ratings." *Journal of Monetary Economics* 56:5, 617–634.

Bolton, Patrick, Xavier Freixas, and Joel Shapiro. 2009. "The Credit Ratings Game." Working Paper 14712. Cambridge, MA: National Bureau of Economic Research.

Bongaerts, Dion, K. J. Martijn Cremers, and William N. Goetzmann. 2009. "Multiple Ratings and Credit Spreads." Working Paper No. 15331. Cambridge, MA: National Bureau of Economic Research.

Coffee, Jr., John C. 2006. *Gatekeepers: The Professions and Corporate Governance.* New York: Oxford University Press.

Damiano, Ettore, Hao Li, and Wing Suen. 2008. "Credible Ratings." *Theoretical Economics* 3:3, 325–365.

Dichev, Ilja D., and Joseph D. Piotroski. 2001. "The Long-Run Stock Returns Following Bond Ratings Changes." *Journal of Finance* 56:1, 173–203.

Doherty, Neil A., Anastasia V. Kartasheva, and Richard D. Phillips. 2009. "Competition among Rating Agencies and Information Disclosure." Working Paper, University of Pennsylvania.

Drake, Pamela Peterson, and Faith R. Neale. 2010. "Financial Guarantee Insurance and the Failures in Risk Management." Working Paper, James Madison University.

Faure-Grimaud, Antoine, Eloïc Peyrache, and Lucía Quesada. 2009. "The Ownership of Ratings." *RAND Journal of Economics* 40:2, 234–257.

Fitch Ratings. 2010. *Definitions of Ratings and Other Forms of Opinion*. Available at http://www.fitchratings.com/creditdesk/public/ratings_defintions/index.cfm.

Gerding, Erik F. 2009. "Code, Crash, and Open Source: The Outsourcing of Financial Regulation to Risk Models and the Global Financial Crisis." *Washington Law Review* 84:2, 127–198.

Hand, John R. M., Robert W. Holthausen, and Richard W. Leftwich. 1992. "The Effect of Bond Rating Agency Announcements on Bond and Stock Prices." *Journal of Finance* 47:2, 733–752.

Hill, Claire A. 2009. "Why Did Agencies Do Such a Bad Job Rating Subprime Securities?" *University of Pittsburgh Law Review* 71:2, 585–608.

Hite, Gailen, and Arthur Warga. 1997. "The Effect of Bond-Rating Changes on Bond Price Performance." *Financial Analysts Journal* 53:3, 35–51.

Hull, John, Mirela Predescu, and Alan White. 2004. "The Relationship between Credit Default Swap Spreads, Bond Yields, and Credit Rating Announcements." *Journal of Banking & Finance* 28:11, 2789–2811.

Hunt, John Patrick. 2009a. "Credit Rating Agencies and the 'Worldwide Credit Crisis': The Limits of Reputation, the Insufficiency of Reform, and a Proposal for Improvement." *Columbia Business Law Journal* 2009:1, 109–209.

Hunt, John Patrick. 2009b. "One Cheer for Credit Rating Agencies: How the Mark-to-Market Accounting Debate Highlights the Case for Rating-Dependent Regulation." *South Carolina Law Review* 60:4, 749–778.

Jaffee, Dwight M. 2009. "Monoline Restrictions to Control the Systemic Risk Created by Investment Banks and GSEs." *B.E. Journal of Economic Analysis and Policy* 9:3, Article 17.

Jorion, Philippe, and Gaiyan Zhang. 2007. "Information Effects of Bond Rating Changes: The Role of the Rating Prior to the Announcement." *Journal of Fixed Income* 16:4, 45–59.

Kisgen, Darren J., and Philip Strahan. 2009. "Do Regulations Based on Credit Ratings Affect a Firm's Cost of Capital?" Working Paper, Boston College.

Klein, Benjamin, and Keith Leffler. 1981. "The Role of Market Forces in Assuring Contractual Performance." *Journal of Political Economy* 89:4, 615–641.

Langohr, Herwig M., and Patricia T. Langohr. 2009. *The Rating Agencies and Their Credit Ratings: What They Are, How They Work, and Why They Are Relevant*. Chichester, UK: John Wiley & Sons.

Listokin, Yair, and Benjamin Taibleson. 2010. "If You Misrate then You Lose: Improving Credit Rating Accuracy through Incentive Compensation." *Yale Journal on Regulation* 27:1, 91–113.

Lizzeri, Alessandro. 1999. "Information Revelation and Certification Intermediaries." *RAND Journal of Economics* 30:2, 214–231.

Manns, Jeffery. 2009. "Rating Risk after the Subprime Mortgage Crisis: A User Fee Approach for Rating Agency Accountability." *North Carolina Law Review* 87:4, 1011–1089.

Mathis, Jérôme, James McAndrews, and Jean-Charles Rochet. 2009. "Rating the Raters: Are Reputation Concerns Powerful Enough to Discipline Rating Agencies?" *Journal of Monetary Economics* 56:5, 657–674.

Moody's Investors Service. 2010. *Rating Symbols and Definitions*. Available at http://v3.moodys.com/ratings-process/Ratings-Definitions/002002.

Nanda, Vikram, and Rajdeep Singh. 2004. "Bond Insurance: What Is Special about Munis?" *Journal of Finance* 59:5, 2253–2259.

New York Insurance Law. 2010. New York: McKinney's.

Norden, Lars, and Martin Weber. 2004. "Informational Efficiency of Credit Default Swap and Stock Markets: The Impact of Credit Rating Announcements." *Journal of Banking and Finance* 28:11, 2813–2843.

Opp, Christian C., Marcus M. Opp, and Milton Harris. 2010. "Rating Agencies in the Face of Regulation—Rating Inflation and Regulatory Arbitrage" Working Paper, University of Chicago.

Partnoy, Frank. 1999. "The Siskel and Ebert of Financial Markets? Two Thumbs Down for the Credit Rating Agencies." *Washington University Law Quarterly* 77:3, 619–714.

Partnoy, Frank. 2001. "The Paradox of Credit Ratings." In Richard M. Levich, Giovanni Majnoni, and Carmen Reinhart, eds. *Rating Agencies and the Global Financial System*, 65–84. Boston: Kluwer Academic Publishers.

Partnoy, Frank. 2009. "Overdependence on Credit Ratings Was a Primary Cause of the Crisis." Proceedings of the 2008 International Banking Conference: The First Credit Turmoil of the 21st Century. Hackensack, NJ: World Scientific Publishers.

Pinches, George E., and J. Clay. Singleton. 1978. "The Adjustment of Stock Prices to Bond Rating Changes." *Journal of Finance* 33:1, 29–44.

Robbé, Jan Job de Vries. 2008. *Securitization Law and Practice in the Face of the Credit Crunch*. Alphen aan den Rijn: Kluwer Law International.

Schwarcz, Steven L. 2002. "Private Ordering of Public Markets: The Rating Agency Paradox." *University of Illinois Law Review* 2002:1, 1–27.

Sinclair, Timothy J. 2005. *The New Masters of Capital: American Bond Rating Agencies and the Politics of Creditworthiness*. Ithaca, NY: Cornell University Press.

Skreta, Vasiliki, and Laura Veldkamp. 2009. "Ratings Shopping and Asset Complexity: A Theory of Ratings Inflation." *Journal of Monetary Economics* 56:5, 678–695.

Standard & Poor's. 2010. *About Credit Ratings*. Available at http://www.standardandpoors.com/ratings/en/us/.

Stanton, Richard, and Nancy Wallace. 2010. "CMBS Subordination, Ratings Inflation, and the Crisis of 2007–2009." Working Paper, University of California at Berkeley.

Stolper, Anno. 2009. "Regulation of Credit Rating Agencies." *Journal of Banking and Finance* 33:7, 1266–1273.

Thakor, Anjan. 1982. "An Exploration of Competitive Signaling Equilibria with 'Third Party' Information Production: The Case of Debt Insurance." *Journal of Finance* 37:3, 717–739.

United States Code (U.S.C.) Annotated. 2010. Minneapolis: West.

United States Code of Federal Regulations (C.F.R.). 2010. Washington, DC: Office of the Federal Register.

United States Congress. 2010. Dodd-Frank Wall Street Reform and Consumer Protection Act, Public Law 111-203. Washington, D.C.: Government Printing Office.

U.S. Department of Labor. 2002. "Amendment to Prohibited Transaction Exemption (PTE) 2000-58." Federal Register 67:163 54,487-54,495. Washington, DC: Office of the Federal Register.

U.S. Securities and Exchange Commission. 2008a. References to Ratings of Nationally Recognized Statistical Rating Organizations, RIN 3235-AK17. Washington, DC: Securities and Exchange Commission.

U.S. Securities and Exchange Commission. 2008b. Security Ratings, RIN 3235-AK18. Washington, DC: Securities and Exchange Commission.

U.S. Securities and Exchange Commission. 2008c. References to Ratings of Nationally Recognized Statistical Rating Organizations, RIN 3235-AK19. Washington, DC: Securities and Exchange Commission.

U.S. Securities and Exchange Commission. 2009. Annual Report on Nationally Recognized Statistical Rating Organizations. Washington, DC: Securities and Exchange Commission.

Weinstein, Mark I. 1977. "The Effect of a Rating Change Announcement on Bond Price." *Journal of Financial Economics* 5:3, 329–350.

White, Lawrence, J. 2002. "An Industrial Organization Analysis of Rating Agencies." In Richard M. Levich, Giovanni Majnoni, and Carmen Reinhart, eds. *Rating Agencies and the Global Financial System*, 41–64. Boston: Kluwer Academic Publishers.

ABOUT THE AUTHOR

John Patrick Hunt is Acting Professor of Law at the University of California, Davis School of Law, where he teaches contracts, finance, and financial regulation. Professor Hunt has published on rating agencies and rating-dependent regulation, governmental responses to the financial crisis that began in 2007, and financial bubbles. Before entering academia, he worked for several years at major law firms and as a credit derivatives analyst. Professor Hunt holds an AB from Harvard College, a JD from Yale Law School, and a MFE (Masters in Financial Engineering) from the Haas School of Business at the University of California, Berkeley.

CHAPTER 18

Secured Financing

HUGH MARBLE III
Assistant Professor of Finance, University of Vermont

INTRODUCTION

To inform capital structure choices, this chapter attempts to synthesize current theory and evidence about secured debt, borrowers using secured debt, and reasons for using secured debt. Secured debt use is widespread. For example, Barclay and Smith (1995), who analyze the liabilities of a comprehensive sample of industrial firms over an 11-year period, find that 63 percent of the observations have some secured debt. Despite their widespread use, security provisions are strongly related to the funding source and to whether the debt is public or private. Publicly-issued bonds are rarely secured. Julio, Kim, and Weisbach (2008) find that no more than 3 percent of a comprehensive sample of public debt issues by nonfinancial firms between 1971 and 2004 were secured. In contrast, loans from banks and finance companies are very often secured. Nini, Smith, and Sufi (2009) find that approximately 65 percent of a large sample of private credit agreements between 1996 and 2005 were secured. This pattern and the relative magnitudes are generally consistent across the literature.

However, substantial within-firm liability structure variation exists including variation in debt security provisions. Firms cannot be neatly divided into private debt issuers and public debt issuers, where the former mostly use secured debt and the latter rarely use secured debt. Roughly half of the private credit agreements studied by Nini, Smith, and Sufi (2009) involve firms with a credit rating. While Barclay and Smith (1995) find that 63 percent of their sample had some secured debt, only 11 percent relied solely on secured debt. This highlights the importance of distinguishing between borrowers and debt instruments when analyzing the use of secured debt.

Although a wide range of theoretical and empirical research is available to explain the motivations for using security, research has not found a single, unifying framework to explain using secured debt. Possible motivations include mitigating agency problems between stockholders and lenders, signaling firm quality, improving incentives to monitor or liquidate the borrower, and expropriating wealth from other creditors.

Incentive conflicts between bondholders and stockholders can lead a firm to make suboptimal investment decisions, and firms can use secured debt to lessen some problematic incentives. The two most well-known bondholder–stockholder incentive conflicts are asset substitution and underinvestment. First, a firm can engage in asset substitution, which transfers wealth from bondholders to stockholders by increasing the riskiness of the firm or its assets after borrowing money (Jensen and Meckling 1976). Second, a firm can underinvest, or reject positive net present value (NPV) projects, when the benefits of a good investment would flow to bondholders (Myers 1977). Smith and Warner (1979b) argue that using security provisions can mitigate the asset substitution problem. Stulz and Johnson (1985) propose a model under which firms can use secured debt to lessen the underinvestment problem. Although not unanimous, some empirical support is available for using secured debt to mitigate bondholder–stockholder agency conflicts. Berkovitch and Kim (1990) put forth a more comprehensive model than Stulz and Johnson. Their model considers overinvestment, which includes asset substitution, and underinvestment. Berkovitch and Kim find that nonrecourse secured debt can minimize debt-related investment distortions if the borrower and lender have similar information about project quality. When there is asymmetric information, recourse secured debt can mitigate some underinvestment problems.

Numerous studies address using secured debt to signal borrower quality. The fundamental idea regarding secured debt is that granting a lender a security interest can be rational for a higher-quality borrower and irrational for a lower-quality borrower. Chan and Kanatas (1985) and Chan and Thakor (1987) find that using collateral improves problems related to information asymmetry. Igawa and Kanatas (1990) present evidence that using collateral can mitigate ex-ante information problems but can lead to moral hazard in the maintenance of the collateral.

In contrast to the studies noted above, which report a straightforward relationship between the use of collateral and the mitigation of information asymmetry, Boot, Thakor, and Udell (1991) find that either higher- or lower-quality firms may use collateral. Empirically, the role of secured debt in signaling borrower quality is less positive. Berger and Udell (1990) present evidence that the use of collateral is typically associated with higher-risk borrowers, higher-risk loans, and higher-risk lenders. Barclay and Smith (1995) find limited support for using secured debt as a signaling mechanism to resolve information asymmetry. However, a caveat exists in linking some of the theory and empirics. Several theoretical papers on using secured debt to mitigate information asymmetry model the use of outside collateral. Barclay and Smith analyze firms in Compustat that are highly unlikely to rely on outside collateral.

Secured debt serves a role in promoting effective monitoring and efficient liquidation of borrowers. Several studies, including Levmore (1982) and Triantis (1992), support the use of security interests to reduce free-riding and to improve coordination among monitors. Free-riding occurs when some of the benefit of a lender's monitoring effort accrues to another lender, reducing every lender's incentive to monitor. Rajan and Winton (1995) note a second route through which security interests promote effective monitoring. When a lender is unsecured, the lender will fare better if it takes a security interest before the firm reaches financial distress. Bankruptcy rules can lead to rejecting a security interest created immediately preceding financial distress. As Rajan and Winton note, this leads the lender to vigilantly monitor for early signs of trouble so the lender can optimally protect its interest.

Both monitoring and efficient liquidation influence debt structure because firms and their lenders are trying to structure optimal ex-ante contracts. Efficient liquidation refers to the lender not only monitoring the borrower but also forcing the borrower to liquidate when continuation would be economically dissipative. Repullo and Suarez (1998) and Gorton and Kahn (2000) present models explaining the senior and secured pattern of bank debt being driven by the better abilities of banks to monitor, renegotiate, and force liquidation. Habib and Johnsen (1999) consider a specialized lender with superior skill at monitoring the borrower and redeploying assets in unfavorable economic conditions. The efficiency in redeploying the assets implies superior liquidation decisions by the lender. The optimal contract in this case is nonrecourse secured debt. Welch (1997) makes a novel argument for the seniority of bank debt, which is consistent with bank debt being secured. Banks are better able to contest allocations in bankruptcy, which implies that giving them priority ex-ante leads to more efficient outcomes.

A final proposed rationale for using secured debt is that it may transfer wealth from other creditors to the firm's equity holders and secured lenders. Scott (1977), who raised this possibility in his analysis, shows that using more secured debt reduces the amount available to potential litigants, increasing the combined value of the claims of the equity holders and secured lenders. LoPucki (1994) and Bebchuk and Fried (1996) extend the consideration of this issue to include creditors and claimants for whom thorough analysis of the firm's liability structure is simply not economically rational. These authors raise this issue to question the fairness of the priority of secured debt, not to guide firm behavior.

In addition to finance, accounting, and economics journals, law journals contain studies of secured debt. The legal scholarship and finance scholarship are not completely independent and reveal differences as well as unreconciled areas of disagreement. Although oriented to a finance audience, the current discussion attempts to incorporate some legal writings, particularly where they disagree with the extant finance literature and raise issues not fully addressed therein. This is not an exhaustive examination of the legal literature on secured debt, much of which focuses on broad questions involving the fairness and appropriateness of the priority given to secured creditors. While a binary categorization as finance research or legal research is an oversimplification, it facilitates a clearer exposition of the current state of knowledge.

The remainder of the chapter has the following organization. The next section examines the meaning of secured debt and is followed by a discussion of the use of secured private and public debt. Various theories that explain the use of secured debt are presented along with empirical support for these explanations. The final section provides a summary and conclusions.

TYPOLOGY AND DEFINITIONS OF SECURED DEBT

Secured debt is not a single uniform type of debt instrument. Understanding and synthesizing what is known and recognizing what is unknown about using secured debt require a general understanding of the basic institutional details of secured debt. This process also requires attention to what definition of secured debt is operative in a particular model or empirical analysis. The definition of secured debt is an area of meaningful disagreement between the finance and legal research. Also, finance scholars generally recognize the variation in secured debt to a lesser degree than do their legal counterparts.

Corporate finance-oriented research typically recognizes differences in secured debt in two dimensions that are fundamental to the meaning of security: (1) recourse versus nonrecourse, and (2) inside versus outside collateral. Although private debt is far more likely than public debt to be secured, the public-private dimension does not fundamentally change the meaning of security the way variations in recourse and collateral do.

Nonrecourse secured debt isolates a project from the firm. The lender would have a security interest in the project but would not have the ability to recover against any other assets of the firm. Recourse secured debt allows the lender to recover against other assets of the firm if the collateral is insufficient to repay the debt. The portion of a recourse secured claim that exceeds the value of the collateral becomes an unsecured claim. The seniority of that unsecured claim varies across debt contracts.

Inside collateral generally refers to firm assets used as security for borrowing, while outside collateral typically refers to assets that would not ordinarily be part of a firm's bankruptcy estate. Berger and Udell (1998) discuss the two types of collateral. They note that outside collateral is commonly considered in analyses of moral hazard and adverse selection problems, while analyses of the use of secured debt to address asset substitution and underinvestment problems generally focus on inside collateral.

Firms can use outside collateral for small business loans, but using outside collateral in loans to larger firms, especially those with outside equity, would be surprising. This has important implications for the interface of theoretical models and empirical tests. For example, an analysis of firms covered by Compustat would not be expected to provide empirical support for theoretical models that depend on outside collateral because the firms included in Compustat are large and typically have listed securities. Although Compustat data are compiled from various sources, much of the data is collected from filings made by companies that have issued, or plan to issue, some type of public equity or debt.

Although exceptions such as Berger and Udell (1998) exist, corporate finance analyses of secured debt rarely make even casual direct comparisons along either the collateral or the recourse dimensions. Collectively, the literature recognizes the heterogeneity of secured debt noted above, but the heterogeneity of secured debt is not typically an area of analysis. Rather, most consideration of secured debt compares it with unsecured debt or other claims.

Compared with the corporate finance literature, the legal literature recognizes more variation within secured debt. With this recognition, some legal scholars have been critical of finance scholarship for generally treating secured debt as more homogeneous than warranted by the facts. Mann (1997) and Hill (2002) argue that not only is secured debt more varied than suggested by the two-dimensional characterization but also that research on secured debt cannot be built upon a base that ignores the nuanced variation of secured debt contracts. Mann first stressed the importance of recognizing the heterogeneity within secured debt contracts. Hill provides a discussion of the variation in both secured debt and various leasing structures. Secured debt can be backed by a particular asset, by a blanket lien on all assets, or by a firm's receivables. Debt backed by a particular asset can be either recourse or nonrecourse. As Hill notes, debt backed by all assets is inherently recourse while debt backed by receivables is inherently nonrecourse.

USING SECURED DEBT

Firms widely use secured debt, and its use is especially common among smaller firms, those with lower credit quality, and firms without bond market access. Secured debt is also an important source of capital for large firms and for those with access to bond markets. This highlights the importance of drawing a distinction between firms and debt contracts. Security is a common feature of private debt and an uncommon feature of public debt. For reference, Faulkender and Petersen (2006) estimate that between 69 and 93 percent of the debt of issuers with public debt market access is public debt.

Barclay and Smith (1995) catalog and analyze the variation in the components of firms' fixed claims. Their sample data from Compustat include 36,845 industrial firm-year observations between 1981 and 1991. The authors find widespread use of secured debt, with some secured debt on 63 percent of the firm-year balance sheets. For 11 percent of the observations, secured debt is the sole fixed claim. This implies that more than half of the observations in the sample use secured debt with at least one other type of fixed claim.

Using Secured Private Debt

Private debt contracts, which represent the majority of secured borrowings, span the range of borrowings from loans to small businesses through large private placements. At the small-business end of the spectrum, outside collateral is common. Leeth and Scott (1989) use data from two surveys of small businesses to analyze the use of secured debt among those responding firms that reported borrowing from a commercial bank in a six-and-a-half-year period preceding the survey. The 1980 and 1982 surveys generated 1,432 and 1,177 observations for analysis, respectively. The mean loan size in both surveys is slightly more than $60,000. The authors find that 61 percent of the loans reported in the 1980 survey and 62 percent of the loans in the 1982 survey are secured. In both surveys, 51 percent of the secured loans have only business collateral. Personal collateral is the only source of security for 30 and 29 percent of the 1980 and 1982 responses, respectively. Both business and personal collateral secure the remaining loans.

Carey, Post, and Sharpe (1998), who study the different lending practices of banks and finance companies, find that banks lend to lower-risk borrowers and finance companies lend to higher-risk borrowers. The analysis uses Dealscan data on 14,735 loans between 1987 and 1993. Security and Exchange Commission (SEC) filings represent a substantial source of the Dealscan data, implying that the majority of the borrowers are either publicly traded or have public debt outstanding. For loans with only one lender, 70 percent of the loans made by banks are secured, and 92 percent of the loans made by finance companies are secured. The proportions are lower for loans underwritten by a group of lenders. When the lending group includes only banks, 52 percent of loans are secured. The proportion rises to 80 percent when the lending group includes at least one finance company. While Leeth and Scott (1989) find that about 60 percent of commercial bank loans in their sample are secured, they note other analyses that put the percentage secured around 80 percent when considering all loan sources.

Nini, Smith, and Sufi (2009) examine the terms of 3,720 private credit agreements entered between 1996 and 2005. The authors are able to conclusively determine if the debt is secured for 3,117 of the agreements. Across both rated and unrated borrowers, 64.7 percent of the agreements are secured. Among the 1,822 agreements with rated firms, the fraction of the agreements that are secured increases monotonically with lower credit ratings. For firms rated A or above, 6.5 percent of the agreements are secured. For firms rated CCC or below, all of the agreements are secured. The proportion of agreements that are secured jumps sharply at the investment grade threshold from 21.8 percent of the agreements with BBB rated firms to 80.8 percent of the agreements with BB rated firms. Although not explicitly reported, an inference from their reported statistics is that about 85 percent of the agreements with unrated firms are secured.

Using a proprietary sample of 658 non–Rule 144A private placements bonds issued between 1985 and 1994, Kwan and Carleton (2010) find that 32.5 percent of the private placements are secured. The effective distinction between non–Rule 144A private placements and Rule 144A private placements is that the latter can be traded among qualified institutional parties, making the private placements more like public bonds.

Using Secured Public Debt

In contrast to private debt contracts, public debt issues are rarely secured. Julio, Kim, and Weisbach (2008) examine nearly 15,000 public debt issues between 1971 and 2004, representing all nonfinancial public debt issues during the sample period. The mean size of secured issues is smaller than the mean size of unsecured issues. While 3 percent of the issues are secured, firms raised only 2 percent of the proceeds from secured issues. Julio, Kim, and Weisbach (p. 20) find that "firms issuing secured debt tend to be smaller and much more highly levered than unsecured issuers. Firms also tend to issue secured debt after periods of low cash flows and stock returns. Additionally, [their] results suggest that firms tend to issue secured debt when growth options are low." Using a similar sample of public debt issues, Billett, King, and Mauer (2007) find that nearly 19 percent of public debt issues are secured. Although not explicitly addressed in Julio, Kim, and Weisbach, the difference in the proportion of secured public debt issues is likely attributable to issues by regulated firms.

No single accepted explanation is available as to why public debt is rarely secured when security is a common feature of nonpublic debt contracts. However, some theories suggest that using secured debt could be reasonably linked to the public-private debt dimension. The strongest link between security provisions and private or bank debt occurs where debt structure is framed in terms of its influence on the incentives of the lender to monitor or liquidate the borrower. The next section provides further discussion of this link.

THEORIES EXPLAINING THE USE OF SECURED DEBT

Both the finance and legal literatures offer analyses and explanations for using secured debt. While the two groups of scholarship are connected, they do not necessarily agree on some key issues. Because a full reconciliation of the positions does not exist (i.e., neither body of scholarship has fully addressed and explained the other), understanding the differing views is worthwhile. The discussion herein is oriented to financial economists. The current discussion of the legal literature is not exhaustive and focuses on areas of meaningful differences in assumptions and empirical analysis.

A key difference in assumptions concerns what are often called nonadjusting or involuntary creditors. In the finance literature, Scott (1977) considers involuntary creditors, which might arise from litigation. Articulating the position that is more common in financial analyses, Smith and Warner (1979a) argue that efforts by shareholders and prospective lenders to transfer expected wealth from involuntary creditors leads to changes in terms of trade and cannot be relied on as an explanation for using secured debt. The possibility of nonadjusting and involuntary creditors is much more central to the analysis of secured debt in the legal scholarship. For example, LoPucki (1994) and Bebchuk and Fried (1996) address the issue of involuntary creditors as part of an analysis of the problems with secured debt.

A unique feature of the empirical work in the legal scholarship on secured debt is using practitioner interviews as a means to understand the patterns of use of secured debt and to gain insights into the various theories explaining the use of secured debt. Mann (1997) and Hill (2002) use practitioner interviews to better understand the use of secured debt. Existing work had treated secured debt as a basically uniform type of financing and built analyses of its use upon that presumption of uniformity. Interviews promote a more nuanced understanding of what secured debt looks like in practice. A second contribution of the interviews is direct insight into the motivations for the choice of security structure. As discussed in the section on nonadjusting creditors, some interviewed lenders reject the importance of expropriation in choosing secured debt. While interviews are subject to reporting bias and generally cannot provide statistically significant results, their potential contributions are simply unavailable in the traditional financial economics strand of secured debt scholarship.

Mitigating Bondholder–Stockholder Agency Conflicts

Explanations of secured debt often appeal to two seminal agency cost papers, Jensen and Meckling (1976), analyzing asset substitution, and Myers (1977), analyzing underinvestment. Jensen and Meckling model the wealth transfer that can occur from bondholders to stockholders if the firm makes investment decisions after borrowing money. According to Jensen and Meckling (p. 335), when faced with a choice between a low-variance project and a high-variance project, an owner-manager can "[promise] to take the low variance project, [sell] bonds and then [take] the high variance project, [transferring] wealth from the (naïve) bondholders to himself as equity holder." The authors also note the challenge and costs of contracting around the possibility of the firm engaging in asset substitution.

Myers (1977) models the distorted incentives that can lead a firm to pass up positive NPV projects. Firms with risky debt outstanding may reject valuable investment opportunities when some of the benefits of those investments would accrue to bondholders. Although he does not discuss secured debt in detail, Myers (p. 156) notes "that lenders often protect themselves by obtaining security in the form of specific assets for which secondary markets exist."

Stulz and Johnson (1985) present a model under which secured debt can reduce the underinvestment problem considered by Myers (1977), but not the asset substitution problem considered by Jensen and Meckling (1976). For a firm with outstanding risky debt, if secured debt can be used to fund the purchase of a new asset, the firm will take some positive-NPV projects that would be passed up if the firm was required to fund the purchase with either equity or unsecured debt.

Hennessy (2004) develops a model of debt overhang and empirically tests it using a sample of 278 manufacturing firms in a balanced panel between 1992 and 1995. All firms have credit ratings each year because the ratings are necessary for the construction of proxies. Hennessy (p. 1735) notes that the "results provide strong evidence in favor of the existence of debt overhang and against the notion that firms utilize additional secured debt issuance as a device for mitigating the problem."

A few authors have proposed that firms can use secured debt to limit Jensen and Meckling's (1976) asset substitution problem (Jackson and Kronman 1979; Smith and Warner 1979b). Smith and Warner (p. 128) make two predictions about the use of secured debt to address asset substitution problems.

> *The Costly Contracting Hypothesis leads to two predictions about the use of secured debt. First, if the firm goes into bankruptcy proceedings and the collateral is judged necessary for the continued operation of the firm, the bankruptcy judge can prohibit the bondholders from taking possession of the property. Thus for firms where liquidation is more likely than reorganization (e.g., for smaller firms), the issuance of secured debt will be greater. Second, we would expect more frequent use of secured debt the less specialized the firm's resources. To the extent the assets (such as a patent right) are highly specialized and firm-specific, their value is greater to the firm than in the market place. Consequently, it will be costly to the stockholders if they dispose of such assets in order to engage in asset substitution. The more specialized the assets, the more costly is asset substitution to stockholders, the tighter the implicit constraint on asset sale, and thus the less likely is the use of secured debt.*

Empirically, Barclay and Smith (1995) find limited support for the idea that firms subject to underinvestment and asset substitution problems have a higher proportion of senior debt claims relative to their fixed obligations. Their evidence supports using capitalized leases, but not secured debt, to mitigate the incentive problems. In their analysis of small business loans, Leeth and Scott (1989) find loan-maturity-based support for asset substitution considerations influencing the choice of security provisions. In an analysis of Compustat firms, Brown and Marble (2007) provide some evidence consistent with using secured debt to mitigate the effects of asset substitution on leverage.

Berkovitch and Kim (1990) model the optimal structure of debt contracts, balancing underinvestment and overinvestment incentives. *Overinvestment* refers to taking any negative-NPV project, which would include engaging in asset substitution. They find that the presence of asymmetric information affects the best contract choice. When the lender and the borrower have the same information about the new project, nonrecourse secured debt, or project financing, is optimal. Berkovitch and Kim note that nonrecourse secured debt has economic properties more similar to leasing than to recourse secured debt.

In the presence of asymmetric information, the seniority of the new debt should depend on the riskiness of the project. Less risky projects should be given seniority to best address underinvestment considerations. This can be achieved through recourse secured debt, which effectively grants a senior claim on the new asset and a parity or junior claim on the existing assets (Berkovitch and Kim 1990). This approach to mitigating underinvestment is similar to that of Stulz and Johnson (1985).

According to Berkovitch and Kim (1990), firms should finance projects that are ex-ante riskier with subordinated debt because overinvestment is a more likely problem than underinvestment. This conclusion is not inconsistent with Smith and Warner (1979b), who consider whether having a security interest protects a lender against future asset substitution. The contracts considered by Berkovitch and Kim would be struck with lenders for new projects.

Morellec (2001) provides a theoretical argument that security provisions are chosen to optimally limit the firm's ability to sell its assets to the detriment of the lender. A firm's debt capacity will be lower if the firm's assets can be easily sold without a substantial liquidity discount. Using the assets to secure some of the firm's debt can limit the negative effects of the asset liquidity. However, using secured debt adversely constrains the firm's operating choices. Thus, the firm will choose secured debt levels based on this trade-off.

Information Problems and Signaling

Several papers consider using security interests to resolve information asymmetry problems. The basic idea is that using collateral or secured debt can signal borrower or loan riskiness and mitigate ex-ante information asymmetry. Using collateral can also mitigate or aggravate moral hazard problems.

Chan and Kanatas (1985) model the use of outside collateral when there is asymmetric information but no potential for moral hazard. Because offering collateral is not costless, higher-quality borrowers will offer collateral. Chan and Thakor (1987), who analyze the use of collateral with the existence of moral hazard and adverse selection problems, find that collateral can mitigate both problems. Igawa and Kanatas (1990) find that higher-quality firms use secured debt because it can mitigate information problems about firm quality. However, using secured debt can actually induce moral hazard problems in maintenance of the collateral securing the loans. While several of the information asymmetry models support the positive signal of a borrower choosing a secured debt contract, Boot, Thakor, and Udell (1991) find a more nuanced result. They model secured lending when both moral hazard and ex-ante asymmetric information are present and find that either higher- or lower-risk borrowers may post collateral.

Barclay and Smith (1995) find statistically significant, but economically small, evidence for using secured debt as a signaling mechanism. Firms with higher abnormal earnings tend to have more secured debt in their capital structure. However, moving from the 10th to the 90th percentile of abnormal earnings only increases secured debt as a fraction of firm value by 2.5 percent of the mean ratio of secured debt to firm value. Because Barclay and Smith conduct their empirical analysis using Compustat data, the chance that any of the firms use outside collateral to secure their loans is highly unlikely. To the extent that some of the signaling power comes from bringing in outside collateral, the economic magnitude of the signaling effect for Compustat firms would be limited. In their study of bank loans to small businesses, Leeth and Scott (1989) find some empirical patterns consistent with the use of collateral to mitigate information asymmetry.

Although some models of information asymmetry such as Boot, Thakor, and Udell (1991) find that higher-risk firms might choose secured debt, the models tend to support using secured debt to signal higher quality. The empirical evidence leans the other way. In contrast to the signaling argument, Berger and Udell (1990) provide empirical evidence that compared with the average unsecured loan, the average secured loan is made to a riskier borrower, represents a riskier loan, and is held by a riskier financial institution. They consider this pattern, rather than the one predicted by most signaling models, to be consistent with practitioner expectations. Berger and Udell suggest that the likely explanation for the difference is that observable risk drives the empirical pattern while unobservable risk drives the signaling models.

Improved Incentives to Monitor or Liquidate

As discussed above, bank loans and other private credit agreements are far more likely to be secured than are public debt issues. A central argument for using bank debt is that banks can monitor the borrower more effectively and can make better liquidation decisions. The incentives around monitoring and efficient liquidation are the most significant nexus between secured debt and bank debt.

While discussion in this section focuses on that nexus, the relationship is imperfect. Some counterevidence is provided in an analysis of bank debt and capital structure by Johnson (1998, p. 53), who notes: "bank debt use is not merely reflecting a secured debt effect." Johnson's analysis, however, does not focus on the difference between bank debt and secured debt. In fact, this precise relationship has not been an object of any major empirical study.

Both monitoring and efficient liquidation drive debt structure because lenders and borrowers are seeking ex-ante optimal arrangements. Monitoring will be considered first because monitoring is expected to occur before liquidation, although the two activities are closely related and could even be considered synonymous. Diamond (1984), who attributes the general idea of delegated monitoring to Schumpeter (1939), shows that financial intermediaries such as banks have a fundamental cost advantage in monitoring borrowers. Fama (1985) and James (1987) provide evidence that bank loans have inherent advantages over other sources of debt. James finds that equity returns to firms announcing bank loans are significantly positive while the equity returns to firms announcing private placements are negative. Further, he finds negative announcement returns to non–bank-loan debt used to retire bank loans.

Diamond (1991) finds that the benefits of monitoring in reducing borrower moral hazard vary with firm quality. Reputational effects constrain the behavior of the highest-quality borrowers and mitigate moral hazard problems, reducing the need for monitoring. For the lowest-quality firms, bank monitoring cannot sufficiently reduce moral hazard problems. This leads middle-quality firms to borrow from a source that can monitor effectively.

Using secured debt can promote effective monitoring in several ways. First, security interests can reduce free-riding and improve coordination among monitors (Levmore 1982; Triantis 1992). Second, Rajan and Winton (1995) contend that collateral can improve a lender's incentive to monitor. If a lender is fully secured and the collateral value exceeds the lender's claim, there is no incentive to monitor. However, if the lender is unsecured, the lender will fare better if it takes a security interest before the firm reaches financial distress. Rajan and Winton note that bankruptcy rules could effectively disallow a security interest created too close to the onset of financial distress. Therefore, a lender needs to be sufficiently vigilant and effective in monitoring the borrower to be able to perfect its security interest early enough to protect the lender's interests.

The central thesis of the efficient liquidation argument is that firms choose debt structures that are ex-ante more likely to lead to correct liquidation decisions. Repullo and Suarez (1998) and Gorton and Kahn (2000) present models explaining the senior and secured pattern of bank debt. As a single lender, the bank is better able to monitor and renegotiate. According to Gorton and Kahn (p. 358), when needed, "in addition to their ability to act unilaterally, banks' status as senior claimants puts them in the position to gain the most in the event of liquidation."

Habib and Johnsen (1999) model the efficient redeployment of specific assets. In their model, an asset redeployer is a specialist lender that can maximize the value of the asset in unfavorable states where the entrepreneur might default. In this case, the lender is making a nonrecourse secured loan against the specific assets. The redeployer has superior skill at both monitoring the assets and placing the assets into their next best use if the borrower defaults. The efficiency in redeploying the assets implies superior liquidation decisions by the lender.

Welch (1997) makes a novel argument for the seniority of bank debt, which is consistent with bank debt typically being secured. Because bank debt is more concentrated than public debt and banks are better organized than public bondholders, banks will be better able to contest priorities in liquidation. Giving priority to the strongest party ex-ante increases efficiency and reduces expected costs. Although this model raises a unique consideration, its implications are similar to those of models of efficient liquidation decisions.

Post–Chapter 11 debt structure choices provide empirical support for the efficient liquidation argument. Alderson and Betker (1995) use filings of 88 firms that reorganized under Chapter 11 to estimate liquidation costs as the percentage of going-concern value that would be lost if the firm liquidated. Firms with the highest liquidation costs are less likely to use secured debt. Conditional on using secured debt, firms with the highest liquidation costs are far more likely to grant security interests in specific assets rather than security interests in all assets. Among the 22 firms in the lowest liquidation cost quartile, 20 firms used secured debt, with 18 of the 20 granting an interest in all firm assets. For the 22 firms in the highest liquidation cost quartile, 16 firms used secured debt, with only six granting an interest in all firm assets.

A comprehensive analysis of recovery rates by Bris, Welch, and Zhu (2006) provides additional evidence consistent with the efficient liquidation hypothesis. The authors manually collect data on nearly all unique bankruptcy filings between 1995 and 2001 in the Arizona and New York federal bankruptcy courts. Secured creditors do not fare particularly well in Chapter 7 cases, with a low-end recovery rate estimate of only 32 percent. However, the fate of the unsecured creditors is far worse, with a 1 percent recovery rate. Despite the poor recovery, the relative position of the secured creditors is consistent with a strong incentive to liquidate rather than continue.

Some final evidence on the interplay among liquidation decisions, secured debt, and bank debt comes from the analysis of loans by banks and finance companies by Carey, Post, and Sharpe (1998). They find some support for the hypothesis that reputational considerations are one reason banks lend to less-risky borrowers while finance companies lend to riskier borrowers. Finance companies lend to riskier borrowers and have a reputation for tougher negotiation and greater readiness to force liquidation. As highlighted in the section on using private secured debt, Carey, Post, and Sharpe find that finance company loans are even more likely than bank loans to be secured. For loans with only one lender, 70 percent of the loans made by banks are secured and 92 percent of the loans made by finance companies are secured.

Expropriation from Nonadjusting or Involuntary Creditors

Some researchers have hypothesized that the economic benefits of secured debt may derive from reducing the value of other claims in bankruptcy. Scott (1977) argues that using secured debt can increase a firm's value because secured debt effectively has a higher priority than legal claims and tax claims, while unsecured debt does not. By granting a security interest to lenders, stockholders can increase the proportion of expected firm value that is divided between themselves and the lenders. Smith and Warner (1979a) present the opposing argument: Customers and other potential litigants would adjust the terms of trade with a firm that has used secured debt and hence limited the possible recovery in litigation. This issue has not been completely settled, but it has been more prominent in the legal literature than in the finance literature.

Bebchuk and Fried (1996) discuss a range of nonadjusting creditors including the potential litigants and the tax authorities noted above. Their analysis focuses on questioning the appropriateness of priority given to secured debt claims, not on making capital structure choices. They maintain that many voluntary creditors with economically small interests will be nonadjusting because the information costs of adjusting are not offset by the benefits of adjusting. Finally, they also contend that practical monitoring and covenant-enforcement limitations exist even for creditors with economically large interests. Those creditors may also be unable to adjust to secured debt that is subsequently issued.

Limited empirical evidence supports or refutes secured debt incentives associated with nonadjusting creditors. Hill (2002) generally argues that nonadjusting creditors are unlikely to be an important influence on the decision to use secured debt. Legal equity considerations could limit the effects on involuntary creditors.

Further, Hill notes that interviewed lenders are confident of their ability to avoid being harmed as nonadjusting voluntary creditors.

SUMMARY AND CONCLUSIONS

The patterns of secured debt usage are consistent across many studies. In the public-private dimension, firms are far more likely to secure private debt. Public debt is rarely secured, with the fraction of secured debt between 3 percent and 19 percent, depending upon definitions, methodology, and the unit of measurement. Omitting debt issues by regulated firms, the fraction secured likely falls toward the lower end of that range. Private debt is frequently secured. In a proprietary sample of non–Rule 144A private placements, Kwan and Carleton (2010) find that 32.5 percent of the issues are secured. By almost any measure, the majority of bank and finance company loans are secured. More than 60 percent of small business loans from commercial banks were secured in each of two surveys (Leeth and Scott 1989). In a comprehensive analysis of six years of loans in Dealscan, the proportion of the loans secured ranged between 52 percent and 90 percent depending on the number of lenders and whether the lenders were banks or finance companies (Carey, Post, and Sharpe 1998). One exception to the private-loans-are-usually-secured rule is found in an analysis of private credit agreements sorted by firm credit rating. For firms with an A or better credit rating, only 6.5 percent of the agreements are secured. For firms with a BBB credit rating, only 21.8 percent of the agreements are secured. For unrated firms and firms with credit ratings below BBB, the clear majority of the agreements are secured (Nini, Smith, and Sufi 2009).

The backdrop for the variation in security provisions between private debt and public debt is within-firm debt structure heterogeneity. In a large sample of Compustat industrial firms between 1981 and 1991, 63 percent of firm-year observations reflected some secured debt. For 52 percent of the overall sample, the liability structure included secured debt and at least one other fixed claim (Barclay and Smith 1995).

Four general explanations are available for using secured debt. First, secured debt can mitigate agency conflicts between bondholders and stockholders. Empirical support for using secured debt to reduce underinvestment or overinvestment, including asset substitution, is limited. Patterns of small business bank loans are consistent with using secured debt to address agency conflicts (Leeth and Scott 1989).

Second, secured debt can address information asymmetries between the lender and borrower. Several models use the pledging of collateral to signal firm quality or to address moral hazard. In some cases, the models assume that firms pledge outside collateral to resolve information asymmetry, limiting the expected predictive power for public firms. For smaller firms, the patterns of secured debt are consistent with efforts to mitigate information asymmetry (Leeth and Scott 1989). Empirical evidence also shows that firms use secured debt to mitigate information asymmetry in the universe of Compustat firms, but the magnitude of the economic effect is limited (Barclay and Smith 1995). Berger and Udell (1990) show that secured loans and borrowers are riskier, which is counter to the information asymmetry argument. Their explanation turns on the relative importance of observable and unobservable borrower risk.

Third, secured debt can improve the incentives of lenders to monitor and efficiently liquidate the borrower. The evidence generally supports a monitoring and efficient liquidation argument. Empirically, firms with higher liquidation costs use less secured debt (Alderson and Betker 1995).

Fourth, secured debt can represent a mechanism for secured lenders and borrowers to transfer wealth from other claimants (Bebchuk and Fried 1996; Scott 1977). Smith and Warner (1979a) argue that the other claimants are rational and will adjust the terms of trade to account for the level of secured debt. However, limited evidence supports or rejects this possibility. Hill (2002) argues on two bases that nonadjusting creditors should not be a significant factor in using secured debt. First, legal equity may limit the economic impact on nonadjusting creditors if the firm reaches bankruptcy. Second, interviewed lenders express confidence in their ability to avoid being disadvantaged as a nonadjusting creditor.

DISCUSSION QUESTIONS

1. What is secured debt?
2. What is the link between bank debt and secured debt?
3. How strong is the evidence supporting the use of secured debt to signal borrower quality?
4. How does evidence from bankruptcies support using secured debt to improve monitoring and efficient liquidation?

REFERENCES

Alderson, Michael J., and Brian L. Betker. 1995. "Liquidation Costs and Capital Structure." *Journal of Financial Economics* 39:1, 45–69.

Barclay, Michael J., and Clifford W. Smith Jr. 1995. "The Priority Structure of Corporate Liabilities." *Journal of Finance* 50:3, 899–916.

Bebchuk, Lucian Ayre, and Jesse M. Fried. 1996. "The Uneasy Case for the Priority of Secured Claims in Bankruptcy." *Yale Law Journal* 105:4, 857–934.

Berger, Allen N., and Gregory F. Udell. 1990. "Collateral, Loan Quality and Bank Risk." *Journal of Monetary Economics* 25:1, 21–42.

Berger, Allen N., and Gregory F. Udell. 1998. "The Economics of Small Business Finance: The Roles of Private Equity and Debt Markets in the Financial Growth Cycle." *Journal of Banking & Finance* 22:6–8, 613–673.

Berkovitch, Elazar, and E. Han Kim. 1990. "Financial Contracting and Leverage Induced Over- and Under-Investment Incentives." *Journal of Finance* 45:3, 765–794.

Billett, Matthew T., Tao-Hsien Dolly King, and David C. Mauer. 2007. "Growth Opportunities and the Choice of Leverage, Debt Maturity, and Covenants." *Journal of Finance* 62:2, 697–730.

Boot, Arnoud W. A., Anjan V. Thakor, and Gregory F. Udell. 1991. "Secured Lending and Default Risk: Equilibrium Analysis, Policy Implications and Empirical Results." *Economic Journal* 101:406, 458–472.

Bris, Arturo, Ivo Welch, and Ning Zhu. 2006. "The Costs of Bankruptcy: Chapter 7 Liquidation versus Chapter 11 Reorganization." *Journal of Finance* 61:3, 1253–1303.

Brown, David T., and Hugh Marble III. 2007. "Secured Debt Financing and Leverage: Theory and Evidence." Working Paper, University of Vermont.

Carey, Mark, Mitch Post, and Steven A. Sharpe. 1998. "Does Corporate Lending by Banks and Finance Companies Differ? Evidence on Specialization in Private Debt Contracting." *Journal of Finance* 53:3, 845–878.

Chan, Yuk-Shee, and George Kanatas. 1985. "Asymmetric Valuations and the Role of Collateral in Loan Agreements." *Journal of Money, Credit and Banking* 17:1, 84–95.

Chan, Yuk-Shee, and Anjan V. Thakor. 1987. "Collateral and Competitive Equilibria with Moral Hazard and Private Information." *Journal of Finance* 42:2, 345–363.

Diamond, Douglas W. 1984. "Financial Intermediation and Delegated Monitoring." *Review of Economic Studies* 51:3, 393–414.

Diamond, Douglas W. 1991. "Monitoring and Reputation: The Choice between Bank Loans and Directly Placed Debt." *Journal of Political Economy* 99:4, 689–721.

Fama, Eugene F. 1985. "What's Different About Banks?" *Journal of Monetary Economics* 15:1, 29–39.

Faulkender, Michael, and Mitchell A. Petersen. 2006. "Does the Source of Capital Affect Capital Structure?" *Review of Financial Studies* 19:1, 45–79.

Gorton, Gary, and James Kahn. 2000. "The Design of Bank Loan Contracts." *Review of Financial Studies* 13:2, 331–364.

Habib, Michel A., and D. Bruce Johnsen. 1999. "The Financing and Redeployment of Specific Assets." *Journal of Finance* 54:2, 693–720.

Hennessy, Christopher A. 2004. "Tobin's Q, Debt Overhang, and Investment." *Journal of Finance* 59:4, 1717–1742.

Hill, Claire A. 2002. "Is Secured Debt Efficient?" *Texas Law Review* 80:5, 1117–1177.

Igawa, Kazuhiro, and George Kanatas. 1990. "Asymmetric Information, Collateral, and Moral Hazard." *Journal of Financial and Quantitative Analysis* 25:4, 469–490.

Jackson, Thomas H., and Anthony T. Kronman. 1979. "Secured Financing and Priorities among Creditors." *Yale Law Journal* 88:6, 1143–1182.

James, Christopher. 1987. "Some Evidence on the Uniqueness of Bank Loans." *Journal of Financial Economics* 19:2, 217–235.

Jensen, Michael C., and William H. Meckling. 1976. "Theory of the Firm: Managerial Behavior, Agency Costs and Ownership Structure." *Journal of Financial Economics* 3:4, 305–360.

Johnson, Shane A. 1998. "The Effect of Bank Debt on Optimal Capital Structure." *Financial Management* 27:1, 47–56.

Julio, Brandon, Woojin Kim, and Michael S. Weisbach, 2008. "What Determines the Structure of Corporate Debt Issues?" Fisher College of Business Working Paper No. 2008-03-010. Dice Center WP 2008-11.

Kwan, Simon H., and Willard T. Carleton. 2010. "Financial Contracting and the Choice between Private Placement and Publicly Offered Bonds." *Journal of Money, Credit and Banking.* Forthcoming.

Leeth, John D., and Jonathan A. Scott. 1989. "The Incidence of Secured Debt: Evidence from the Small Business Community." *Journal of Financial and Quantitative Analysis* 24:3, 379–394.

Levmore, Saul. 1982. "Monitors and Freeriders in Commercial and Corporate Settings." *Yale Law Journal* 92:1, 49–83.

LoPucki, Lynn M. 1994. "The Unsecured Creditor's Bargain." *Virginia Law Review* 80:8, 1887–1965.

Mann, Ronald J. 1997. "Explaining the Pattern of Secured Credit." *Harvard Law Review* 110:3, 625–683.

Morellec, Erwan. 2001. "Asset Liquidity, Capital Structure, and Secured Debt." *Journal of Financial Economics* 61:2, 173–206.

Myers, Stewart C. 1977. "Determinants of Corporate Borrowing." *Journal of Financial Economics* 5:2, 147–175.

Nini, Greg, David C. Smith, and Amir Sufi. 2009. "Creditor Control Rights and Firm Investment Policy." *Journal of Financial Economics* 92:3, 400–420.
Rajan, Raghuram, and Andrew Winton. 1995. "Covenants and Collateral as Incentives to Monitor." *Journal of Finance* 50:4, 1113–1146.
Repullo, Rafael, and Javier Suarez. 1998. "Monitoring, Liquidation, and Security Design." *Review of Financial Studies* 11:1, 163–187.
Schumpeter, Joseph A. 1939. *Business Cycles*. New York: McGraw-Hill.
Scott, Jr., James H. 1977. "Bankruptcy, Secured Debt, and Optimal Capital Structure." *Journal of Finance* 32:1, 1–19.
Smith, Clifford W., and Jerold B. Warner. 1979a. "Bankruptcy, Secured Debt, and Optimal Capital Structure: Comment." *Journal of Finance* 34:1, 247–251.
Smith, Clifford W., and Jerold B. Warner. 1979b. "On Financial Contracting : An Analysis of Bond Covenants." *Journal of Financial Economics* 7:2, 117–161.
Stulz, René M., and Herb Johnson. 1985. "An Analysis of Secured Debt." *Journal of Financial Economics* 14:4, 501–521.
Triantis, George G. 1992. "Secured Debt under Conditions of Imperfect Information." *Journal of Legal Studies* 21:1, 225–258.
Welch, Ivo. 1997. "Why Is Bank Debt Senior? A Theory of Asymmetry and Claim Priority Based on Influence Costs." *Review of Financial Studies* 10:4, 1203–1236.

ABOUT THE AUTHOR

Hugh Marble III received his PhD from the University of Florida in 2007 and then joined the faculty of the University of Vermont as an Assistant Professor of Finance. He teaches introductory and corporate finance to undergraduate and MBA students. His research focuses on credit ratings and debt contracts. Recent work focuses on the frequency with which the underlying causes of corporate credit rating changes are within management control.

CHAPTER 19

Sale and Leasebacks

KYLE S. WELLS
Professor of Finance, Dixie State College

INTRODUCTION

A sale-and-leaseback (SLB) transaction occurs when the owner of a previously purchased asset contracts to sell the asset and to lease it back from the buyer. Thus, an SLB provides a means of raising money based on an asset while continuing to use the asset (Seitz and Ellison 2005). In essence, the firm is changing its mind about the lease-versus-buy decision. When a firm makes the initial investment decision, it decides to buy the asset. However, due to unexpected changes within the company or in the economy, the firm later finds that leasing the asset is more advantageous. Airborne Freight Corporation (1990, p. 5) acknowledged such a decision process in its 1989 annual report as follows:

> *The Company has historically elected to own virtually all of its aircraft, the only carrier in the industry to do so. In 1989 the Company made a strategic decision to leverage the significant equity it has in its aircraft fleet. With this objective in mind, the Company completed two sale-leaseback financing transactions involving a total of nine aircraft, five DC-8 aircraft and four DC-9 aircraft. Proceeds from these transactions totaled $83.9 million and were used to pay down the bank lines of credit.*

Thus, when a firm needs capital and alternative sources are unavailable or are cost prohibitive, SLBs represent an alternative to traditional financing.

In addition to raising capital, a firm may also use an SLB to optimize the use of its assets. For example, the *Wall Street Journal* (1992) reported the following:

> *Bell Atlantic Corp. said it entered into an agreement to sell and lease back its 51-story corporate headquarters building in Philadelphia. Under the agreement, Bell Atlantic Properties will transfer the building to joint-venture formed by units of Dana Corp. and Textron Inc. Bell Atlantic, the Bell telephone company serving the mid-Atlantic region, will lease the tower for a minimum of 20 years, retain ownership of the land and continue to manage the building.*

In both examples, a firm that once owned an asset sold and leased it back from a buyer. In the first example, the corporation reports its intent to unlock equity in its assets and use the proceeds for other purposes. In the second, ownership of the asset changed but property rights or operating control did not. These motives are common in SLB transactions in contrast to direct leasing.

SLBs differ from direct leasing in that the operating assets of the company remain unchanged. In essence, an SLB is a financing decision, not an operating decision. From the financial manager's position, the question is "How do the costs of a sale and leaseback transaction compare to the costs of traditional financing?" In 1987, National Semiconductor completed a $92 million dollar SLB transaction in which the firm used the proceeds from the sale in an expansion project yielding 20 percent annually. The implied yield on the lease was only 11 percent annually netting a 9 percent difference while reducing plant, property, and equipment from 57.4 percent of total assets to 38.5 percent of total assets (Knutsen 1990).

In the academic literature, the decision to enter in an SLB is similar to the lease-versus-buy decision and is typically analyzed under a Modigliani and Miller (1958) framework of financial structure irrelevance. These studies largely focus on tax-related incentives when perfect market assumptions are removed (Miller and Upton 1976). Sharpe and Nguyen (1995) test additional reasons for leasing beyond tax minimization strategies. They find that the propensity to lease increases when financial contracting costs are high. Increases in these costs occur when the firm suffers from asymmetric information and agency problems. When a firm can fully utilize the tax benefits of ownership and the contracting costs are minimized through ownership, the optimal decision is to buy rather than lease an asset. If the firm cannot fully utilize the tax benefits of ownership or financing costs are high, a firm prefers leasing to owning (Schallheim 1994).

Miller and Upton (1976) analyze the leasing decision from a capital budgeting perspective using perfect capital market assumptions and find no financial advantages to leasing. In other words, the lease-versus-buy decision is irrelevant. Using the irrelevance approach, they relax the assumptions of perfect capital markets and find that the lease-versus-buy decision becomes quite complicated. Much of the existing finance literature focuses on the benefit of differential taxation between the lessee and the lessor. Brealey and Young (1980) show that leasing may dominate both debt and equity for companies in temporary nontax positions. In a world with differential taxation, the government may suffer a loss equal to the present value of the tax differential, which creates gains for the firms involved (Myers, Dill, and Bautista 1976; Franks and Hodges 1978).

Smith and Wakeman (1985) identify eight nontax incentives to lease or buy. Many of the nontax incentives focus on the financial contracting costs faced by the firm. Sharpe and Nguyen (1995) find that a firm's informational contracting costs influence its propensity to lease. The informational contracting costs include asymmetric information (Myers and Majluf 1984), agency problems (Smith and Warner 1979), and the underinvestment problem (Myers 1977). Although this chapter includes an examination of traditional motives in the lease-versus-buy decision, it also explores alternative hypotheses that stem from the unique nature of SLBs. SLBs differ from direct leases in that they can provide additional cash, whereas direct leases do not. When financing is scarce and/or the firm is credit-impaired, external financing costs may be high. An SLB can provide needed liquidity and can be a practical alternative to other forms of external financing.

The chapter has the following organization. The next section presents a summary of the accounting rules of leasing and SLBs. This is followed by the possible benefits and costs of SLBs that are posited in the extant literature. A stylized example of an SLB transaction is then presented to show how this transaction may affect a firm's financial statements and financial ratios. Empirical studies examining market reactions to SLBs are discussed. Although the referenced studies make important contributions to the finance literature, they are not intended to be exhaustive. The final section offers a summary and conclusions.

ACCOUNTING FOR SALE AND LEASEBACKS

In response to the increase in leasing transactions in the 1970s, the Financial Accounting Standards Board (FASB) issued Statement 13 in May 1976. Although the intent of this statement was to provide guidance on accounting for leases, FASB 13 was vague on many issues, especially involving accounting guidance about SLBs. As a result, the FASB issued several amendments to FASB 13. In accordance with FASB 13, a lease is considered a capital lease and must be included on the balance sheet if any of the following four conditions apply: (1) the lease automatically transfers ownership of the property to the lessee by the end of the term; (2) the lease contains a bargain-purchase option; (3) the lease term is equal to 75 percent or more of the estimated economic life of the leased property; and (4) the present value of the lease payments at the beginning of the lease term equals or exceeds 90 percent of the fair-market value of the property.

The FASB recognizes an SLB as a financing vehicle that allows the seller/lessor to capitalize on the value of its lease. It allows the corporation to realize the cash value of the equity impounded in an asset in addition to the excess value available when the asset is attached to a lease. According to Milnes and Pollina (1992), the SLB transaction offers corporations an important opportunity to achieve their financial goals but the economic and accounting issues of the proposed transactions must be carefully evaluated and structured.

Besides other changes, FASB 98 addresses SLBs specifically but limits explicit guidance to those transactions involving real estate. When a transaction qualifies as an SLB according to FASB 98, the seller/lessor is allowed to keep the property and related debt off its books. According to FASB 98, SLB accounting rules apply to those transactions meeting all of the following requirements.

First, the SLB must meet the test of being a normal or operating leaseback. The property (commonly interpreted as any asset in an SLB transaction whether real estate or not) must be in active use in the trade or business of the seller/lessee. The statement does allow the subleasing of a certain portion of the property, but it must be limited to a minor amount. A minor amount is defined as not more than 10 percent of the present market value of the asset at the time of the SLB transaction. A normal leaseback also requires the payment of rent, which may include a fixed amount or scaled depending based on the future operations of the business.

Second, the transaction must meet certain criteria concerning the sale of real estate. Namely, it must meet down payment requirement percentages for different types of property. FASB 98 also requires that the buyer must make annual payments of principal and interest in an amount sufficient to amortize any seller financing over a customary first mortgage loan term for that type of property.

Finally and most importantly, the terms of the sale must also provide for a transfer of all risks and rewards of ownership from the seller to the buyer. There can be no continuing involvement with the property except through the normal lease of the property. Types of transactions that imply continuing involvement may include an obligation or option to repurchase the property. However, a first right of refusal clause is not prohibited under SLB accounting requirements as long as the offer is based on a bona fide third-party offer.

The seller/lessor cannot guarantee the buyer/lessor any return on the investment of any type for either a limited or extended period of time. This includes any profit-sharing arrangements or operational subsidies. The seller is not allowed to provide nonrecourse financing to the buyer/lessor for any portion of the sales price. This restriction is important because it differs from the accounting rules relating to sales of real estate not involving leasebacks, which permits nonrecourse seller financing. The seller/lessor must be relieved of any obligations under any existing debt related to or secured by the property. Under these conditions, the sale of the asset is considered to be an "arm's length" transaction, and the resulting lease agreement is considered a true or operating lease.

BENEFITS OF A SALE AND LEASEBACK

A critical question for a corporation considering an SLB is, Do the benefits of the SLB transaction outweigh the contracting costs and the loss of fee ownership of the asset? In other words, do the advantages of receiving the net cash proceeds from the sale and the removal of the asset from the balance sheet outweigh the rent paid, plus the loss of depreciation and residual value? Cohen (1988) summarizes several reasons that a firm might be interested in pursuing an SLB. These factors are not necessarily independent and are certainly not exhaustive. Cohen suggests that when a firm finds one or more of the following, the benefits to leasing may outweigh the contracting costs and benefits of ownership.

Cost of Capital

When the implied costs of capital in a lease is less than alternative forms of financing, the asset creates a higher present value through leasing versus purchasing contracts. When does leasing reduce the costs of capital? Sharpe and Nguyen (1995) hypothesize that firms facing high costs of external funding may be able to economize on fixed capital costs by leasing. In their study, they focus on how leasing alleviates informational contracting constraints. The cost of debt increases when a high level of informational asymmetry exists between borrowers and lenders. This occurs primarily because the borrower is unsure of the future prospects of the lender. Leasing helps mitigate the information asymmetry problem because the lessor has a higher priority than secured debt if default occurs.

Jensen and Meckling (1976) show that agency problems exist between managers and debt holders. If the firm is near default, managers might accept negative net present value (NPV) projects that they otherwise might reject in a world with no information asymmetries. Another agency problem of underinvestment occurs when managers have more information than the owners. According to Myers (1977), managers will reject positive NPV projects that owners would force them to accept a world of perfect information. A pecking order of financial securities arises in these models where internal capital is the least costly form of financing followed by debt and then equity. Myers shows that firms can mitigate this problem by securing debt. In bankruptcy, a lessor can more easily regain control of an asset than it is for a secured lender to repossess it. In this way, a lessor has a priority claim to assets in the event of bankruptcy. Thus, when firms are subject to asymmetric information costs, leasing may be a less costly form of financing than either debt or equity.

Eisfeldt and Rampini (2005) argue that the ability of the lessor to repossess an asset is a major benefit of leasing. In the event of bankruptcy, leases defined by the courts as "true leases" are senior to both debt and equity. Thus, a leased asset is simpler to repossess. When a lease can be structured so that it fails the test of FASB 13, it is considered an operating or "true lease" and assumes that ownership of the asset resides with the lessor. In this case, the lessor can implicitly extend more credit than a lender whose claim may be secured by the same asset, lowering the implied cost of capital in a lease relative to other sources of capital.

Tax Incentives

When a firm cannot take full advantage of depreciation tax shields, an SLB creates a vehicle for the firm to transfer depreciation tax shields. Brealey and Young (1980) show that leasing may dominate debt and equity for companies in temporary nontax positions. In a world with differential taxation, the government may suffer a loss equal to the present value of taxes, which creates gains for the firms involved (Myers, Dill, and Bautista 1976; Franks and Hodges 1978). To the extent that the lessee has a lower tax rate than the lessor, the lessee may be able to transfer this tax allowance under the U.S. tax code. Leasing offers the opportunity to transfer or "sell" nondebt tax shields. If the lessee firm can locate a buyer (lessor) who has a higher probability of using these tax deductions, this buyer may pay more for them than they are worth to the lessee. The lessor "buys" these tax shields by reducing the implied cost of capital in the lease through lower lease payments, a higher salvage value, and better terms, thus lowering the financing costs of the asset.

The tax benefit of leasing is maximized when the difference between the marginal tax rate of the lessor and the lessee is the greatest. Graham, Lemmon, and Schallheim (1998) find that marginal tax rates, defined as the present value of current and expected future taxes paid on an additional dollar of income earned today are inversely proportional to leasing. This suggests that firms with lower marginal tax rates are more likely to lease assets than similar firms with higher marginal tax rates (Graham 1996).

Off-Balance Sheet Effects

Although the operating asset base remains unchanged, off-balance sheet considerations such as debt ratings and financial ratios may influence financing decisions. When a firm can structure a lease as an operating lease, the lessee shows the lease obligations in a footnote rather than in the body of the audited financial statements as both an asset and corresponding liability. By reducing the amount of assets on the balance sheet, the firm may be able to improve its return on assets (ROA). Once again, reducing the assets on the balance sheet by qualifying an asset as an operating rather than a capital lease can reduce the denominator on in the ROA equation.

This motivation for leasing may be questionable. Corporations may assume that rating agencies and shareholders are rational and will add back leases as a contingent liability to the balance sheet thereby nullifying the benefits of off-balance sheet financing. Copeland, Koller, and Murrin (1990) suggest that the focus of valuation should therefore not be on ownership risk but rather on property rights (i.e., who controls the future benefits of the assets). Ezzell and Vora (2001) show a statistically significant increase to the lessee's equity value upon SLB announcements. Yet, they find no statistically significant change resulting from the announcement of direct leases, suggesting that the market values these changes to the balance sheet, even if they are only aesthetic.

Earnings Management

A firm may sell assets to enhance its earnings. When the company is capital constrained and/or has negative earnings, an SLB can help improve earnings temporarily. Once again, most shareholders implicitly discount earnings by the gain on the sale, but it may not discourage a chief financial officer (CFO) from using an SLB to "smooth" earnings. To date, no study has explicitly looked at the relationship between SLBs and earnings management. Wells and Whitby (2006), however, hypothesize that firms with higher financial distress costs, as measured by relatively higher debt to value and lower interest coverage ratios, have a higher propensity to use SLBs. They find some evidence supporting this hypothesis but it is not statistically significant. This result may also be interpreted as resulting from the need of capital-constrained firms for additional financing and not as a way to manage earnings.

Capital Constraints

Through an SLB, a company can convert equity to cash and avoid tying up capital in poor-performing assets. Because most firms are not in the business of asset ownership, owning assets that may have lower returns on invested capital than other operating assets does not make sense. An SLB is unique in that it provides the release of capital for redeployment while maintaining operational control of the asset. Selling and leasing back assets that fail to meet internal hurdle rates enable corporations to use funds to enhance liquidity, expand operations, and invest in core businesses. The firm may also use the funds from an SLB to pay down debt in order to improve its balance sheet and to reduce financial distress costs. Avoiding market penalties due to a dividend reduction may also be a motive for capital-constrained firms to engage in SLBs (Lintner 1956).

SLBs may also provide avenues of financing for credit-constrained firms. According to Shaw (2002, p. 1), "In an environment where corporate financing has been hard to get, especially for smaller, credit-impaired companies, sale-leaseback transactions, an alternative form of financing that is tied to real property or equipment, has been gaining popularity." For companies with short operating histories, financing terms are usually short, maturing in 5 to 10 years or less with call provisions and annual review requirements. An SLB usually provides a 20-to-25-year term.

Barris (2002) considers SLB transactions in Europe. His evidence shows that raising funds is the main motive behind SLBs but fails to consider that taxes and transaction costs may also be a factor. Wells and Whitby (2006) find that after controlling for tax rates and information asymmetries, capital needs in tandem with capital constraints may motivate firms to seek a buyer/lessor to engage in an SLB. When financing is scarce and/or the firm is credit-impaired, external financing costs may be high and selling and leasing back can provide a practical alternative to other forms of external financing.

Debt Covenants

Restrictive covenants may exacerbate financial distress costs. Most corporate financing is structured with restrictive covenants requiring that they periodically meet certain tests or else the loan can be in default. These covenants often take the form of financial ratios negotiated between the corporation and lender when making the loan. For example, the lender may restrict the payment of dividends unless the firm maintains a specific debt-to-equity ratio. By using an SLB, a firm can improve its interest coverage and other ratios related to debt covenants by reducing the amount of secured debt on the balance sheet.

Sharpe and Nguyen (1995) show that relative to secured debt, leasing has a greater potential to reduce the costs of financial distress. Bankruptcy is a legal mechanism that distributes the assets of the firm to claims against the firm in the event of default on contracted obligations. When the probability of default is high, the firm can reduce bankruptcy costs ex-ante by using contracts that limit legal involvement. Relative to secured debt, leasing has the potential of reducing financial distress costs by tying the claim of the debt holder directly to the asset. An SLB typically does not require such covenants. By selling poor-performing assets such as real estate and nonspecialized equipment, the firm can maintain operating control of the asset while reducing its debt, improve its financial ratios, and free up capital and/or debt capacity for use in higher-yielding assets. With this type of financing, the corporation is required to maintain the asset but is not burdened with financing and operational requirements.

Hidden Value

Asset appreciation may not be reflected in a firm's financial statements. A distinguishing characteristic between an SLB and direct leasing is the ability to capture the difference between the market value of an asset and the claims held against that asset. When the market value of an asset exceeds its book value, an SLB allows the firm to capture this value while maintaining the operational capacity of the asset. Grönlund, Louko, and Vaihekoski (2008) suggest that a firm can use SLBs as a mechanism to reveal the hidden value of its assets to the market. Capital yields on real estate and general use equipment have been historically low. By changing the asset from low-yielding assets to a more liquid form and investing it in the core business, a firm's return to equity (ROE) increases.

Many corporations find cost efficiencies exist when real estate property management is outsourced. Additionally, an owner-occupier has a fixed cost structure where a new owner can competitively market and rent free space not used by the lessee, therefore reducing the implied costs of the lease.

Tender Defense

Another incentive for an SLB may be to avoid a takeover by another corporation. Testing this hypothesis is difficult, but the prime motivation for many takeovers is the capitalization of unrealized value. According to Knutsen (1990), between 15 to 20 percent of the net worth of U.S. corporations is typically tied to real estate assets. In older, more established organizations, those assets can approach 30 to 35 percent and may be valued based on outdated book values rather than current market values. A firm could use an SLB to access the unrealized equity in these assets.

An SLB could also be a motivation for a takeover. While the effects of a bump in earnings would be short lived, an SLB transaction may diminish the takeover appeal. Although not tested explicitly, firms facing high financing costs due to asymmetric information have a greater propensity to use SLB transactions (Sharpe and Nguyen 1995). These firms are also correlated with higher abnormal returns from SLB announcements (Ezzell and Vora 2001).

COSTS OF SALE AND LEASEBACKS

Contracting costs can vary and typically are a smaller percentage in larger transactions. Knutsen (1990) estimates contracting costs at about 3 percent of the transaction and can require as long as 9 to 12 months to complete, depending on the size and complexity of the deal. A firm can usually finance these costs as part of the transaction. Nonetheless, burdens created in the event that the transaction does not materialize or the firm encounters false starts must be addressed.

Although leasing can mitigate informational asymmetry problems by securing the asset in the case of bankruptcy, it creates additional agency problems by separating the use from the ownership of the asset. This may lead to a higher cost of capital. In a world of perfect information, the lessor knows *ex-ante* whether the lessee will properly use and maintain the asset. Due to this information asymmetry, the lessor assumes that the lessee will mistreat the asset. Thus, the lessor either charges a premium for assets that require higher maintenance or insists that the lessee fund the creation of a maintenance reserve account.

The cost of the lease will be higher than the costs of ownership when the owner cannot monitor the use of the asset. The risks to the lessor include responsibility for loss, wear, tear, and obsolescence. These risks and the associated implied lease rates imposed by the lessor are then evaluated based on the ownership benefits, which include the right of use, gains from asset appreciation, and ultimate possession of the asset. When the moral agency problem created by asymmetric information cannot be mitigated, the cost of leasing is prohibitive, and the propensity is to own rather than lease the asset.

Klein, Crawford, and Alchian (1978) maintain that firms are likely to own assets with more firm-specific use (vertical integration) and to lease more general-purpose assets. Similarly, Grossman and Hart (1986) and Williamson (1988) suggest that asset specificity plays a crucial role in ownership and financing decisions. Eisfeldt and Rampini (2005) contend that asset type is related to the cost of leasing. They show that if an asset is general in use, its resale value in the event of default will be more liquid and easily resold or leased and should be leased on more favorable terms. Eisfeldt and Rampini argue that firms leasing specific assets either have high external financing costs and/or have a low probability of default reducing the possibility that the lessee will return the leased asset. Ben-David (2005) finds that financially solvent firms often use specific assets in SLB transactions, whereas firms that are not financially solvent tend to lease general assets.

THE SALE AND LEASEBACK: AN EXAMPLE

Exhibit 19.1 presents a simplified statement of income and balance sheet for a hypothetical company and shows the potential effects of an SLB transaction. The second column represents the financial statements before or without the SLB transaction. The third column reflects the assumption that the SLB transaction occurs on the final day of the fiscal period. This example is structured specifically to illustrate the potential incentives for the SLB while holding all else constant and does not necessarily represent the benefits accrued to an individual or average company.

In this example, the firm's management sells real estate with a book value of $400,000 for $470,000 after selling expenses and simultaneously enters into an operating lease agreement on the property. By doing so, the firm can remove both a $340,000 mortgage note on the property and the asset from its balance sheet.

Assuming the company is in a temporary no-tax position due to operating losses (without carry-backs or carry-forwards), operating losses mostly offset the resulting tax on the gain. In this example, the effective tax rate is 20 percent on positive earnings after the transaction and with no taxable earnings before the transaction. Although operating earnings remain unaffected, a gain on the sale of the asset results in investing income of $70,000. The gain from the sale, minus the tax effect, is added to cash and marketable securities on the balance sheet.

The difference between the debt service and lease payments does not affect net income until the next period. Further, the implied interest rate on the lease does not have to be less than the interest rate on the mortgage debt in order to create value for the company. When the firm is capitally constrained or alternative sources of capital are cost prohibitive, exchanging secured debt for lease payments can create value if properly invested.

The SLB transaction effectively unlocks equity previously unavailable to the company and should therefore be compared to the firm's opportunity cost of capital. The firm does not complete the transaction in isolation and usually pairs it with an intended use for the capital, such as reducing debt, buying fixed assets, increasing net working capital, or purchasing stock. Thus, the SLB differs from a direct lease in that a firm's operating assets remain unchanged, but the financing changes.

Exhibit 19.1 Sale and Leaseback: An Example

Income Statement ($ Thousands)				
		20xx		20xx
Sales	$	2,050	$	2,050
Cost of goods sold		(1,050)		(1,050)
Gross profit		1,000		1,000
Fixed expenses		(975)		(975)
Gain (loss) on sale of assets*		–		70
Earnings before interest and taxes		25		95
Depreciation		(16)		(16)
Interest expense		(29)		(29)
Earnings before taxes		(20)		50
Tax expense		–		(10)
Net income		(20)		40
Balance Sheet ($ Thousands)				
Current assets				
Cash	$	18	$	78
Accounts receivable		498		498
Inventory		186		186
Total current assets		702		762
Property and equipment				
Machinery and equipment		240		240
Real estate		400		–
Accumulated depreciation		(146)		(93)
Total property and equipment		494		147
Total assets		1,196		909
Current liabilities				
Accounts payable	$	270	$	270
Current portion of long-term debt		97		97
Total current liabilities		367		367
Long-term liabilities				
Long-term debt		411		71
Total liabilities		778		438
Stockholders' equity				
Common stock		120		120
Accumulated retained earnings		311		351
Total stockholders' equity		431		471
Total liabilities and stockholders' equity	$	1,209	$	909
Select Financial Ratios				
Current ratio		1.91		2.08
Total asset turnover		1.71		2.26
Debt ratio		65%		48%
Coverage ratio		0.87		3.28
Return on equity (ROA)		–1.66%		4.41%
Return on equity (ROE)		–4.60%		8.51%
Long-term debt to earnings		NA		1.77

Note: This exhibit represents the income statement and balance sheet of a hypothetical company before and after a sale and leaseback transaction. The second column represents the financial statements before the transaction. The third column reflects the assumption that the transaction occurs on the final day of the fiscal period. In the transaction, the company sells a real estate asset for $470,000 that has a book value of $400,000 after selling expenses. Using the proceeds of the sale, the firm pays down a $340,000 mortgage note on the property.

Effects on Cost of Capital

Due to negative earnings and low coverage ratios resulting from an SLB, the marginal cost of capital is likely high. If the cost of leasing was once greater than the cost of capital, the situation has likely changed making leasing, and specifically an SLB, an attractive form of financing. Comparing the implied rate on the lease to alternative financing sources may be appropriate for direct leasing. However, when evaluating an SLB, the financial manager should compare the cost of leasing to the firm's marginal weighted average cost of capital (WACC) because, unlike direct leasing, an SLB transaction is a source of financing.

Tax Effects

Before an SLB, the firm may be in a temporarily low or no-tax position due to low operating earnings, depreciation, and financing expenses. After the SLB, the firm's taxable earnings are positive, but operating losses reduce the effective tax rate on the gain on sale. If the firm were taxed the full statutory rate of 35 percent on the gain on sale, the tax burden would have been \$24,500 or (\$70,000 × 0.35). Due to the low tax rate and operating losses, the tax burden on the sale was only \$10,000, creating an effective rate on the gain on sale of 14.3 percent or (\$10,000/\$70,000). For simplicity, this example omits important tax details such as passive activity loss rules, alternative minimum tax, accelerated depreciation schedules, and investment tax credits relating to the leasing decision. Although future depreciation tax shields have been sold in the transaction as well as claims to residual value, the lease expense provides a future tax shield benefit.

Off Balance Sheet Effects

Since the lease is structured as an operating versus a capital lease, the book value of the asset is removed from the balance sheet. As a result, return on assets (ROA) increases from −1.66 percent before the SLB transaction to 4.41 percent after the transaction. The asset turnover ratio increases from 1.70 to 2.26. This increase benefits from both an increase in operating earnings and a decrease in invested capital.

Earnings Management

Net income shows an increase from a \$20,000 loss to a \$40,000 gain but operating profits remain unchanged. The return on equity (ROE) increased from −4.6 percent to 8.5 percent due to the change in leverage. However, an informed investor may recognize the gain as an extraordinary event and make the necessary adjustments to net income for nonreoccurring earnings.

Capital Constraints

Without additional information about the firm's credit environment, assessing any capital limitations the company may face is difficult. Yet, assuming a relatively high leverage ratio, negative earnings, a relatively high portion of account receivables, and a low current ratio, the firm would probably have difficulty raising funds. After the SLB transaction, the debt ratio falls from 65 percent to 48 percent, the current ratio climbs from 1.91 to 2.08, and cash more than quadruples. These changes are likely to reduce the firm's marginal cost of capital.

Debt Covenants

Exhibit 19.1 does not present the specifics of the debt covenants. However, assuming that typical debt covenants require an interest coverage ratio of more than 2.0 and a long-term debt-to-earnings ratio of no more than 5.0, the firm appears to be in default of the debt covenants before the SLB. After the transaction, the coverage ratio increases from 0.87 to 3.28 and the long-term debt-to-earnings ratio changes from negative to 1.77. Thus, the firm is no longer in violation of these covenants. The change in the latter ratio benefits from both an increase in earnings and a decrease in long-term debt.

Hidden Value

Due to the difference between the market value and the book value of the asset, the equity captured by the SLB is equal to the difference minus the tax effects of the SLB transaction. Depending on the opportunity costs, by changing the asset from low-yielding assets to a more liquid form and investing it in the core business, the ROE will increase in direct relation to the difference between the yield on invested capital and the market capitalization rate of the lease. The lessee may also benefit from outsourcing its facility ownership and maintenance to a third party who specializes in these services. This may in turn reduce the implied cost of the lease. The release of this hidden capital reduces the takeover threat, which may also be a motivation for the transaction from the manager's perspective.

In summary, the SLB transaction allows the firm to increase net income, reduce fixed assets, and reduce debt. These changes result in an increase in both ROA and ROE, a reduction in debt-to-value, and a sharp increase in interest coverage. Additionally, the sale of the depreciated asset at a market price higher than the current book value captures hidden value. The firm can reinvest those funds in higher yielding assets.

MARKET REACTION TO SALE AND LEASEBACKS

For the lessee firm, the securities issuance literature indicates that the market typically responds negatively to announcements of external financing regardless of how the firm uses the proceeds. Thus, if the market views an SLB as a form of secured financing, it should generate nonpositive returns upon announcement (Myers and Majluf 1984; Miller and Rock 1985). The market may treat an announcement of an SLB as if the firm announced an issue of secured debt and, thus, can be taken as a signal of an unexpected shortfall in the firm's earnings from its current projects. This would have a negative impact on the shareholder wealth of the lessee.

Slovin, Sushka, and Polonchek (1990) were the first to test the market reaction to leasebacks. Contrary to theory, they find a positive market reaction to the announcement of an SLB for lessee firms. Due to the ability of the lessor to structure the transaction, there should be sufficient benefits to make an SLB a positive NPV transaction. The authors find that lessors experience a positive but insignificant market reaction to the purchase and lease under an SLB contract. Assuming that the lessor is in the leasing business, the market is likely to perceive the announcement as a fully anticipated event, which may explain why the market value is not significant upon announcement for the lessor.

Ezzell and Vora (2001) find that the lessee's tax rate is significantly negatively related to the lessee's return. That is, the lower the lessee's tax rate, the greater is the return from the SLB. The market gains experienced in an SLB are the net of the tax revenues from the sale and the present value of the depreciation tax shields. In essence, a low–tax rate firm cannot use the depreciation tax shields and can access the capital gains in the asset at a low tax rate by selling the depreciation tax shields to a firm that can use them more fully. The authors also find that equity value increases are greater for non–dividend-paying lessees than for dividend-paying lessees. Ezzell and Vora interpret this result as evidence that leasing reduces the adverse selection problem arising when high information asymmetry firms attempt to raise capital. The authors also find that equity values increase more for firms with low interest coverage ratios, suggesting that capital-constrained firms may use SLBs as an alternative source of funding.

Wells and Whitby (2006) find evidence supporting the primary theoretical reason for leasing, namely taxes, and mixed support for asymmetric information costs and bankruptcy costs relating to leasing. However, contrary to theory, they find that these firms are typically large and solvent with high growth potential but have low interest coverage and high leverage suggesting that the need for cash in tandem with capital constraints is driving these transactions. Many firms in their sample pay a substantial dividend yet find themselves facing a cash shortage.

Grönlund, Louko, and Vaihekoski (2008) examine European firms and also find that firms using SLBs are met with positive market reactions and are motivated by potential tax and efficiency gains. Controlling for credit constraints, Wells and Whitby (2006) find abnormal market returns are positively correlated with the price-earnings (P/E) ratio and negatively correlated with debt structure. They hypothesize that firms perceived as using an SLB transaction to finance growth in tight credit markets are enhancing value. Firms using SLBs for growth are characterized by having higher-than-average P/E multiples and profit margins while spending more than the average firm in their industry on research and development (R&D). The same SLB transaction perceived as being motivated by a need to cover existing debt or meet current financial obligations has an opposite response from the market. Thus, the market perceives such a transaction as value destroying. Firms that are likely to use funds to meet debt obligations characterized by low coverage and high debt ratios experience lower event returns.

SUMMARY AND CONCLUSIONS

This chapter provides a synthesis of both anecdotal and empirical support for the potential motives for SLBs. SLBs differ from direct leasing in that the operating assets essentially remain unchanged and represent a substitute for other financing sources available to firms. A decision to sell and leaseback is a financing decision. SLBs can provide needed liquidity and can be a practical alternative to other forms of external financing for capital-constrained or credit-impaired firms.

The extant literature in this area primarily focuses on the tax incentives of leasing. Empirical studies find several other nontax incentives for leasing such as a reduced cost of capital, off–balance sheet effects, earnings management, capital constraints, debt covenants, and hidden value. Although not tested in empirical studies, another possible reason for SLBs is the tender defense. A prime motivator in takeovers is the unrealized value of a corporation's asset holdings. An SLB provides a vehicle to unlock the equity and relinquishes ownership while maintaining the asset's operational capacity.

While not an exhaustive list, these factors represent the focus of academic research are not necessarily independent and may affect firms differently. Whereas leases are normally structured to meet the operational needs of the company, an SLB should be evaluated from principally a financial perspective. If structured properly, an SLB transaction can enable a corporation to tap into the equity and cash value of its assets without losing operational control. A corporation may also find an SLB to be an effective and cost-beneficial means of financing its business especially when traditional sources of financing are unavailable or cost prohibitive.

DISCUSSION QUESTIONS

1. Consider a firm that purchased its headquarters with a low interest rate mortgage loan. Why might the firm want to sell the building and lease it back, even if the implied rate of interest on the lease is greater than the current mortgage rate of interest?
2. Some dismiss earnings management and manipulation of financial ratios as dubious motives for SLB transactions. Why might a financial manager still choose to use them for these reasons?
3. Are SLB transactions likely to increase or decrease during a recession? Why?
4. Empirical evidence shows an abnormally positive and statistically significant return for lessee firms that announce an SLB but not a significant return for the lessor. What explains this difference?

REFERENCES

Airborne Freight Corporation. 1990. *Airborne Freight Corporation 1989 Annual Report*. Seattle, WA.

Barris, Roger D. 2002. "Sale-Leasebacks Move to the Forefront: What Is Motivating Buyers and Sellers and What Are Their Preferred Methods?" *Briefings in Real Estate Finance* 2:2, 103–112.

Ben-David, Itzhak. 2005. "Company Performance and Leased Assets in Sale-and-Leaseback Transactions." *Journal of Equipment Lease Financing* 23:2, 1–8.

Brealey, Richard A., and Charles M. Young. 1980. "Debt, Taxes and Leasing—A Note." *Journal of Finance* 35:5, 1245–1250.

Cohen, Gerald S. 1988. "Sale/Leasebacks: How They Can Benefit the Corporation." *Site Selection & Industrial Development* 33:6, 18–20.

Copeland, Tom, Tim Koller, and Jack Murrin. 1990. *Valuation: Measuring and Managing the Value of Companies*. New York: John Wiley & Sons.

Eisfeldt, Andrea L., and Adriano A. Rampini. 2005. "Leasing, Ability to Repossess, and Debt Capacity." Working Paper, Northwestern University.

Ezzell, John R., and Premal P. Vora. 2001. "Leasing versus Purchasing: Direct Evidence on a Corporation's Motivations for Leasing and Consequences of Leasing." *Quarterly Review of Economics and Finance* 41:1, 33–47.

Franks, Julian R., and Stewart D. Hodges. 1978. "Valuation of Financial Lease Contracts: A Note." *Journal of Finance* 33:2, 657–669.

Graham, John R. 1996. "Debt and the Marginal Tax Rate." *Journal of Financial Economics* 41:1, 41–73.

Graham, John R., Mike Lemmon, and James S. Schallheim, 1998. "Debt, Leases, Taxes, and the Endogeneity of Corporate Tax Status." *Journal of Finance* 53:1, 131–161.

Grönlund, Tomi, Antti Louko, and Mika Vaihekoski. 2008. "Corporate Real Estate Sale and Leaseback Effect: Empirical Evidence from Europe." *European Financial Management* 14:4, 820–843.

Grossman, Sanford J., and Oliver D. Hart. 1986. "The Costs and Benefits of Ownership: A Theory of Vertical and Lateral Integration." *Journal of Political Economy* 94:4, 691–719.

Jensen, Michael C., and William H. Meckling. 1976. "Theory of the Firm: Managerial Behavior, Agency Costs and Ownership Structure." *Journal of Financial Economics* 3:4, 305–360.

Klein, Benjamin, Robert G. Crawford, and Armen A. Alchian. 1978. "Vertical Integration, Appropriable Rents, and the Competitive Contracting Process." *Journal of Law and Economics* 21:2, 297–326.

Knutsen, Kenneth C. 1990. "The Impact of Real Estate on Operational and Financial Statements: Sale/Leaseback Transactions." *Industrial Development* 159:6, 27–30.

Lintner, John. 1956. "Distribution of Incomes of Corporations among Dividends, Retained Earnings, and Taxes." *American Economic Review* 46:2, 97–113.

Miller, Merton H., and Kevin Rock. 1985. "Dividend Policy under Asymmetric Information." *Journal of Finance* 40:4, 1031–1051.

Miller, Merton H., and Charles W. Upton. 1976. "Leasing, Buying, and the Cost of Capital Services." *Journal of Finance* 31:3, 761–786.

Milnes, Raymond, and Ronald Pollina. 1992. "Sale/Leasebacks: Are They Right for Your Company?" *Industrial Development* 161:2, 23–26.

Modigliani, Franco, and Merton H. Miller. 1958. "The Cost of Capital, Corporation Finance and the Theory of Investment." *American Economic Review* 48:3, 655–669.

Myers, Stewart C. 1977. "Determinants of Corporate Borrowing." *Journal of Financial Economics* 5:2, 147–175.

Myers, Stewart C., David A. Dill, and Alberto J. Bautista. 1976. "Valuation of Financial Lease Contracts." *Journal of Finance* 31:3, 799–819.

Myers, Stewart C., and Nicholas S. Majluf. 1984. "Corporate Financing and Investment Decisions When Firms Have Information That Investors Do Not Have." *Journal of Financial Economics* 13:2, 187–221.

Schallheim, James S. 1994. *Lease or Buy? Principles for Sound Decision Making*. Boston: Harvard Business School Press.

Seitz, Neil, and Mitch Ellison. 2005. *Capital Budgeting and Long-Term Financing Decisions*, 4th Ed. Cincinnati, Ohio: Southwestern.

Sharpe, Steven A., and Hien H. Nguyen. 1995. "Capital Market Imperfections and the Incentive to Lease." *Journal of Financial Economics* 39:2, 271–294.

Shaw, Joy C. 2002. "Sale-Leasebacks Gain Popularity." *Wall Street Journal*. December 11, 1.

Slovin, Myron B., Marie E. Sushka, and John A. Polonchek. 1990. "Corporate Sale-and-Leasebacks and Shareholder Wealth." *Journal of Finance* 45:1, 289–299.

Smith, Jr., Clifford W., and L. MacDonald Wakeman. 1985. "Determinants of Corporate Leasing Policy." *Journal of Finance* 40:3, 895–908.

Smith, Jr., Clifford W., and Jerold B. Warner. 1979. "Bankruptcy, Secured Debt, and Optimal Capital Structure: Comment." *Journal of Finance* 34:1, 247–251.

Wall Street Journal. 1992. "Equitable Loss Narrows by Profit at Investment Business." August 14, 14.

Wells, Kyle S., and Ryan Whitby. 2006. "Evidence of Motives and Market Reactions to Sale and Leasebacks." Working Paper, Dixie State College.

Williamson, Oliver E. 1988. "Corporate Finance and Corporate Governance." *Journal of Finance* 43:3, 567–591.

ABOUT THE AUTHOR

Kyle Wells is a professor of finance at Dixie State College. He previously taught courses in finance and statistics at the University of Utah and University of New Mexico. His research interests are in empirical corporate finance, leasing, and pedagogical methods for online instruction. He received a BS in Civil and Environmental Engineering from the University of Utah in 1998, an MBA from the University of Arizona in 2002, and a PhD in Finance from the University of Utah in 2008.

PART IV

Special Topics

CHAPTER 20

Financial Distress and Bankruptcy

KIMBERLY J. CORNAGGIA
Associate Professor of Finance, American University

INTRODUCTION

The static trade-off theory, which traces back to Modigliani and Miller (1963), suggests that the optimal level of debt financing weighs the benefits of debt, such as the tax deductibility of interest payments, against the costs of debt including financial distress and bankruptcy. Therefore, it is critical to understand the sources, likelihoods, and costs of financial distress, which vary by industry and firm when considering the optimal capital structure. Specifically, product type (commodities versus highly specific production technologies), industry concentration, product and labor market power, and ease of asset redeployment all affect both the risk and costs of bankruptcy. A comprehensive analysis considers exogenous factors such as contagion among rival firms and along the supply chain as well as internal factors such as investment opportunities, financing policies, corporate governance, and risk management.

This chapter explores a host of methods for estimating the expected likelihood of distress, surveys the literature regarding direct and indirect costs of distress, and discusses distress resolution including formal bankruptcy. Additional attention is given to the conflicts of interest inherent in a negotiation-based restructuring process and common consequences for incumbent management as well as creditors and shareholders. The chapter provides a brief discussion of the role of "too big to fail" and other regulatory considerations. Jensen (1991, p. 26) argues that regulatory changes in the late 1980s and early 1990s "substantially increased the frequency and costs of financial distress and bankruptcy." These arguments are again relevant as regulators consider amendments to a host of securities market and financial institution regulation. The chapter also comments on the 2005 amendments to the U.S. Bankruptcy Code and their implications for the role of certain prodebtor features of Chapter 11 including violations of an Absolute Priority Rule (APR) in favor of incumbent shareholders and Key Employee Retention Programs (KERP) that favor incumbent management.

PREDICTING DISTRESS

There exist a host of metrics predicting the bankruptcy event, with varying usefulness as early indicators of potential distress. This section discusses the ubiquitous use of credit ratings as triggers in debt contracts and as the benchmark of credit quality by regulators and institutional investors. Also explored are Merton (1974) structural models that rely on market data as well as models that rely exclusively on accounting data obtained from audited financial statements. Finally, the chapter discusses the emergence of independent commercial credit analysis as traditional credit ratings come under fire in the face of global credit crises.

Credit Ratings

The role of a credit rating is to assess the likelihood of receiving promised payments from a financial security. Ordinal scales serve as mnemonics for financial risk and have historically been assumed by regulators and a host of market participants to provide an efficient summary to the market. As discussed below, these assumptions are presently being tested. But the ubiquitous reliance on these ratings by regulators, institutional investors, and in corporate contracts suggests that credit ratings will continue to serve as benchmarks for financial risk assessment.

This section refers both to Credit Rating Agencies (CRAs) and to Nationally Recognized Statistical Ratings Organizations (NRSROs). The latter are a special subset of the former, and these terms are not interchangeable. Following 2006 reform legislation, the U.S. Securities and Exchange Commission (SEC) opened the process from designation to application. As a result, 10 firms now carry the NRSRO designation. The insurance specialty of one (A. M. Best) and the heretofore trivial market share of others (DBRS Ltd., Egan-Jones, Japan Credit Rating Agency, LACE Financial Corp, Rating and Investment Information, Inc., and Realpoint LLC) result in an industry commonly referred to as an oligopoly with "two and a half" players: Moody's, S&P, and Fitch.

One reason markets have historically relied heavily on credit ratings as a measure of financial risk is their ease of use; ratings by the large traditional CRAs are intuitive and readily obtained. A second reason for the reliance on credit ratings is the expectation that credit ratings convey information not otherwise observable to the market. Indeed, the SEC exempts NRSROs from Regulation FD (Fair Disclosure) based on the expectation that rating analysts converse with issuers in order to incorporate nonpublic information.

Perhaps the primary reason for the ubiquitous use of credit ratings is due to regulatory requirements. Only ratings purchased from an NRSRO qualify for regulatory compliance. Money market funds must hold short-term securities (typically commercial paper) rated AAA. The SEC sets net capital requirements for broker dealers based on NRSRO ratings of their securities. Banking regulators base capital adequacy requirements on ratings. The Department of Labor enforces the Employee Retirement Income Savings Act (ERISA) prohibiting pension funds from holding speculative-grade securities. Insurance regulators have similar prudent investment requirements. Finally, issuers obtaining stronger credit ratings enjoy preferential treatment when registering securities with the SEC; that is, "short form" registration.

Following a host of bankruptcies by firms considered "investment grade" by the primary NRSROs, such as Enron and WorldCom, critics questioned whether the conflicts of interest inherent in the compensation of NRSROs by issuing firms resulted in inflated credit ratings. These concerns became acute following the 2007 crisis in structured finance markets originating with Residential Mortgage Backed Securities (RMBS) backed by subprime mortgages and spreading along the leverage chain to Collateralized Debt Obligations (CDOs), culminating in the ultimate global economic turmoil in 2008–2009. Coval, Jurek, and Stafford (2009) discuss the role of credit rating error in the collapse of structured finance markets.

Regulatory requirements based on the NRSRO ratings are currently the subject of debate. At the time of this writing, regulators have not found a viable alternative. But even if regulators are able to remove the regulation-induced reliance on these ratings, decades of debt covenants employing these ratings as triggers for restructuring remain. The prohibitive cost of rewriting debt covenants and other corporate contracts suggests that these ratings will persist as risk metrics into the foreseeable future.

Bankruptcy Prediction Models

Quantitative default prediction models have been published for decades. Early discriminant analysis by Altman (1968) and the maximum likelihood logistic model of Ohlson (1980) are still widely employed as financial risk metrics. Shumway (2001) published a parsimonious discrete hazard model that has been shown to outperform credit ratings predicting default in corporate bonds. Unlike qualitative analyst ratings, these published models are based on input data that are publicly available, readily obtained, and easily transferred. Therefore, these tools are commonly employed by academics and practitioners analyzing large numbers of firms.

However, accounting-based models utilize income statement and balance sheet data, making them sensitive to accounting reporting standards. Franzen, Rodgers, and Simin (2007) document the impact of conservative accounting treatment of investment in research and development (R&D) on Altman's Z-Score and Ohlson's O-Score. Because R&D in the United States is expensed rather than capitalized, these research assets (most valuable for firms such as pharmaceuticals marked by high R&D expenditures) are off the books and thus not reflected in capital structure. This conservative accounting treatment results in balance sheets and income statements falsely indicating financial distress.

The GAAP treatment of operating leases also distorts accounting-based models. Cornaggia, Franzen and Simin (2010) demonstrate a remarkable increase in off-balance-sheet (OBS) lease financing and a simultaneous decrease in capital (on-balance-sheet) lease financing. Because these obligations are long term and noncancellable, they are essentially debt. The authors document that the increase in OBS financing is in addition to, rather than in lieu of, traditional debt. These results suggest that common risk metrics that rely on balance sheets and income statements will increasingly underestimate the risk of such firms as the lower debt ratios may be associated with higher OBS debt financing. The authors employ straightforward methodologies to compute the impact on leverage ratios, return on capital, and levered beta estimates.

Sensitivity to accounting reporting standards leads some to employ more sophisticated structural models following Black and Scholes (1973) and Merton (1974), as discussed by Vassalou and Xing (2004). However, critics of these models argue that they require strong assumptions regarding the completeness of equity market information, produce unrealistic probabilities, and imply default spreads (to risk-free Treasury bonds) that vary significantly from those observed empirically (Kim, Ramaswamy, and Sunderasan 1993; Stein 2005). Hillegeist et al. (2004) conclude that market-based, option-pricing models have more explanatory power than strictly accounting-based models, but that O- and Z-Scores still contribute significant incremental information. Perhaps a more notable drawback of the option-pricing models is their binary nature. While they appear to outperform predicting bankruptcy in the next period (a binary indicator), they are less useful than continuous scores to observe a continuum of financial health. Franzen, Rodgers, and Simin (2007) employ a simple procedure to capitalize the R&D investment and improve accounting-based scores.

Independent Commercial Analysis

Increased concern about conflicts of interest in the traditional credit ratings business ignited a new crop of independent commercial credit research. Formed in November 2000, CreditSights (producer of BondScore) provides independent capital structure research and strategy and has already received industry recognition, including four consecutive years as "Best Independent Credit Research Provider" as ranked by *Credit* magazine. Other new entrants include RapidRatings (formed in 1991) and Center for Financial Research & Analysis (CFRA), founded in 1994 and subsequently acquired by RiskMetrics in 2007. These firms are compensated by end users rather than securities issuers. To date, none have applied for the once-coveted NRSRO designation. Fairly or not, traditional credit ratings have faced considerable scrutiny concerning inflated ratings following the global credit crises and the collapse of structured finance markets. This scrutiny has further fuelled growth in the independent credit analysis sector. RapidRatings, for example, reports 550 percent customer growth in 2009.

EXPECTED COST OF DISTRESS

Estimated direct costs of bankruptcy vary widely from 1.5 percent to 9.5 percent of firm value (Warner 1977; Altman 1984; Weiss 1990; Betker 1997; Lubben 2000; LoPucki and Doherty 2004; Bris, Welch, and Zhu 2006). These costs include legal counsel and valuation expertise. Such costs are offset to some extent by direct benefits of court protection such as reprieve from interest payments and delayed principal repayment. However, empirical studies suggest direct costs of bankruptcy pale in comparison to *indirect* costs, though the latter are more difficult to quantify (Altman 1984; Asquith, Gertner, and Scharfstein 1994; Gilson 1997; Hotchkiss 1995; LoPucki and Whitford 1993; Hertzel, Li, Officer, and Rodgers 2008). Estimates of combined direct and indirect costs of distress are much higher, between 10 percent and 20 percent of firm value (Andrade and Kaplan 1998).

Indirect costs include lost revenues, as customers concerned with guarantees and warranties take their business to nondistressed rivals. Distressed auto manufacturers offer substantial rebates in an effort to retain customers. On May 6, 2009, CNN.Money.com reported: "Chrysler announced a new sales incentive plan Wednesday as the carmaker seeks to spur sales while it works through bankruptcy.... Chrysler is immediately offering up to $4,000 in cash rebates...." General Motors and Ford offered similar rebates and zero percent financing to stymie customer loss, according to CBS MoneyWatch.com in July 2009. Eastern Airlines priced tickets well below the cost of flying in order to retain customers over their years spent in bankruptcy. Beyond implications for creditors and shareholders, the price impact on rivals is an example of the contagion documented by Lang and Stulz (1992) and Hertzel et al. (2008).

Additional indirect costs include less favorable credit terms. Firms that have historically enjoyed 2/10, net 30 terms may face collect on delivery or risk losing their suppliers. As Cutler and Summers (1988, pp. 167–168) note, Texaco cited less favorable supply terms as a substantial burden in their 1987 bankruptcy:

> *The most important evidence for the adverse effects of the dispute is an affidavit Texaco submitted with its bankruptcy.... The affidavit asserted that some suppliers had demanded cash payments before performance or insisted on secured forms of repayment. Others halted crude shipments temporarily or cancelled them entirely. A number of banks had also refused to enter into, or placed restrictions on, Texaco's use of exchange-rate futures contracts. The affidavit concluded: The increasing deterioration of Texaco's credit and financial condition has made it more and more difficult, with each passing day, for Texaco to continue to finance and operate its business.... As normal supply sources become inaccessible and other financing is unavailable, Texaco's operations will begin to grind to a halt. In fact, Texaco is already having to consider the prospect of shutting down one of its largest domestic refineries because of its growing inability to acquire crude and feedstock.*

Indirect costs most difficult to quantify are associated with lost product innovation due to distracted or departing employees. Employees who were once tasked with capital budgeting, project valuation, and R&D are instead consumed with restructuring. Skilled employees concerned about employment longevity and potential pay cuts may be more easily lured by rivals.

These costs vary by industry and firm. Retaining key employees is likely of greatest concern in highly technical industries with substantial R&D such as software or pharmaceuticals. Because costs of distress are a function of asset specificity, industries marked by tangible, readily redeployed, fixed assets are expected to have higher debt capacity (higher optimal levels of debt financing in their capital structure) than those marked by intangible, firm-specific assets.

In a related way, the duration of the good or service provided impacts the risk of lost consumers. Consumers were rationally wary of Oldsmobile after General Motors announced it would discontinue the line. In contrast, consumers of short-lived goods and services such as books, inexpensive children's toys, and hair cuts are less concerned about the going concern of the provider. Industries providing higher cost, longer-term goods and services are subject to greater lost revenue in distress and thus, ceteris paribus, have lower debt capacity.

Expected costs of distress also vary within industries. Specifically, firms that enjoy brand loyalty are less likely to lose customers. Additionally, firms that impose higher switching costs are potentially insulated. For example, passengers remain loyal to particular commercial airlines through bankruptcy due to frequent flier rewards programs. Without such entrenchment, switching carriers rather than risking cancelled flights may have been prudent. Indeed, U.S. Airways cancelled multiple routes during their restructuring, imposing costs of rebooking or flight transfers on customers previously accustomed to direct flights. Competitive advantage of brand loyalty or customer switching cost lowers both the likelihood and expected costs of distress and thus translates into higher debt capacity.

Perhaps size is the greatest firm-level determinant of distress costs. While total costs are higher for larger firms, they are lower as a percentage of firm value. For the largest firms, the expectation of "too big to fail" policies lowers at least the *expected* costs of financial distress. A history of government intervention (early railroad bankruptcies, airlines, the U.S. steel and auto industries, and most recently the financial services sector) may result in the expectation of assistance among large firms. Arguments in favor of government intervention include employment considerations and the potential contagion to counter-parties. Arguments against intervention include the moral hazard problem, wherein firms retain the benefit of risky projects that pay off but share with taxpayers the costs of those that do not. Government intervention remains contentious among academics and politicians, but the expectation of intervention—good or bad—affects perceived costs of distress and thus optimal debt levels.

Predefault Cost of Distress

Existing literature speaks primarily to costs associated with bankruptcy or default. However, Ruback (1984, p. 643) argues that "at least some of the costs of financial distress are likely to be incurred prior to the actual default." Indeed, distress is not best considered a binary state but rather a continuum of financial health. Many firms take actions that have wealth implications for employees, customers, suppliers, creditors, and shareholders long before default or bankruptcy. Airlines cancel undersold flights and entire routes to cut costs in the early stages of distress. Delivery services add extra fuel surcharges. Cash rebates and zero-percent financing were offered not only by bankrupt Chrysler and General Motors but also by Ford, which avoided bankruptcy in 2009. With a sample of 1695 firms filing bankruptcy over the period 1978 to 2004, Hertzel et al. (2008) document substantial wealth effects to these firms, their rivals, customers, and suppliers months before filing bankruptcy.

Financial versus Economic Distress

The 1980s were marked by high-leverage corporate restructuring. The popularity of original-issue, high-yield bonds facilitated the buyouts of many firms including high profile Safeway, Unocal, and R. J. R. Nabisco. These highly levered buyouts (LBOs) resulted in substantial tax savings, but the resulting debt burden led to financial distress including bankruptcy for many. Kaplan and Stein (1993a, 1993b) find that more than 30 percent of management buyouts completed after 1985 later defaulted. An unintended consequence of this spike in Chapter 11 filings was a laboratory to distinguish between the costs of strictly financial distress (associated with suboptimal capital structure) and economic distress (associated with poor product development and marketing, for example).

Wruck (1990) similarly distinguishes between insolvency on a flow basis (inability to meet current cash requirements) and insolvency on a stock basis (where the present value of cash flows is less than the present value of debt obligations). Andrade and Kaplan (1998) distinguish practically by comparing bankruptcies resulting from suboptimal capital structures following highly leveraged transactions (HLT) against other non-HLT bankrupt firms. These authors conclude that the apparently inefficient outcomes of bankruptcy (continued operating losses and subsequent bankruptcies) are largely attributable to economically distressed firms. Andrade and Kaplan estimate the costs of economic distress range from 10 to 20 percent of firm value but find the cost of purely financial distress associated with excessive debt is "negligible." This evidence suggests a need not only to predict distress but also to characterize it.

Denis and Rodgers (2007) report that firms entering bankruptcy with higher operating margins (relative to respective industries) and firms that improve margins during their restructuring emerge successfully and profitably. This finding is important given that 48 percent of their sample emerges unprofitably and 12 percent refile Chapter 11. These results suggest that operating performance metrics are useful indicators of economic viability.

Financial distress and economic distress are not mutually exclusive, but neither is a subset of the other. A firm producing only VHS tapes is likely to be both financially and economically distressed, while a state-of-the-art media technology firm with excessive debt may be considered strictly financially distressed (but economically viable). Firms with too little debt in their capital structures may suffer economic distress (eroding shareholder value), even while meeting current debt obligations. This leads Jensen (1986) to an agency cost argument for debt financing apart from tax implications.

Duration

Both direct and indirect costs increase over time in bankruptcy. Weiss (1990), Franks and Torous (1994), and Hotchkiss (1995) report an average of 2 to 2.5 years from Chapter 11 petition to resolution. But duration in bankruptcy court (and thus cost) is generally declining. Denis and Rodgers (2007) report a median duration of 20 months, and Bharath, Panchapegesan, and Werner (2007) report an average 16 months for firms filing petitions during the period 2000 to 2005.

Denis and Rodgers (2007) analyze factors that influence this duration. They find that firms spend less time in Chapter 11 the smaller they are, the stronger their industries, and the better their prefiling operating performance. This is consistent with the results reported by Heron, Lie, and Rodgers (2009, p. 1) that "firms that reported positive operating income leading up to Chapter 11 emerge faster, suggesting that it is quicker to remedy strictly financial distress than economic distress."

EXTERNAL SOURCES OF FINANCIAL RISK

The substantial operating losses experienced by Eastern Airlines while bankrupt clearly had implications for other firms. Eastern's creditors lost collateral value as the court approved the sale of aircraft to fund operating losses. Competitors suffered price pressure as Eastern sold deeply discounted flights. External sources of financial risk are often referred to as contagion. Lang and Stulz (1992) estimate contagion among rivals and Hertzel et al. (2008) estimate contagion along the supply chain. These authors report negative wealth effects for customers and suppliers to financially distressed firms. These negative wealth effects are worse for suppliers than for customers, suggesting that distress flows upstream. Supplier wealth effects are most negative when intra-industry contagion is most severe. Potential contagion from distressed rivals, customers, and suppliers suggests that appropriate risk management considers potential distress of counter-parties as well as the firm's own capital structure.

RESOLUTION OF DISTRESS

In a frictionless Modigliani and Miller (1958) world, resolution of financial distress is costless. In reality, conflicts of interest among parties with asymmetric information result in a lengthy and costly resolution process that may include formal court proceedings.

Title 11

Title 11 of the U.S. Code, enacted by the Bankruptcy Reform Act of 1978, provides a framework for court-supervised distress resolution. Chapter 7 details procedures for the liquidation of firm assets and Chapter 11 allows for debt- and asset-restructuring for a going concern. Under Chapter 7, the court appoints a trustee to oversee asset sales and distribute proceeds according to absolute priority rule: senior creditors are paid in full before junior creditors receive payment (implying that shareholders generally receive nothing).

Title 11 has historically been held as prodebtor (Bradley and Rosenzweig 1992). Provisions in Chapter 11 designed to continue distressed firms as going concerns favor incumbent management and shareholders. An automatic stay (a moratorium on debt collection and collateral foreclosure) favors debtors in negotiation with prepetition creditors, as does the superpriority of postpetition financing. Section 364 of the Bankruptcy Code (hereafter The Code) grants debtor-in-possession (DIP) lenders superseniority status that effectively negates seniority covenants in original (prepetition) debt. This status clearly reduces the risk to new (postpetition) lenders and encourages marginal loans. Whether this exacerbates overinvestment or mitigates Myers's (1977) underinvestment problem depends on the investment opportunity set of the distressed firm (i.e., whether the firm is economically viable).

Other noteworthy prodebtor features of the Code include the right to convert involuntary Chapter 7 filings into Chapter 11 reorganizations, managers' exclusive right to file restructuring plans for 120 days (plus an additional 60 days to obtain creditor support), and the creditor classification provision requiring only majority (two-thirds by value and one-half in number) assent to confirm management's reorganization plans, which often violate absolute priority rules (APR). The interpretation of the Code appears to vary among districts and perhaps also among judges. LoPucki and Whitford (1991) document routine extension of incumbent managers' exclusive right to file reorganization plans and forum shopping for judges believed to favor debtors. The priority of claims is violated in an overwhelming majority of cases studied by Franks and Torous (1989); Eberhart, Moore, and Roenfeldt (1990); and Weiss (1990). Because the sample of firms with APR violation is large, Cornaggia, Simin, and Upneja (2009) provide a robust model for predicting priority violation. In the remarkable case of Eastern Airlines, Weis and Wruck (1998) document court-sponsored asset stripping where firms sold creditor collateral to fund operating losses. Evidence from larger samples also suggests a system bent towards the continuation of nonviable firms (Hotchkiss 1995; Denis and Rodgers 2007).

The prodebtor nature of Chapter 11 (as opposed to more creditor-oriented bankruptcy laws of the United Kingdom) should, ceteris paribus, result in higher debt ratios in U.S. firms. However, the Bankruptcy Abuse Prevention and Consumer Protection Act (BAPCPA) of 2005 curbed the prodebtor nature to some extent. New rules limit the discretion of judges to extend the exclusivity period to 18 months, limit automatic stay for repeat filers, restrict managerial retention bonuses and severance packages, and reduce the flexibility of bankrupt firms to put leased assets back to lessors. Apparently, this new regime may also adhere more strictly to the notion of absolute priority (Bris et al. 2006; Bharath, Panchapegesan, and Werner 2007). To the extent that a prodebtor system favoring incumbent management and shareholders resulted in higher debt ratios, this trend might be expected to reverse under more creditor-oriented rules.

Private Workouts

Many firms resolve financial distress without filing formal bankruptcy petitions. Of 169 distressed public U.S companies studied by Gilson, John, and Lang (1990), 80 successfully restructured outside of court and 89 filed Chapter 11. These proportions are similar to those reported later by Franks and Torous (1994). Private workouts appear less costly than formal bankruptcy (Betker 1997; Gilson, John, and Lang 1990). However, this finding is at least partially attributable to a sample selection issue. As Heron, Lie, and Rodgers (2009) report, financial distress is resolved more readily than economic distress in bankruptcy court. Intuitively, economically viable firms with suboptimal capital structures are better able to privately renegotiate the terms of their debt, leaving nonviable firms to file for the court's protection from creditor-forced liquidation. Consistent with this explanation, Franks and Torous find the firms able to complete successful private workouts are more solvent, liquid, and have less negative stock returns before restructuring than firms filing Chapter 11. Likewise, Chatterjee, Dhillon, and Ramirez (1995) find the firms successfully restructuring out of court have stronger operating performance than those filing Chapter 11.

Even among viable firms, impediments to successful workouts reflect asymmetric information (between managers and creditors) and conflicts of interest among classes of claimants (shareholders and creditors) and managers. Even when all creditors are better off with restructured claims (as opposed to lower recovery rates from fire sale liquidation), individual creditors are better off holding out for full and timely payment while other creditors restructure (Grossman and Hart 1981).

The LTV bankruptcy apparently exacerbated this holdout problem. After the private workout proved insufficient, the firm filed bankruptcy. Creditors who cooperated with the private workout lost out in bankruptcy court. The court ruled that bondholders who participated in the early exchange could claim only market value while holdouts could claim full face value. Tashjian, Lease, and McConnell (1996) suggest that this ruling gave rise to the boom in prepackaged bankruptcies (prepacks), where managers negotiate with key creditors outside of court. The pre-approved reorganization plan is then filed simultaneously with the Chapter 11 petition. The lower costs of private workouts are combined with the Chapter 11 solution to the holdout problem (grouping creditors into classes and requiring only majority acceptance by class). The court overturned the controversial ruling in the LTV case, but the prepackaged bankruptcy remains popular. Baird and Rasmussen (2003) report that one-quarter of their 2002 sample of bankruptcies were prepacks.

Not all firms can achieve the private restructuring required for prepacks. Firms with more complicated debt structures may find creditor coordination difficult (Gertner and Scharfstein 1991). For such firms, the costly option of hiring an investment bank as an intermediary in the exchange offer appears expedient (Mooradian and Ryan 2005).

Debt Restructuring

Once in bankruptcy court, prepetition claims are classified based on priority and maturity. Reorganization plans reallocate claims, specifying what each class receives in exchange for prepetition claims. Delayed interest, lengthened maturity to principal repayment, and unilateral write-down of principal are all common. In many cases, senior claims in the prepetition firm are exchanged for subordinated claims in the restructured firm. Indeed, some forgiveness of debt is required in order to meet the expectations of the Code that only plans resulting in firms unlikely to require subsequent bankruptcy should be confirmed by the court.

Roe (1983) and Bebchuk (1988) argue that the Chapter 11 process imposes barriers to reducing debt and thus needs reform. Alternatively, Alderson and Betker (1995, p. 47) contend that the choice of capital structure for firms emerging from Chapter 11 is "free of the holdout and hidden information problems that might otherwise restrict a complete capital structure rearrangement." Gilson's (1997, p. 163) empirical study concludes that "transaction costs do not appear to be a major deterrent to reducing debt in Chapter 11." His results suggest that post-restructuring debt ratios are unrelated to pre-restructuring debt ratios and that a new capital structure is completely re-established. However, Gilson employs a small sample of 51 reorganizations and the number of observations in his regressions ranges from 14 to 42. Heron, Lie, and Rodgers (2009) examine a larger and more recent sample of 172 firms that emerged from Chapter 11 after 1990 under "fresh-start" accounting rules. These authors find that firms generally do not fully reset their capital structures in line with industry-based expectations. Rather, higher-than-optimal debt ratios appear "sticky." Firms emerge with more debt than suggested by their comparative industry counterparts. This finding is consistent with critics' contention that inefficiencies in the Chapter 11 process inhibit complete restructuring.

The results of Heron, Lie, and Rodgers (2009) are also consistent with a clientele effect. Certain pre-investors preferred fixed income claims before bankruptcy and are similarly reluctant to hold residual claims thereafter. This preference may reflect investor tax or income status or regulatory requirements. For example, while federal and state banking laws permit U.S. banks to take equity claims when restructuring nonperforming loans, regulators base capital requirements for banks and insurance companies on the financial risk of their assets.

In practice, Asquith, Gertner, and Scharfstein (1994) report that banks waive covenants but rarely reduce principal. James (1995) also reports that banks are reluctant to make concessions. In his sample of 102 distressed restructurings, only 31 percent of deals result in banks taking equity. Given relatively illiquid markets for equity claims on emerging firms, prepetition creditors may rationally prefer a fixed income claim on a firm with a suboptimal capital structure.

Kahl (2002) views repeated Chapter 11 filings as part of a creditor-controlled dynamic liquidation process. As an old adage suggests: Borrow $1,000 and you have a creditor; borrow $1,000,000 and you have a partner. Kahl contends that while economic viability remains uncertain, creditors have an incentive to allow the going concern (as opposed to forcing liquidation) but allow managers limited discretion. The "short rope" Kahl suggests is short-term debt, which allows creditors to monitor progress and force liquidation if operations do not return to positive profitability.

Asset Restructuring

In addition to debt restructuring, many reorganization plans require asset sales. Before Chapter 11, a firm can liquidate tangible assets in order to generate cash to meet current obligations and avoid bankruptcy (Asquith, Gertner, and Scharfstein 1994). Lang, Poulsen, and Stulz (1995) document asset sales following poor stock performance before bankruptcy. Once a Chapter 11 petition is filed, the automatic stay (interest and principal moratorium) should enable firms to make only strategic divestitures. Yet, firms continue to divest (Hotchkiss 1995; Denis and Rodgers 2007). The answer to the question of whether to sell assets (and which assets to sell) is ultimately a function of market value. Strategically, the firm may want to divest their least profitable assets, but these assets generate the least cash. By "selling crown jewels," firms may generate more cash but then restructure around underperforming assets.

Shleifer and Vishny (1992) argue that the market value of distressed assets may be extraordinarily depressed if the distress is industry-wide. When higher-value users are cash constrained, firms must entertain bids by lower-value users. But when the distress catalyst is idiosyncratic, industry rivals may offer higher bids. Industry organization is crucial in this matter. Competitive industries with multiple well-capitalized players bid against one another while industries comprised of fewer players result in lower bids. Denis and Rodgers (2007) characterize weak players in both strong and weak industries and report, not surprisingly, that weak players suffer most in weak industries. Consistent with this result, Pulvino

(1998) documents fire sales of distressed assets in a distressed industry (commercial airlines).

Once in bankruptcy court, Denis and Rodgers (2007) find that firms are more likely to emerge as going concerns and achieve positive profitability if they significantly reduce assets in Chapter 11. These results are consistent with those of Maksimovic and Phillips (1998), who report that bankrupt firms in growth industries are better able to sell assets than those in declining industries and the productivity of such assets increases under new management (but only in higher-growth industries).

Conflicts of Interest and Managerial Incentives

The negotiation-based Chapter 11 process exacerbates conflicts of interest (Wruck 1990). Because the residual claim on a distressed firm is essentially an option, shareholders of financially distressed firms prefer increasingly risky (possibly negative net present value (NPV)) investments that afford them (unlimited if unlikely) upside potential, while creditors bear the increased risk. In contrast, creditors prefer relatively safe (or no) marginal investment. Thus, distressed firms face simultaneously an overinvestment problem (funding risky negative NPV investment) and an underinvestment problem (passing on relatively safe positive NPV investment) associated with what Myers (1977) refers to as a debt overhang.

Certain prodebtor features of Title 11 (the automatic stay, exclusive right to file reorganization plans, creditor voting classification, and superpriority of DIP financing) influence the balance of negotiating power. Other important factors include Section 382 limitations, which significantly limit (and possibly eliminate) tax breaks associated with net operating loss carry-forwards (NOLC), given an ownership change within two years of emergence. For many distressed firms, NOLC are valuable assets but are lost when prebankruptcy shareholders lose control. Furthermore, beginning in 1990, "fresh start" accounting rules apply when reorganizations result in the transfer of 50 percent or more of prebankruptcy ownership. Heron, Lie, and Rodgers (2009) provide a detailed explanation of fresh start accounting. These features of the Code enable incumbent management to retain value for prebankruptcy shareholders. LoPucki and Doherty (2004) contend that venue choice also plays an important role.

Historically, APR violation (where prebankruptcy shareholders retain claims in the reorganized firm) was the rule. Eberhart, Moore, and Roenfeldt (1990), Weiss (1990), and Franks and Torous (1989) report APR violations in about 75 percent of cases. Betker (1995) reports that violations reflect nontrivial sums: Shareholders received, on average, 2.86 percent of the postbankruptcy assets. This is approximately equal to the direct costs of bankruptcy reported by both Weiss and Betker. However, this evidence does not necessarily suggest inefficiency in the Chapter 11 process. In the model of Gertner and Scharfstein (1991), deviations from APR increase value by increasing investment in financially distressed firms facing Myers's (1997) underinvestment problem. Whether or not increased investment enhances value, the evidence of Bharath, Panchapegesan, and Werner (2007) suggests that APR violations have become less routine. With a large sample of firms filing bankruptcy in the period 1991 to 2005, these authors find that 26 percent of cases in the 1990s violated APR, while only 9 percent did so in the years 2000 to 2005.

When firms are solvent, managers have a fiduciary duty to shareholders, who favor riskier marginal investment once the firm is "under water" (Wruck 1990). However, those concerned with employment longevity may become increasingly risk averse as the firm's financial health deteriorates. Eckbo and Thorburn (2003) make a similar argument. Additionally, Bradley and Rosenzweig (1992) make a compelling argument that Chapter 11 shields incompetent management from forced turnover. Anecdotal evidence, including the infamous Eastern Airlines case documented by Weiss and Wruck (1998), supports their claim. However, a host of empirical papers suggests that incumbent management is rationally concerned about future employment prospects. Gilson (1989) reports that 49 of 69 bankrupt firms in his sample turn over the chief executive officer (CEO), chairman, and/or president in the four-year period around the Chapter 11 filing. Moreover, he reports that none of these replaced executives is employed by another publicly-traded firm in the United States within the three-year window following termination. Later papers indicate similar or higher rates of turnover among CEOs (Betker1995; Ayotte and Morrison 2007). Should CEOs retain their positions, they are likely to face substantial pay cuts (Gilson and Vetsuypens 1993).

Once the firm approaches default, Aghion, Hart, and Moore (1992) suggest that fear of termination in bankruptcy perversely leads managers to increasingly risky negative NPV projects. This incentive is perverse as it coincides with the shift in fiduciary duty from prebankruptcy shareholders (ex-ante ownership) to prebankruptcy creditors (ex-post ownership) (Branch 2000). In any case, managers interested in preserving their jobs rationally seek to continue operations, even if liquidation (or an acquisition by a more efficient management team) is more efficient. Thus, the opposing perspectives of creditors and shareholders are in addition to the conflict of interest between management (agent) and residual claimants (principal).

One way in which creditors (residual claimants in the newly restructured firm) may combat perverse managerial incentives is through Key Employee Retention Programs (KERP). Such plans pay substantial bonuses to executives and employees perceived to be especially valuable to the firm in order to combat lucrative (and less uncertain) employment opportunities elsewhere. The results of Bharath, Panchapegesan, and Werner (2007) show a simultaneous increase in KERP over the period of decline in APR. One (perhaps cynical) interpretation of these results is that creditors can more cheaply "buy off" managers directly, rather than appeasing an entire class of shareholders through APR violations. Because the 2005 amendments to Title 11 now severely limit the use of KERP, one might expect a resulting increase in APR back to earlier levels. Should this prove to be the case, the model of Cornaggia, Simin, and Upneja (2009) should be especially useful to investors in distressed equity.

Success

Are distressed reorganization attempts successful? The evidence here is mixed and open to interpretation. Most attempts to restructure debt out-of-court fail to avoid bankruptcy (Gilson et al. 1990; Franks and Torous 1994). But even the "failed" negotiations may save time and money in Chapter 11. One definition of a successful Chapter 11 filing is emergence as a going concern, which reflects half of the sample employed by Denis and Rodgers (2007). Weiss (1990); LoPucki and Whitford (1993); Bris, Welch, and Zhu (2006); and Kalay, Singhal, and Tashjian (2007) provide similar evidence on Chapter 11 outcomes. However, firms emerging with suboptimal capital structure, reporting continued operating losses, and subsequent restructuring—including subsequent Chapter 11 petitions—call this definition of success into question. For example, 49 percent of the emerging firms in Denis and Rodgers' sample experience operating losses in the first two years after emergence, and 18 percent subsequently restructure, refile Chapter 11, and/or liquidate. Only 43 percent of emerging firms, which is 22 percent of filing firms, exist as an independent-going concern three years post-emergence, do not require subsequent reorganization over that period, and exhibit positive operating margin in at least two of three years following reorganization. Under this definition of success, 78 percent of Chapter 11 filings fail. To place this ultimate cost of distress in perspective, these firms (with consistent negative operating income) are characterized as economically distressed (Wruck 1990; Andrade and Kaplan 1998). Financially distressed firms that are more clearly economically viable are among those successful with private workouts or Chapter 11 reorganizations.

SUMMARY AND CONCLUSIONS

The static trade-off theory suggests a balance between benefits and costs of debt financing. Tax savings from interest payments are quantifiable, as are the likelihood and expected costs of financial distress and bankruptcy. A host of empirical studies suggests that these costs are significant and thus optimizing capital structure requires a thorough understanding of factors influencing both the likelihood and the expected costs of distress. These factors include product type, industry concentration, and ease of asset redeployment. Beyond the factors specific to the firm, careful consideration of financial health of rivals, customers, suppliers, and other counter-parties is essential given evidence of contagion within industries and along the supply chain. There are several methods for gauging financial risk including credit ratings, traditional accounting-based bankruptcy prediction models, Merton-style structural models, and proprietary risk metrics from the growing set of firms providing independent credit analysis. The increasing use of off-balance-sheet financing is an important consideration when employing any risk metrics that rely on balance sheets and income statements.

Financial distress is often resolved through private exchange offers. However, in many cases with complex debt structures and/or economic distress, private workouts fail and firms result to formal bankruptcy. The notion of success in Chapter 11 remains a matter of academic debate. Many firms do not emerge, and among emerging firms many experience continued operating losses and require further distressed restructuring. The bias toward the continuation of such firms leads many to contend that the U.S. Bankruptcy Code is inefficiently prodebtor. Others contend that failure in Chapter 11 is a reflection of economically distressed firms who cannot achieve a private workout rather than of the process itself. In any case, amendments to the U.S. Bankruptcy Code in 2005 impose limits on certain prodebtor features of the Code that favor incumbent management and shareholders. Changes in these features impact the ex-ante costs to shareholders of potential default and thus affect the use of debt financing. Recent bailouts of firms considered "too big to fail" similarly influence the ex-ante trade-off between the benefits of debt (which accrue to shareholders in real time) and the perceived costs (which, if incurred at all, are borne also by taxpayers) of such firms.

DISCUSSION QUESTIONS

1. Why has Chapter 11 historically been characterized as "prodebtor"? How might the amendments to the U.S. Bankruptcy Code in 2005 alter this characterization?
2. Explain the conflicts of interest among stakeholders in a financially distressed firm and how these conflicts potentially destroy firm value.
3. Explain the importance of considering the financial risk of rivals, customers, suppliers, and other counter-parties. What evidence suggests these considerations are material?
4. Explain the impact of "too big to fail" and similar bailout policies on the optimal capital structure, ex-ante.

REFERENCES

Aghion, Philippe, Oliver Hart, and John Moore. 1992. "The Economics of Bankruptcy Reform." *Journal of Law, Economics and Organization* 8:3, 523–546.

Alderson, Michael J., and Brian L. Betker. 1995. "Liquidation Costs and Capital Structure." *Journal of Financial Economics* 39:1, 45–69.

Altman, Edward I. 1968. "Financial Ratios, Discriminant Analysis and the Prediction of Corporate Bankruptcy." *Journal of Finance* 23:4, 589–609.

Altman, Edward I. 1984. "A Further Empirical Investigation of the Bankruptcy Cost Question." *Journal of Finance* 39:4, 1067–1089.

Andrade, Gregor, and Steven N. Kaplan. 1998. "How Costly Is Financial (not Economic) Distress? Evidence from Highly Leveraged Transactions that Became Distressed." *Journal of Finance* 53:5, 1443–1493.

Asquith, Paul, Robert Gertner, and David Scharfstein. 1994. "Anatomy of Financial Distress: An Examination of Junk Bond Issuers." *Quarterly Journal of Economics* 109:3, 625–658.

Ayotte, Kenneth M., and Edward R. Morrison. 2007. "Creditor Control and Conflict in Chapter 11." Working Paper, Columbia Law School.

Baird, Douglas G., and Robert K. Rasmussen. 2003. "Chapter 11 at Twilight." *Stanford Law Review* 56:3, 673–699.

Bebchuk, Lucian A. 1988. "A New Approach to Corporate Reorganization." *Harvard Law Review* 101:4, 775–804.

Betker, Brian L. 1995. "Management's Incentives, Equity's Bargaining Power, and Deviations from Absolute Priority in Chapter 11 Bankruptcies." *Journal of Business* 68:2, 161–183.

Betker, Brian L. 1997. "The Administrative Costs of Debt Restructurings: Some Recent Evidence." *Financial Management* 26:4, 56–68.

Bharath, Sreedar T., Venky Panchapegesan, and Ingrid Werner. 2007. "The Changing Nature of Chapter 11." Working Paper, University of Michigan.

Black, Fischer, and Myron Scholes. 1973. "The Pricing of Options and Corporate Liabilities." *Journal of Political Economy* 81:3, 637–659.

Bradley, Michael, and Michael Rosenzweig. 1992. "The Untenable Case for Chapter 11." *Yale Law Journal* 101:5, 1043–1095.

Branch, Ben S. 2000. "Fiduciary Duty: Shareholders versus Creditors." *Financial Practice and Education* 10:2, 8–13.

Bris, Arturo, Ivo Welch, and Ning Zhu. 2006. "The Costs of Bankruptcy: Chapter 7 Liquidation versus Chapter 11 Reorganization." *Journal of Finance* 61:3, 1253–1303.

Chatterjee, Sris, Upinder S. Dhillon, and Gabriel G. Ramirez. 1995. "Coercive Tender and Exchange Offers in Distressed High-Yield Debt Restructurings: An Empirical Analysis." *Journal of Financial Economics* 38:3, 333–360.

Cornaggia, Kimberly. J., Laurel A. Franzen, and Timothy T. Simin. 2010. "Manipulating the Balance Sheet? Implications of Off-Balance-Sheet Financing." Working Paper, Pennsylvania State University.

Coval, Joshua, Jakub Jurek, and Erik Stafford. 2009. "The Economics of Structured Finance." *Journal of Economic Perspectives* 23:1, 3–25.

Cutler, David M., and Lawrence H. Summers. 1988. "The Costs of Conflict Resolution and Financial Distress: Evidence from the Texaco-Pennzoil Litigation." *Rand Journal of Economics* 19:2, 157–172.

Denis, Diane K., and Kimberly J. Rodgers. 2007. "Chapter 11: Duration, Outcome and Post-Reorganization Performance." *Journal of Financial and Quantitative Analysis* 42:1, 101–118.

Eberhart Allan C., William T. Moore, and Rodney L. Roenfeldt. 1990. "Security Pricing and Deviations from the Absolute Priority Rule in Bankruptcy Proceedings." *Journal of Finance* 45:5, 1457–1469.

Eckbo, B. Espen, and Karin S. Thorburn. 2003. "Control Benefits and CEO Discipline in Automatic Bankruptcy Auctions." *Journal of Financial Economics* 69:1, 227–258.

Franks, Julian R., and Walter N. Torous. 1989. "An Empirical Investigation of U.S. Firms in Reorganization." *Journal of Finance* 44:3, 747–769.

Franks, Julian R, and Walter N. Torous. 1994. "A Comparison of Financial Recontracting in Distressed Exchanges and Chapter 11 Reorganizations." *Journal of Financial Economics* 35:3, 349–370.

Franzen, Laurel A., Kimberly J. Rodgers, and Timothy T. Simin. 2007. "Measuring Distress Risk: The Effect of R&D Intensity." *Journal of Finance* 62:2, 2931–2967.

Gertner, Robert, and David Scharfstein. 1991. "A Theory of Workouts and the Effects of Reorganization Law." *Journal of Finance* 46:4, 1189–1222.

Gilson, Stuart C. 1989. "Management Turnover and Financial Distress." *Journal of Financial Economics* 25:2, 241–262.

Gilson, Stuart C. 1997. "Transactions Costs and Capital Structure Choice: Evidence from Financially Distressed Firms." *Journal of Finance* 52:1, 161–196.

Gilson, Stuart C., Kose John, and Larry H. P. Lang. 1990. "Troubled Debt Restructurings: An Empirical Study of Private Reorganization of Firms in Default." *Journal of Financial Economics* 27:2, 315–353.

Gilson, Stuart C., and Michael R. Vetsuypens. 1993. "CEO Compensation in Financially Distressed Firms: An Empirical Analysis." *Journal of Finance* 48:2, 425–458.

Grossman, Sanford J., and Oliver D. Hart. 1981. "The Allocational Role of Takeover Bids in Situations of Asymmetric Information." *Journal of Finance* 36:2, 253–270.

Heron, Randall A., Erik Lie, and Kimberly J. Rodgers. 2009. "Financial Restructuring in Fresh Start Chapter 11 Reorganizations." *Financial Management* 38:4, 727–745.

Hertzel, Michael G., Zhi Li, Micah S. Officer, and Kimberly J. Rodgers. 2008. "Inter-Firm Linkages and the Wealth Effects of Financial Distress along the Supply Chain." *Journal of Financial Economics* 87:2, 374–387.

Hillegeist, Stephen A., Elizabeth K. Keating, Donald P. Cram, and Kyle G. Lundstedt. 2004. "Assessing the Probability of Bankruptcy." *Review of Accounting Studies* 9:1: 5–34.

Hotchkiss, Edith S. 1995. "Postbankruptcy Performance and Management Turnover." *Journal of Finance* 50:1, 3–21.

James, Christopher. 1995. "When Do Banks Take Equity in Debt Restructurings?" *Review of Financial Studies* 8:4, 1209–1234.

Jensen, Michael C. 1986. "Agency Costs of Free Cash Flow, Corporate Finance, and Takeovers." *American Economic Review* 76:2, 323–329.
Jensen, Michael C. 1991. "Corporate Control and the Politics of Finance." *Journal of Applied Corporate Finance* 4:2, 13–33.
Kahl, Matthias. 2002. "Economic Distress, Financial Distress, and Dynamic Liquidation." *Journal of Finance* 57:1, 135–168.
Kalay, Avner, Rajeev Singhal, and Elizabeth Tashjian. 2007. "Is Chapter 11 Costly?" *Journal of Financial Economics* 84:3, 772–796.
Kaplan, Steven, and Jeremy Stein. 1993a. "The Evolution of Buyout Pricing and Financial Structure in the 1980s." *Quarterly Journal of Economics* 108:2, 313–358.
Kaplan, Steven, and Jeremy Stein. 1993b. "The Evolution of Buyout Pricing and Financial Structure (or What Went Wrong) in the 1980s." *Journal of Applied Corporate Finance* 6:1, 72–88.
Kim, Joon, Krishna Ramaswamy, and Suresh Sunderasan. 1993. "Does Default Risk in Coupons Affect the Valuation of Corporate Bonds? A Contingent Claims Model." *Financial Management* 22:3, 117–131.
Lang, Larry, Annette Poulsen, and René Stulz. 1995. "Asset Sales, Firm Performance, and the Agency Costs of Managerial Discretion." *Journal of Financial Economics* 37:1, 3–37.
Lang, Larry H. P., and René M. Stulz. 1992. "Contagion and Competitive Intra-Industry Effects of Bankruptcy Announcements: An Empirical Analysis." *Journal of Financial Economics* 32:1, 45–60.
LoPucki, Lynn M., and Joseph W. Doherty. 2004. "The Determinants of Professional Fees in Large Bankruptcy Reorganization Cases." *Journal of Empirical Legal Studies* 1:1, 111–141.
LoPucki, Lynn M., and William C. Whitford. 1991. "Venue Choice and Forum Shopping in the Bankruptcy Reorganization of Large Publicly Held Companies." *Wisconsin Law Review*, 11–63.
LoPucki, Lynn M., and William C. Whitford. 1993. "Patterns in the Bankruptcy Reorganization of Large, Publicly Held Companies." *Cornell Law Review* 78:4, 597–618.
Lubben, Stephen J. 2000. "The Direct Costs of Corporate Reorganization: An Empirical Examination of Professional Fees in Large Chapter 11 Cases." *American Bankruptcy Law Journal* 74:4, 509–552.
Maksimovic, Vojislav, and Gordon. M. Phillips. 1998. "Asset Efficiency and the Reallocation Decisions of Bankrupt Firms." *Journal of Finance* 53:5, 1495–1532.
Merton, Robert C. 1974. "On the Pricing of Corporate Debt: The Risk Structure of Interest Rates." *Journal of Finance* 29:2, 449–470.
Modigliani, Franco, and Merton H. Miller. 1958. "The Cost of Capital, Corporation Finance, and the Theory of Investment." *American Economic Review* 48:3, 261–297.
Modigliani, Franco, and Merton Miller. 1963, "Corporation Income Taxes and the Cost of Capital: A Correction." *American Economic Review* 53:3, 433–443.
Mooradian, Robert M., and Harley E. Ryan, Jr. 2005. "Out-of-Court Restructurings and the Resolution of Financial Distress: Section 3(a)(9) Compared to Investment-Bank-Managed Exchange Offers." *Journal of Business* 78:4, 1593–1624.
Myers, Stewart C. 1977. "Determinants of Corporate Borrowing." *Journal of Financial Economics* 5:2, 147–175
Ohlson, James A. 1980. "Financial Ratios and the Probabilistic Prediction of Bankruptcy." *Journal of Accounting Research* 18:1, 109–131.
Pulvino, Todd C. 1998. "Do Asset Fire Sales Exist? An Empirical Investigation of Commercial Aircraft Transactions." *Journal of Finance* 53:3, 939–978.
Cornaggia, Kimberly J., Timothy T. Simin, and Arun Upneja. 2009. "Role of Deviations from Absolute Priority Regulations in Equity Valuation at Bankruptcy Filing." Working Paper, Pennsylvania State University.

Roe, Mark J. 1983. "Bankruptcy and Debt: A New Model for Corporate Reorganization." *Columbia Law Review* 83:3, 527–602.
Ruback, Richard. 1984. "Estimation of Implicit Bankruptcy Costs: Discussion." *Journal of Finance* 39:3, 643–645.
Shleifer, Andrei, and Robert W. Vishny. 1992. "Liquidation Values and Debt Capacity: A Market Equilibrium Approach." *Journal of Finance* 47:4, 1343–1366.
Shumway, Tyler. 2001. "Forecasting Bankruptcy More Accurately: A Simple Hazard Model." *Journal of Business* 74:1, 101–124.
Stein, Roger M. 2005. "Evidence on the Incompleteness of Merton-Type Structural Models for Default Prediction." Technical Report 1-2-1-2000. New York: Moody's KMV.
Tashjian, Elizabeth, Ronald C. Lease, and John J. McConnell. 1996. "Prepacks: An Empirical Analysis of Prepackaged Bankruptcies." *Journal of Financial Economics* 40:1, 135–162.
Vassalou, Maria, and Yuhang Xing. 2004. "Default Risk in Equity Returns." *Journal of Finance* 59:2, 831–868.
Warner, Jerold B. 1977. "Bankruptcy Costs: Some Evidence." *Journal of Finance* 32:2, 337–347.
Weiss, Lawrence A. 1990. "Bankruptcy Costs and Violation of Claims Priority." *Journal of Financial Economics* 27:2, 285–314.
Weiss, Lawrence A., and Karen H. Wruck. 1998. "Information Problems, Conflicts of Interest, and Asset Stripping: Chapter 11's Failure in the Case of Eastern Airlines." *Journal of Financial Economics* 48:1, 55–97.
Wruck, Karen Hopper. 1990. "Financial Distress, Reorganization, and Organizational Efficiency." *Journal of Financial Economics* 27:2, 419–444.

ABOUT THE AUTHOR

Kimberly J. Cornaggia is an Associate Professor of Finance at the Kogod School of Business at American University. Professor Cornaggia's primary research interests include financial distress, corporate bankruptcy, capital structure, and credit ratings. Her work has been published in the *Journal of Finance*, *Journal of Financial Economics*, *Journal of Financial and Quantitative Analysis*, and *Financial Management* and has won various recognitions including the Fama–DFA Prize for Best Paper published in the *JFE*. Professor Cornaggia earned her PhD in finance from the Krannert Graduate School at Purdue University in 2000, joined the Smeal College of Business faculty at the Pennsylvania State University, and later taught at the Stern School of Business at New York University. She has taught a wide array of courses to graduate students including corporation finance, corporate restructuring, equity valuation, and capital markets. She joined the Office of Economic Analysis (OEA) at the U.S. Securities and Exchange Commission in 2003, and later in 2007, to study the credit ratings industry. Professor Cornaggia continues to provide OEA with periodic assistance on this topic.

CHAPTER 21

Fiduciary Responsibility and Financial Distress

REMUS D. VALSAN
Doctor of Civil Law Candidate, Faculty of Law, McGill University

MOIN A. YAHYA
Associate Professor of Law, University of Alberta

INTRODUCTION

The field of corporate finance has much to offer to corporate law. One such area is the doctrine of fiduciary duties. In the context of corporate law, there are four players: shareholders, creditors, directors, and managers. This chapter examines the role financial distress can play involving the fiduciary duties owed by some of these parties to others.

Consider the following scenario. A firm is on the verge of insolvency with little cash left on hand. The directors, or the managers, of the firm may be tempted to invest the cash in a very risky venture in the hopes of generating a large return. If the investment pays off, the corporation is rescued, and everyone is happy. If the investment does not yield the desired payoffs, the corporation goes bankrupt. While the shareholders have no returns, they would not have had any returns if no action were taken, as the firm was on the verge of bankruptcy. Similarly, the directors and managers are no worse off now than before. The creditors, on the other hand, may be worse off as very little cash may be left to satisfy their claims due to the high-risk nature of the last investment.

This scenario initially suggests that the law ought to prevent the directors from instigating risky investments when a firm is close to insolvency. The law that would most likely proscribe such risky behavior is the law of fiduciary duties. Indeed, several cases in the United States, Canada, and other countries suggest this proscription, while other cases do not impose any prohibitions. These cases in the United States and Canada have sparked a heated debate about the fiduciary duties of directors to creditors, especially in the "vicinity of insolvency." The concern regarding directors and creditors is sometimes summarized as follows. Since shareholders elect the directors, the directors are beholden to the shareholders. When the firm is in the vicinity of insolvency, the shareholders would prefer that directors engage in risky projects that have a large upside potential much to the chagrin of creditors who would rather the directors engage in less-risky activities so that they may recover some of their principal. Hence, the courts have expressed concern that directors may sometimes gamble away creditors' money.

The scenario was numerically illustrated in the seminal Delaware Court of Chancery decision in *Credit Lyonnais Bank Nederland, N.V. v. Pathe Comm. Corp.*, 1991 WL 277613 (Del. Ch. 1991). A simplified version of the example is as follows. Consider a corporation that is funded by $50 million of debt. The firm can invest in one project that pays $100 million or $0 with equal probability or another project that pays $25 million or $75 million with equal probability. Shareholders would prefer the first project because they have an expected payoff of $25 million in contrast with $12.5 million in the second project. Creditors, on the other hand, would prefer the second as they have an expected payoff of $37.5 million as opposed to $25 million in the first.

The question is, therefore, should the law direct the board of directors, acting in the interest of shareholders, to choose one of the two projects? This chapter argues that there is no need for such a legal intervention (Valsan and Yahya 2007). The board of directors should continue to invest in projects that increase the firm's value, leaving the corporate constituencies to look after their own specific interests. The remainder of the chapter has the following organization. The first part analyzes several economic and financial principles that explain and contrast the interests of the corporation with those of the corporate constituencies. The second part discusses the solutions adopted by various courts regarding the duties of corporate managers in financial distress. The last part integrates the economic principles with the dominant judicial approach to show that increasing the firm's value should remain the managers' focus when the firm becomes financially troubled.

FIVE BACKGROUND ECONOMIC PRINCIPLES

Many scholars and numerous court decisions argue that the managers' purpose is to look after the best interests of the firm. Regrettably, some of these opinions are beset with confusion between the interests of the corporation and those of the stakeholders. This section appeals to several economic principles to demonstrate that the corporation has a distinct economic interest that can be furthered by directors without investigating stakeholders' particular expectations. Furthermore, the section shows acting in the best interests of the firm effectively meets the economic interests of corporate constituencies and, therefore, aligns such interests with those of the firm itself.

The Law and Economics of Fiduciary Duties

The association between directors and managers, on the one hand, and corporation, on the other, is a fiduciary relationship. A fiduciary relationship usually arises when one party (the fiduciary) enters into a relationship with another party where the fiduciary has some degree of control or superiority in information or position over the second party. Such a relationship requires the highest duties of care, good faith, candor, and loyalty from the fiduciary. The terms of the relationship are dictated primarily by law and not by contract.

The historical legal origins of these duties are instructive. Imagine that, in his will, a dying father, with a very young son unable to provide for himself, leaves his assets to his brother, and asks that he use the assets to provide for his son. The brother, or the son's uncle, however, has different plans, as he wants to consume the assets. Through a variety of mechanisms, such as equity, trusts, and liens, the law imposed "fiduciary duties" on the uncle towards his nephew. The uncle could no longer do with the assets as he wished. Rather, he owed the nephew a duty of loyalty and had to exercise his best judgment in looking after the assets for the nephew's benefit.

Sometimes contracts, or at least the way the contract law is enforced, cannot achieve certain privately and socially desirable outcomes. The law imposes certain duties in order to protect the rights of certain parties that may not have the ability to adequately contract themselves. It is the equivalent to imposing the result of a hypothetical bargain on parties had they had the ability to properly negotiate the contract in the first place (Coase 1960; Cooter and Freeman 1991).

In the case of the young son, the rationale for why the law would impose such duties on the uncle is obvious. But the law also imposes such duties on lawyers to their clients, doctors to their patients, and directors and managers to the corporation and, maybe even the shareholders and creditors. One argument for these duties is increased transaction costs. These costs may preclude the parties to conclude a complete contract that would address every contingency that may occur and every action that may be feasible in any possible situation. Stated differently, the high transaction costs and the bounded rationality of the parties cause the contracts between the firm and stakeholders to be incomplete.

These fiduciary duties entail both positive and negative duties. Directors have an obligation to avoid conflicts of interest and not to compete with the corporation, engage in self-dealing, usurp the firm's opportunities, and disclose confidential information. Directors also have the obligation to act in the best interests of the corporation (and possibly shareholders and creditors).

The Firm as a Black Box: A Coasean Perspective

Starting with Coase (1937), economists have viewed a corporation as a nexus of contracts, which offers a more efficient alternative for various stakeholders to pursue their economic activities. This extends to creditors and shareholders as well (Jensen and Meckling 1976; Bainbridge 2002; Klein and Coffee 2004). The corporation is neither an entity nor something capable of being owned. Rather, the firm is a network of both explicit and implicit contracts among various suppliers of inputs acting together to produce goods or to provide services.

These contracts comprise the details of the claims of various parties over the assets of the firm. If the corporation is regarded as a collection of claims over a universality of assets, the particular features of this universality, such as limited liability, differentiate this "nexus" from a regular network of contracts between various persons. In the corporate setting, however, many of the "nexus" stakeholders do not contract directly with each other. If they could efficiently and costlessly do so, the resources generated by the business would be allocated in the most efficient way and identifying the purpose of fiduciary duties would be pointless.

The constituencies contract directly with the corporation and have claims against the corporation, rather than against each other. Therefore, the corporation can be pictured as a "black box" that receives the inputs of various constituencies and produces the expected outputs. The existence of the black box is independent from the continuous shifts in the mass of stakeholders and creditors alike. Once the corporation is regarded as a distinct entity, affirming that directors must defend the best interests of the corporation they are managing is highly intuitive.

The Firm as a Black Box: The Fisher Separation Theorem

Fisher (1930) introduced the separation theorem, which Hirshleifer (1964 1965, 1966) further developed. The theorem's main result is that physical production and financial decisions concerning the firm can be separated. The firm's managers do not need to inquire into the financial preferences of their investors. All that the manager has to do is invest in those projects that have the highest net present value (NPV). If the corporation is pictured as a pie, one way of expressing the Fisher separation is to say that the firm's managers should maximize the size of the pie, thereby allowing the shareholders and creditors the maximum flexibility to decide on how to spend the earnings from their share of the pie.

The theorem is styled in terms of a consumer-investor who owns a firm and who faces the decision of investing some capital in the firm or consuming the capital. Obviously, the consumer's preferences regarding savings, consumption, and financial investments are all intertwined. Shareholders and creditors are also consumers. An investor who invests capital in a firm is ultimately interested in how much cash will be returned in order for the investor qua consumer to decide on how much of the cash to spend on consumption and how much to save. Some investors have a higher preference for immediate consumption, while others may be more patient. Some investors may be more risk averse and would prefer that the firm invest in safe projects, while others may be more risk loving and prefer the firm to take more risks.

A firm whose management can achieve high rates of return, for example, may induce many of the investors to demand more investments at the expense of current consumption. Such investors also want the firm to engage in riskier projects that yield higher rates of return. Other investors, who are extremely risk averse, do not care too much about the high rates of return, and rather they would care more about a constant stream of dividends.

The problem this poses for management, therefore, is whose wishes to follow? The Fisher separation theorem states that management need not concern itself with this question. Rather, all that management has to do is invest in those productive activities that yield the highest NPV for the firm. Those risk-preferring investors will invest in the firm, while those risk-averse investors will become creditors. In this manner, the investors sort themselves out.

The Irrelevance of Capital Structure

The Modigliani-Miller theorem, set forth by Modigliani and Miller (1958 1963), is a foundational theorem in finance and economics. It stands for the proposition that, under certain highly restrictive conditions such as no taxes, the value of the firm is independent of its capital structure. The value of a corporation depends on its profitability and not on how the firm is financed.

When corporate taxes are taken into account, the analysis gets complicated. Because interest payments are tax deductible, the value of the firm is increasing in the amount of debt and this suggests that the firm should be fully leveraged. In practice, this is neither observed nor would anyone believe this to be a reasonable strategy.

Various authors have sought to explain what could be constraining the leverage decisions of a firm, with a view to determining the optimal debt level (Kane, Marcus, and McDonald 1984; Altman 1984). For example, according to Altman, as the firm borrows more, bankruptcy costs rise. These costs can be direct, such as the expenses that need to be paid to lawyers when liquidating the assets of a firm. They can also be indirect, such as lost profits, the disruption of supplies, managers demanding higher compensation for potential unemployment, and other such costs that may result if the firm declared bankruptcy. In fact, bankruptcy costs can be taken to be a metaphor for all such disadvantages that a highly leveraged firm may signal to market participants.

Debt also has nontax advantages. Agency costs, those costs that arise from the inability of shareholders to perfectly monitor the firm's managers, are one such advantage of debt. Jensen and Meckling (1976) introduced this insight to finance literature. They identify two sources of conflicts: one between the shareholders and the managers and the second between the shareholders and creditors. The authors contend that increasing the ratio of debt to equity can solve both of these conflicts. More debt means that managers now have a higher percentage of ownership in the firm, thereby increasing their incentives to act in the best interests of the remaining shareholders. More debt also means that the firm needs more cash flow to service the interest payments, and this forces the managers to focus on increasing cash flows by seeking higher NPV projects.

The more debt the firm accumulates, however, the higher is the potential for shareholders to want the managers (who now also own an increasing share of the firm) to invest in riskier projects. Creditors who anticipate this behavior will either saddle the debt with restrictive covenants or increase the interest rate charged, thereby making debt costly. At some point, an optimal or target debt equity ratio exists that balances the benefits and costs of debt. Similar to the trade-off between taxes and bankruptcy costs, a trade-off also exists between managers controlling and being controlled by creditors. Harris and Raviv (1991) provide a comprehensive survey of the various theories of capital structure including those relating to agency costs. Although the article is somewhat dated, the principal results remain valid and comprehensive today.

An increased level of debt is associated with the perspective of a costly winding up and liquidation process (i.e., with bankruptcy costs). A high debt-to-equity ratio may also trigger managers' incentive to underinvest in profitable projects. The underinvestment incentive is the mirror image of the "going for broke" scenario (i.e., investing in highly risky projects). Managers may have less of an incentive to invest in highly profitable projects due to the greater possibility of bankruptcy, which will mean that the managers will not reap much benefit from those projects.

These concerns regarding shareholders, managers, and creditors arise because shareholders and creditors have difficulty monitoring the managers. Asymmetric information prevents the various parties from being "honest" players in the market, forcing creditors to attach covenants and shareholders to issue debt. Reputation is one way to solve these concerns.

Diamond (1989) and Hirshleifer and Thakor (1992), for example, suggest that reputation can overcome many of the concerns that creditors may have regarding the temptation to undertake risky projects. Older firms with reputations for investing in safe and less-risky projects will be able to attract more debt financing at lower rates, while newer firms will struggle to raise debt without incurring higher interest rates reflecting creditors' fears regarding the "going for broke" strategy. Additionally, managers themselves may want to have a reputation for undertaking safe projects as this will enhance their personal reputations in the event that they are fired from their current firm due to insolvency or other reasons. Therefore, managers will be more conservative in their investment strategies as the market for managers will evaluate them on how successful their projects are, as opposed to shareholders who might only be concerned with the expected payoff.

In fact, risk aversion by managers can defeat any desires by the shareholders for the pursuit of riskier projects. Since managers are risk-averse, they will want to signal to the market the quality of their investment projects by taking on more debt and having a greater share in the firm's equity (Leland and Pyle 1977). Although the higher debt will mean more risk for the manager, the positive signal this and the managers' ownership in the firm sends to the market allows for cheaper credit and a higher valuation of the remaining equity. This compensates the manager and alleviates the concerns from any risk aversion.

Myers and Majluf (1984) argue that managers can also overcome the market's concerns regarding asymmetric information by using a "pecking order" when financing the firm. When managers want to finance a project, issuing more equity may not result in an enthusiastic response by investors. Investors will attach a probability that the project has a large expected payoff as claimed by the manager. They will also attach another probability that the project is not as great as the managers claim it is. The result is that the managers may have difficulty raising the extra cash and the project may have to be forgone. According to pecking order theory, the managers will, therefore, first finance their project using retained earnings. If the cash on hand is insufficient, then debt will be preferred over new equity, as this signals to the creditors that the project is truly worthy and the managers do not fear default. Finally, equity will be a last resort if debt and retained earnings are insufficient. Debt, therefore, raises the value of the firm since the shareholders who do not want to infuse more equity in the company do not suffer a dilution in the value of their shares each time the firm decides to finance a new project.

When firms can balance the costs and benefits of debt, they can achieve an optimal or at least a target debt level. Thus, creditors and shareholders arrive at a balance that protects the creditors who have also adequately priced their credit while allowing shareholders to achieve their returns.

How Do Creditors Protect Themselves?

The discussion above highlights the fact that firm value is invariant to the amount of debt beyond what might be optimal. Creditors will price any risk beforehand, and shareholders will be therefore disciplined. But what if, after borrowing the money for one project, the shareholders decide to undertake a second project that is riskier than the original project? Creditors would then be underpricing the risk, and the shareholders' equity will emerge with a higher value at the expense of the creditors. This example is analogous to the example at the beginning of this chapter from *Credit Lyonnais*.

This scenario is not equilibrium under rational expectations. Given that those specifying the model of the entrepreneur's behavior anticipate that he would choose the riskier project after representing to the creditor that the first project would be chosen, the creditor would also anticipate this behavior. To say that the entrepreneur could fool the creditor would not be rational. Furthermore, any model that specifies such behavior does not describe an economic equilibrium. Such moral hazard behavior will result in the creditors always assuming that the shareholder will invest in the riskier project. Creditors will now charge a higher risk-adjusted interest rate, and the shareholder will have to invest in that project.

Therefore, an entrepreneur who genuinely wants to only undertake the less-risky project would have to design a debt contract, or covenant, in such a way as to indicate credible commitment to undertaking only the less-risky project. Similarly, the creditor could finance the less-risky project at the lower interest rate by designing the debt contract so that the entrepreneur would only choose the less-risky project. Such contracts may specify a huge penalty for choosing the riskier project. They may also require the maintenance of certain financial ratios or even specify the nature of projects undertaken. This ability by creditors to specify restrictions on the firm's behavior is the reason the courts and legal scholars have resisted adding fiduciary duties to creditors as another layer of protection.

Debt covenants have existed for hundreds of years (Rodgers 1965; Simpson 1973; Smith and Warner 1979; McDaniel 1983; Lloyd 1991). Smith and Warner show that debt contracts solve the bondholder–shareholder conflict by providing specific covenants that give shareholders the incentives to follow a strategy that maximizes the value of the firm. They identify the main sources of this potential conflict as dividend payment, claim dilution, asset substitution, and the incentive for underinvestment. Rational bondholders anticipate shareholders' incentives and therefore include restrictive covenants in the bond indentures. Although restrictive covenants involve costs, they can increase firm value by reducing the opportunity loss caused by stockholders' incentive to pursue projects that do not maximize firm value.

Smith and Warner (1979) look at covenants and classify them into four broad categories: (1) production/investment covenants, (2) dividend covenants, (3) financing covenants, and (4) bonding covenants. By using one or more of the four covenants, bondholders can effectively control shareholder and managerial opportunism. These covenants usually have acceleration clauses that state that the debt payments can be accelerated upon the occurrence of certain events or a violation of the terms of the covenant.

The production/investment covenants usually specify restrictions on the firm's purchase of other financial assets, disposition of assets, or restrictions on merger activities. The restrictions on the purchase of other financial assets represent an attempt to prevent asset substitution, that is, the transformation of the cash raised by debt into another asset thereby leaving the creditor at the mercy of new asset's uncertain value. Similarly, the restriction on the firm's disposition of assets protects the creditor against an opportunistic sale of collateral (if the debt is secured) or potential assets to seize in the event of insolvency (if the debt is unsecured).

The restriction on merger activities achieves the same goals as the prohibition on asset disposition. Specifically, mergers usually open up the potential for mixing of secure or liquid assets with other assets making the creditors' job of finding his security much harder than before the merger. Other covenants in this category can also require the maintenance of certain assets or restrict what can be done with them. All of these restrictions are imposed to protect the firm's assets from waste or opportunistic liquidation. The effect of these restrictions is to keep the firm from liquidating assets and declaring them as dividends or to prevent the firm from undertaking risky projects that will put the assets at risk.

The dividend covenants restrict payments of dividends by defining an inventory of funds available for dividend payments over the life of the bonds. These covenants do not restrict payment of dividends per se, but the distribution of dividends financed by issuing debt or by sale of the firm's existing assets (either of which would reduce the value of the debt).

Bratton (2006) shows that creditors also use dividend covenants to address indirectly shareholders' underinvestment incentives. In financially distressed firms, shareholders have the incentives to forgo the projects whose benefits accrue entirely to creditors. If the project yields no net gains to shareholders, from their point of view such an investment is worthless. Underinvestment is prejudicial for creditors because of the heightened default risk, and to the extent that no other firm can pursue the project society as a whole also loses. Including a covenant that blocks dividend payments addresses this problem indirectly by forcing the firm to reinvest its free liquid assets or, if no profitable projects are available, to repay the loan's principal amount. The dividend covenants have some disadvantages. An outright prohibition or a tight restriction on dividends increases the firm's incentives to engage in asset substitution and claim dilution. Furthermore, when the firm is doing poorly, the dividend constraint is incapable of controlling indirectly the investment/financing policy.

The efficiency of bond covenants is ensured by the default remedies available to bondholders. In case of default, bondholders can seize the collateral, trigger the acceleration of debt maturity or commence bankruptcy proceedings. Because such actions are costly, the debt contract is usually renegotiated to eliminate the default.

The bond covenants increase firm value by reducing the costs associated with the conflict of interests between stockholders and bondholders. Such costs are reduced both by decreasing the agency costs associated with risky debt and by establishing an optimal amount of debt that reduces the benefits of wealth transfer from bondholders to stockholders. The benefits of bond covenants, however, are impaired by the direct and opportunity costs of complying with the contractual restrictions.

Although the Smith and Warner (1979) study is dated, Billett, King, and Mauer (2007) confirm its results. The authors investigate the use of covenants by firms by examining more than 15,000 debt issues between 1960 and 2003. They find that lower-priority, lower-rated, and shorter maturity debt have more covenant protections. Such debt is most vulnerable when compared to higher-priority and higher-rated debt. They also find that debt issued by regulated firms (and hence whose investment activities are limited in scope) has less covenant protections. Their evidence shows that firms with more leverage and more growth opportunities (and hence the potential for riskier investment projects) have more covenant protections, but firms with growth opportunities that have covenant protections have higher debt levels. Because of the covenant protections, creditors are willing to lend more to firms that have high payoff (but high-risk) investment opportunities if they feel protected. This, of course, is good news for shareholders who can see higher value to their shares from the higher growth opportunities. Where firms do not use long-term debt laden with covenants, they use short-term debt that acts as a substitute for covenant protected long-term debt. Hence, Billet et al. find that firms with higher growth opportunities use more short-term debt and that convertible debt has fewer covenant restrictions. The convertibility allows the creditors to stave off the potential conflict with the shareholders by converting the debt to shares if the high payoffs are realized.

DIRECTORS AND STAKEHOLDERS IN AND OUT OF INSOLVENCY: A REVIEW OF DOCTRINE AND CASE LAW

In a solvent firm, the interests of the main corporate constituencies are usually congruent. The shareholders, as residual beneficiaries, prefer projects that maximize the present value of the expected income of the firm. Creditors are indifferent to the level of risk of managerial decisions as long as the firm can pay its debts as they come due. When the firm becomes financially distressed, however, the interests and risk preferences of these constituencies change. As shown in the previous sections, equity depletion increases the shareholders' appetite for risk since they have nothing more to lose and everything to gain. The creditors, in contrast, prefer a course of action that does not endanger the remaining corporate assets. As the fortune of the firm dwindles, the diverging views of the main corporate constituencies as to the proper business trajectory bring to the forefront the following question: To whom are directors and managers beholden in times of financial distress? From a legal standpoint, this question involves identifying the direct beneficiary of directors' and managers' fiduciary duties. This section analyzes the Delaware jurisprudence (Delaware being the state whose jurisprudence is the most relevant for corporate law in the United States) and the underlying doctrinal principles concerning the substance of the fiduciary duties and the effect that the threat of insolvency has on the beneficiaries of such duties.

A preliminary terminological clarification is required at this stage. From a strict legal point of view, the bearers of fiduciary duties are corporate directors and officers. Other key employees of the firm, who, from a finance perspective fall in the category of "managers," may owe fiduciary duties to the firm in the capacity of agents thereof, and not qua managers. For the purpose of the present discussion, a detailed discussion of the potential differences in the legal regime of the fiduciary duties of all these corporate actors would be unproductive. Therefore, the present section refers to the fiduciary duties of directors, with the specification that, with a few exceptions, the same principles apply to officers and other fiduciary managers of the firm.

The Content of the Fiduciary Duties

What does it mean to say that directors are fiduciaries? This is a central issue in Delaware, as it is in Canada, and many aspects of directors' fiduciary role remain controversial. The Delaware and Canadian courts, however, have gone to great lengths to emphasize that, as fiduciaries, directors must act in what they perceive to be the best interests of the corporation and must decide on an informed basis. These two main duties, referred to as the duty of loyalty and the duty of care, respectively, are the two components of the "fiduciary duties" notion.

In Delaware, recent Chancery and Supreme Court jurisprudence has elucidated much of the incertitude that surrounds the fiduciary duties. The traditional point of view of the Delaware Supreme Court was that directors owed a "triad" of fiduciary duties: good faith, loyalty, and care (*Cede & Co. v. Technicolor Inc.*, 634 A.2d 345 (Del. 1993)). The Delaware Court of Chancery has expressed repeatedly its disagreement with this classification of directors' duties and stated that the duty of good faith cannot exist separately from a duty of loyalty (*Guttman v. Huang*, 823 A.2d 492 (Del. Ch. 2003)).

In 2006, the Delaware Supreme Court put to an end to the dispute over the content of directors' fiduciary duties, in its seminal decision *Stone v. Ritter*, 911 A.2d 362 (Del. 2006). The Supreme Court finally confirmed that, under Delaware law, the obligation to act in good faith does not establish an independent fiduciary duty that stands on the same footing as the duties of care and loyalty. The *Stone* case also brought substantial clarifications concerning the meaning of the fiduciary duty of loyalty. The court explained that a director acts disloyally whenever he does not believe in good faith that his actions are in the best interests of the corporation. Acting in the best interests of the corporation does not mean simply avoiding a financial or other cognizable conflict of interests between directors' own interests and those of the corporation. Any conscious action that is not in the firms' interest is disloyal, irrespective of directors' motivation (Bainbridge, Lopez, and Oklan 2008).

Recent Delaware jurisprudence has also brought clarifications regarding the other fiduciary duty, the duty of care. With few exceptions, the courts were reluctant to interfere in the management of a business by substituting their judgment on the substantial merits of a decision for that of the directors. The deference that the courts show to directors' business expertise is manifested in the so-called business judgment rule. This rule established a presumption that "in making a business decision the directors of a corporation acted on an informed basis, in good faith and in the honest belief that the action taken was in the best interest of the company" (*Aronson v. Lewis*, 473 A.2d 805, 812 (Del. 1984)). The rationale behind the business judgment rule resides in the recognition that investors' wealth would be lower if managers' decisions were routinely subjected to strict judicial review (Easterbrook and Fischel 1996).

To benefit from the protection of the business judgment rule, directors must inform themselves, before making a business decision, of all material information reasonably available to them. In order to remove the presumption of proper business judgment and hold directors liable for breach of the duty of care, stakeholders of Delaware firms must prove that directors did not comply with minimalist procedural standards of attention and displayed gross negligence. In other words, an investment decision that, in hindsight, proved "foolishly risky! stupidly risky! egregiously risky!—you supply the adverb" will not trigger liability for breach of fiduciary duties, absent bad faith or gross negligence (*Gagliardi v. TriFoods Int'l, Inc.*, 683 A.2d 1049, 1052 (Del. Ch. 1996); Allen, Jacobs, and Strine 2002).

Fiduciary Duties and the Interests of Corporate Constituencies

When the firm is financially sound, the courts will not interfere to censure directors' decisions as to what are the best interests of the corporation, as long as they act loyally and with care. In the case of financially distressed firms, however, the doctrine and the case law offer various, often conflicting answers as to the proper beneficiary of directors' fiduciary duties.

According to one current of thought, directors of financially troubled firms owe their fiduciary duties to creditors. The concept of fiduciary duties owed directly to creditors originated in the "trust fund doctrine," which states that, when a corporation becomes insolvent, its assets are held in trust for the benefit of creditors. Thus, directors, as trustees, have the fiduciary duty to preserve the firm's remaining assets for the benefit of creditors. Conversely, creditors acquire an equitable lien on the assets improperly distributed to shareholders or transferred to third parties without consideration, prior to satisfaction of creditor claims.

The Delaware Supreme Court endorsed this doctrine in *Bovay v. H.M. Byllesby & Co.*, 38 A.2d 808 (Del. 1944), where it stated that, upon insolvency, a trust arises and the property of the corporation must be administered for the benefit of creditors. In this case, the Delaware Supreme Court emphasized that the scope of the trust fund doctrine was limited to situations involving self-dealing and misappropriation of corporate assets. Over time, the American courts have expanded this doctrine beyond its original scope. Most notably, in *Geyer v. Ingersoll Publications Co.*, 621 A.2d 784 (Del. Ch. 1992), the Delaware Court of Chancery invoked *Bovay* to argue that the insolvency in fact triggers fiduciary duties for the benefit of creditors, regardless of whether or not the debtor had filed for bankruptcy (Barondes 1998).

The debate concerning fiduciary duties to creditors shifted from insolvency in fact to the so-called vicinity of insolvency, in the wake of the seminal Court of Chancery decision in *Credit Lyonnais*. The court argued that, when a firm "is operating in the vicinity of insolvency" the fiduciary duties require directors to take into account creditors' interests as well as the claims of all other constituencies that contribute to the firm's well-being. The decision in *Credit Lyonnais* raised more questions than it answered. First, the court did not provide any guidelines for determining the vicinity of insolvency zone. Second, it failed to identify clearly the recipient of fiduciary duties by referring successively to the best interests of the firm and to the interests of all constituencies. Third, the court provided no explanations as to what are the best interests of the corporation or the collective interests of stakeholders and how the directors are supposed to further such interests.

Due to these ambiguities, some courts have interpreted *Credit Lyonnais* as providing a sword for creditors to challenge the boards' decisions for breach of fiduciary duty not only when the firm is insolvent but also when there is a threat of insolvency (e.g., *Official Comm. of Unsecured Creditors of Buckhead Am. Corp. v. Reliance Capital Group, Inc. (In re Buckhead Am. Corp.)*, 178 B.R. 956 (Bankr. D. Del. 1994)).

The Delaware Court of Chancery disapproved of this interpretation of *Credit Lyonnais* in *Production Resources Group, L.L.C. v. NCT Group, Inc.*, 863 A.2d 772 (Del. Ch. 2004). In this decision, the court reasoned that, in insolvency in fact, creditors may assert breach of fiduciary duty claims only on behalf of the debtor corporation (derivative actions), for the harm the board had caused to the debtor corporation. The court reaffirmed that there is no direct duty to creditors either in insolvency in fact or in the so-called vicinity of insolvency. The boards' duties do not undergo significant changes as the firm nears insolvency. The fiduciary duties continue to run to the benefit of the corporation, with an accompanying shift in the weight of the interests of shareholders and creditors (Ribstein and Alces 2007).

The Delaware Supreme Court recently endorsed the conclusion of *Production Resources* in *North American Catholic Educational Programming Foundation, Inc. v. Gheewalla*, 930 A.2d 92 (Del. 2007). The Delaware Supreme Court indicated that creditors of a Delaware corporation that is either insolvent or in the zone of insolvency have no right, as a matter of law, to assert direct claims for breach of fiduciary duty against corporate directors. Creditors can protect their interests by introducing derivative claims on behalf of the insolvent corporation by enforcing their contractual rights or by asserting any nonfiduciary duty claims based on other legal sources of creditor protection, such as implied covenants of good faith and fair dealing, fraudulent conveyance law, or bankruptcy law (Veasey 2008).

The Supreme Court of Canada adopted a similar approach to the "vicinity of insolvency" theory in *Peoples Department Stores Inc. (Trustee of) v. Wise* 2004 SCC 68. In this case, the Court argued that the concept of "vicinity of insolvency" is impossible to be defined and is void of any legal meaning. Therefore, directors' fiduciary duties do not change when the firm is in the nebulous "vicinity of insolvency." In other words, the shifts in the interests of corporate constituencies that occur as the corporation's fortune changes do not affect the content of the fiduciary duties. Such duties are owed at all times to the corporation, and the interests of the corporation are not to be confused with the interests of the creditors or those of any other stakeholders.

Many scholars regard the theories promoting the shift of fiduciary duties to creditors as unpersuasive attempts to depart from the traditional shareholder wealth maximization norm. According to such authors, the long-established American corporate law tradition imposes on directors the obligation to maximize shareholder wealth. Several theories have been put forward to justify the primacy of the shareholders' interests.

One argument states that fiduciary duties should be owed exclusively to shareholders because, in their capacity as residual claimants, they have the best incentives to maximize the value of the firm (Easterbrook and Fischel 1996). Other authors contend that the purpose of fiduciary duties is to protect shareholders against the agency costs generated by the separation between ownership and control, specific to public corporations (Berle and Means 1932). The separation between ownership and control implies an open-ended delegation of powers from shareholders to directors. In large public corporations, such separation results in acquiring by the board of a largely autonomous position in relation to shareholders, which creates incentives for the former to abuse their powers. Since monitoring and effectively disciplining the directors' performance would be costly or impracticable for the shareholders, the statutory fiduciary duties must be imposed on the latter for the benefit of the former. Another theory states that the fiduciary duty for the benefit of shareholders is a bargained-for contractual term in the nexus of contracts setting that represents the corporation (Bainbridge 1993). The shareholder wealth maximization is a bargained-for obligation of the board-shareholder contract. Stated differently, in a hypothetical bargain setting, the shareholders would negotiate for contractual terms imposing on directors fiduciary duties that incorporate the shareholder wealth maximization norm.

The shareholder primacy theory is sustained by several court decisions. One of the most influential cases endorsing the shareholder wealth-maximization norm is *Dodge v. Ford Motor Co.*, 170 N.W. 668 (Mich. 1919). In response to Henry Ford's affirmation that the corporation had an obligation to benefit the public, the employees, and the customers, the court argued that business corporations are organized and carried on primarily for the profit of the shareholders. Moreover, the court stated that shaping the business of the corporation for the merely incidental benefit of the shareholders would fall beyond the lawful powers of a board of directors. In a more recent decision, the Delaware Court of Chancery found that directors' attempt to maximize the long-run interests of the shareholders at the expense of other constituencies does not amount to a "cognizable legal wrong" and does not constitute a breach of duty, despite the corporation's declining financial condition (*Katz v. Oak Industries Inc.*, 508 A.2d 873 (Del. Ch. 1986); Hu and Westbrook 2007).

Despite the various theories and court decisions advocating fiduciary duties for the benefit of creditors or shareholders in financial distress, the recent Delaware jurisprudence reinforces the idea that directors have a continuing duty to act in the best interests of the corporation (Strine et al. 2010). Directors, therefore, do not have to assess and balance the interests of all groups that contribute to the firm's well-being, as suggested by some of the court decisions previously mentioned. Such a task would render the board's task overwhelmingly complex and eventually would impair the quality of its decisions.

SUMMARY AND CONCLUSIONS

Shareholder primacy is usually a key mantra in modern corporate law. When stated in a more refined manner, it is called the primacy of the board of directors who act for the shareholders. Despite the confusing case law that sometimes suggests that the board of directors owes duties to shareholders, sometimes to the corporation, and sometimes to others, the courts all act as if the duties are owed to the corporation (Ribstein and Alces 2007; Bainbridge 2007; Feasby 2009). Although the cases speak sometimes of duties to various constituencies, the value of the firm is simply the sum of the value of equity and debt. Hence, maximizing one necessarily means the maximization of the other. This means that the courts are speaking about the same thing.

Given the Modigliani-Miller theorem, the Fisher separation theorem, the associated observations on debt covenants, and the black box approach to corporations, this result should not be controversial from an economist's perspective. The goal of firm value maximization can be achieved by pursuing the projects having the highest expected NPV, which does not require the managers to evaluate the expectations of different corporate constituencies. The result of this policy serves the interests of both fixed and residual claimants. Positive NPV projects align the best interests of the corporation, regarded as a separate legal entity, with the economic interests of shareholders and creditors.

Hence, the directors' obligation to maximize the value of the firm can be construed as the obligation to select the projects that generate the highest discounted value of future cash flow streams (the projects that have the highest expected NPV). This in turn means that the directors will satisfy the interests of shareholders and creditors at the same time.

This understanding of fiduciary duties accommodates the interests of the corporation with those of its constituencies. Once an optimum level (from the firm's value perspective) of debt is reached, directors or managers' decisions regarding the maximization of firm's value are independent of the specific interests of creditors and shareholders. In terms of fiduciary duties, the firm value maximization goal requires directors to pursue the best interests of the corporation, without investigating the stakeholders' particular expectations.

DISCUSSION QUESTIONS

1. What is the economic justification for fiduciary duties if the parties can freely contract?
2. What is the fear courts have regarding the relationship among directors, shareholders, and creditors?
3. What economic principles can be used to disperse the fear that shareholders may use debt for opportunistic behavior?
4. How can the differing cases on fiduciary duties be reconciled?

REFERENCES

Allen, William T., Jack B. Jacobs, and Leo E. Strine, Jr. 2002. "Realigning the Standard of Review of Director Due Care with Delaware Public Policy: A Critique of *Van Gorkom* and Its Progeny as a Standard of Review Problem." *Northwestern University Law Review* 96:2, 449–466.

Altman, Edward I. 1984. "A Further Empirical Investigation of the Bankruptcy Cost Question." *Journal of Finance* 39:4, 1067–1089.

Bainbridge, Stephen M. 1993. "In Defense of the Shareholder Wealth Maximization Norm: A Reply to Professor Green." *Washington and Lee Law Review* 50:4, 1423–1448.

Bainbridge, Stephen M. 2002. *Corporation Law and Economics*. New York: Foundation Press.

Bainbridge, Stephen M. 2007. "Much Ado about Little? Directors' Fiduciary Duties in the Vicinity of Insolvency." *Journal of Business and Technology Law* 1:2, 335–370.

Bainbridge, Stephen M., Star Lopez, and Benjamin Oklan. 2008. "The Convergence of Good Faith and Oversight." *UCLA Law Review* 55:3 559–606.

Barondes, Royce de R. 1998. "Fiduciary Duties of Officers and Directors of Distressed Corporations." *George Mason Law Review* 7:1, 45–104.

Berle, Adolf A., and Gardner C. Means. 1932. *Modern Corporation and Private Property*. New York: Commerce Clearing House.

Billett, Matthew T., Tao-Hsien D. King, and David C. Mauer. 2007. "Growth Opportunities and the Choice of Leverage, Debt Maturity, and Covenants." *Journal of Finance* 62:2, 697–730.

Bratton, William W. 2006. "Bond Covenants and Creditor Protection: Economics and Law, Theory and Practice, Substance and Process." *European Business Organization Law Review* 7:1, 39–87.

Coase, Ronald H. 1937. "The Nature of the Firm." *Economica* 4:16, 386–405.

Coase, Ronald H. 1960. "The Problem of Social Cost." *Journal of Law and Economics* 3:1, 1–69.

Cooter, Robert, and Bradley J. Freeman. 1991. "The Fiduciary Relationship: Its Economic Character and Legal Consequences." *New York University Law Review* 66:4, 1045–1076.

Diamond, Douglas W. 1989. "Acquisition in Debt Markets." *Journal of Political Economy* 97:4, 828–862.

Easterbrook, Frank H., and Daniel R. Fischel. 1996. *The Economic Structure of Corporate Law.* Cambridge: Harvard University Press.

Feasby, Colin. 2009. "Bond holders and Barbarians: *BCE* and the Supreme Court on Directors' Duties, Oppression, and Plans of Arrangement." In Todd L. Archibald and Randall S. Echlin, eds., *Annual Review of Civil Litigation 2009*, 83–126. Toronto: Carswell.

Fisher, Irving. 1930. *The Theory of Interest as Determined by Impatience to Spend Income and Opportunity to Invest It.* New York: Macmillan.

Harris, Milton, and Artur Raviv. 1991. "The Theory of Capital Structure." *Journal of Finance* 46:1, 297–355.

Hirshleifer, David, and Anjan V. Thakor. 1992. "Managerial Conservatism, Project Choice, and Debt" *Review of Financial Studies* 5:3, 437–470.

Hirshleifer, Jack. 1964. "Efficient Allocation of Capital in an Uncertain World." *American Economic Review* 54:3, 77–85.

Hirshleifer, Jack. 1965. "Investment Decision under Uncertainty: Choice-Theoretic Approaches." *Quarterly Journal of Economics* 79:4, 509–536.

Hirshleifer, Jack. 1966. "Investment Decision under Uncertainty: Applications of the State-Preference Approach." *Quarterly Journal of Economics* 80:2, 252–277.

Hu, Henry T. C., and Jay Lawrence Westbrook. 2007. "Abolition of the Corporate Duty to Creditors." *Columbia Law Review* 107:6, 1321–1403.

Jensen, Michael C., and William H. Meckling. 1976. "Theory of the Firm: Managerial Behavior, Agency Costs and Ownership Structure." *Journal of Financial Economics* 3:4, 305–360.

Kane, Alex, Alan J. Marcus, and Robert L. McDonald. 1984. "How Big Is the Tax Advantage to Debt?" *Journal of Finance* 39:3, 841–853.

Klein, William A., and John C. Coffee Jr. 2004. *Business Organization and Finance: Legal and Economic Principles.* New York: Foundation Press.

Leland, Hayne E., and David H. Pyle. 1977. "Information Asymmetries, Financial Structure, and Financial Intermediation." *Journal of Finance* 32:2, 371–387.

Lloyd, Robert M. 1991. "Financial Covenants in Commercial Loan Documentation: Uses and Limitations" *Tennessee Law Review* 58:3, 335–366.

McDaniel, Morey W. 1983. "Are Negative Pledge Clauses in Public Debt Issues Obsolete?" *Business Lawyer* 38:3, 867–882.

Modigliani, Franco, and Merton H. Miller. 1958. "The Cost of Capital, Corporate Finance and the Theory of Investment." *American Economic Review* 48:3, 261–297.

Modigliani, Franco, and Merton H. Miller. 1963. "Corporate Income Taxes and the Cost of Capital: A Correction." *American Economic Review* 53:3, 433–443.

Myers, Stewart C., and Nicholas S. Majluf. 1984. "Corporate Financing and Investment Decisions When Firms Have Information That Investors Do Not Have." *Journal of Financial Economics* 13:2, 187–221.

Ribstein, Larry E., and Kelli Alces. 2007. "Directors' Duties in Failing Firms." *Journal of Business and Technology Law* 1:2, 529–552.

Rodgers, Churchill. 1965. "The Corporate Trust Indenture Project." *Business Lawyer* 20:3, 551–572.

Simpson, David. 1973. "The Drafting of Loan Agreements: A Borrower's Viewpoint." *Business Lawyer* 28:3, 1161–1196.

Smith, Clifford W., and Jerold B. Warner. 1979. "On Financial Contracting: An Analysis of Bond Covenants." *Journal of Financial Economics* 7:3, 117–161.

Strine, Leo E., Lawrence A. Hamermesh, R. Franklin Balotti, and Jeffrey Gorris. 2010. "Loyalty's Core Demand: The Defining Role of Good Faith in Corporation Law." *Georgetown Law Journal* 98:3, 629–697.
Valsan, Remus D., and Moin A. Yahya. 2007. "Shareholders, Creditors, and Directors' Fiduciary Duties: A Law and Finance Approach." *Virginia Law and Business Review* 2:1, 1–52.
Veasey, E. Norman. 2008. "Counseling the Board of Directors of a Delaware Corporation in Distress." *American Bankruptcy Institute Journal* 27:5, 61–65.

ABOUT THE AUTHORS

Remus D. Valsan is a doctoral candidate at McGill University and an associate lawyer at Pachiu & Associates, Romania. He received his JD from Nicolae Titulescu University, Bucharest, Romania, and his LLM from the University of Alberta. Mr. Valsan also studied comparative law in Strasbourg, European antitrust law in Turin, and Austrian Economics in New York. His research interests include corporate law, equity and trusts and legal history. In his doctoral thesis Mr. Valsan analyzes the development of legal relationships based on confidence, from a historical and comparative perspective.

Moin A. Yahya is an associate professor of law at the University of Alberta. Currently, he is on leave to the Alberta Utilities Commission, where he is one of the Commissioners. The views here are personal, do not reflect that of the Commission, and are based on work done before joining the Commission. He obtained his BA (Hons) in Economics from the University of Alberta, where he also obtained his MA in Economics. Professor Yahya received his PhD in Economics from the University of Toronto, and his JD is from George Mason University School of Law, where he graduated *summa cum laude* and was the Robert A. Levy Fellow in Law & Liberty. His research is focused on the law of economics of corporate law, antitrust law, securities law, and criminal law.

CHAPTER 22

The Lease versus Buy Decision

SRIS CHATTERJEE
Professor of Finance, Fordham University

AN YAN
Associate Professor of Finance, Fordham University

INTRODUCTION

A *lease* is a contract that allows the lessor to retain ownership of an asset and the lessee to enjoy the services of the asset over a stipulated time period (usually longer than a year but less than the economic life of the asset) in return for stipulated rental payments to the lessor. This general definition hides an important difference between a capital (or financial) lease and an operating lease. In a *capital* or *financial lease*, the lessee may acquire ownership of the leased asset at the end of the lease-term, and a single lessee can guarantee an economic return to the lessor. In an *operating lease*, the lessor must arrange several transactions to generate adequate economic returns that can cover the capital cost of the asset. The differences are discussed later in the chapter.

Smith and Wakeman (1985) provide a good description of the unique contractual features in leasing. Schallheim (1994) illustrates numerous stylized facts and features of leasing, including the fact that certain equipment such as aircraft, computers, and office machines, and certain industries such as trucking and telecommunications, dominate the leasing market. In the United States, about one-third of all assets are leased, and this fraction has remained quite stable. Leasing by small firms substantially exceeds that of large firms, particularly in manufacturing. Eisfeldt and Rampini (2009) as well as Gavazza (2007, 2010) provide a more recent overview of leased capital and a review of related theoretical literature.

As with the analysis of the debt versus equity choice, the lease versus buy decision has been analyzed first by invoking the Modigliani and Miller (1958) (hereafter MM) framework of capital structure irrelevance in an ideal world with zero imperfections and zero taxes. The analysis then incorporates real-world features such as corporate and personal taxes, agency costs, asymmetric information, and the existence of incomplete contracts. Indeed, the post-MM models of capital structure provide a useful roadmap to the analytical models of the lease versus buy decision. Again, consistent with the history of capital structure research, the earlier research on leasing emphasizes the importance of corporate taxes. Lewis and Schallheim (1992) point out that the analysis of the tax effects can be complex, even under the assumption of complete markets. Earlier research on tax-based models includes Lewellen, Long, and McConnell (1976); Miller and Upton (1976); Myers, Dill, and Bautista (1976); Franks and Hodges (1978); and Brealey and Young (1980). Later research emphasizes the importance of transaction costs and embedded options in the leasing contracts (Flath 1980; McConnell and Schallheim 1983; Smith and Wakeman 1985). More recent work on leasing analyzes the effects of information asymmetry and asset specificity (Gavazza 2007, 2010; Eisfeldt and Rampini 2009; Chemmanur, Jiao, and Yan 2010).

This chapter provides an overview of the models that help to explain the contractual features of leases. It discusses several models from the leasing literature including models based on taxes, asymmetric information, and incomplete contracts and/or contracting costs. The overview also summarizes the empirical findings in leasing research and investigates why some firms decide to lease an asset instead of buying it, and why certain assets seem to be more amenable to leasing than others. The chapter does not cover the research on certain categories of leases (for example, real estate leases) and the effect of leasing on computing financial ratios. The interested reader can review Grenadier (2002) for real estate leases and Damodaran (2009) for ratio computation.

The chapter has the following organization. The next two sections examine tax-based and nontax models of leasing, respectively. The nontax section examines models based on incomplete contracts, contracting costs, and asset specificity. Next, the chapter summarizes key empirical evidence about leasing. The final section provides a summary and conclusions.

TAX-BASED MODELS OF LEASING

Textbooks in finance typically emphasize the fact that leases displace debt (Ross, Westerfield, and Jaffe 2010; Emery, Finnerty, and Stowe 2011). The underlying reason for this approach is that lease payments are contractually similar to payments to debt holders. The discussion in this section is based largely on Emery, Finnerty, and Stowe (2011) and focuses only on capital leases or financial leases.

If the lessee misses a scheduled payment, the lessor has the right to reclaim the asset and take legal actions. In the event of a missed lease payment, the lessor has the same default rights as creditors. Emery, Finnerty, and Stowe (2011) define this approach as the debt service parity (DSP) approach. The main idea in evaluating leases is that the firm's total cash flows after taxes (CFATs) should be the same under either leasing or buying the asset with debt. From the lessee's perspective, the relevant incremental cash flows associated with a lease versus borrow-and-buy decision include (1) the cost of the asset (savings); (2) the lease payments (cost); (3) the depreciation tax deductions (forgone benefit); (4) the expected net residual value (forgone benefit); (5) any incremental differences in operating or other expenses between leasing and buying alternatives (cost or savings); and (6) any investment tax credit or other tax credits (forgone benefit).

The net advantage to leasing equals the purchase price minus the present value of the incremental CFATs associated with the lease. The net advantage to leasing (NAL) can be expressed as:

$$\text{NAL} = \text{P} - \text{PV(CFATs)} \tag{22.1}$$

where P denotes the purchase price and PV(CFATs) is the present value of the CFATs. Smith and Wakeman (1985) provide a more detailed discussion of marginal tax rates and other costs, including contracting costs, for both the lessor and the lessee.

The appropriate discount rate for determining the present value of the lease payments, any after-tax change in operating or other expenses (due to the lessor becoming responsible for paying them under the terms of the lease), and the depreciation tax deductions is the lessee's after-tax cost of similarly secured debt, assuming 100 percent debt financing for the asset. This is the required rate of return for the lease payments because a firm's lease payments belong to the same risk class as debt payments. Additionally, the lease obligation is secured because the lessor retains ownership of the asset.

However, some differences exist between a lease and a secured debt. On the one hand, the lessee is effectively borrowing 100 percent of the purchase price. That is, the financial lease obligation is not overcollateralized as is typically the case with conventional secured debt financing. Typically, the amount of the secured loan is less than the initial market value of the asset. Thus, the collateral value exceeds the amount of the loan. On the other hand, in the event of Chapter 11 bankruptcy reorganization, the lessor has the option of rejecting a "true" lease and may immediately recover possession of the leased asset and re-lease it or sell it. The lessor may also file an unsecured claim against the lessee for any economic losses suffered, while secured creditors are prevented from immediately repossessing the collateralized asset because of the provision of automatic stay. The provision of an "automatic stay" in Chapter 11 of the Bankruptcy Code allows the debtor firm to stop all payments of interest and principal to creditors and also prevents secured creditors from foreclosing on their collateral. Eisfeldt and Rampini (2009) analyze the ability of the lessor to repossess a leased asset and the agency problem of caring for the leased asset. This issue is discussed later in the chapter. In practice, the required rate of return in present value calculations is a weighted average of the cost of fully secured debt and the cost of unsecured debt.

The present value of the expected residual value of the asset (i.e., the salvage value) is determined by discounting at a higher rate of return to reflect its greater riskiness. Residual value is more closely related to overall project economic risk than to financing risk. Therefore, analysts typically use a project's required rate of return to determine the present value of the expected residual value. The net advantage to leasing can be rewritten as:

$$NAL = P - \sum \frac{((1 - T_c)L_t - \Delta e_t) + T_c(Dep_t)}{(1 + (1 - T_c)k_d)^t} - \frac{SAL}{(1 + k)^N} - ITC \qquad (22.2)$$

where:

NAL = net advantage to leasing
P = purchase price of the asset
T_c = lessee's (asset user's) marginal ordinary income tax rate
L_t = lease payment in year t
Δe_t = total incremental difference in operating or other expenses in year t between the lease and buy alternatives

Dep_t = depreciation deduction (for tax purposes, not financial reporting purposes) in year t;
k_d = pretax cost of debt, assuming 100 percent debt financing for the asset (typically, this is a weighted average of fully secured and unsecured debt rates)
SAL = expected residual value of the asset at the end of the lease
k = required rate of return for the asset (after tax weighted cost of capital)
N = number of periods in the life of the lease
ITC = investment tax credit, if available

The above equation is written from the lessee's perspective. A similar equation can be written for the lessor (Smith and Wakeman 1985). The equation assumes that the lessee makes the lease payments in arrears (i.e., at the end of each period), not in advance (at the beginning of each period), and that the lessor claims any investment tax credit (ITC). Lease agreements often provide for lease payments to be made in advance, which requires adjusting the equation appropriately to reflect the exact timing of the lease payments. When the ITC is available, lease agreements sometimes allow the lessee to claim it, which requires making an appropriate adjustment. The option to allocate the ITC to the party that values it more highly provides an additional tax advantage to leasing. The relative valuation is linked to the effective marginal tax rates. For the lessor to be indifferent between keeping the ITC and passing it to the lessee, the net present value (NPV) of the lease payments where the ITC is passed to the lessee must exceed the NPV of retaining the ITC by $ITC/(1 - T_{lessor})$. Similarly, for the lessee to be indifferent, the difference in NPV must equal $ITC/(1 - T_{lessee})$. Thus, allocating the ITC to the party in the higher tax bracket reduces the total tax bill. Further, the ITC (when available) provides a partial explanation as to why assets with higher ITC are more amenable to leasing.

In a market characterized by perfect competition, fixed real activity choices for a firm, no taxes and contracting costs, and no other frictions, the user of an asset should be indifferent between owning and leasing the asset. Alternatively, if corporate taxes are not zero, the assumption is that the lessor and the lessee have the same effective marginal tax rate. This is simply a special case of the Modigliani and Miller (1958) theorem on capital structure irrelevance.

Smith and Wakeman (1985) point out three conditions that must be met for an asset to be leased: (1) the NPV of the leasing alternative must be non-negative for the lessor; (2) the NPV of leasing must be non-negative for the lessee; and (3) the NPV of leasing must be equal to or greater than the NPV of buying the asset. Therefore, the main contribution of the tax-based models is to show that leasing is beneficial when the lessor and the lessee face different effective marginal tax rates, thus reducing the total tax bill. If marginal tax rates are exogenous, a firm with a low marginal tax rate will be the lessee and a firm with a high marginal tax rate will be the lessor.

Another important contribution of tax models is their ability to explain why manufacturers and third-party lessors offer leases for some assets. Smith and Wakeman (1985) suggest that the provisions in the tax code are important in explaining this variation. The basis for calculating the ITC and the depreciation for the manufacturer-lessor is the manufacturing cost (C), while for the third-party lessor, it is the sale price (P) of the asset. Further, the manufacturing profit P – C need not be immediately recognized for tax purposes. The combined effect of these two provisions is ambiguous, which explains the existence of both manufacturer-lessor and third-party lessor for some assets.

NONTAX MODELS OF LEASING

Despite their contribution to understanding the economic rationale behind leasing and the rationale of why a firm may choose to be a lessor or a lessee, the tax models fail to explain many other contractual features of leasing. For example, tax-based models do not explain why certain assets are more amenable to leasing than others. Chemmanur, Jiao, and Yan (2010) report that in a survey of entrepreneurs by the Small Business Administration (SBA), 13 percent cite the ability to access the latest technology in the least risky way as the main motivation behind leasing, and another 13 percent mention maintenance options and costs. In contrast, only 9 percent cite tax advantages as the main motivation behind leasing. Smith and Wakeman (1985) provide a list of eight nontax characteristics that may influence the leasing decision. The failure of the tax models to explain the relationship between leasing and asset characteristics has spawned several nontax models that build upon some characteristics listed by Smith and Wakeman. Some of these models are discussed below.

Information Asymmetry Models

Starting with Myers and Majluf (1984), financial economic theory has recognized the role of capital structure in alleviating the adverse selection problems created by asymmetric information. Sharpe and Nguyen (1995) show that firms can reduce the cost of external funds arising from asymmetric information problems through leasing and that firms facing a high contracting cost have a greater propensity to lease.

Chemmanur, Jiao, and Yan (2010) provide a well-developed theoretical model of double-sided information asymmetry that attempts to explain many stylized features of leasing contracts. They assume that a manufacturer of capital goods has private information about the quality of these goods and that users of capital goods differ in their cost of providing maintenance for these goods. The maintenance cost is private information to each user who, in turn, comes to learn the quality of capital goods only through time. Leasing emerges as an equilibrium solution to this double-sided information asymmetry and various contractual provisions in leasing contracts also emerge as equilibrium solutions under alternative scenarios. In particular, depending on the nature of the capital equipment and the characteristics of the lessor and lessee, the following provisions emerge as equilibrium solutions: (1) both short-term and long-term operating leases, with noncancellation provisions; (2) leases that grant the lessee the option to buy the asset at termination; (3) service leases, where the manufacturer agrees to maintain the leased asset; and (4) leases involving metering, where the lease payment is a function of the intensity of the asset usage.

The model developed by Chemmanur, Jiao, and Yan (2010) is particularly useful in understanding the leasing market for capital equipment that uses newer technology, where the information asymmetry is likely to be more pronounced. The model's prediction is consistent with the observation by practitioners that leasing allows the transfer of technological risk from lessors to lessees. One limitation of the model is that it cannot explain the prevalence of leasing in the new car market because more information asymmetry exists about old cars. Also, the model cannot explain the presence of third-party lessors who are not manufacturers.

Hendel and Lizzeri (2002) as well as Johnson and Waldman (2003) develop theoretical analyses of leasing contracts focusing on the relationship between the new and used car markets. Hendel and Lizzeri study a setting with two types (levels of quality) of cars with consumers having heterogeneous valuations for quality. Neither the manufacturer nor the consumer knows the true quality of a new car, so no adverse selection exists in the new car market. However, because consumers can observe the quality of a car through using it over time, the used car market is characterized by adverse selection. A leasing contract in their setting specifies not only the rental payment for the car but also the option price at which a consumer can purchase the car at lease maturity.

In the above setting, Hendel and Lizzeri (2002) demonstrate two important results. First, leasing and selling can co-exist in the new car market: consumers with a high valuation for quality prefer to lease a car while those with a low valuation prefer to buy. Leasing thus allows the manufacturer to increase profits by segmenting the new car market between the two kinds of consumers. Second, consumers who lease cars and observe that their cars are of a low quality return them to the manufacturers, while those observing a high quality purchase their cars at the buyback (or option) price. The latter result implies that the manufacturer can set the option price specified in the lease for a new car above the market clearing price in the used car market to reflect the higher quality of off-lease cars. The analysis of Johnson and Waldman (2003) also generates results broadly similar to those of Hendel and Lizzeri (2002).

In another strand of the research on information asymmetry, Beatty, Liao, and Weber (2010) investigate the impact of financial reporting quality on the leasing decision, where higher reporting quality mitigates the effect of information asymmetry. The authors extend Fazzari, Hubbard, and Petersen (1988), who examine the impact of information asymmetry on optimal investment decisions, and build on Biddle and Hilary (2006), who suggest that the role of accounting quality in capital investment decisions depends on the firm's use of other monitoring mechanisms that reduce information asymmetry. Beatty et al. find that firms with worse financial reporting have a greater propensity to lease their assets. The main result is that accounting quality and leasing are substitute mechanisms in reducing financing constraints.

Models Based on Incomplete Contracts, Contracting Costs, and Asset Specificity

Explaining the patterns of asset ownership has been a hallmark of incomplete contracts theory. For example, Baker and Hubbard (2003) provide an insightful application to trucking. One strand of the contracting theories argues that more liquid assets decrease the cost of external financing, thus making leasing more attractive. The reason is that more liquid assets are more redeployable (Shleifer and Vishny 1992) and less specific (Klein, Crawford, and Alchian 1978; Williamson 1979). Indeed, the liquidation value of an asset has received much attention in the incomplete contract theory.

Based on this intuition, Gavazza (2010) examines the commercial aircraft leasing market, which is an ideal candidate for investigating asset specificity and incomplete contracts. More than half of all commercial aircraft is leased, and an active secondary market exists. Additionally, finding a valid proxy for the liquidity of a given aircraft is possible. Gavazza finds that more liquid aircraft is more likely to be leased and to be under an operating lease, commands lease rates with lower mark-ups over prices, and has shorter operating leases than longer capital leases.

An Agency Cost Model of Leasing

Perhaps no other theory has received more recognition in the capital structure literature than the theory of agency costs. Leasing gives rise to an agency problem regarding the care with which the lessee uses or maintains the leased asset. On the other hand, the ability of the lessor to repossess the leased asset is a major benefit of leasing. The U.S. Bankruptcy Code treats leasing and secured lending quite differently under Chapter 11 because the lessee can reject the lease and return the asset to the lessor while the collateral of a secured lender is subject to automatic stay. The provision of an "automatic stay" allows the debtor to stop all payments of interest and principal to the creditors, and also prevents the secured creditors from foreclosing on their collateral. This implicit ability to repossess allows the debt capacity of leasing to exceed the debt capacity of secured lending. Eisfeldt and Rampini (2009) argue that the basic trade-off between the agency cost of maintenance and the benefit of repossession determines whether an asset will be leased. Using data from Compustat and the U.S. Census of Manufactures, Eisfeldt and Rampini show that small firms and credit-constrained firms lease a considerably larger fraction of their capital. Further, firms that pay lower dividends and have lower cash flows (compared to assets) and those with higher Tobin's q lease a significantly larger fraction of their capital. Even for large firms, the fraction of leased capital is 16 percent in their sample, which is comparable to the long-term debt-to-assets ratio of 19 percent. These findings raise important research questions about the effect of weak legal environments on the relative merits of leasing versus secured lending and about the possibility of using leasing data, particularly regarding operating leases, as a revealed-preference indicator of financial constraints.

EMPIRICAL STUDIES ON LEASES

The previous sections reviewed several theoretical models that try to explain why leasing is a valuable financing option for a firm. The following section reviews some empirical findings that focus on the relationship between leasing and debt financing. The empirical findings are mixed on this issue. This section provides a brief review of these findings and a discussion of a comprehensive testing procedure.

The Relationship between Leases and Debt

The current literature contains numerous studies on the relationship between leases and debt. Traditional theories typically treat leases and debt as substitutes. For example, most models discussed above, such as the tax model, the information asymmetry model, and the agency cost model, all predict that a greater use of lease financing should be associated with a lower level of conventional debt financing. However, Lewis and Schallheim (1992) note that leases and debt can be complements because a lessee can sell its tax shields to a lessor through leases. Thus, more leases reduce the potential redundancy of tax shields and hence the cost of debt.

Most early empirical studies provide mixed evidence on the relationship between leases and debt. In particular, Ang and Peterson (1984) present a leasing puzzle by showing that leases and debt are complements even after controlling for differences in debt capacity. By contrast, Marston and Harris (1988) and Krishnan and Moyer (1994) provide evidence suggesting that leases and debt are substitutes. Adedeji and Stapleton (1996) find an insignificant positive relationship between leases and debt for a sample of UK firms.

Smith and Wakeman (1985) point out that this empirical ambiguity may reflect the difficulty of empirically controlling for debt capacity. Another possible explanation for this empirical controversy is the identification problem that may have incurred in previous studies. As a result, the relationship found between leases and debt in those studies could be an unidentified mix of both the true relation and the factors that simultaneously affect leasing and debt financing. To avoid this identification problem, Bayless and Diltz (1988) use an experimental setting in which banks are queried about the amount of funds they would be willing to lend under various hypothetical circumstances. The authors find that banks do not treat outstanding capitalized leases and debt differently.

To resolve the conflicting empirical evidence, Yan (2006) re-examines the relationship between leases and debt. He first incorporates different theories on the relationship between leases and debt into a simple structural model. Yan uses this model to conceptualize the relationship between leasing and debt financing and to capture, in a reduced form, the effects of asymmetric information, moral hazard, and taxes on the relationship between leases and debt. The author then uses the model to derive and test the hypotheses under which leases and debt are substitutes or complements.

In the model, Yan (2006) examines a risk-neutral firm (entrepreneur) that is planning to invest in a new project. The firm has no other existing projects. The firm has available to it an amount of internal capital W, which is insufficient to fund the new project to the first-best level. Thus, the firm needs to finance externally. The firm can raise extra funds through lease or debt financing. In debt financing, the firm borrows from banks or other similar financial institutions, while in leasing, the firm obtains financing from manufacturers or leasing companies. The firm chooses between these two financing alternatives in order to maximize the NPV of its investment in the new project (and thus the firm's value). Therefore, the firm faces the following maximization problem:

$$\begin{aligned} &\max_{d.l.i} M(i) - C(D+d,\ L+l) \\ &s.t.\ W+d+l=i \end{aligned} \tag{22.3}$$

where:

i = amount of investment in the project
D = amount of existing deteriorated debt
d = amount of new debt raised to fund the new investment
L = amount of existing deteriorated leases
l = amount of new leases raised
M = payoff function of the investment
C = financing cost function

The first-order conditions for the above model are:

$$M' - C_1 = 0, \text{ and } M' - C_2 = 0 \tag{22.4}$$

The solutions to these two equations are denoted as $l(D, L)$ and $d(D, L)$. Taking the derivatives of the first-order conditions with respect to L yields:

$$\frac{\partial d}{\partial L} = \frac{M''(C_{12} - C_{22})}{H} \tag{22.5}$$

Similarly, taking the derivatives of the first-order conditions with respect to D yields:

$$\frac{\partial l}{\partial D} = \frac{M''(C_{21} - C_{11})}{H} \text{ where } H = (M'' - C_{11})(M'' - C_{22}) - (M'' - C_{12})^2. \tag{22.6}$$

Here, C_{11} (C_{22}) represents the change in the cost of debt financing (leasing) in response to an extra amount of debt (leases); $C_{11} > 0$ and $C_{22} > 0$. C_{12} is the change in the cost of debt financing in response to an extra amount of existing leases; C_{21} is the change in the cost of leasing in response to an extra amount of existing debt; and $C_{11} = C_{22}$. H is the determinant of the Hessian matrix; $H > 0$.

Yan (2006) interprets the substitutability/complementarity between leases and debt based on the financing cost C. Leases and debt are substitutes when a firm's marginal cost of new debt or new leases increases with fixed-claim obligations in place, that is, $C_{12} > 0$ and $C_{21} > 0$. This interpretation is consistent with the trade-off theory of capital structure. The trade-off theory suggests that each firm has its own optimal leverage ratio, which is determined by the trade-off between the benefits and the costs of fixed-claim obligations. The benefits of fixed-claim obligations come primarily from the tax deductibility of fixed payments. The primary costs are those related to financial distress, personal income taxes, and agency problems. According to this theory, any additional fixed-claim obligation, such as debt or leases, would increase the possibility of financial distress or the possibility of underinvestment (Myers 1977), which leads to a larger cost of further external financing.

Yet, leases and debt are complements when the marginal cost of debt decreases in the use of leases, that is, $C_{12} < 0$ or when the marginal cost of leases decreases in the amount of existing debt, that is, $C_{21} < 0$. This interpretation is consistent with Lewis and Schallheim (1992). If the lessee uses more leases and thereby sells more of its nondebt tax shields, the potential redundancy of its tax shields will be reduced. Consequently, the lessee's tax benefits from issuing debt will be increased, which leads to a reduced marginal cost of debt for the lessee. Or if a firm issues more debt, its effective marginal tax rate can be reduced, so that the firm is more likely to locate a lessor with a higher effective marginal tax rate. Because such a lessor places a greater value on tax shields than does the firm, the lessor is willing to pay for tax shields by demanding smaller lease payments from the firm, which reduce the firm's cost of leasing.

Based on these interpretation, Yan (2006) shows that $\frac{\partial d}{\partial L}$ and $\frac{\partial l}{\partial D}$ are positive if leases and debt are complements but ambiguous if they are substitutes. These are also the empirical hypotheses that Yan tests. To test these hypotheses, he uses a GMM framework to control for endogeneity and firm fixed effects. The empirical evidence generally shows that debt and leases are substitutes on average. Yan also examines the variation between leases and debt in different firms, and concludes that the substitutability between debt and leases is more pronounced in firms (1) paying zero dividends and thus facing a greater degree of information asymmetry; (2) having more investment opportunities and growth options, thus facing higher agency costs; and (3) facing high before-financing marginal tax rates.

Transaction Cost Explanation on Lease versus Buy

Several other papers bypass the direct estimation of this relationship by assuming the substitutability between leases and debt, and explore the role of leasing in firms' financing policies. Smith and Wakeman (1985) provide an informal but insightful analysis of the determinants of corporate leasing policy. They argue that leases can reduce the transaction costs that arise when the asset's physical life exceeds the firm's economic life. Smith and Wakeman informally discuss several possible rationales for some common provisions in leasing contracts. Sharpe and Nguyen (1995) hypothesize that firms facing high financial contracting costs can alleviate these costs by leasing. They present evidence indicating that such firms have a high propensity to lease. Krishnan and Moyer (1994), Barclay and Smith (1995), and Graham, Lemmon, and Schallheim (1998) provide similar results supporting the financial contracting cost explanation of lease versus buy decisions.

Tax Explanation of Lease versus Buy

Graham, Lemmon, and Schallheim (1998) find supporting evidence for the tax theory's prediction of a negative relationship between leasing and the tax rate. Based on the before-financing marginal tax rate, which is a direct measure of tax rates and not endogenously affected by the financing decision, the authors document a negative relationship between a firm's use of operating leases and its marginal tax rate. They find little association between capital leases and the firm's tax rate, a result which they interpret as evidence that capital leases are a mixture of true and nontrue leases from the perspective of the Internal Revenue Service (IRS).

Other Empirical Findings

Several papers study other explanations of the lease versus buy decision. For example, Barclay and Smith (1995) focus on the maturity and priority structure of corporate external obligations, and examine three prevailing explanations for corporate financing choices including leasing and debt financing. They discuss and test the contracting-cost, the information or signaling, and the tax hypotheses. Barclay and Smith do not find any statistically significant evidence for the signaling and the tax explanations, although they provide evidence for the incentive-contracting explanation. The basic tenet of signaling theory is that undervalued (or high-quality) firms will issue more higher-priority claims compared to overvalued (low-quality) firms. Because capitalized leases have a higher priority of claims compared to debt (even secured debt), signaling theory predicts that higher-quality firms have more capitalized leases. But the data examined by Barclay and Smith show that the coefficient of capitalized leases is insignificantly correlated with the quality proxy.

Finally, several studies examine how to value leasing contracts. For example, McConnell and Schallheim (1983) value various provisions in leasing contracts using the redundant-assets methodology of option pricing models. However, because they use the arbitrage-free option pricing methodology, they, by definition, do not study issues of the optimality of these provisions. Grenadier (1995, 1996) also takes a valuation approach to leasing contracts.

SUMMARY AND CONCLUSIONS

The vast literature on leasing and the earlier analytical models have almost exclusively focused on the relative tax incentives of leasing. The first section of this chapter reviews these tax incentives. Despite providing many important insights, the tax models fail to explain several stylized facts about leasing. Recent research attempts to fill this gap by building models based on information asymmetry, incomplete contracts, and agency problems. A review of these models shows that important insights are provided by a specific model in understanding and predicting one or more contractual features for a specific leasing situation. But no single model is sufficiently general to explain all or even most features of leasing. For example, a model that explains why certain kinds of firms (e.g., small firms) have a proclivity for leasing may not be a good model to explain why certain kinds of assets are more amenable to leasing, and vice versa. While researchers have made much progress in helping to understand leasing, many questions still remain unanswered.

DISCUSSION QUESTIONS

1. What are the unique features of lease contracts as described in Smith and Wakeman (1985), Schallheim (1994), Eisfeldt and Rampini (2009), and Gavazza (2010)?
2. What are the arguments for and against treating leases as a substitute for debt?
3. What are the strengths and weaknesses of the tax-based models in explaining leasing?
4. What are the strengths and weaknesses of the different nontax models in explaining the empirical data on leasing?

REFERENCES

Adedeji, Abimbola, and Richard C. Stapleton. 1996. "Leases, Debt, and Taxable Capacity." *Applied Financial Economics* 6:1, 71–83.

Ang, James, and Pamela P. Peterson. 1984. "The Leasing Puzzle." *Journal of Finance* 39:4, 1055–1065.

Baker, George, and Thomas N. Hubbard. 2003. "Make or Buy in Trucking: Asset Ownership, Job Design, and Information." *American Economic Review* 93:3, 551–572.

Barclay, Michael J., and Clifford W. Smith, Jr. 1995. "The Priority Structure of Corporate Liabilities." *Journal of Finance* 50:3, 899–916.

Bayless, Mark E., and J. David Diltz. 1988. "Debt Capacity, Capital Leasing, and Alternative Debt Instruments." *Akron Business and Economic Review* 19:4, 77–88.

Beatty, Anne, Scott Liao, and Joseph Webber. 2010. "Financial Reporting Quality, Private Information, Monitoring and the Lease-versus-Buy Decision." *Accounting Review* 85:4, 1215–1238.

Biddle, Gary C., and Gilles Hillary. 2006. "Accounting Quality and Firm Level Capital Investment." *Accounting Review* 81:5, 963–982.

Brealey, Richard A., and C. M. Young. 1980. "Debt, Taxes, and Leasing—A Note." *Journal of Finance* 35:5, 1245–1250.

Chemmanur, Thomas, Y. Jiao, and An Yan. 2010. "A Theory of Contractual Provisions in Leasing." *Journal of Financial Intermediation* 19:1, 116–142.

Damodaran, Aswath. 2009. "Leases, Debt and Value." Working Paper, New York University. Available at http://ssrn.com/abstract=1390280.

Eisfeldt, Andrea, and Adriano A. Rampini. 2009. "Leasing, Ability to Repossess, and Debt Capacity." *Review of Financial Studies* 22:4, 1621–1657.

Emery, Douglas R., John D. Finnerty, and John Stowe. 2011. *Corporate Financial Management*, 4th ed. Morristown, NJ: Wohl Publishing, Inc.

Fazzari, Steven M., R. Glenn Hubbard, and Bruce C. Petersen. 1988. "Financing Constraints and Corporate Investment." *Brookings Papers on Economic Activity* 1, 141–195.

Flath, David. 1980. "The Economics of Short-Term Leasing." *Economic Inquiry* 18:2, 247–259.

Franks, Julian R., and Stewart D. Hodges. 1978. "Valuation of Financial Lease Contracts: A Note." *Journal of Finance* 33:2, 657–669.

Gavazza, Alessandro. 2007. "Leasing and Secondary Markets: Theory and Evidence from Commercial Aircraft." Working Paper, New York University.

Gavazza, Alessandro. 2010. "Asset Liquidity and Financial Contracts: Evidence from Aircraft Leases." *Journal of Financial Economics* 95:1, 62–84.

Graham, John R., Michael L. Lemmon, and James S. Schallheim. 1998. "Debt, Leases, Taxes and the Endogeneity of Corporate Tax Status." *Journal of Finance* 53:1, 131–162.

Grenadier, Steven R. 1995. "Valuing Lease Contracts a Real-Options Approach." *Journal of Financial Economics* 38:3, 297–331.

Grenadier, Steven R. 1996. "Leasing and Credit Risk." *Journal of Financial Economics* 42:3, 333–364.

Grenadier, Steven R. 2002. "An Equilibrium Analysis of Real Estate Leases" Available at http://ssrn.com/abstract=369780 or doi:10.2139/ssrn.369780.

Hendel, Igal, and Alessandro Lizzeri. 2002. "The Role of Leasing under Adverse Selection." *Journal of Political Economics* 110:1, 113–143.

Johnson, Justin P., and Michael Waldman. 2003. "Leasing, Lemons, and Buybacks." *RAND Journal of Economics* 34:2, 247–265.

Klein, Benjamin, Robert G. Crawford, and Armen Alchian. 1978. "Vertical Integration, Appropriable Rents, and the Competitive Contracting Process." *Journal of Law and Economics* 21:2, 297–326.

Krishnan, V. Sivarama, and R. Charles Moyer. 1994. "Bankruptcy Costs and the Financial Leasing Decision." *Financial Management* 23:2, 31–42.

Lewellen, Wilbur G., Michael S. Long, and John J. McConnell. 1976. "Asset Leasing in Competitive Capital Markets." *Journal of Finance* 31:3, 787–798.

Lewis, Craig M., and James S. Schallheim. 1992. "Are Debt and Leases Substitutes?" *Journal of Financial and Quantitative Analysis* 27:2, 497–511.

Marston, Felicia, and Robert S. Harris. 1988. "Substitutability of Leases and Debt in Corporate Capital Structures." *Journal of Accounting, Auditing and Finance* 3:2, 147–170.

McConnell, John J., and James S. Schallheim. 1983. "Valuation of Asset Leasing Contracts." *Journal of Financial Economics* 12:2, 237–261.

Miller, Merton H., and Charles W. Upton. 1976. "Leasing, Buying, and the Cost of Capital Services." *Journal of Finance* 31:3, 761–786.

Modigliani, Franco, and Merton H. Miller. 1958. "The Cost of Capital, Corporation Finance and the Theory of Investment." *American Economic Review* 48:3, 261–297.

Myers, Stewart C. 1977. "Determinants of Corporate Borrowing." *Journal of Financial Economics* 5:2, 147–175.

Myers, Stewart C., David A. Dill, and Alberto J. Bautista. 1976. "Valuation of Financial Lease Contracts." *Journal of Finance* 31:3, 799–819.

Myers, Stewart C., and Nicholas S. Majluf. 1984. "Corporate Financing Decisions When Firms Have Information That Investors Do Not." *Journal of Financial Economics* 13:1, 187–220.

Ross, Stephen, Randolph Westerfield, and Jeffrey Jaffe. 2010. *Corporate Finance*. New York: McGraw-Hill Irwin.

Schallheim, James S. 1994. *Lease or Buy? Principles for Sound Corporate Decision Making*. Boston: Harvard Business Press.

Sharpe, Steven A., and Hien H. Nguyen. 1995. "Capital Market Imperfections and the Incentive to Lease." *Journal of Financial Economics* 39:2–3, 271–294.

Shleifer, Andrei, and Robert W. Vishny. 1992. "Liquidation Values and Debt Capacity: A Market Equilibrium Approach." *Journal of Finance* 47:4, 1343–1366.

Smith Jr., Clifford. W., and L. MacDonald Wakeman. 1985. "Determinants of Corporate Leasing Policy." *Journal of Finance* 40:3, 895–908.

Williamson, Oliver E. 1979. "Transaction-Cost Economics: The Governance of Contractual Relations." *Journal of Law and Economics* 22:2, 233–261.

Yan, An. 2006. "Leasing and Debt Financing: Substitutes or Complements?" *Journal of Financial and Quantitative Analysis* 41:3, 709–731.

ABOUT THE AUTHORS

Sris Chatterjee is a Professor in the Finance and Business Economics Area at Fordham University's Schools of Business where he is currently the Area Chair. He has taught various courses including mergers and acquisitions, principles of modern finance, and behavioral finance for the graduate and undergraduate levels. Professor Chatterjee's main research interests are in corporate finance and futures and options. He has published in the *Journal of Banking and Finance*, *Journal of Financial Economics*, *Financial Management*, *Journal of Financial and Quantitative Analysis*, and *Journal of Futures Markets*. Professor Chatterjee serves on several editorial boards including the *International Journal of Banking, Accounting and Finance*, and *International Journal of Behavioral Accounting and Finance*. He received his MPhil and PhD degrees from Columbia University's Graduate School of Business.

An Yan is an Associate Professor in the Finance and Business Economics Area at Fordham University's Schools of Business where he also serves as the Director of the Center for Research in Contemporary Finance. Professor Yan teaches the core corporate finance course at the graduate level and also teaches in Fordham's Executive MBA and Master in Quantitative Finance programs. He often serves as a faculty advisory for consulting and internship projects. His main research interest is in theoretical and empirical corporate finance. He has published in scholarly journals including the *Journal of Financial Economics, Journal of Financial and Quantitative Analysis, Journal of Banking and Finance, Journal of Financial Intermediation,* and *Financial Management*. Professor Yan received his undergraduate degree from Tsinghua University, China, and his PhD degree from Boston College.

CHAPTER 23

Private Investment in Public Equity

WILLIAM K. SJOSTROM JR.
Professor of Law, University of Arizona

INTRODUCTION

Private investment in public equity (PIPE) refers to the private sale to a limited number of investors of equity or securities convertible into equity by a company whose stock is publicly traded. *Private* in this context means that the company's sale is structured so that it is exempt from registration with the U.S. Securities and Exchange Commission (SEC). Generally, investors must hold securities issued in an exempt offering (also known as a private placement) for at least six months from the date of issuance. In a typical PIPE transaction, however, the company agrees to promptly register the resale of the PIPE shares (the common stock issued in the private placement, or issued upon conversion of the convertible securities issued in the private placement) following the closing of the private placement. This means that the investors do not have to wait six months to sell their shares but can instead sell them as soon as the SEC declares the resale registration statement effective, which is normally within a few months of the closing of the private placement. During 2009, companies raised a total of $39.7 billion in 1,100 U.S. PIPE deals. While companies of all sizes have used PIPEs to raise money, PIPE deals have emerged as a vital financing source for small public companies with the majority of deals being completed by companies with market capitalizations of $250 million or less. This is driven by the reality that PIPEs represent the only available financing option for many small public companies.

PIPE TYPES

Because PIPE transactions are highly negotiated, considerable variation exists among deals regarding the attributes of the PIPE securities. PIPE securities may consist of common stock or securities convertible into common stock, such as convertible preferred stock or convertible notes, and may be coupled with common stock warrants. Regardless of the type of securities involved, PIPE deals are categorized as either traditional or structured. With a *traditional PIPE*, the PIPE shares are issued at a price fixed on the closing date of the private placement. This fixed price is typically set at a discount to the trailing average of the market price of the issuer's common stock for some period of days before closing of the private placement. As mentioned above, securities regulations generally prohibit investors from selling PIPE shares before the SEC declares the resale registration statement effective. Thus, because the deal price is fixed, investors in traditional PIPEs assume price risk, which is the risk of future declines in the market price of the issuer's common stock during the pendency of the resale registration statement.

With a *structured PIPE*, the issuance price of the PIPE shares is not fixed on the closing date of the private placement. Instead, it adjusts (often downward only) based on future price movements of the issuer's common stock. For example, investors may be issued convertible debt or preferred stock that is convertible into common stock based on a floating or variable conversion price; that is, the conversion price fluctuates with the market price of the issuer's common stock. Hence, with a structured PIPE, investors do not assume price risk during the pendency of the resale registration statement. If the market price declines, so too does the conversion price, and therefore the PIPE securities will be convertible into a greater number of shares of common stock.

For example, say an investor purchases a $1 million convertible note in a PIPE transaction. The note provides that the principal amount is convertible at the holder's option into the issuer's common stock at a conversion rate of 90 percent of the stock's per share market price on the date of conversion. Thus, if the market price of the issuer's common stock is $10 per share, the note is convertible at $9 a share into 111,111 shares of common stock. If the market price drops to $8 per share, the note is then convertible at $7.20 per share into 138,889 shares of common stock. Regardless of how low the price drops, upon conversion the investor will receive $1 million of common stock based on the discounted market price of the stock on the day of conversion.

Some structured PIPEs contain floors on how low the conversion price can adjust downward or caps on how many shares can be issued upon conversion. If a structured PIPE has neither a floor nor cap, it can potentially become convertible into a controlling stake of the PIPE issuer. Continuing the example from above, if the market price dropped to $0.01, the note would then be convertible into more than 100 million shares, which would constitute a controlling stake unless the issuer had at least 200 million shares outstanding. Hence, structured PIPEs lacking floors or caps are pejoratively labeled "death spirals" or "toxic converts" because investors in these deals may be tempted to circulate false negative rumors or engage in other types of market manipulation to push down the issuer's stock price so that their structured PIPEs become convertible into a controlling stake of the issuer (Hillion and Vemaelen 2004).

REGISTRATION REQUIREMENT

As mentioned above, a key feature of a PIPE transaction is the company's agreement to register the resale of the PIPE shares with the SEC. This registration requirement can be either concurrent or trailing. With a concurrent registration requirement, investors commit to buy a specified dollar amount of PIPE securities in the private placement, but their obligations to fund are conditional on the SEC indicating that it is prepared to declare the resale registration statement effective. If the SEC never gets to this point, the investors do not have to go forward with the deal. Thus, the issuer bears the registration risk; that is, the risk that the SEC will refuse to declare the resale registration statement effective.

With a trailing registration rights requirement, which is much more common, the parties close on the private placement, and then the issuer files a registration statement. Consequently, the investors bear the registration risk. If the issuer never files or the SEC never declares the registration statement effective, the investors will be unable to sell their PIPE shares into the market for at least six months. As a result, PIPE deals that include such trailing registration requirements typically obligate the issuer to file the registration statement within 30 days of the private placement closing date and require that it be declared effective within 90 to 120 days of such date. If these deadlines are not met, the issuer is obligated to pay the investors a penalty of 1 to 2 percent of the deal proceeds per month until filing or effectiveness.

PIPE ISSUERS

Public companies of all sizes use PIPE deals as a source of financing but for different reasons. This section discusses why PIPE financing is attractive to both small and large capitalization firms.

Small Capitalization Firms

As mentioned above, small public companies undertake the majority of PIPE deals. These companies generally pursue PIPEs not because they offer advantages over other financing alternatives but because the companies have no other financing alternatives (Chaplinsky and Haushalter 2006; Brophy, Ouimet, and Sialm 2009; Chen, Dai, and Schatzberg 2010). PIPE issuers are not only small in terms of market capitalization but also have a weak cash flow and poorly performing stocks. A study of PIPE issuers by Chaplinsky and Haushalter (2006, p. 4) finds that "more than 84% of PIPE issuers have negative operating cash flow and over 50% of the issuers have falling stock prices in the year prior to issue." Further, a majority of PIPE issuers will run out of cash within a year unless they obtain additional financing. Thus, traditional forms of financing are simply not an option. Few, if any, investment banking firms are willing to underwrite follow-on offerings for small, distressed public companies. Further, these companies lack the collateral and financial performance to qualify for bank loans and the upside potential to attract traditional private equity financing.

Small private companies with limited financing options often go public in order to have access to PIPE financing. These companies probably do not go public through a traditional underwritten initial public offering (IPO) because no underwriter is willing to take them public. Instead, they use reverse mergers. A company goes public through a reverse merger by working with a shell promoter to locate a suitable nonoperating or shell public company. The private company then merges with the shell company thereby succeeding to the shell company's public status. Oftentimes the reverse merger is coupled with PIPE financing, meaning both transactions are closed simultaneously (Sjostrom 2008).

Given the distressed status of PIPE issuers, PIPE financing can be very expensive. Not only does the company typically issue common stock or common stock equivalents at a discount to market price, but PIPE deals often involve other cash flow rights such as dividends or interest (typically paid in kind, not in cash) and warrants. After taking into account these cash flow rights and protective features, such as floating conversion prices, Chaplinsky and Haushalter (2006) find that the "all-in net purchase discount" for PIPE deals ranges from 14.3 percent to 34.7 percent.

Not surprisingly, small capitalization (cap) PIPE issuers continue to perform poorly following PIPE financings. Chaplinsky and Haushalter (2006) also find negative abnormal returns to existing shareholders of PIPE issuers of –16 percent after 12 months (with a median of –43 percent) and –33 percent after 24 months (with a median of –70 percent). Additionally, the stock of 28 percent of issuers was delisted within 24 months after the PIPE financing.

Large Capitalization Firms

In recent years, larger companies have increasingly opted for PIPE financing. While these companies generally have other financing alternatives (unlike many smaller public companies), they presumably pursue PIPE financing because it represents the best financing alternative at a given point in time. For example, during the financial crisis, Citigroup, Goldman Sachs, and Morgan Stanley all raised capital through PIPE transactions.

For a larger cap public company, PIPE financing can involve lower transaction costs and can be completed on a quicker timeframe than, for example, an underwritten follow-on or secondary equity offering (SEO). Additionally, firms can use PIPE financing on a confidential basis because they do not need to file a registration statement with the SEC or make a public announcement until the financing is closed. Contrast this to an SEO where the issuer must file a registration statement or prospectus supplement preclosing, thereby alerting the marketplace to the deal preclosing. This disclosure typically triggers the well-known negative SEO announcement effect, increasing the issuer's floatation costs for the offering (Ritter 2003). Firms need to weigh these advantages against the disadvantages of PIPE financing, including the big disadvantage of the issuer likely having to sell PIPE securities at a discount to the then-current market price of its stock.

PIPE INVESTORS

PIPE investors pursue PIPE deals for different reasons. This section discusses the different types of investors that invest in PIPE deals of small capitalization and large capitalization firms and their typical reasons for investing.

Small Capitalization Investors

The dismal post-PIPE performance of small cap companies raises the question of who invests in PIPEs. According to Brophy, Ouimet, and Sialm (2009), hedge funds invest for the obvious reason: Their returns from PIPE investments meet or beat market benchmarks. Chaplinsky and Haushalter (2006, p. 4) estimate PIPE investors' excessive returns using various benchmarks and find that "from three to twelve months post-issue, average returns consistently exceed benchmark returns, often by double digits."

Hedge funds can obtain these returns notwithstanding the poor performance of PIPE issuers through a relatively straightforward trading strategy. They sell short the issuer's common stock promptly following public disclosure of the PIPE deal (Brophy, Ouimet, and Sialm 2009). To execute a short sale, a fund borrows stock of the PIPE issuer from a broker-dealer and sells this borrowed stock in the market. The fund then closes out or covers the short sale at a later date by buying shares in the open market and delivering them to the lender. By shorting stock against the PIPE shares, the fund locks in the PIPE deal purchase discount. With a traditional PIPE, if the market price of the issuer's common stock drops below the discounted price after a PIPE transaction, the fund takes a loss on the PIPE shares. However, the gains exceed the loss when the hedge fund closes out its short position because it can buy shares in the market to cover the position at a lower price than it earlier sold the borrowed shares. If the market price of the issuer's common stock rises after the PIPE transaction, the fund incurs a loss when closing out the short position because it has to buy shares to cover the position at a higher price than it earlier sold the borrowed shares. The increase in the value of the PIPE shares exceeds this loss because the fund purchased them at a discount to the prerise market price.

For example, say an issuer negotiates a traditional PIPE deal for the sale of $1 million of common stock to a hedge fund at a 15 percent discount to market price as shown in Exhibit 23.1. The issuer then discloses the deal to the market, and its stock drops from $11 to $10 per share. Shortly thereafter, the parties close the private placement, the fund wires $1 million to the issuer, the issuer issues 117,647 shares of common stock to the fund ($1 million divided by $8.50), and the fund sells short 117,647 shares of the issuer's common stock at an average price of $9.50 or $1,117,646.50 in the aggregate. Three months later, the PIPE resale registration statement is declared effective, and the fund unwinds its position, that is, it sells its PIPE shares at the prevailing market price of, say, $7.00 per share, and covers its short position at $7.00 per share resulting in a profit of $117,646.50 on the transaction, excluding transaction fees such as legal fees and brokerage commissions.

The above example assumes, among other things, that the fund can sell its PIPE shares and cover its short position at the same price per share, which is probably

Exhibit 23.1 An Example of a Traditional PIPE Deal

Initial Investment	–$1,000,000.00
Proceeds from short sales	1,117,646.50
Proceeds from sales of PIPE shares	823,529.00
Cost to cover short position	–823,529.00
Profit	$117,646.50
90-day return	11.76%
Annualized return	47.04%

Note: This exhibit illustrates a how a PIPE deal conducted by a hedge fund can result in a profit. The example assumes that the fund can sell its PIPE shares and cover its short position at the same price per share, which is probably unrealistic.

Exhibit 23.2 An Example of a Structure PIPE Deal

Initial Investment	–$1,000,000.00
Proceeds from short sales	1,117,646.50
Proceeds from sales of PIPE shares	1,215,683.00
Cost to cover short position	–823,529.00
Profit	$509,800.50
90-day return	50.98%
Annualized return	203.92%

Note: This exhibit illustrates a structured PIPE deal for the sale of a $1 million convertible note to a hedge fund resulting in a profit.

an unrealistic assumption. However, even if the fund covers its short position at $7 per share and sells its PIPE shares at $6.50 per share, it would still make $58,823.50 on the deal, yielding a 90-day return of 5.88 percent and an annualized return of 23.53 percent.

The strategy can be even more profitable for hedge funds in a structured PIPE deal with a floating conversion price. If the issuer's stock price drops, a fund profits on its short sales dollar for dollar. At the same time, it also profits on the PIPE shares because the conversion price of the PIPE securities is based on a discount to market price on the date of conversion; that is, the conversion price floats down with the market price. Hence, the fund makes money on both sides of the trade, subject only to unwinding risk.

For example, assume that an issuer negotiates a structured PIPE deal for the sale of a $1 million convertible note to a hedge fund as illustrated in Exhibit 23.2. The note bears interest at 10 percent per annum and provides that the principal amount and interest is convertible at the holder's option into the issuer's common stock at 85 percent of the per share market price on the date of conversion. The issuer then discloses the deal to the market, and its stock drops from $11 to $10 per share. Shortly thereafter, the parties close the private placement, the fund wires $1,000,000 to the issuer, the issuer issues the note, and the fund sells short 117,647 shares of the issuer's common stock at an average prices of $9.50 or $1,117,646.50 in the aggregate. Three months later, the PIPE resale registration statement is declared effective, at which time the issuer's stock is trading at $7 per share. The fund converts the note into 173,669 shares of common stock based on $5.95 conversion price (85 percent of $7), sells these shares into the market at $7 per share, and covers its short position at $7 per share resulting in a profit of $509,800.50 on the transaction, excluding transaction fees.

This strategy is obviously dependent on a fund being able to borrow shares to sell short. For various reasons, a limited supply of PIPE issuer shares is often available in the equity lending market. Thus, a fund may be unable to borrow enough shares to fully lock in the discount through standard short sales. Some funds, however, have allegedly dealt with this issue by engaging in naked short selling. A *naked short sale* is simply the sale of shares for the account of an investor who neither owns nor has borrowed the shares. Naked short selling is not necessarily illegal but may constitute illegal stock manipulation, depending on intent.

Besides short selling, many hedge funds retain upside potential by negotiating for warrants as part of a PIPE transaction. Hedge funds typically hold on to these warrants even after unwinding their PIPE shares positions, so that they can profit further in the event the issuer's stock happens to rise above the warrant exercise price. In sum, hedge funds can garner superior returns through PIPE investments because they purchase the PIPE shares at a substantial discount to market, manage their downside risk through short sales and floating conversion prices, retain upside potential through warrants, and liquidate their positions a relatively short time after closing on the private placement.

Large Capitalization Investors

Investors in larger cap PIPEs include mutual funds, private equity funds, and sovereign wealth funds. These investors are typically long-term and are attracted to a particular PIPE offering because of issuer fundamentals. For them, a big advantage to PIPE investing as opposed to buying shares in the open market is that they can make a large investment at a discount and without having to concern themselves with moving the market.

SECURITIES LAWS COMPLIANCE

PIPE transactions raise numerous legal issues. This section discusses compliance with federal securities laws. The Securities Act of 1933 requires that every offer and sale of a security either be registered with the SEC or qualify for an exemption from registration. A PIPE involves two offerings—an exempt or private offering by the issuer to the PIPE investors and a registered or public offering by the PIPE investors to the public.

Private Offering

A private offering, by definition, is conducted in compliance with an exemption from registration as opposed to being registered with the SEC. The Securities Act and rules promulgated there under contain numerous registration exemptions. PIPE issuers generally rely on the exemption provided by Section 4(2) of the Securities Act. Section 4(2) exempts from registration "transactions by an issuer not involving any public offering." Thus, the application of Section 4(2) turns on the definition of "public offering," but the Securities Act does not define the term. The SEC has, however, promulgated Rule 506, which serves as a Section 4(2) "safe harbor"; that is, if a private offering complies with the conditions specified in Rule 506, the offering will be deemed exempt under Section 4(2).

To fall within the safe harbor, the offering must be limited to accredited investors and have no more than 35 nonaccredited investors. Virtually all hedge funds and the like qualify as accredited investors because Rule 501(a) defines "accredited investor" as, among other things, any business "not formed for the specific purposed of acquiring the securities offered, with total assets in excess of $5,000,000." The issuer has to furnish any nonaccredited investors who purchase securities in the offering with certain specified information about the issuer and the offering a reasonable time before the purchase and has to reasonably believe that all nonaccredited investors are sophisticated, either alone or with their purchaser representatives. Typically, PIPE deals are marketed only to accredited investors, so that the issuer does not have to contend with meeting these disclosure and sophistication requirements.

Neither the issuer nor anyone acting on its behalf can solicit investors in an offering made in reliance on Rule 506 through any form of "general solicitation" or "general advertising." For a communication to a potential investor not to be considered general solicitation or advertising, the SEC requires a pre-existing, substantive relationship between the solicitor and potential investor. The SEC considers a relationship pre-existing if it is established before the solicitation for the particular offering. The SEC considers a relationship substantive if it "would enable the issuer (or a person acting on its behalf) to be aware of the financial circumstances or sophistication of the persons with whom the relationship exists or that otherwise are of some substance and duration" Mineral Lands Research & Mktg. Corp., SEC No-Action Letter, 1985 SEC No-Act. LEXIS 2811at *2 (December 4, 1985).

The only filing that must be made with the SEC for a Rule 506 offering is a nine-page Form D setting forth some basic information about the offering. The company must file the Form D no later than 15 days after the first sale of securities. Securities issued in reliance on Rule 506 are considered "restricted securities." This means a PIPE investor cannot generally sell the PIPE shares for at least six months from the closing of the PIPE, unless the subsequent sale is registered with the SEC.

Public Offering

As mentioned above, PIPE deals include a requirement that the issuer file a registration statement regarding the resale or secondary offering of the PIPE shares. The issuer typically registers the resale on Form S-3 under the Securities Act unless it does not meet the eligibility requirements of the form. Form S-3 is an abbreviated registration form that allows a public company to incorporate by reference the information contained in its existing and future quarterly, annual, and other required SEC reports under the Securities Exchange Act of 1934 ("Exchange Act"). This means that much information about the company is not actually set forth in the registration statement, but instead the registration statement contains a cross reference to the company's Exchange Act reports. As a result of incorporation by reference, frequently a Form S-3 prospectus will be short, containing only very abbreviated financial and business disclosure about the issuer.

To be eligible to use Form S-3 for a secondary offering, among other things, a company must have been a reporting company for at least the previous year and have filed all Exchange Act reports timely during the previous year. Additionally, the company must (1) have securities of the same class as those being registered "listed and registered on a national securities exchange or . . . quoted on the automated quotation system of a national securities association" (Securities Act of 1933, Form S-3, General Instructions I.B.3.) or (2) have a common stock public float of at least $75 million. Many PIPE issuers, however, fail to meet the first requirement because their shares are listed on the OTC Bulletin Board or the Pink Sheets, and the SEC has stated that these markets do not fall within the authorized exchanges or quotation systems. Further, many PIPE issuers do not have a sufficient public float to meet the second requirement.

If a company is ineligible to use Form S-3, it will have to register the resale on Form S-1. Form S-1 is a full-blown registration statement; that is, much more information is actually set forth in the registration statement as compared to a registration statement on Form S-3. Using Form S-1 will likely result in higher transaction costs for a PIPE issuer as compared to a registration statement on Form S-3. Because Form S-1 requires more elaborate disclosure, it takes more time and effort to prepare, which results in higher professional fees. Additionally, the SEC is more likely to review a Form S-1 registration statement, which would further delay effectiveness. Hence, PIPE investors often demand an additional discount or higher penalty to compensate them for the fact that, as compared to an S-3, a Form S-1 takes longer for the company to file the registration statement and involves greater risk that effectiveness will be delayed by SEC review.

Firms file the resale registration statement for a PIPE as a shelf registration statement under Securities Act Rule 415. Rule 415 allows a registration statement to cover sales that will be made over a period of time. This provides investors with the flexibility to sell their PIPE shares into the market over an extended period of time. Generally for a PIPE shares registration statement to qualify under Rule 415, the registration statement must pertain only to "[s]ecurities which are to be offered or sold solely by or on behalf of a person or persons other than the registrant, a subsidiary of the registrant or a person of which the registrant is a subsidiary" Securities Act of 1933, Rule 415(a)(1)(i).

Integration

Under the concept of integration, the SEC may "integrate" or treat two or more offerings, which an issuer structured and views as separate and discrete, as one larger offering. Integration is generally intended to prevent an issuer from circumventing the registration requirements of the Securities Act by structuring a large offering for which an exemption is unavailable as two or more smaller exempt offerings. If the SEC integrates a series of apparently exempt offerings, the integrated offering must qualify for an exemption. If it does not, since by definition the integrated offering was not registered, all sales in connection therewith will have been made in violation of Section 5 of the Securities Act, resulting in, among other things, each purchaser in the offering having a right to rescind the transaction.

Integration is relevant to a PIPE deal because the deal involves a private placement followed shortly thereafter by a public offering. If these two offerings are integrated and treated as one larger offering, the issuer violates Section 5 of the Securities Act. Rule 506 would not exempt the larger offering because the public offering component involves general solicitation. The registration statement does not save a violation because it covers the resale of the underlying securities by the PIPE investors and not the issuance of the PIPE securities to the investors. Hence, the integrated offering is neither fully registered nor exempt, and therefore violates Section 5.

Fortunately for PIPE issuers, integration issues are easy to manage because of Securities Act Rule 152. Rule 152 dates back to 1935 and "makes clear that offerings made prior to the filing of the registration statement and made under circumstances which did not necessitate registration or contemplate registration, do not by the fact of registration become the type of offerings which are prohibited by the Securities Act" Securities Act Release No. 305, (March 2, 1935). Under SEC interpretations of the rule, as long as the private offering is completed before the filing of the registration statement for the secondary offering, the offerings will not be integrated even if the registration statement is filed shortly after the closing of the private placement.

In fact, SEC interpretations allow an issuer to file a resale registration statement before closing the related private offering without integration concerns, provided the private offering meets each of the following three conditions:

1. The private offering investors are "irrevocably bound to purchase a set number of securities for a set purchase price that is not based on market price or a fluctuating ratio, either at the time of effectiveness of the resale registration statement or at any subsequent date."
2. There are "no conditions to closing that are within an investor's control or that an investor can cause not to be satisfied." Examples of prohibited closing conditions include those "relating to the market price of the company's securities or the investor's satisfactory completion of its due diligence on the company."
3. "The closing of the private placement of the unissued securities must occur within a short time after the effectiveness of the resale registration statement" SEC Division of Corporate Finance, 1999, Sec. 35b.

Hence, a PIPE can be structured so that the PIPE investors' obligations to close on the private placement are conditional on the effectiveness of the resale registration statement for the underlying common stock. Having the SEC declare a resale registration statement effective is considered outside the control of the PIPE investors.

SEC PIPE ENFORCEMENT ACTIONS

Considering the popularity of PIPE investments among hedge funds, some of which routinely push the legal envelope with their trading strategies, finding that the SEC has uncovered PIPE investors that have engaged in some questionable practices is not surprising. In the last five years, the SEC has brought numerous enforcement actions relating to PIPE deals. Most of these actions involve claims that the defendants engaged in insider trading and/or violated Section 5 of the Securities Act of 1933 (Securities Act).

Insider Trading

The SEC has leveled insider trading allegations against defendants that sold short shares of PIPE issuers in the open market before public disclosure of the PIPE financing. Under the misappropriation theory of insider trading, a person violates Section 10(b) of the Securities and Exchange Act of 1934 (Exchange Act) and Rule 10b-5 "when he misappropriates confidential information for securities trading purposes, in breach of a duty owed to the source of the information" *United States v. O'Hagan*, 521 U.S. 642, 652 (1997). To prevail on an insider trading claim under the misappropriation theory, the SEC must prove that the defendant traded on material, nonpublic information in breach of a duty of trust or confidence owed by the defendant to the information source.

Information is considered material with respect to insider trading if a substantial likelihood exists that a reasonable investor would consider the information important in making an investment decision. Put differently, "there must be a substantial likelihood that the disclosure of the [information] would have been viewed by the reasonable investor as having significantly altered the 'total mix' of information made available" *TSC Indus., Inc. v. Northway, Inc.*, 426 U.S. 438, 449 (1976). In a 2000 release, the SEC specifically listed "private sales of additional securities" as an event "that should be reviewed carefully to determine whether [it is] material" Selective Disclosure and Insider Trading, SEC Release No. 34-43154, 2000 WL 1201556 at *10 (August 15, 2000).

A duty of trust or confidence is deemed to arise from any fiduciary or fiduciary-like relationship, such as an employer/employee, attorney/client, and doctor/patient relationship. Outside of this context, Rule 10(b)(5)-2 under the Exchange Act is relevant. Rule 10(b)(5)-2 "provides a non-exclusive definition of circumstances in which a person has a duty of trust or confidence for purposes of the 'misappropriation' theory of insider trading." Among other things, the rule provides that a duty of trust or confidence exists "[w]henever a person agrees to maintain information in confidence."

The December 12, 2006, complaint filed by the SEC in the United States District Court for the Southern District of New York against Edwin Buchanan Lyon IV, Gryphon Master Fund, L.P., and related entities, provides a good example of the application of the misappropriation theory in the context of PIPE deals: *SEC v. Lyon* (S.D.N.Y. filed December 12, 2006). According to the complaint, defendants engaged in illegal insider trading by selling short the securities of four PIPE issuers before the public announcements of their PIPE offerings. The SEC alleged that information concerning the four PIPE offerings was material because "the announcement typically precipitates a decline in the price of a PIPE issuer's securities due to the dilutive effect of the offering and the PIPE shares being issued at a discount to the then prevailing market price of the issuer's stock." Hence, "[a] reasonable investor would have considered information concerning each of the four PIPEs—including the date of the PIPE offering, the discounted price of the stock, and the number of shares issued—important to his or her investment decision and a significant alteration of the total mix of information available to the public."

The SEC alleged that the defendants owed a duty of trust or confidence to the PIPE issuers because defendants "received offering documents with language requiring them to maintain the information contained therein in confidence and/or to refrain from trading prior to the public announcement of the offering." Hence, the SEC appears to be asserting that the defendants agreed to keep information concerning the impending PIPE deals in confidence, and therefore the requisite duty of trust or confidence is established under Rule 10(b)(5)-2. The SEC alleged that defendants breached this duty when they sold short the issuers' securities before each of the four PIPE deals were publicly announced.

Section 5 Violations

Section 5 of the Securities Act requires that every offer and sale of a security be registered with the SEC, although a number of exemptions from registration are available. The SEC has recently asserted Section 5 violations against several PIPE investors. The factual basis is functionally the same in all these cases, and *SEC v. Joseph J. Spiegel* provides a representative example. *See SEC v. Spiegel, Inc.*, No. 03C-1685, 2003 U.S. Dist. 17933 (N.D. IL 2003). Spiegel was the portfolio manager for a hedge fund that invested in several PIPE deals. In three of these deals, Spiegel hedged the fund's PIPE investment by selling short the PIPE issuers' securities before the resale registration statements for the PIPE shares were declared effective. Spiegel then covered some or all of these short sales with PIPE shares.

According to *SEC v. Spiegel, Inc.*, the SEC views the short sales as Section 5 violations "because shares used to cover a short sale are deemed to have been sold when the short sale was made." Hence, Spiegel, in effect, sold the PIPE shares into the market before registration statements for these sales were declared effective, thus violating Section 5.

The reason this allegedly constitutes a violation of Section 5 is somewhat convoluted. The PIPE shares were issued in a transaction not involving a public offering and were therefore "restricted." Restricted securities can be sold only if the sale is registered with the SEC or if an exemption from registration is available. Typically, the resale of securities is exempt from registration under Section 4(1) of the Securities Act. Section 4(1) exempts from registration "transactions by any person other than an issuer, underwriter, or dealer." In the SEC's view, however, Section 4(1) is unavailable to Spiegel because he is an underwriter. Section 2(a)(11) of the Securities Act defines the term "underwriter," among other things, as "any person who has purchased from an issuer with a view to . . . the distribution of any security." Under SEC interpretations, anyone who sells restricted securities is generally presumed to be an underwriter unless the sale is made in compliance with Securities Act Rule 144. Rule 144 sets forth conditions under which a person who sells restricted securities "shall be deemed not to be engaged in a distribution of such securities and therefore not to be an underwriter thereof within the meaning of Section 2(a)(11) of the [Securities] Act" Securities Act of 1993, Rule 144. Because Spiegel, in effect, sold the restricted shares (the PIPE shares) in an unregistered transaction and out of compliance with Rule 144, he is presumed to be an underwriter. Hence, Section 4(1) does not exempt the sales and neither does any other exemption. Thus, Spiegel violated Section 5 because the sales were neither registered nor exempt.

This line of reasoning rests on characterizing Spiegel's pre-effectiveness short sales as sales of PIPE shares. Such a characterization makes sense in Spiegel's case because he allegedly "executed 'naked' short sales by, among other things, selling short without borrowing unrestricted shares to deliver" *SEC v. Spiegel, Inc.* No. 03C-1685, 2003 U.S. Dist. 17933 (N.D. IL 2003). However, the analysis would be the same even if Spiegel had borrowed unrestricted shares to sell short. The SEC has long taken the position that a short sale cannot be covered with securities that were restricted on the date of the short sale.

A PIPE investor can sell short a PIPE issuer's securities before effectiveness of the resale registration so long as the short position is covered with shares purchased in the open market. As the SEC stated in a recent order from an administrative proceeding:

> *Many PIPE investors "hedge" their investment by selling short the PIPE issuer's securities before the resale registration statement is declared effective. There is nothing per se illegal about "hedging" a PIPE investment by selling short the issuer's securities. Such short sales do not violate the registration provisions of the Securities Act if, among other things, the investor closes out the short position with shares purchased in the open market (*In re Spinner Asset Management, LLC, *SEC Order, Securities Act Release No. 8763, Investment Advisers Act Release No. 2573 (December 20, 2006)).*

In this situation, the investor would still be viewed as selling the shares it used to cover the short position into the market on the date it effected the short sale. However, because these shares were purchased in the open market and are therefore unrestricted, the investor will not have violated Section 5; the sales will be exempt under Section 4(1) because the investor will not be considered an underwriter.

The SEC's position may make sense conceptually. It does not, however, appear to further the policy behind Section 5. The policy behind Section 5 is "to provide investors with full disclosure of material information concerning public offerings of securities in commerce," *Ernst & Ernst v. Hochfelder*, 425 U.S. 185 (1976), so that they can make informed investment decisions. To that end, Section 5 generally requires that all public offerings of securities be registered with the SEC and that each investor in the offering have access to a prospectus. Whether a PIPE investor covers short sales with PIPE shares or open-market purchases has no impact on a seller's disclosure obligations. Disclosure regarding the resale of PIPE shares will be set forth in the resale registration statement, and this disclosure will be the same regardless of the type of shares used by a PIPE investor to cover a short position.

In the PIPE context, the SEC's position is apparently based on the fact that allowing a PIPE investor to sell short an issuer's stock and then later cover the short position with PIPE shares would enable PIPE investors "to invest in PIPE offerings without incurring market risk." There are at least two problems with this justification. First, Section 5 is about ensuring disclosure, not preventing investors from avoiding market risk. Second, the SEC allows PIPE investors to avoid market risk by short selling so long as the short position is covered by shares purchased in the open market. If the issue really is about market risk, should not the SEC interpret Section 5 to prohibit this as well? Notably, two courts have recently dismissed Section 5 violation claims in PIPE cases brought by the SEC involving investors who covered short sales with PIPE shares.

Rule 105 of Regulation M under the Exchange Act prohibits an investor from selling shares short within five business days of the pricing of a firm commitment public offering and then covering the short sales with shares purchased in the public offering. This prohibition, however, is not based on Section 5 but on the antifraud and antimanipulation provisions of the securities laws. Regardless, the prohibition does not apply to PIPE-related transactions because they do not involve firm commitment underwritings.

At any rate, by prohibiting a PIPE investor from covering a short position with PIPE shares, the SEC is not ensuring that PIPE investors are subject to market risk. What it is ensuring is that the investors will be subject to increased unwinding risk. Unwinding risk is the risk that unwinding or closing out a hedged position is difficult and expensive. Unwinding risk is minimal if a PIPE investor can use PIPE shares to close out its position. It simply delivers the PIPE shares to cover the short position once the resale registration statement for the PIPE shares is declared effective. Since the SEC does not allow this, the investor will instead need to have a broker execute a sale order for the PIPE shares and a buy order for market shares. Hence, the PIPE investor will have to pay a brokerage commission on each order and will also likely lose money on the bid/ask spread.

This assumes that the orders can be executed simultaneously. Simultaneous execution, however, will be difficult with respect to the shares of many PIPE issuers because their stocks are thinly traded. Hence, PIPE investors also have to bear the risk of potential adverse price movement following execution of one order but before execution of the other, and the thinner the market for a PIPE issuer's shares, the greater the risk. The end result is that PIPE issuers will have to compensate investors for this unwinding risk through such means as greater market discount and increased warrant coverage. Alternatively, PIPE investors may insist on a floating PIPE deal because the repricing mechanism would provide a built-in hedge, thereby reducing unwinding risk. That is, PIPE investors will be hedged against market risk without having to engage in short selling.

REGULATORY ARBITRAGE

Hedge funds can reap positive abnormal risk-adjusted returns from investing in PIPEs in part because they are engaging in regulatory arbitrage. This becomes apparent when a PIPE transaction is compared to an underwritten, firm-commitment, follow-on public offering of common stock or SEO.

In an SEO, an issuer sells shares of common stock at a market discount to a syndicate of underwriters. The syndicate then promptly resells the shares to the public. In a typical PIPE transaction, an issuer sells common stock or securities convertible into common stock at a market discount to a "syndicate" of hedge funds. The "syndicate" then promptly resells the PIPE shares to the public—directly, if the closing is conditional on the effectiveness of the resale registration, or if not, indirectly through short sales.

The regulatory implications for the underwriters of a follow-on public offering as compared to those for investors in a PIPE, however, are much different. For example, Regulation M under the Exchange Act places a whole host of trading restrictions on underwriters at specified times during the public offering. Regulation M generally has no application to PIPE investors. Further, the Financial Industry Regulatory Authority (FINRA) (formerly known as the National Association of Securities Dealers, Inc. (NASD)), the self-regulatory organization of which virtually every investment banking firm in the United States is a member, and hence subject to its rules, regulates public offering underwriting compensation.

Specifically, FINRA Rule 5110 provides that "no member or person associated with a member shall receive an amount of underwriting compensation in connection with a public offering which is unfair or unreasonable." Under the rule, an underwriter is required to make certain filings with FINRA specifying the underwriter's proposed compensation. FINRA then adds up all "items of value" to be received by the underwriters in connection with the offering including discounts, commissions, expense reimbursements, and warrants, and then notifies the underwriters as to whether it finds the proposed compensation unfair or unreasonable. FINRA presumably uses a multifactored formula to make the determination but refuses to provide the specific formula out of concern that doing so "would tend to encourage members to charge issuers the maximum compensation allowed. . ." Exchange Act Release No. 30,587 (April 15, 1992).

FINRA has indicated that the gross dollar amount, type of underwriting (firm commitment or best efforts), and type of offering (initial or follow-on) are relevant to the calculation. In a 1992 Notice to Members, the NASD indicated that "generally accepted levels of underwriting compensation" for a firm commitment follow-on offering as a percentage of gross dollar amount of the offering was 14.57 percent for a $1 million deal, 10.72 percent for a $5 million deal, and 8.18 percent for a $10 million deal: NASD Notice to Members 92-53 (1992). A PIPE deal does not fall within the ambit of Rule 5110. Thus, there are no restrictions on the "compensation" hedge funds can receive for doing the deal. As mentioned above, the "All-in" discount for PIPE deals ranges from 14.3 percent to 34.7 percent, well above the maximum FINRA would allow an underwriter to charge for a follow-on public offering.

Additionally, underwriters face potential liability under Section 11 of the Securities Act for material misstatements in, or omissions from, registration statements of offerings they underwrite, subject to the due diligence defense. Hence, a standard part of an SEO is a due diligence investigation of the issuer by the lead underwriter and its counsel. This investigation is necessary not only to preserve the due diligence defense but also to protect the underwriter's reputational capital. By bringing an offering to the market, an underwriter implicitly certifies the legitimacy of the offering to the marketplace. If the certification turns out to be misplaced, the underwriter's reputational capital will take a hit. Therefore, an underwriter will not proceed with a deal if the investigation uncovers major problems with the issuer. Conversely, a hedge fund generally does not face potential liability under Section 11 when investing in a PIPE deal nor is its investment in a deal viewed as an implicit certification of the issuer. Hence, the hedge fund can get away with performing minimal due diligence.

The bottom line is that hedge funds are engaging in regulatory arbitrage when they invest in PIPE deals. They are in essence underwriting SEOs but avoiding many of the regulations applicable to traditional underwriters. Hence, hedge funds can sell short stock in PIPE issuers at any time during the "distribution," can charge as much in "compensation" as the PIPE issuer is willing to pay, and can choose to perform minimal due diligence. Further, they do not have to compete for deals against SEO underwriters. Virtually no investment banking firms underwrite SEOs for small companies. The economics simply does not make sense because the FINRA cap on underwriting compensation is too low. Underwriters cannot charge enough to make up for the small deal size, heightened liability, and reputational concerns associated with small company offerings. Therefore, they do not do them (Sjostrom 2010).

SUMMARY AND CONCLUSIONS

Companies of all sizes use PIPE financing. For larger companies, PIPE deals offer quick and confidential access to equity financing and attract the interest of long-term investors, such as mutual funds and pension funds. For smaller companies, PIPE deals are a financing option of last resort and mainly attract hedge funds looking to make short-term profits. By legally skirting various regulations, hedge funds can earn market-beating returns through PIPE investing.

PIPE deals raise numerous securities regulation issues, but all of them are manageable. Because hedge funds regularly push the legal envelope, the SEC has brought several enforcement actions against them in recent years, with mixed success.

In conclusion, PIPE deals demonstrate the dynamism of our capital markets. They have filled a financing gap for small public companies while adding another financing option for larger public companies.

DISCUSSION QUESTIONS

1. What benefits does a PIPE offering provide an issuer over a traditional private placement?
2. At whose expense are hedge funds profiting through PIPE deals?
3. Why do PIPE shares sell at a discount?
4. Why does an issuer's stock price typically drop following the announcement of a PIPE financing?

REFERENCES

Brophy, David J., Paige P. Ouimet, and Clemens Sialm. 2009. "Hedge Funds as Investors of Last Resort." *Review of Financial Studies* 22:2, 541–574.

Chaplinsky, Susan, and David Haushalter. 2006. "Financing under Extreme Uncertainty: Contract Terms and Returns to Private Investments in Public Equity." Working Paper, University of Virginia.

Chen, Hsuan-Chi, Na Dai, and John D. Schatzberg. 2010. "The Choice of Equity Selling Mechanisms: PIPEs versus SEOs." *Journal of Corporate Finance* 16:1, 104–119.

Ernst & Ernst v. Hochfelder, 425 U.S. 185 (1976).

Exchange Act Release No. 30,587 (Apr. 15, 1992).

FINRA Rule 5110.

Hillion, Pierre, and Theo Vermaelen. 2004. "Death Spiral Convertibles." *Journal of Financial Economics* 71:2, 381–415.

In re Spinner Asset Management, LLC, SEC Order, Securities Act Release No. 8763, Investment Advisers Act Release No. 2573 (Dec. 20, 2006).

Mineral Lands Research & Mktg. Corp., SEC No-Action Letter, 1985 SEC No-Act. LEXIS 2811at *2 (December 4, 1985).

NASD Notice to Members 92-53. 1992.

Ritter, Jay R. 2003. "Investment Banking and Securities Issuance." In George M. Constantinides, Milton Harris, and René Stulz, eds., *Handbook of the Economics of Finance*, vol. 1A, 255–306. Amsterdam: Elsevier B.V.

SEC Division of Corporate Finance. 1999. *Manual of Publicly Available Telephone Interpretations*, Sec. 35b.

SEC v. Lyon (S.D.N.Y. filed December 12, 2006). Available at http://www.sec.gov/litigation/complaints/2006/comp19942.pdf.
SEC v. Spiegel, Inc., No. 03C-1685, 2003 U.S. Dist. 17933 (N.D. IL 2003). Available at http://www.sec.gov/litigation/complaints/comp18020.htm.
Securities Act of 1933, 15 U.S.C. §§ 77a et seq.
Securities Act of 1933 Form S-1.
Securities Act of 1933 Form S-3, General Instructions I.B.3.
Securities Act of 1993, Rule 144.
Securities Act of 1933 Release No. 305 (March 2, 1935).
Securities Act of 1933, Rule 10(b)(5)-2.
Securities Act of 1933, Rule 152.
Securities Act of 1933, Rule 415.
Securities Act of 1933, Rule 415(a)(1)(i).
Securities Act of 1933, Rule 501(a).
Securities Act of 1933, Rule 506.
Securities Exchange Act of 1934, 15 U.S.C. §§ 78a et seq.
SEC Division of Corporate Finance, 1999, Sec. 35b.
Selective Disclosure and Insider Trading, SEC Release No. 34-43154, 2000 WL 1201556 at *10. August 15, 2000.
Sjostrom Jr., William K. 2008. "The Truth about Reverse Mergers." *Entrepreneurial Business Law Journal* 2:2, 743–759.
Sjostrom Jr., William K. 2010. "The Untold Story of Underwriter Compensation Regulation." *UC Davis Law Review.* Forthcoming.
TSC Indus., Inc. v. Northway, Inc., 426 U.S. 438, 449 (1976).
United States v. O'Hagan, 521 U.S. 642 (1997).

ABOUT THE AUTHOR

William K. Sjostrom Jr. is a professor of law at the University of Arizona, James E. Rogers College of Law, where he teaches business organizations, securities regulation, and mergers and acquisitions. His scholarship focuses on securities regulation and corporate law. He has published in the *UCLA Law Review*, *Boston College Law Review*, and *Washington and Lee Law Review*, among others. Before entering academia, Professor Sjostrom was an attorney with Fredrikson & Byron in Minneapolis, Minnesota. His practice included public and private securities offerings, venture capital financing, mergers and acquisitions, and corporate governance. He holds a B.S. in finance with high honors from the University of Illinois at Urbana-Champaign and a J.D. *magna cum laude* from Notre Dame Law School.

CHAPTER 24

Financing Corporate Mergers and Acquisitions

WOLFGANG BESSLER
Professor, Center for Finance and Banking, Justus-Liebig-University Giessen,

WOLFGANG DROBETZ
Professor, Institute of Finance, University of Hamburg,

JAN ZIMMERMANN
Research Assistant and PhD student, Center for Finance and Banking, Justus-Liebig-University Giessen,

INTRODUCTION

Mergers and acquisitions (M&As) are one of the most important and largest investment decisions that companies and corporate decision makers face. They are also one of the more complex transactions usually involving simultaneous decisions on how to engage in a merger or acquisition, how to finance and pay for an M&A, and how to align the financing requirements with the target capital structure. To convince management and shareholders of the acquisition target to agree to a proposed merger or to tender their shares in an acquisition, the bidder not only must make a financially attractive offer but also must disclose the terms of the proposed M&A, thereby offering valuable insights for an empirical analysis.

The main objective of this chapter is to analyze the financial aspects of corporate M&As. This issue can be addressed from several different perspectives. Exhibit 24.1 graphically presents these perspectives. In many empirical studies on financing M&As, the method of payment (2), that is either stock (2.2) or cash (2.3), is often the focus of the analysis, given that it is clearly a pivotal element in the acquisition process. Another approach is to concentrate solely on the financing aspect of an M&A and analyze the internal and external financing alternatives (3) that are available for the bidder. A closely related issue is how the financial requirements and the specific financing choices affect the capital structure (4) of the acquirer in the short- and long-run before (4.2) and after (4.3) an M&A. The structure of this chapter follows these basic ideas.

However, focusing only on these three main aspects may be too narrow because it omits other important facets of the M&A process. In fact, most practitioners view the method of payment, financing alternatives, and capital structure choices

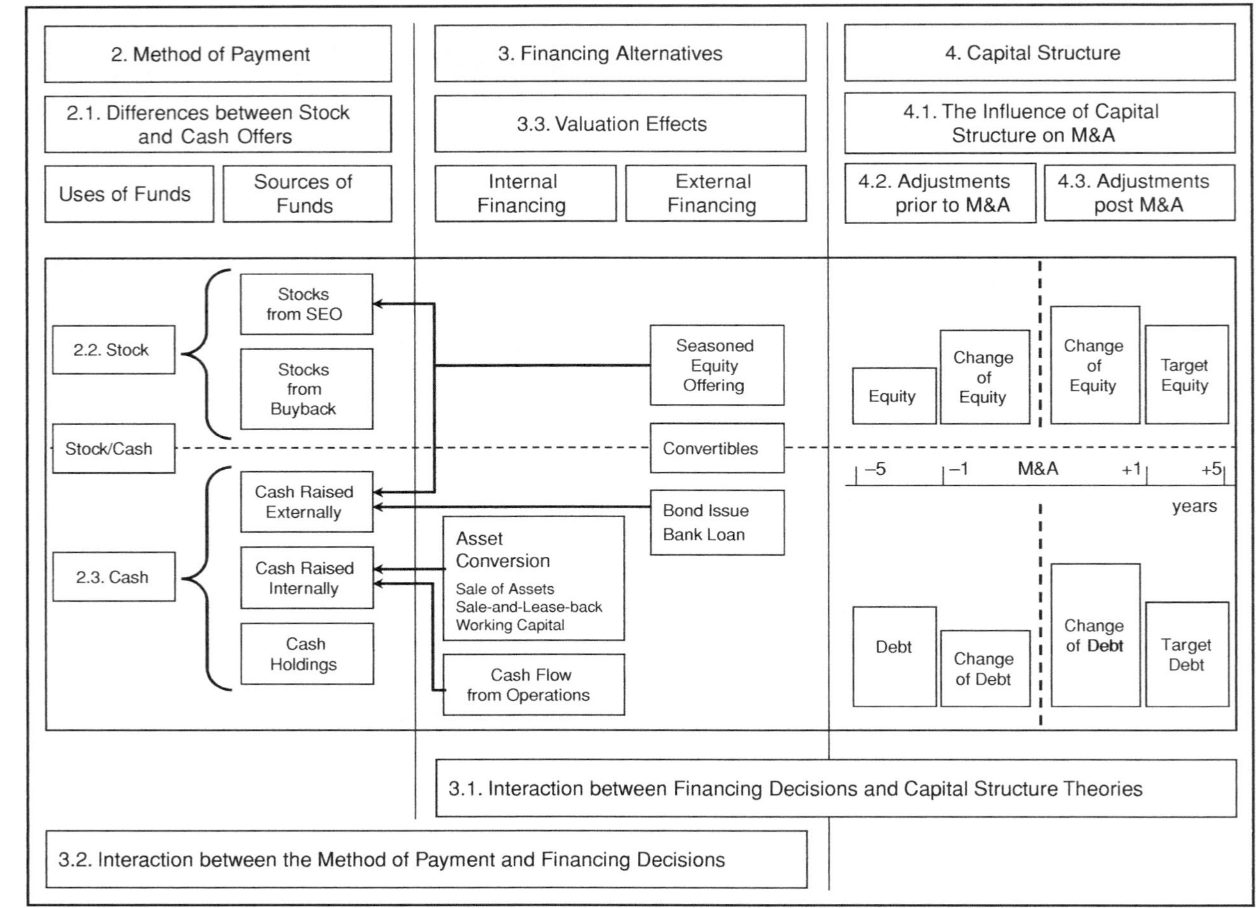

Exhibit 24.1 The Link among Method of Payment, Financing, and Capital Structure

Note: This exhibit illustrates the relationship among the method of payment, financing alternatives, and capital structure effects of M&As. This motivates the structure of this chapter, which first examines the method of payment decision, followed by the financing alternatives, and finally by the interactions between takeovers and the capital structures of both the acquirer and target.

as a joint decision in setting the terms of a deal (Bruner 2004). Because financing decisions may be related to the method of payment, investigating whether any interactions occur between the method of payment and the financing decisions in a takeover (3.2) is necessary. Obviously, financing decisions are also intertwined with the capital structure choice so that the possible interaction between financing and capital structure changes needs to be explored as well (3.1). On the one hand, these analyses should offer valuable insights into whether and how investment and financing decisions of M&As are independent of each other or interrelated. On the other hand, they can indicate whether interdependencies exist between the financing and the capital structure decisions. This chapter also addresses these issues.

In addition to these fundamental questions, even more complex and challenging issues need to be considered. For example, most takeover bids offering stock are typically financed with equity, whereas cash offers are usually financed with internally generated funds or debt (Eckbo 2009). However, when paying with stocks, the bidder may (1) issue new equity, (2) use already repurchased shares, or (3) convert cash holdings or cash inflows from issuing debt into stock by repurchasing shares. Consequently, the method of payment is the result of the sequencing of various financing activities with the objective of minimizing agency costs and maximizing shareholder value. Bidders may also first raise the financial sources necessary for an M&A and then proceed with the offer or alternatively may first approach the target and then address the financing of the deal. Therefore, the pivotal question remains whether a specific method of payment results in certain financing activities or whether a certain financing decision ultimately leads to a specific form of payment. In contrast to this view, another possibility is that the financing and investment decisions are, in the sense of Modigliani and Miller (1958), independent.

Nevertheless, either a separated or an interrelated set of well-known agency problems exists about paying with cash or stock and to financing with debt or equity. Consequently, agency costs are related to the method of payment and to the issuance of equity and debt. Most likely costs are also associated with the adjustment of the current capital structure. The deviation from some target leverage ratio may either constrain companies to engage in an M&A or support M&A activities. Finally, another possibility is that corporate takeovers are employed to exploit some unused debt capacity or to serve as a means for adjusting the capital structure towards its long-term target.

The rest of this chapter first discusses the advantages and disadvantages of cash versus stock as the method of payment and then examines in greater detail the acquirers' financing alternatives, which may themselves depend on the method of payment. The following section then provides a discussion of capital structure theories and analyzes how acquirers can make adjustments before and after an M&A. Finally, the interactions between financing and capital structures of both acquirer and target are investigated. This chapter ends with a summary and conclusions.

METHOD OF PAYMENT

The bidder in a corporate takeover usually has to decide on the method of payment before making an offer. Therefore, the bidder faces the dilemma of overpaying for the target or risks the possibility that the offer is too low, which may result in the target rejecting the offer or attracting competing bidders. Deciding on the method of payment is therefore an important issue because cash and stock offers differ regarding these transaction risks. These differences are due to information asymmetries and variation in their pricing mechanisms. Stock and cash offers are also different from a governance perspective because stock offers may substantially change the ownership structure of the acquirer. These factors explain the preference for a particular method of payment as well as the difference in valuation effects of stock and cash deals.

Differences between Stock and Cash Offers

When deciding on the method of payment, the negotiating parties must settle on the price that the target shareholders receive in exchange for their shares as well as on the allocation of control rights they hold when the deal is closed. To convince the target shareholders to agree on the terms of the takeover and to prevent competition from other bidders, the offer price has to exceed the target's stock price before the announcement by a substantial margin. Empirical studies report that the required premium is around 30 percent but in some cases can reach 45 to 50 percent (Eckbo 2009). Theoretically, the offer premium should reflect the potential gains from expected synergies or other factors of the merger and also how these gains are allocated between the bidder and the target companies. The premium will also depend on the relative bargaining positions of bidder and target. In an empirical study, Andrade, Mitchell, and Stafford (2001) find that the target's stock price increases on average by 16 percent in the three-day interval surrounding the takeover announcement. In contrast, the bidder's stock price declines insignificantly by about 1 percent on average. When weighted by the companies' relative market values, the combined abnormal returns increase to 2 percent. Hence, most of the gains accrue to the target shareholders, while the acquirer shareholders merely break even, at least in the short run, indicating that not all deals are expected to generate value for the shareholders of the bidder.

Significant differences exist between cash and stock offers regarding the risk and return trade-offs as well as the allocation of control rights. When using cash as the method of payment, the bidding company offers a fixed amount it is willing to pay in exchange for the target shares. When the deal is closed, the target shareholders divest from the firm in exchange for cash. However, they are not prevented from investing money in the bidder's stock and continue to be shareholders. In contrast, when stocks are offered as the method of payment, there is uncertainty about the actual price the target shareholders receive. Typically, they are offered a specific number of shares of the bidder or of the newly combined company in exchange for their shares. Consequently, the precise price that is paid in these deals is conditional on the stock price movements of the bidder's shares until closing and is therefore a contingent claim. Furthermore, when the deal is closed, the target shareholders become shareholders of the newly combined company so that their return depends on the performance of the newly created company and the potential gains from synergies. Nevertheless, investors always have the opportunity to exit and sell their shares at the prevailing market price before or after the deal is closed. While all-stock or all-cash offers are the two principal methods of payment in M&As, another approach is to combine both forms of payment.

In a perfect capital market, the method of payment should have no impact on the valuation of an M&A. With symmetric information between all parties, the level and distribution of takeover gains is therefore independent of the method of payment. A potential acquirer may estimate the realizable synergies and offer a certain fraction of the expected gains to the target. However, when uncertainty exists about the fair value of the target and the potential synergies being generated from the merger, the method of payment becomes important. Moreover, when a firm's ownership structure is crucial as a consequence of agency problems, the market reaction will also reflect changes in the acquirer's ownership structure. Therefore, market imperfections must be included when analyzing the method of payment decision and its consequences for the valuation of corporate takeovers.

Exhibit 24.2 provides an overview of the empirical studies regarding the valuation effects of the method of payment. The magnitude of these effects may depend on the bidder's size, the development stage of the target, and whether the bidder is trying to acquire a public or a private target. The next sections present and discuss these empirical results in greater detail.

Motives and Valuation Effects of Stock Deals

When the shares of the bidder are perceived, at least from the management perspective, as being overvalued, or when risk-sharing motives dominate the method of payment decision, stock deals are generally preferred to cash deals. This is also the case when the bidder wants to retain the management or shareholders of the target and when the bidder plans to dilute the influence of its current blockholders. However, stock payments may be constrained by the institutional features and characteristics of both bidder and target. Nevertheless, the relevant aspects to consider when analyzing the pros and cons of stock deals are market timing, risk sharing, and corporate control motives.

Market Timing

When managers of the bidder perceive their own company's stock as overvalued, they may attempt to exploit this situation and "time" the market. When offering overvalued stock, the intention is to acquire the target company at an effective discount. Because the bidder's incentive to pay with overvalued stock is well known, the target is generally reluctant to accept such offers. However, the target may easily agree to such deals if its shareholders have a short investment horizon and quickly sell the shares of the bidder after the closure of the deal or if its managers receive additional payments or golden parachutes for their approval (Shleifer and Vishny 2003). An alternative explanation is that the target may be more inclined to accept a stock payment from a bidder with high valuation levels when its institutional investors have a preference for growth stocks (Burch, Nanda, and Silveri 2009). Additionally, target management may systematically overestimate synergies during periods of high market-wide overvaluation (Rhodes-Kropf and Viswanathan 2004). Nevertheless, when the bidder offers stock to the target, the market often interprets this as a signal of overvaluation. Consequently, for public targets this generally results in a negative market reaction and lower bidder returns for stock

Exhibit 24.2 Valuation Effects of the Method of Payment

Study	Sample	Subgroup	Returns (−1,+1)%	Returns (−1,+1)%
Andrade, Mitchell, and Stafford (2001)	3,688 M&As	Stock payment	**Acquirers**	**Targets**
	Period: 1973 to1998	No stock payment	−1.50***	13.00***
	U.S. public firms		0.40	20.10***
Eckbo (2009)	15,987 takeover bids (including unsuccessful)	**Public targets**	**Large bidders**	**Small bidders**
	Period: 1980 to 2005	Stock payment	−2.21***	−0.06
	U.S. public bidders	Cash payment	−0.30***	3.06***
		Private targets	**Large bidders**	**Small bidders**
		Stock payment	0.10	6.46***
		Cash payment	0.26***	1.76***
Officer, Poulsen, and Stegemoller (2009)	1,944 M&As	**Development stage targets**		
	Period: 1995 to 2004	Stock payment	5.80*	
	U.S. public bidders and private targets	No stock payment	−5.80*	
			Pre-announcement (−60,−2)%	**Post-announcement (+2,+60)%**
Martynova and Renneboog (2009)	1,361 M&As	Cash payment	1.04	−2.21***
	Period: 1993 to 2001	Cash and stock payment	−0.73	−4.11***
	European public firms	Stock payment	3.09***	−5.15***

Note: This exhibit provides an overview of bidders' short-run valuation effects reported in various takeover studies grouped by the method of payment. Cumulative abnormal returns (CARs) are calculated for the event window of (–1, +1) days around the announcement date, except Martynova and Renneboog (2009) who also examine pre-announcement CARs (–60, –2) and post-announcement CARs (+2, +60). ***, **, * denote statistical significance at the 0.01, 0.05, and 0.10 level, respectively.

deals compared to cash deals (Exhibit 24.2). In contrast, when a private target with few owners, who presumably possess superior information, accepts a stock payment, this usually conveys a positive signal to the market. This fact may explain why for private targets bidder returns are typically higher in stock deals than in cash deals (Chang 1998).

Risk Sharing

If the management of the target has reliable private information about its own value, it will not accept any offer that is below this value. Furthermore, expected synergies generally involve considerable uncertainty. Hence, when offering a fixed amount of cash, the bidder usually faces the risk of overpayment. By offering stock, the bidder may hope to share this risk with the target. The benefits from the contingent-pricing mechanism of stock offers will be especially high if information asymmetries concerning the target are severe and if the target is relatively large compared to the bidding company (Hansen 1987). A group of companies for which information asymmetries are particularly pronounced are research and development (R&D) intensive, high-technology, and private firms. In the case of private targets, the beneficial effect of risk sharing becomes even more evident due to the lower level of bidder competition and regulatory requirements in private markets (Officer, Poulsen, and Stegemoller 2009). This may explain why for start-up firms and private targets the bidder returns are often higher in stock offers than in cash offers.

Corporate Control Motives

While the previous two motives focus on the information asymmetries that influence the desirability of the contingent pricing mechanism of stocks, corporate control motives are another important determinant when deciding on the method of payment. In this respect, payments with stock may be motivated by two different objectives. First, the bidder may want to retain the target managers who are in a strong bargaining position to negotiate a stock deal when they have sufficient voting power in the target company. Thereby, the target management may gain influence in the combined firm and at the same time increase their chances of retaining their jobs (Ghosh and Ruland 1998). The target blockholders may also exert influence on management to negotiate a stock deal in order to preserve their position in the combined firm. Second, the bidder may use stock deals as a means to intentionally dilute the share holdings of its current blockholders, such as hedge funds or private equity firms, in order to limit their monitoring and influence. Such a strategy may be feasible when these blockholders lack the power to negotiate a cash deal (Harris, Madura, and Glegg 2010). In this case, the target will also be more inclined to accept a stock payment given the existence of active monitors in the bidder.

Limiting Factors

While stock may be the preferred method of payment in situations described above, numerous factors may limit the ability to conduct a stock deal. For example, due to regulatory reasons affecting the speed of the offer process, most tender offers are made entirely with cash (being the fastest mechanism), while mergers often involve a stock payment. Furthermore, in the context of cross-border transactions, the bidder has to take into account that the shareholders of a foreign target may be less willing to hold foreign equity (Gaughan 2007). To overcome this difficulty, the potential acquirer may consider cross-listing in the foreign country to obtain an acquisition currency. Otherwise, it will have to rely on a cash payment. Further, the shareholders of private targets may be less inclined to accept a stock payment because their sale of assets is often motivated by liquidity or restructuring reasons (Faccio and Masulis 2005). Finally, some difficulties may arise when the dividend policies of the bidder and the target are fundamentally different (Ligon, Jeon, and Soranakom 2010). For example, if the target shareholders are accustomed to a different dividend policy than that of the bidder, they may sell their shares before or after the deal closes, causing negative valuation effects.

Motives and Valuation Effects of Cash Deals

Cash deals are often preferred to stock deals in cases of bidder competition or when the bidder wants to preserve its prevailing ownership structure and therefore needs to prevent a dilution or the creation of a blockholder stake. Furthermore, and similar to offering overvalued equity, a bidder with private information prefers a cash offer when its stock price is relatively depressed. Therefore, the relevant aspects to consider when analyzing the pros and cons of cash deals are preempting competition, preventing dilution of voting rights or blockholder creation, and realizing the tax effects.

Preempt or Win Bidder Competition

In case of information asymmetries regarding the value of a proposed takeover, signaling through the method of payment is relevant for potential or actual bidder competition. By offering a substantial premium and payment in cash, the initial bidder not only signals his high valuation of the target but also tries to preempt possible competition. This is due to the fact that any rival bidder has to incur a cost in evaluating its gains from a takeover and will advance a competing offer only when the probability to win and the payoff conditional on winning are sufficiently high (Fishman 1989). The advantage and success of preempting competition is particularly high for targets with severe information asymmetries. Chemmanur, Paeglis, and Simonyan (2009) present evidence that cash offers are more likely to deter rival bids. Furthermore, when there are already multiple bidders competing for a target, to outbid its rivals any bidder may signal a higher private valuation of the target by increasing the cash component of the offer. This strategy follows from the incentive to offer a higher amount of cash and hence share less of the expected synergies and risks with the target than rival bidders. This most likely occurs when the bidder has private information that its proposed takeover will result in higher synergies (Berkovitch and Narayanan 1990).

Prevent Dilution or Blockholder Creation

Similar to the idea of stock payments being preferred for certain corporate control reasons, cash payments may be motivated by the strong preference to preserve the bidder's existing ownership structure. This mechanism works in two ways. First, bidders with managerial ownership prefer a cash payment to prevent dilution and to protect the voting power of their managers (Amihud, Lev, and Travlos 1990). Also, when the control of the bidder's dominant shareholder or other blockholders is threatened when making a stock offer, they try to block a stock deal and convince the bidder's management to make a cash offer (Martin 1996; Faccio and Masulis 2005). Second, cash offers prevent creating a new blockholder in the acquiring company when the target has a concentrated ownership structure (Chang and Mais 2000). This may explain why bidder returns are higher in stock deals than in cash deals for private targets. The intent to prevent blockholder creation is particularly important for targets that have experienced aggressive monitors who may actively engage in internal and operative decision processes (Harris, Madura, and Glegg 2010). An alternative explanation is that the target blockholders may prefer a cash deal to cash out on their investment rather than being forced to monitor the combined company. Thus, the method of payment may not only be influenced by the equity stakes of the blockholders but also by the extent of their monitoring.

Tax Effects

A frequently cited preference for stock deals relative to cash deals is the different tax treatment that could also influence the valuation. After a cash deal, the target shareholders have to pay taxes on their capital gains immediately, while the acquirer may have the opportunity to increase its tax shield. In contrast, when stock is offered to the target, capital gains taxes are deferred until the shares are sold, and the acquirer may not be able to increase its tax shield. Hence, this might be one explanation why the target often receives higher payments in cash deals (Bruner 2004). Evidence from the United Kingdom, however, shows that the bid premiums were higher in cash than in stock deals even before the introduction of a capital gains tax in 1965 (Franks, Harris, and Mayer 1988). Thus, the tax effect may not fully explain the different valuation effects.

FINANCING ALTERNATIVES

In deciding on the source of funds for a corporate takeover, the bidder has to consider both the benefits and costs associated with various financing alternatives. These may arise from information asymmetries and agency costs. If the decisions on the method of payment and the financing alternatives are related, then the bidder should make both decisions simultaneously because they will affect each other, though the direction of the causality is not obvious. Furthermore, a sequencing of the takeover and financing decisions is often observed and may be considered as an alternative strategy for a corporate takeover. In these cases, the bidder first starts a takeover attempt and then assesses different financing alternatives. Alternatively, the bidder first gathers cash or secures sufficient financing sources and then approaches a takeover target. This first section provides a review of the most relevant capital structure theories and discusses how they relate to M&As. The next section then reviews different financing sources and discusses their valuation effects.

Interaction between Financing Decisions and Capital Structure Theories

Over the last several decades, financial economists have advanced various alternative hypotheses that attempt to explain the financing behavior of a firm. These hypotheses build on the seminal work of Modigliani and Miller (1958), who derived that in a frictionless capital market, corporate financing and investment decisions are independent. Consequently, firms can finance all positive net present value (NPV) projects including takeovers without any restrictions on the instrument or the level of financing. Therefore, the capital structure and the financing instrument do not affect firm value. Subsequent work relaxed several restrictive assumptions of their model and allowed for capital market frictions such as taxes, financial distress costs, and information asymmetries.

The trade-off theory suggests that firms consider the benefits and costs of debt in their financing decisions. This trade-off gives rise to an optimal capital structure that minimizes the cost of capital and thereby maximizes firm value. In the model of Kraus and Litzenberger (1973), the benefits of debt are the result of tax savings, while the increase in the costs of debt is due to expected bankruptcy costs. In the agency models of Jensen (1986) and Stulz (1990), benefits of debt arise from a reduction of the overinvestment problem in firms with high free cash flows, while the costs of debt result from the risk-shifting problem and the underinvestment problem faced by firms with high growth opportunities. These concepts are also related to as the free cash flow hypothesis (Jensen 1986) and the debt overhang problem (Myers 1977), respectively. Because debt financing constrains managerial discretion over funds, agency conflicts between managers and shareholders may be reduced for firms without good investment opportunities. In contrast, debt financing may aggravate the agency conflicts between shareholders and debt holders in firms with high growth opportunities.

Myers' (1984) pecking order theory builds on information asymmetries between managers and shareholders. Due to adverse selection costs associated with security issuance, firms follow a financing hierarchy in that they first use internally generated funds, then debt, and issue new equity only as a financing means of "last resort." In such a world financial slack, or cash on hand and unused debt capacity, may be valuable because informational frictions make external financing costly (Myers and Majluf 1984). According to the pecking order theory, there is no optimal capital structure or it is only of secondary importance. Hence, the pecking order and the trade-off theories of capital structure are often regarded as contesting theories (Bessler, Drobetz, and Grüninger 2010). Finally, the market timing hypothesis predicts that firms issue equity when their market values are relatively high and avoid issuing equity when their market values are relatively low as measured by the market-to-book ratio (Baker and Wurgler 2002). Accordingly, capital structure is the cumulative outcome of a firm's past attempts to "time" the market.

In an empirical study, Welch (2004) challenges the idea that companies efficiently adjust their capital structure. He finds that leverage measured at market values, which generally provide a more meaningful economic measure than historical accounting values, is largely driven by stock returns. However, rather than counterbalancing return-induced changes to market leverage, managers exacerbate deviations from target leverage through their financing activities, i.e., by attempting to "time" the market. However, these effects may be less important in the long run. This is consistent with a dynamic trade-off theory that allows for costly adjustment towards the target capital structure over time (Bessler, Drobetz, and Pensa 2008).

With transaction-specific motives (as explained above) primarily driving the method of payment decision, the following questions arise: Which financing theories best explain acquirers' financing decisions and is the financing decision related to the method of payment? The next section investigates these issues.

Interaction between the Method of Payment and Financing Decisions

In order to finance a takeover, bidders may use internally generated funds that require no additional financing or access the capital market in those cases when the current cash holdings or cash flows from operations are insufficient. Outside financing usually becomes necessary and more likely the larger the target and the lower the acquirer's profitability and consequently its level of cash holdings and operating cash flows. The usual alternatives for external funding involve financing with bank loans or issuing bonds, convertibles, or equity, as presented in Exhibit 24.1. In these cases, the firm needs to evaluate the specific costs and benefits associated with each financing source. Alternatively, asset sales and divestitures of divisions or other forms of asset conversion, such as sale-and-lease-back or working capital conversion, are means to provide the company with additional cash holdings. Divestitures may also complement a strategy of refocusing the firm or mitigating antitrust concerns arising from a takeover.

Independence of the Method of Payment and Financing Decisions

One approach to analyze the method of payment and the financing decision is to assume that they are not interrelated but independent and therefore can be viewed separately. A justification for such an approach is to provide evidence that any financing source can be converted into any method of payment. This is the perspective taken in this section and may be similar to the arbitrage arguments of Modigliani and Miller (1958). Liquidity that has been generated internally from operations or asset conversion or that is the result of issuing new equity and debt may be used for an all-cash payment (Exhibit 24.1). Alternatively, the bidder may prefer an all-stock payment when the firm has issued new equity, especially for financing the acquisition or when transaction-specific motives promote the use of shares instead of cash as the method of payment in order to mitigate certain risks associated with the takeover, such as the risk of overpayment. In this case, share buybacks provide an alternative to cash payments (Exhibit 24.1). By first repurchasing shares, a company may convert its cash holdings into shares, which it may then use for a cash-and-stock or an all-stock payment in a takeover. While share buybacks are typically limited to a certain fraction of a company's shares, they may provide the firm with a sufficient number of shares, as long as the target company or the fraction of the deal that is paid for with equity is not too large. Thus, cash holdings, cash generated internally from operations and asset conversion, or cash raised by external financing does not necessarily have to be employed only for an all-cash payment.

Similarly, when a company issues equity to finance a takeover, it may use the proceeds from a seasoned equity offering (SEO) to pay with cash or directly exchange the newly-issued stocks for the stocks of the target company in a so-called stock swap merger. In this case, share buybacks may also provide a mechanism that potentially influences the financing decision. When a firm has issued seasoned equity, the market typically interprets this as a signal of overvaluation, which usually results in a negative stock price reaction (Myers and Majluf 1984). Hence, a sequence of first buying back shares to reduce information asymmetries between management and shareholders followed by an equity issue to fund the investment, such as a takeover, may reduce the information costs of a new equity issue (Billett and Xue 2007). Because a company could obtain the preferred method of payment from several alternative financing sequences, one could argue that the method of payment and the financing decisions are independent.

Dependence of the Method of Payment and Financing Decisions

However, some empirical evidence suggests that a link between the method of payment and the source of financing exists. First, the majority of cash payments are financed with internally generated funds. Second, when a cash payment is offered in a takeover, there is often additional financing by issuing new debt. This is particularly the case for deals involving relatively large targets for which internally generated funds are usually insufficient (Harford, Klasa, and Walcott 2009). Finally, an all-stock payment usually requires a new equity issuance unless share repurchases provide enough shares for payment. In contrast, cash payments financed with equity are less commonly observed (Martynova and Renneboog 2009). The reason is that issuing equity is generally more costly than debt due to higher information and flotation costs. For example, besides triggering a negative market reaction, an SEO typically requires a shareholder vote and registration, which are both time and money consuming. Hence, this financing behavior for cash payments is consistent with the predictions of the pecking order theory. Unless firms try to exploit their favorable market valuations or are already highly leveraged, debt financing of cash payments is often used when internally generated funds are insufficient.

As the target management and stockholders will certify the value of the bidder's stock in a stock-for-stock merger, the costs of raising equity while pursuing a merger may be lower than in an SEO with substantial asymmetric information between the management and outside shareholders (Alshwer and Sibilkov 2009). Moreover, from a market-timing perspective, issuing new equity through a merger may be a more efficient means than through an SEO as "a merger more effectively hides the underlying market timing motive from investors" (Baker, Ruback, and Wurgler 2007, p. 157). In this case, the bidder may argue that it needs to make a stock offer for a transaction-specific reason. Additionally, investors who would not actively participate in an SEO may passively accept stock in a takeover (Baker, Coval, and Stein 2007). Therefore, the negative valuation effects of issuing additional equity may be less severe and the information costs lower when equity financing is used for a stock payment instead of cash payment, as suggested in the models of Shleifer and Vishny (2003) and Rhodes-Kropf and Viswanathan (2004). Overall, cash as the method of payment is mainly associated with debt financing or internally generated funds. In contrast, stock as the method of payment is closely linked with equity financing.

Does the Method of Payment Determine the Financing Decision or Vice Versa?
The arguments so far raise the question of whether the method of payment determines the financing decision or whether the financing decision influences the method of payment decision. Empirical results for a study of European takeovers indicate that strategic preferences for a certain method of payment may influence an acquirer's financing decision (Martynova and Renneboog 2009). Consistent with the pecking order theory, acquirers that have high internally generated cash flows do not raise external funds and prefer debt to equity financing when they have a high debt capacity and do not suffer from a debt overhang problem. In line with the market timing hypothesis, acquirers raise equity rather than employing internally generated funds when their stock prices have recently performed well. These results hold when restricting the sample to all-cash payments for which all financing sources are possible. Hence, they are independent of the method of payment. However, the threat of a change in control and risk-sharing incentives may influence the financing decision indirectly through the method of payment decision. While these factors appear to have a significant effect on the financing decision, they lose their significance when restricting the sample to cash payments, which means that their impact is conditional on the method of payment. Thus, the method of payment seems to have an impact on the financing decision.

In contrast, the method of payment may also depend on the financing decision. Consistent with the trade-off theory, acquirers that are overleveraged are less likely to finance a relatively large takeover with debt and pay with cash, particularly when they are more prone to a debt overhang problem (Harford, Klasa, and Walcott 2009; Uysal 2009). Hence, when the deviation from the target capital structure becomes too large, firms are constrained in their choice of financing alternatives, which then indirectly influences the method of payment. Moreover, the target will most likely not be in favor of equity payment when the bidder cannot justify equity financing on the basis of the trade-off theory, i.e., when the bidder is underleveraged. In this case, the target shareholders will interpret a stock swap merger immediately as a signal of overvaluation. Vermaelen and Xu (2009) confirm this notion in their study of 3,261 takeovers. While acquirers' financing decisions are mostly consistent with a target leverage model, deviations from the predictions of the trade-off theory are almost entirely driven by underleveraged firms, which are reluctant to pay with undervalued equity. In contrast, firms find that capitalizing on their overvalued stock is difficult when the trade-off theory predicts cash payment. Overall, a fair conclusion seems to be that the method of payment may have an impact on a firm's financing decision and that a firm's financing decision may also be influenced by the method of payment decision.

Valuation Effects of Takeover Financings

Due to market imperfections, the capital market reaction at the time of a takeover announcement will reflect both the market's assessment of the value of the acquisition and the effect of the financing decision. This is due to the fact that the use of internally generated funds, on the one hand, and debt and equity financing, on the other hand, differ with respect to information asymmetries and agency costs. This should also have an impact on the market value of the acquiring firm. The empirical findings and the literature presented in Exhibit 24.3 suggest that the source of financing influences the valuation effects of takeovers.

When there is a sequence of first financing and then announcing an M&A, the valuation effects of the bidding company at the time of the financing announcement will reflect both the overvaluation signal and investment opportunities. Consequently, the stock price reaction to the M&A decision will reflect the resolution of the market's uncertainty about the firm's ability to realize investment opportunities and whether the financing decision was merely driven by overvaluation. In this case, the takeover announcement reduces some of the uncertainty about the motivation for a firm's decision to issue equity, which is either overvaluation or the funding of great investment opportunities (Schlingemann 2004). In contrast, when the sequence is first announcing an M&A and then financing, the use of funds may be credibly signaled, so that raising funds may be less costly.

Internal Financing

Takeovers financed with internally generated funds offer the advantage of avoiding informational frictions and costs associated with external financing (Myers and Majluf 1984), while increasing the risk of allowing management to pursue its own objectives, for example empire building, which often means investing in negative NPV projects (Jensen 1986). Hence, determining which of these two effects dominates in the market's perception requires an empirical analysis. Harford (1999) finds that cash-rich firms are more likely to become bidders and that bidder announcement returns decrease with the amount of excess cash holding, particularly when the takeover announcement is unexpected. This result also holds for firms with good investment opportunities as measured by a high market-to-book ratio. Differentiating by firms' investment opportunities, Schlingemann (2004) finds a negative relationship between acquirers' announcement returns and their free cash flow levels, which is even stronger for firms with low Tobin's q. This evidence is consistent with the agency costs of free cash flow dominating the benefits from financial slack. Without the capital market's external control associated with the financing decision, cash-rich firms may be less constrained to undertake unprofitable or even value-destroying takeovers. This agency conflict is reflected in the negative market reaction to takeovers that are financed with internally generated funds. This also implies that the market reaction to financing decisions made before a takeover announcement may be more adversely affected by agency problems when the management is unable to credibly signal that the funds raised will be employed to implement profitable investment opportunities.

External Financing

Any kind of external funding, both debt and equity financing, has the positive effect of giving the market an opportunity to control and constrain management. In contrast to equity financing, however, debt financing usually conveys a positive signal that the bidder's shares are not overvalued. In case of overvaluation, the firm should have a preference for issuing equity (Martynova and Renneboog 2009). Furthermore, debt financing may signal a more profitable takeover opportunity to

Exhibit 24.3 Valuation Effects of the M&A Financing

Study	Sample	Subgroup	Returns (−1,+1)%	
Bharadwaj and Shivdasani (2003)	115 cash tender offers	**Bank debt**		
	Period: 1990 to 1996	No financing	0.54	
	U.S. public bidders	Partially financed	−0.27	
		Entirely financed	3.81***	
Martynova and Renneboog (2009)	1,361 M&As	Internal financing	0.79***	
	Period: 1993 to 2001	Debt financing	1.32***	
	European public firms	Mixed financing	1.10***	
		Equity financing	0.49***	
			Pre-announcement (−60,−2)%	**Post-announcement (+2,+60)%**
		Internal financing	0.42	−1.35***
		Debt financing	1.92**	−0.28
		Mixed financing	−1.85***	−3.14***
		Equity financing	1.87***	−5.73***

Note: This exhibit provides an overview of bidders' short-run valuation effects reported in various takeover studies grouped by the source of financing. Cumulative abnormal returns (CARs) are calculated for the event window of (−1, +1) days around the announcement date, except Martynova and Renneboog (2009) who also examine pre-announcement CARs (−60, −2) and post-announcement CARs (+2, +60). ***, **, * denote statistical significance at the 0.01, 0.05, and 0.10 level, respectively.

investors than equity financing because the profits mainly accrue to the current shareholders. In contrast, in issuing new equity the new shareholders share the losses in case the takeover does not generate the expected cash inflows (Schlingemann 2004).

As Exhibit 24.4 shows, the empirical evidence is generally consistent with these predictions. First, in line with the agency costs of free cash flow hypothesis, Martynova and Renneboog (2009) document that debt-financed cash payments result in significantly higher announcement returns for the bidder than those financed with internally generated funds. Second, Bharadwaj and Shivdasani (2003) report that acquirers' returns are positively related to the fraction of the deal value that is financed with bank debt. Thus, in addition to the monitoring function of the capital market, banks also perform an important certification and monitoring role for acquirers. Finally, Martynova and Renneboog (2009) find that equity financing is associated with negative bidder returns irrespective of the method of payment. Hence, sufficient empirical evidence exists to conclude that in takeovers, debt financing is more value enhancing than equity financing.

Sequence of Financing and Acquisition Decisions

With respect to sequential financing and M&A decisions, bidder gains at the time of the takeover announcement are positively related to the amount of cash that was raised through equity offerings during the year prior to the M&A. This is consistent with a resolution of uncertainty at the time of the takeover announcement (Schlingemann 2004). This effect is even stronger for firms with high Tobin's q, for which equity issuance could be interpreted as a signal of overvaluation rather than funding of profitable investment opportunities at the time of the financing decision. Overall, these valuation effects provide empirical evidence that the stock market reaction to takeover announcements reflects both the decision with respect to the method of payment and the decision with respect to the source of financing. Moreover, a sequence of first financing and then investing in an M&A may be more adversely affected by uncertainty about the appropriate use of funds at the time of the financing decision, which presumably makes funding more costly.

CAPITAL STRUCTURE EFFECTS OF MERGERS AND ACQUISITIONS

The current capital structure of a firm may impact its future financing opportunities as well as its subsequent M&A decisions, especially when its financial flexibility is constrained by capital market frictions such as information asymmetries and agency costs. Consequently, a large deviation from a target leverage ratio as well as general market conditions may determine the timing and terms of a takeover. Most importantly, it may even determine which companies are in a position to engage in M&A activities. These factors may also provide the financial rationale for corporate takeovers and for determining which company will be the bidder and which will be the target. Furthermore, an analysis of the short- and long-term capital structure changes before and after a takeover may provide insight into the relevance of alternative capital structure theories for M&A (Exhibit 24.1). This is due to the fact that takeovers are typically major investment decisions for companies

Exhibit 24.4 Valuation Effects of the Method of Payment and M&A Financing

Study	Sample	Subgroup	Returns (−1,+1)%	
Martynova and Renneboog (2009)	1,361 M&As	**Cash payment**		
	Period: 1993 to 2001	Internal financing	0.79^{***}	
	European public firms	Debt financing	1.32^{***}	
		Mixed financing		
		Cash payment	0.81^{***}	
		Mixed payment	1.22^{***}	
		Equity financing		
		Cash payment	1.21^{***}	
		Mixed payment	1.01^{***}	
		Stock payment	−0.16	
			Pre-announcement (−60,−2)%	**Post-announcement (+2,+60)%**
		Cash payment		
		Internal financing	0.42	-1.35^{***}
		Debt financing	1.92^{**}	−0.28
		Mixed financing		
		Cash payment	2.64^{***}	-4.52^{***}
		Mixed payment	-3.82^{***}	-1.09^{***}
		Equity financing		
		Cash payment	2.66^{***}	-6.25^{***}
		Mixed payment	0.42	-4.91^{***}
		Stock payment	3.09^{***}	-5.15^{***}

Note: This exhibit provides an overview of bidders' short-run valuation effects reported in Martynova and Renneboog (2009) grouped by the combination of method of payment and source of financing. Cumulative abnormal returns (CARs) are calculated for the event window of (−1, +1) days around the announcement date as well as for the pre-announcement period (−60, −2) and the post-announcement period (+2, +60). ***, **, * denote statistical significance at the 0.01, 0.05, and 0.10 level, respectively.

and most information on the method of payment and the source of financing quickly becomes publicly available. Finally, the magnitude of the valuation effects at the time of the takeover announcement may depend on current leverage ratios and deviations from the target capital structure of bidder and target companies before the takeover as well as on changes resulting from the takeover.

The Influence of the Capital Structure on M&A Activity

In imperfect capital markets, the decision to acquire another company may be interrelated to the decision of how to finance the takeover. When firms have exhausted their internally generated funds, they need to access external funding sources. However, when a firm is constrained in its financing opportunities—for example, because its current capital structure deviates considerably from the target capital structure or the transaction requires a certain method of payment, which in turn may be linked to a specific financing source—the takeover decision may depend on the capital structure.

This conflict will be particularly severe when a firm is currently overleveraged and does not have sufficiently large cash holdings or is not generating sufficient cash flows from operations. In this case, more costly equity financing is required. Consequently, overleveraged firms are less likely to engage in takeover activities given their financing constraints. However, if they decide to make an offer, both the premium and the cash component most likely will have to be lower, thus decreasing the probability of success. In these cases, the targets are also usually smaller (Uysal 2009). In contrast, companies with sufficient cash holdings, cash flows from operations, or some unused debt capacity are well equipped to engage in corporate takeovers. Thus, most often bidders are firms with some financial slack.

In contrast, firms currently facing financial constraints that restrict them in financing their growth opportunities are often ideal takeover candidates. If raising capital is costly due to information asymmetries, becoming a target and subsequently being acquired by a cash-rich company may be the best strategy if the firm has valuable projects and if the firm cannot finance these projects alone (Myers and Majluf 1984). This strategy may be particularly important for small R&D–intensive firms, for which financing is generally more costly and difficult to obtain. Thus, when the bidder provides the needed funds to finance the target's positive NPV projects, this should result in value creation. These financial synergies provide a rationale for firms to offer themselves for sale to another firm with sufficient financial slack in order to get the required funding unless they can go public and raise the necessary equity in the capital market.

While a combination of cash-rich firms and cash-poor firms with growth opportunities may create value in general, a financially restricted bidder will have difficulty obtaining sufficient funding to finance a takeover, compared to bidders with sufficient financial slack (Bruner 1988). Furthermore, this combination may mitigate both the underinvestment problem of the slack poor target and the potential overinvestment problem of the slack rich bidder (Smith and Kim 1994). Accordingly, firms with financial slack are more likely to acquire another firm due to ease of financing, particularly those in need of funding, thus profiting from possible financial synergies.

Capital Structure Adjustments before an M&A

When the capital structure is an important factor in determining whether a company becomes a target or is in a position to act as a bidder in a corporate takeover, the leverage ratios of bidder and target may differ before a takeover. The leverage ratios may not only be different between bidders and target firms but may also differ from industry averages or from comparable firms that are not involved in takeover activities. Moreover, if the capital structure influences M&A activity, bidders may adjust their leverage in advance for future takeovers so that they are not constrained in their decision-making process if the opportunity arises. In this case, they first secure financing and then engage in an M&A.

Leverage before an M&A

Given the theoretical arguments and empirical observations, it is expected that bidders may have more financial slack than targets and other companies that do not engage in takeovers, while targets are expected to have less financial slack than bidders or other firms. Exhibit 24.5 shows several studies dealing with capital structure adjustments around M&As. Consistent with these predictions Bruner (1988) finds that bidders have significantly lower leverage ratios and larger financial slack before the takeover. Further, targets are significantly more levered than bidding firms or a control sample. These differences are more pronounced for successful takeover offers. Hence, this evidence is consistent with the idea that firms with financial slack often acquire financially constrained companies. Thus, capital structure is an important factor in M&As, and available financing alternatives are more than a means of raising funds.

Because some bidders have higher leverage ratios and less financial slack than other bidders, this may require them to finance the takeover by issuing seasoned equity. Although these highly leveraged firms are constrained in their activities, they may nevertheless become acquirers when the benefits from adjusting towards the target capital structure outweigh the costs of issuing new equity. Thus, according to the trade-off theory, the leverage of bidding companies before the takeover will be higher when equity financing is used rather than debt financing. Evidence that the leverage of bidders is generally higher in takeovers with equity payment compared to takeovers with cash payment is consistent with this view (Vermaelen and Xu 2009). Nevertheless, Harford, Klasa, and Walcott (2009) find that the median bidder in large takeovers has lower leverage even when payment is made with equity, thus supporting the idea that bidders are usually slack-rich companies.

Short-Term Adjustments before an M&A

While the previous predictions focus on the capital structures of bidding and target firms at the time of the takeover, another question is whether firms also adjust their capital structure before an M&A. Specifically, the issue is whether bidders actively build up financial slack, such as cash and unused debt capacity, in order to be in a superior position for future acquisitions. Although Bruner (1988) finds that acquirers have relatively high levels of financial slack before the takeover, they apparently do not actively buffer liquidity. Nevertheless, there may be explanations for leverage decreases before a takeover. First, as a lower leverage can influence the timing and terms of a takeover, managers of highly leveraged firms will actively

Exhibit 24.5 Capital Structure Adjustments Pre- and Post–M&As

Study	Sample	Variable	Subgroup	−2%	−1%	0%	+1%	+2%	
Bruner (1988)	75 M&As	Debt-to-assets	Successful	30	24	25	25		
	Period: 1955 to1979		Unsuccessful	37	30	31	32		
	Bidders in *Fortune*	Net debt-to-assets	Successful	15	14	17	17		
	1000 list of 1979		Unsuccessful	21	19	22	23		
Safieddine and Titman (1999)	573 failed M&A bids Period: 1982 to1991 U.S. public targets	Debt-to-assets	**Targets:**		59.8	64.3	71.5		
				−5	**−4**	**−3**	**−2**	**−1**	
Ghosh and Jain (2000)	239 M&As	Debt-to-assets	Unadjusted	36.8	34.3	31.5	28.3	30.7	
	Period: 1978 to 1987 U.S. public firms		Industry and size-adjusted	−0.2	−4.5	−3.6	−2.2	−4.4	
				0	**+1**	**+2**	**+3**	**+4**	**+5**
			Unadjusted		36.6	36.6	38.4	34.2	35.8
			Adjusted		2.3	6.3	9.5	3.1	2.6
				−5	**−4**	**−3**	**−2**	**−1**	
Harford, Klasa, and Walcott (2009)	1,188 M&As	Actual - predicted market leverage	Cash payment	−4.19	−6.27	−6.67	−6.38	−7.03	
	Period: 1981 to 2000 U.S. public bidders, large targets		Stock payment	−5.53	−8.77	−6.90	−7.69	−7.34	
				0	**+1**	**+2**	**+3**	**+4**	**+5**
			Cash payment	6.92	5.16	4.14	6.48	4.57	2.27
			Stock payment	−7.60	−5.91	−6.23	−5.10	−6.07	−2.82

Note: This exhibit provides an overview of bidders' leverage and leverage deviation in the years before and after M&As as reported in various takeover studies. The stated figures are percentage points and report the sample median, except Bruner (1988) who reports the sample mean. Fiscal years are numbered relative to the year when the M&A is completed, i.e., year 0.

rebalance their capital structure before a takeover to mitigate constraints from being overleveraged. Otherwise they will be limited to pursue only selective transactions and even forego profitable investment opportunities (Uysal 2009). Second, due to stock price or interest rate movements, the market leverage of a firm may change even in the absence of financing activities (Bessler, Drobetz, and Pensa 2008). Thus, leverage measured at market values may decrease during periods of stock market increases, that is, without additional financing decisions. Supporting the idea of active rebalancing to facilitate takeovers, Uysal (2009) reports that overleveraged bidders, (i.e., firms with a positive difference between their actual and predicted or target leverage) reduce their leverage deficit even more than other overleveraged firms when the opportunity and likelihood of a takeover is relatively high. This effect is not observed for underleveraged bidders. Hence, the capital structures of both bidder and target firms before the takeover have an impact on the takeover decision.

Valuation Effects

The leverage ratios at the time of the takeover announcement may also influence the valuation effects because the market reaction includes differences in agency and other costs associated with differing levels of leverage at both the bidder and the target. First, abnormal returns of the bidder are significantly positively related to their leverage ratio before the takeover, consistent with the benefits of debt hypothesis (Maloney, McCormick, and Mitchell 1993). Second, overleveraged bidders have the highest abnormal returns and these returns increase significantly with their leverage deviation. The reason is that these firms are most constrained in their takeover decision and, hence, can be expected to pursue only the most value-enhancing takeovers. Finally, with higher leverage ratios of the target, takeovers become more complex, which means that they take longer and more often involve multiple bidders and increased bids (Jandik and Makhija 2005). These factors are associated with higher abnormal returns for the target as well as for both firms combined. Thus, the capital structures of both the bidder and the target before a takeover also impact the valuation effects.

Capital Structure Adjustments Post–M&A

Following a takeover, the capital structure of the combined firm may change relative to the pretakeover leverage ratios of the acquiring and the target firm for various reasons. These may include changes in leverage ratios, which result purely from the combination of the firms without any adjustments. However, there may also be an active strategy to pursue a new target leverage ratio, for instance, to exploit unused debt capacity. Thus, takeover-induced leverage changes may be temporary, for example, when companies become overleveraged due to the financing of the takeover, but often they are adjusted toward the target capital structure in the following years.

Leverage Post–M&A

After an M&A, leverage may increase due to unused debt capacity from the pre-takeover period. First, underleveraged firms may finance a takeover with debt in order to adjust the leverage ratio towards their target capital structure. Second, firms with financial slack may provide funding for the unrealized projects of a financially constrained firm and thereby increase the leverage ratio of the combined firm. Further, leverage may rise as a consequence of an increase in debt capacity. This "coinsurance effect" results from the combination of imperfectly correlated earnings streams, which provide diversification benefits and hence risk reduction for the combined firm, particularly when the firms operate in different lines of business (Lewellen 1971). To capture the economic gains from an increase in debt capacity and mitigate wealth transfers from shareholders to bondholders when the value of outstanding debt increases as a consequence of the takeover, the combined firm should lever up following the takeover (Kim and McConnell 1977).

In contrast, leverage may also decrease after the takeover when highly leveraged firms finance the takeover with equity to adjust toward their target capital structure. Leverage may also decrease when financial synergies from combining two firms with different risks and default costs are negative, thereby reducing the debt capacity of the combined firm (Leland 2007). Whether the leverage-increasing or the leverage-decreasing effects dominate is an empirical question.

Overall, the empirical evidence suggests that combined firms often lever up permanently after the merger or acquisition and that the announcement period abnormal returns are significantly positively related to this increase in leverage (Bruner 1988; Ghosh and Jain 2000). However, the general increase in leverage may be limited to deals with cash payments, which mostly imply debt financing when the target is relatively large. In contrast, equity financing does not necessarily lead to a significant decrease in leverage because the debt of the target is usually assumed as a consequence of the takeover, which then reduces the amount of net equity issued. Explaining the reasons for the leverage increase, empirical support is stronger for the increased debt capacity argument. In particular, Harford, Klasa, and Walcott (2009) provide evidence that in financing decisions for large takeovers bidders incorporate more than two-thirds of the change to the combined firm's target leverage. Nevertheless, they also find that the takeover-induced change in leverage is significantly negatively associated with the bidder's leverage deviation before the takeover. This supports the unused debt capacity argument. Both effects are even stronger for growth firms that are more likely to suffer from a debt overhang problem, and hence more closely monitor their leverage and leverage deviation. However, Ghosh and Jain (2000) do not find a significant influence of unused debt capacity on the takeover-induced change in leverage. Finally, and contrary to the prediction of Myers and Majluf (1984) that takeover targets are slack-poor firms, targets significantly increase their leverage subsequent to the termination of a takeover offer (Safieddine and Titman 1999).

Long-Term Adjustments Post–M&A

With respect to the question of whether the general increase in leverage after takeovers is permanent or only temporary, the overall evidence is more in line with a permanent change. The significant increase in leverage in the year of the takeover is maintained over a period of up to five years after the takeover (Bruner 1988; Ghosh and Jain 2000). Furthermore, the permanent effect of the capital structure change through takeovers is also supported by the fact that the increase in leverage particularly results from an increase in long-term debt (Ghosh and Jain 2000).

Nevertheless, some evidence also supports a temporary effect in line with the trade-off theory. This is based on the intuition that when bidders finance the merger or acquisition in a way that moves them away from their target leverage they will actively rebalance toward their target capital structure after the takeover (Harford, Klasa, and Walcott 2009). Specifically, in cash deals overleveraged bidders on average reverse 75 percent of the takeover-induced change in leverage within a period of five years. The extent of rebalancing increases with the degree of leverage deviation before and immediately after the takeover. Thus, bidders include in their decision-making process changes in the capital structure resulting from the takeover.

SUMMARY AND CONCLUSIONS

M&As are major corporate investment decisions that are likely to have a considerable impact on a company's financial flexibility and success. Sufficient information on the method of payment as well as on the financing decisions is generally available at the time of the announcement of a takeover. Therefore, takeovers provide an interesting setting to examine whether corporate financing and investment decisions are independent or whether they are interrelated and therefore need to be analyzed as joint decisions.

Empirical evidence suggests that takeovers are largely financed in a way that is consistent with the predictions of the pecking order hypothesis and the trade-off theory. Specifically, companies usually rely on internal funding for a takeover and only access the external capital market when internally generated funds are insufficient. Furthermore, companies take into account deviations from their target capital structure in that underleveraged bidders face difficulties when they attempt to offer overvalued equity. Overleveraged bidders are constrained in the timing and terms of a takeover, which may even decrease their ability to conduct M&As. Moreover, consistent with dynamic models of the trade-off theory, firms adjust their capital structure before and after takeovers in the short- and long-run in a way that reduces their deviation from the target capital structure and hence maximizes shareholder value. Thus, the empirical result that bidders permanently increase leverage subsequent to an M&A is in line with the finding that most bidders are slack-rich before the takeover and that M&As may lead to an increase in debt capacity.

Moreover, in the context of corporate takeovers, interactions between the method of payment and the financing decision are of interest. Empirical evidence suggests that these two decisions are not independent of each other. They can influence each other due to capital market frictions such as asymmetric information and agency costs. Specifically, cash payments are mostly financed with debt or internally generated funds due to the higher cost of issuing equity, whereas equity payments are mainly associated with equity financing due to specific limitations on the use of share repurchases. Hence, when a takeover requires a certain method of payment to mitigate transaction risks, such as overpayment or bidder competition, or when a firm's financing decision is constrained to a certain source of financing—for example, when the bidder is overleveraged—interactions exist between the method of payment and the financing decisions. The analysis clearly suggests that financing M&As involves a more complex system of dependencies and interactions than just determining the sources of funding. It has to include the interactions between the method of payment and the financing decision as well as the interaction between the financing decision and the capital structure choices.

DISCUSSION QUESTIONS

1. What are the main motives for payments with stock or cash in corporate takeovers?
2. Which combination of the method of payment and the source of financing prevails empirically, and what is the reasoning for this observation?
3. Does the current capital structure influence who is in a position to be the bidder or who becomes the target in an M&A?

REFERENCES

Alshwer, Abdullah A., and Valeriy Sibilkov. 2009. "The Method of Payment in Mergers and Acquisitions and the Opportunity Cost of Cash." Working Paper, University of Wisconsin-Milwaukee.

Amihud, Yakov, Baruch Lev, and Nickolaos G. Travlos. 1990. "Corporate Control and the Choice of Investment Financing: The Case of Corporate Acquisitions." *Journal of Finance* 45:2, 603–616.

Andrade, Gregor, Mark Mitchell, and Erik Stafford. 2001. "New Evidence and Perspectives on Mergers." *Journal of Economic Perspectives* 15:2, 103–120.

Baker, Malcolm, Joshua Coval, and Jeremy C. Stein. 2007. "Corporate Financing Decisions When Investors Take the Path of Least Resistance." *Journal of Financial Economics* 84:2, 266–298.

Baker, Malcolm, Richard S. Ruback, and Jeffrey Wurgler. 2007. "Behavioral Corporate Finance." In B. Espen Eckbo, ed. *Handbook of Corporate Finance: Empirical Corporate Finance*, vol. 1, 145–186. New York: Elsevier/North Holland.

Baker, Malcolm, and Jeffrey Wurgler. 2002. "Market Timing and Capital Structure." *Journal of Finance* 57:1, 1–32.

Berkovitch, Elazar, and M. P. Narayanan. 1990. "Competition and the Medium of Exchange in Takeovers." *Review of Financial Studies* 3:2, 153–174.

Bessler, Wolfgang, Wolfgang Drobetz, and Matthias C. Grüninger. 2010. "Information Asymmetry and Financing Decisions." *International Review of Finance*. Forthcoming.

Bessler, Wolfgang, Wolfgang Drobetz, and Pascal Pensa. 2008. "Do Managers Adjust the Capital Structure to Mrket Value Changes? Evidence from Europe." *Zeitschrift für Betriebswirtschaft* Special Issue 6, 113–145.

Bharadwaj, Anu, and Anil Shivdasani. 2003. "Valuation Effects of Bank Financing in Acquisitions." *Journal of Financial Economics* 67:1, 113–148.

Billett, Matthew T., and Hui Xue. 2007. "Share Repurchases and the Need for External Finance." *Journal of Applied Corporate Finance* 19:3, 42–55.

Bruner, Robert F. 1988. "The Use of Excess Cash and Debt Capacity as a Motive for Merger." *Journal of Financial and Quantitative Analysis* 23:2, 199–217.

Bruner, Robert F. 2004. *Applied Mergers and Acquisitions*. Hoboken, NJ: John Wiley & Sons.

Burch, Timothy R., Vikram Nanda, and Sabatino Silveri. 2009. "Does Style Matter? The Effect of Target Shareholder Preferences on Bid Composition and Premiums." Working Paper, University of Miami.

Chang, Saeyoung. 1998. "Takeovers of Privately Held Targets, Methods of Payment, and Bidder Returns." *Journal of Finance* 53:2, 773–784.

Chang, Saeyoung, and Eric Mais. 2000. "Managerial Motives and Merger Financing." *Financial Review* 35:4, 139–152.

Chemmanur, Thomas J., Imants Paeglis, and Karen Simonyan. 2009. "The Medium of Exchange in Acquisitions: Does the Private Information of Both Acquirer and Target Matter?" *Journal of Corporate Finance* 15:5, 523–542.

Eckbo, B. Espen. 2009. "Bidding Strategies and Takeover Premiums: A Review." *Journal of Corporate Finance* 15:1, 149–178.

Faccio, Mara, and Ronald W. Masulis. 2005. "The Choice of Payment Method in European Mergers and Acquisitions." *Journal of Finance* 60:3, 1345–1388.

Fishman, Michael J. 1989. "Preemptive Bidding and the Role of the Medium of Exchange in Acquisitions." *Journal of Finance* 44:1, 41–57.

Franks, Julian R., Robert S. Harris, and Cohn Mayer. 1988. "Means of Payment in Takeovers: Results for the United Kingdom and the United States." In Alan J. Auerbach, ed., *Corporate Takeovers: Causes and Consequences*, 221–264. Chicago: University of Chicago Press.

Gaughan, Patrick A. 2007. *Mergers, Acquisitions, and Corporate Restructurings*. Hoboken, NJ: John Wiley & Sons.

Ghosh, Aloke, and Prem C. Jain. 2000. "Financial Leverage Changes Associated with Corporate Mergers." *Journal of Corporate Finance* 6:4, 377–402.

Ghosh, Aloke, and William Ruland. 1998. "Managerial Ownership, the Method of Payment for Acquisitions, and Executive Job Retention." *Journal of Finance* 53:2, 785–798.

Hansen, Robert G. 1987. "A Theory for the Choice of Exchange Medium in Mergers and Acquisitions." *Journal of Business* 60:1, 75–95.

Harford, Jarrad. 1999. "Corporate Cash Reserves and Acquisitions." *Journal of Finance* 54:6, 1969–1997.

Harford, Jarrad, Sandy Klasa, and Nathan Walcott. 2009. "Do Firms Have Leverage Targets? Evidence from Acquisitions." *Journal of Financial Economics* 93:1, 1–14.

Harris, Oneil, Jeff Madura, and Charmaine Glegg. 2010. "Do Managers Make Takeover Financing Decisions that Circumvent More Effective Outside Blockholders?" *Quarterly Review of Economics and Finance* 50:2, 180–190.

Jandik, Tomas, and Anil K. Makhija. 2005. "Leverage and the Complexity of Takeovers." *Financial Review* 40:1, 95–112.

Jensen, Michael C. 1986. "Agency Costs of Free Cash Flow, Corporate Finance, and Takeovers." *American Economic Review* 76:2, 323–329.

Kim, E. Han, and John J. McConnell. 1977. "Corporate Mergers and the Co-Insurance of Corporate Debt." *Journal of Finance* 32:2, 349–365.

Kraus, Alan, and Robert H. Litzenberger. 1973. "A State-Preference Model of Optimal Financial Leverage." *Journal of Finance* 28:4, 911–922.

Leland, Hayne E. 2007. "Financial Synergies and the Optimal Scope of the Firm: Implications for Mergers, Spinoffs, and Structured Finance." *Journal of Finance* 62:2, 765–807.

Lewellen, Wilbur G. 1971. "A Pure Financial Rationale for the Conglomerate Merger." *Journal of Finance* 26:2, 521–537.

Ligon, James, Jin Jeon, and Charn Soranakom. 2010. "Dividend Policy and the Method of Payment in Mergers and Acquisitions." Working Paper, University of Alabama.

Maloney, Michael T., Robert E. McCormick, and Mark L. Mitchell. 1993. "Managerial Decision Making and Capital Structure." *Journal of Business* 66:2, 189–217.

Martin, Kenneth J. 1996. "The Method of Payment in Corporate Acquisitions, Investment Opportunities, and Management Ownership." *Journal of Finance* 51:4, 1227–1246.

Martynova, Marina, and Luc Renneboog. 2009. "What Determines the Financing Decision in Corporate Takeovers: Cost of Capital, Agency Problems, or the Means of Payment?" *Journal of Corporate Finance* 15:3, 290–315.

Modigliani, Franco, and Merton H. Miller. 1958. "The Cost of Capital, Corporation Finance and the Theory of Investment." *American Economic Review* 48:3, 261–297.

Myers, Stewart C. 1977. "Determinants of Corporate Borrowing." *Journal of Financial Economics* 5:2, 147–175.
Myers, Stewart C. 1984. "The Capital Structure Puzzle." *Journal of Finance* 39:3, 575–592.
Myers, Stewart C. and Nicholas S. Majluf. 1984. "Corporate Financing and Investment Decisions When Firms Have Information That Investors Do Not Have." *Journal of Financial Economics* 13:2, 187–221.
Officer, Micah S., Annette B. Poulsen, and Mike Stegemoller. 2009. "Target-Firm Information Asymmetry and Acquirer Returns." *Review of Finance* 13:3, 467–493.
Rhodes-Kropf, Matthew, and S. Viswanathan. 2004. "Market Valuation and Merger Waves." *Journal of Finance* 59:6, 2685–2718.
Safieddine, Assem, and Sheridan Titman. 1999. "Leverage and Corporate Performance: Evidence from Unsuccessful Takeovers." *Journal of Finance* 54:2, 547–580.
Schlingemann, Frederik P. 2004. "Financing Decisions and Bidder Gains." *Journal of Corporate Finance* 10:5, 683–701.
Shleifer, Andrei, and Robert W. Vishny. 2003. "Stock Market Driven Acquisitions." *Journal of Financial Economics* 70:3, 295–311.
Smith, Richard L., and Joo-Hyun Kim. 1994. "The Combined Effects of Free Cash Flow and Financial Slack on Bidder and Target Stock Returns." *Journal of Business* 67:2, 281–310.
Stulz, René M. 1990. "Managerial Discretion and Optimal Financing Policies." *Journal of Financial Economics* 26:1, 3–27.
Uysal, Vahap B. 2009. "Deviation from the Target Capital Structure and Acquisition Choices." Working Paper, University of Oklahoma.
Vermaelen, Theo, and Moqi Xu. 2009. "Acquisition Finance, Capital Structure and Market Timing." Working Paper, Institut Européen d'Administration (INSEAD).
Welch, Ivo. 2004. "Capital Structure and Stock Returns." *Journal of Political Economy* 112:1, 106–131.

ABOUT THE AUTHORS

Wolfgang Bessler is Professor of Finance and Banking at the Justus-Liebig University Giessen. He holds a doctorate from the University of Hamburg and was a faculty member at Syracuse University, Rensselaer Polytechnic Institute, and the Hamburg School of Economics. His research interests are corporate finance, financial markets and institutions, and asset management. He serves as a member on the editorial board of various international finance journals including the *European Journal of Finance, Journal of International Financial Markets, Institutions & Money,* and *Journal of Multinational Financial Management.*

Wolfgang Drobetz is Professor of Finance at the University of Hamburg. He holds a doctorate from the University of St. Gallen and a Habilitation from the University of Basel. His research interests are corporate finance, asset pricing, and asset management. He is a member of the editorial board of the *European Journal of Finance* and served as co-president of the European Financial Management Association (EFMA).

Jan Zimmermann is a research assistant and PhD student in finance at the Justus-Liebig University Giessen. He graduated in business administration at the Justus-Liebig University Giessen and received an M.A. in economics from the University of Wisconsin-Milwaukee. His research interests are corporate finance and M&As.

Answers to Chapter Discussion Questions

CHAPTER 2 FACTORS AFFECTING CAPITAL STRUCTURE DECISIONS

1. The trade-off theory is based on the premise that equity gains are taxed at the firm level, while interest payments can be expensed and hence are tax-advantaged. This unequal treatment of debt and equity creates the so-called tax shield of debt. Without offsetting costs, the tax advantage of debt would lead to pure debt financing. However, the tax advantage of debt is limited because firms have to consider two kinds of costs: bankruptcy and agency costs.

   Obviously, the higher a firm's leverage ratio, the higher is its probability of going bankrupt. Since bankruptcy or being near bankruptcy (financial distress) involves costs such as legal fees and loss in consumer confidence among others, firms cannot drive their leverage ratios excessively high. Accordingly, the trade-off theory predicts that firms pursue a target leverage ratio, where the marginal gains from the tax shield are equal to the marginal costs of bankruptcy.

   A similar argument can be made about agency problems. For example, managers have an incentive to maximize shareholder value at the expense of bondholders by engaging in risk shifting. Since bondholders anticipate this behavior, they will demand a risk premium on the issuing firm's cost of debt. Therefore, another version of the trade-off theory contends that firms have a target leverage ratio at which the marginal gains from the tax shield are equal to the marginal costs of incurring agency problems.

2. The pecking order theory assumes that managers have superior information compared to shareholders. Therefore, it predicts that firms prefer financing instruments with a low degree of information asymmetry because the compensation investors require for bearing adverse selection costs is smallest when information discrepancies are negligible. According to the pecking order theory, managers will prefer internal financing (without adverse selection costs) over debt financing and debt financing over equity financing (with the highest adverse selection costs of all financing instruments).

   The negative announcement returns of equity issues are the result of adverse selection. Rational investors assume that managers do not have an incentive to issue equity when they feel that their stock is undervalued. They only issue equity when they think that the firm is in a bad state and its equity is overvalued. Investors anticipate this behavior and perceive the announcement as a signal that firm insiders feel that the firm's equity is overvalued, and hence they sell the announcing firm's stock.

3. Rajan and Zingales (1995) suggest four different empirical measures of leverage:
   1. The ratio of total (non-equity) liabilities to total assets
   2. The ratio of short- and long-term debt to total assets
   3. The ratio of debt to net assets, where net assets are total assets less accounts payable and other current liabilities
   4. The ratio of total debt to capital

   One advantage of using book values of leverage is that they are more closely related to a firm's assets in place than to a firm's growth opportunities. Also, book values better resemble the relationship between investments and their source of capital. Moreover, book values are less volatile than market values, which make them a better proxy for a firm's target leverage ratio. A major problem that arises from using book values is that book equity is simply the difference between the left-hand and the right-hand side of the balance sheet and hence a mere plug-number. Further, book measures are backward looking because they measure what happened in the past. By contrast, market values are forward-looking as are firms' financial managers. Accordingly, market values serve as a better proxy for the decision-making of financial managers.

4. Frank and Goyal (2009) identify six factors to be driving forces behind capital structure decision. They call these factors "the core model of leverage."
   1. Firms with high growth opportunities tend to have low levels of leverage.
   2. Firms with considerable tangible assets tend to have high levels of leverage.
   3. Large firms tend to have high levels of leverage.
   4. Profitable firms tend to have less leverage.
   5. When expected inflation is high, firms tend to have high levels of leverage.
   6. Firms that belong to industries in which the median leverage ratio is high tend to have higher leverage.

CHAPTER 3 CAPITAL STRUCTURE AND CORPORATE STRATEGY

1. Different factors affect underinvestment and overinvestment by firms. The existence of risky debt and scarce growth opportunities, coupled with the lack of internal financial resources (cash flow), provides the context for debt overhang problems, related to the rejection of positive net present value (NPV) investment projects. In the same way, managers, acting in shareholder interests, could decide to promote high-risk investment policies that take away value from debt holders and maximize equity value (risk-shifting problems). In a similar context, but with highly relevant future growth opportunities, managers may choose conservative investment policies to avoid the risk of losing their control over the firm today and be able to enjoy of future benefits (risk avoidance problems). By contrast, managerial overinvestment problems are basically generated when firms have low debt levels and a high availability of cash liquidity but low prospects for growth opportunities.

In the case of underinvestment and risk avoidance problems, the main source of distortion is related to the presence of risky debt, that is, high levels of debt whose market value is lower than the nominal one and therefore difficult for the firm to handle (e.g., crisis situations or financial distress). With managerial overinvestment, an increase in leverage disciplines management behavior (Jensen 1986; Stulz 1990). In fact, the presence of debt obliges managers to pay interest and meet deadlines, which increases their commitment toward more efficient company management and reduces opportunism. A benefit of using debt is that it enables management to foresee and prevent problems of managerial overinvestment. Instead, the costs of debt lie in the risk of not being able to undertake positive NPV investment projects because of debt overhang problems or incentives to accept excessively risky projects.

2. Financial distress, related to a high level of debt in the capital structure, affects the decisions and behaviors of employees. Because of the high likelihood of liquidation, financial distress may impose costs to workers. In particular, because of the possibility that high-debt firms fail, employees could lose their jobs. In particular, highly qualified employees will avoid making more firm-specific investments and will start looking for jobs elsewhere. Moreover, potential employees will avoid seeking jobs in these firms. Thus, the firm might have an interest in maintaining a low debt level to avoid the probability of distress. By contrast, some studies such as Sarig (1998) argue that skilled employees of highly leveraged firms can negotiate better contract terms than can employees of identical but less leveraged firms. This is because highly leveraged firms are more susceptible to employee threats to seek alternative employment than are less leveraged firms.
3. A firm's reputation on the product market concerns the public feelings that customers have about the reliability of the firm and the quality of its products. The product market reputation, acquired after a long period of time, is the firm's most valuable intangible asset because it affects corporate financing decisions. Reputation is at the base of customer loyalty and simplifies the decision-making process of customers. A firm's reputation signals its quality, discourages opportunistic decision-making by managers, and allows a firm greater ease in obtaining required financing. Thus, firms that strive to maintain a good reputation to ensure long-run profitability generally have more opportunities to obtain needed financing. Although an incentive exists to be short-term-oriented in times of financial distress, this can negatively affect a firm's reputation. The long-run value of a good reputation may be less important to managers than the short-run need to generate enough cash to avoid bankruptcy.
4. Low-debt and cash-rich firms can prey upon high-debt and cash-poor rivals by adopting a predation strategy. A predator may voluntarily lose money in the short-run to eliminate a rival in the market after which point the reduction in competition will allow the predator to more than recoup the short-term loss in earnings. The behavior may concern strategic choices that can hurt the rival's bottom line and prospects based on such factors as low or selective price cuts, intense advertising, and close positioning. These strategies can exhaust highly leveraged firms that are vulnerable to predation from low-levered competitors and drive them out of the market. Thus, debt weakens the competitive position

of firms especially regarding entrant firms or those operating in industries in which customers are interested in long-term support after a sale.

CHAPTER 4 CAPITAL STRUCTURE AND FIRM RISK

1. Empirical findings show that financial leverage amplifies negative economic shocks. Hence, arguing that excessive financial leverage has made the economic crisis more severe would be reasonable. Financial leverage increased the vulnerability of banks to liquidity shocks, and made firms and consumers more vulnerable to the tightening of credit constraints. However, financial leverage alone is unlikely to have caused the crisis. It cannot easily account for the availability of cheap money that helped fuel the real estate bubble. Neither can financial leverage account for the eagerness with which market participants suspended their belief in basic economic principles. Deregulation, financial innovation, the failure of corporate governance, and Keynes' "animal spirits" are just a few of the other likely culprits.
2. In the presence of capital market imperfections, efficiency no longer guarantees survival. Efficient firms may be forced to exit the market because they cannot secure financing in certain states of the world. Inefficient firms can survive if they happen to have more funds when credit constraints become binding. Further, well-capitalized but inefficient firms actually have incentives to drive efficient but financially distressed firms out of business. When the barriers to entry in the industry are high, inefficient firms can survive even in the long run, and may end up dominating the market. The evidence presented by Zingales (1998) and Khanna and Tice (2005) is consistent with this view.
3. The literature often discusses financial constraints as imposing significant costs on the firm. However, such arguments rely on the implicit assumption that firms would always choose efficient investments. Situations exist when this assumption is clearly violated, such as when managers pursue growth for the sake of their own interests and against the interest of shareholders. In such cases, financial constraints can be beneficial to the firm by preventing managers from making suboptimal investments. Financial constraints can also provide valuable information to managers. Specifically, tightening financial constraints often coincides with slower economic growth. By restricting the availability of funds, financial constraints can automatically reduce the firm's output when demand is dropping. This may provide an important competitive advantage in markets with greater uncertainty as to optimal investment policy.
4. In Modigliani and Miller (1958), financial leverage is not a separate risk factor; it only magnifies existing risks to equity such as beta risk. Two conditions must be met for financial leverage to be a separate risk factor. First, it must affect the risk of the firm. Since financial leverage has been shown to increase operating risk, this condition is easily met. Second, the risk associated with financial leverage must not be diversifiable. Here the evidence is less straightforward. Highly levered firms are likely to become distressed in tandem because of cyclical variations in credit constraints. However, the losses experienced by high-debt firms may be offset by equally large gains to low-debt firms. In this case, financial

distress is unlikely to have any effect on well-diversified portfolios and financial leverage risk will not be priced.

CHAPTER 5 CAPITAL STRUCTURE AND RETURNS

1. Proposition II states that return on equity is an increasing function of leverage. Debt increases the riskiness of the stock and hence equity shareholders demand a higher return on their stocks. Modigliani and Miller (1958) define returns as the sum of interest, preferred dividends, and stockholders' income net of corporate income taxes. They find a positive and linear relationship between leverage and returns in their cross-sectional estimations in the electric utilities and oil and gas sectors. Their work led to the development of different theories on capital structure including the trade-off theory, pecking order theory, agency theory, market timing theory, corporate control theory, and product cost theory.
2. The trade-off theory states that debt in a firm's capital structure is beneficial to equity investors as long as they are rewarded up to the point where the benefit of the tax deductibility of interest offsets potential bankruptcy costs. The trade-off theory consists of two parts: static trade-off theory and dynamic trade-off theory. According to the static trade-off theory, firms select an optimal capital structure that balances the advantages and disadvantages of using debt and equity. Dynamic trade-off theory suggests that firms may move away from their target capital structure adjusting leverage only when it strays beyond extreme bounds due to fixed cost of issuing equity. Firms only periodically make large readjustments to capture the tax benefits of leverage.

   The pecking order theory is based on the notion that management favors using internally generated versus externally generated funds. Firms obtain financing based on a series of pecking order decisions. If firms are required to finance new projects by issuing equity, underpricing may be so severe that new investors capture more than the net present value (NPV) of the new project resulting in a net loss to existing shareholders. In such a case, the firm will reject the project despite having a positive NPV. A firm can avoid this underinvestment if the firm can finance the new project using a security that is not so badly undervalued by the market. To avoid this distortion, managers follow a pecking order. They finance projects first using retained earnings, which involve no asymmetric information, followed by low-risk debt for which the asymmetric information problem is negligible, and then risky debt. The firm issues equity only as a last resort when the investment so far exceeds earnings that financing with debt would produce excessive leverage.
3. Empirical evidence on the relationship between leverage and stock returns is mixed. For example, Hamada (1972) and Bhandari (1988) show that returns increase with leverage, while Hall (1967), Dimitrov and Jain (2008), Korteweg (2010), and Muradoglu and Sivaprasad (2009a, 2009b, 2011) show that returns decrease with leverage.
4. Contradictory empirical results may stem from differences in samples, methodologies in calculating returns, and definitions of leverage in various studies. Hence, the results appear sensitive to such differences. Researchers use the different samples and methodologies in calculating stock returns. For example

Arditti (1967) uses the geometric average of returns, and his sample of firms includes industrials, railroads, and utilities. Hall and Weiss (1967) define returns as returns on equity, which means profits after tax. Their sample includes the 500 largest industrial corporations. Hamada (1972) tests the link between a firm's leverage and its common stock's systematic risk over a cross-section of all firms. He uses 304 U.S. firms from 1948 to 1967. He applies the market model to test the relationship between leverage and stock returns. Masulis (1983) studies daily stock returns following exchange offers and recapitalizations where recapitalizations occur at a single time. Bhandari (1988) uses inflation-adjusted returns. He controls for idiosyncratic risk through size and beta. Bhandari's sample consists of all firms including financial companies. Nissim and Penman (2003) examine the effect of leverage on profitability rather than stock returns. Muradoglu and Sivaprasad (2009) use abnormal returns measured in excess of market.

Definitions of leverage vary considerably as well. Changes in debt levels are commonly used among recent researchers. Dimitrov and Jain (2008) study how changes in the levels of debt are negatively associated with contemporaneous and future-adjusted returns. Hull (1999) measures the market reaction to common stock offerings with the sole purpose of debt reduction. Korteweg (2004) also bases tests on pure capital structure changes (i.e., exchange offers). He controls for business risk by assuming nonzero debt betas and uses a time series approach. Studies using levels of leverage differ in terms of using book versus market leverage. Early work uses market leverage (Masulis 1983; Bhandari 1988). Recent work uses book values (Nissim and Penman 2003; Muradoglu and Sivaprasad 2009a, 2009b, 2011).

CHAPTER 6 CAPITAL STRUCTURE AND COMPENSATION

1. The result is important because it indicates when finding an optimal capital structure should not be possible, that is, where not to look for the determinants of optimal capital structure. For example, before Modigliani and Miller's (1958) analysis, some thought that debt financing was optimal because it could lead to an increase in earnings. Consider a manager who identifies a project with an expected return of 6 percent. Suppose that the firm's weighted average cost of capital is 7 percent but its cost of debt is 5 percent. Since the expected return is 6 percent, the project is expected to increase after tax earnings by 1 percent. Modigliani and Miller illustrate that, despite the increase in expected earnings, this project would decrease value. Thus, value-maximizing managers should reject this project. Earnings-based compensation, however, could cause managers to accept the project because the increase in earnings would increase their compensation.
2. The different settings can lead to substantially different implications regarding the investment, financing, and compensation policies. In the combined manager-owner setting, the objective is to find policies that maximize the utility of the manager. In John and John (1993), the objective is to maximize shareholder wealth subject to a reservation level of utility for the manager; and in Zwiebel

(1996) the objective is again to maximize manager utility, but this time subject to keeping corporate raiders at bay. While each analysis has a different focus in general the distinct settings can lead to differing conclusions regarding some common issues. Consider the incentive for monitoring the manager's decisions. In Jensen and Meckling (1976), the manager has an incentive to set up monitoring to get better prices for its securities and increase manager welfare. In John and John's setting, monitoring will not affect the manager's reservation utility, so the manager is in some sense indifferent. In Zwiebel, monitoring is likely to reduce the manager's utility. Thus, the interpretation of monitoring activity potentially differs across settings.

Consider also leverage levels. In the first setting, leverage is likely to be limited by shareholder-bondholder conflicts. In the second, it need not be limited by shareholder-bondholder conflicts, because the manager's payoffs can be adjusted to alleviate these conflicts. In the third, leverage levels are limited by managerial preferences to avoid discipline: lower leverage is chosen by entrenched managers to maintain flexibility (versus to maximize value). Compensation levels should also differ: to the extent that the board supports entrenched managers, their compensation should be higher and subject to less risk. Similar differences arise regarding investment decisions.

3. Although this issue has many dimensions, a somewhat provocative, cynical view that might spark some debate is as follows. The arguments in Jensen (1986) and Jensen and Murphy (1990) suggest that managers were doing very well in the 1980s, having substantial power and perquisite suites with little risk or discipline, except from outside raiders with the ability to profit from taking control and improving incentives. Some illustrate that the takeover threat has subsequently relaxed in part due to management-led lobbying that resulted in regulations that impede hostile takeovers. Even with the threat relaxed, however, managers may have embraced the concerns over low pay-for-performance. Indeed, possibly as a response to this concern, the amount of stock and options granted to top management has increased substantially, increasing pay-for-performance significantly.

   For example, the sensitivity of CEO wealth to stock prices tripled between 1980 and 1994 (Hall and Liebman 1998), and then doubled again between 1994 and 2000 (Bergstresser and Philippon 2006). The greater pay sensitivity may have increased managerial effort and decreased perquisite consumption. At the same time, compensation payments have risen enormously, and arguably top management is still doing quite well (possibly even better than in the 1980s). The top management position appears to remain highly valuable especially in large, diffusely held corporations as in North America.

4. In general, designing compensation to maximize shareholder wealth is consistent even when some investors are bondholders. However, as discussed below, problems can arise from shareholder-bondholder incentive conflicts. Firms typically focus on maximizing shareholder wealth because shareholders are the residual claimants—all others claimants are paid first. Also, all other claimants must receive at least their opportunity cost, at least in expectation. This makes maximizing the residual claim efficient. Further, the residual payment is the riskiest. Shareholders can efficiently take on this risk because shares are easily

traded in financial markets enabling them to diversify risk better than other claimants (although bond markets are a close second). Still, incentive conflicts can cause problems through time. After issuing debt contracts, managers have an incentive to take self-serving actions such as asset substitution or under-investment choices described in the chapter. Bond contracts are designed to minimize this risk and indeed the use of compensation plans may increase the difficulty for shareholders to convince the board to induce suboptimal actions through the compensation plan. That is, managerial compensation adds another layer of complication in pursuing these actions. As the links between compensation and the costs of debt indicate, the concern with expropriating actions remains substantial.

CHAPTER 7 WORLDWIDE PATTERNS IN CAPITAL STRUCTURE

1. Evidence shows that firm-specific factors identified as main determinants of leverage ratios for U.S. firms influence the leverage ratios for non–U.S. firms. Leverage ratios are positively related to both the tangibility of assets and firm size and negatively related to profitability, growth opportunities, interest rates, and share price performance. However, some determinants vary across various countries such as the equity premium, effective tax rates, payout ratios, and merger and acquisition (M&A) activity. For example, in Germany the tax rate on dividends is lower than on retained earnings, which explains why German firms have a higher payout ratio relative to French firms. British firms have the highest payout ratio among all G5 countries. This ultimately affects the financing hierarchy in that firms use less internal financing and more external financing. M&A activity influences capital structure decisions in Japan, the United Kingdom, and the United States but has no impact on French and German firms. This finding is consistent with the view that hostile takeovers are more frequent in market-based economies relative to bank-based economies.
2. Legal systems provide investors with a certain level of protection for their rights. Therefore, shareholders and bondholders make their investment decisions based on the level of protection various legal systems offer. The common law system offers the strongest protection for investors, while the French civil law system offers the weakest protection, with Scandinavian and German civil law systems falling between the two extremes. On average, firms in civil law countries carry more debt than do firms in common law countries. The components of debt vary with legal systems. Firms in common law countries have more long-term debt and less short-term debt relative to firms in civil law countries. Firms in civil law countries rely more on internally generated funds to finance their investments. In contrast, firms in common law countries depend more on external financing, particularly more on equity than debt to finance their investment opportunities.
3. Firms maintain an optimal capital structure by balancing the benefits and costs of debt. Because legal and institutional features affect the benefits and costs of debt,

the rate of adjustment toward an optimal capital structure varies significantly across countries. Firms in common law countries adjust to optimal leverage much faster than do firms in civil law countries. With respect to the financial orientation of the economy, firms in market-based economies adjust to optimal leverage faster than do firms in bank-based economies. This is because a market-based structure imposes lower adjustment costs and higher benefits of adjusting to an optimal capital structure.

4. Firms in less-developed markets, bank-based economies, and civil law countries have higher information asymmetry and therefore higher costs of raising equity and lower costs of financial distress due to opaqueness, illiquid capital markets, and lower protection to creditor rights. As a result, these firms rely more on internally generated funds or on borrowing from the banking system to meet their financing needs. The pecking order theory predicts a positive relationship between the debt ratio and financing deficit. Evidence shows that when controlling for the deviation from target leverage, firms across various countries have a positive and significant relationship between debt level changes and financing deficit, with a higher magnitude in civil law countries. This is consistent with the argument that information asymmetry and legal systems play an important role in explaining debt levels around the world.

CHAPTER 8 CAPITAL STRUCTURE THEORIES AND EMPIRICAL TESTS: AN OVERVIEW

1. Harris and Raviv (1991) find that leverage increases with fixed assets, non-debt tax shields, investment opportunities, and firm size. By contrast, leverage decreases with volatility, advertising expenditure, probability of bankruptcy, profitability, and uniqueness of the product. Frank and Goyal (2009) separate the most important factors from the less important ones. The core model is composed of a positive relation to median industry debt ratio, tangible assets, size, and expected inflation, in addition to a negative relation to market-to-book, profitability, and dividends.
2. After Modigliani and Miller (1958), researchers investigated the assumptions made in their irrelevance theorem. This research yielded models that today provide arguments for the relevance of capital structure in a real world. The empirical literature has developed from static, single-equation regression models on capital structure determinants to dynamic models that nest several relations and estimate target debt ratios. Important parameters such as speed of adjustment of capital structure are made contingent on macroeconomic variables such as in Cook and Tang (2010).
3. The tax-shield on interest paid on debt, cost of financial distress, product market commitments, asymmetric information costs, and agency costs can help explain capital structure choice. Transactions costs can make debt adjustments too costly compared to the benefits within a range of optimal debt ratio. The debt overhang theory of Myers (1977), which states that firms can forgo positive net present value investments because profits must be shared with debt

holders already invested in the firm, can explain why growth firms have low debt ratios.

4. The contest between the two main theories of capital structure is not determined yet. Under different methods and data samples, both theories show significant signs of being important for firm financing. Until further evidence is brought forward, these theories should be considered as partner theories that both have relevance for the capital structure choice.
5. A significant positive speed of adjustment (SOA) would favor the trade-off theory and not the pecking order or market timing theory. A simple partial adjustment model used in many SOA studies cannot differentiate between pecking order and market timing theory. If an average estimate of the SOA found in several studies is 25 percent, the firm will use 2.5 years to adjust half of the deviation from the target debt ratio. This slow adjustment cannot support the trade-off theory, which leaves pecking order and market timing as possible theories for capital structure choice.
6. Stakeholder theory predicts that firms with unique products such as computer and automobile manufacturers should have lower leverage. An automobile company in financial trouble will experience a drop in sales. A high debt ratio can signal high competitiveness and an aggressive stance towards other firms. Firms tend to follow the usual practice in each industry but with clear variation. A high debt ratio can reduce agency costs and benefit shareholders.

CHAPTER 9 CAPITAL STRUCTURE IRRELEVANCE: THE MODIGLIANI-MILLER MODEL

1. The cost of debt is not independent of leverage but rather increases with debt because creditors accept a portion of risk in all-equity financed cash flows. At the extreme, at very high levels of leverage, and under perfect market conditions, the cost of debt will approach the cost of unlevered equity. The cost of debt cannot exceed the cost of unlevered equity as in the case of an all-debt financed firm because the creditors turn out to be the firm's owners and accept nothing more than the risk of an all-equity financed cash flow. At the same time, as debt displaces equity, the residual risk is redistributed to a lesser amount of equity, and shareholders should require a proportionate increase in the cost of levered equity. This cost increases according to Modigliani and Miller's (1958) Proposition II, although not in a linear way, but in a concave curve according to the increase in the cost of debt. Managers should consider the relationship between the cost-of-debt and the cost-of-equity functions when choosing a firm's optimal or target capital structure.
2. The problem of tax savings was the stumbling block in the Modigliani and Miller (1963) constructions for the cost of levered equity and the cost of capital for levered firms. Although MM recognize the advantages of tax deductibility of interest expense, they confuse the riskiness of tax savings flow and get entangled in determining an appropriate discount rate for this savings. Later Modigliani (1988) concludes that the risk of the tax shield depends on such matters as the riskiness of the firm's cash flow, the displacement of nondebt tax shields, and the

risk of changes in interest rates. In contrast, loss carry-forwards reduce the risk. The risk of the tax savings increases with leverage, as the debt coverage ratio decreases. Therefore, the appropriate discount rate varies from nearly the risk-free rate to the rate exceeding the cost of unlevered equity because of additional risks associated with unused nondebt tax shields.

Calculating an appropriate discount rate of the tax savings is controversial. One approach is to examine possible risks separately and apply reasonable assumptions. Another way is to use probabilistic simulations of an advanced financial model with interactions of relevant variables that influence riskiness of tax savings stream.

The costs of financial distress also occur in the real world and take the form of professional fees or an indirect reduction in revenues or an increase in operational costs shortly before and after the default. Estimating the costs of financial distress requires researching possible costs relative to nominal debt or value of the firm and identifying the probability of default.

3. There is no active market for shares of closely-held firms, and prices observed in mergers and acquisitions of these firms usually contain large discounts relative to publicly-held firms. The assumption of a perfect capital market is invalid for closely-held firms. Investors have a considerable proportion of their wealth invested in a single firm and do not have the benefits of diversification. Discounts for low liquidity may reach a third of the value of the firm's expected cash flows. Thus, the arbitrage argument does not apply to closely-held firms and market imperfections should be considered.
4. Market imperfections are common in practice. The reliability of investment evaluation crucially depends on the distinction between the assumption of fixed investment policy and the assumption of possible changes in future investment opportunities. Although the fixed investment policy assumption simplifies valuation, growth opportunities are not without interest and often require analysis using a real option valuation framework. An adverse selection problem arises because managers have discretion in choosing the firm's future policies, while investors can only guess about such policies. Consequently, capital structure becomes relevant to a firm's value.

   The unifying framework suggested in this chapter involves considering risk shifting between shareholders and creditors. The levered equity and its cost are determined as the difference between an all-equity financed firm and the value of debt from the shareholders' viewpoint. The direct and potential cash flows created by debt (e.g., tax benefits, cost of financial distress, and agency costs) are evaluated at separate discount rates. Although little theory or guidance exists on how to estimate these rates, the traditional formulas found in textbooks (e.g., costs of equity and the weighted average cost of equity) fail to solve the problem and conceal several flaws. Another problem is that practitioners often rely on conventional formulas and do not understand their restrictions. Thus, widely-used textbooks produce incorrect estimates for finite cash flows and assume a constant amount of debt or the constant ratio of debt-to-market value of equity. In practice, clearly expressing all of a model's assumptions is important. Generalized approaches and formulas provide appropriate flexibility and prevent errors by requiring that relevant assumptions be explicitly stated.

CHAPTER 10 TRADE-OFF, PECKING ORDER, SIGNALING, AND MARKET TIMING MODELS

1. Long-term underperformance of firms issuing equity involves two aspects. One regards the operating performance of these firms. Operating performance of firms issuing equity decreases relative to operating performance of non-issuing firms. The second aspect involves the controversial topic of stock underperformance. Some evidence shows that stock returns of companies issuing new shares underperform in the long run compared to the returns of non-issuing firms (Ritter and Welch 2002). However, financial leverage increases a firm's financial risk, its beta, and the financial risk of investments in equity. Companies issuing shares have lower leverage compared to non-issuing firms. Eckbo, Masulis, and Norli (2007) and Carter, Dark, and Sapp (2009) argue that no such puzzle exists regarding the long-term underperformance of newly issued stocks because risk changes after capital structure changes.
2. "Target reversion" or "mean reversion" is the continuous process of adjusting capital structure toward the target ratio (Shyam-Sunder and Myers 1999; Frank and Goyal 2003). Trade-off theory provides an explanation for mean reversion. Namely, debt changes should be dictated by the difference between the current level of debt and the level predicted by Equation 10.2. The difficulty of conducting econometric research is that the target debt-to-equity ratio is unobservable. Chang and Dasgupta (2007) argue that if the historical average debt-to-equity ratio is taken as a target debt-equity ratio, alternative explanations may exist for mean reversion. The pecking order theory, for example, predicts a negative correlation between debt and profitability. Because free cash flows vary over the business cycle, the mean reversion can be observed if the average debt ratio is taken as the target. Leverage increases above the average level in the years of poor earnings, and it falls below the average level in the years of surpluses (Shyam-Sunder and Myers). Chang and Dasgupta show that even with random financing and with no apparent target, leverage may appear to be mean reverting. They show that this mechanical rebalancing can lead to mean reversion in simulated data where the financing is purely random.
3. The existence of regulation that requires more reliable financial information such as the Sarbanes–Oxley Act reduces the effect of managerial entrenchment. Firms do not have to use leverage as a disciplinary device for managers as much as this was necessary before the Sarbanes–Oxley Act. Thus, firms reduced their leverage after the Sarbanes–Oxley Act (Bertus, Jahera, and Yost 2008). Regulation that requires more reliable financial information also reduces the extent of asymmetric information. Evidence by Bertus et al. indicates that firms should issue more equity when information asymmetry is reduced.
4. Zero debt in Microsoft capital structure is consistent with a negative correlation between debt and profitability. According to pecking order theory, firms will not use external financing unless they are financially constrained. Because large, profitable firms are typically not financially constrained, their financing strategy with low or zero leverage is consistent with the sole pecking order theory. According to trade-off theory, firms with a high level of intangible assets and

research projects should not have large debt because of high expected bankruptcy costs. Firms such as Microsoft that have an important founder who is still part of the firm may be less subject to discipline problems compared to firms where ownership is largely dispersed. This reduces the advantage of debt financing as a disciplinary device for managers. Yet, asset substitution problems and bankruptcy costs are high for firms operating in an environment with considerable intangible assets, research projects, and the like. This also makes debt financing less attractive. If Microsoft expands globally, the disciplinary effect of debt financing may become more important because Microsoft will create more business units worldwide.

CHAPTER 11 ESTIMATING CAPITAL COSTS: PRACTICAL IMPLEMENTATION OF THEORY'S INSIGHTS

1. A firm's existing WACC only measures the rate of return investors require from a company, given the firm's existing business risk and financial strategy. If the firm were to move into more risky ventures, then its current WACC would reflect neither investors' reaction to the increased risk nor the appropriate benchmark for existing investments (e.g., a project or division) if that investment's use of funds does not fit the firm's average risk profile. Good practice would be to use the WACC for another company, which is primarily in the riskier (safer) line of operations as a better risk-adjusted benchmark. Thus, a firm's WACC is not always the appropriate hurdle rate for its investments.
2. Ideally analysts should find firms that match the company in question on all dimensions. Because this is impractical, analysts should take the following steps. First, they should find comparable firms with similar business risk. This means finding companies in the same industry with similar business models. Second, if possible, they should match on a proxy for capital structure such as the debt-to-equity ratio or bond ratings. Third, they should try to find companies of comparable size whose shares have comparable liquidity in the market. In working with private firms, analysis should look for publicly-traded companies that best fit these criteria.
3. Because most firms obtain funding with a mix of sources, primarily common equity and various forms of debt, thinking of an average cost of these sources is useful. The firm's overall WACC is thus the cost of raising funds, given the financing mix the firm has chosen. This cost to the firm reports the rate of return investors require to supply that pool of funds to the firm. Analysts tend to use market values because they reflect the values that investors see and can buy in markets.
4. The market risk premium should capture forward-looking attitudes of investors. Past returns may not be a good gauge for future expectations. Additionally, both intuition and research suggest that equity market risks and risk premiums change over time. Using a historical risk premium will either under- or overestimate the cost of equity capital depending on whether investors currently

demand higher or lower than the historical market premium. When dealing with the cost of debt, changes in the risk premiums on bonds can be observed as the spread between yields on corporate and government yields changes. Estimating these changes is difficult in equity markets.

5. Even assuming that the theory underlying the CAPM is accurate, estimating some of the CAPM's components presents substantial challenges because the theory calls for forward-looking data. Analysts typically estimate beta from past data. Yet, there is no guarantee that the past will mirror the future. Moreover, beta for a single company is likely measured with substantial error. The result is that estimating beta involves sometimes difficult judgments. The task of estimating a forward-looking market risk premium is also challenging.
6. The practice of unlevering and relevering betas attempts to separate the business and financial risk that affects beta. The logic of this approach is compelling and provides several advantages. That is, the approach incorporates the statistical advantages of averages and controls for the impacts of the debt-equity mix on shareholder risks. While using unlevered betas has its appeal, the method has drawbacks. One concern is that capital structure choices are unlikely to be independent of business risk even within an industry. Such a pattern can clearly emerge within an industry if higher business risk firms target a particular bond rating by using less debt. Some analysts avoid averaging unlevered betas across companies based on this concern. Another concern is the mechanics of unlevering. The formulas rely on theory that captures debt's tax advantages but does not deal well with some of the offsetting costs such as financial distress. Moreover, disagreements exist on which version of the theory to apply. The specific formula used is especially important if one extrapolates to beta levels far from debt levels seen in an industry.

CHAPTER 12 ECONOMIC, REGULATORY, AND INDUSTRY EFFECTS ON CAPITAL STRUCTURE

1. There are three main theories that explain the observed capital structure choices of firms. First, the trade-off theory suggests that as firms increase leverage, they "trade-off" the tax benefits of debt with the increased potential for financial distress. Second, the pecking order theory by Myers (1984) and Myers and Majluf (1984) states that a firm's capital structure is determined by its preference ordering for various types of financing options available. That is, firms prefer to use internal funds first, followed by debt, and then equity. However, these two theories assume the incentives of managers are aligned with that of shareholders through the use of optimal inventive contracts. Because incentive contracts cannot perfectly align these interests, managers may act in their own self-interest. Jensen's (1986) free cash flow theory takes this into account. This theory posits that a firm with large amounts of free cash flow substantially exceeding its profitable investment opportunities may hold higher levels of debt. This forces managers to pay out the extra cash instead of investing it in inefficient "empire building," that is, investing in projects that enhance their own position within the firm but may not be value-enhancing for shareholders.

The capital structure choices of regulated firms differ substantially from those of nonregulated firms. Regulation appears to increase leverage. The prevailing wisdom is that regulated firms choose high debt levels to induce rate (price) increases. High debt levels induce regulators to set high rates that account for the firm's costs including the cost of debt, thereby insuring the firm against possible financial distress. Taggart (1985), who provides a second explanation, attributes the high debt levels primarily to the "safer business environment" created by regulation. Spiegel and Spulber (1997), however, argue that the capital structure of regulated firms is the product of balancing two opposing incentives: using high leverage to signal high cost to regulators to induce rate increases, and using low leverage to signal low cost and high value to the capital markets. Yet, De Fraja and Stone (2004) show that a higher leverage carried by regulated firms may be a product of regulator's inducing firms to take more debt rather than firm's independently using greater debt to increase rates. Thus, regulation changes the playing field for firms and alters the primary motives using debt.

2. Industry and firm characteristics have important implications for the capital structure choice of firms. Firm characteristics such as being an entrant versus an incumbent and a technology leader versus a laggard, as well as aggregate industry-level factors such as market concentration, product market competition, and industry characteristics influence the financing decision of firms. The product market fundamentally affects the type of equilibrium in the capital market, and firms alter their capital structure to affect their competitive position in the product market. Additionally, market structure, mode of competition within the industry, such as price or quantity competition, R&D races, and other dimensions of competition and uncertainty, all influence the mix of financing options that firms use. These strategic factors influencing debt primarily apply to oligopolies and not to monopolies or perfectly competitive markets.

   The effect of industry concentration on firm financial leverage depends on the degree of competition within the industry. On one hand, concentrated industries with "intense rivalry" are more likely to have low financial leverage, while a lack of competition may lead to a high leverage. Intense rivalry leads to lower leverage because firms may signal their "toughness" with a low debt level in order to avoid being preyed upon by other firms. With strong product market competition, firms will not need to use debt as a disciplining mechanism, and hence may have low leverage. On the other hand, if concentrated industries are collusive, a positive relationship may exist between industry concentration and firm leverage because shareholders (owners) may use debt as a disciplining mechanism to prevent managers from using the free cash flow for empire-building purposes. Also, high debt levels in concentrated industries may be a result of large firm size and industry stability. Other industry effects, such as whether the firm is high or low tech and the existence of tariffs, may influence a firm's financing decision. Because industry factors can only partially explain the observed differences in leverage among firms, a focus on firm-specific characteristics is also needed.

   Complex interactions between industry and firm attributes shape the capital structure decision of firms. The relative position of the firm within the industry, the actions of industry peers, and its status as an entrant, incumbent, or exiting firm have important implications for capital structure. Within competitive industries, firms that diverge from the median industry capital-to-labor ratio use more debt relative to firms whose capital-to-labor ratios are comparable to industry medians. Besides the position of firms vis-à-vis their peers, other factors such as the nature of assets under governance determine both the availability and use of different forms of financing. Firms that can adjust their production aspects without much difficulty, such as factor intensity or product level or mix, generally use less debt. Also, firms tend to hold less debt if they have specific assets tailored to their specific needs, relation-specific investments, bilateral buyer-supplier relationships, and unique products. However, greater investment flexibility, such as a greater amount of liquid assets, increases financial leverage.

Besides the above factors, other informational and strategic considerations may influence the financing decision of firms. Both theoretical and empirical studies show that firms alter their leverage decisions when attempting to signal information to outside investors. Another major influence on capital structure is whether the firm is subject to some form of government regulation. Regulation changes the types and nature of risks faced by the regulated firm. For example, with rate regulation, the firm is not free to set market prices, and some external regulatory body determines the rate the firm charges its customers. This type of regulation usually leads to high leverage as firm's attempt to induce higher rates from regulators. Other firm attributes such as its newness or size may influence capital structure choice. Large firms use more debt. Also, a positive relationship exists between debt levels and firm incorporation. For new startups, entrepreneur attributes such as education, race and ethnic ties, gender, strategic alliances and networks, risk-return preferences, and experience of the founding team influence the use of different forms of financing, and hence a firm's capital structure.

3. Although the capital structure of firms differs depending on the country of origin and operation, there are certain broad similarities. At best, the empirical evidence is mixed depending on the countries in the sample. One empirical regularity that emerges from the literature is that firms in countries with stronger legal institutions and safeguards hold more debt and have greater access to external finance. Conversely, firms in less developed countries rely more on internal sources.

   Two related strands of literature attempt to explain these findings. One explanation traces the dissimilarities between countries to the differences in institutional and legal frameworks and regulatory environment. These include differences in bankruptcy laws and availability of various financing opportunities (Booth et al. 2001); better creditor protection (Fan, Titman, and Twite 2008); information asymmetries, creditor conflict resolution policies, tax policies and agency problems (Wald 1999); variations in the national culture of countries (Chui, Lloyd, and Kwok 2002); and government policies such as privatization, financial liberation leading to increased real interest rates, and the declining cost of equity capital due to rising price-earnings ratios (Singh 1995). Using a sample of 49 countries with different legal systems, La Porta, Lopez-de-Silanes, Shleifer, and Vishny (1998) find that firms in countries with stronger legal safeguards have more external debt and equity financing available to them.

Glen and Pinto (1994) and Demirguc-Kunt and Maksimovic (1996) offer a second related explanation. They find that development of capital markets, the effectiveness of legal systems, and the strength of the banking sector together influence the capital structure of firms in developing countries. Firms display a higher leverage in countries with more developed capital markets and strong legal institutions. Studying the affiliates of multinational firms, Desai, Foley, and Hines (2004) find that capital market conditions and tax incentives of the host country have a large influence on the capital structure of an affiliate. Firms rely less on external debt and more on internal sources in countries with underdeveloped capital markets and poor creditor protections.

4. Traditionally, the electric utility industry in the United States has been organized as a vertically integrated regulated monopoly with for-profit, investor-owned utilities that had service monopolies in particular geographical regions, which were overseen by the Federal Energy Regulatory Commission and state regulators. The primary purpose of regulating the utilities was to set prices based on the "cost of service ratemaking" principle where the rates were fixed and could not be changed without regulator authorization. Such rate-regulation has typically been associated with high leverage ratios, which have alternatively been attributed to utilities attempting to influence regulators to set higher rates (Dasgupta and Nanda 1993; Hagerman and Ratchford 1978; Spiegel and Spulber 1994). Conversely, regulators themselves may implicitly incentivize utilities to carry more debt because debt is cheaper than equity and allows the regulators to decrease rates (De Fraja and Stones 2004). Other explanations are that utility managers react to unfavorable regulation (Rao and Moyer 1994), a safer business environment under regulation that implies a greater debt capacity for firms (Taggart 1985), or regulatory quality (Rao and Moyer 1994).

   During the 1980s and 1990s, this regulatory structure changed when "cost-based" regulation paradigms gave way to competitive electricity markets. The onset of restructuring altered the nature of financial distress costs by increasing bankruptcy probability. Sanyal and Bulan (2009) find that leverage decreases between 25 and 27 percent post deregulation. They show that any policy that decreases earnings stability, or increases competition and threatens market share, lowers debt levels. Specifically, utilities in states that encouraged the divestiture of generation assets, that is, encouraged or mandated that utilities would have to sell off their generation plants if they wanted to operate in the regulated transmission and distribution sectors, reduced leverage. Firms facing higher market uncertainty have lower leverage. If the utility had the opportunity to gain potential customers from neighboring states due to a lack of default provider policies in those states, leverage increased. However, if the market gain opportunity arose because of divestiture policies in the neighboring states, leverage declined. Last, if utilities expected to exercise greater market power in the future, they were more likely to take on higher debt compared to utilities in states where there was no potential for exercising market power. These findings highlight the complexities surrounding the financing decisions of the electric utility industry and provide a window into firms transitioning from a regulated to a competitive market.

CHAPTER 13 SURVEY EVIDENCE ON FINANCING DECISIONS AND COST OF CAPITAL

1. The survey method has several limitations. First, surveys measure beliefs and not necessarily actions of managers. Second, the respondents may not represent the population because of nonresponse bias. Third, managers may misunderstand some questions, give wrong or "politically correct" answers, or make decisions on different criteria than asked in survey questions.

   Researchers can address some of these issues using several techniques. For example, they can examine sample representativeness by comparing population and respondent firm characteristics such as firm size and industry. Researchers could also ask both structured (closed-ended) and open-ended questions on the same topic to minimize the risk that respondents may not properly understand some questions. They can check the robustness of survey findings through one-on-one interviews with a sample of managers and with the results of other survey and empirical studies in different time periods and samples. Despite these potential limitations, surveys are a valuable tool and a complementary method to other types of empirical studies that rely on secondary data in linking theory and practice of finance.
2. The evidence shows that large firms use different criteria in their cost of capital and financing decisions and adhere more closely to textbook teachings than do small firms. For example, compared to small firms, large firms are more concerned about their credit rating and target debt-to-equity ratio. Large firms also generally use more sophisticated methods and techniques for risk management. These differences could be driven by several factors that differ between the two groups, such as access to capital markets, ownership structure, and public listing. Small firms are often private firms and have limited access to public capital markets because of higher information asymmetry and ownership concentration. By contrast, large firms are generally publicly-listed firms and have access to both private and public capital markets. Another difference could be the CEO education level. Most large firm CEOs have an MBA (or an equivalent diploma) and are likely to be more familiar with sophisticated financial techniques compared to their small firm peers. Finally, large firms are more likely to have sophisticated treasury departments, which help managers analyze their financing and risk management choices, whereas small firms are likely to devote fewer resources for risk management techniques.
3. A country's legal and institutional system can directly or indirectly influence corporate financing decisions. La Porta et al. (1997, 1998) show that countries with better quality of investor protection tend to have larger capital markets, which, in turn, can affect the access and availability of external financing for corporations in different countries. The quality of investor protection can also influence the ownership structure and corporate governance system, which can indirectly influence corporate financing decisions. For example, banks have a strong influence on corporate governance in Germany through ownership of several German firms. The legal system of a country can also facilitate the development of a quality banking system or quality securities markets, or both, which can affect the potential determinants of financing decisions. For example,

survey evidence shows that managers in market-oriented countries are less concerned about financial flexibility and more concerned about equity dilution compared to their peers in bank-based system countries. However, legal and institutional factors are less important in explaining cross-country variation in determinants of financing decisions compared to firm-specific factors, such as firm size and ownership structure.

4. The survey evidence shows that both U.S. and European managers try to time the market to minimize their financing costs. More than 40 percent of responding managers issue debt when interest rates are low or when the firm's equity is undervalued by the market. Both U.S. and European managers also consider the amount of stock overvaluation or undervaluation and a rise in the firm's stock price as important factors in their equity issuance decision. Market timing is also an important consideration in convertible issuance decision. The survey evidence that managers use market timing for financing decisions is generally consistent with empirical findings. Studies also document that managers select the timing of financing decisions opportunistically to take advantage of temporarily favorable market conditions and attractive stock prices. For example, Kim and Weisbach (2008) show that firms around the world use market timing in their initial public offering and seasoned equity offering decisions. Baker and Wurgler (2002) find that market timing has a persistent effect on firms' capital structure.

CHAPTER 14 SURVEY EVIDENCE ON CAPITAL STRUCTURE: NON-U.S. EVIDENCE

1. Survey research offers several strengths. First, survey research directly assesses the decision maker's opinions, whereas other research derives their motivations from estimation between variables that are the outcomes of the decision making. Second, survey research allows the measurement of insights and variables, which are only known to the firm's insiders. In particular, information asymmetries and agency problems are unknown to outside observers.

   Survey research has several potential drawbacks. First, the results may be biased by limited representativeness or respondents providing socially desired responses. Second, the answers of the chief financial officers (CFOs) may reflect what they *think* they do but not their *actual* decisions. A common critique is that CFOs may not know the precise motivations for their decisions but still make optimal decisions.

2. Graham and Harvey (2001) and Brounen, de Jong, and Koedijk (2006) ask (where 0 is not important to 4 is very important) respondents to indicate the importance that they attached to the following statement: "We limit debt so our customers/suppliers are not worried about our firm going out of business." In all countries the scores for this question are low: from a low of 0.96 in the Netherlands, to 1.24 in the United States, and a maximum of 1.62 in the United Kingdom. De Jong and Van Dijk have two questions that measure uniqueness. The first is uniqueness towards customers: "The products and services of my firm are easily replaceable by customers for products and services of another

firm" (7 points scale, fully agree/fully disagree). The second is uniqueness towards employees: "My employees depend upon the continuity of my firm, because it is difficult for them to find a suitable position in another firm" (7 points scale, fully agree/fully disagree). They do not find these two questions to be significantly related to leverage.

3. Fan and So (2004) survey managers of Hong Kong firms both before and after the 1997 Asian crisis. Before the crisis, they find that more than three-quarters of managers prefer the pecking order theory over the static trade-off theory. In this setting they finance expansion first from retained earnings, then from debt, and finally from equity issues. After the crisis, less than half the managers prefer the pecking order theory, which implies that setting a healthy debt level has become much more important. More than 77 percent of the managers indicate that the Asian financial crisis has made equity look more favorable relative to debt as a source of capital. Fan and So's study shows that managers' views can change fairly rapidly.

CHAPTER 15 THE ROLES OF FINANCIAL INTERMEDIARIES IN RAISING CAPITAL

1. Borrowing to pay off a bank loan could be good or bad news for shareholders. By switching to public funds, the firm forgoes the monitoring benefits of banks. This is bad news for shareholders if they rely on bank monitoring. The switch away from banks also reduces hold-up problems, which may be good news for shareholders. The net effect depends on which of the forces is stronger for a given firm.
2. A commercial bank might offer the following deal to a low-quality borrower: take a bank loan, issue a new security to pay back the bank loan and interest quickly, and keep the additional funds. Since bank relationships appear to reduce the yield on new securities, the firm will borrow relatively cheaply without the bank taking a risky position. The evidence that commercial bank–underwritten securities do not have higher default rates provides support against this conflict of interest.
3. Because price stabilization requires underwriters to take positions in risky securities, a danger exists that losses to those assets will reduce the ability of banks to cover their demand deposits. Covering the losses in securities can make demand deposits risky, which can lead to a bank run, or can force banks to forgo lending opportunities to prevent a run.
4. Banks provide important services in reducing information asymmetries, especially when other information sources are unavailable. In times of uncertainty, the ability of banks to screen and monitor is arguably more important to prevent economic stagnation. Moreover, banks have relative information advantages because of borrower relationships. When times are already uncertain, these borrowers may be cut off entirely from funding because other banks cannot establish a relationship quickly.

CHAPTER 16 BANK RELATIONSHIPS AND COLLATERALIZATION

1. A bank relationship can prove costly to the bank if it faces a soft-budget constraint problem. This problem occurs when a lender in a relationship is compelled to provide additional credit when the borrower faces default to protect its previous loans. The borrower, knowing that the lender is so compelled, may be motivated to engage in risky behaviors in which it would otherwise not engage had the bank not been constrained. The bank relationship can prove costly to the borrower if it faces a hold-up problem, where the bank's information monopoly can lead to undesirable outcomes such as higher borrowing rates, or a reluctance on the borrower's part to borrow further from the bank in order to limit the monopolizing effect.
2. An explanation for an observed positive relation between loan maturity and rate spreads is as follows: First, from the borrower's perspective longer-maturity loans are more desirable as they limit refinancing costs. Second, lenders prefer shorter-term loans to minimize agency costs. Hence, the borrower is willing to pay more for longer-term loans, while the lender demands greater compensation for longer-term loans. Both of these effects suggest a positive relationship between loan maturity and rate spreads. An explanation for an observed negative relationship between loan maturity and rate spreads follows. Lenders direct lower-risk borrowers to longer-maturity loans and direct higher-risk borrowers to shorter-term loans. This will result in lower-risk, longer-term loans, and higher-risk shorter-term loans. The combination of these effects suggests a negative relationship between loan maturity and rate spreads.
3. Offering collateral is a bonding activity by borrowers that reduces monitoring costs for lenders and lowers bankruptcy costs by increasing recoveries in the event of liquidation. Secured borrowing also attenuates agency costs of asset substitution and underinvestment. For these reasons, a given borrower with a choice of either a secured or unsecured bank loan would find the secured loan offered at a lower spread. If, however, a shift occurs from comparing two loans to a single borrower to examining the difference between a two pools of loans, one secured and the other unsecured, the result is the opposite. Pledging collateral is an activity associated with riskier borrowers, many of which would not qualify for unsecured bank borrowing. As result, loans with collateral are riskier and offer higher yields than unsecured borrowing. In order to sort out these two effects, researchers require more sophisticated econometric models that control for the probability that a loan will be secured.
4. Scoring technology offers a low-cost way for banks headquartered outside a market to compete with local banks. Screening by scoring is a good strategy for the distant banks because the inputs to scoring models are "hard" information that is verifiable and does not require a relationship with the borrower. Since such transaction loans generally do not involve collateral, to the extent that distant banks take business from local banks, the use of collateral will decline. When facing such competition, local bankers may find controlling monitoring costs by taking collateral advantageous. This increases the use of collateral. The

overall result depends on the joint impact of the two effects and research has produced mixed results.

CHAPTER 17 RATING AGENCIES AND CREDIT INSURANCE

1. Determining whether rating agencies do or do not do a good job relative to what they should accomplish is problematic given the inherent uncertainty of financial outcomes. This complicates efforts to hold agencies liable for poor-quality ratings for two reasons. First, considerable difficulty exists in establishing a minimum quality level. Second, the major rating agencies argue that they have appropriate quality incentives because they want to preserve good reputations. If quality cannot be observed even in hindsight, then a reputation for quality is not meaningful.

   The main measure of rating quality that supposedly does what agencies say the ratings are intended to do is the accuracy ratio. Comparing the accuracy ratios across agencies to arrive at a relative assessment of quality potentially could support arguments that particular agencies do or do not deserve a reputation for quality. However, such an approach has received little attention in either academic literature or in practice.

2. Private users rely extensively on credit ratings to meet regulatory requirements and as reference benchmarks for agreements and investment mandates. As an example of the former, insurance companies may choose to have their credit risk of the bonds they own assessed for regulatory purposes by rating agencies or by the NAIC's Securities Valuation Office. Most insurance companies choose to use the bonds' credit ratings, although a special third approach was created to deal with mortgage-backed securities in the wake of the financial crisis. As an example of the latter, consider the infamous trading arrangements between AIG and Goldman Sachs, which exempted AIG from posting collateral as long as it maintained a AAA credit rating.

   Whether investors rely on credit ratings as a measure of credit risk in selecting investments is less clear. Event studies suggesting that rating changes are associated with market price changes could be explained by regulatory effects of ratings rather than by investor reliance, even discarding the studies that find no effect. Rigorous direct studies of actual investor reliance appear rare, although participants in the money-market fund industry comment that they find credit ratings useful in the context of the SEC's proposal to eliminate regulatory reliance on ratings in this context.

3. Any risk-based capital regulatory system needs some measure of credit risk. Despite the recent high-profile issues with credit ratings, determining whether credit ratings are generally of high or low quality relative to what their quality should have been is difficult. Moreover, the continued private use of credit ratings as reference points for investment mandates suggests that no clearly superior alternative to agency ratings is available. The alternatives also have problems. Market prices impound many factors besides credit risk. Government provision of ratings is often viewed as inefficient, and a government rating agency would likely be underfunded during a boom. The history of the NAIC's

Securities Valuation Office (SVO) illustrates this; the NAIC decided to outsource most of its evaluative duties to private rating agencies because it was felt that the SVO duplicates effort.

At the same time, regulators should recognize that regulatory use of ratings poses a kind of externality in the form of a risk of creating problems for rating-agency quality. Regulatory use of ratings produces demand for ratings that is independent of rating quality and thus blunts incentives for high-quality ratings. It also heightens pressure on rating agencies to inflate ratings and could create a feedback loop in which rating changes produce defaults. Rating agencies may not be well-equipped to deal with this endogeneity, and they do not seem to want this responsibility. For example, S&P has taken the position that ratings should not be incorporated into financial regulation. Of course, most of these points apply to purely private "reference uses" of credit ratings such as the Goldman-AIG trading arrangements.

Regulatory uses of credit ratings that are not tied purely to credit risk are especially problematic. The SEC's Rule 15c3-1 for broker-dealers uses high credit ratings as a proxy for liquidity. The ERISA rules treat a high credit rating as a proxy for the absence of a conflict of interest between the underwriter and pension funds with which it may interact. Even if such proxies are empirically justified in that high ratings usually result in liquidity or, more questionably, reduce conflicts of interest, they are dangerous in that rating agencies do not undertake to preserve those empirical relationships.

4. Competition in ratings may be good because it sharpens the reputational mechanism. Users who want to use ratings can reduce their reliance on ratings produced by an agency that is of poor quality. Moreover, competing firms may be more likely to bring competing models and approaches to bear.

   Competition in ratings may be bad because it reduces the benefits of having a good reputation (i.e., if prices are competed down to cost, there is no way to exploit a reputation for high quality) and because it facilitates ratings shopping (i.e., issuers can more easily find an agency that will give them the ratings they want, especially if they can hide the fact that they solicited ratings they didn't use). The empirical evidence to date is mixed, although no definitive studies have been completed.

   If rating agencies serve a certification function via rating-dependent regulation (i.e., if instruments need one or two high ratings to satisfy regulatory requirements), then that seems to exacerbate the ratings-shopping part of the story and suggests that competition-boosting initiatives should be accompanied by efforts to reduce rating-dependent regulation.

CHAPTER 18 SECURED FINANCING

1. *Secured debt* generally refers to a borrowing for which the lender has been granted a security interest in some or all of the borrower's assets until the borrower repays the debt. Considerable variation exists in secured debt arrangements. Secured debt can be recourse or nonrecourse, with recourse indicating the lender has a claim against the borrower that is not limited to the value of the specific pledged collateral. A borrower can pledge all of its assets making recourse

irrelevant, or some of its assets. When borrowers pledge receivables as security, the debt is nonrecourse.

2. While there is not a perfectly tight empirical link between secured debt and bank debt, the two are highly correlated. Public debt is rarely secured, but bank and finance company debt is usually secured. The strongest theoretical tie between secured debt and bank debt is in the area of monitoring and efficient liquidation. Levmore (1982) and Triantis (1992) suggest that secured debt improves coordination and efficiency in monitoring. Given the central role of monitoring in explaining the use of bank debt, using secured debt to promote monitoring is consistent with the frequent coexistence of bank lenders and security provisions. Analysis of liquidation incentives more strongly supports a link between bank debt and secured debt. Models by Repullo and Suarez (1998) and Gorton and Kahn (2000) show that bank debt should be senior and secured because the ability of a bank to act unilaterally, combined with the liquidation incentives of seniority, lead to efficient liquidation choices. The pattern of bank and finance company loans in Carey, Post, and Sharpe (1998) is generally consistent with the efficient liquidation argument.
3. The evidence supporting the use of secured debt to signal borrower quality is mixed. Leeth and Scott (1989) find evidence consistent with using secured debt to mitigate information asymmetry. Their sample of bank loans to small businesses finds significant use of outside collateral, which is a feature of some signaling models. Barclay and Smith (1995) find statistically significant but economically small effects of signaling on the use of secured debt. While the general predictions of signaling models are that higher-quality firms use secured debt to signal borrower or loan quality, Berger and Udell (1990) find that secured loans and the associated borrowers are riskier. They suggest this may be driven by the relative importance of observable versus unobservable risk.
4. The clearest bankruptcy-based evidence supporting the use of secured debt to promote monitoring and efficient liquidation comes from Alderson and Betker (1995). They use a sample of companies emerging from bankruptcy to analyze the relationship between liability structure choices and liquidation costs. Firms with the highest liquidation costs are less likely to use secured debt. When they do use secured debt, it is more likely to be secured by specific assets rather than a blanket lien on all assets. In a comprehensive sample of bankruptcies, Bris, Welch, and Zhu (2006) find that secured creditors do far better than unsecured creditors when firms reach Chapter 7. This is generally consistent with secured creditors having incentives to liquidate efficiently.

CHAPTER 19 SALE AND LEASEBACKS

1. The rate of interest in the mortgage is irrelevant. To optimize shareholder value, the financial manager should compare the leasing rate to the firm's marginal cost of capital. This is especially true if the manager wants to raise funds to expand existing business. The firm should base the net present value (NPV) on a weighted average cost of capital (WACC), not on any individual source of financing.

2. Although the academic literature assumes that the marginal investor is rational, behavioral research shows that this may not be the case. Also, debt covenants may not cover all contingencies. Thus, using an SLB to meet contractual obligations may be an optimal decision depending on the contractual language of the debt covenants.
3. In a recessionary environment, capital constraints may be high, even if the cost of capital is low. The demand for funds will increase. For this reason, an increase in alternative forms of financing such as SLBs may arise. However, the demand for these assets might decrease when opportunity costs are low and rates of returns fall. Even though demand from the seller/lessees may increase, the supply from buyers/lessors may decrease. The seller may be forced to discount the value of the asset and accept stringent leasing terms to incentivize a buyer to take the risk.
4. A substantial portion of third-party buyers/lessors are real estate holding companies or leasing agencies that are in the business of leasing assets. The market may perceive the transaction as a regular action of the business and thus not lead to abnormal increases or decreases in stock price. Competition may preclude lessors from charging lessees any more than the minimum required rate of return for a specific transaction so the lessor would not enjoy an excess return.

CHAPTER 20 FINANCIAL DISTRESS AND BANKRUPTCY

1. Certain features of the U.S. Bankruptcy Code favor incumbent management, shareholders, and the continuation of the distressed firm. These features include the automatic stay, the exclusive right to file a plan of reorganization, classification of creditors for majority voting rules, and the superpriority claim of postpetition financing. Additionally, violations of APR that benefit shareholders were commonplace. The Bankruptcy Abuse Prevention and Consumer Protection Act of 2005 limits the discretion of judges to extend the exclusivity period to 18 months, limits automatic stay for repeat filers, restricts managerial retention bonuses and severance packages, and reduces the flexibility of bankrupt firms to put leased assets back to lessors. This new regime may also adhere more strictly to the notion of absolute priority. To the extent that a prodebtor system favoring incumbent management and shareholders resulted in higher debt ratios, this trend to reverse under new more creditor-oriented rules might be expected.
2. Because the residual claim on a financially distressed firm is essentially an option, shareholders prefer increasingly risky (possibly negative net present value (NPV)) investments that afford them (unlimited if unlikely) upside potential while creditors bear the increased risk. Creditors, on the other hand, prefer relatively safe (or no) marginal investment. Thus, financially distressed firms may face simultaneously an overinvestment problem (funding risky negative NPV investments) and an underinvestment problem (passing on relatively safe positive NPV investments) associated with what Myers (1977) refers to as a debt overhang. Also, managers concerned with employment longevity may

depart from firm value maximization toward investment policies that ensure the continuation of the firm under their control.

3. Lang and Stulz (1992) and Hertzel, Li, Officer, and Rodgers (2008) document contagion of financial distress within an industry and along the supply chain. Real wealth effects for shareholders exist at the bankruptcy filing by a rival, supplier, or customer. These wealth effects are also discernable at the onset of financial distress, often well in advance of the initial default event.
4. An important firm-level determinant of direct and indirect costs is firm size. Direct costs include both fixed and variable costs. Thus, while total costs are higher for larger firms, they are lower as a percentage of firm value. For the largest of firms, the expectation of "too big to fail" policies lowers at least the expected costs of financial distress. A history of government intervention (early railroad bankruptcies, airlines, the U.S. steel and auto industries, and most recently the financial services sector) may result in the expectation of assistance among the largest firm in distress. Arguments in favor of government intervention include employment considerations and potential contagion of distress to counter parties. Arguments against intervention include the moral hazard problem where firms retain the benefit of risky projects that pay off but share with taxpayers the costs of risky projects that do not pay off. Whether government intervention is efficient remains widely contested by academics, politicians, and pundits, but the expectation of the intervention—good or bad—affects perceived costs of distress and thus optimal debt levels.

CHAPTER 21 FIDUCIARY RESPONSIBILITY AND FINANCIAL DISTRESS

1. Sometime parties cannot contract properly either due to inability (such as a contract between a minor and adult) or asymmetric information (such as between a doctor and a patient), or when there are transaction costs (such as between shareholders and the board of directors). The law imposes these duties as what it envisions a hypothetical bargain would have been between the two parties if the impediments to free contracting were removed.
2. When a firm is close to insolvency, shareholders may want to engage in much more risky investments than what the creditors had anticipated when lending the corporation money. The shareholders have no downside to this since they will lose all their money anyway if the firm goes bankrupt. The creditors would prefer a less-risky venture so that some assets remain if the firm is liquidated. Hence, the courts fear opportunistic moral hazard behavior on the shareholders' part at the expense of creditors.
3. Creditors can contract in advance and monitor in order to mitigate this sort of behavior. The contract can specify the appropriate risk-adjusted interest rate or specific metrics of performance. Failure to perform will trigger advanced liquidation. Creditors can anticipate those fears that the courts have and adequately price and specify shareholder behavior. The literature on capital structure and the Fisher separation theorem provides the best justification for this view.

4. Although the cases speak sometimes of duties to various constituencies, the value of the firm is simply the sum of the value of equity and debt. Hence, maximizing one necessarily means the maximization of the other. This means that the courts are speaking about the same thing.

CHAPTER 22 THE LEASE VERSUS BUY DECISION

1. Smith and Wakeman (1985) describe some of the unique provisions in lease contracts including (1) deposits and penalty clauses; (2) restrictions on subleasing and use; (3) service versus net lease; (4) metering and tie-in sales; and (5) options to extend or purchase or cancel. Schallheim (1994) provides a list of popular reasons for leasing of which many are dubious when subjected to careful scrutiny of economic logic. According to Schallheim (p. 15), one strong economic reason is that "equipment leasing provides customized financing with potentially unique tax features." He also describes eight factors that determine lease payments and shows how lease contracts can be divided into eight general categories. These categories include the terms of the lease payments, equipment procurement and delivery, use and maintenance, obligations at expiration, warranties and default procedures, among others. The uniqueness of a lease contract derives from the interaction among these categories. Another unique feature of leasing is the treatment of the lessor when the lessee is in bankruptcy. Eisfeldt and Rampini (2009) point out that the U.S. Bankruptcy Code treats leasing and secured lending differently. Regarding the aircraft leasing market, Gavazza (2010) notes that the U.S. Bankruptcy Code provides lessors with stronger claims on aircraft than any other asset in bankruptcy.
2. Most early literature on leasing treats leasing as a substitute for secured lending. Schallheim (1994, p. 93) states that "lease contracts, especially financial leases, commit the lessee to a series of fixed payments as does a loan contract." Emery, Finnerty, and Stowe (2011) advocate a similar premise in implementing their debt-service-parity model. Yan (2006) explains why leases and debt are substitutes from the perspective of the trade-off theory of capital structure. The trade-off theory predicts that leases and debt are substitutes because a firm's marginal cost of new debt or new leases increases with the fixed claims obligations that are already in place. However, the trade-off theory does not consider the opportunity of tax-arbitrage in lease transactions. Leases and debt can be complements because the lessee can sell excess tax-shields to the lessor.

   Schallheim (1994) also states that the fundamental difference between leasing and debt concerns the residual value. Eisfeldt and Rampini (2009) elaborate on this issue and point out that the U.S. Bankruptcy Code treats leasing and secured lending differently. Eisfeldt and Rampini (p. 2) note that "in bankruptcy it is much easier for a lessor to regain control of an asset than it is for a secured lender." As Gavazza (2010) points out, this is true only for an operating lease. For a capital lease, the lessor is treated as a secured lender in a Chapter 11 reorganization. Gavazza further adds that, regarding the aircraft leasing market, the U.S. Bankruptcy Code provides lessors with stronger claims on aircraft than any other asset in bankruptcy. According to Section 1110 of the Bankruptcy Code, aircraft are not subject to automatic stay, and lessors can foreclose an aircraft if the lessee fails to make lease payments within 60 days.

3. Smith and Wakeman (1985) note that the biggest strength of the tax-based models is that provisions in the tax code are important in explaining the fact that for some assets, leases are offered both by manufacturers and third-party lessors. Tax-based models are also important in estimating lease payments that would make the NPV of leasing equal to zero in equilibrium.

   But the tax-based models cannot explain the maturity structure of leases. Nor can these models explain why small firms resort to leasing much more than large firms and why certain industries and assets (such as trucking and aircraft) are more amenable to leasing.

4. The nontax models examine the effects of contracting costs, agency costs, liquidity, and information asymmetry. The fact that the nontax models capture many aspects of reality (that are not captured by the tax-based models) is their biggest strength. The nontax models can explain many observed facts about leasing that are not explained by the tax-based models. For example, Chemmanur, Jiao, and Yan (2010) show that various contractual provisions, such as short-term versus long-term leases with noncancellation clauses, option to buy at lease termination, and service leases, emerge as equilibrium solutions in their double-sided asymmetric information model. Their model also shows that leases with metering provisions may be used when, in addition to maintenance costs, lessees differ in their intensity of usage of the capital goods.

   A weakness of the nontax models is that no single model can explain all contractual features observed in practice. Chemmanur, Jiao, and Yan (2010) point to the puzzle that their asymmetric information model cannot explain, namely, why new cars are leased much more than used cars despite more asymmetric information in the used car market. Their model also cannot explain the prevalence of third-party lessors.

CHAPTER 23 PRIVATE INVESTMENT IN PUBLIC EQUITY

1. In a traditional private placement, the issuer relies on an exemption from Securities and Exchange Commission (SEC) registration requirements to issue securities to investors but does not promise to promptly register the resale of the securities, which distinguishes a traditional private placement from a PIPE. By doing a PIPE, that is agreeing to promptly register the resale, the issuer can sell the shares at a smaller discount, reflecting a shorter period of illiquidity for the investor. Additionally, offering an investment with a shorter period of illiquidity increases the pool of potential investors because they can more quickly turn a short-term profit through the hedge fund strategy described in the chapter.

2. The profit that hedge funds earn through PIPE deals is at the expense of the issuer's existing shareholders because the discounted sales to hedge funds dilute the financial claim of the existing shares. The counter is that if a PIPE deal is the issuer's only financing option, suffering dilution is better than the issuer having

to cease operations due to a lack of funds, at which point its stock would be worthless.

3. An issuer has to sell PIPE shares at a discount to attract investors. The hedge fund strategy only works if the fund can buy shares at a price below which it can short the shares in the market. Thus, the hedge fund will only invest and provide the issuer with the needed funds if the issuer adequately discounts the shares. The discount also needs to reflect the unwinding risk assumed by the hedge fund. With PIPE deals by larger companies, the discount reflects illiquidity because an investor cannot immediately resell the shares as it could if the shares were sold in a registered offering or purchased in the open market. The investor has to wait until the resale registration statement is declared effective and thus assume the risk of delay. Also, the discount probably reflects a volume discount as PIPE deals typically involve a larger block of stock.
4. A partial answer appears in a quote included in the chapter from the *SEC v. Lyon* complaint (see SEC PIPE Enforcement Actions/Insider Trading): "the announcement typically precipitates a decline in the price of a PIPE issuer's securities due to the dilutive effect of the offering and the PIPE shares being issued at a discount to the then prevailing market price of the issuer's stock." For PIPEs by smaller companies, the drop in an issuer's stock price also reflects the negative signal of having to resort to PIPE financing; that is, the company is not in good enough shape to attract any other types of financing.

CHAPTER 24 FINANCING CORPORATE MERGERS AND ACQUISITIONS

1. Payments with stock or cash differ with respect to transaction risks arising from information asymmetries such as overpayment or bidder competition, as well as their implications for the acquirer's ownership structure and related agency problems. Stock payments are mainly motivated by market timing and risk-sharing motives. Furthermore, corporate control considerations may also favor stock payments, for example, when the bidder's intention is to retain target managers or shareholders, or when the bidder wants to dilute the influence of its current block holders. In contrast, cash payments are preferred when the bidder's stock price is depressed or to preempt or win bidder competition when combined with a relatively high takeover premium. Additionally, cash payments may be motivated by the acquirer's intention to preserve its prevailing ownership structure.
2. Some contend that the method of payment and financing decisions are independent, as any financing source can be converted into any method of payment. However, empirical evidence suggests a link between the method of payment and the source of financing. Cash payments are mainly financed with internally generated funds or debt, while equity payments usually require new equity issuance unless share repurchases provide enough shares for payment. In contrast, cash payments financed with new equity are less commonly observed. This financing behavior is consistent with the pecking order theory as issuing equity is generally more costly than debt regarding both information and

flotation costs. For example, equity financing typically triggers a negative market reaction and requires a shareholder vote and registration. Moreover, when a firm issues new equity to finance a merger or acquisition, stock payment (i.e., a stock swap merger) may be less costly than cash payment. This is because target management and shareholders will certify the value of the bidder's stock and investors who would not participate in a seasoned equity offering may passively accept stock in a takeover. Also, issuing new equity through a stock swap merger can be an effective means to hide an underlying market timing motive, as the bidder may argue that it needs to make a stock payment for transaction-specific reasons.

3. In imperfect capital markets, the decision to acquire another company may not be independent of the capital structure when firms are constrained in their financing opportunities or when the transaction requires a certain method of payment, which may be linked to a specific source of financing. Particularly, overleveraged firms without sufficient cash holdings or cash flows from operations may be constrained in their timing and terms of takeovers. This may even decrease their ability to conduct M&As, for example, due to a lower premium and cash component. Therefore, bidders are most often firms with financial slack, which they may also actively build up before a merger or acquisition. In contrast, small R&D–intensive firms, which face difficulties in financing their growth opportunities, are often ideal takeover targets. In this case, the bidder may provide the required funding for the unrealized positive NPV projects of the target that it cannot finance itself. Thus, firms with financial slack are more likely to acquire another firm due to ease of financing, particularly those in need of funding, and thereby profit from financial synergies.

Index

D

E

Lightning Source UK Ltd.
Milton Keynes UK
UKHW032152210220
359070UK00002B/37